NOTABLE BRITISH NOVELISTS

MAGILL'S CHOICE

NOTABLE BRITISH NOVELISTS

Volume 2

E. M. Forster — Walter Pater

351 – 706

edited by

CARL ROLLYSON

SALEM PRESS, INC.

Pasadena, California   Hackensack, New Jersey

Essays originally appeared in *Critical Survey of Long Fiction,
Second Revised Edition*, 2000; new material has been added.

∞ The paper used in these volumes conforms to the American
National Standard for Permanence of Paper for Printed Library Materials, Z39.48-1992 (R1997).

Library of Congress Cataloging-in-Publication Data
Notable British novelists / editor, Carl Rollyson
      p.   cm. — (Magill's choice)
  Includes bibliographical references and index.
ISBN 0-89356-204-1 (set : alk. paper). —
ISBN 0-89356-208-4 (v. 1 : alk. paper). —
ISBN 0-89356-209-2 (v. 2 : alk. paper). —
ISBN 0-89356-237-8 (v. 3 : alk. paper)
  1. English fiction—Bio-bibliography—Dictionaries. 2. Nov-
elists, English—Biography—Dictionaries. 3. English fiction— Dic-
tionaries I. Rollyson, Carl E. (Carl Edmund) II. Series.
PR821.N57   2001
820.9′0003—dc21
[B]   00-046380

First Printing

Contents – Volume 2

Notable British Novelists

Complete List of Contents

Contents—Volume 1

Contents—Volume 2

Contents—Volume 3

Notable British Novelists

E. M. Forster

Born: London, England; January 1, 1879
Died: Coventry, England; June 7, 1970

Principal long fiction · *Where Angels Fear to Tread,* 1905; *The Longest Journey,* 1907; *A Room with a View,* 1908; *Howards End,* 1910; *A Passage to India,* 1924; *Maurice,* 1971 (wr. 1913).

Other literary forms · In addition to his novels, E. M. Forster wrote short stories, travel books, biographies, essays, and criticism. A number of these works, as well as his novels, have already appeared in the standard Abinger Edition, in progress. *The Celestial Omnibus and Other Stories* (1911) includes his frequently anthologized story "The Road from Colonus" and five other stories written in a fantastic vein that is found much less frequently in his novels. *Aspects of the Novel* (1927) remains one of the most widely read discussions of that genre, while the essays of *Abinger Harvest–A Miscellany* (1936) and *Two Cheers for Democracy* (1951) have also found many receptive readers. In *Marianne Thornton: A Domestic Biography, 1797-1887* (1956) Forster recalls his great-aunt, a woman whose long life plunged him into the social history of a milieu going back to the closing years of the eighteenth century. A useful description of Forster's uncollected writings by George H. Thomson may be found in *Aspects of E. M. Forster* (1969), a *Festschrift* honoring the author on his ninetieth birthday. In the same volume, Benjamin Britten recounts one more Forster achievement: the libretto he coauthored with Eric Crozier for Britten's opera *Billy Budd* (1951).

Achievements · Forster will continue to stand a little apart from other major novelists of the twentieth century. Because he made it difficult to decide by which standards his work should be judged, assessing it fairly presents problems. Unlike many of his Bloomsbury friends, he did not rebel against the Victorians or their literary habits; neither did he embrace the literary trends of his own time with any great enthusiasm. He lamented the encroachment of a commercial culture, but he did not war on the modern world. Although he composed a set of lectures on the novel, its plural title, *Aspects of the Novel,* anticipates his refusal to develop therein any single theory of the form in which he distinguished himself. On the one hand, his work is impossible to pigeonhole; on the other hand, his six novels do not entitle him to a lonely eminence overshadowing his most able contemporaries.

Readers of the novel will not lose sight of Forster, however, because the very ambiguities and inconsistencies which frustrate efforts to find a niche for him continue to intrigue critics. Forster lived long enough to see his reputation fade and then rebound strongly. He had gained critical acclaim while still in his twenties, written a masterpiece in midlife, and published no fiction for nearly two decades before Lionel Trilling's *E. M. Forster* (1943) swung critical attention back to him. Since that time, a formidable body of books and articles dealing with Forster has formed, and many aspects of his work have been studied in great detail. While incapable of putting Forster in a specific place, his critics agree overwhelmingly that he deserves a place of honor among English novelists.

Archive Photos

Forster's critics, fortunately, do not hold his unusually protracted silence against him. The author's failure to write a novel in the final forty-six years of his life has been explained in various ways—for example by noting that instead of exercising his talents in succession, husbanding his resources, exhausting one mode before moving to another, Forster put all of himself into the first six novels and then ceased at an age when many novelists are just reaching their prime. Whatever the reason for his early retirement from a literary form successfully practiced by so many older writers, he furnished his critics no occasion to regret the decline of his powers.

Those powers yielded fiction marked by a blend of qualities—intelligence, wit, sensitivity, compassion, and alert moral imagination—that few other writers can match. No doubt, many readers begin *A Passage to India* in the line of duty, for it has attained the rank of "classic," but they are likely to complete it, and then begin the earlier ones, out of a desire to know better a man who could write so movingly and yet so tough-mindedly about the climate created by racial and religious prejudice. Few such readers are disappointed, for while the earlier novels are less fine, the distance between *Where Angels Fear to Tread* and *A Passage to India* is not nearly so great as that between the apprentice and masterworks of most writers. Even if his final novel is, as one critic puts it, "Forster's sole claim upon posterity," those who delve into his other works will continue to reap rewards in proportion to the attention they bestow on them, for neither wit nor wisdom is ever far away.

The critical consensus is that Forster's most successful mode is comic irony, and his name is often coupled with those of Jane Austen and George Meredith, whose test for comedy—"that it shall awaken thoughtful laughter"—Forster passes with flying colors. Critics invariably hasten to point out that Forster refused to confine himself to this mode; in the midst of deploring these deviations from high comedy, they find in Forster's odd blends of comedy, melodrama, fantasy, lyricism, and tragedy a distinctiveness they would not willingly relinquish.

Biography · Edward Morgan Forster lived a long but rather uneventful life. Born on New Year's Day, 1879, he was reared by his possessive mother and worshipful great-aunt (whose biography he later wrote) after the death of his father from tuberculosis before Forster turned two. Happy, protected, and dominated by women in his early years, he suffered painfully the transition to the masculine, athletically oriented

Tonbridge School–later the model for Sawston School in *The Longest Journey.* After a more congenial four years, 1897 to 1901, at King's College, Cambridge, he took a second-class degree. In the next few years, he wrote seriously, traveled in Italy and Greece, tutored the children of a German countess, and also indulged in walking tours of his native land.

His first novel, *Where Angels Fear to Tread,* much of which is set in Italy, received favorable reviews in 1905, and Forster produced three more novels in the next five years, of which *A Room with a View* drew also on his Italian experience, while *The Longest Journey* and *Howards End* both reflect his keen delight in the English country-side. Thereafter, having attained a considerable reputation as a novelist, he slowed his pace. He began, but could not finish, a novel called *Arctic Summer,* completed a novel about homosexuality, his own orientation, which he knew to be unpublishable; and brought out a volume of short stories. Among his many friends he numbered Virginia Woolf, as well as others of the Bloomsbury group, of which, however, he was never more than a fringe member. World War I found him in Egypt as a Red Cross worker. Although he disliked Egypt, his life there led to the writing of two nonfiction books.

Forster had first visited India in 1912, but his second sojourn there as personal secretary to the Maharaja of Dewas gave him the opportunity to observe the political and social life closely enough to inspire him to write another novel. *A Passage to India,* which appeared in 1924, increased his fame and led to an invitation to deliver the Clark Lectures at Trinity College, Cambridge, in 1927, published later that year as *Aspects of the Novel.* Although he continued to write for several more decades, he published no more novels. Forster received a number of honors, culminating in the Order of Merit, presented to him on his ninetieth birthday. He died in June of 1970.

Analysis · E. M. Forster's most systematic exposition of the novelist's art, *Aspects of the Novel,* is no key to his own practice. Written three years after the publication of *A Passage to India,* the work surveys neither his achievement nor intentions. While full of the insights, charm, and homely but colorful metaphors which also distinguish Virginia Woolf's *Common Reader* volumes (1925, 1932), the book is an enthusiast's, rather than a working writer's, view of the novel, as if Forster were already distancing himself from the form which earned him his fame as a writer.

A lecture given twenty years later by Lionel Trilling, who had already published his book on Forster, gives a better sense of Forster's achievement. In "Manners, Morals, and the Novel," later published in *The Liberal Imagination* (1950), Trilling explains the novel as the writer's response to the modern world's besetting sin of snobbery, which he defines as "pride in status without pride in function." Europeans, and perhaps especially the English, familiar with snobbery as a manifestation of class structure, require less explanation than do Americans of the novel's relation to snobbery. The central tradition of the English novel from Henry Fielding through Jane Austen, Charles Dickens William Makepeace Thackeray, and George Meredith– and indeed English comedy as far back as Geoffrey Chaucer's *The Canterbury Tales* (1387-1400)–stands as evidence.

In Forster's time, however, that tradition was being modified. For one thing, the greatest English novelists at work during Forster's formative years were a wealthy American expatriate and a retired Polish mariner. No one as sensitive as Forster could escape the influence of Henry James and Joseph Conrad, but these men made curious heirs to Dickens and Thackeray and George Eliot. James, while intensely interested in the textures of society, focused his attention on the relations between the English (and Continental) leisure class and those American travelers that Mark Twain had christened "innocents abroad," thus limiting his social scrutiny, in Forster's opinion, to the narrow perceptions of a few wealthy idlers. Conrad diverged even more sharply from the path of previous English novelists, for he neither understood nor cared to understand any level of English society. A man of his temperament and interest might be imagined as a literary force in the midcentury United States of Nathaniel Hawthorne's *The Scarlet Letter* (1850) and Herman Melville's *Moby Dick* (1851), but not in the England of Thackeray's *Vanity Fair* (1847-1848) and Dickens's *Bleak House* (1852-1853). Nevertheless, Conrad was more in tune with his own literary milieu than Meredith, who at the end of the century reigned as the grand old man of English letters, and Conrad's work, like that of James, diverted the creative energy of many of the new century's novelists into new channels.

Of native English novelists still regarded as substantial, the most active at the time of Forster's entry into the field were Arnold Bennett, H. G. Wells, and John Galsworthy—all men born in the 1860's and all inheritors of the native tradition of the novel, albeit on a somewhat reduced scale. The next generation of novelists, born slightly after Forster in the 1880's, included Woolf, James Joyce, and D. H. Lawrence, all of whom published their initial works after Forster had already written five of his six novels. This latter group obviously belongs to a new literary dispensation. Society and its network of snobbery, though still significant, have receded into the background, and the conflicts of the protagonists are waged at a more personal, intimate, sometimes semiconscious level. Clearly the work of psychologists such as Sigmund Freud and Henry James's brother William influenced these later writers and drove them to develop literary techniques adequate to the task of a more truly psychological novel.

Forster, as has been suggested, stands in the middle. A friend of Virginia Woolf and in her mind, certainly, no part of the decaying tradition she trounced so severely in her essay "Mr. Bennett and Mrs. Brown," Forster nevertheless anticipated few of the technical innovations of the novelists who reached their maturity after World War I. His last novel stands with the post-Freudian achievements. *Howards End,* his most ambitious novel, is in most respects a novel of the old school. It is denser, symbolically richer, than the characteristic work of Bennett, Wells, and Galsworthy, but the same might be said of *Bleak House,* written more than half a century earlier.

Only around the time of Forster's birth did novelists begin to insist on the novel as an art form and write theoretical defenses of it. Meredith delivered a lecture on "The Idea of Comedy and the Uses of the Comic Spirit" (1877), which, though mentioning Miguel de Cervantes and Fielding, has more to say of Aristophanes and Molière; Henry James's essay "The Art of Fiction" appeared in 1884. By the century's end, novelists had achieved respectability, and Conrad could soberly echo Longinus: "Art is long and life is short, and success is very far off."

Such new expressions of the novelist's kinship with poet and playwright did not end the nineteenth century habit of producing loose, baggy narratives in a diversity of modes, punctuated by their author's abrupt changes of direction, interpolated moral essays, and episodes introduced for no better reason than a hunch that readers, who cared nothing for artistic integrity, would enjoy them. Stock literary devices that storytellers had accumulated over the centuries—bizarre coincidences, thoroughly improbable recognition scenes thrust into "realistic" contexts, the bundling forth of long-lost (often supposedly deceased) personages in the interests of a happy or surprising denouement, all devices that twentieth century novels would shun–still flourished in Forster's youth, and he used many of them unashamedly.

If Forster's moment in literary history partly explains his wavering between Victorian and modern canons, his skeptical, eclectic temperament must also be cited. His astute analyses of the morals and manners of society involved him in comedy, tragedy, romance, and fantasy–the sort of "God's plenty" that the supposedly neoclassical John Dryden admired in Chaucer and Ben Jonson in William Shakespeare. Such men would write any sort of work and take up with any sort of character. Forster was similarly indiscriminate. His veneration for Leo Tolstoy's *War and Peace* (1865-1869), though "such an untidy book," betrays his Englishman's weakness in believing that God's plenty would overcome the artist's scruples.

Of course Forster's novels are not as long as *War and Peace* or the Victorian ones that readers worked their way through in installments spread over many months. Compared with the seamless garments of Woolf or even the longer works of Joyce and William Faulkner (both of whom exhibit an un-English type of variety but also an astonishing coherence), Forster's juxtapositions of sharply contrasting modes invite criticism by readers who take in his works in two or three successive evenings. Thus, while Forster does not belong with Wells and Galsworthy, neither does he quite keep company with the greatest of his slightly younger contemporaries, for he loved too much the variety and freedom that most earlier English novelists permitted themselves.

Nevertheless, his motto for *Howards End*–"Only connect"–applies to his work generally. If he does not always make the artistic connections, his consistent theme is the necessity of making moral connections with fellow humans, of struggling against the class divisions which so many Englishmen, including a number of his fellow novelists, took for granted. In his novels, prudence is invariably on the side of those who, like Henry Wilcox in *Howards End* and Ronnie Heaslop in *A Passage to India*, resist the breakdown of social barriers; but courage, generosity, friendship, and sympathy are found among Forster's liberal opponents of snobbery. In the world of Forster's novels, the closed class is always sterile and corrupt.

Forster's eclecticism, his versatility, his refusal to ignore the claims either of heart or head make the reading of his novels an ambiguous but rich experience. Never, though, does he seem like a mere exhibitionist. Rather, his openness to life's variety amounts to a perpetual invitation to the participation of alert and open-minded readers. He is far less afraid of a gaucherie than of a missed opportunity to "connect."

Where Angels Fear to Tread · Forster's shortest and most tightly focused novel is *Where Angels Fear to Tread*. A young man named Philip Herriton is commissioned by his mother and sister Harriet to bring back from Italy the infant son of Lilia Carella, the widow of another of Mrs. Herriton's sons. Within a year after marrying Gino Carella, the aimless son of a small-town dentist, Lilia died giving birth to a son. Aided by Harriet and by Caroline Abbott, who as Lilia's traveling companion had been able to do nothing to ward off the offensive marriage, Philip finds Gino resistant to Mrs. Herriton's pocketbook and ultimately becomes involved in a shabby kidnapping venture engineered by Harriet–a venture that ends with the accidental death of the child. On the way home, Philip finds himself drawn emotionally to Caroline, who reveals that she too has fallen in love with Gino. In the common effort to minister to the pitifully unregenerate Harriet, however, Philip and Caroline become friends.

Thus summarized, the novel bears some resemblance to one by Henry James.

Forster enjoys contrasting Anglo-Saxon and Italian mores, and he shares James's fascinated horror over the machinations and intrigues of sophisticated schemers. He may have owed the idea of centering the story on a somewhat detached emissary to James, whose novel *The Ambassadors* (1903) appeared shortly before Forster began work on his own book.

Forster's handling of his material, however, differs substantially from James's. He cannot resist scathing treatment of the characters whose company he expects his readers to keep and with whom they are to sympathize. Harriet, appalled by Italy's uncleanliness, carries a bottle of ammonia in her trunk, but Forster has it "burst over her prayer-book, so that purple patches appeared on all her clothes." Prayer brings out the worst in many of Forster's characters, an exception being Caroline, who is able to pray in the church in Gino's hometown, "where a prayer to God is thought none the worse of because it comes next to a pleasant word to a neighbor." For Philip to develop neighborliness is a struggle. Not only is he much less experienced and resourceful than Strether or any other Jamesian ambassador, he is also decidedly unattractive: callow, priggish, and cowardly. Caroline's assessment of him in the final chapter, though tardily arrived at, is accurate enough: "You're without passion; you look on life as a spectacle, you don't enter it; you only find it funny or beautiful." By the time he hears this, however, Philip has learned what neither his mother nor his sister ever suspects: that the son of an Italian dentist can love his child more than wealth, that he is capable of trust and friendship, that he can be not merely angered but also hurt by a betrayal. Philip has also felt enough by this time to be hurt by Caroline's words.

Though selfish and short-sighted, Gino is without the treachery of a Jamesian Italian such as Giovanelli in *Daisy Miller* (1878). Indeed, Forster makes him morally superior to the Herriton women. Fixing on a domestic vignette of a sort impossible in any well-appointed English household (or in a James novel, for that matter)–Gino bathing his infant son–Forster draws Caroline into helping him and lets Philip come upon them so engaged, "to all intents and purposes, the Virgin and Child, with Donor." Forster's heroes tend to idealize people who are only behaving a little better than expected, but the capacity to idealize is a symptom of their regeneration.

Harriet tricks Philip into the kidnapping; he discovers the ruse only after the baby has died and his own arm has been broken in a carriage accident. He returns to confess the transgression, only to have the grief-stricken Gino cruelly twist his broken arm and then nearly choke him to death before Caroline appears to stop him. In a typically Forsterian piece of symbolism, she persuades Gino and Philip together to drink the milk that had been poured for the child. In a pattern that Forster repeats in later novels, Philip, though excessive in his estimate of Caroline's goodness, is nevertheless "saved" by it. Salvation is at least partly illusion, but such an illusion serves him better than the cynicism that Philip has spent his youth imbibing.

The Longest Journey · Like Philip, Rickie Elliot of *The Longest Journey* is frail and aesthetic. In addition, a deformed foot which he has inherited from his father marks him as different from his Cambridge classmates. At the beginning of the novel, both his father, whom he despised, and his beloved mother are dead; his father's sister, Mrs. Failing, is his closest relative. On her Wiltshire estate lives a young man, Stephen Wonham, an illegitimate half-brother to Rickie. Rude, truculent, undiscriminating in his choice of companions, and more or less a habitual drunkard, Stephen also proves loyal and almost pathetically trusting. The relationship between the two brothers forms the core of the novel.

The title of the book, from Percy Bysshe Shelley's poem *Epipsychidion* (1821), alludes to the folly of denying the rest of the world for the sake of "a mistress or a friend," with whom, in consequence, one must "the dreariest and longest journey go." In the midst of mulling over the poem, Rickie ironically decides to take his journey with Agnes Pembroke, a girl whose first lover, a strapping athlete, has died suddenly of a football injury. Death, it may be noted, always strikes with unexpected suddenness in Forster's novels. The marriage disgusts Rickie's closest friend, Stewart Ansell, and Rickie himself comes soon enough to regret it. Discouraged by Agnes and her elder brother Herbert from pursuing a career as a writer, Rickie takes a teaching post at Sawston School, where Herbert is a master. By a strange coincidence, a maladjusted boy at the school writes a letter to Stephen Wonham, among other total strangers, asking Stephen to "pray for him." Agnes's practical mind senses trouble if Stephen appears at the school, but mercifully the boy withdraws before Stephen can carry out an offer to come visit him. Rickie, while not fond of Stephen, is willing for him to receive his aunt's property when she dies; not so Agnes. When Mrs. Failing sends the troublesome Stephen packing, he decides to visit Sawston and inform Rickie of their relationship—about which Rickie already knows.

Outside the school, Stephen meets Stewart Ansell, on hand to verify for himself the death of his friend's spirit in his loveless union with the Pembrokes, and, after receiving an insult, knocks him down. Before Stephen can see Rickie, Agnes intercepts him and offers him the money she is sure he wants in return for leaving Sawston and sparing Rickie the embarrassment of acknowledging him. Stunned and stung, the utterly unmercenary Stephen leaves, but Ansell, won over not only by Stephen's fist but also by his principles, breaks into the Sawston dining hall during Sunday dinner and, in front of masters, students, and all, rebukes Rickie for turning away his own brother in the latter's deepest distress. As the assemblage gapes, Ansell reveals what he has correctly intuited: that Stephen is not the son of Rickie's father, as Rickie had supposed, but of his beloved mother. At this news Rickie faints.

Although wildly improbable, the scene has an electric intensity about it. Ansell, with all the clumsy insistence of a true egalitarian and all the insight of a true friend, has, while mistakenly charging Rickie with complicity in Agnes's treachery, stripped away the hypocrisy behind which the couple has hidden. There is about this revelation something of the quality of the recognition scene of a tragedy such as Sophocles' *Oedipus Tyrannus* (c. 429), with Rickie the lame protagonist faced with the consequences of his disastrous marriage and of his unjust assumption about his father, as well as of his denial of his brother.

From the time Rickie listened mutely to his classmates' discussion of whether the cow in the field was "there" if no one was present to perceive her, he has searched unavailingly for reality. He has misinterpreted his love for Agnes as real, watched his son—inevitably deformed like his father and himself—die in infancy, and seen his attempt at a schoolmaster's life tumble. Now he tries, none too successfully, to effect a reconciliation with his brother. He leaves Agnes and the school and tries to rekindle the flame of his short-story writing. When Stephen disappoints him on a visit to Mrs. Failing by breaking a promise not to drink, Rickie concludes that people are not "real." Finding Stephen sprawled drunkenly across the tracks at a railroad crossing, Rickie finds the strength to move him from the path of an oncoming train—but not the strength to save himself.

Rickie's aunt and brother-in-law, incapable of seeing his rescue of Stephen as worthwhile, see him as a failure whose life is mercifully over. Stephen, who is no thinker, is not so sure. In the final chapter, he feels himself to be in some sense the future of England, for he is now the father of a girl who bears the name of his and Rickie's mother. Dimly, he acknowledges that his salvation is from Rickie.

Not only does *The Longest Journey* run to melodrama, but it also incorporates some rather tedious moralizing, both on the part of Mrs. Failing and in an interpolated essay by Forster which forms the whole twenty-eighth chapter (although the chapter is a short one). Probably the greatest burden, however, is the one Stephen Wonham is forced to carry. First of all, he is the disreputable relative who knocks people down and falls down drunk himself. He serves a contrasting and complementary purpose as a kind of spiritual extension of Rickie, particularly after Rickie, recognizing him as his mother's son, begins to invest him with her excellencies, as recollected. In the final chapter, Stephen becomes the consciousness of the novel itself.

Without Stephen, however, Forster's brilliant portrait of Rickie is not only incomplete but also depressing, for Rickie dies, sad to say, murmuring agreement with Mrs. Failing's antihumanist convictions that "we do not live for anything great" and that "people are not important at all." Stephen exists and procreates and retains the idea of greatness to prove Rickie wrong.

A Room with a View · Forster sends his principals off to Italy again in *A Room with a View*. The room in question is one which Lucy Honeychurch and her elder cousin Charlotte Bartlett do not enjoy at the beginning of their stay in a Florentine hotel but which two other travelers, the elderly Mr. Emerson and his son George, are more than willing to exchange for the one that furnishes the ladies with only a disappointing view of the courtyard. Characteristic of Forster's well-bred characters, they lose sight of Emerson's generosity in their horror at the directness and bluntness of his offer, for he has interrupted their conversation at dinner before other guests: "I have a view, I have a view." Having defied the convention that forbids hasty and undue familiarity with a stranger, Mr. Emerson must be certified by an English clergyman, after which the ladies somewhat stiffly accept the view. Mr. Emerson, of course, has throughout the novel a "view" which the cousins, who hate the darkness but blanch at openness, achieve only with difficulty.

Soon an unexpected adventure literally throws Lucy and George Emerson more closely together. While enthusiastically and uncritically buying photographs of Italian masterpieces, Lucy witnesses a stabbing in a public square. She faints; George catches her and, after throwing her blood-spattered photographs into the River Arno, conducts her away gently. Later, Lucy puzzles over the affair and comes to the conclusion that, despite his kind intentions, George Emerson is devoid of "chivalry."

When circumstances throw them together again, George impulsively kisses Lucy. Such behavior drives Lucy and Charlotte to Rome, where they meet Cecil Vyse. He is propriety itself, never once offering to kiss Lucy, and back in England Lucy and Vyse become engaged. By coincidence, Vyse has met the Emersons and introduces them to the neighborhood where Lucy and her mother live. Though well-intentioned, Vyse is one of Forster's snobs. He is also a drab lover, and when Lucy finally tastes one of his unsatisfactory kisses, she is thrown into a panic by the prospect of another meeting with George. They meet again, and George kisses her again, with the result that Lucy deems George impossible and Vyse intolerable and breaks her engagement to the latter with the resolve never to marry anyone.

Clearly Forster is on a different, more wholeheartedly comic, course in this novel, and the denouement fulfills the tradition of romantic comedy, the inevitable marriage of Lucy and George being brought about through the ministrations of a lady who casts off her role as an apparently irredeemable snob–cousin Charlotte. What Forster says of the Honeychurch house, Windy Corner, might almost be said of the novel: "One might laugh at the house, but one never shuddered." Despite the play of Forster's wit throughout the novel and the sympathy he extends to a girl as silly as Lucy, the reader does shudder occasionally. Two murders, the real one Lucy sees and a supposed one, interrupt the proceedings. The latter is a rumor, bruited about by a clergyman named Eager, that Mr. Emerson has murdered his wife. The charge is baseless and seems to have been injected to deepen Emerson's character as a man of sorrows. The real death is even more gratuitous–unless it is meant to validate George Emerson's seriousness and dependability.

Events lead Lucy into a series of lies which she supposes to be little white ones but which threaten general unhappiness, until Mr. Emerson, whom she has led to believe that she still intends to marry Vyse, induces heart's truth and persuades her to marry George. The novel ends with the honeymooners back in Florence speculating on Charlotte's motive in bringing about Lucy's climactic meeting with Mr. Emerson. They conclude that "she fought us on the surface, and yet she hoped."

Mr. Emerson, in two respects at least, echoes the writer of the same name. He is convinced of the importance of discovering Nature, and he is an apostle of self-trust. A good man, he grows tedious after the initial chapter, functioning finally as his son's advocate. George himself never quite comes into focus, and the reader is forced to accept on faith Charlotte's change of heart. The lightest of Forster's novels, *A Room with a View*–had it been lighter yet and avoided the rather heavy-handed symbolism of the "view" and the dark–might not have turned out to be the weakest of the five novels Forster published in his lifetime.

Howards End · *Howards End*, Forster's most ambitious novel, recounts the adventures of two sisters, Margaret and Helen Schlegel, after two encounters with people not of their quiet, cultivated London set. At the beginning, while a guest at the country home of the Wilcoxes (a family the Schlegels had met while traveling abroad), Helen has become engaged–at least in her own mind–to one of the Wilcox sons, Paul. Her visit and engagement end awkwardly when her aunt whisks her back to London. The second incident grows out of Helen's inadvertently taking home from the theater the umbrella of a bank clerk named Leonard Bast. Standing "at the extreme verge of gentility," Leonard wishes to approach closer. The idealistic Schlegels appreciate the impulse and strike up an acquaintance. Meanwhile, the Wilcox connection is reestablished when the Wilcoxes rent a flat across from the house where the Schlegels, including younger brother Tibby, live, and Margaret, the oldest Schlegel, comes to know Mrs. Wilcox.

A quiet, even dull woman, Ruth Wilcox is an utterly charitable person who conveys to Margaret "the idea of greatness." Her husband Henry, a prosperous businessman, and the three Wilcox children–young adults like Helen and Tibby–radiate energy, good humor, and physical health but lack wit, grace, and any sense of beauty. Suddenly, a quarter of the way through the novel, Ruth Wilcox dies.

In marrying Henry Wilcox, Margaret proves very nearly as improvident as Lilia Herriton or Rickie Elliot. The two have little in common, and before long a series of fortuitous events shakes their precarious union. As a result of offhand bad advice from Henry, duly passed on by the Schlegel sisters, Leonard Bast loses his job. Leonard makes a pilgrimage to Oniton, one of several Wilcox estates on which Henry and

Margaret are living. Unfortunately, Leonard chooses to bring along his unbecoming common-law wife, who turns out to be a former mistress of Henry Wilcox. When Henry angrily turns the Basts away, the conscience-stricken Helen insists on trying to compensate Bast. Like Stephen Wonham, he indignantly refuses her money. The impulsive and emotionally overwrought Helen refuses to abandon him. Later Helen disappears into Germany for a time; on her return Margaret discovers that she has conceived a son by Leonard.

When Margaret relays to her husband Helen's request that she be permitted to stay at the unused Howards End for one night, he indignantly refuses, and Margaret realizes that Henry, the betrayer of his own first wife, is unrepentant in his maintenance of a moral double standard. One tragic scene remains. Leonard appears at Howards End to beg forgiveness for sinning with Helen, Charles Wilcox (Henry's other son) totally misunderstands the intruder's motive and strikes him down with the flat of a sword, and Leonard's weak heart gives way. Charles is convicted of manslaughter, and at the end, Margaret, Helen and her child, and the broken-spirited Henry are living together at Howards End.

The reader will have noted similarities to Forster's first two published novels—the melodrama, the improbable coincidences, the often awkward modulations between comic and tragic tone, and so on. The pattern of events in *Howards End*, on the other hand, is both more richly and less intrusively symbolic. As many critics have observed, this is a novel about England, written in the uneasy pre-World War I years of growing antagonism between Germany and England. Forster permits himself a series of meditations on, paeans of praise to, his native isle in the manner of John of Gaunt's "This blessed plot, this earth, this realm, this England" speech in William Shakespeare's *Richard II* (1595-1596). At the same time, Forster clearly intimates that England is also the Wilcoxes—insular in their outlook, stolid in their prejudices, merciless in their advocacy of the class structure. The Schlegel sisters spring from a German father and revere German Romantic culture. Chapter 5 of the novel celebrates their (and Forster's) extraordinary sensitivity to Ludwig van Beethoven; it is after a performance of the *Fifth Symphony* that Helen takes Leonard's umbrella.

Margaret also loves England, typified by Howards End, which is no ancient seat of the Wilcoxes but a property which had belonged to Mrs. Wilcox herself, even though she sometimes seems to be amid alien corn there. England, Forster seems to say, needs to unite the best in its Wilcoxes, its providers and healthy consumers of material goods, with the Schlegel principle, expressed in the love of art and civilized discussion. By themselves the Schlegels are ineffectual. They can only watch helplessly as commercial development dooms their London house. After Helen has been carried away by her feeling for Leonard's plight, she flees to her father's ancestral home but cannot live there. Only at Howards End can she live securely and watch her child grow up.

As a symbol for England and for the possibilities of a balanced life, Howards End might seem to have some deficiencies. It is lacking in beauty and tradition. It has become the seat of a philistine family, for even the saintly Ruth demonstrates no artistic interest more highly developed than a fondness for flowers and for a certain adjacent meadow in the early morning. On her first visit to Howards End, Helen Schlegel sees more of nature's beauties than any of the Wilcoxes, who are preoccupied with croquet, tennis, and "calisthenic exercises on a machine that is tacked on to a greengage-tree," ever perceive.

The agent who renders Howards End truly habitable is an uneducated farm woman who refuses to accept her "place." When Margaret first visits Howards End, where, it is thought, they will *not* make their home, she finds Miss Avery there. The old woman, who for a second mistakes Margaret for the first Mrs. Wilcox, has taken it upon herself to guard the empty house. Her presumptuousness, which in the past has taken the form of wedding gifts to both Henry's daughter and daughter-in-law—gaucheries the Wilcoxes are quick to condemn—extends shortly thereafter to unpacking the Schlegel books and other personal belongings, which have been stored there following the expiration of the lease on the London house. After ranging the Schlegel library in bookcases and arranging the Schlegel furniture to suit herself, the woman declines to accept even polite criticism: "You think that you won't come back to live here, Mrs. Wilcox, but you will."

Thus it is an intuitive country person who joins the half-foreign Schlegel culture to the native Wilcox stock. Miss Avery also sends over a country boy, Tom, after Helen and Margaret, in defiance of Henry, spend a night together at Howards End. "Please, I am the milk," says Tom, speaking more truth than he knows. As in *Where Angels Fear to Tread*, the milk is spiritual as well as physical nourishment. Peopled with such life-affirming folk, Howards End becomes a sustaining place, an embodiment of what English life might yet be if the deepening disorder of 1910 is somehow averted. Finally won over to permitting Helen to reside there—and thus at least tacitly acknowledging his own fornication—Henry decrees that at his death the property will pass to Margaret; Ruth Wilcox herself had wanted to give it to her.

The motto of *Howards End* is "Only connect." In the house, "the prose and passion" of life, the Wilcox and Schlegel principles, are joined through the ministrations of another of Forster's characters willing to defy the class system in the interests of a nobler order.

The central symbol of *Howards End* is hay. Ruth Wilcox is first observed "smelling hay," a product that the naturally fertile estate produces in abundance. The rest of the Wilcoxes, Miss Avery at one point observes maliciously, all suffer from hay fever. Forster uses the hay very much as Walt Whitman, whom he occasionally quotes and from whom he appropriated the title of his final novel, uses the grass: to suggest life, sustenance, hope, democracy. At the end of the novel, the chastened Henry's case of hay fever seems to have subsided when Helen, her baby, and Tom burst in from the meadow, with Helen exclaiming, "It'll be such a crop of hay as never!"

Maurice · Written a few years after *Howards End*, *Maurice* did not see print until the year following Forster's death. In a later "terminal note" to this novel of a homosexual, Forster observed a change in the public's reaction to this subject from one of "ignorance and terror" at the time he wrote it to "familiarity and contempt" in his old age, so he continued to withhold the work. Maurice Hall also defies the class system, for his sexual partner is a gamekeeper on a college classmate's estate. Given the rigid penal code of the time, the novel is also about criminality.

Aside from his sexual orientation, Maurice resembles his creator very little, being rather ordinary in intellect, little drawn to the arts, and rather robust physically. Whereas Rickie Elliot had been effeminate, his deformed foot a symbolic impediment to satisfactory heterosexuality, Maurice seems quite "normal" to his friends. His college friend Clive Durham, leaning somewhat to homosexuality in college, ironically changes after an illness and a trip to Greece, and marries. The Durhams are gentlefolk, though somewhat reduced, and Maurice has gotten on well with them, but Clive's marriage drives a wedge between them. After indulging in, and apparently escaping from, a furtive but passionate affair with Alec Scudder, their gamekeeper, Maurice suffers a blackmail threat from his former lover, but in the end Alec proves true, and instead of emigrating with whatever conscience money he might have extracted, Alec returns to the Durham estate, where, in the boathouse, the two come together again. At the end, Maurice's revelation to the conventionally horrified Clive leaves the latter trying "to devise some method of concealing the truth from Anne"– his wife.

Maurice demonstrates Forster's conviction that the desire for loving human rela- tions is proof against the snobbery of all social classes. Although it could not be printed when it was written, the novel now seems more dated than Forster's other works, perhaps because its style is plain and drab. It obviously suffers from its lack of a contemporary audience, although Forster showed it to Lytton Strachey and received some constructive advice. Significantly, when Oliver Stallybrass, the editor of the Abinger Edition of Forster's works, assembled his favorite quotations from Forster, he could find nothing in *Maurice* worth including.

A Passage to India · Although Forster committed himself wholeheartedly to friend- ship, it cannot be called the central theme of any of his novels until *A Passage to India.* The friendship of Rickie Elliot and Stewart Ansell, while vital to the former's devel- opment and self-discovery, is subordinated to the theme of brotherhood, in its familial sense, and Rickie can find no basis for friendship with Stephen. The incipient friendship of Margaret Schlegel and Ruth Wilcox is aborted by the latter's death. *A Passage to India*, while treating of brotherhood in its largest sense, is at heart a novel of friendship and its possibilities in the context of a racially and religiously fragmented society.

Beginning with the visit to India of the mother and fiancé of Ronnie Heaslop, the young colonial magistrate, and the complications of their encounters with a few educated natives, the narrative comes to focus on the friendship that, as a conse- quence, waxes and wanes between the English schoolmaster Cyril Fielding and the young Muslim Dr. Aziz. Forster dedicated the book to another Anglo-Indian friend- ship: his own with Syed Ross Masood, who first knew Forster as his tutor in Latin prior to Masood's entrance to Oxford in 1906, and who provided the impetus for Forster's own initial passage to India a few years later. Since Anglo-Indian prejudice was one of the loquacious Masood's favorite subjects, Forster understood it well by the time he came to write the novel. Indeed, his friendship with Masood demonstrated the possibility of such a relationship surviving the strains imposed on it by one partner's determination to pull no punches in discussing it.

Aziz, accused by Ronnie's fiancé Adela Quested of assaulting, or at least offending her (for she remains vague about the matter throughout), in a cave they are exploring, is a less masterful and self-confident figure than Masood, and the reader knows all along that there must be some mistake. Adela has seen how Ronnie's Indian service has exacerbated the weaker aspects of his character, and she has broken off their engagement, but she is not, as Aziz affects to believe, a love-starved female—at least not in the crude sense Aziz intends.

Forster draws an unforgettable picture of the tensions between the colonial rulers and the Indian professional class. The most idealistic Englishmen, it seems, succumb to the prevailing intolerance. It is an effort to consider the natives as human, as when Ronnie, told by his mother, Mrs. Moore, of her meeting with a young doctor, replies: "I know of no young doctor in Chandrapore," though once he learns that his mother has actually been consorting with a Muslim, he identifies him readily enough.

An exception to the rule is Fielding, already over forty when he came to India and a continuing believer in "a globe of men who are trying to reach one another." When Aziz' trial divides the community more openly and dangerously than usual, Fielding supports the young doctor–a move that assures the enmity of the English without guaranteeing the affection of the skeptical Indians. After Adela withdraws her charges against Aziz, the intimacy between the two men reaches its height; almost immediately, however, they quarrel over Aziz' determination to make his tormentor pay damages.

Fielding cannot persuade Aziz to show mercy, but Mrs. Moore can, even though she has left the country before the trial and in fact has died on her return passage. For the sake of the mother of the detested man whom Aziz still believes Adela will marry, he spares the young woman, knowing that the English will interpret this decision as an indication of guilt. With Adela finally gone, Aziz mistakenly assumes that Fielding, now contemplating a visit to England, intends to marry her himself. When the friends meet again two years later, the old frankness and intimacy has been shattered. Although Fielding has married, his bride is the daughter of Mrs. Moore.

The final chapter is a particularly excellent one. As Aziz and Fielding ride horses together, the former vowing that they can be friends but only after the Indians "drive every blasted Englishman into the sea," the horses swerve apart, as if to counter Fielding's objection. Not religion, land, people, even animals want the friendship now. It is difficult to escape the conclusion that under imperial conditions no rapprochement is possible.

Much of the interest in this novel has centered on Mrs. Moore, a rather querulous old woman with a role not much larger than Mrs. Wilcox's in *Howards End.* Although she joins the roster of Forster's admirable characters who defy the taboos that divide people, she refuses to involve herself in the Aziz trial. Nevertheless, the Indians make a legend out of her and invest her with numinous powers. Critics have tended to regard her as a more successful character than Mrs. Wilcox. Part of the explanation may lie in Forster's decision to allow the reader to see her not only at first hand but also through the eyes of the Indians. If their view of Mrs. Moore is partly illusion, the illusion itself–like the more familiar illusions of the English–becomes itself a part of the truth of the situation. It is one of Forster's virtues that he knows and communicates the often conflicting values and attitudes of native Indians.

Nor is the Indian version of Mrs. Moore completely illusory, for in addition to her openness and candor, Mrs. Moore in one respect surpasses all the Europeans, even the gentle Fielding. She loves and respects life, especially unfamiliar life. It is illuminating to contrast her attitude with that of two incidental characters–missionaries who live among the people and never come to the whites' club. They measure up to their calling very well for Forster clergymen, allowing that God has room in his mansions for all people. On the subject of animals they are not so sure; Mr. Sorley, the more liberal of the two, opts for monkeys but stumbles over wasps. Mrs. Moore, more alert to the native birds and animals than she is to many people, is even sympathetic to a wasp ("Pretty dear") that has flown into the house. It is doubtless significant that the wasp is very different from the European type. Long after she is gone, Professor Godbole, Aziz' Hindu friend, remembers her in connection with the wasp. Love of humble forms of life, which the other Westerners in the novel notice only as irritations if at all, is for the Indians of Forster's *A Passage to India* a reliable indication of spirituality.

The sensitivity of Mrs. Moore and the good will of Fielding seem like frail counterweights to the prevailing cynicism and prejudice which stifle the necessarily furtive social initiatives of well-intentioned victims such as Aziz. If these flawed but genuine human beings have little impact on the morally bankrupt society in which they move, they have for more than half a century heartened readers of like aspirations.

Robert P. Ellis

Other major works
SHORT FICTION: *The Celestial Omnibus and Other Stories,* 1911; *The Eternal Moment and Other Stories,* 1928; *The Collected Tales of E. M. Forster,* 1947; *The Life to Come and Other Stories,* 1972; *Arctic Summer and Other Fiction,* 1980.
PLAY: *Billy Budd,* pb. 1951 (libretto; with Eric Crozier).
NONFICTION: *Alexandria: A History and a Guide,* 1922; *Pharos and Pharillon,* 1923; *Aspects of the Novel,* 1927; *Goldsworthy Lowes Dickinson,* 1934; *Abinger Harvest—A Miscellany,* 1936; *Virginia Woolf,* 1942; *Development of English Prose Between 1918 and 1939,* 1945; *Two Cheers for Democracy,* 1951; *The Hill of Devi,* 1953; *Marianne Thornton: A Domestic Biography, 1797-1887,* 1956; *Commonplace Book,* 1978.

Bibliography
Beauman, Nicola. *E. M. Forster: A Biography.* New York: Knopf, 1994. A well-informed biography drawing on new archival material. Includes a family tree.
Crews, Frederick J. *E. M. Forster: The Perils of Humanism.* Princeton, N.J.: Princeton University Press, 1962. This comprehensive, readable introduction to Forster's novels and short stories argues that, although Forster's mind is anchored in liberalism, he is always aware of the liberal tradition's weaknesses. Claims that "his artistic growth runs parallel to his disappointments with humanism." Although he is agnostic and anti-Christian, Forster's "books are religious in their concern with the meaning of life" and the virtues of private freedom, diversity, personal relationships, sincerity, art, and sensitivity to the natural world and its traditions. Indexed.
Furbank, P. N. *E. M. Forster: A Life.* London: Secker & Warburg, 1978. This major biographical study written by another famous novelist is readable and perceptive in its analyses of the novels, short stories, and criticism. Finds pertinent influences on Forster's writing in his childhood, adolescent, and early adult years. An index is included.
Gransden, K. W. *E. M. Forster.* 1962. 2d ed. New York: Grove Press, 1970. This insightful study summarizes Forster's career, the influences of Samuel Butler, George Meredith, and Jane Austen, and his novels and short fiction. Included is a postscript to the 1970 revised edition which celebrates Forster's tenacious hold on his readers as well as selective primary/secondary bibliographies and an index.
Iago, Mary. *E. M. Forster: A Literary Life.* New York: St. Martin's Press, 1995. A succinct study of Forster's novels and work for the BBC. Helpful notes.
McConkey, James. *The Novels of E. M. Forster.* Hamden, Conn.: Archon Books, 1957. This historically important study looks forward to the 1960's emphasis on textual and philosophical criticism of Forster's writings. Analyzes the author's use of point of view, fantasy, images, symbols, and rhythms and demonstrates that both the transcendent and the physical worlds are always present in Forster. Selective primary and secondary bibliographies and an index conclude the book.
Trilling, Lionel. *E. M. Forster.* Norfolk, Conn.: New Directions, 1943. This is one of

the most important, most influential assessments of Forster ever written. Trilling's discussion of Forster and the liberal imagination went far to influence a revival of interest in the work. Considers Forster's novels, short fiction, and criticism to show that his work is to be explained in terms of his emphasis upon the disastrous effects of "the undeveloped heart." An index is included.

John Fowles

Born: Leigh-on-Sea, England; March 31, 1926

Principal long fiction · *The Collector*, 1963; *The Magus*, 1965, 1977; *The French Lieutenant's Woman*, 1969; *Daniel Martin*, 1977; *Mantissa*, 1982; *A Maggot*, 1985.

Other literary forms · In addition to his novels, John Fowles has written philosophy, essays for scholarly and popular audiences, criticism, poetry, and short fiction. He has also translated several other writers into English. *The Aristos: A Self-Portrait in Ideas*, published in 1964, is his philosophical "self-portrait in ideas." Patterned after writings of Heraclitus, the fifth century B.C.E. Greek philosopher, it reflects Fowles's philosophical stance, outlining many of the views which Fowles expresses more fully and artistically in his fiction. His collected poetry is published in *Poems* (1973); much of it reflects his period of residence in Greece, the major setting for *The Magus*. His longer nonfiction pieces reflect his love for and interest in nature: *Shipwreck* (1974), a text to accompany the photographs of shipwrecks along the English coast near Fowles's home, and *Lyme Regis Camera* (1990), a text to accompany photographs of the town, its inhabitants, and its immediate environs; *Islands* (1978), about the Scilly Islands off the English coast, but more about the nature of islands as a metaphor for literature and the writer; *The Tree* (1980), an extension of the same theme with emphasis on the tree as representative of all nature; and *The Enigma of Stonehenge* (1980), a further extension of nature to encompass the mystery of a sacred place. All these themes are touched on in the varied pieces collected in *Wormholes: Essays and Occasional Writings* (1998). These themes find definition and elaboration in his fiction. Fowles's only collection of short fiction, *The Ebony Tower*, includes a novella from which the title is taken, three short stories, and a translation of a medieval romance with a "Personal Note" that comments on its relation to his fiction. The collection, entitled *Variations* in manuscript, also reflects Fowles's central themes in the longer fiction.

Achievements · Fowles's place in literary history is difficult to assess. He has established an excellent reputation as a writer of serious fiction, one who will continue to be read. He continues to receive the notice of numerous critics; more than a dozen books have been published about him. Fowles, however, is no "ivory tower" author; he enjoys a wide readership, and several of his novels have been made into motion pictures, including *The Collector*, *The Magus*, and *The French Lieutenant's Woman*. Readers can expect to find in Fowles's works a good story with a passionate love interest, complex characters, a healthy smattering of philosophy, all presented within the context of the plot. Critics can slice away multiple layers to get at the wheels-within-wheels of meaning on existential, historical, philosophical, psychological, and myriad other levels.

Because Fowles rarely tells the same story in the same way, genre is a topic of much discussion among his critics. His fiction reflects not only his experimentation with genre, but also his questioning of authorial voice, the continuum of time, moments out of time, split viewpoint, a story without an ending, a story with a choice of endings, and still another with a revised ending. Despite such experimentation, most of the novels are in many ways quite old-fashioned, reflecting the ancient boy-meets-girl, boy-loses-girl, boy-seeks-to-find-girl-again-and-in-so-doing-finds-himself quest motif that characterizes so much fiction. They are fairly straightforward "good reads" without the dizzying experimentation of a James Joyce to make them virtually inaccessible to all but the most diligent reader. On any level, Fowles is enjoyable, and what reserves him a place among memorable writers is that he is discoverable, again and again.

Biography · John Fowles was born in Leigh-on-Sea, Essex, England, on March 31, 1926, to Robert and Gladys Richards Fowles. During World War II, his family was evacuated to the more remote village of Ippeplen, South Devon, and it was there that Fowles discovered the beauty of the country of Devonshire, his "English Garden of Eden" that figures so prominently in other guises in his fiction. During that same period, he was a student at the exclusive Bedford School, where he studied German and French literature, eventually rising to the stature of head boy, a position of great power over the other boys in the school. It was there that he got his first taste of literature, which he loved, and power, which he despised. The knowledge of both was influential in his own writing.

From Bedford, he went into military service, spending six months at the University of Edinburgh and completing training as a lieutenant in the merchant marine just as the war was ending. Following the war, he continued his education in German and more particularly French literature at New College, Oxford University; he graduated in 1950 with a B.A. with honors. His fiction owes many debts to his study of French literature, particularly his interest in existentialism as espoused by Jean-Paul Sartre and Albert Camus and his knowledge of the Celtic romance, from which stems his expressed belief that all literature has its roots in the theme of the quest.

Upon graduation, Fowles taught English at the University of Poitiers. After a year at Poitiers, he took a job teaching English to Greek boys on the island of Spetsai in the Aegean Sea. The school, the island, the aura of Greece, and the thoughts of the young teacher became the material for *The Magus*, his first novel (although not published first). It was also on Spetsai that he met Elizabeth Whitton, whom he married three years later. For Fowles, Greece was the land of myth, the other world, the place of the quest. Leaving Greece, Fowles suffered the loss of another Eden, but that loss inspired him to write. While writing, he continued to teach in and around London until the publication of *The Collector* in 1963, the success of which enabled him to leave teaching and devote himself full time to writing. The following year he published *The Aristos*, and in 1965 he finally published *The Magus*, twelve years after its conception.

A year later, he and Elizabeth moved to Lyme Regis in Dorset, a small seaside town away from London where they have continued to live. First living on a rundown farm, the Fowleses later moved to an eighteenth century house overlooking Lyme Bay. The dairy, the house, and the town of Lyme figure prominently in his third novel, *The French Lieutenant's Woman*, a work that established his international reputation. Following its success were his *Poems, The Ebony Tower, Daniel Martin*, the revised version of *The Magus, Mantissa*, and *A Maggot*.

Fowles's love of nature is evident in his writing as well as his life, especially in such nonfiction works as *Islands* and *The Tree*. At his home in Lyme Regis, he oversees a large, wild garden overlooking Lyme Bay and fosters the natural development of the flora, passions that have not died since boyhood. One that has died, however, is the collection of living things. Once a collector of butterflies, like his character Frederick Clegg in *The Collector*, Fowles now abhors such activities. Rather, he collects Victorian postcards and antique china, reads voluminously, goes to London infrequently, and shares a very private life with his wife, who is his best critic. It was a life he very much enjoyed until he suffered a mild stroke in early 1988. Although the stroke caused no permanent damage, it left him depressed by the sudden specter of death and by a resulting loss of creative energies. By the mid-1990's most readers who had followed Fowles's career did not expect him to add to his body of work, but he said at the Fowles seminar in Lyme Regis in 1996 that he was again at work.

Analysis · John Fowles's fiction has one theme: the quest of his protagonists for self-knowledge. Such a quest is not easy in the modern world because, as many other modern authors have shown, the contemporary quester is cut off from the traditions and rituals of the past that gave people a purpose and sense of direction. Still, desiring the freedom of individual choice which requires an understanding of self, the Fowlesian protagonist moves through the pattern of the quest as best he can.

Following the tradition of the quest theme found in the medieval romance, which Fowles sees as central to his and all of Western fiction, the quester embarks on the journey in response to a call to adventure. Because the quester is in a state of longing for the adventure, oftentimes not recognized as such by him, he readily responds to the call. The call takes him across a threshold into another world, the land of myth. For Fowles's questers, this other world is always described as a remote, out-of-the-way place, often lush and primeval. In this place the quester meets the usual dragons, which, in modern terms, are presented as a series of challenges that he must overcome if he is to proceed.

Guided by the figure of the wise old man who has gone before him and can show the way, the quester gradually acquires self-knowledge, which brings freedom of choice. For Fowles's heroes, this choice always centers around the acceptance of a woman. If the quester has attained self-knowledge, he is able to choose the woman— that is, to know and experience love, signifying wholeness. Then, he must make the crossing back into the real world and continue to live and choose freely, given the understanding the quest has provided.

What separates the journey of the Fowlesian hero from the journey of the medieval hero is that much of it has become internalized. Where the quester of old did actual battle with dragons, monsters, and mysterious knights, the modern quester is far removed from such obvious obstacles. He cannot see the enemy in front of him, since it is often within him, keeping him frozen in a state of inertia that prevents him from questing. The modern journey, then, can be seen in psychological terms; while the events are externalized, the results are measured by the growth of the protagonist toward wholeness or self-knowledge. Thus, as Joseph Campbell describes in *The Hero with a Thousand Faces* (1949), "The problem is . . . nothing if not that of making it possible for men and women to come to full human maturity through the conditions of contemporary life."

Each of Fowles's protagonist/heroes follows the pattern of the mythic quest. Each journeys to a strange land (the unconscious): the Greek island of Phraxos and Conchis's more secret domain for Nicholas Urfe, the isolated countryside house for Frederick Clegg, the primitive Undercliff of Lyme Regis for Charles Smithson, the hidden manor in the forests of Brittany for David Williams, the lost landscape of his youth and the journey up the Nile for Daniel Martin, the interior space of the mind of Miles Green, and the ancient landscape of Stonehenge plus the mystery of the cave for Bartholomew and Rebecca. Each undergoes a series of trials (the warring aspects of his personality) intended to bring him to a state of self-consciousness. With the exception of Clegg, whose story represents the antiquest, each has the aid of a guide (the mythical wise old man): Conchis for Nicholas, Dr. Grogan for Charles, Breasley for David Williams; Professor Kirnberger, Georg Lukács, a Rembrandt self-portrait, and others for Daniel Martin; the various manifestations of the muse for Miles Green; and Holy Mother Wisdom for Bartholomew and Rebecca. Each has an encounter with a woman (representative of "the other half" needed for wholeness): Alison for Nicholas, Miranda for Frederick, Sarah for Charles, the "Mouse" for David, Jane for Daniel, Erato for Miles, Holy Mother Wisdom for Bartholomew, and Bartholomew for Rebecca. The ability of the quester to calm or assimilate the warring aspects within him, to come to an understanding of himself, and as a result reach out to the experience of love with the woman, represents the degree of growth of each.

Feeling strongly that his fiction must be used as "a method of propagating [his] views of life" to bring a vision of cosmic order out of modern chaos, Fowles sees himself on a journey to accomplish this task. An examination of his fiction reveals the way in which he tackles the task, providing his readers with a description of the journey that they, too, can take.

The Magus · *The Magus* was Fowles's first novel (although it was published after *The Collector*), and it remains his most popular. Fowles himself was so intrigued by the novel that he spent twelve years writing it, and even after publication, produced a revised version in 1977 because he was dissatisfied with parts of it. While some critics see changes between the original and the revision, there is little substantive difference between the two books beyond the addition of more explicit sexual scenes and the elaboration of several sections; thus the discussion of one suffices for the other.

The story derives from Fowles's period of teaching in Greece, and its protagonist, Nicholas Urfe, is much like Fowles in temperament and situation. As is often the case with Fowles, his fiction describes protagonists of the same age and temperament as himself at the time of his writing; thus an examination of the corpus reveals a maturing hero as well as a maturing author. In this first novel, Nicholas is twenty-five, Oxford-educated, attracted to existentialism, and bored with life. He is the typical Fowlesian protagonist, wellborn and bred, aimless, and ripe for the quest.

Discontented with his teaching job in England, he, like Fowles, jumps at the opportunity to teach in Greece. His subconscious desire is for a "new land, a new race, a new language," which the quest will provide. Just before going, he meets Alison, who is to become the important woman in his life, although it takes many pages and much questing through the labyrinth of self-knowledge on Phraxos for Nicholas to realize this. Alison, as the intuitive female, the feeling side Nicholas needs for wholeness, recognizes the importance of their relationship from the beginning, while Nicholas, representing reason, does not. In discussing the elements of the quest that bring Nicholas to an understanding and acceptance of the feeling side of himself which allows him to experience love, one can chart the pattern of the quest which Fowles presents in variations in all his fiction.

On Phraxos, Nicholas responds to the call to adventure embodied in the voice of a girl, the song of a bird, and some passages of poetry, especially four lines from T. S. Eliot: "We shall not cease from exploration/ And the end of all our exploring/ Will be to arrive where we started/ And know the place for the first time." These lines state the mystery of the journey that awaits him: to quest outside so as to come back to himself with understanding. Put another way, it is the yearning in humankind for the return to the harmony of the Garden of Eden. It is, as well, the thesis of *Four Quartets* (1943), which solves for Eliot the problem of the wasteland. Finally, it is the concept that motivates almost all of Fowles's questers, beginning with Nicholas.

Crossing the threshold beyond the *Salle d'Attente*, or Waiting Room, to the domain of myth at Bournai, Nicholas meets Conchis, his guide through the quest. Under Conchis's tutelage, Nicholas's "discoveries" begin. Nicholas understands that something significant is about to happen, that it is somehow linked to Alison, and that it restores his desire to live. Conchis exposes Nicholas to a series of experiences to teach and test him. Some he describes for Nicholas; others make Nicholas an observer; and still others give him an active, sometimes frightening role. In all, whether he is repulsed, fascinated, or puzzled, Nicholas wants more, allowing himself to be led deeper and deeper into the mysteries. These culminate in the trial scene, during which Nicholas is examined, his personality dissected, his person humiliated. Finally, he is put to the test of his ability to choose. Longing to punish Lily/Julie, the personification of woman Nicholas romantically and unrealistically longs for, he is given the opportunity at the end of the trial to flog her. His understanding that his freedom of choice gives him the power to resist the predictable, to go against the dictates of reason alone and follow the voice of the unconscious, signifies that he has become one of the "elect." Nicholas emerges from the underground chamber reborn into a higher state of consciousness. He must then make the return crossing into the real world.

To begin the return journey, he is given a glimpse of Alison, although he has been led to believe that she has committed suicide. Realizing that she is alive and that she offers him "a mirror that did not lie" in her "constant reality," he understands that the remainder of the quest must be toward a reunion with Alison. Apparently, however, he is not yet worthy of her, being dominated still by the ratiocinative side of himself, that part that seeks to unravel logically the mystery that Conchis presents. Thus, on his return to London he is put through additional tests until one day, completely unsuspecting of her arrival, he sees Alison again and follows her to Regents Park for their reunion.

Signifying the experience of the Garden of Eden when man and woman existed in wholeness, the park provides an appropriate setting for their reunion. Echoing lines from Eliot, Nicholas has arrived where he started. Now he must prove that he is worthy of Alison, that he can accept the love she once offered freely, but that he must win her just as Orpheus attempted to win Eurydice from the dead. Becoming his own magus, he acts out a drama of his own making, challenging Alison to meet him at Paddington Station, where their journey together will begin. Unlike Orpheus, who was unsuccessful in bringing Eurydice from the dead, Nicholas has the confidence gained in his quest to leave Alison and not look back, knowing that she will be at the train station to meet him. While there is some question among critics as to whether Nicholas and Alison do meet and continue their journey together, Fowles has indicated that "Alison is the woman he will first try to love." Certainly, in either case it is the element of mystery that is important, not whether Nicholas wins this particular woman. The significance is in his yearning for her, demonstrating that he has learned to accept and give love, that he has journeyed toward wholeness.

What makes such a journey significant for the reader is that he or she can partake of the experience as an insider, not as an outsider. This results from the narrative technique Fowles employs. In Fowles's first-person narrative, Nicholas reveals only what he knows at any particular point on his journey; thus the reader sees only what Nicholas sees. Not able to see with any more sophistication than Nicholas the twistings and turnings of Conchis's "godgame," the reader must do exactly what Nicholas does: try to unravel the mystery in its literal sense rather than understand the "mystery" in its sacred sense. Believing every rational explanation Nicholas posits, one learns as he learns. As his own magus, Nicholas leads the reader into the mystery he was led into, not spoiling one's sense of discovery as his was not spoiled, and providing one with the experience of the journey as he experienced it. Of course, behind Nicholas is the master magus Fowles, whose design is to lead each reader to his own essential mysteries. The technique provides an immediacy that allows each reader to take the journey toward self-discovery; the novel provides a paradigm by which the mystery of Fowles's other novels can be deciphered.

The Collector · *The Collector*, in sharp contrast to *The Magus*, presents the other side of the coin, sounding a warning. Here the protagonist is the antihero, his captured lady, the heroine. She goes on the journey he is incapable of taking, which, in his incapacity to understand her or himself, he aborts.

Frederick Clegg, the protagonist, shares many similarities with Nicholas of *The Magus*. Each is orphaned, in his twenties, and aimless. Each forms an attachment to a blond, gray-eyed woman, and each goes to a remote land in which the relationship with this woman is explored. Each is given the opportunity to become a quester in that land, and each tells a first-person narrative of the experience. In each, the narrative structure is circular, such that the novel arrives where it started.

The major difference, of course, is that Nicholas journeys toward wholeness; Clegg, while given the same opportunities, does not. The reason for Clegg's failure lies in the fact that he cannot understand the mythic signals; thus, he cannot move beyond his present confused state. The novel begins and ends in psychic darkness; the hero does not grow or develop. Yet, while Clegg remains unchanged, the captive Miranda, trapped as Clegg's prisoner, undergoes a transforming experience that puts her on the path of the quest Clegg is unable to take. The tragedy is not so much Clegg's lack of growth as it is the futility of Miranda's growth in view of the fact that she cannot apply in the real world the lessons learned in her quest. She is incapable even of having any beneficial effect on her captor.

Part of the problem between Miranda and Clegg lies in the differences in their cultural backgrounds. Miranda has the background of a typical Fowlesian quester in terms of education and social standing; Clegg's, however, is atypical in his lower-class roots and lack of education. Part of the thesis of this novel is the clash between these two as representative of the clash between the "Many" and the "Few," which Fowles describes in detail in *The Aristos*. The novel, presented as a divided narrative told first by Clegg and then by Miranda, depicts in its very structure the division between Miranda and Clegg that cannot be bridged.

The first problem for Clegg as a quester is that he captures the object of his quest, keeping her prisoner in a hidden cellar. In psychological terms, Miranda, the feeling side of Clegg, is kept in the cellar "down there," which disallows the possibility of union. Clegg remains a divided man, living above in the house, with Miranda imprisoned below. Miranda, however, discovers that her "tomb" becomes a "womb" in which she grows in self-consciousness and understanding. Thus, the quest centers on her and the antiquest centers on Clegg.

As a butterfly collector, Clegg sees Miranda as his prize acquisition. He hopes that she will come to love him as he thinks he loves her, but what he really prizes is her beauty, which he has hoped to capture and keep as he would a butterfly's. When she begins to turn ugly in her vitality and lack of conformity to his preconceived notions of her, she falls off the pedestal on which he has placed her, and he then feels no compunction about forcing her to pose for nude photographs.

Clegg's problems are many. On a social level, he identifies too closely with what he sees as the judgment of the middle class against his lower-class background. On a psychological level, he is possessed by images from his past, the negative influences of his aunt, and his upbringing. His sexual fears and feelings of personal inadequacy combine to lock him into his own psychological prison in the same way that he locks Miranda in hers. Trapped in his internal prison, the outward presence of Miranda remains just that, outside of himself, and he cannot benefit from her proximity. She, however, while externally imprisoned by Clegg, is not prevented from making the inward journey toward self-discovery. At the same time, there is within Clegg, although deeply buried, a desire to break away and move onto the mythic path, and Miranda sees that aspect of him, his essential innocence, which has caused him to be attracted to her in the first place. Nevertheless, it is too deeply buried for Miranda to extract, and his power over her becomes his obsession. When he blurts out, "I love you. It's driven me mad," he indicates the problem he faces. Love is madness when it takes the form of possession, and Clegg is possessed by his feelings in the same way that he possesses Miranda. As Miranda asserts her individuality and Clegg becomes repulsed by her, he is able to shift blame for her death to her as a direct consequence of her actions.

While Clegg learns nothing from his experience and uses his narrative to vindicate himself, Miranda uses her narrative to describe her growing understanding and sense of self-discovery, aborted by her illness and subsequent death. After her death, Clegg cleans out the cellar, restoring it to its original state before Miranda's arrival. This circular structure, returning the reader to the empty cellar, echoes the circular structure of *The Magus*, except that Clegg has learned nothing from his experience, and Nicholas has learned everything. It is not that Nicholas is essentially good and Clegg essentially bad; rather, it is that Clegg cannot respond to the good within him, rendered inert by the warring aspects of his personality. Clegg's failure to respond to the elements of the quest is, in some respects, more tragic than Miranda's death, because he must continue his death-in-life existence, moving in ever-decreasing circles, never profiting or growing from the experience of life. In his next conquest, he will not aim so high; this time it will not be for love but for "the interest of the thing."

Reflecting the bleakness of Clegg's situation, the novel is filled with images of darkness. The pattern of *The Collector* is away from the light toward the darkness. Miranda's dying becomes a struggle against "the black and the black and the black" and her last words to Clegg—"the sun"—are a grim reminder of the struggle between them: the age-old struggle of the forces of light against those of darkness. Miranda's movement in the novel is upward toward light, life, and understanding; Clegg's is one of helpless descent toward darkness, evil, and psychic death.

The French Lieutenant's Woman · With *The French Lieutenant's Woman*, Fowles returns to the theme of the successful quest. Here the quester is Charles Smithson, much like Nicholas in social standing and education. The important differences between the novels are that *The French Lieutenant's Woman* is set in Victorian England and that

Charles, in his thirties, a decade older than Nicholas, reflects the older viewpoint of the author. Like Nicholas, his twentieth century counterpart, Charles is representative of his age and class. Also like Nicholas, Charles is somewhat bored with his circumstances, despite the fact that he is finally taking the proper course of marriage to the proper lady, Ernestina. Not nearly so aware of his boredom as is Nicholas, Charles is nevertheless immediately attracted to Sarah upon their first meeting, sensing instantly that she is not like other women. Meeting her again in Ware Commons and its more secret Undercliff, Charles finds in this "other world" the mythic encounter for which he unconsciously yearns. A seeker after fossils, he subconsciously fears his own extinction in the receding waters of the Victorian age, a gentleman left behind in the face of the rising tide of the Industrial Revolution.

Sarah, having recognized her uniqueness in a world of conformity, relishes her position apart from others, particularly in its ability to give her a freedom other women do not possess. As the French lieutenant's woman (a euphemism for whore), she is outside society's bonds. Capitalizing on her position, she has already begun her own quest when she meets Charles; thus, she leads him to his own path for the journey. Ernestina represents the known, the predictable, the respectable; Sarah, the opposite: the unknown, the mysterious, the forbidden. Torn between the two choices, Charles eventually comes to know himself well enough to be able to make the more hazardous choice, the one more fraught with danger, yet far more likely to lead to wholeness.

The feeling and reasoning aspects of Charles's psyche war within him. Seeking advice from Dr. Grogan, he gets the proper scientific viewpoint of Sarah and is prescribed the proper course of action: return to Ernestina. One side of Charles, the rational, longs to do so; the other side, the feeling, cannot. Thus, after much wrestling with the problem, Charles chooses Sarah, breaks his engagement to Ernestina, and returns to Sarah for what he thinks will be the beginning of their beautiful life in exile together—only to find her gone. At this point, Charles's real journey begins. Sarah has brought him to the point of resisting the predictable and recognizing his feeling side; he must now learn to live alone with such newfound knowledge.

Such a choice is not a simple one, and the reader must choose as well, for there are three "endings" in the novel. The first is not really an ending, as it comes in the middle of the book. In it, Charles rejects Sarah, marries Ernestina and lives, as it were, happily ever after. One knows, if only by the number of pages remaining in the book, that this is not really the ending; it is merely Victorian convention, which the author-god Fowles quickly steps in to tell the reader is not the actual ending. Thus, the reader passes through another hundred pages before he comes to another choice of endings, these more realistic.

The first is happy; the second is not. The endings themselves indicate the evolutionary process that Charles, as well as the novel, takes; for if one includes the hypothetical early ending, one moves from the traditional Victorian view to the emancipated view of Charles's and Sarah's union to the final existential view of the cruelty of freedom which denies Charles the happy ending. Fowles wanted his readers to accept the last ending as the right choice, but feared that they would opt for the happy ending; he was pleased when they did not.

In the first ending, the gap between Charles and Sarah is bridged through the intercession of Lalage, the child born of their one sexual encounter. The assertion that "the rock of ages can never be anything but love" offers the reader a placebo that does not effect a cure for the novel's dilemma. Fowles then enters, turns the clock back, and sets the wheels in motion for the next ending. In this one, the author-god Fowles drives off, leaving Sarah and Charles to work out their fate alone in much the same way that Conchis absconds from the "godgame" when Nicholas and Alison are reunited in *The Magus*. In both cases, Fowles is trying to demonstrate that the freedom of choice resides with the individual, not with the "author." Since Sarah fears marriage for its potential denial of her hard-won freedom and sense of individuality, she cannot accept Charles's offer to marry, nor can he accept hers of friendship in some lesser relationship. Sarah then gives Charles no choice but to leave, and in his leaving he is released from his bonds to the past, experiencing a new freedom: "It was as if he found himself reborn, though with all his adult faculties and memories." Like Nicholas in *The Magus*, the important point is not whether he wins this particular woman but that he has learned to know himself and to love another. This is what sets him apart as an individual, saves him from extinction, and propels him into the modern age.

The Ebony Tower · Intending to name his collection of short works *Variations* because of its reflection of various themes and genres presented in his longer fiction, Fowles changed the name to *The Ebony Tower* (after the title novella) when first readers thought the original title too obscure. Anyone familiar with Fowles's themes, however, immediately sees their variations in this collection. The volume contains the title novella, followed by a "Personal Note," followed by Fowles's translation of Marie de France's medieval romance *Eliduc* (c. 1150-1175), followed by three short stories: "Poor Koko," "The Enigma," and "The Cloud." In his "Personal Note," Fowles explains the inclusion of the medieval romance, relating it first to "The Ebony Tower," more generally to all of his fiction, and finally to fiction in general.

The title story describes a quester who inadvertently stumbles into the realm of myth only to find that he cannot rise to the challenge of the quest and is therefore ejected from the mythic landscape. The other three stories are all centered on enigmas or mysteries of modern life. These mysteries arise because "mystery" in the sacred sense no longer appears valid in modern humanity's existence. The movement of the stories is generally downward toward darkness, modern humankind being depicted as less and less able to take the journey of self-discovery because it is trapped in the wasteland of contemporary existence. Thus, the variations in these stories present aspects of the less-than-successful quest.

David Williams of "The Ebony Tower" leaves his comfortable home and lifestyle in England and enters the forests of Brittany, the land of the medieval romance, to face an encounter with Henry Breasley, a famous (and infamous) painter. Because David is a painter himself, he is interested in the journey from an artist's perspective; he does not anticipate the mythic encounter that awaits him in this "other" world. Within this other world, Breasley attacks the "architectonic" nature of David's work in its abstraction, in contrast to Breasley's art, which has been called "mysterious," "archetypal," and "Celtic." In defaming David's art for its rigidity and lack of feeling, Breasley serves as a guide to David. David also finds the essential woman here in the figure of Diana, "The Mouse." The two characters offer him the potential of becoming a quester. The story represents the forsaken opportunity and its aftermath.

David's problem, like that of Nicholas and Charles at the beginning of their quests, is that he is so caught up with the rational that he cannot understand the emotional, in others or in himself. To all that he finds bewildering, he tries to attach a rational explanation. When finally confronted with pure emotion in his meeting with Diana in the Edenic garden, he hesitates, fatally pausing to consider rationally what his course of action should be. In that moment, he loses the possibility of responding to his innermost feelings, failing to unite with the woman who represents his feeling side; as a result, he is evicted from the mythic landscape.

Caught between two women, his wife and Diana, David cannot love either. His situation is in sharp contrast to that of Eliduc, who also encounters two women, and can love both. For Eliduc, love is a connecting force; for David, a dividing force. Thus, when David leaves the Brittany manor, he runs over an object in the road, which turns out to be a weasel. Here the weasel is dead with no hope of being restored to life. In *Eliduc*, love restores the weasel to life.

The rest of the story is David's rationalization of his failure. Like Clegg of *The Collector*, David first recognizes his failure but knows that he will soon forget the "wound" he has suffered and the knowledge of his failure. Already the mythic encounter seems far away. By the time he arrives in Paris, he is able to tell his wife that he has "survived." Had David succeeded in his quest, he would have done far more than survive: He would have lived.

The remaining stories in the collection are connected to the title story by the theme of lost opportunities. In "Poor Koko" the narrator, a writer, is robbed by a young thief who burns his only possession of value, his manuscript on Thomas Love Peacock. The story is the writer's attempt to understand the seemingly meaningless actions of the thief, which he finally comes to realize extend from the breakdown in communication between them. On a larger scale, the clash between the boy and the old man is the clash between generations, between a world in which language is meaningful and one in which it is empty.

In the succeeding story, "The Enigma," a mystery of a different kind is presented: the disappearance of John Marcus Fielding, member of Parliament, and the subsequent investigation by Sergeant Jennings. The first mystery focuses on the reason behind the disappearance of Fielding, whose body is never discovered and whose motive is never revealed. What is hinted at by Isobel Dodgson, the former girlfriend of Fielding's son and the last person to have seen Fielding before he disappeared, is that Fielding absconded from life because it offered no mystery; thus he provided his own by disappearing.

The second and more engaging mystery is seen in the developing relationship between Jennings and Isobel. While theirs is not of the dimensions of the relationship between Charles and Sarah, Nicholas and Alison, or even David and Diana, since they are not on the mythic journey, it is nevertheless interesting because it provides a sense of mystery. In a world that motivates a Fielding to walk out, it will have to suffice.

The last story, "The Cloud," is probably the most mysterious in the literal sense, although it describes a world most lacking in mystery in the sacred or mythic sense. The setting is a picnic with two men, Peter and Paul, and two women, sisters, Annabel and Catherine. While the setting describes an idyllic day, one senses from the outset that this is not paradise, because the women are lying in the sun, "stretched as if biered," an image of death that pervades the story. Catherine has apparently suffered the loss of a loved one, presumably her husband, and is in deep depression. She seems unable to make the crossing back into the world. Language does not serve as a bridge, and her feelings elicit no depth of response from the others. Thus, by the end of the story, she enters a myth of her own making, which is described in the story she invents for her niece about the princess abandoned by her prince. Catherine remains behind, unbeknown to the others when they leave the woods, and the reader is left with the assumption that she commits suicide, symbolized by the presence of the dark clouds rolling over the scene. Thus, the dark image of the ebony tower in the first story is replaced by the dark cloud in the last, and the reader has come full circle once again.

Daniel Martin · Having described aspects of the failed quest in *The Ebony Tower*, Fowles once again returns to the theme of the successful quest in *Daniel Martin*. This time the quester is a mature man in his forties, as was the author at the time of the novel's composition, and this time Fowles is able to write the happy ending that had eluded him in his other fiction. The first sentence of the novel contains its thesis and the summation of Fowles's philosophy: "WHOLE SIGHT OR ALL THE REST IS DESOLATION." Like the questers in *The Magus* and *The French Lieutenant's Woman*, Daniel Martin must take the mythic journey to learn the meaning of whole sight and to change his world from a place of desolation to one of fulfillment.

While the first sentence of the novel states the thesis, the epigraph states the problem: "The crisis consists precisely in the fact that the old is dying and the new cannot be born; in this interregnum a great variety of morbid symptoms appears." Trapped in the wasteland of contemporary existence, Daniel experiences "morbid symptoms" in his failure to feel deeply and to be connected to a meaningful past. It is the movement of the novel from the crisis to whole sight that constitutes the quest.

The call to adventure comes with a phone call announcing the impending death of Anthony, an old friend. In going to England to be at his friend's bedside, he returns to the land of his youth and to the time when love was real. That love was with Jane, who later married Anthony, forcing both Daniel and Jane to bury their true feelings for each other. With Anthony's death, Daniel is once again faced with the dilemma of his own happiness and the role that Jane can play in it. At the same time, Daniel is wrestling with the problem of his desire to write a novel; subsequently, as the story unfolds, Daniel's novel unfolds, such that at the completion of the story one also has the completion of Daniel's novel, the demonstrable product of his successful quest.

Moving in and out of time, the novel skips from Daniel's boyhood to his present life in Hollywood with Jenny, a young film actress, to his memories of happy days at Oxford, and to his continuing relationship with Jane in the present. It also has several narrative points of view: Daniel tells certain sections, the omniscient author tells others, and still others are told by Jenny.

Daniel is aided on his journey by several wise old men: among them, Otto Kirnberger, the professor he and Jane meet on their trip up the Nile; and the Hungarian Marxist literary critic Georg Lukács, whose writings explain Daniel's choices as a writer. Daniel also describes several Edenic settings which he calls the experience of the "*bonne vaux.*" Remembrance of these experiences at Thorncombe, at Tsankawi, and at Kitchener's Island reinforce his desire to bring them more fully into his life; thus he quests on.

Realizing that the essential element of the quest is his ability to express his love for Jane, he worries that he will be rejected by her. Jane, less certain of her ability to choose her own future, tries to retreat from his declaration of love, telling him that she sees love as a prison. Jane is not yet ready to accept Daniel, but they journey on together, this time to Palmyra, a once beautiful but now desolate and remote outpost. In this wasteland, they experience the renewal of love. The catalyst comes in the form of a sound, "a whimpering, an unhappiness from the very beginning of existence." The sound is that of a litter of forlorn puppies, followed by another sound from their bedraggled mother, who tries to protect her puppies by acting as a decoy to distract the couple. The scene propels Jane out of her own wasteland into an enactment of a private ritual. Burying her wedding ring in the sand, she symbolically severs herself from her restrictive past to connect with the present and Daniel.

On his return to England, Daniel then severs himself from his remaining past by rejecting Jenny, recognizing all the while the importance of compassion in his relations with her and others. Following their last meeting, he enters a nearby church and is confronted with a living picture of all that he has learned: the famous late Rembrandt self-portrait. In this vision of compassion and whole sight, Daniel sees how far he has come and where the path into the future will lead. In Daniel's experience of the happy ending, the reader sees also a beginning. Thus, the last sentence of the novel one reads becomes the first sentence of the novel that Daniel will write. Again the experience is a circle, arriving where it started, with the circle expanding as it does in *The Magus* and in *The French Lieutenant's Woman.*

The movement of Fowles's fiction through *Daniel Martin* suggested the completion of a cycle: from a statement of the thesis in *The Magus,* to a statement of its opposite in *The Collector,* to an examination of the thesis from a different historical perspective in *The French Lieutenant's Woman,* to variations in *The Ebony Tower,* and to arrival at the long-sought happy ending in *Daniel Martin.* One could easily anticipate that the next novel would be very different, and so it was. *Mantissa,* which Fowles defines in a footnote, is a term meaning "an addition of comparatively small importance, especially to a literary effort or discourse." The novel's critical reception was mixed, some critics applauding the obvious departure from Fowles's customary style and others deploring its seeming frivolousness. Fowles contends that it should be taken as "mantissa," a kind of lark on his part. In it, he explores the role of creativity and freedom for the author, expressed through his protagonist Miles Green, as he wakes up to find himself an amnesiac in a hospital. The action of the novel, although it appears to have numerous characters entering and leaving the hospital, is really taking place in the protagonist's head, with the various characters representing manifestations of the muse Erato. The debate between muse and author gives Fowles the opportunity to turn the essential question of "freedom to choose," which he makes the object of the quest for his protagonists in his novels, into the object of the quest for the author/protagonist in this one. It also gives Fowles the opportunity to poke fun at the literary-critical approaches of the day, especially deconstruction. Finally, it gives Fowles the perfect opportunity to write graphically about sexual encounter, which he claims is one of the reasons he revised *The Magus:* to correct a "past failure of nerve."

A Maggot · In his next novel, *A Maggot,* he again chooses a title that requires explanation, his use of the term being in the obsolete sense of "whim or quirk." He goes on to explain in his prologue that he was obsessed with a theme arising out of an image from his unconscious of an unknown party of riders on horseback, and his desire was to capture this "remnant of a lost myth." This same obsession with an image is what led to the writing of *The French Lieutenant's Woman,* the historical novel set in the nineteenth century. In *A Maggot,* the temporal setting is the eighteenth century, and, as in *The French Lieutenant's Woman,* the struggle of a man and a woman to break out of their trapped existence is once again the focus. The man is Bartholomew, the son of a wealthy lord, and the woman is a prostitute named Fanny whose real name is Rebecca Lee. Bartholomew leads Rebecca into the quest, but he disappears, and the remainder of the novel becomes a search for the truth behind the events leading to his disappearance. To conduct this investigation, Bartholomew's father hires the lawyer Henry Ayscough, and the form of the novel shifts from third-person omniscient to first-person depositions, as Ayscough locates and questions everyone connected with the journey leading to the mysterious disappearance of Bartholomew. Everyone has a different view of the event, none of which Ayscough finds convincing. His desire for the truth is based on a belief that there is a rational, logical explanation; yet, despite the thoroughness of his inquiries, he cannot come up with one, finally concluding, without the evidence to prove it, that it must have been a murder.

The crux of the problem lies in his statement to Rebecca, "There are two truths, mistress. One that a person believes is truth; and one that is truth incontestible. We will credit you with the first, but the second is what we seek." Rebecca's belief, that Bartholomew has been transported by a maggot-shaped spaceship to June Eternal and that she has been reborn into a new life, frees her to break out of the trap of her existence by founding what will become the Shaker Movement, which the daughter to whom she gives birth at the end of the novel will take to America. The mystery of Bartholomew's disappearance is never solved, and the reader is left to decide where the truth lies. For Rebecca, the central quester, the truth she experienced in the cave gives her the freedom to choose a new life, which is the object of the quest.

Carol M. Barnum, updated by David W. Cole

Other major works

POETRY: *Poems*, 1973.

NONFICTION: *The Aristos: A Self-Portrait in Ideas*, 1964; *Shipwreck*, 1974; *Islands*, 1978; *The Tree*, 1980; *The Enigma of Stonehenge*, 1980 (with Barry Brukoff); *A Brief History of Lyme*, 1981; *Lyme Regis Camera*, 1990; *Wormholes: Essays and Occasional Writings*, 1998; *Conversations with John Fowles*, 1999 (Diane L. Vipond, editor).

MISCELLANEOUS: *The Ebony Tower*, 1974 (novella, 3 short stories, and translation of a French medieval romance).

Bibliography

Acheson, James. *John Fowles*. New York: St. Martin's Press, 1998. An excellent introduction to the life and works of Fowles.

Aubrey, James R. *John Fowles: A Reference Companion*. New York: Greenwood, 1991. An indispensable tool for the student of Fowles. Contains a biography, summary descriptions of Fowles's principal works and their receptions, a perceptive and judicious survey of the principal secondary works treating the Fowles canon, an extensive set of explanatory notes on Fowles's fiction, and a comprehensive bibliography.

Baker, James R., and Dianne Vipond, eds. "John Fowles Issue." *Twentieth Century Literature* 42 (Spring, 1996). A collection of essays on Fowles's work, together with two poems by Fowles and an interview with Fowles conducted by Dianne Vipond.

Barnum, Carol M. *The Fiction of John Fowles: A Myth for Our Time*. Greenwood, Fla.: Penkevill, 1988. Discusses six novels and the short-story collection from the point of view of the quest motif, which unites the seemingly disparate approaches of the fiction under a central theme. Includes notes, index, and a subdivided bibliography.

Foster, Thomas C. *Understanding John Fowles*. Columbia: University of South Carolina Press, 1994. An accessible critical introduction to Fowles's principal works. Contains an annotated bibliography.

Huffaker, Robert. *John Fowles*. Boston: Twayne, 1980. A good overview and introduction to Fowles, including chronology through 1980. Discusses fiction through *Daniel Martin*, focusing on the theme of naturalism. Includes notes, selected bibliography, and index.

Loveday, Simon. *The Romances of John Fowles*. New York: St. Martin's Press, 1985. Includes a chronology through 1983 plus an introductory chapter on the author's life and work. Discusses the fiction through *Daniel Martin*, with a concluding chapter that places Fowles in the romance tradition. Notes, subdivided bibliography, and index.

Palmer, William J., ed. "Special Issue: John Fowles." *Modern Fiction Studies* 31 (Spring, 1985). An excellent collection of essays on the fiction through *Daniel Martin*, plus an interview and a good, selected bibliography, subdivided by individual works, as well as general essays and interviews.

Pifer, Ellen, ed. *Critical Essays on John Fowles*. Boston: G. K. Hall, 1986. A collection of essays previously published elsewhere in journals. A good introduction by the editor is followed by essays organized under two themes: the unity of Fowles's fiction and discussions of individual works. Coverage through *Mantissa*. Includes notes and an index.

Tarbox, Katherine. *The Art of John Fowles*. Athens: University of Georgia Press, 1988. Discusses the novels through *A Maggot* with emphasis on Fowles's dictum to "see whole." Does not include a chapter on *The Ebony Tower*. The last chapter is an interview with the author. Notes, subdivided bibliography, and index.

John Galsworthy

Born: Kingston Hill, England; August 14, 1867
Died: London, England; January 31, 1933

Principal long fiction · *Jocelyn*, 1898 (as John Sinjohn); *Villa Rubein*, 1900 (as Sinjohn); *The Island Pharisees*, 1904; *The Man of Property*, 1906; *The Country House*, 1907; *Fraternity*, 1909; *The Patrician*, 1911; *The Dark Flower*, 1913; *The Freelands*, 1915; *Beyond*, 1917; *The Burning Spear*, 1919; *Saint's Progress*, 1919; *In Chancery*, 1920; *To Let*, 1921; *The Forsyte Saga*, 1922 (includes *The Man of Property*, "Indian Summer of a Forsyte," "Awakening," *In Chancery*, and *To Let*); *The White Monkey*, 1924; *The Silver Spoon*, 1926; *Swan Song*, 1928; *A Modern Comedy*, 1929 (includes *The White Monkey*, *The Silver Spoon*, *Two Forsyte Interludes*, and *Swan Song*); *Maid in Waiting*, 1931; *Flowering Wilderness*, 1932; *Over the River*, 1933; *End of the Chapter*, 1934 (includes *Maid in Waiting*, *Flowering Wilderness*, and *Over the River*).

Other literary forms · John Galsworthy attempted and succeeded at writing in all major literary forms. His earlier short fiction is collected in *Caravan: The Assembled Tales of John Galsworthy* (1925); among the individual collections, some of the best known are *A Man of Devon* (1901), published under the pseudonym "John Sinjohn," *Five Tales* (1918), *Two Forsyte Interludes* (1927), and *On Forsyte 'Change* (1930). His plays made him, along with George Bernard Shaw, James M. Barrie, and Harley Granville-Barker, a leading figure in British drama during the early decades of the twentieth century. Galsworthy's most enduring plays include *The Silver Box* (1906), *Justice* (1910), *The Skin Game* (1920), and *Loyalties* (1922). Collections of Galsworthy's literary sketches and essays include *A Motley* (1910), *The Inn of Tranquility* (1912), and *Tatter-demalion* (1920). Galsworthy wrote poetry throughout his life, and the *Collected Poems of John Galsworthy* were published in 1934.

Achievements · Galsworthy was a writer who reaped the rewards of literary acclaim in his own time—and suffered the pangs that attend artists who prove truer to the tastes of the public than to an inner vision of personal potential. Galsworthy won the esteem of his countrymen with a play, *The Silver Box*, and a novel, *The Man of Property*, published in his *annus mirabilis*, 1906. From that time on, he was a major figure in the British literary establishment, even winning the Nobel Prize in Literature in 1932. Idealist, optimist, and activist, Galsworthy was a perennial champion of the under-privileged in his works. Women (especially unhappily married ones), children, prisoners, aliens, and animals (especially horses and dogs) engaged Galsworthy's sympathies. His literary indictments of the injustices forced upon these victims by an unfeeling society helped to arouse public support for his causes and frequently resulted in elimination of the abuses. After World War I, Galsworthy's crusading spirit was somewhat dampened. Despite his disillusionment, though, Galsworthy's conscience remained sensitive to inequities of all sorts.

Although popular as a writer of fiction and influential as a spokesman for humane, enlightened personal behavior and public policy, Galsworthy was not the sort of writer who changes the course of literature. His early works contain some powerful satire and some interesting experiments in probing and expressing his internal conflicts. By upbringing and inclination, however, Galsworthy was too "gentlemanly" to be comfortable with self-revelation or even with introspection. Thus, while the English novel was becoming increasingly psychological because of Joseph Conrad, Virginia Woolf, and D. H. Lawrence, Galsworthy continued in the nineteenth century tradition of Ivan Turgenev and Guy de Maupassant, carefully describing social phenomena and assessing their impact on private lives. Most of his characters are individualized representatives of particular social classes, whether the rural gentry, the aristocracy, the intelligentsia, or the London professional elite. He excelled at presenting the fashions, politics, manners, and phrases peculiar to certain milieus at certain times. In creating the Forsytes—and most notably Soames, "the man of property"—Galsworthy's talent transcended that of the memorialist or mere novelist of manners and provided England with a quintessential expression of the shrewd, rich, upright middle class of Victorian London, a group whose qualities subsequent generations found easy to mock, possible to admire, but difficult to love.

Biography · John Galsworthy, son and namesake of a solicitor, company director, and descendant of the Devonshire yeomanry, was born into the rich Victorian middle class he so accurately describes in *The Forsyte Saga*. His early years followed the prescribed pattern of that class. Having spent his childhood at a series of large, grand, ugly country houses outside of London, Galsworthy was graduated from Harrow School and New College, Oxford. Called to the bar in 1890, he commenced a languid practice of maritime law and traveled widely, to Canada, Australia, and the Far East. On returning to England, he committed an unpardonable breach of middle-class manners and morals: He openly became the lover, or more accurately husband *manqué*, of Ada, the unhappy wife of his cousin Major Galsworthy.

Having placed themselves beyond the pale, the lovers traveled abroad and in England and, with Ada's encouragement and assistance, Galsworthy began his literary career by writing books under the pen name "John Sinjohn." In 1905, after Ada's divorce, the Galsworthys were able to regularize their relationship, and, in 1906, public acclamation of *The Man of Property* and *The Silver Box* gave Galsworthy a secure place in the British literary establishment. Sub-

stantial resources permitted the Galsworthys to maintain London and country residences and to continue what was to be their lifelong habit of extensive traveling.

A kindly, courtly, almost hypersensitive person concerned throughout his life with
altruistic ventures large and small, Galsworthy was distressed that his age and physical
condition precluded active service in World War I. During these years, Galsworthy
donated half or more of his large income to the war effort, wrote patriotic pieces, and
for some time served as a masseur for the wounded at a hospital in France.

Friends observed that neither John nor Ada Galsworthy ever truly recovered from
the war, and the last decade or so of Galsworthy's life was, beneath a smooth surface,
not particularly happy. He had achieved all the trappings of success. Born rich,
married to a woman he adored, he owned an elegant town house at Hampstead and
an imposing country place at Bury, in Sussex. He was president of the International
Association of Poets, Playwrights, Editors, Essayists and Novelists (PEN). The public
honored him as a humanist and philanthropist, acknowledged him as one of the
foremost British men of letters, and even—thanks to the nostalgic novels written
during the 1920's which, along with *The Man of Property*, constitute *The Forsyte Saga* and
its sequel *A Modern Comedy*—made him a best-selling author. Nevertheless, Galsworthy
keenly felt that he had never made the most of his talent or fulfilled the promise of
his early works.

Furthermore, though he was the sort of gentleman who found complaints and even
unarticulated resentment "bad form," Galsworthy must have felt some unconscious
hostility toward his wife, who, for all her devotion, was superficial, hypochondriacal,
demanding, and possessive in the Forsyte way that Galsworthy found deplorable (at
least in people other than Ada) and who, by obliging him to live life on her terms,
was perhaps the principal force in the circumspection of his talents. He also felt
anxious realizing that the intense, even claustrophobic bond of love that had joined
him and Ada would eventually be severed by the death of one or the other. Ironically,
in 1932, it became evident that the "stronger" of the two would not survive his "frail"
companion. Galsworthy was stricken with an initially vague malaise that, though
never satisfactorily diagnosed, was very likely a brain tumor. Galsworthy died at
home in London on January 31, 1933, two months after having been awarded in
absentia the Nobel Prize in Literature.

Analysis · John Galsworthy is one of those authors whose works are valued most
highly by their contemporaries. Once placed in the first rank by such discriminating
readers as Joseph Conrad, Edward Garnett, Gilbert Murray, and E. V. Lucas (though
Virginia Woolf despised him as a mere "materialist"), Galsworthy is now remembered
as the workmanlike chronicler of the Forsyte family. Most of his other works are
ignored. Changing fashions in literature do not suffice to explain this shift in critical
esteem. Rather, the way Galsworthy chose to employ his talents—or the way his
upbringing and personal situation obliged him to use them—guaranteed him the
esteem of his peers but in large measure lost him the attention of posterity.

Galsworthy's literary strengths are impressive. His works are acutely observant
and intensely sympathetic. In his novels, one finds carefully detailed presentations of
the manners, codes, pastimes, and material surroundings of England's ruling classes
as well as enlightened consideration of the diverse injustices these classes deliberately
and inadvertently inflicted on those below them. Temperamentally inclined to support the "underdog"—whether an unhappily married woman, a poor workingman less
honest than those in happier circumstances would like him to be, an ostracized

German-born Londoner in wartime, or a badly treated horse–Galsworthy does not treat his characters as stereotypes of good or evil. Even when he is a partisan in one of the ethical dilemmas he presents (such as Soames Forsyte's sincerely enamored but brutally proprietary attitude toward Irene, the woman who passively marries him but actively repents of that decision), he strives to show the mixture of good and bad, commendable and culpable, in all parties.

Galsworthy writes best when he deals with characters or situations from his own experience (for example, the various loves in *The Dark Flower*), comments on his own background or family history (as in the satirical group portrait of the Forsytes), or attempts to externalize the intricate course of motivations and ambivalences in his own mind (as does his study of Hilary Dallison, a prosperous writer suffering under the curse of "over-refinement," in *Fraternity*). Nevertheless, Galsworthy's reserve and stoicism, innate qualities further cultivated by his gentlemanly upbringing, made him increasingly unwilling to look within himself and write. His peripatetic existence and desire to grind out work for good causes must have made concentration on truly ambitious projects difficult. His wife's wishes and values, closer than he ever acknowledged to the more blighting aspects of Forsyteism, cut him off from many of the experiences and relationships that writers tend to find enriching. As a result, most of his carefully crafted literary works remain topical productions: He fails to confer suggestions of universality or living particularity on the social types and situations he describes, and thus, as novels of manners tend to do, his works seemed more profound and interesting to the age and society whose likenesses they reflect than they have to succeeding generations.

The first of the Forsyte novels, *The Man of Property*, is generally agreed to be Galsworthy's finest work, and the excellence of this book in great measure guaranteed that its less skillfully realized sequels and the peripheral Forsyte collections such as *Two Forsyte Interludes* and *On Forsyte 'Change* would attract and interest readers. If these social novels typify Galsworthy's achievement, two other works deserve mention, not for their continued popularity or complete artistic success but because they indicate the other avenues Galsworthy might have explored had he not directed his talent as he chose to do. *The Dark Flower*, one of Galsworthy's favorites among his works, displays his ability to handle emotional relationships; *Fraternity*, which he termed "more intimate than anything I've done . . . less *machinery* of story, less history, more life," is his most complex psychological study, a flawed but ambitious attempt at writing a "modern" novel.

Fraternity · In the spring of 1909, ensconced in the Devonshire countryside he loved, Galsworthy worked on the study of London life that would be *Fraternity*. The book's first title, however, was *Shadows*, a word that gives perhaps a clearer indication of the novel's ruling concern. In *Fraternity*, Galsworthy presents two adjacent but contrasting neighborhoods, elegant Campden Hill (where he and Ada then had their town residence) and disreputable Notting Hill Gate, and two sets of characters, the genteel, prosperous, enlightened Dallisons and their "shadows," the impoverished Hughs family.

Aware of the existence of their less fortunate brothers (Mrs. Hughs does household chores for Cecelia, wife of Stephen Dallison, and the Hughses' tenant models for Bianca, the artist wife of Hilary Dallison) and rationally convinced of the unity of humankind and the falseness of the divisions fostered by the class system, the Dallisons would like to take positive actions to help their "shadows" but find themselves unable to succeed at putting their theories into practice. Hilary in particular–like his creator Galsworthy a fortyish writer with a comfortable income and an uncomfortably sensitive conscience–is willing but unable to do some good. Discovering in one of many episodes of self-scrutiny that his benevolent intentions toward his wife's "little model" are far from disinterested and, worse yet, learning that the poor girl loves him, Hilary suffers a fit of repulsion. He is, as Catherine Dupre observes in *John Galsworthy: A Biography* (1976), "horrified by the prospect of any sort of union with someone whose difference of class and outlook would doom from the start their relationship." For Hilary and all the Dallisons, the common bond of shared humanity is ultimately less significant than the web of social life that separates the privileged from their "shadows," that permits observation without true empathy.

Galsworthy's friend Joseph Conrad was not alone in appraising *Fraternity* as "the book of a moralist." The great danger and difficulty of such a novel, Conrad argued to Galsworthy, is that its "negative method" of stressing a moral problem without prescribing a remedy leaves the reader dissatisfied: "It is impossible to read a book like that without asking oneself–what then?" In that sentence, Conrad characterizes a recurrent quality of Galsworthy's writing. Except in specific cases (and there were many of these–among them women's suffrage, slaughterhouse reform, docking of horses' tails, vivisection, slum clearance, the condition of prisons, the state of zoos), Galsworthy tended to be a moralist without a gospel. His scrutiny of human behavior and social conditions detracted from the artistic success of his novels without providing anything but a sense of unease. Still, as Galsworthy explained to another critic of *Fraternity*, cultivating this awareness of moral problems is a step, albeit an oblique one, toward "sympathy between man and man."

The Dark Flower · *The Dark Flower* was one of Galsworthy's particular favorites among his novels. His professed intention in writing the book was to offer "a study [I hoped a true and a deep one] of Passion–that blind force which sweeps upon us out of the dark and turns us pretty well as it will." The book was taken by various readers, the most articulate among them being Sir Arthur Quiller-Couch, who reviewed it in *The Daily Mail*, as a case for free love, an assertion that commitment to a marriage should end when love ends. Interestingly, as Catherine Dupre suggests, the gist of *The Dark Flower* is something less general than either the authorial statement of purpose or the critical view would have it be: It is an emotionally faithful representation of Galsworthy's own loves, most immediately, of his 1912 infatuation with a young actress and dancer named Margaret Morris.

The Dark Flower is divided into three parts, "Spring," "Summer," and "Autumn," each depicting a romantic experience in the life of the protagonist, Mark Lennan. Attracted to his tutor's wife in "Spring," the youthful Lennan is rejected and advised to find a woman of his own age. In "Summer," he meets and comes to love a beautiful, charming married woman, Olive Cramier, whose unyielding antipathy for the man to whom she has unwisely yoked herself obviously parallels Ada's revulsion for Major Galsworthy. Olive, the great love of Lennan's life, drowns; in "Autumn" he is happily but not passionately married to a wife of fifteen years, Sylvia, and infatuated with a lovely young girl, Nell. The middle-aged lover fondly hopes that he can retain Sylvia without giving up Nell. Like Ada in real life, Sylvia says she can be broad-minded but clearly demonstrates that she cannot. Lennan, like Galsworthy, accordingly sacrifices the more intense love for the long-standing one–in fact, his speeches and Nell's are, as Margaret Morris recalls in *My Galsworthy Story* (1967), accurate quotations of real-life dialogue. It is not surprising that having laid out his emotional autobiography, discreetly veiled though it may have been, and having been charged with promoting the sentimental and irresponsible sort of spiritual polygamy advocated by the very young Percy Bysshe Shelley, the reserved and dutiful Galsworthy was afterward reluctant to commit his deepest feelings to print.

The Man of Property · The trilogy for which Galsworthy is principally known was launched with the publication of *The Man of Property* in 1906. Although Galsworthy thought at the time of continuing his satirical work and mentioned various possibilities in his letters to Conrad, not until 1917, when he returned to England from his stint of hospital service in France and began writing "Indian Summer of a Forsyte," did Galsworthy resume the work that would be his magnum opus.

The Man of Property, the finest and fiercest of the Forsyte novels, combines portraiture of a whole gallery of Galsworthy's Victorian relations with a particular focus on one example of the tenacious Forsyte instinct for possession: Soames Forsyte's refusal to free his beautiful and intensely unhappy wife Irene from a marriage she sees as dead; Irene's affair with a "bohemian" (June Forsyte's fiancé Bosinney); and the grim but temporary victory of Soames over Irene, of Victorian convention over love. The triangular romance can be seen as symbolic or schematic—the two men, representing the possessive spirit and the creative temperament, both aspire in their different ways for Beauty—but it is also Galsworthy's thinly disguised account of Ada's tragic marriage with his cousin. The personal involvement results in what is least satisfactory about a fine book: Galsworthy's inability, despite an attempt to be philosophical, to moderate his extreme sympathy for Irene and his emotional if not rational assignment of total guilt to Soames, a man both sinned against and sinning.

The Man of Property begins with an "At Home" at the house of Old Jolyon, eldest of the Forsyte brothers and head of the family. At this gathering on June 15, 1886, a party honoring the engagement of old Jolyon's granddaughter June to the architect Philip Bosinney, the reader is privileged to observe "the highest efflorescence of the Forsytes." In the senior generation, the sons and daughters of "Superior Dosset" Forsyte, who had come from the country and founded the family's fortunes, are a variety of Victorian types, among them Aunt Ann, an ancient sybil tenaciously holding onto the life that remains to her; Jolyon, imperious and philosophical; Soames's father James, milder than Jolyon but even more single-minded in his devotion to the Forsyte principles of property and family; James's twin Swithin, an old pouter-pigeon of a bachelor whose hereditary prudence is tinged with antiquated dandyism; and Timothy, the youngest of the ten brothers and sisters and perhaps the Forsyte's Forsyte. He is a man whose caution and whose saving nature are so highly developed that he has retired early and placed all his resources in gilt-edged "Consols," retreating so successfully from the world's demands that even at his own house, the "Exchange," where Forsytes meet and gossip, his presence is felt more often than seen or heard.

The common bond that unites these superficially variegated characters and makes them representative of their whole class is described by young Jolyon, Galsworthy's mouthpiece in the novel: "A Forsyte takes a practical—one might say a common-sense—view of things, and a practical view of things is based fundamentally on a sense of property." The Forsytes, who know good things when they see them, who never give themselves or their possessions away, are the "better half" of England—the "cornerstones of convention."

The novel's principal demonstration of the Forsyte "sense of property" centers on the marriage of Soames, a prospering young solicitor, and the mysterious and lovely Irene. Troubled by his wife's chilly indifference to his strong and genuine love for her and the fine possessions which are his way of showing that feeling, Soames engages June's fiancé Bosinney to design and erect an impressive country house for him and Irene at Robin Hill, in the Surrey countryside outside of London. While building this house, a process which posits Bosinney's aesthetic scorn for base monetary matters against Soames's financial precision and passion for a bargain, the architect falls in love with Irene. She, seeing him as an emblem of all that her detested husband is not, reciprocates. The two of them betray their respective Forsytes and enter into a clandestine relationship.

These complicated circumstances pit Soames, determined to retain his property, against Irene, equally determined in her stubbornly passive way to be free of her enslaver. The outcome is tragedy. Bosinney, bankrupt because Soames has justly but vengefully sued him for overspending on the house, and crazed with jealousy and sorrow because Soames has forcibly exercised his conjugal rights, falls under a cab's wheels in a fog and is killed. As the novel ends, the errant Irene has returned to her prison-home, not out of inclination but because like a "bird that is shot and dying" she has nowhere else to fall. Young Jolyon, arriving with a message from his father, has one glimpse into the well-furnished hell that is Soames and Irene's abode before Soames slams the door shut in his face.

Galsworthy's friends and literary advisers Edward and Constance Garnett felt that this ending was unsuitable and wished for the telling defeat of Forsyteism that would be afforded by Irene and Bosinney succeeding in an elopement. Galsworthy, with better instincts, stuck to his "negative method" as a stronger means of arousing public feeling against the possessive passion he attacked. Still, if the crushing forces of property were allowed a victory, albeit a comfortless one, at the novel's end, Soames's triumph was to prove short-lived, though contemporary readers would have to wait eleven years to make the discovery. In "Indian Summer of a Forsyte," Old Jolyon, who has bought Robin Hill from Soames and lives there with his son and grandchildren, encounters Irene, now living on her own, and makes her a bequest that enables her to enjoy a comfortable independence.

In Chancery · *In Chancery* continues the conflict between the two hostile branches of the Forsyte clan. Soames, who feels the need for a child and heir to his property, is still in love with Irene and hopeful of regaining her. Young Jolyon, made Irene's trustee by his father's will, opposes Soames in his efforts and finds himself attracted by more than sympathy for the lovely, lonely woman. At length, Soames's persistent importunities drive Irene to elope with Jolyon. The infidelity gives Soames grounds for a divorce. Freed at last from any connection with the man she loathes, Irene marries Jolyon. Soames in his turn makes a convenient match with a pretty young Frenchwoman, Annette. The novel ends with the birth of children to both couples.

To Let · *To Let*, the final volume of the trilogy, brings the family feud to a new generation. Fleur, daughter of Annette and Soames, and Jon, son of Irene and Jolyon, meet first by chance, then, mutually infatuated, by strategy. The cousins intend to marry but are dramatically separated by the dead hand of the past enmity. Jon goes off to America, where after some years he marries a Southern girl. Fleur, as passionately proprietary in her feeling for Jon as her father was toward Irene, believes that she has lost her bid for love and settles for a milder sort of happiness. She accepts the proposal of Michael Mont, the amiable, humorous, eminently civilized heir to a baronetcy.

A Modern Comedy · The second Forsyte series, *A Modern Comedy* (consisting of *The White Monkey, The Silver Spoon, Two Forsyte Interludes*, and *Swan Song*) centers on the adventures of the fashionable young Monts–Michael's stints in publishing and politics, Fleur's career as society hostess, femme fatale to a promising poet, canteenkeeper during the General Strike, mother, and most of all spoiled daughter to a fond yet wise father. In his love for his child, old Soames proves as selfless and giving as young Soames was possessive in his passion for Irene. Some twenty years after introducing Soames to the world, Galsworthy had come to admire, and at moments even to like, aspects of this gruff, practical, scrupulous incarnation of the possessive instinct, a character who as the years passed had usurped the place of Irene in the artist's imagination. Soames's death at the end of *Swan Song*–he succumbs to a blow on the head inflicted by a falling painting from which he saves Fleur–is at once an ironically appropriate end to the career of a man of property and a noble gesture of self-sacrifice.

When Galsworthy chose to terminate the life of Soames Forsyte, he symbolically presented the close of an age but also implicitly acknowledged the end of what was finest in his own literary career. However wide-ranging his talent might have been if possessed by another man, his personal temperament, training, and circumstances constrained it to a certain limited excellence. Galsworthy the artist was at his best depicting conflicts typical of the Victorian period, that consummate age of property, and relevant to his own life: the contradictory urges of artistic integrity and worldly wisdom, the foolish desire to possess beauty at war with the wise inclination to contemplate and appreciate it, the altruistic motto "do good" contending with the sanely middle-class imperative "be comfortable." Because he knew the overfurnished Victorian and post-Victorian world of the Forsytes and their kind from the inside, Galsworthy's best moral fables are credibly human as well, but when the old order he comprehended, if never endorsed, gave way to a new and unfathomable one, the novelist of principle dwindled to a kind of literary curator.

Peter W. Graham

Other major works

SHORT FICTION: *From the Four Winds*, 1897 (as John Sinjohn); *A Man of Devon*, 1901 (as Sinjohn); *Five Tales*, 1918; *Captures*, 1923; *Caravan: The Assembled Tales of John Galsworthy*, 1925; *Two Forsyte Interludes*, 1927; *On Forsyte 'Change*, 1930; *Soames and the Flag*, 1930; *Forsytes, Pendyces, and Others*, 1935.

PLAYS: *The Silver Box*, pr. 1906; *Joy*, pr. 1907; *Strife*, pr., pb. 1909; *Justice*, pr., pb. 1910; *The Little Dream*, pr., pb. 1911; *The Eldest Son*, pr., pb. 1912; *The Pigeon*, pr., pb. 1912; *The Fugitive*, pr., pb. 1913; *The Mob*, pr., pb. 1915; *A Bit o' Love*, pr., pb. 1915; *The Little Man*, pr., pb. 1915; *The Foundations*, pr. 1917; *Defeat*, pr. 1920; *The Skin Game*, pr., pb. 1920; *A Family Man*, pr. 1921; *The First and the Last*, pr., pb. 1921; *Hall-marked*, pb. 1921; *Punch and Go*, pb. 1921; *The Sun*, pb. 1921; *Loyalties*, pr., pb. 1922; *Windows*, pr., pb. 1922; *The Forest*, pr., pb. 1924; *Old English*, pr., pb. 1924; *The Show*, pr., pb. 1925; *Escape*, pr., pb. 1926; *Exiled*, pr., pb. 1929; *The Roof*, pr., pb. 1929.

POETRY: *The Collected Poems of John Galsworthy*, 1934 (Ada Galsworthy, editor).

NONFICTION: *A Commentary*, 1908; *A Motley*, 1910; *The Inn of Tranquility*, 1912; *A Sheaf*, 1916; *Another Sheaf*, 1919; *Tatterdemalion*, 1920; *Castles in Spain*, 1927; *Candelabra: Selected Essays and Addresses*, 1932; *Letters from John Galsworthy, 1900-1932*, 1934 (Edward Garnett, editor).
MISCELLANEOUS: *The Works of John Galsworthy*, 1922-1936 (30 volumes).

Bibliography

Batchelor, John. *The Edwardian Novelists*. New York: St. Martin's Press, 1982. Begins by defining "Edwardian" literature and discusses Galsworthy in terms of his surprising similarities to D. H. Lawrence. *The Man of Property* and *Fraternity* are analyzed in detail, and the overall attitude toward Galsworthy is very positive. Contains an excellent bibliography of Edwardian fiction.
Dupre, Catherine. *John Galsworthy: A Biography*. New York: Coward, McCann & Geoghegan, 1976. A well-written and well-researched account of Galsworthy's life, relying heavily on letters and other primary sources. Also contains information about the writing of his literary works. Provides an excellent index, bibliographic notes, and several photographs.
Gindin, James. *John Galsworthy's Life and Art*. Ann Arbor: University of Michigan Press, 1987. Utilizing new sources, Gindin has written a masterful literary biography, particularly appropriate since Galsworthy's fiction is itself so closely tied to his personal life, social criticism, and historic times. Galsworthy moved from apprenticeship to "public edifice," but that image was tarnished and he became a "private edifice." This well-researched biography succeeds in relating Galsworthy's literary work to his life.
Mottram, Ralph H. *For Some We Loved: An Intimate Portrait of Ada and John Galsworthy*. London: Hutchinson University Library, 1956. This informal, undocumented account of Galsworthy's life, written by a personal friend of his, is anecdotal and laudatory. Mottram's focus is biographical, not critical, and he devotes little attention to Galsworthy's literary work. Contains a serviceable index.
Rønning, Anne Holden. *Hidden and Visible Suffrage: Emancipation and the Edwardian Woman in Galsworthy, Wells, and Forster*. New York: Peter Lang, 1995. See chapter 1, "The Social Context of Edwardian Literature," chapter 4, "Marriage in Galsworthy, Wells, and Forster," and chapter 6, "Galsworthy's View on Suffragism." Includes notes and bibliography.
Ru, Yi-ling. *The Family Novel: Toward a Generic Definition*. New York: Peter Lang, 1992. Examines Galsworthy's Forsyte saga as an example of the family novel. Other authors, including Roger Martin du Gard and Chin Pa, are examined as well.
Sternlicht, Sanford. *John Galsworthy*. Boston: Twayne, 1987. The most helpful critical volume on Galsworthy's literary and dramatic works despite being relatively brief. Four chapters are devoted to his novels, some of which, notably *A Modern Comedy*, are analyzed in some depth. His short stories, plays, and literary criticism are the subjects of three additional chapters. Provides a chronology, a biographical chapter, an excellent bibliography, including annotated secondary sources, and a helpful index.

Elizabeth Gaskell

Born: Chelsea, London, England; September 29, 1810
Died: Holybourne, England; November 12, 1865

Principal long fiction · *Mary Barton*, 1848; *Cranford*, 1851-1853; *Ruth*, 1853; *North and South*, 1854-1855; *Sylvia's Lovers*, 1863; *Cousin Phillis*, 1863-1864; *Wives and Daughters*, 1864-1866.

Other literary forms · The novels of Mrs. Elizabeth Gaskell appeared in serial form in journals such as *Household Words* and *All the Year Round* edited by Charles Dickens and *Cornhill Magazine* edited by William Makepeace Thackeray. During the years of novel-writing, she also published travel sketches, essays, and short stories. Her collections of stories which appeared in serial as well as hardcover form were *Lizzie Leigh and Other Tales* (1855); *Round the Sofa* (1859), containing also the separate tales inset in "My Lady Ludlow"; *Right at Last and Other Tales* (1860); *Lois the Witch and Other Tales* (1861); and *Cousin Phillis and Other Tales* (1865). Sketches of Manchester life appeared as *Life in Manchester* (1847) under the pseudonym "Cotton Mather Mills, Esq." A biography of Charlotte Brontë, still regarded as a standard source, appeared in 1857. The standard edition of Gaskell's work is the Knutsford edition (1906), which includes both fiction and nonfiction. *The Letters of Mrs. Gaskell* (1966) was edited by Arthur Pollard and J. A. V. Chapple.

Achievements · The reputation of Gaskell sank in the modernist reaction to Victorian literature in the post-World War I period, and she was relegated to the status of a second- or third-rate novelist, markedly inferior to Dickens, Thackeray, George Eliot, George Meredith, and Anthony Trollope, and even placed below Charles Kingsley and Wilkie Collins. With the reassessment of Victorian writers that has gone on since World War II, her reputation has risen, and the concerns of the feminist movement in the 1970's have led to such a revaluation that the scholar Patricia M. Spacks refers to her as "seriously underrated" in the twentieth century. Other writers about the women's movement, including Elaine Showalter, Jenni Calder, and Ellen Moers, have praised Gaskell for detailing faithfully in her fiction the relation between women and marriage, the struggle for self-achievement, and the intermixture of women's careers and public history. The sense in her work of women of all classes as victims of economic and social restrictions has caused scholars to study her work and life more closely in the last decade. She has been elevated to the ranks of the major Victorian novelists.

Biography · Elizabeth Gaskell's life was divided between the industrial Midlands of the north and London and rural Hampshire in the south of England, as was that of her heroine, Margaret Hale, in *North and South*. Her mother's family, the Hollands, substantial landowners, were established near Knutsford, Cheshire, which became the "Cranford" of her best-known work. Elizabeth Cleghorn Stevenson was born on September 29, 1810, in Chelsea, then just outside London, where the family had settled after a period in Scotland. Because of her mother's death, Elizabeth was taken to Knutsford, where she spent the next thirteen years in the care of her aunt, Mrs. Hannah Lumb. The years at Knutsford were very happy ones, and her affection for the town is indicated by the tales in *Cranford* about its inhabitants. Her brother, John, twelve years older, went into the merchant navy but simply disappeared on a voyage to the Far East in 1823, an event marked in Gaskell's fiction by various lost and recovered brothers.

Her father remarried, having two more children, and at fourteen Elizabeth was sent to Avonbank School in Stratford, which was kept by the Byerley sisters, her stepmother's aunts. It was a progressive school by Victorian standards of feminine education, serving Unitarian and other liberal religious groups. She left school at seventeen to tend her paralyzed father, the relationship between the two having been somewhat strained in the preceding years. From 1827 until his death in 1829, she faithfully nursed him, her dedication to the task bringing forth a grateful testimony from her stepmother. The experience furnished the basis for Margaret Hale's nursing of her critically ill mother.

The experience of Margaret in the fashionable home of her London relations appears to parallel the months spent by Elizabeth with her uncle, Swinton Holland, a banker, and her cousin, Henry Holland, a London physician. Following the fashion for educated and leisured Victorian women, she visited various places during the next few years: in and out of Knutsford (like her narrator, Mary Smith, in *Cranford*), two winters in Newcastle with a minister, William Turner (the model for the kindly Unitarian minister, Thurstan Benson, in *Ruth*), and his daughter, Anne, a visit to Manchester to Anne's sister, Mary, and a winter in Edinburgh with the intellectual and artistic company there. At Manchester, she met William Gaskell, assistant minister of Cross Street Unitarian Chapel, and their warm relationship eventuated in marriage at Knutsford in August, 1832. At her various residences in Manchester, to whose busy industrial life and brusque manners she had to adjust, Gaskell became the mother of four daughters and a son: Marianne, Margaret Emily, Florence, Julia, and William, whose death at the age of ten months caused her great sorrow and resulted in the writing of an idealized portrait of a boy, found in her novel *Ruth*.

Gaskell's husband, who became senior minister in 1854, had a solid reputation as a public speaker, teacher of English history and literature, editor of church publications, and preacher. Despite the uncomfortable weather and atmosphere of Manchester, it was a gathering place for well-educated Unitarians and other non-Anglicans, Cross Street Chapel being a center of lively discussion and numbering many self-made mill-owners among its members. It was also true, however, that class divisions between owners and mill-workers were strongly evident to Gaskell, whose character, Margaret Hale, wonders why two groups dependent upon each other regard their interests as opposed.

To understand Gaskell's preoccupation with social problems in her fiction, one must note her constant involvement in social welfare with Sunday and weekday schools for children of workers, her visits to working-class homes in the course of parish duties, and her concern for victims of the social system such as unwed mothers. The depression of 1839 to 1840, the Chartist movement aimed at gaining more political power for workers, the Factory Act of 1832 opposed by industrialists and widely evaded in its purpose of restricting hours of labor for women and children—all these conditions provided Gaskell with subject matter.

Gaskell's immediate impulse to write came from grief over her son's death, a decision which her husband hoped to channel constructively by encouraging her in her efforts. Her first attempt at a diary and further encouragement from publisher friends resulted in sketches about *Life in Manchester,* but this was a prelude to her first success as a novelist, *Mary Barton.* This novel presented the sufferings of the workers during labor unrest, the resistance of the mill-owners, the failure of parliament to respond to labor grievances, and the need for reconciliation. The book was praised by Friedrich Engels and Karl Marx and condemned as unfair by the wealthy parishioners of Cross Street Chapel, a denouncement which led Gaskell to present what she considered an account more favorable to the industrialists in *North and South.*

Library of Congress

The acclaim and damnation of *Mary Barton* made Gaskell rather visible among British intellectuals such as Thomas Carlyle, the social critic; Walter Savage Landor, the poet; Benjamin Jowett, the classicist; John Ruskin, the reformer of industrial ugliness; Charles Kingsley, author of *Alton Locke* (1850) and *Yeast* (1851) and a founder of Christian socialism; Antony Cooper, Earl of Shaftesbury, the prime mover of legislative reform in mid-Victorian England; and Dickens. Thus, Gaskell joined the reforming group bent on altering the unsatisfactory living and working conditions among the laboring class in Britain.

Gaskell's friendship with Dickens inspired her to produce a story about an unmarried mother, "Lizzie Leigh," for Dickens's journal *Household Words* and created a writer-editor relationship that lasted more than a dozen years. Having become interested in the fate of the "fallen woman," she used, as the basis for her novel *Ruth* (first serialized and then published in 1853), the actual case of a sixteen-year-old female dressmaking apprentice who had been seduced, abandoned, and then imprisoned for theft in trying to keep herself alive. In the novel, a similar young girl is saved from a parallel disgrace by the intervention of a kindly minister and his sister and brought back to respectability and social usefulness by their tender concern. The presentation of Ruth's case, mild by modern standards, became almost instantly controversial, various prudish fathers refused to allow their wives and daughters to read it, and even Gaskell kept the book from her own daughters. Gaskell had already interested herself in promoting immigration by unwed mothers to the colonies as a practical way of restoring their reputations and building new futures; the book was an outcome of her own concern, though Ruth is rehabilitated within the community rather than leaving it and must still suffer unfair stigmatization, precisely the kind which the novel itself received.

While visiting another reformer, James Kay-Shuttleworth, who promoted educational advancements for the workers, Gaskell met Charlotte Brontë, who had recently risen to prominence with *Jane Eyre* (1847); a strong friendship developed from this meeting and continued until Brontë's death in 1855. In fact, the riot of the working-men against their employer in *North and South* has similarities to a scene in Brontë's *Shirley*, which appeared six years before Gaskell's novel.

While *Ruth* was exciting controversy, *Cranford*, the work which for a long time overshadowed Gaskell's reputation as a social critic, created a nostalgic and melancholic mood. Yet even in this novel, Gaskell expresses a concern for lives that are close to poverty, genteel survivors of once lively and secure families. To please Dickens, in 1863 Gaskell added one more story to the collection for *All the Year Round*, his second magazine. Gaskell had by then established the parameters of her work: the creation of moving depictions of life under an industrializing social order; the alertness to social injustice; the longings for a more rural, innocent, and organic world of natural feelings and associations; and the melancholy strain of hopes unrealized because of social or financial constraints.

In *North and South*, completed two years after *Cranford*, Gaskell made a determined effort to present the mill-owner, Thornton, as a man with integrity, initiative, and humanitarian concern for his workers, a sort of Samuel Greg who weathers the financial crisis both with the support of his wife, Margaret Hale, newly rich, and that of his workers, drawn to him by his philanthropy. Northern energy, brusque efficiency, and the rough democracy of industrialists sprung from the humble origins of their own workers are set against the arduous toil and isolation of Southern farm laborers and the class-consciousness of Southern workers, town-dwellers, and professional people. In the same year, Gaskell drew upon memories of Avonbank School for stories, which she inset in a frame story narrated by an aristocrat, Lady Ludlow. These appeared as "My Lady Ludlow," later added to and published as *Round the Sofa*. During these years, Gaskell also wrote various sketches, such as "Cumberland Sheep Shearers" with its Wordsworthian setting of rough toil among natural beauties, and Christmas stories, some with ghostly apparitions in the style of Dickens's own stories, which appeared in *Household Words*. Dickens's *Hard Times* (1854) provoked some anxiety in Gaskell since it dealt in part with union agitation and industrial unrest, as did *North and South*. What strained the relationship with Dickens, however, was the leisurely description and extended characterization in *North and South* together with difficulties of episodic compression for weekly publication in his journal. Though Dickens eventually came to appreciate the virtues of *North and South*, the editorial struggle over it induced Gaskell to look for publication elsewhere in more prestigious journals run on a monthly basis.

Upon the death of Charlotte Brontë in March, 1855, Gaskell undertook to write the authorized biography, using Brontë's words where possible but interpreting the facts somewhat freely. The biography, published in March, 1857, led to a continuing friendship with her new publisher, George Smith, Jr., whose firm, Smith, Elder, and Company, had been Brontë's publishers. Smith's support proved most helpful when questions of libelous statements in the biography necessitated apologies and vexatious changes in the third edition. Despite the partisanship evident in certain passages, the feeling for its subject and the general fairness in its presentation make it a good study of a writer by another writer.

Gaskell's work from 1858 to 1863 was uneven. She desired sales apparently to pay for increasing amounts of travel with her daughters, expenses of weddings for two of them, and new property. In Rome, in 1857, a new friend and major correspondent appeared, an American, Charles Eliot Norton, future president of Harvard University, who probably gave her information on Puritan New England to add to her lore of withcraft and demonism on which she drew for the stories found in *Lois the Witch and Other Tales*. A trip to Heidelberg, Germany, provided legendary matter for *Right at Last and Other Tales*. At this time, there was much interest in Great Britain in folklore materials and romantic wonders derived from ghostly and spiritual legends, and Gaskell, among others, was willing to fictionalize this type of literature.

Writing in another contrary strain, Gaskell employed rural settings in her next two novels, *Sylvia's Lovers* and *Cousin Phillis*; the novel or novella following these two was *A Dark Day's Night*, intended to capture part of the market for intriguing mystery-and-suspense stories. As *Cousin Phillis* was winding up its serial publication in August, 1864, Gaskell started what some critics consider her major work, *Wives and Daughters*, an exploration of the role of women in Victorian intellectual and social life. It was never completed. Gaskell's unceasing activity, including essays for the *Sunday School Magazine*, was taking its physical toll. She had already had fainting spells. Hoping to retire to Holybourne, Hampshire, which she had used a decade earlier as Margaret Hale's beloved home community, she had purchased a home there as a surprise for her husband. While spending a trial weekend with family and guests there, she suffered a sudden and fatal stroke on November 12, 1865. She was buried at Brook Street Chapel, Knutsford, where her husband was also buried in June, 1884.

Analysis · Despite her own creativity, which certainly had the support of her husband, Elizabeth Gaskell, when questioned by a young writer, insisted that a woman's first duty was to husband and family. Friends recollected her carrying out her early career in the midst of household activities. Later, however, she often went traveling alone or with her daughters but—except for jaunts to a beloved vacation spot near Manchester—never with her husband. The traveling periods gave her isolation for writing, suggesting that her own practice ran counter to her advice.

Enid L. Duthie has found in Gaskell's fiction a strong interest in natural scenery, in country customs, crafts, and tales; a sympathy for conservative small towns, yet equally a concern for working men and women; a desire for practical knowledge to enhance living; a focus upon the family as the stable social unit where affections are close but able, on occasion, to extend to others in need; and an insistence that violence is futile, the human condition precarious, faith necessary. John McVeagh sees Gaskell as insisting that absolute judgments become meaningless when related to concrete human situations requiring compromise. In Gaskell's treatment of the laboring element, Jenni Calder sees her as avoiding the duality of other portrayers of working-class families—sympathetic yet condescending—and refers to Gaskell as one of the few major Victorian writers showing marriage from a woman's viewpoint and not simply as an escape, a bid for social status, or a profitable contract. Gaskell has been praised for her concrete presentation of social milieus, in the spirit of seventeenth century Dutch genre painters, and her gift for recording the relationship between work and home and between husbands and wives is a special one. Patricia M. Spacks refers to a "steady integrity of observation" and "penetrating accuracy," especially as Gaskell draws, tacitly, the analogy between the plight of women in their dependency and that of workers in relation to their employers.

Gaskell's dilemma for a feminist such as Elaine Showalter lies in Victorian expectations of feminine domesticity and marriage as an end to intellectual creativity. Gaskell herself surmounted the problem, but her characters find it a difficult challenge. Spacks points out that Margaret Hale, Gaskell's greatest heroine, from *North and South,* tries to mediate between an impoverished working class which really does respect its own labor and an enlightened upper-class self-interest which enjoys emotional and cultural richness. In the end, however, Margaret must inherit property as a defense for her own introspective feeling and the diminution of her former social vitality. It is her way of surviving in a materialistic world.

Mary Barton · The titular heroine of *Mary Barton* has a true lover, Jem Wilson, and a potential seducer, Henry Carson, son of a textile mill-owner. The love interest is established as the background for a social problem which Gaskell treats with historical accuracy. John Barton, Mary's father, aware of the sufferings of his fellow mill-workers during a lockout by the employers, is enraged by the death of the wife of his friend, Davenport, while the masters enjoy leisure, modernize their mills, and keep up profits by using scabs and decreasing wages when they reopen. Barton is hopeful that the workers will find redress for their grievances from a sympathetic parliament, to which the unionists will present the Chartist Petition. The charter is rejected, however, and the embittered workers are further incensed by Henry Carson's casual caricature of the striking workers, which he passes around at a meeting of employers. He is selected as the target of assassination, Barton being chosen to murder him. Jem is accused of the murder, and Mary faces a conflict, since she can clear Jem only by exposing her father. Though Jem's acquittal makes this step unnecessary, the other workers shun him (a situation Gaskell borrowed from the true story of a former convict ostracized by those in the workplace), and he and Mary are forced to emigrate. Her father, still publicly innocent, confesses, somewhat implausibly, to Carson, Sr., and gains forgiveness. The solution to class conflict comes through mutual goodwill, recognition of wrongdoing, and restitution.

Ruth · The heroine of *Ruth,* which takes issue with Victorian hostility toward the unmarried mother, is seduced among the romantic clouds and mountains of Wales. The idyllic moment turns to desperation when she is abandoned by her lover, Bellingham. A kindly, crippled Unitarian minister, Thurstan Benson, and his sister, Faith, take Ruth into their home and community, modeled on Knutsford, and deceive people about her condition to protect her reputation. The lie is the price of social respectability. Ruth's discreet conduct from this point on gains her admittance to the mill-owning Bradshaw family as companion to their daughter, Jemima. The electoral reforms of 1832 give Bellingham a chance to stand for political office, his reappearance in Ruth's life leading to a renewal of his interest in her and a new temptation for her to forgo her independence by accepting an offer of marriage. Her pride in her child, Leonard, makes Ruth reject Bellingham. Unfortunately, Bradshaw learns the truth about Ruth, and his self-righteous indignation leads him to repel Ruth and denounce his friend, Thurstan. Denied the opportunity for further cultural development in the Bradshaw family, Ruth must turn to nursing to establish her social usefulness. As a visiting nurse, her conscientious assistance during a typhoid epidemic brings the praise of the community.

Critics have said that Gaskell, having made her point that unmarried mothers should be treated humanely so that their talents can be made productive, should have ended her novel. Unfortunately, three-volume publication, extended serialization, and a tendency toward melodrama fostered by Charles Dickens, led Gaskell to have Bradshaw's son forge a signature on some stocks entrusted to him by Thurstan.

Bradshaw denounces his son, comes back ignominiously to the chapel worship he has furiously abandoned, and eventually breaks down and is reconciled to Thurstan, having repented of his harshness toward Ruth. Ruth, however, is not permitted to live since Gaskell apparently felt that her rehabilitation was not enough to gain sympathy. Wearied by constant care of the sick, Ruth falls sick while somewhat improbably tending her former lover, Bellingham. She dies possessing an aura of sanctity, and perhaps it was this martyrdom which Victorian critics found too much to accept.

North and South · In *North and South*, the protagonist Margaret Hale must adjust to life in industrial Darkshire (Derbyshire) after living in rural Hampshire, and, through her perceptions, Margaret guides the reader to a major issue: the way in which a money-oriented competitive society challenges a more leisured, socially stratified one. The abrasive confrontations of Margaret and John Thornton, a mill-owner being tutored in classics by Margaret's father, define the mutual incomprehension of north and south in England. Thornton wants to have a "wise despotism" over his workers; Margaret contends for understanding based upon common destiny in the mills. The question of authority is raised in another dimension in the Hale family's personal travail over the enforced exile of Margaret's brother, Frederick, because of charges, unwarranted, of inciting the crew of his naval vessel to mutiny. Through friendship with Bessy Higgins, a mill girl dying of a disease fostered by textile manufacturing, Margaret, the central consciousness of the novel, is able to observe the sufferings of the working class during a strike caused by union efforts to prevent wage cuts, which the mill-owners justify because of American competition. The owners themselves, while cooperating in opposition to workers, fight one another for economic survival, according to Thornton, who sees an analogy with the theory of survival of the fittest. Though Margaret can see the closeness of working men and women in their common suffering, a riot, instigated without union approval by Nicholas Boucher, a weak agitator, against Irish scab labor, seriously compromises the position of the union in terms of its own self-discipline. The issue is posed whether coercive tactics to enlist worker support of unions can be justified when a weak leader can jeopardize legitimate demands. Margaret terminates the riot, in fact, by heroically intervening between Thornton and the rioters. She quite literally mediates between the two sides.

The difficulty of reconciliation is made evident, however, when Bessy's father, Nicholas Higgins, a unionist, argues that Christian forbearance will not answer the industrialists, though he admits that workers and employers might compromise if they could understand one another. The blacklisting of Nicholas by other employers leads to Margaret's intervention, encouraging Thornton to rehire him, his own persistence equally helping to regain a job. Thornton realizes that employer responsibility must be broadened. The turmoil of the riot, in which Margaret must confront social disruption, has its counterpart in her own turmoil over the approaching death of her mother and the secret reappearance of her brother to be with their mother. Unfortunately, Frederick's departure from town involves a scuffle with a drunken informer which later requires that Margaret lie to protect Frederick. This lie, like that in *Ruth*, produces its painful outcome when Thornton, who has observed the scuffle, thinks that she is lying to protect a lover, thus causing further altercations. Margaret realizes, however, that her moral condemnation of manufacturers has been too harsh. Indeed, to an Oxford don, an old family friend who comes to her mother's funeral, she suggests that it would be well if intellectuals associated with manufacturers.

Margaret's opinions about the south as a preferable society also undergo change.

She counsels Nicholas that his going to the south, when he is blacklisted, would lead to deadening toil, no real companionship, and intellectual decay because of the rural isolation. Visiting Helstone, her old home, Margaret encounters an old native superstition when a live cat is boiled to avert a curse. A meeting with her former lover, Lennox, confirms that Thornton is the more vital man. A fortunate inheritance from the Oxford don, Mr. Bell, enables Margaret to save Thornton, who is faced with mounting debts because of competition. He, too, has faced a moral dilemma: whether it is right to borrow money to keep himself afloat knowing that the lenders are at a strong risk. Thornton wishes to start again, seeking an opportunity for social interchange with his workers beyond the cash nexus. Margaret, now an heiress, helps Thornton stay afloat and marries him. Higgins, providentially having witnessed the scuffle, knows who Frederick really is. Thus, north and south are united, and Thornton becomes a philanthropist.

Wives and Daughters · In *Wives and Daughters*, Gaskell explores the question of the middle-class woman seeking to define herself and her goals in an atmosphere uncongenial to intellectual independence. Molly Gibson, whose mother has died, must cope in her teens with the remarriage of her father, who has sought a wife as much to guide Molly as out of real love. Her father's new wife, Hyacinthe Kirkpatrick, is the epitome of the parasitical woman, a former governess previously married out of necessity and then forced back into supporting herself and her daughter, Cynthia, upon her husband's death. She has become a companion to the newly aristocratic Cumnor family, but, wanting comfort, she can achieve it only by marrying Gibson. Molly receives her moral education, in part, by seeing through her stepmother's pretenses. Cynthia, shuffled off while her mother has pursued Gibson, comes to reside in the household and establishes a close friendship with Molly despite her moral skepticism and social opportunism. Thus, the daughters are contrasted, not in black and white, but as possible responses to the dependency of women.

Cynthia's mother tries to marry her to Osborne Hamley, eldest son of an old family, not knowing that he is already married, and that the child of the marriage has been kept secret for some time. The event has caused Hamley to fail in attaining his degree, and he returns home to mope, thus arousing the antagonism of his father, to whom he cannot acknowledge his liaison. Hamley finally dies, causing Mrs. Kirkpatrick to shift her sights for Cynthia to the second son, Roger. Molly meanwhile has naïvely pledged herself at sixteen to the odious Preston, a situation from which she is rescued by the more forthright Cynthia, who is in love with Roger but also the object of the affections of Walter Henderson, Gaskell's ideal of the practical, creative scientist, a new social type. Cynthia, socially ambitious, realizes that the Hamley family enjoys ancient honor but is materially threatened, and she transfers her affections to a superficial, weak, but socially prominent young man. Molly is left to marry Roger, but the problem remains as to whether she can forge for herself a free life with her husband's support. The lifestyles of the two older women, Lady Harriet Cumnor and Mrs. Hamley, provide alternatives for her development. Lady Harriet is a realist about feminine hypocrisy as the price of dependency and wishes to challenge it, but Mrs. Hamley, despite her efforts to mother Molly, is emotionally sterile. Her death leaves Squire Hamley bereft and helplessly alienated from his infant grandson. The other, older men in the novel fare no better; Mr. Gibson suppresses his feelings about his wife to the point of emotional numbness, Lord Cumnor takes refuge in foolish snobbery, and even the younger Osborne painfully learns the price of romantic impulsiveness. The novel's probing analysis of the dilemma of femininity in a world guided by material values and restricted social consciousness, a world in which men too are caught by the inhibitions of social position and frozen into immobility, gives it peculiar power. It is an indication of what Gaskell could have accomplished if she had lived longer, and it shows her continuing effort to link broader social issues to very specific circumstances with careful attention to detail.

Roger E. Wiehe

Other major works

SHORT FICTION: *The Moorland Cottage,* 1850; *Lizzie Leigh and Other Tales,* 1855; *The Manchester Marriage,* 1858; *Round the Sofa,* 1859; *Right at Last and Other Tales,* 1860; *Lois the Witch and Other Tales,* 1861; *The Cage at Cranford,* 1863; *Cousin Phillis and Other Tales,* 1865.

NONFICTION: *Life in Manchester,* 1847 (as "Cotton Mather Mills, Esq."); *The Life of Charlotte Brontë,* 1857; *The Letters of Mrs. Gaskell,* 1966 (Arthur Pollard and J. A. V. Chapple, editors).

Bibliography

Chapple, J. A. V. *Elizabeth Gaskell: The Early Years.* Manchester, England: Manchester University Press, 1997. A good biography of Gaskell, focusing on her beginning years as a writer.

Craik, W. A. *Elizabeth Gaskell and the English Provincial Novel.* New York: Harper & Row, 1975. A major rehabilitation of Gaskell as an important novelist, comparing her with her contemporaries. Sets her five long fictions within the provincial novel tradition and demonstrates how she expanded the possibilities and universality of that tradition. A short bibliography and a chronology of major nineteenth century provincial novels are included.

Duthie, Enid. *The Themes of Elizabeth Gaskell.* Basingstoke, England: Macmillan, 1980. Despite their contrasting settings and plots, there is a unity of themes in all Gaskell's fiction. Her entire work and letters are drawn upon to reconstruct her imaginative world and the themes central to it. Contains a select bibliography and an index.

Easson, Angus. *Elizabeth Gaskell.* London: Routledge & Kegan Paul, 1979. Examines the relationship of all Gaskell's writings to her life and times, tracing the source of her fiction to her culture. A select bibliography and index are included.

Gerin, Winifred. *Elizabeth Gaskell.* New York: Oxford University Press, 1976. The first biography able to make use of the publication in 1966 of *The Letters of Mrs. Gaskell,* and still one of the best. Contains a select bibliography and an index.

Hughes, Linda K., and Michael Lund. *Victorian Publishing and Mrs. Gaskell's Work.* Charlottesville: University Press of Virginia, 1999. Part of the Victorian Literature and Culture series, this volume puts Gaskell's writing in the context of the Victorian era. Includes bibliographical references.

Spencer, Jane. *Elizabeth Gaskell.* New York: St. Martin's Press, 1993. Chapters on Gaskell's career, *Mary Barton,* her biography of Charlotte Brontë, *Cranford* and *North and South, Sylvia's Lovers,* and *Wives and Daughters.* Includes notes and bibliography.

Stoneman, Patsy. *Elizabeth Gaskell.* Brighton, England: Harvester Press, 1987. This feminist reading claims that previous accounts of Gaskell have seriously misread her and that the interaction of class and gender must be made central in any interpretation of her. A select bibliography and index are provided.

Uglow, Jenny. *Elizabeth Gaskell: A Habit of Stories.* New York: Farrar, Straus & Giroux, 1993. A major critical biography, exploring in detail both Gaskell's life and work. Paying close attention to primary source material, especially letters, Uglow has produced a definitive life. Includes illustrations and notes but no bibliography.

George Gissing

Born: Wakefield, England; November 22, 1857
Died: St. Jean-Pied-de-Port, France; December 28, 1903

Principal long fiction · *Workers in the Dawn,* 1880; *The Unclassed,* 1884; *Isabel Clarendon,* 1886; *Demos,* 1886; *Thyrza,* 1887; *A Life's Morning,* 1888; *The Nether World,* 1889; *The Emancipated,* 1890; *New Grub Street,* 1891; *Denzil Quarrier,* 1892; *Born in Exile,* 1892; *The Odd Women,* 1893; *In the Year of Jubilee,* 1894; *Eve's Ransom,* 1895; *The Paying Guest,* 1895; *Sleeping Fires,* 1895; *The Whirlpool,* 1897; *The Town Traveller,* 1898; *The Crown of Life,* 1899; *Our Friend the Charlatan,* 1901; *The Private Papers of Henry Ryecroft,* 1903; *Veranilda,* 1904; *Will Warburton,* 1905.

Other literary forms · Though George Gissing will be remembered primarily as a novelist, he tried his hand at a variety of literary projects. In the 1890's especially, he found it profitable to write short stories; these were generally published in periodicals, but one volume—*Human Odds and Ends* (1897)—was published during his lifetime. Many of his other short stories, some from his early contributions to Chicago newspapers, have since been collected: *The House of Cobwebs* (1906), *Sins of the Fathers* (1924), *A Victim of Circumstances* (1927), and *Brownie* (1931). Gissing also wrote essays for a number of periodicals. *Notes on Social Democracy* (1968, with an introduction by Jacob Korg), reprints three articles he wrote for the *Pall Mall Gazette* in 1880. *George Gissing: Essays and Fiction* (1970) prints nine prose works published for the first time. Late in his life, Gissing published *Charles Dickens: A Critical Study* (1898) and *By the Ionian Sea* (1901), his "notes of a ramble in southern Italy."

Achievements · During his lifetime, Gissing achieved neither the fame nor the fortune that he would have liked. His reputation, though it grew steadily, especially in the 1890's, was always overshadowed by the powerhouse writers of the late Victorian era. Gissing was nevertheless seriously reviewed and often applauded by the critics for his objective treatment of social conditions in England. After his death, his reputation was eclipsed for many years, and it was only in the late twentieth century that Gissing began to receive the reevaluation needed to determine his place in English literary history. The renewed academic attention, manifested by numerous new editions of his novels, critical biographies, full-length studies of his novels, and several volumes of his correspondence, suggested that Gissing's niche would become more firmly established.

Biography · Born on November 22, 1857, in Wakefield, Yorkshire, George Robert Gissing was the eldest of five children of Thomas Waller and Margaret Bedford Gissing. Thomas Gissing was a chemist in Wakefield and something of a religious skeptic whose extensive library provided the young George with convenient access to a variety of reading material. The early years of financial security and familial harmony were disrupted when Thomas Gissing died in December, 1870. George, only thirteen, and his two brothers were sent to Lindow Grove School at Alderley Edge, Cheshire. There, the young Gissing's studious habits gained for him the first of many academic accolades. His performance on the Oxford Local Examination in 1872 was especially encouraging, but financial circumstances made it necessary for him to attend Owens College in Manchester, where he had won free tuition for three sessions and where he continued with his academic success.

Gissing was not, however, enjoying the same success in his personal life. Living a lonely and studious life in Manchester, he fell in love with a young prostitute named Marianne Helen Harrison ("Nell"). With the zeal of the reformer, Gissing tried to save her from her profession and her penury, apparently not realizing at first that she was an alcoholic as well. Exhausting his own funds, the young Gissing stole miscellaneous property from his fellow students at Owens College. He was soon caught, and the course of his life was radically altered, for he was forced to abandon all thoughts of an academic life. With the aid of friends, he sailed for the United States in the fall of 1876 and worked briefly as a high school teacher in Waltham, Massachusetts. Why he left Waltham, where he apparently enjoyed a reasonably good life, is not known, but in the spring of 1877 he moved to Chicago, where he tried to eke out an existence as a writer. Though he did publish his first work (a short story called "The Sins of the Fathers," in the Chicago *Tribune*, March 10, 1877), he was not well paid for his endeavors and left after only four months. He worked at odd jobs in New England and elsewhere, and then in the fall of 1877 he made his way back to England. In London, he lived in near-poverty, working sporadically as a tutor and drafting his first novels. Nell came to live with him, and in October, 1879, they were married. Despite Gissing's noble intention to reform her apparently self-destructive character, the marriage was not successful. A vivid fictionalized account of the sordidness of their married life is given in *Workers in the Dawn*, Gissing's first published novel. He lived a turbulent life with Nell until he put her in an invalids' home in January, 1882. Even after that, she gave him trouble, both financial and emotional, until she died in 1888.

The direction of Gissing's writings in the 1880's was influenced not only by his failed marriage but also by a number of other lifelong interests which were well established by the end of the decade: his friendship with the budding German writer Eduard Bertz, his reading of Auguste Comte, his unfailing compassion for the poverty of late Victorian England, his friendship with Frederic Harrison, who read his first novel and provided much-needed encouragement, and his friendship with Morley Roberts, who later became Gissing's first biographer with the thinly disguised *The Private Life of Henry Maitland* (1912). Not until 1886, with the publication of *Demos*, did Gissing gain moderate success with his writing. Buoyed by more favorable circumstances, especially the sense of freedom once Nell died, Gissing left for an extended tour of Europe in September, 1888. He also shifted the emphasis of his novels from the working class to the middle class, beginning in 1890 with *The Emancipated*.

The 1890's began auspiciously for Gissing's literary career, particularly with the publication of *New Grub Street* and *Born in Exile*. His personal life, however, was following a different course. On a trip to Italy in 1890, he noticed the first signs of the respiratory illness which would plague him the rest of his life. On February 25, 1891, he married Edith Underwood, a "work-girl," as he described her, with whom he was not in love. The marriage was a complete failure, despite the birth of two sons (Walter Leonard, born 1891, and Alfred Charles, born 1895). Gissing's literary success in the 1890's, as moderate as it was, was achieved in spite of his loveless marriage and domestic unrest. He persevered until September, 1897, when he permanently separated from his wife and went to Italy. In the summer of 1898, he met Gabrielle Fleury, a Frenchwoman who was the complete opposite of his two wives in her refined and cultured manner. Gissing was immediately attracted to her and would have legally married her had a divorce from Edith been possible. Instead, the two sanctified their relationship with each other in a private ceremony on May 7, 1899, in Rouen. Living in France under the most favorable circumstances of his entire life, Gissing continued to write, and in 1903 he saw *The Private Papers of Henry Ryecroft*, his most popular work, go through three editions. His health, however, had been growing steadily worse, and his short-lived happiness came to an end when he died on December 28, 1903, of myocarditis at St. Jean-Pied-de-Port in France.

Analysis · In his personal life, George Gissing was a man of divided mind, and the biographical antitheses were paralleled by the literary and philosophical influences on his work. In private life, he gravitated toward Frederic Harrison's circle of intellectuals and sophisticated people; at the same time, he was drawn into marriages with psychologically, intellectually, and socially unsuitable women. He was attracted, on the one hand, to a scholarly career as a historian, philosopher, and classicist; on the other, he was drawn to journalism, hackwork, and lectures to workingmen's associations with an emphasis on social reform. Like many writers at the end of the nineteenth century, he was caught between the sociological realists with reform instincts and the adherents of an aesthetic movement with their emphasis on the attainment of ideal beauty. His sensuousness conflicted with his intellectual idealism; his desire for popularity and material success with his austere integrity as an artist.

Gissing's career as a novelist, at least until the late twentieth century, has been assessed in the context of nineteenth century realism and naturalism. Certainly, the techniques employed in his novels, especially the early ones, owe much to the Victorian conventions that had become well established by the time of Gissing's first published novel. He was thoroughly acquainted with the work of Charles Dickens; his own novels are often sentimental, cautiously admonitory, and riddled with sub-plots. Gissing, however, never treated his subject matter as humorously as did Dickens in his early novels. Dickens's treatment of poverty, for example, is sometimes used for picturesque effects; Gissing saw poverty in a solemn manner, finding it both lamentable and execrable.

For other literary precedents, Gissing turned to the French and Russian writers, discovering in the French naturalists such as Émile Zola the pervasive effects of physical and social environments and finding in the Russian naturalistic psychologists the precise and complete analysis of character. Like Zola, he described the squalor of poverty, probed the psychology of sex (though with more reserve), and generally ended his novels in dismal defeat. Yet, unlike the naturalists, Gissing was not so much concerned with the particular details of the workshop, with conflicts between capital and labor, but with the whole atmosphere of poverty, especially the resultant loss of integrity on the part of those who struggle to rise beyond and above it.

To divide Gissing's career into neat stages is not an easy task. For the purposes of an overview, however, it is convenient to look at three large, if not always distinct, groups of his novels. In the 1880's, beginning with *Workers in the Dawn* and ending with *The Nether World*, Gissing was most often concerned with the lower class and social reform. In the first half of the 1890's, beginning with *The Emancipated*, Gissing turned to the middle class, examining the whole middle-class ethic and ranging his focal point from the tradesman to the "new woman." In the last half of the 1890's and until his death in 1903, Gissing's work was more varied, ranging from a historical romance to a travel book to reworkings of his early themes. In those last years, his works were not always successful, either commercially or critically, but that was the period of his most popular work, the semiautobiographical *The Private Papers of Henry Ryecroft.*

In an early and important ressessment of Gissing's career, Jacob Korg ("Division of Purpose in George Gissing," in *PMLA*, June, 1955) points out that the dichotomy between Gissing's artistic principles and his anger over Victorian England's social problems is evident in five of his novels published in the 1880's: *Workers in the Dawn, The Unclassed, Demos, Thyrza,* and *The Nether World.* In each of these novels, Gissing the reformer contends with Gissing the artist; in none of them is the tension resolved satisfactorily.

Workers in the Dawn · Most of the material Gissing used in *Workers in the Dawn* can be found repeatedly in the other novels of the 1880's, and most of that material springs from his own experiences. Clearly, his early marriage to a girl from the slums underlined his interest in social themes throughout his life. In the late 1870's and 1880's, he had also become enthusiastic about the radical party, read Comte, promoted positivist doctrines, and spoke at various radicalist meetings. Between 1879 and 1880, Gissing began writing *Workers in the Dawn,* a novel of avowed social protest in which he serves, as he says in a letter of June 8, 1880, as "a mouthpiece of the advanced Radical party." Equally obvious in the novel, however, is the fact that Gissing is perturbed about placing art in service to political and moral dogma. Arthur Goldring, the hero of the novel, is both a painter and a social reformer, but he is clearly upset with this duality in his life. Convinced that the aims of his two avocations are antithetical, he looks for consolation from Helen Norman, the woman he loves. Through the mouth of Helen, George Gissing propounds the ideas that he had gleaned from Percy Bysshe Shelley's *A Defence of Poetry* (1840)—most specifically that art is the true legislator of the moral order. Gissing, however, found it difficult to practice what he held to be intellectually valid; thus, the early Gissing, like Goldring, constantly found difficulty in accepting the tenet that art should not attempt to teach morality directly.

The Unclassed · In *The Unclassed,* Gissing continued to struggle with the intricacies of the artist's world. The result, unfortunately, was a novel in which the fall of the two artist-figures is in one case oversimplified and in the other, muddled. Confused and worried about his own failings, Gissing attempted to analyze the artistic temperament and the forces operating against such a temperament by segmenting the artist into Julian Casti and Osmond Waymark. Casti's story is Gissing's attempt to depict an artist undone by an overriding sense of moral obligation to a shrewish and possessive woman, Harriet Smales, a character with clear similarities to Gissing's own wife Nell. Not until the last chapter is the physically debilitated and intellectually frustrated Casti convinced that his moral obligation to Harriet is futile. He leaves for the Isle of Wight, where he quietly spends his last days plaintively talking of the epic he will never write.

The portrait of Waymark is Gissing's attempt to counterbalance the oversimplified Casti. Waymark is a more complex figure, and his role as an artist is more thoroughly scrutinized by Gissing. Waymark is thwarted in his pursuit of art by a variety of causes: his aborted social consciousness, his vaguely defined ideological tenets, his relationship with women, and his pecuniary predicament. By the end of the novel, after a plethora of complications, Waymark is neither a complete success nor a complete failure. His one published novel receives mediocre reviews, and Waymark himself shows little concern either for its intrinsic value or for its critical reception. By placing his artist-hero in the grips of consuming personal, political, and economic woes, Gissing tries to suggest that art cannot flourish with integrity or purity. The portrait of Waymark, however, is finally very muddled, for it is not clear to which forces Waymark the artist succumbs. Questions about the role of art in the political and moral order continued to dominate Gissing's thinking in much the same way throughout the 1880's, and he entered the 1890's very much in the middle of the two main currents of literary thought, drawn both to the angry didacticism of the realists and naturalists and to the ivory towers of the aesthetes.

In the 1890's, Gissing broadened the range of his novels and produced his best work. At the beginning of the decade, he published *The Emancipated*, the story of a young middle-class widow restricted by religious scruples until she finds release in art. In *Denzil Quarrier*, Gissing tried his hand at a political novel and produced one of his more popular works. In *Eve's Ransom*, a short novel that was first serialized, he focused on the pangs of unrequited love. In *Born in Exile*, Gissing examined the life of one born in the lower classes who has the opportunity to rise to a higher socioeconomic level. In *The Odd Women*, Gissing focused his attention on early feminists, making a careful study of women who never marry but who must support themselves in a male-dominated society.

New Grub Street · The novel on which Gissing's reputation has most depended is *New Grub Street*, his full-length study of the artist's role in society. From Jasper Milvain to Whelpdale to Alfred Yule to Edwin Reardon to Harold Biffin, Gissing offers a finely graduated hierarchy of the late nineteenth century artist. He is particularly interested in characterizing the artist *manqué* and the forces which have contributed to his failure. Unlike the earlier novels, however, *New Grub Street* presents a wider-ranging understanding of the artist's dilemma. It is no longer a simple case of idealized social reform versus an even more idealized artistic purity. In keeping with his social interests of the early 1890's, Gissing sees the factors operating against the artist arising more from without than from within. He concentrates on two particularly potent forces which militate against the artist and ultimately ensure his downfall.

The first force is the woman, and her influence on the artist is subtle, pervasive, and lasting. Often sensitive and frequently lonely, the nascent artists of Gissing's Grub Street are prime targets for the love of a good woman. She appeals particularly to the psychologically insecure artist, promising a lifetime of emotional stability. At the outset, she is a source of inspiration, yet time and disillusionment reveal more distressing realities. It is the age-old femme fatale who lures the artist away from his art into an emotionally draining existence, thwarting his inclination and energy for production. It is "the other woman" who instigates a complicated triangle with like results. It is the husband-hunting woman who tantalizes the frustrated artist with the attraction of domestic security, but soon she either stifles that inexplicable drive to write for the sake of writing or provides a marriage so socially disadvantageous that advancement is precluded.

Economics is the second, equally potent, force militating against the three failed artists (Reardon, Biffen, Yule) of *New Grub Street*. While the force of woman is chiefly felt on a psychological level, her destructive influence within the economic sphere is evident. After all, the necessity of supporting a wife and children increases the financial difficulties the artist must face. Monetary matters also prove a problem in and of themselves. An artist such as Biffen easily falls victim to the myth of so many struggling artists, convinced that poverty and hardship are essential in the experience of any would-be writer. In the portrait of Reardon, however, one quickly sees the artist at odds with real poverty, rarely an inspiration and usually a deterrent to his work.

Edwin Reardon is the novel's central character, and it is Reardon who is subjected to the greatest number of debilitating forces. When he is introduced, it is immediately clear that his marriage to Amy has entangled him in the finely woven web of woman. At the outset, Reardon is thirty-two, has been married two years, and has a ten-month-old child. None of his decisions, artistic or otherwise, can be wholly unaffected by this domestic responsibility. Gissing makes his viewpoint clear in the very first scene with Reardon and Amy. In this scene, largely a heated discussion over Reardon's approach to writing, Amy chides her husband for not compromising his artistic integrity and forcibly reminds him that "art must be practised as a trade, at all events in our time. This is the age of trade." Thus, in this one early scene, the two powerful influences of woman and commerce come together, and there is little doubt that they will take a heavy toll on Reardon the artist. Reardon's failure as an artist, both aesthetically and materially, runs in direct proportion to the failure of his marriage and the decline of his economic status.

Obviously lending itself to autobiographical interpretation, the artist-novel is the means by which the real-life writer works out—or fails to work out—his own aesthetic and personal conflicts. *New Grub Street*, like Gissing's earlier novels, has its share of autobiographical elements, but his analysis of his emotional and intellectual condition is far more perceptive. He has gained tighter control on the raw materials of the artist's world which are treated ambiguously in the early novels. The eleven years between *Workers in the Dawn* and *New Grub Street* were the training ground for an increased self-insight and a more encompassing, objective portraiture of the artist-figure and the gray areas with which he must cope.

The work Gissing produced in the last half of the 1890's has not generally contributed to his critical reputation. Part of his later years he spent on a variety of projects that are not especially characteristic of his overall career. In 1898, he published *Charles Dickens: A Critical Study*. In 1901, he published *By the Ionian Sea*, a travel book about his experiences in Italy. He also worked on a historical novel which was never completed but published posthumously as *Veranilda* in 1904. The novels that Gissing published in his last years are for the most part undistinguished and often are reworkings of his earlier themes. *The Whirlpool* is a study of marriage in the "whirlpool" of modern life. *The Crown of Life* is his paean to the perfect marriage, significantly begun shortly after he met Gabrielle Fleury in 1898.

The Private Papers of Henry Ryecroft · In 1900, Gissing did most of the writing of *The Private Papers of Henry Ryecroft*, though it was not published until 1903. The book is not really a novel. Pretending to be merely the book's editor, Gissing provides a short preface saying that he has come across the papers of his friend Ryecroft and has ordered them in an arbitrary way. There are four main sections, each labeled with one of the seasons, beginning with spring and ending with winter. The book is a mixture of autobiography and reverie, providing the author a platform on which he can discuss sundry subjects. Thus, there are memories of childhood, of poverty in London, of peaceful trips to Italy. There are descriptive sketches of rural scenes in England. There are short essays on philosophical ideas and terse confessions of various preferences, ranging from food to countries. The book provides delightful if not exciting reading and gives a memorable portrait of the aging author who has retired to the calmness of Exeter to ruminate.

When Gissing died in 1903, he left behind an impressive corpus, but the reputation he had at the time of his death did not continue to grow. By some, he was criticized as being too ponderous and undramatic, inclined to publish an analytical study rather than a dramatized story. By others, he was accused of being melodramatic, relying too exclusively on the contrivances of the Victorian "triple-decker." In the second half of the twentieth century, however, especially during the last two decades, Gissing attracted more attention in academic circles. His seriousness as a novelist has slowly been recognized, both for his historic role in the heyday of English realism and for his integrity as an individual novelist.

David B. Eakin

Other major works

SHORT FICTION: *Human Odds and Ends*, 1897; *The House of Cobwebs*, 1906; *Sins of the Fathers*, 1924; *A Victim of Circumstances*, 1927; *Brownie*, 1931.

NONFICTION: *Charles Dickens: A Critical Study*, 1898; *By the Ionian Sea*, 1901; *The Immortal Dickens*, 1925; *Letters of George Gissing to Members of His Family*, 1927; *George Gissing and H. G. Wells: Their Friendship and Correspondence*, 1961; *The Letters of George Gissing to Eduard Bertz*, 1961; *George Gissing's Commonplace Book*, 1962; *The Letters of George Gissing to Gabrielle Fleury*, 1964; *George Gissing: Essays and Fiction*, 1970; *The Diary of George Gissing, Novelist*, 1978.

Bibliography

Connelly, Mark. *Orwell and Gissing*. New York: Peter Lang, 1997. Compares *New Grub Street* with George Orwell's *Keep the Aspidistra Flying* (1936). Also, a chapter on "Doomed Utopias: *Animal Farm* and *Demos*."

Coustillas, Pierre, and Colin Partridge, eds. *Gissing: The Critical Heritage*. London: Routledge & Kegan Paul, 1972. A very important research tool for the study of Gissing, containing a large selection of reviews dating from his own time to the late 1960's. Among the notable essays is a notice by the great Victorian critic George Saintsbury, who claimed that Gissing had an obsessional interest in attacking the social order, but who nevertheless liked Gissing because his writing was difficult to forget. Paul Elmer More argued that Gissing overcame the undue realism of his first novels. Gissing's study of the classics and philosophy tempered his overblown portrayal of society.

Grylls, David. *The Paradox of Gissing*. London: Allen & Unwin, 1986. Maintains that paradox is the key to reading Gissing properly. He was attracted to conflicting points of view on various topics, including women, social reform, poverty, and art. His novels express these contradictions, often by a sharp break in the middle. In *New Grub Street*, Gissing achieved an integration of diverse opinions.

Halperin, John. *Gissing: A Life in Books*. Oxford, England: Oxford University Press, 1982. The most comprehensive life of Gissing. Its dominant theme is that he wrote about his own life in his novels, and much of the book discusses Gissing's fiction from this point of view. Halperin does not confine himself to Gissing's life, devoting considerable attention to the critical reaction to Gissing after his death. Maintains that H. G. Wells launched a campaign of vilification against Gissing. Also includes a section that offers acidulous remarks of other writers about Gissing.

Michaux, Jean-Pierre, ed. *George Gissing: Critical Essays.* New York: Barnes & Noble Books, 1981. This valuable anthology gives a good selection of twentieth century critics' discussions of Gissing. Includes an influential essay by Q. D. Leavis, who praised Gissing's portrayal of the misery of the Victorian world. His careful and realistic observations achieved their culmination in *New Grub Street,* which Leavis places among the outstanding English novels. An essay by George Orwell lauds Gissing's attack on respectability.

Selig, Robert L. *George Gissing.* Rev. ed. New York: Twayne, 1995. An excellent introduction, with chapters on Gissing's major works, his career as a man of letters, and his biography. Includes chronology, notes, and annotated bibliography.

Sloan, John. *George Gissing: The Cultural Challenge.* New York: St. Martin's Press, 1989. Chapters on Gissing's "Hogarthian beginnings," his working-class novels, his career from *The Emancipated* to *New Grub Street,* and *The Odd Women.* Includes detailed notes and bibliography.

William Golding

Born: St. Columb Minor, Cornwall, England; September 19, 1911
Died: Perranarworthal, Cornwall, England; June 19, 1993

Principal long fiction · *Lord of the Flies,* 1954; *The Inheritors,* 1955; *Pincher Martin,* 1956 (also known as *The Two Deaths of Christopher Martin*); *Free Fall,* 1959; *The Spire,* 1964; *The Pyramid,* 1967; *Darkness Visible,* 1979; *Rites of Passage,* 1980; *The Paper Men,* 1984; *Close Quarters,* 1987; *Fire Down Below,* 1989; *The Double Tongue,* 1995.

Other literary forms · William Golding's first and only book of poetry, entitled simply *Poems,* was published in 1934. "Envoy Extraordinary," a 1956 novella, was recast in 1958 in the form of a play, *The Brass Butterfly;* set in Roman times, *The Brass Butterfly* uses irony to examine the value of "modern" inventions. "Envoy Extraordinary" was published along with two other novellas, "The Scorpion God" and "Clonk Clonk," in a 1971 collection bearing the title *The Scorpion God.*

Golding also produced nonfiction; his book reviews in *The Spectator* between 1960 and 1962 frequently took the form of personal essays. Many of his essays and autobiographical pieces were collected in *The Hot Gates and Other Occasional Pieces* (1965). *A Moving Target* (1982) is another set of essays; *An Egyptian Journal* (1985) is a travelogue. Golding also gave numerous interviews explaining his work; these have appeared in a variety of journals and magazines.

Achievements · Sir William Gerald Golding is without doubt one of the major British novelists of the post-World War II era. He depicted in many different ways the anguish of modern humanity as it gropes for meaning and redemption in a world where the spiritual has been all but crushed by the material. His themes deal with guilt, responsibility, and salvation. He depicts the tension between individual fallenness and social advance, or, to put it differently, the cost of progress to the individual.

Golding's work portrays a period in which the last vestiges of an optimistic belief in evolutionary progress collapsed under the threat of nuclear destruction. In doing this, he moved the classic British novel tradition forward both in stylistic and formal technique and in the opening up of a new, contemporary social and theological dialectic.

Golding was a Fellow of the Royal Society of Literature (elected in 1955), and in 1983 he received the Nobel Prize in Literature. He won the James Tait Black Memorial Prize in 1979 for *Darkness Visible* and the Booker Prize in 1980 for *Rites of Passage.* He was knighted in 1989.

Biography · Born in the county of Cornwall in the southwest corner of England, the son of a rationalistic schoolmaster, William Golding had a relatively isolated childhood. Eventually his family moved to Marlborough, in Wiltshire, where his father was a science teacher. There Golding received his high school education, while revisiting Cornwall frequently. He graduated from Brasenose College, Oxford, in science and literature. The choice of arts over science was made at the university, but scientific interests and approaches can be easily discerned in his literary work. Each

407

©The Nobel Foundation

novel is, in a way, a new experiment set up to test a central hypothesis.

After the unsuccessful publication of a book of poetry in 1934, Golding moved to London and participated in fringe theater without achieving anything of significance. In 1939 he married Ann Brookfield and accepted a teaching position at Bishop Wordsworth's School, Salisbury, also in Wiltshire. Soon after the outbreak of war, he joined the Royal Navy, seeing extensive action against German warships, being adrift for three days in the English Channel, and participating in the Normandy landings.

After the war, Golding resumed teaching and tried writing novels. His first four were highly imitative and met only by editorial refusals. He then decided to write as he wanted, not as he thought he should. This shift in approach led to the immediate publication of *Lord of the Flies* in 1954; this work became almost at once a landmark on the British literary scene. Golding was able to follow this achievement with three more novels in the space of only five years, by which time paperback versions were being issued on both sides of the Atlantic. In 1961 he retired from teaching, becoming for two years a book reviewer with *The Spectator*, one of the leading British weekly cultural reviews. In *The Paper Men*, Golding depicts a novelist whose first novel turned out to be a gold mine for him—an autobiographical echo, no doubt.

After the publication of *The Pyramid* in 1967, when Golding was fifty-six years old, there came rather a long silence, and many people assumed that he had brought his career to a close. With the publication of *Darkness Visible* twelve years later, however, a steady stream of new novels emerged, including a trilogy. This second phase also marked the reception of various prizes, including the Nobel Prize in Literature, and his being knighted, a comparatively rare honor for a novelist in Britain.

Golding had one son and one daughter. He and his wife returned to Cornwall to live in 1984. Two years after his death in 1993, a nearly completed novel, *The Double Tongue*, was published.

Analysis · William Golding, like his older British contemporary Graham Greene, is a theological novelist: That is to say, his main thematic material focuses on particular theological concerns, in particular sin and guilt, innocence and its loss, individual responsibility and the possibility of atonement for mistakes made, and the need for spiritual revelation. Unlike Greene, however, he does not write out of a particular

Christian, or even religious, belief system; the dialectic he sets up is neither specifically Catholic (like Greene's) nor Protestant. In fact, Golding's dialectic is set up in specific literary terms, in that it is with other works of literature that he argues, rather than with theological or philosophical positions per se. The texts with which he argues do represent such positions or make certain cultural assumptions of such positions; however, it is through literary technique that he argues—paralleling, echoing, deconstructing—rather than through narratorial didacticism.

Golding's achievement is a literary tour de force. The British novel has never contained theological dialectic easily, except at a superficial level, let alone a depiction of transcendence. Golding has accepted the nineteenth century novel tradition but has modified it extensively. Each novel represents a fresh attempt for him to refashion the language and the central consciousness of that tradition. Sometimes he has pushed it beyond the limits of orthodox mimetic realism, and hence some of his novels have been called fables, allegories, or myths. In general, however, his central thrust is to restate the conflict between individuals and their society in contemporary terms, and in doing this, to question at a fundamental level many cultural assumptions, and to point up the loss of moral and spiritual values in twentieth century Western civilization—an enterprise in which most nineteenth century novelists were similarly involved for their own time.

Lord of the Flies · Golding's first and most famous novel, *Lord of the Flies*, illustrates this thesis well. Although there is a whole tradition of island-castaway narratives, starting with one of the earliest novels in English literature, Daniel Defoe's *Robinson Crusoe* (1719), the text which Golding clearly had in mind to argue with was R. M. Ballantyne's *The Coral Island* (1858), written almost exactly one hundred years before Golding's. The names of Ballantyne's three schoolboy heroes (Ralph, Jack, and Peterkin) are taken over, with Peterkin becoming Simon (the biblical reversion being significant) and various episodes in Ballantyne being parodied by Golding—for example, the pig-sticking.

Ballantyne's yarn relied on the English public-school ethos that boys educated within a British Christian discipline would survive anything and in fact would be able to control their environment—in miniature, the whole British imperialistic enterprise of the nineteenth century. Most desert-island narratives do make the assumption that Western men can control their environment, assuming that they are moral, purposeful, and religious. Golding subverts all these suppositions: Except for a very few among them, the abandoned schoolboys, significantly younger than Ballantyne's and more numerous (making a herd instinct possible), soon lose the veneer of the civilization they have acquired. Under Jack's leadership, they paint their faces, hunt pigs, and then start killing one another. They ritually murder Simon, the mystic, whose transcendental vision of the Lord of the Flies (a pig's head on a pole) is of the evil within. They also kill Piggy, the rationalist. The novel ends with the pack pursuing Ralph, the leader democratically elected at the beginning; the boys are prepared to burn the whole island to kill him.

Ironically, the final conflagration serves as a powerful signal for rescue (earlier watchfires having been pathetically inadequate), and, in a sudden reversal, an uncomprehending British naval officer lands on the beach, amazed at the mud-covered, dirty boys before him. Allegorically it might be thought that as this world ends in fire, a final divine intervention will come. Ironically, however, the adult world that the officer represents is also destroying itself as effectively, in a nuclear war. Salvation remains problematic and ambiguous.

What lifts the novel away from simple allegory is not only the ambiguities but also the dense poetic texture of its language. The description of Simon's death is often quoted as brilliantly heightened prose—the beauty of the imagery standing in stark contrast to the brutality of his slaying. Yet almost any passage yields its own metaphorical textures and suggestive symbolism. Golding's rich narrative descriptions serve to point up the poverty of the boys' language, which can only dwell on basics—food, defecation, fears and night terrors, killings. Golding's depiction of the children is immediately convincing. The adult intervention (the dead airman, the naval officer) is perhaps not quite so, being too clearly fabular. In general, however, the power of the novel derives from the tensions set up between the book's novelistic realism and its fabular and allegorical qualities. The theological dialectic of humanity's fallenness (not only the boys') and the paper-thin veneer of civilization emerges inexorably out of this genre tension.

The Inheritors · The thinness of civilization forms the central thesis of Golding's second novel, *The Inheritors*. The immediate literary dialectic is set up with H. G. Wells's *The Outline of History: Being a Plain History of Life and Mankind* (1920), which propounds the typical social evolutionism common from the 1850's onward. At a more general level, Golding's novel might also be seen as an evolutionary version of John Milton's *Paradise Lost* (1667): Satan's temptation to Eve is a temptation to progress; the result is the fall. Just as Adam and Eve degrade themselves with drunken behavior, so do Golding's Neanderthal protagonists, Lok and Fa, when they stumble over the remains of *Homo sapiens*' cannibalistic "festivities."

Golding has subverted the Wellsian thesis that Neanderthals were totally inferior by depicting them as innocent, gentle, intuitive, playful, and loving. They stand in ironic contrast to the group of *Homo sapiens* who eventually annihilate them, except for a small baby whom they kidnap (again reversing a short story by Wells, where it is Neanderthals who kidnap a human baby). The humans experience terror, lust, rage, drunkenness, and murder, and their religion is propitiatory only. By contrast, the Neanderthals have a taboo against killing anything, and their reverence for Oa, the Earth Mother, is gentle and numinous in quality.

As in *Lord of the Flies*, the conclusion is formed by an ironic reversal—the reader suddenly sees from the humans' perspective. The last line reads, "He could not see if the line of darkness had an ending." It is a question Golding is posing: Has the darkness of the human heart an end?

Golding's technique is remarkable in the novel: He succeeds in convincing the reader that primitive consciousness could have looked like this. He has had to choose language that conveys that consciousness, yet is articulate enough to engage one imaginatively so that one respects the Neanderthals. He explores the transition from intuition and pictorial thinking to analogous and metaphoric thought. The ironic treatment of *Homo sapiens* is done also through the limits of Neanderthal perceptions and consciousness. Unfortunately, humans, as fallen creatures, can supply all too easily the language for the evil that the Neanderthals lack.

Pincher Martin · Golding's third novel, *Pincher Martin* (first published in the United States as *The Two Deaths of Christopher Martin*), returns to the desert-island tradition. The immediate dialectic is perhaps with Robinson Crusoe, the sailor who single-handedly carves out an island home by the strength of his will aided by his faith. Pincher Martin is here the faithless antihero, although this is not immediately apparent. He, like Crusoe, appears to survive a wreck (Martin's destroyer is torpedoed during the war); he kicks off seaboots and swims to a lonely island-rock in the Atlantic. With tremendous strength of will, he appears to survive by eating raw shellfish, making rescue signals, forcing an enema into himself, and keeping sane and purposeful.

In the end, however, his sanity appears to disintegrate. Almost to the end it is quite possible to believe that Christopher Martin finally succumbs to madness and death only after a heroic, indeed Promethean, struggle against Fate and the elements. The last chapter, however, presents an even greater reversal than those in the first two novels, dispelling all of this as a false reading: Martin's drowned body is found washed up on a Scottish island with his seaboots still on his feet. In other words, the episode on the rock never actually took place. The reading of *Pincher Martin* thus becomes deliberately problematic in a theological sense. The rock must be an illusion, an effort of the will indeed, but an effort after physical death. Yet it is not that all of one's life flashes in front of one while one drowns, though that does happen with Martin's sordid memories of his lust, greed, and terror. It is more that the text is formed by Martin's ongoing dialectic with, or rather against, his destiny, which he sees as annihilation. An unnameable god is identified with the terror and darkness of the cellar of his childhood memories. His will, in its Promethean pride, is creating its own alternative. Theologically, this alternative can only be Purgatory or Hell, since it is clearly not heaven. Satan in *Paradise Lost* says, "Myself am Hell": Strictly, this is Martin's position, since he refuses the purgatorial possibilities in the final revelation of God, with his mouthless cry of "I shit on your heaven!" God, in his compassion, strikes Martin into annihilation with his "black lightning."

Free Fall · Golding's first three novels hardly suggested that he was writing from within any central tradition of the British novel. All three are highly original in plot, for all of their dialectic with existing texts, and in style and technique. In his next novel, *Free Fall*, Golding writes much more recognizably within the tradition of both the *Bildungsroman* (the novel of character formation) and the *Künstlerroman* (the novel of artistic development). Sammy Mountjoy, a famous artist, is investigating his past life, but with the question in mind, "When did I lose my freedom?" The question is not in itself necessarily theological, but Sammy's search is conducted in specifically theological categories.

It has been suggested that the literary dialectic is with Albert Camus's *La Chute* (1956; *The Fall*, 1957), a novella published some three years earlier. Camus's existentialism sees no possibility of redemption or regeneration once the question has been answered; his protagonist uses the question, in fact, to gain power over others by exploiting their guilt, so the whole search would seem inauthentic. Golding sees such a search as vital: His position seems to be that no person is born in sin, or fallen, but inevitably at some stage, each person chooses knowingly to sin. At that moment he falls and loses his freedom to choose. The only possibility of redemption is to recognize that moment, to turn from it, and to cry out, "Help me!"

This is Sammy's cry when he is locked in a German prisoner-of-war camp and interrogated. His physical release from his cell is also a spiritual release, a moment of revelation described in Pentecostal terms of renewal and a new artistic vision. His moment of fall, which he discovers only near the end of the book (which is here culmination rather than reversal), was when he chose to seduce Beatrice (the name of Dante's beloved inspiration also), whatever the cost and despite a warning that "sooner or later the sacrifice is always regretted."

Other theological perspectives are introduced. Two of Sammy's teachers form an opposition: the rational, humanistic, likable Nick Shales and the religious, intense, but arrogant Miss Pringle. Sammy is caught in the middle, wanting to affirm the spiritual but drawn to the materialist. The dilemma goes back in the English novel to George Eliot. Though Golding cannot accept Eliot's moral agnosticism, he has to accept her inexorable moral law of cause and effect: Sammy's seduction of Beatrice has left her witless and insane. The scene in the prison cell is balanced by the scene in the mental institution. Redemption costs; the past remains. The fall may be arrested and even reversed, but only through self-knowledge and full confession.

In *Free Fall*, Golding chose for the first time to use first-person narrative. Before that he had adopted a third-person narrative technique that stayed very close to the consciousness of the protagonists. In *The Spire*, Golding could be said to have perfected this latter technique. Events are seen not only through the eyes of Dean Jocelin but also in his language and thought processes. As in Henrik Ibsen's *Bygmester Solness* (1892; *The Master Builder*, 1893), Golding's protagonist has an obsessive drive to construct a church tower, or rather a spire on a tower, for his cathedral lacks both. (Inevitably one takes the cathedral to be Salisbury, whose medieval history is almost identical, although it is not named.) Ibsen's play deals with the motivation for such an obsession, the price to be paid, and the spiritual conflicts. Golding, however, is not so much in a dialectic situation with the Ibsen play as using it as his base, agreeing with Ibsen when the latter talks of "the power of ideals to kill." At the end of the novel, the spire has been built in the face of tremendous technical difficulties, but Jocelin lies dying, the caretaker and his wife have been killed, the master builder, Roger, is a broken man, and the whole life of the cathedral has been disrupted.

Thus Golding raises the question of cost again: What is the cost of progress? Is it progress? The power of the book is that these questions can be answered in many different ways, and each way searches out new richness from the text. The patterning of moral and theological structures allows for almost endless combinations. The novel can also be read in terms of the cost of art—the permanence of art witnessing to humanity's spirituality and vision, as against the Freudian view of art as sublimation and neurotic outlet, the price of civilization.

By staying very close to Jocelin's consciousness, the reader perceives only slowly, as he does, that much of his motivation and drive is not quite as visionary and spiritual as he first thinks. Freudian symbolism and imagery increasingly suggest sexual sublimation, especially centered on Goody Pangall, whom he calls "his daughter in God." In fact, much later one learns that he received his appointment only because his aunt was the king's mistress for a while. Jocelin manipulates people more and more consciously to get the building done and chooses, perhaps unconsciously at first, to ignore the damage to people, especially the four people he regards as his "pillars" to the spire. Ironically, he too is a pillar, and he damages himself, physically, emotionally, and spiritually (he is almost unable to pray by the end, and has no confessor). Yet despite all the false motives, the novel suggests powerfully that there really has been a true vision that has been effected, even if marred by humanity's fallenness and "total depravity," every part affected by the fall.

The Spire · The language of *The Spire* is the most poetic that Golding attempted. The density of imagery, recurring motifs, and symbolism both psychological and theological blend into marvelous rhythms of ecstasy and horror. The interweaving of inner monologue, dialogue, and narrative dissolves the traditional tight bounds of time and space of the novel form, to create an impassioned intensity where the theological dialectic takes place, not with another text, but within the levels of the moral, spiritual, and metaphoric consciousness of the text itself.

The Pyramid · After the verbal pyrotechnics of *The Spire*, Golding's next novel, *The Pyramid*, seems very flat, despite its title. It returns to *Free Fall* in its use of first-person narrative, to a modified form of its structure (flashbacks and memories to provide a personal pattern), and to contemporary social comedy, strongly echoing Anthony Trollope. The language is spare and unadorned, as perhaps befits the protagonist, Olly, who, unlike Sammy Mountjoy, has turned away from art and spirit to become *un homme moyen sensual*. His life has become a defense against love, but as a petit bourgeois he has been protected against Sammy's traumatic upbringing, and so one feels little sympathy for him. Theological and moral dialectic is muted, and the social commentary and comedy have been better done by other novelists, although a few critics have made out a case for a rather more complex structuring than is at first evident.

Darkness Visible · Perhaps the flatness of *The Pyramid* suggests that Golding had for the time being run out of impetus. Only two novellas were published in the next twelve years, and then, quite unexpectedly, *Darkness Visible* appeared. In some ways it echoes Charles Williams, the writer of a number of religious allegorical novels in the 1930's and 1940's. The reality of spiritual realms of light and darkness is made by Golding as explicitly as by Williams, especially in Matty, the "holy fool." Yet Golding never quite steps into allegory, any more than he did in his first novel. His awareness of good and evil takes on a concreteness that owes much to Joseph Conrad. Much of the feel of the novel is Dickensian, if not its structure: The grotesque serves to demonstrate the "foolishness of the wise," as with Charles Dickens.

The book divides into three parts centering on Matty, orphaned and hideously burned in the bombing of London during the war. At times he keeps a journal and thus moves the narrative into the first person. The second part, by contrast, focuses on Sophy, the sophisticated twin daughter of a professional chess-player (the rationalist), and overwhelmingly exposes the rootlessness and anomie of both contemporary youth culture and the post-1960's bourgeoisie (the children of Olly's generation). The third part concerns a bizarre kidnapping plot where Matty and Sophy nearly meet as adversaries; this is the "darkness visible" (the title coming from the hell of *Paradise Lost*). The end remains ambiguous. Golding attempts a reversal again: The kidnap has been partially successful. Matty has not been able to protect the victims, nor Sophy to complete her scheme, but still children are kidnapped.

Central themes emerge: childhood and innocence corrupted; singleness of purpose, which can be either for good or for evil (contrast also Milton's single and double darkness in *Comus*, 1634); and the foolishness of the world's wisdom. Entropy is a key word, and Golding, much more strongly than hitherto, comments on the decline of Great Britain. Above all, however, Golding's role as a novelist of transcendence is reemphasized: Moments of revelation are the significant moments of knowledge. Unfortunately, revelation can come from dark powers as well as from those of the light. Ultimately, Golding's vision is Miltonic, as has been suggested. The theological dialectic is revealed as that between the children of light and the children of darkness.

Rites of Passage · When *Rites of Passage* followed *Darkness Visible* one year later, Golding had no intention of writing a trilogy (now generally called *To the Ends of the*

Earth: A Sea Trilogy). It was only later he realized that he had "left all those poor sods in the middle of the sea and needed to get them to Australia." The trilogy was well received, perhaps because the plot and themes are relatively straightforward and unambiguous, and the social comedy is more obvious than the theological dialectic. The trilogy fits well into the *Bildungsroman* tradition of Dickens's *Great Expectations* (1860-1861), in that it follows the education of a snob, Edmund Talbot, who, under the patronage of an aristocratic and influential godfather, is embarking on a political career by taking up an appointment in the new colony of New South Wales, Australia, in 1810. It is also enlivened by Golding's wide knowledge of sailing ships and life at sea; the trilogy is the fullest literary expression of this interest he has allowed himself.

The narrative proceeds leisurely in the first person as Edmund decides to keep a diary. In *Rites of Passage*, the plot focuses on the death of one of the passengers, a ridiculous young clergyman, the Reverend Robert James Colley. He is made the butt of everyone's fun, including that of the ordinary sailors. As the result of the shame of a joke, where he is made drunk and then engages in homosexual activities, he more or less wills himself to die. Captain Anderson covers up the incident–at which Edmund, for the first time, feels moral outrage and vows to expose the captain to his godfather when he can. The moral protest is vitiated, however, by Edmund's use of power and privilege.

Close Quarters · In *Close Quarters*, Edmund's education continues. As conditions on board ship deteriorate, he increases in stature, losing his aristocratic bearing and becoming willing to mix socially. His relationship with Summers, the most morally aware of the ship's lieutenants, is good for him in particular. He also shows himself sensitive: He weeps at a woman's song, he falls in love (as opposed to the lust in *Rites of Passage*), and he admires Colley's written style (Colley, too, has left behind a journal). He suffers physically and shows courage. His falling in love is delightfully described, quite unselfconsciously. He learns, too, the limits of his power: The elements control everything. The speed of the ship runs down as weeds grow on its underside, reintroducing the entropy motif of *Darkness Visible*. He cannot prevent suicide or death. As the novel proceeds, the "ship of fools" motif of late medieval literature becomes very strong. Edmund is no more and no less a fool than the others.

Fire Down Below · *Fire Down Below* closes the trilogy as the ship docks in Sidney Cove, and Edmund is reunited happily with the young lady he met. The ending seems to be social comedy, until one realizes that Summers's fear, that a fire lit below decks to forge a metal band around a broken mast is still smoldering, is proved true. The anchored ship bursts into flame, and Summers is killed, having just been given promotion, partly through Edmund's efforts. Despite this tragedy, the ending is Dickensian, for the voyage has turned into a quest for love for Edmund, and love has helped mark his way with moral landmarks. Edmund has learned much, although at the end he has still far to go. The ending is perhaps the most mellow of all Golding's endings: If Australia is not "the new Jerusalem," it is not hell either, and if Edmund lacks spirituality, he is yet more than *un homme moyen sensual.*

The Paper Men · *The Paper Men* is, like *Free Fall*, a *Künstlerroman*. The style is much more akin to that of twentieth century American confessional literature, especially Saul Bellow's. Golding's Wilfred Barclay could easily be a Henderson or a Herzog, with the same energetic, somewhat zany style, and with the themes of flight and pursuit in a frantic search for identity. Unusually for Golding, the novel seems to be repeating themes and structures, if not style, and perhaps for that reason has not made the same impact as his other novels. Wilfred's revelation of the transcendent in an ambiguous spiritual experience of Christ (or Pluto) marks the high point of the novel.

The Double Tongue · Golding's final novel, *The Double Tongue*, was still in its third draft at the time of his death. For the first time he uses a female first-person voice; also for the first time, there is a classical Greek setting. Arieka is the prophetess, or "Pythia," of the renowned Delphic oracle, but during a period of its decline after the Roman occupation. She tells of her own calling, her first experience of the prophetic, and of the continuing marginalization of the oracle. The male presence is represented by Ionides, the high priest of Zeus and master in charge of the sacred complex of Delphi and its wider network. The only other full character is the slave-librarian, Perseus.

The style of the novel is sparer and more relaxed than that of Golding's earlier novels, with few characters and minimal plot. Its interest lies, as in *The Paper Men*, with the nature of epiphany and with whether the experience of transcendence actualizes anything of significance in an increasingly secular world. The political genius of Rome, and even the literary legacy of the Ancient Greek writers, seem much more powerful influences. The sacred is reduced almost to superstition: The questions posed to the oracle become more and more trivial.

Ionides, while institutionally having to acknowledge the sacred, behaves as if the human spirit is the ultimate source of the prophetic. Arieka, having been seized, or "raped," by Dionysos, the god of prophecy, knows the truth to be otherwise, but even she increasingly feels that her prophetic gift has ceased to be supernatural and has become a natural expression of her human wisdom. In a way, this concern with the prophetic can be traced back to Simon in *The Lord of the Flies*, and then to the form of the *Künstlerroman*. Unlike the latter, however, the context here is specifically sacred, and it would be a mistake to deconstruct the novel in terms of the nature of artistic inspiration. Nevertheless, the problematic nature of inspiration, whether divine or poetic, is as real to Golding in his last novel as in, say, *The Spire*.

The setting of a declining Greece continues the concern with entropy so powerfully expressed in *Darkness Visible*. Signs of cultural entropy include the growth of "copying" manuscripts rather than creating texts, the marginalization of the transcendent, and the *trahison des clercs*–Ionides is found to be plotting a pathetic revolt against Roman hegemony. Politics has undermined any integrity he had.

There would not appear to be a specific subtext with which Golding is arguing. *The Double Tongue* bears remarkable similarities to C. S. Lewis's final, and most literary, novel, *Till We Have Faces* (1956), also set in classical Greek times. In both, a female consciousness aware of its own physical ugliness, yet possessing real power, undergoes a spiritual journey with multifarious symbolic levels. Lewis's novel, however, ends with epiphany as closure; Golding's begins with it, and the rest of the novel seeks ambiguously to give it meaning. Golding's epiphany here is the god's laughter, at least that laughter of which Arieka is aware.

Although each Golding novel, with a few exceptions, is a new "raid on the inarticulate," certain thematic and technical features remain constant over the years. Golding's moral and didactic concerns consistently sought theological grounding out of which to construct a critique of the lostness and fallenness of humankind, and specifically of contemporary Western civilization, with its spiritual bankruptcy. In this quest there is a line of continuity back to George Eliot and Charles Dickens in the

English novel tradition. In his affirmation of the primacy of the spiritual over the material he echoes not only them but also, in different ways, Thomas Hardy and D. H. Lawrence. In his vision of the darkness of the human soul, unenlightened by any transcendent revelation, he follows Joseph Conrad.

He also seeks, as did E. M. Forster and Lawrence, to find a style that escapes the materiality of prose and attains to the revelatory transcendence of poetry. The result is usually dramatic, incarnational metaphors and motifs. The mode is usually confessional, almost Augustinian at times, coming from a single consciousness, though often with a sudden reversal at the end to sustain an ambiguous dialectic.

There is in Golding no articulated framework of beliefs: Transcendence lies ultimately beyond the articulate. God is there, and revelation is not only possible but indeed necessary and salvific. Yet the revelation remains ambiguous, fleeting, and numinous, rather than normative. In the end, this often means that Golding's social critique, of the moral entropy of Britain in particular, comes over more powerfully than the darkness that is the refusal of the terror of believing in God.

David Barratt

Other major works
SHORT FICTION: *The Scorpion God,* 1971.
PLAY: *The Brass Butterfly,* pr., pb. 1958.
RADIO PLAYS: *Miss Pulkinhorn,* 1960; *Break My Heart,* 1962.
POETRY: *Poems,* 1934.
NONFICTION: *The Hot Gates and Other Occasional Pieces,* 1965; *A Moving Target,* 1982; *An Egyptian Journal,* 1985.

Bibliography
Baker, James R., ed. *Critical Essays on William Golding.* Boston: G. K. Hall, 1988. A collection of the best essays on Golding's novels through *The Paper Men.* It also includes Golding's Nobel Lecture and an essay on trends in Golding criticism.
Bloom, Harold, ed. *Lord of the Flies.* Broomall, Pa.: Chelsea House, 1998. Of the many collections of essays on Golding's best-known novel, this is probably the best.
Boyd, S. J. *The Novels of William Golding.* New York: St. Martin's Press, 1988. Provides a chapter on each of Golding's novels through *The Paper Men.* Includes a full bibliography.
Dick, Bernard F. *William Golding.* Boston: Twayne, 1987. Excellent introduction to Golding's life and works.
Dickson, L. L. *The Modern Allegories of William Golding.* Tampa: University of Southern Florida Press, 1990. Renewed theoretical interest in fantasy and allegory have produced this reading of Golding's novels, suggesting a useful balance to earlier studies that looked to psychological realism.
Gindin, James. *William Golding.* Basingstoke, England: Macmillan, 1988. Golding's novels are paired in essays that compare them. Additional chapters examine themes in Golding's work and its critical reception.
Kinkead-Weekes, Mark, and Ian Gregor. *William Golding: A Critical Study.* New York: Harcourt, Brace & World, 1967. Still one of the standard critical accounts of Golding. A full analysis of the first five novels, showing imaginative development and interconnection. An added chapter deals with three later novels.
McCarron, Kevin. *The Coincidence of Opposites: William Golding's Later Fiction.* Shef-

field, England: Sheffield Academic Press, 1995. Analyzes Golding's late works, from *Darkness Visible* to *Fire Down Below*.

Page, Norman, ed. *William Golding: Novels, 1954-1967*. New York: Macmillan, 1985. Part of the excellent Casebook series, this volume consists of an introductory survey, several general essays on Golding's earlier work, and eight pieces on specific novels through *The Pyramid*.

Redpath, Philip. *William Golding: A Structural Reading of His Fiction*. Totowa, N.J.: Barnes & Noble, 1986. Redpath explores the way the novels create meaning, especially through their structures. The novels are treated thematically, not chronologically as in most studies. The final chapter offers suggestions for the future of Golding criticism.

Oliver Goldsmith

Born: Pallas, County Longford(?), Ireland; November 10, 1728 or 1730
Died: London, England; April 4, 1774

Principal long fiction · *The Citizen of the World,* 1762 (collection of essays first published in *The Public Ledger,* 1760-1761); *The Vicar of Wakefield,* 1766.

Other literary forms · Oliver Goldsmith contributed significantly to several literary genres. His works of poetry include *The Traveller: Or, A Prospect of Society* (1764) and *The Deserted Village* (1770), a classic elegiac poem of rural life. He wrote the biographies *Memoirs of M. de Voltaire* (1761), particularly interesting for its anecdotes, and *The Life of Richard Nash of Bath* (1762), especially valuable as a study in the social history of the period. Goldsmith developed principles of literary criticism in *An Enquiry into the Present State of Polite Learning in Europe* (1759), a history of literature in which he laments the decline of letters and morals in his own day. Specimens of his literary journalism are found in *Essays. By Mr Goldsmith* (1765), which includes well-written humorous studies of London society. He wrote two comic plays, *The Good-Natured-Man* (1768) and *She Stoops to Conquer: Or, The Mistakes of a Night* (1773), a rollicking lampoon of the sentimental comedy then in vogue, which is still performed today. In addition, Goldsmith published translations, histories, and even a natural history, *An History of the Earth, and Animated Nature* (1774), containing some quaint descriptions of animals.

Achievements · Goldsmith's contemporaries and posterity have been somewhat ambivalent about his literary stature, which is epitomized in English writer Samuel Johnson's estimate of him: "Goldsmith was a man who, whatever he wrote, did it better than any other man could do." However, Johnson demurred on Goldsmith's *The Vicar of Wakefield,* judging it "very faulty." Yet there can be little dispute over critic A. Lytton Sells's judgment that Goldsmith's "versatility was the most remarkable of his gifts."

Although the novel *The Vicar of Wakefield* has usually been considered his best work, Goldsmith despised the novelist's art and regarded himself principally as a poet. His most famous poem is the reflective and melancholic *The Deserted Village,* a serious piece in heroic couplets; however, perhaps his real poetic gift was for humorous verse, such as *The Haunch of Venison* (1776) and *Retaliation* (1774). Indeed, humor and wit are conspicuous in all his major works: There is the gentle irony of *The Vicar of Wakefield,* the comic portraits and satirical observations in *The Citizen of the World,* and the outright farce of *She Stoops to Conquer.*

Goldsmith was not a Romantic but a classicist by temperament, whose taste was molded by the Latin classics, the Augustan poetry of John Dryden and Alexander Pope, and seventeenth century French literature, and for whom the canons of criticism laid down by Nicolas Boileau and Voltaire were authoritative. Reflecting that background, Goldsmith's style is, in Johnson's words, "noble, elegant, and graceful."

Biography · Oliver Goldsmith was born of English stock to Ann Jones and the Reverend Charles Goldsmith, an Anglican curate. He first attended the village school of Lissoy and was taught by Thomas Byrne, a veteran of the War of the Spanish Sucession. Byrne, a versifier who regaled his pupils with stories and legends of old Irish heroes, perhaps inspired Goldsmith with his love of poetry, imaginative romance, and adventure. In 1747, Goldsmith attended Patrick Hughes's school at Edgeworthstown, where he received a thorough grounding in the Latin classics. While there he probably first heard Turlogh O'Carolan, "the last of the bards," whose minstrelry left a lasting impression on him. In 1745, he entered Trinity College, Dublin, as a sizar, a position which required him to do menial work in exchange for room, board, and tuition. Goldsmith

Library of Congress

earned his B.A. degree in either 1749 or 1750. In 1752, he journeyed to Edinburgh to study medicine, pursuing his medical studies in Leyden in 1754. The next year he set out on a grand tour of the Continent. In February, 1756, he arrived in London, where he briefly taught in Dr. Milner's school for nonconformists and eked out a living doing hack writing.

A reversal of his fortune occurred in 1759, with the publication of his first substantial work, *An Enquiry into the Present State of Polite Learning in Europe.* Goldsmith subsequently befriended such luminaries as the great critic and writer Johnson, the Scottish novelist Tobias Smollett, the actor David Garrick, the writer and statesman Sir Edmund Burke, and the aesthetician and portraitist Sir Joshua Reynolds. In 1763, they formed themselves into the famous Literary Club, which is memorialized in James Boswell's great biography of Johnson. Goldsmith died in 1774, possibly of Bright's disease exacerbated by worry over debts, and was buried in Temple Churchyard. Two years later, the Club erected a monument to him in Poet's Corner of Westminster Abbey, for which Johnson wrote an inscription.

Analysis · Themes that run through Goldsmith's long fiction are his philosophical inquiries into human nature, the problem of evil, the vying of the good and the bad within the human breast, and the conflict between "reason and appetite." His fiction addresses at its deepest level the perennial problem of theodicy, or why God allows the innocent to suffer so grievously. Lien Chi in *The Citizen of the World* exclaims, "Oh, for the reason of our creation; or why we were created to be thus unhappy!" Dr. Primrose in *The Vicar of Wakefield* ruminates, "When I reflect on the distribution of good and evil here below, I find that much has been given man to enjoy, yet still more to suffer." Both come to terms with the conundrum of evil practically, by resolving, in Lien Chi's words, "not to stand unmoved at distress, but endeavour to turn every disaster to our own advantage."

The Citizen of the World · The ninety-eight essays of *The Citizen of the World* were originally published as the "Chinese Letters" in various issues of *The Public Ledger* from January 24, 1760, to August 14, 1761. They were subsequently collated and published in book form in 1762. These essays purport to be letters from Lien Chi Altangi, a Mandarin philosopher from Peking who is visiting London, to his son Hingpo and to Fum Hoam, first President of the Ceremonial Academy of Peking. What qualifies this work as long fiction are the well-delineated characters it creates and the interwoven stories it relates. The principal character is Lien Chi, a type made familiar in the eighteenth century by Charles de Montesquieu's *Lettres persanes* (1721; *Persian Letters*, 1722). Lien Chi represents the man who, through travel, has overcome provincialism and prejudice and has achieved a cosmopolitan outlook. More specifically, perhaps, he represents the sociable, sanguine, and rational side of Goldsmith, who himself had traveled extensively in Europe.

To reinforce the notion that these are the letters of a Chinese man, Goldsmith studs them with Chinese idioms and makes references throughout to Asian beliefs, manners, and customs. Lien Chi cites the philosopher Confucius, and he compares the enlightenment of the East with the ignorance and folly of the West. *The Citizen of the World* capitalizes on the enthusiasm in eighteenth century England for anything Eastern—particularly Chinese—in the way of literature, fashion, design, and art, a vogue which Goldsmith satirizes through the bemused observations of Lien Chi.

Through the character of Lien Chi, a naïve but philosophically astute observer of the human scene, Goldsmith presents a full-blown satire of English society (reminiscent of his compatriot Jonathan Swift's *Gulliver's Travels* [1726], but not so savage). In his letters, Lien Chi gives his impressions of the English, particularly of London society—their institutions, traditions, customs, habits, manners, foibles, and follies. He describes for readers a series of charming and funny pictures of London life in the eighteenth century, the literary equivalent of a William Hogarth painting. He shows us the coffeehouses, literary clubs, theaters, parks and pleasure gardens, churches, and private homes. Two scenes are particularly memorable: In one, Lien Chi describes a church service at St. Paul's Cathedral, where he mistakes the organ for an idol and its music for an oracle. In another scene, he attends a dinner for some clergy of the Church of England and is shocked to find that their sole topic of conversation is nothing more spiritual than the merits of the victuals they are intent on devouring. Aside from the entertainment and edification they afford, these letters are a document in social history, much like Samuel Pepys's diary.

While touring Westminster Abbey, Lien Chi meets and befriends the Man in Black, who represents the "melancholy man," a stock character of the Renaissance. He more particularly can be seen to represent Goldsmith's introverted and melancholy side. Through the Man in Black, Lien Chi meets Beau Tibbs, "an important little trifler" who is a rather shabby, snobbish, and pathetic fop who lives by flattering the rich and the famous. A particularly comic scene describes the visit of Lien Chi, the Man in Black, the pawnbroker's widow, Beau Tibbs, and his wife to Vauxhall Gardens. The Tibbses insist upon having supper in "a genteel box" where they can both see and be seen. The pawnbroker's widow, the Man in Black's companion, heartily enjoys the meal, but Mrs. Tibbs detests it, comparing it unfavorably to a supper she and her husband lately had with a nobleman. Mrs. Tibbs is asked to sing but coyly declines; however, with repeated entreaties she obliges. During her song, an official announces that the waterworks are about to begin, which the widow is especially bent on seeing. Mrs. Tibbs, however, continues her song, oblivious to the discomfort she is causing, right through to the end of the waterworks. Goldsmith here anticipates Charles Dickens in his comic portrayal of character. In addition to the stories featuring the above characters, there are Asian fables interspersed throughout the book, inspired no doubt by English translations of the *The Arabian Nights' Entertainments* (fifteenth century).

The *British Magazine* aptly described *The Citizen of the World* as "light, agreeable summer reading, partly original, partly borrowed." Sells regards the work as fundamentally a parody of the genre of satiric letters, to which Montesquieu and Jean-Baptiste de Boyer had earlier contributed. It reveals Goldsmith at the top of his form as a humorist, satirist, and ironist.

The Vicar of Wakefield · *The Vicar of Wakefield*, Goldsmith's only true novel, was published in 1766. It is a first-person narrative set in eighteenth century Yorkshire. It is largely autobiographical, with Dr. Primrose modeled on Goldsmith's father and brother, and George modeled on Goldsmith himself. It was likely intended to satirize the then-fashionable sentimental novel, particularly Laurence Sterne's *Tristram Shandy* (1759-1767). Its style and conventions, such as the digressions, charming pastoral scenes, and mistaken identities, are those of the eighteenth century English novel.

Dr. Charles Primrose, the vicar, narrates the story of his family's misfortunes. In addition to his wife, there are six children, among whom George, Olivia, and Sophia figure most prominently in the story. The vicar loses most of his inherited wealth to an unscrupulous banker, necessitating the removal of him and his family to a humbler abode. Their new landlord is Squire Thornhill, a notorious rake, whose uncle is Sir William Thornhill, a legendary benefactor. There they are befriended by a Mr. Burchell and cheated by an Ephraim Jenkinson.

Olivia is then abducted. After a search, her father finds her in an inn, where she informs him that the squire had arranged her abduction and married her, as he had other women, in a false ceremony. The squire visits and invites Olivia to his wedding with a Miss Wilmot, assuring Olivia that he will find her a suitable husband. Dr. Primrose is outraged, insisting that he would sanction only the squire's marriage to Olivia. He is subsequently informed of Olivia's death and of Sophia's abduction. Presently Mr. Burchell enters with Sophia, whom he had rescued from her abductor. It is now that Mr. Burchell reveals his true identity as Sir William Thornhill. Witnesses testify that the squire had falsely married Olivia and was complicit in Sophia's abduction. However, on the occasion of the squire's marriage to Olivia, the squire was tricked by Jenkinson with a real priest and marriage license. Jenkinson produces both the valid license and Olivia, having told Dr. Primrose that Olivia was dead in order to induce him to submit to the squire's terms and gain his release from prison.

The Vicar of Wakefield can be read on many levels. First, it is a charming idyll depicting the joys of country life. Second, it dramatizes the practical working-out of virtues such as benevolence and vices such as imprudence. Third, it severely tests seventeenth century German philosopher Gottfried Wilhelm Leibniz's dictum that we live in the best of all possible worlds where all things ultimately work for good. Thus, *The Vicar of Wakefield* is a philosophical romance, like Voltaire's *Candide* (1759) and Johnson's *Rasselas* (1759), which challenges the shallow optimism of the Enlightenment.

The Vicar of Wakefield has been criticized for its overly sentimentalized and idealized picture of English country life, its virtuous characters whose displays of courage in the face of adversity strain credulity, and its villains bereft of any redeeming virtue.

However, some commentators see these apparent faults as being integral to Goldsmith's ironic intention. E. A. Baker was the first to recognize that the work is ironic and comic. Robert Hopkins went further by claiming that Goldsmith intended Dr. Primrose "to satirise the complacency and materialism of a type of clergy."

Richard A. Spurgeon Hall

Other major works

PLAYS: *The Good Natured-Man*, pr., pb. 1768; *She Stoops to Conquer: Or, The Mistakes of a Night*, pr., pb. 1773.

POETRY: "An Elegy on the Glory of Her Sex: Mrs. Mary Blaize," 1759; "The Logicians Refuted," 1759; *The Traveller: Or, A Prospect of Society*, 1764; "Edwin and Angelina," 1765; "An Elegy on the Death of a Mad Dog," 1766; *The Deserted Village*, 1770; "Threnodia Augustalis," 1772; "Retaliation," 1774; *The Haunch of Venison: A Poetical Epistle to Lord Clare*, 1776; "The Captivity: An Oratoria," 1820 (wr. 1764).

NONFICTION: *An Enquiry into the Present State of Polite Learning in Europe*, 1759; *The Bee*, 1759 (essays); *Memoirs of M. de Voltaire*, 1761; *The Life of Richard Nash of Bath*, 1762; *A History of England in a Series of Letters from a Nobleman to His Son*, 1764 (2 volumes); *Essays. By Mr. Goldsmith*, 1765; *Life of Bolingbroke*, 1770; *Life of Parnell*, 1770; *An History of the Earth, and Animated Nature*, 1774 (8 volumes; unfinished).

MISCELLANEOUS: *The Collected Works of Oliver Goldsmith*, 1966 (5 volumes; Arthur Friedman, editor).

Bibliography

Dixon, Peter. *Oliver Goldsmith Revisited*. Boston: Twayne, 1991. An updated introduction to the life and works of Goldsmith.

Ginger, John. *The Notable Man: The Life and Times of Oliver Goldsmith*. London: Hamilton, 1977. Possibly the most engrossing of the modern biographies of Goldsmith.

Irving, Washington. *Oliver Goldsmith: A Biography*. New York: Putnam, 1849. A biography of one distinguished man of letters by another. Goldsmith and Irving were kindred spirits.

Mikhail, E. H., ed. *Goldsmith: Interviews and Recollections*. New York: St. Martin's Press, 1993. Contains interviews with Goldsmith's friends and associates. Includes bibliographical references and index.

Sells, A. Lytton. *Oliver Goldsmith: His Life and Works*. New York: Barnes & Noble Books, 1974. The author sets out to remedy the defects in many of the earlier biographies of Goldsmith that omit facts or tend to overlook or diminish his faults. Sells particularly criticizes Goldsmith for plagiarism.

Wardle, Ralph Martin. *Oliver Goldsmith*. Lawrence: University of Kansas Press, 1957. A scholarly and thorough study by one who is sympathetic to Goldsmith.

Robert Graves

Born: Wimbledon, England; July 24, 1895
Died: Deyá, Majorca, Spain; December 7, 1985

Principal long fiction · *My Head! My Head!*, 1925; *No Decency Left*, 1932 (as Barbara Rich, with Laura Riding); *I, Claudius*, 1934; *Claudius the God and His Wife Messalina*, 1934; *"Antigua, Penny, Puce,"* 1936 (also known as *The Antigua Stamp*, 1937); *Count Belisarius*, 1938; *Sergeant Lamb of the Ninth*, 1940 (also known as *Sergeant Lamb's America*); *Proceed, Sergeant Lamb*, 1941; *The Story of Marie Powell, Wife to Mr. Milton*, 1943 (also known as *Wife to Mr. Milton, the Story of Marie Powell*); *The Golden Fleece*, 1944 (also known as *Hercules, My Shipmate*, 1945); *King Jesus*, 1946; *Watch the North Wind Rise*, 1949 (also known as *Seven Days in New Crete*); *The Islands of Unwisdom*, 1949 (also known as *The Isles of Unwisdom*); *Homer's Daughter*, 1955; *They Hanged My Saintly Billy*, 1957.

Other literary forms · Robert Graves considered himself primarily a poet. Beginning with *Over the Brazier* (1916) and ending with *New Collected Poems* (1977), he published more than fifty books of poetry. His poems during and for some years after World War I explored themes of fear and guilt, expressive of his experience of trench warfare in France. He later became more objective and philosophical. Since he developed his theory of the White Goddess in the 1940's, he wrote love poetry almost exclusively.

Graves also had more than fifty publications in the nonfiction category, including literary criticism, books about writing and language, an autobiography (*Goodbye to All That*, 1929), a biography of T. E. Lawrence (*Lawrence and the Arabs*, 1927), social commentaries, and studies in Greek and Hebrew myths. In addition, he translated such writers as Suetonius, Homer, Hesiod, Lucius Apuleius, and Lucan. He had one volume of *Collected Short Stories* (1964).

Achievements · Graves was one of the most versatile writers of the twentieth century, known not only as an excellent poet but also as a mythologist, novelist, translator, lecturer, and persistent intellectual maverick. He has perhaps the clearest claim among twentieth century poets as the inheritor of the Romantic tradition, although he purified his poetry of the kind of flowery elaboration that is often associated with Romanticism. He avoided fads and schools in poetry, perfecting a delicate craftsmanship generally outside the modernist trends inspired by T. S. Eliot and Ezra Pound.

For the novel *I, Claudius*, Graves received the Hawthornden Prize, oldest of the famous British literary prizes, and the James Tait Black Memorial Prize, administered through the University of Edinburgh for the year's best novel. Collections of his poetry brought the Loines Award for Poetry (1958), the William Foyle Poetry Prize (1960), the Arts Council Poetry Award (1962), and the Queen's Gold Medal for Poetry (1968).

The White Goddess: A Historical Grammar of Poetic Myth (1948) and Graves's other studies in mythology, particularly *The Greek Myths* (1955, 2 volumes), *Hebrew Myths: The Book of Genesis* (1964, with Raphael Patai), and *The Nazarene Gospel Restored* (1953, with Joshua Podro), together with his novels based on myth, have undoubtedly had a subtle and pervasive influence on modern literature. He was a prominent spokesperson for the view that women and matriarchal values were much more prominent in the ancient world than once realized and that civilization has suffered from the overthrow of women as social and spiritual leaders. The demotion of women from their former prominence, Graves said, is recorded and rationalized in Hebrew texts and classical Greek mythology.

Biography · Robert Graves was born in Wimbledon (outside of London) on July 24, 1895, to Alfred Percival Graves and Amalie von Ranke Graves. His father was an inspector of schools, a Gaelic scholar, and a writer of poetry of a conventional sort. His mother was German, descended from Leopold von Ranke, whom Graves has called the first modern historian. Graves had a conventional Victorian home and upbringing, with summer visits to German relatives. These included an aunt, Baronin von Aufsess, who lived in an imposing medieval castle in the Bavarian Alps.

Because his name was listed as R. von R. Graves, his obvious German connections became an embarrassment during his years at Charterhouse, a private boarding school for boys, during the period before World War I when anti-German sentiment was on the rise. He finally earned his classmates' respect, however, by becoming a good boxer. He also became friends with George Mallory, a famous mountaineer who later died on Everest. Mallory interested Edward Marsh, patron of the contemporary Georgian school of poetry, in the poetry Graves was writing. Marsh encouraged Graves in his writing but advised him to modernize his diction, which was forty years behind the time.

When World War I began, Graves joined the Royal Welsh Fusiliers and soon went to France as a nineteen-year-old officer. In his autobiography, written when he was thirty-five, he provides one of the best descriptions of trench warfare to come out of the war—a gritty, objective account of a soldier's daily life. He was badly wounded, however, both physically and mentally, by his war experiences. The autobiography, which followed a long siege of war neurasthenia during which his poetry was haunted by images of horror and guilt, was a conscious attempt to put that part of his life behind him forever. Graves continued to use his gift for narrating war experiences, however, in subsequent novels, such as *Count Belisarius*, the Sergeant Lamb novels, and the Claudius novels.

©Washington Post; reprinted by permission of the D.C. Public Library

During the war, Graves married Nancy Nicholson, a young painter, socialist, and vehement feminist. They were in essential agreement about the ruinous effect of male domination in modern society. Graves, along with his wartime friend, the famous war poet Siegfried Sassoon, was already thoroughly disillusioned with war and the leaders of society who supported it.

Graves and his wife parted company in 1929 after a shattering domestic crisis involving the American poet Laura Riding. Riding was Graves's companion for the next thirteen years. They established themselves in Deyá, Majorca, Spain, published the critical magazine *Epilogue* on their own Seizin Press, and devoted themselves to writing both poetry and prose. Graves wrote his best historical novels during that period—the Claudius novels and *Count Belisarius*.

After Riding met and married the American poet Schuyler Jackson, Graves—during the Spanish Civil War, when British nationals were evacuated from Majorca—married Beryl Hodge. Graves returned to Majorca with his new wife, where he stayed until his death in 1985. Graves had eight children, four by Nancy Nicholson, four by his second wife.

During the 1940's, Graves became fascinated with mythology. While he was doing research for his novel about Jason and the Golden Fleece, he became engrossed in the ubiquitous presence of a great goddess associated with the moon, the earth, and the underworld. She was not only the source of life and intuitive wisdom, but also, as Muse, the patron of the poets and musicians. She bound humans both to the seasons of nature and the demands of the spirit.

When Graves discovered a similar pattern in Celtic folklore and literature and correlated the findings of such anthropologists as Robert Briffault, J. J. Bachofen, James Frazer, Jane Harrison, and Margaret Murray and some of the recent discoveries in archaeology, he was convinced that the goddess cult once permeated the whole Western world. In this pattern of myth, as explained in *The White Goddess*, Graves found the unified vision he needed to animate his poetry and much of his subsequent prose for the rest of his life. It not only inspired some of the best love poetry of his time, but also led to some lively treatments of Greek and Hebrew myth in both fiction and nonfiction.

Analysis · The novels of Robert Graves are usually a curious combination of detective work in history, legend, or myth and a considerable gift for narration. He never claimed any particular ability to invent plots, but he could flesh out imaginatively the skeletal remains of adventures he discovered in the past. Thus, the Emperor Claudius lives again as the gossipy information in Suetonius and other Roman chroniclers passes through Graves's shaping imagination. Sometimes, as in *King Jesus*, a traditional tale takes on a startling new dimension through an unconventional combination with other legendary material.

My Head! My Head! · Graves's first attempt at converting ancient history or myth into fiction was a short novel about Elisha and Moses, somewhat inauspiciously entitled *My Head! My Head!* It was begun, as most of Graves's subsequent novels were, because the original accounts were somewhat mysterious, leaving much unsaid about what really happened and why. The novel elaborates on the biblical story of Elisha and the Shunamite woman (2 Kings, Chapters 8-37) and, secondarily, through Elisha's narration, on the career of Moses.

The novel demonstrates both Graves's tendency to explain miracles in naturalistic terms and his contrary fascination with a certain suprarational possibility for special persons. The writer's curious views on magic are not entirely consistent with his debunking of miracles. The inconsistency is quite noticeable here because of the omniscient point of view. In most later novels, Graves wisely used a first-person narrator, which makes seeming inconsistencies the peculiar bias of a persona, rather than of the author. Thus, *King Jesus* is told by a first century narrator who is neither Jewish nor Christian. In such a person, rational skepticism about specific miracles such as the virgin birth might well coexist with a general acceptance of magic.

In spite of its technical shortcomings, *My Head! My Head!* shows Graves's interest in a number of themes which would continue to concern him for the rest of his life: the changing relationships between men and women, the nature of the gods, and the way in which knowledge of the past and of the future must depend upon an understanding of the present.

No Decency Left · On those two occasions when Graves did not depend on mythological or historical sources for his fiction, the results were strange, satirical compositions, lucidly told, but somehow disquieting. The first of these, a collaboration with Laura Riding, appeared under a pseudonym as *No Decency Left* by "Barbara Rich." It is a satirical potpourri of events, drawing on such discordant elements as the rise of dictators, the man in the iron mask, the miraculous feeding of the multitude in the Bible, and comic-opera romance. The ideas in his fantasy may be attributable more to Riding than to Graves, though the attitudes displayed are quite consistent with Graves's views on the follies of men and the hidden strengths of women. The action occurs in one day, the twenty-first birthday of Barbara Rich, who decides that on this special day she is going to get everything she wants. She forthwith crashes high society, becomes incredibly rich, marries the heir to the throne, feeds a multitude of hungry unemployed people by invading the zoo and arranging for the slaughter and cooking of zoo animals, captures the Communists who try to take over the country when the old king dies, and becomes a dictator in her own almost-bloodless revolution.

If the tone of this outrageous fable were lighter and its protagonist more lovable, it could be converted into Hollywood farce or Gilbert and Sullivan operetta, but everyone in it is disagreeable. People are either uniformly stupid and cowardly or utterly unscrupulous. The book was probably written primarily to make money when Riding and Graves were short of cash. (Graves has always claimed that he wrote novels primarily to support himself while he wrote poetry.) It is obviously accidental that the novel, written in 1932, might seem to satirize the blanket powers given to Adolf Hitler by the Reichstag in 1933, or the famous love affair of King Edward with the commoner Wallis Simpson in 1936.

The Antigua Stamp · The view of the human animal, male or female, as vicious, with superior cleverness and ingenuity the mark of the female, also dominates Graves's novel *The Antigua Stamp*. The everlasting battle of the sexes is dramatized here as sibling rivalry that is never outgrown—a controversy over the ownership of an exceedingly valuable stamp. A long-standing, sour feud between brother and sister ends with the latter's victory because she is by far the more clever and conniving of the two. *The Antigua Stamp* and *No Decency Left* are potboilers, though interesting for the eccentric attitudes they exhibit toward human character and social affairs. These biases concerning the essential stupidity and greed of men and the intelligence and ruthlessness of women emerge in a somewhat softened form in Graves's better novels.

Eight of Graves's novels are based, at least in part, upon historical characters and events. The first of these is still the best—*I, Claudius,* which is probably also the best known because of the sensitive portrayal of Claudius by Derek Jacoby in the British Broadcasting Corporation (BBC) television series based on the Claudius novels. *Count Belisarius*, about the brilliant general to the Byzantine Emperor Justinian, is also a fascinating excursion into an exciting time, even though the character of Belisarius is not so clearly drawn as that of the stuttering Claudius.

They Hanged My Saintly Billy · Although *Count Belisarius* deserves more attention than it has received, the other historical novels appeal to a rather limited audience. The exception is the last, *They Hanged My Saintly Billy*, which Graves facetiously described in lurid terms: "My novel is full of sex, drink, incest, suicides, dope, horse racing, murder, scandalous legal procedure, cross-examinations, inquests and ends with a good public hanging–attended by 30,000. . . . Nobody can now call me a specialized writer."

The novel is hardly as shocking as this dust-jacket rhetoric implies. The case of Dr. William Palmer, convicted of poisoning his friend, John Parsons Cook, and executed in 1856, instigated a popular protest against capital punishment in Britain. The notorious case was rife with vague, unsubstantiated suspicions about Dr. Palmer's past and irrelevant disapproval of his taste for gambling and race horses. Moreover, supposed medical experts could never agree about the actual cause of Cook's death.

The novel's best feature is the technique by which Graves preserves the confusion and ambiguity of the case. Most of the novel consists of personal testimony from persons who had known Palmer. Thus, each speaker talks from his or her own biases and limited contact, some insisting that "he never had it in him to hurt a fly." Others reveal an incredibly callous schemer who takes out insurance on his brother's life, knowing him to be an alcoholic, then arranges that he drink himself to death. No sure conclusion is ever reached about the justice of the case.

As a member of the Royal Welsh Fusiliers during World War I, Graves became interested in the history of his regiment and discovered the makings of two novels in the career of Roger Lamb, who served in the Ninth Regiment during the American Revolution but joined the Fusiliers after the surrender of General Burgoyne and the incarceration of the Ninth.

Sergeant Lamb's America · Graves is more chronicler than novelist in the two books about Roger Lamb, much of which are devoted to details of military life, curious anecdotes about the colonists, the Indians, the French Canadians, the fiascos and triumph of generals. Graves explains in his foreword to *Sergeant Lamb's America* that this story is not "straight history," though he has invented no main characters. The reader has no way of knowing exactly how accurately he conveys the texture of life in the colonies. "All that readers of an historical novel can fairly ask from the author," Graves writes, "is an assurance that he has nowhere willfully falsified geography, chronology, or character, and that information contained in it is accurate enough to add without discount to their general stock of history." This is a statement to remember, perhaps, in connection with any of Graves's historical novels. Although Graves seemed to have no particular rancor against Americans, the books do reveal a very iconoclastic attitude toward the Founding Fathers. His view of such notables as Benedict Arnold, Major André, and George Washington at least challenges the American reader's preconceptions.

Sergeant Lamb, like Count Belisarius, seems a bit wooden for all his military ingenuity. The protagonist's on-and-off love affair with Kate Harlowe provides only a tenuous thread on which to hang the semblance of a plot. The novels seem to be a scholar's compilation of interesting anecdotes and factual data about the time. Of course, this unimpassioned tone could be defended as exactly appropriate, since the novels are ostensibly the memoirs of a much older Roger Lamb, written when he is a schoolmaster in Dublin. This cool, dispassionate tone is often typical of Graves's style, however, even when he is describing his own experience in warfare in his autobiography, *Goodbye to All That.*

The Islands of Unwisdom · *The Islands of Unwisdom* celebrates, or rather exposes in its pettiness and greed, an abortive sixteenth century Spanish expedition to colonize the Solomon Islands. The leader of the expedition, Don Alvaro de Mendaña y Castro, had discovered the islands many years before. He called them the Isles of Solomon, thinking perhaps they were the location of the famous gold mines of the biblical King Solomon. The natives adorned themselves with gold. When the King of Spain finally gave permission for the expedition, therefore, a great many avaricious participants joined in the venture ostensibly devoted to Christianizing the heathen.

Though a few devout persons, such as the three priests and the chief pilot, tried to maintain the Christian charity of their mission, their feeble efforts were in vain. Practically all the islanders greeted the Spaniards with affection and open hospitality, but sooner or later, the senseless slaughter of innocents converted friends into enemies. The combined stupidity and violence of the military and of the three Barretos, Don Alvaro's brothers-in-law, insured disaster wherever they went. Moreover, Doña Ysabel Barreto, Don Alvaro's beautiful wife, was as proud and cruel as her arrogant brothers. Don Alvaro was devout but indecisive and unable to control the stubborn wills that surrounded him.

Graves uses the narrator, Don Andrés Serrano, an undersecretary to the general, to propose a theory to account for the superiority of the English over the Spanish in such situations. The English soldier could and often did do a sailor's work when help was needed on shipboard. The more rigid class structure of the Spanish, however, prevented a Spanish soldier from doing anything but fighting. During long and hazardous voyages, the Spanish soldier was idle and bored, while the Spanish sailor was overworked and resentful. When a new land was reached, the Spanish soldier felt impelled to demonstrate his function by killing enemies. If none existed, he soon created them.

Graves was particularly drawn to this sordid bit of history not so much because of the too often repeated folly of bringing civilization to the heathen by murdering them, but because of a truly unique feature of this historical event. After the death of her husband, Doña Ysabel achieved the command of a naval vessel—surely an unusual event in any age, and unprecedented in the sixteenth century. Doña Ysabel is not the conventional kind of heroine, to be sure, but a kind that Graves finds most fascinating: beautiful, cruel, and ruthless. This novel was published in the year following *The White Goddess*, and the reader who is familiar with that study may see an uncanny resemblance between Doña Ysabel and the moon goddess in her most sinister phase.

The Story of Marie Powell, Wife to Mr. Milton · *The Story of Marie Powell, Wife to Mr. Milton* is also rooted in history, yet it echoes Graves's own views of feminine nature, as well as his antipathy to John Milton, both as a poet and as a man. That Milton did, indeed, have some marital problems is clear; they were the inspiration for his pamphlet arguing that incompatibility should be sufficient grounds for divorce, which was followed by his brilliant "Areopagitica" against censorship of the press. (Graves notes that in spite of the admitted wisdom of the latter, Milton himself became an official censor under Cromwell.)

In Graves's treatment, Milton is the epitome of the self-righteous, dominating male, drawn to the poetic, half-pagan rural England from which his young wife emerges but determined in his arid Calvinism to squelch these poetic yearnings in himself and his bride. Milton chooses head over heart, always a mistake in a poet, from Graves's point of view. Though Milton desires love, like any man, he has a preconceived set of rules that would define and coerce love, which can only be freely given. He resolutely divorces sexuality from pleasure, for example, knowing his wife only when trying to impregnate her–in compliance, presumably, with God's orders.

Marie is the weakest of Graves's fictional women, a kind of dethroned queen, a person of independent mind doomed to mental and emotional starvation in Milton's household. T. S. Matthews, in his autobiography *Jacks or Better* (1977), makes the provocative suggestion that Graves poured his frustration and resentment about the marriage of Laura Riding to Schuyler Jackson into the book. It was written immediately after Graves fled to England, bereft of his longtime companion. Matthews has considerable background for this opinion, since he and his wife were living in America with the group (including Riding, Graves, Alan and Beryl Hodge, Schuyler and Kit Jackson) when the fruit basket was upset. Even though Graves and Riding were not lovers at that time, according to James McKinley in his introduction to Graves's last book, Graves was profoundly shocked at what he may have perceived as Riding's abdication from her proper role. Whether this explanation is valid or not, this novel seems to touch a more personal vein of frustration, resentment, and sadness than his other historical novels.

Moreover, Graves indulges in a bit of romantic mysticism in this novel, more characteristic of his poetic than his prose style. Marie Milton falls into a three-day swoon during her third pregnancy, at the precise moment that her secret "true love" is killed in Ireland. According to her own account, she spends those three days with her beloved. When she awakens she knows that her cousin, with whom she had fallen in love at the age of eleven, is dead. The child she bears thereafter, her first son, looks like her cousin, not Milton, and Marie is more peaceful than she has ever been. Perhaps this touch of fantasy expresses more about Graves than about Marie Powell Milton, but the author is careful to note in the epilogue that when Marie died giving birth to a third daughter, the one son followed her to the grave shortly after.

Readers may find the style of this novel somewhat ponderous, but Graves tries to adjust his diction to the times about which he writes. He has deliberately used some archaic, seventeenth century terms, for which he provides a glossary at the end; most of these words are easily understood in context.

Count Belisarius · If the pathetic Marie Milton shows the White Goddess in her pitiable decline, one need only return to the powerful women in *Count Belisarius* to see her in her glory. This is true, despite the fact that Graves had not yet formulated his theory of the monomyth which he expressed in *The White Goddess*. In retrospect, his fictional women suggest that the goddess haunted his psyche before he knew her name. In *Count Belisarius*, not one but two striking women demonstrate the strength of the female. These are the Empress Theodora, wife to Justinian, and Antonina, Belisarius's wife. Both had been carefully educated, pagan courtesans, but they acquired Christianity when it became possible to marry prominent Christians. They inevitably display more good sense than most of the men around them. More than once, Theodora saves Belisarius from the vindictive jealousy of Justinian or convinces the negligent monarch that he should send some relief in troops or supplies to his champion on the frontier. When Belisarius's situation becomes desperate because he is almost always vastly outnumbered on the battlefield and short of supplies as well, Antonina sends a private letter to Empress Theodora, who manages, by flattery or guile, to cajole Justinian into at least some action not altogether disastrous.

Of the two prominent men in the novel, Justinian is the more carefully characterized, even though he is invariably presented in a negative light. After Theodora dies and Belisarius throws out Antonina, because of the emperor's campaign to discredit her virtue, nothing remains to protect Belisarius from Justinian's jealousy and fear. Like Samson shorn of his hair, Belisarius is imprisoned and blinded.

Belisarius, the central figure, is the least understandable in psychological terms. Though his exploits against the Persians and against the many tribes that threatened early Christendom are truly remarkable and well told, he himself seems larger than life in moral terms as well as in his undoubted military genius. He is seemingly incorruptible in a world riddled with intrigue and deception, and as such, almost too good to be true. The jealousy of Justinian is more understandable than Belisarius's unswerving loyalty, devotion, and piety. The reader never knows what preserves Belisarius from the corrupting influence of power and popular adulation.

Ultimately, the effect of the novel is ironic, in spite of the total absence of ambiguity in Belisarius's character. The irony rests in the observation that for all the lifelong efforts of one of history's military geniuses, his accomplishments mattered little, since they were so soon negated by Justinian's bad judgment after the death of his greatest general. All the drama and the pageantry of war cannot compensate for its futility and incredible waste and its glorification of destruction in the name of true religion.

For his portrait of Claudius, grandchild of Mark Antony and grandnephew of Octavius Augustus, Graves had rich sources of information on which to draw; perhaps that accounts for the greater depth and complexity Claudius seems to exhibit in comparison with Belisarius. Both *The Annals of Tacitus* (c. 119) and Suetonius's *Lives of the Caesars* (c. 120, a book that Graves translated from the Latin in 1957) contain much of the gossipy, possibly slanted history that fills Graves's *I, Claudius* and *Claudius the God.*

I, Claudius · I, Claudius is a more successful novel than its sequel. It builds to a natural climax as the protagonist, who calls himself "the cripple, the stammerer, the fool of the family," is proclaimed emperor by riotous Roman soldiers after the assassination of Caligula. Claudius captures the sympathy of the reader in this novel as a survivor of a fifty-year reign of terror in which all the more likely prospects for promotion to emperor are eliminated by Livia, Augustus's wife, to assure the elevation of her son Tiberius to the throne. Claudius owes his survival mostly to his physical defects, which seemingly preclude his being considered for high office, and to a ready intelligence and wit which protect him somewhat from the cruelties of Caligula, who is the first to give him any role at all in government. The caprice of the troops in choosing the "fool of the family" as emperor is as great a surprise to Claudius as to anyone else. Presumably the terrified Claudius acquiesces to the whim of the military because the only other alternative is assassination along with the rest of Caligula's close relatives.

Claudius the God and His Wife Messalina · With *Claudius the God and His Wife Messalina*, the reader can no longer cheer the innocent victim of the vicious intrigues of court life. Claudius now has power and, in some respects, wields it effectively and humanely. He acquires, however, many of the tastes and faults of his class. The man who, as a boy, fainted at bloodshed now has a taste for violent entertainment. The scholar who despised ostentatious show now invades Britain so he may have a glorious triumph on his return. Worse yet, the unassuming person who knew how to survive the formidable machinations of Livia now foolishly succumbs to younger women, as ruthless as Livia but without her intelligence and executive ability. He dies of poison administered by a faithless wife.

Graves seems to be making a case for the older Claudius as a kind of tragic hero, who has come to a realization of his own shortcomings as well as those of his contemporaries. He had once idealistically hoped for the return of the Republic, but in his later years he understands that he has actually made self-government less attractive, simply because his rule has been more benevolent than that of his predecessors, Tiberius and Caligula. He decides that the Rupublican dream will not arise until the country again suffers under an evil emperor. The government must be worse before it can be better.

Graves attributes to Claudius a rather improbable scheme of secluding his son from the temptations of court life by sending him to Britain, then letting his ambitious second wife secure the throne for her own son, Nero, whose cruelty and decadence Claudius foresees. In the debacle that will occur in the reign of Nero, Claudius hopes his own son can come back as a conquering hero and reestablish the Republic.

This rather fanciful scheme misfires because Claudius's son refuses to cooperate, confident that he can deal with his foster brother, Nero, himself. Actually, Claudius's son was assassinated after his father's death, presumably at Nero's orders.

This attempted explanation of Claudius's seeming gullibility in his last days is probably intended to lend dignity to his unfortunate decline into a rather foolish old age. Part of the problem with the second novel is simply the intractability of historical facts, which do not necessarily make the most effective plots. One of the usual requirements of tragic heroes is that they attain some measure of self-knowledge and that they are at least partially responsible for their own fall from greatness. Graves has tried to retain empathy for a well-intentioned, thoughtful man who foresaw and accepted his fate, to be murdered by his wife, as a means to a greater good. This attempt to salvage a fading protagonist is understandable, but not wholly successful.

Hercules, My Shipmate · As Graves's historical novels depend partially upon the intrinsic interest of a historical period, so do his novels based on myth depend upon an intrinsic interest in myth interpretation. Quite aside from the familiar story of Jason and the Argonauts, for example, *Hercules, My Shipmate* offers sometimes believable explanations of some of the common ideas found in myth. The centaurs, for example, were not half-horse, half-men, but a barbaric tribe whose totem animal was the horse. They wore horses' manes and worshiped a mare-headed mother goddess. Many of Jason's shipmates were demigods; that is, one parent was a deity. This convention has a nonsupernatural explanation as well: Their births were traceable to the ancient custom of temple prostitutes or priests whose offspring were attributed to the god or goddess under whose auspices they were conceived.

This does not mean that all supernaturalism is rooted out of Graves's treatment of mythic material. Hercules has exaggerated powers analogous to those of Paul Bunyan, a parody of the Greek ideal of the hero, a man so strong he is dangerous to foe and friend as well. Nor does Graves eliminate all supernaturalism from his *King Jesus*, the most controversial of his novels, which fuses biblical myth with his own ideas about the ancient goddess cult.

King Jesus · *King Jesus* creates a new myth about Jesus–a Jesus who is literally the King of the Jews, or at least the proper inheritor of that title. He is inheritor as the grandson of King Herod (through a secret marriage between Mary and Antipater, Herod's son), but also because he is annointed by God's prophet, John the Baptist, which was the traditional Hebrew way of choosing a king. In the latter sense, Herod had less right to the throne than Jesus, since Herod derived his authority from the Romans, not from ancient Hebrew custom. Moreover, Jesus fulfills other expectations built into what Graves presents as ancient Hebrew ritual, such as a marriage to the inheritor of the land. Graves claims that ownership of the land was matrilinear and that in order to become a king, a man had to marry the youngest daughter of the hereditary line, in this case Mary, the sister of Martha and Lazarus. (Graves points out that this matrilinear descent accounts for Egyptian pharaohs marrying their sisters and King David marrying a woman from each of the tribes of Israel in order to unify the tribes.)

Jesus is an ascetic, however, and refuses to cohabit with Mary. Moreover, one of his chief adversaries in the novel is the cult of the goddess, whose chief priestess is yet another Mary, called the Hairdresser–the character known in the bible as Mary Magdalene. It is no accident that the three vital women who attend Jesus in his crucifixion conveniently represent the Triple Goddess: Mary the mother, Mary the wife, and Mary the crone, who lays out the mythic hero in death. The irony of the situation is that in spite of consciously choosing the pattern of the Suffering Servant, described in Isaiah, and trying his best to overthrow the cult of the fertility goddess, Jesus nevertheless fulfills the role of the sacrificial hero in the goddess mythology. Though some may be offended by the liberties Graves has taken with a sacred story, those who are fascinated by the whole of the mythic heritage from the ancient world will appreciate this imaginative retelling.

Watch the North Wind Rise · If *King Jesus* is the most serious of Graves's treatments of the goddess mythology, the most lighthearted is *Watch the North Wind Rise*, a futuristic utopian novel in which the great goddess cult has been revived in Crete (its stronghold in the ancient world) as a social experiment. The protagonist is a time traveler, conjured into the future by a witch, in obedience to the goddess. He also serves a Pandora-like function, bringing unrest into a land made dull by continuous peace. Great art, after all, demands conflict, which this ideal land has left behind. The novel is entertaining as a satire of utopian ideas, but also provides an interesting exploration of the relationship between an artist (the protagonist) and his muse (the goddess).

Homer's Daughter · Graves's last novel on a mythic theme, *Homer's Daughter*, borrows heavily from Homer's *Odyssey* (c. 800 B.C.) and from Samuel Butler's *The Authoress of the "Odyssey"* (1897), which argues that the *Odyssey* must have been written by a woman. Graves's protagonist is the princess Nausicaa, who in the *Odyssey* befriended the shipwrecked Odysseus. In the novel, it is Nausicaa who endures many rude and insistent suitors as Penelope does in Homer's epic. A shipwrecked stranger rescues her in a manner attributed to Odysseus, by shooting the unwanted suitors and winning the fair lady for himself. She is the one who composes the *Odyssey*, incorporating her experience into the story.

In spite of the fact that Graves himself dismissed his fiction as a means of providing support for his writing of poetry, his best novels deserve to live on as imaginative treatments of history and myth. While he may not always have captured the "real" past, he helped to make the past important in a time when many people considered it irrelevant. He showed how ancient symbol-systems may still capture the imagination of one of the most versatile writers of our time. He also helped to overthrow the stereotype of women as weak in intelligence and will. This does not mean that Graves was particularly accurate in his perception of women, but his biases do offer a welcome antidote to the more insipid variety of fictional women. He must be partially responsible for the contemporary interest in mythology and the beginnings of civilization. Part of this is the result of his nonfiction works, such as *The White Goddess, The Greek Myths,* and *Hebrew Myths,* but his use of myth in popular novels has probably reached an even wider audience.

Katherine Snipes

Other major works

SHORT FICTION: *The Shout,* 1929; *¡Catacrok! Mostly Stories, Mostly Funny,* 1956; *Collected Short Stories,* 1964.

POETRY: *Over the Brazier,* 1916; *Goliath and David,* 1916; *Fairies and Fusiliers,* 1917; *Treasure Box,* 1919; *Country Sentiment,* 1920; *The Pier-Glass,* 1921; *The Feather Bed,* 1923; *Whipperginny,* 1923; *Mock Beggar Hall,* 1924; *The Marmosite's Miscellany,* 1925 (as John Doyle); *Welchman's Hose,* 1925; *Poems: 1914-1926,* 1927; *Poems: 1914-1927,* 1927; *Poems: 1929,* 1929; *Ten Poems More,* 1930; *Poems: 1926-1930,* 1931; *To Whom Else?,* 1931; *Poems: 1930-1933,* 1933; *Collected Poems,* 1938; *No More Ghosts: Selected Poems,* 1940; *Work in Hand,* 1942 (with others); *Poems: 1938-1945,* 1946; *Collected Poems: 1914-1947,* 1948; *Poems and Satires: 1951,* 1951; *Poems: 1953,* 1953; *Collected Poems: 1955,* 1955; *Poems Selected by Himself,* 1957; *The Poems of Robert Graves Chosen by Himself,* 1958; *Collected Poems: 1959,* 1959; *The Penny Fiddle: Poems for Children,* 1960; *Collected Poems,* 1961; *More Poems: 1961,* 1961; *The More Deserving Cases: Eighteen Old Poems for Reconsideration,* 1962; *New Poems: 1962,* 1962; *Ann at Highwood Hall: Poems for Children,* 1964; *Man Does, Woman Is,* 1964; *Love Respelt,* 1965; *Collected Poems: 1965,* 1965; *Seventeen Poems Missing from "Love Respelt,"* 1966; *Colophon to "Love Respelt,"* 1967; *Poems: 1965-1968,* 1968; *The Crane Bag,* 1969; *Love Respelt Again,* 1969; *Beyond Giving: Poems,* 1969; *Poems About Love,* 1969; *Advice from a Mother,* 1970; *Queen-Mother to New Queen,* 1970; *Poems: 1969-1970,* 1970; *The Green-Sailed Vessel,* 1971; *Poems: Abridged for Dolls and Princes,* 1971; *Poems: 1968-1970,* 1971; *Poems: 1970-1972,* 1972; *Poems: Selected by Himself,* 1972; *Deyá,* 1972 (with Paul Hogarth); *Timeless Meetings: Poems,* 1973; *At the Gate,* 1974; *Collected Poems: 1975,* 1975 (2 volumes); *New Collected Poems,* 1977.

NONFICTION: *On English Poetry,* 1922; *The Meaning of Dreams,* 1924; *Poetic Unreason and Other Studies,* 1925; *Contemporary Techniques of Poetry: A Political Analogy,* 1925; *Another Future of Poetry,* 1926; *Impenetrability: Or, The Proper Habit of English,* 1926; *The English Ballad: A Short Critical Survey,* 1927; *Lars Porsena: Or, The Future of Swearing and Improper Language,* 1927; *A Survey of Modernist Poetry,* 1927 (with Laura Riding); *Lawrence and the Arabs,* 1927 (also known as *Lawrence and the Arabian Adventure,* 1928); *A Pamphlet Against Anthologies,* 1928 (with Riding, also known as *Against Anthologies*); *Mrs. Fisher: Or, The Future of Humour,* 1928; *Goodbye to All That: An Autobiography,* 1929;

T. E. Lawrence to His Biographer Robert Graves, 1938; *The Long Week-End: A Social History of Great Britain, 1918-1938*, 1940 (with Alan Hodge); *The Reader over Your Shoulders: A Handbook for Writers of English Prose*, 1943 (with Hodge); *The White Goddess: A Historical Grammar of Poetic Myth*, 1948; *The Common Asphodel: Collected Essays on Poetry, 1922-1949*, 1949; *Occupation: Writer*, 1950; *The Nazarene Gospel Restored*, 1953 (with Joshua Podro); *The Crowning Privilege: The Clark Lectures, 1954-1955*, 1955; *Adam's Rib and Other Anomalous Elements in the Hebrew Creation Myth: A New View*, 1955; *The Greek Myths*, 1955 (2 volumes); *Jesus in Rome: A Historical Conjecture*, 1957 (with Podro); *Five Pens in Hand*, 1958; *Greek Gods and Heroes*, 1960; *Oxford Addresses on Poetry*, 1962; *Nine Hundred Iron Chariots: The Twelfth Arthur Dehon Little Memorial Lecture*, 1963; *Hebrew Myths: The Book of Genesis*, 1964 (with Raphael Patai); *Majorca Observed*, 1965 (with Paul Hogarty); *Mammon and the Black Goddess*, 1965; *Poetic Craft and Principle*, 1967; *The Crane Bag and Other Disputed Subjects*, 1969; *On Poetry: Collected Talks and Essays*, 1969; *Difficult Questions, Easy Answers*, 1972.

CHILDREN'S LITERATURE: *The Big Green Book*, 1962; *The Siege and Fall of Troy*, 1962; *Two Wise Children*, 1966; *The Poor Boy Who Followed His Star*, 1968.

TRANSLATIONS: *Almost Forgotten Germany*, 1936 (Georg Schwarz; trans. with Laura Riding); *The Transformation of Lucius, Otherwise Known as "The Golden Ass,"* 1950 (Lucius Apuleius); *The Cross and the Sword*, 1954 (Manuel de Jesús Galván); *Pharsalia: Dramatic Episodes of the Civil Wars*, 1956 (Lucan); *Winter in Majorca*, 1956 (George Sand); *The Twelve Caesars*, 1957 (Suetonius); *The Anger of Achilles: Homer's "Iliad,"* 1959; *The Rubáiyát of Omar Khayyám*, 1967 (with Omar Ali-Shah).

EDITED TEXTS: *Oxford Poetry: 1921*, 1921 (with Alan Porter and Richard Hughes); *John Skelton: Laureate*, 1927; *The Less Familiar Nursery Rhymes*, 1927; *The Comedies of Terence*, 1962; *English and Scottish Ballads*, 1975.

MISCELLANEOUS: *Steps: Stories, Talks, Essays, Poems, Studies in History*, 1958; *Food for Centaurs: Stories, Talks, Critical Studies, Poems*, 1960; *Selected Poetry and Prose*, 1961.

Bibliography

Bloom, Harold, ed. *Robert Graves*. New York: Chelsea House, 1987. Essays on Graves's historical novels, autobiography, and major themes. Includes chronology and bibliography.

Canary, Robert H. *Robert Graves*. Boston: Twayne, 1980. A good general introduction to Graves's work. Emphasizes Graves the poet, but also contains helpful information on his novels and literary criticism. Includes a chronology, notes, a selected bibliography, and an index.

Day, Douglas. *Swifter than Reason: The Poetry and Criticism of Robert Graves*. Chapel Hill: University of North Carolina Press, 1963. The first full-length study of Graves's poetry and criticism. Graves's work is examined chronologically in four major phases, concluding with his emerging concept of the "White Goddess." Includes a bibliography, secondary reading materials, and an index.

Quinn, Patrick J., ed. *New Perspectives on Robert Graves*. Selinsgrove, Pa.: Susquehanna University Press, 1999. A thoughtful, updated volume on the works of Graves. Includes bibliographical references and an index.

Seymour-Smith, Martin. *Robert Graves: His Life and Works*. New York: Paragon House, 1988. Intimate, fascinating glimpse of Graves the man. Seymour-Smith had known Graves since 1943 and has written extensively on him since 1956. An excellent introduction to Graves's remarkable life and literary career.

Graham Greene

Born: Berkhamsted, England; October 2, 1904
Died: Vevey, Switzerland; April 3, 1991

Principal long fiction · *The Man Within*, 1929; *The Name of Action*, 1930; *Rumour at Nightfall*, 1931; *Stamboul Train: An Entertainment*, 1932 (pb. in U.S. as *Orient Express: An Entertainment*, 1933); *It's a Battlefield*, 1934; *England Made Me*, 1935; *A Gun for Sale: An Entertainment*, 1936 (pb. in U.S. as *This Gun for Hire: An Entertainment*); *Brighton Rock*, 1938; *The Confidential Agent*, 1939; *The Power and the Glory*, 1940 (reissued as *The Labyrinthine Ways*); *The Ministry of Fear: An Entertainment*, 1943; *The Heart of the Matter*, 1948; *The Third Man: An Entertainment*, 1950; *The Third Man and The Fallen Idol*, 1950; *The End of the Affair*, 1951; *Loser Takes All: An Entertainment*, 1955; *The Quiet American*, 1955; *Our Man in Havana: An Entertainment*, 1958; *A Burnt-Out Case*, 1961; *The Comedians*, 1966; *Travels with My Aunt*, 1969; *The Honorary Consul*, 1973; *The Human Factor*, 1978; *Dr. Fischer of Geneva: Or, The Bomb Party*, 1980; *Monsignor Quixote*, 1982; *The Tenth Man*, 1985.

Other literary forms · In addition to his novels, Graham Greene published many collections of short stories, including *The Basement Room and Other Stories* (1935); *Nineteen Stories* (1947); *Twenty-one Stories* (1954), in which two stories from the previous collection were dropped and four added; *A Sense of Reality* (1963); *May We Borrow Your Husband? and Other Comedies of the Sexual Life* (1967); and *Collected Stories* (1972). He also wrote plays, including *The Living Room* (1953), *The Potting Shed* (1957), *The Complaisant Lover* (1959), *Carving a Statue* (1964), and *Yes and No* (1980). With the exception of his first published book, *Babbling April: Poems* (1925), he did not publish poetry except in two private printings, *After Two Years* (1949) and *For Christmas* (1950). He wrote some interesting travel books, two focusing on Africa, *Journey Without Maps: A Travel Book* (1936) and *In Search of a Character: Two African Journals* (1961), and one set in Mexico, *The Lawless Roads: A Mexican Journal* (1939). He published several books of essays and criticism, including *British Dramatists* (1942); *The Lost Childhood and Other Essays* (1951); *Essais Catholiques* (1953); *Collected Essays* (1969); and *The Pleasure Dome: The Collected Film Criticism, 1935-40, of Graham Greene* (1972), edited by John Russell-Taylor. He also wrote a biography, *Lord Rochester's Monkey: Being the Life of John Wilmot, Second Earl of Rochester* (1974), and two autobiographical works, *A Sort of Life* (1971), carrying the reader up to Greene's first novel, and *Ways of Escape* (1980), bringing the reader up to the time of its writing. A biographical-autobiographical work, *Getting to Know the General* (1984), spotlights Greene's relationship with General Omar Torrijos Herrera of Panama. Finally, he also wrote four children's books: *The Little Train* (1946), *The Little Fire Engine* (1950), *The Little Horse Bus* (1952), and *The Little Steam Roller: A Story of Mystery and Detection* (1953).

Achievements · Greene's style has often been singled out for praise. He learned economy and precision while with *The Times* in London. More than anything else, he struggled for precision, "truth" as he called it, in form as well as in substance. *The Power and the Glory* won the Hawthornden Prize in 1941. Additionally, his experience as a film reviewer seems to have given him a feel for cinematic technique.

What Greene's reputation will be a century hence is difficult to predict. Readers will certainly find in him more than a religious writer, more—at least—than a Catholic writer. They will find in him a writer who used for his thematic vehicles all the pressing issues of his era: the Vietnam War, Papa Doc Duvalier's tyranny over Haiti, the struggle between communism and capitalism, apartheid in South Africa, poverty and oppression in Latin America. Will these issues seem too topical for posterity, or will they prove again that only by localizing one's story in the specifics of a time and place can one appeal to readers of another time, another place?

Biography · Graham Greene was born on October 2, 1904, in the town of Berkhamsted, England. The fourth of six children, he was not especially close to his father, perhaps because of his father's position as headmaster of Berkhamsted School, which Greene attended. Some of the boys took sadistic delight in his ambiguous position, and two in particular caused him such humiliation that they created in him an excessive desire to prove himself. Without them, he claimed, he might never have written a book.

Greene made several attempts at suicide during these unhappy years; he later insisted these were efforts to avoid boredom rather than to kill himself. At Oxford, he tried for a while to avoid boredom by getting intoxicated each day of an entire semester.

During these Oxford days, Greene met Vivien Dayrell-Browning, a young Catholic woman who had written to him of his error in a film review in referring to Catholic "worship" of the Virgin Mary. He inquired into the "subtle" and "unbelievable theology" out of interest in Vivien and concluded by becoming a Catholic in 1926. Greene married Vivien, and the couple had two children, a boy and a girl. He separated from his parents' family after the wedding and was scrupulous about guarding his own family's privacy.

In 1926, Greene moved from his first, unsalaried, position writing for the Nottingham *Journal* to the position of subeditor for *The Times* in London. There, he learned writing technique, pruning the clichés of reporters and condensing their stories without loss of meaning or effect. Moreover, he had mornings free to do his own writing. When, in 1928, Heinemann accepted Greene's first novel, *The Man Within*, for publication, Greene rashly quit *The Times* to make his living as a writer.

Greene's next two novels, *The Name of Action* and *Rumour at Nightfall*, failed, and he later suppressed them. Still, in trying to understand what went wrong with these works, he discovered that he had tried to omit the autobiographical entirely; as a result, the novels lacked life and truth. He would not make that mistake again.

In 1934, Greene took the first of a seemingly endless series of trips to other parts of the world. With his cousin Barbara, he walked without maps across the heart of Liberia. Recorded in his *Journey Without Maps*, this hazardous venture became a turning point in his life. He had once thought death desirable; in the desert, he became a passionate lover of life. He came even to accept the rats in his hut as part of life. Perhaps more important for his writing, he discovered in Liberia the archetypal basis for his earliest nightmares. The frightening creatures of those dreams were not originally evil beings but rather devils in the African sense of beings who control power. Humankind, Greene came to believe, has corrupted these primitive realities and denied its inherited sense of supernatural evil, reducing it to the level of merely human evil. To do so is to forget "the finer taste, the finer pleasure, the finer terror on which we might have built." Greene had found the basis for themes that made their way into his novels.

Greene began his great fiction with *Brighton Rock*, the publication of which, in 1938, followed a trip to Mexico that delighted him much less than the one to Africa. Nevertheless, his observations in Mexico provided the substance of what many consider his finest achievement, *The Power and the Glory*. For the reader interested in a genuine insight into the way Greene moves from fact to fiction, the travel book that emerged from the Mexican journey, *The Lawless Roads*, is very rewarding, showing for example how his fictional whiskey priest was an amalgam of four real-life priests.

©Amanda Saunders

With the outbreak of the second world war, Greene was assigned to the Secret Intelligence Service, or MI6, as it was then called. The experience–including his work for the notorious spy Kim Philby– gave him the material for several later works, including *Our Man in Havana* and *The Human Factor*, and nurtured in him that "virtue of disloyalty" which informs his novels.

Greene ceased his writing of explicitly religious novels with *The End of the Affair* in 1951, when people began to treat him as a guru. Although his novels continued to treat religious concerns, none–with the possible exception of *A Burnt-Out Case* in 1961–was a religious problem novel. Increasingly, Greene turned to political concern in novels such as *The Quiet American* and *The Comedians*, but these political concerns transcend the topical and speak more enduringly of human involvement.

In his later years, Greene slowed his production somewhat. He continued, however, to write two hundred words every morning, then corrected in great detail in the evening. His practice was to dictate his corrected manuscript into a tape recorder and send the tapes from his home in Antibes, on the French Riviera, to England, where they were typed and then returned. Greene also continued to indulge his taste for travel: He visited Fidel Castro in Cuba, General Omar Torrijos Herrera in Panama, and Ho Chi Minh in Vietnam. A full catalog of his travels would be virtually endless. Despite the reductive label critics have applied to his settings–"Greeneland"– Greene's novels have more varied settings than those of almost any other novelist, and his settings are authentic. Greene died on April 3, 1991, at the age of eighty-six.

Analysis · In an address he called the "Virtue of Disloyalty," which he delivered at the University of Hamburg in 1969, Graham Greene contended that a writer is driven "to be a protestant in a Catholic society, a catholic in a Protestant one," or to be a communist in a capitalist society and a capitalist in a communist one. While loyalty confines one to accepted opinions, "disloyalty gives the novelist an extra dimension of understanding."

Whatever the reader may think of Greene's theory, it is helpful in explaining most of his own novels. From *The Man Within* in 1929, which justified a suicide in the face of Catholic morality's abhorrence for such an act, to *The Human Factor*, forty-nine years later, which comes close to justifying treason, Greene practiced this "virtue of disloyalty."

Most of Greene's obsessions originated in his childhood. Where did the desire to be "disloyal," to play devil's advocate, arise? Certainly his serving in MI6 under the authority of Kim Philby was a factor. Greene admired the man in every way except for what appeared to be a personal drive for power. It was this characteristic of Philby that caused Greene finally to resign rather than accept a promotion and become part of Philby's intrigue. Yet Greene later came to see that the man served not himself but a cause, and all his former admiration of Philby returned. Greene continued his friendship even after Philby's treason. As he saw it, Philby had found a faith in Communism, and he would not discard it because it had been abused by Joseph Stalin any more than Catholics would discard a faith that had been abused by the Inquisitors or the Roman Curia.

Clearly, however, Greene's "disloyalty" or sympathy for the rebel did not originate here. It too must be traced to his childhood, to his isolation at school, where neither the students nor his headmaster father could treat him unambiguously; it can be traced also to his love of poet Robert Browning, who very early instilled in him an interest in the "dangerous edge of things," in "the honest thief, the tender murderer." It was an influence more lasting, Greene said, than any religious teaching. Religiously, though, Greene's fierce independence manifested itself when, upon conversion to Catholicism, he took the name Thomas, not after the angelic doctor but after the doubter.

Though Greene wrote in so many genres, the novel is the form upon which his reputation will rest. His strengths in the genre are many. Like all novelists who are more than journeymen, he returns throughout his oeuvre to certain recurring themes. Another strength is his gift for playing the devil's advocate, the dynamics that occur when his character finds himself divided between loyalties. In Greene's first novel, *The Man Within*, that division was handled crudely, externalized in a boy's attraction to two different women; in later novels, the struggle is internalized. Sarah Miles of *The End of the Affair* is torn between her loyalty to God and her loyalty to her lover. Fowler of *The Quiet American* cannot decide whether he wants to eliminate Pyle for the good of Vietnam or to get his woman back from a rival. The characters are shaded in, rendered complex by internal division.

Brighton Rock · Because he was a remarkable self-critic, Greene overcame most of his early weaknesses. He corrected an early tendency to distrust autobiographical material, and he seemed to overcome his difficulty in portraying credible women. In his first twenty-four years as a novelist, he depicted perhaps only two or three complex women: Kate Farrant of *England Made Me*, Sarah Miles of *The End of the Affair*, and possibly Ida Arnold of *Brighton Rock*. His later novels and plays, however, feature a host of well-drawn women, certainly the best of whom is Aunt Augusta of *Travels with My Aunt*. If there is one weakness that mars some of Graham Greene's later novels, it is their prolixity. Too often in his late fiction, characters are merely mouthpieces for ideas.

Brighton Rock was the first of Greene's novels to treat an explicitly religious theme. Moreover, in attempting to play devil's advocate for *Brighton Rock*'s protagonist,

Pinkie, the author had chosen one of his most challenging tasks. He made this Catholic protagonist more vicious than he was to make any character in his entire canon, yet Greene demonstrated that Catholic moral law could not condemn Pinkie, could not finally know "the appalling strangeness of the mercy of God."

Pinkie takes over a protection-racket gang from his predecessor, Kite, and must immediately avenge Kite's murder by killing Fred Hale. This murder inspires him to commit a series of other murders necessary to cover his tracks. It also leads to Pinkie's marrying Rose, a potential witness against him, and finally to his attempt to induce Rose to commit suicide. When the police intervene, Pinkie takes his own life.

Vicious as he is, with his sadistic razor slashings, his murders to cover murders, and his cruelty to Rose, Pinkie's guilt is nevertheless extenuated, his amorality rendered somewhat understandable. Pinkie's conscience had not awakened because his imagination had not awakened: "The word 'murder' conveyed no more to him than the word 'box,' 'collar,' 'giraffe'. . . . The imagination hadn't awoken. That was his strength. He couldn't see through other people's eyes, or feel with their nerves."

As with so many of Greene's characters, the explanation for Pinkie's self-destructive character lies in his lost childhood: "In the lost boyhood of Judas, Christ was betrayed." In a parody of William Wordsworth's "Ode: Intimations of Immortality" (1807), Greene said that Pinkie came into the world trailing something other than heavenly clouds of his own glory after him: "Hell lay about him in his infancy." Though Wordsworth might write of the archetypal child that "heaven lay about him in his infancy," Greene saw Pinkie in quite different terms: "Heaven was a word: hell was something he could trust." Pinkie's vivid memory of his father and mother having sexual intercourse in his presence has turned him from all pleasures of the flesh, tempting him for a while with thoughts of the celibate priesthood.

When Pinkie is seventeen, Kite becomes a surrogate father to him. Pinkie's lack of conscience, his unconcern for himself, his sadomasochistic tendencies, which early showed themselves as a substitute for thwarted sexual impulses, stand the youth in good stead for a new vocation that requires unflinching loyalty, razor slashings, and, if necessary, murder. His corruption is almost guaranteed. To say this is not to reduce the novel from a theological level to a sociological one on which environment has determined the boy's character. Rose survives somewhat the same circumstances. Pinkie's guilt is extenuated, never excused.

Pinkie, however, is not the only character in the novel on whose behalf Greene invoked his "virtue of disloyalty." Rose is a prefiguration of the unorthodox "saint" that Greene developed more subtly in his later novels, in the Mexican priest of *The Power and the Glory*, in Sarah Miles of *The End of the Affair*, and to some extent in Scobie of *The Heart of the Matter*. Like Scobie, Rose wills her damnation out of love. She is not so well drawn as Scobie, at times making her naïve goodness less credible than his, but she is motivated by selfless concern for another. When she refuses to reject Pinkie and when she chooses to commit suicide, Rose wants an afterlife with Pinkie. She would rather be damned with him than see him damned alone: Rose will show "them they couldn't pick and choose." This seems unconvincing, until one hears the old priest cite the actual case of Charles Peguy, who would rather have died in a state of sin than have believed that a single soul was damned. In her confession to the old priest, Rose learns of God's mercy and also of the "saintly" Peguy, who, like Rose, preferred to be damned rather than believe that another person had been.

One is asked, then, to be sympathetic both to a character who has willed her own damnation and to one who leads a life of thorough viciousness, to believe that the salvation of both is a real possibility. In asking for this sympathy, for this possibility, Greene is not doctrinaire. As an effective problem novelist, Greene makes no assertions but merely asks questions that enlarge one's understanding. Greene does not equate the Church with Rose's official moral teaching, suggesting that the old priest in this novel and Father Rank in *The Heart of the Matter* are as representative as the teachers of Rose and Pinkie. Still, the moral doctrine provided Greene with the material that he liked to stretch beyond its customary shape.

The Heart of the Matter · In *The Heart of the Matter*, Greene achieved the genuine tragedy that he came close to writing in many of his other novels. His protagonist, Major Scobie, is a virtuous man whose hamartia lies in an excess of pity. In Scobie, pity exceeds all bounds and becomes as vicious as Macbeth's ambition. His pity wrecks a marriage he had wanted to save, ruins a lover he had hoped to help, kills his closest friend—his "boy," Ali—and brings about his own moral corruption. Compared with Aristides the Just by one character and to the Old Testament's Daniel by another, Scobie becomes guilty of adultery, smuggling, treason, lies, sacrilege, and murder before he kills himself.

A late edition of the novel restores to the story an early scene between the government spy, Wilson, and Louise Scobie. Greene had written it for the original, then withdrew it since he believed that, told as it was from Wilson's point of view, it broke Scobie's point of view prematurely. When this scene is restored, Louise is seen in a more sympathetic light, and one can no longer see Scobie as hunted to his death by Louise. Though the reader still likes Scobie and is tempted to exonerate him, it is difficult to read the restored text without seeing Scobie's excess of pity for what it is.

The novel's three final, anticlimactic scenes effectively serve to reduce the grandeur of Scobie's act of self-sacrifice, showing the utter waste of his suicide and the fearful pride contained in his act. It is not that the final scenes make Scobie seem a lesser person. On the contrary, his wife and Helen are made to appear more unworthy of him: Louise with her unkind judgments about Scobie's taking money from Yusef when that very money was borrowed to send her to South Africa as she wanted, and Helen giving her body to Bagster immediately after Scobie's death. Nevertheless, the very criticism of these women makes Scobie's suicide more meaningless and even more effectively shows the arrogance of his action.

Scobie's suicide, then, is not meant to be seen as praiseworthy but rather as the result of a tragic flaw—pity. In this respect, it differs from Elizabeth's suicide in *The Man Within*. Still, though his suicide is presented as wrong, the final fault in a good man disintegrating spiritually, the reader is compelled to feel sympathy for Scobie. Louise's insistence on the Church's teaching that he has cut himself off from mercy annoys the reader. One is made to see Scobie through the eyes of Father Rank, who angrily responds to Louise that "the Church knows all the rules. But it doesn't know what goes on in a single human heart." In this novel's complex treatment of suicide, then, Greene does not use the "virtue of disloyalty" to justify Scobie's act, but rather "to comprehend sympathetically [a] dissident fellow."

The Human Factor · The epigraph for *The Human Factor* is taken from Joseph Conrad: "I only know that he who forms a tie is lost. The germ of corruption has entered into his soul." Maurice Castle's soul is corrupted because a tie of gratitude exists between him and a Communist friend.

The Human Factor may, in part, have been suggested by Greene's friend and former superior in British Secret Intelligence, Kim Philby, although Greene had written twenty-five thousand words of the novel before Philby's defection. When Philby wrote his story, *My Silent War* (1968), Greene put the novel aside for ten years. In any case, Greene anticipated the novel long before the Philby case in his 1930 story, "I Spy," in which a young boy watches his father being whisked off to Russia after the British have detected his spying.

The Human Factor was Greene's first espionage novel since *Our Man in Havana* in 1958. Greene's protagonist, Maurice Castle, works for the British Secret Service in London and has, the reader learns halfway through the novel, become a double agent. He has agreed to leak information to the Russians to help thwart "Uncle Remus," a plan devised by England, the United States, and South Africa to preserve apartheid, even to use nuclear weapons for the purpose if necessary. Castle has not become a Communist and will not support them in Europe, but he owes a Communist friend a favor for helping his black wife, Sarah, escape from South Africa. Also, he owes his wife's people something better than apartheid.

Castle's spying is eventually discovered, and the Russians remove him from England. They try to make good their promise to have his wife and child follow, but the British Secret Service makes it impossible for Sarah to take the boy when it learns that Sam is not Castle's boy, but the boy of an African who is still alive. The novel ends in bleak fashion when Maurice is permitted to phone from Moscow and learns that his family cannot come. He has escaped into a private prison.

The Human Factor exemplifies again the "virtue of disloyalty," but even more, it demonstrates that Greene does not merely flesh out a story to embody that disloyalty. Though he does everything to enlist the reader's sympathies for Castle, demonstrating his superiority to those for whom he works, Greene ultimately condemns his actions as he condemned Scobie's. As Scobie had been a victim of pity, Castle is a victim of gratitude. In chatting with his wife, Sarah, before she learns that he has been spying, Castle defends his gratitude, and his wife agrees it is a good thing "if it doesn't take you too far." Moreover, as Scobie had an excessive pity even as a boy, Maurice Castle had an exaggerated gratitude. At one point, he asks his mother whether he was a nervous child, and she tells him he always had an "exaggerated sense of gratitude for the least kindness." Once, she tells him, he gave away an expensive pen to a boy who had given him a chocolate bun. At novel's end, when Castle is isolated in Russia, Sarah asks him in a phone conversation how he is, and he recalls his mother's words about the fountain pen: "My mother wasn't far wrong." Like Scobie as well, Castle is the most appealing character in the book, and many a reader will think his defection justified.

The Power and the Glory · The novels considered above are perhaps extreme examples of Greene's "virtue of disloyalty," but the same quality can be found in most of his novels. In his well-known *The Power and the Glory*, for example, Greene sets up a metaphorical conflict between the powers of God and the powers of atheism, yet it is his "disloyalty" that prevents the allegory from turning into a medieval morality play. The forces of good and the forces of evil are not so easily separated. Although his unnamed priest acquires a real holiness through suffering, the author depicts him as a much weaker man than his counterpart, the atheistic lieutenant. The latter is not only a strong man, but also a good man, who is selflessly devoted to the people. His anti-Catholicism has its origin in his boyhood memory of a Church that did not show a similar concern for its people. Perhaps Greene's fairness to Mexico's dusty rationalism, which he actually despised, can be seen by contrasting the novel with its film version. In John Ford's 1947 film, renamed *The Fugitive*, the viewer is given a hero, the priest, played by Henry Fonda, opposed by a corrupt lieutenant.

The Quiet American · That writer's judgment, so firmly founded on "disloyalty," also helped Greene to overcome his tendency to anti-Americanism in *The Quiet American*. While Greene is critical of the naïve and destructive innocence of the young American, Pyle, he is even more critical of the English narrator, Fowler, who is cynically aloof. In the end, Greene's "disloyalty" permits him to show Vietnam suffering at the hands of any and all representatives of the Western world.

Greene's painstaking attempt to see the other side, and to be as "disloyal" as possible to his own, animated his fictional worlds and gave both him and his readers that "extra dimension of understanding."

Henry J. Donaghy

Other major works

SHORT FICTION: *The Basement Room and Other Stories*, 1935; *The Bear Fell Free*, 1935; *Twenty-four Stories*, 1939 (with James Laver and Sylvia Townsend Warner); *Nineteen Stories*, 1947; *Twenty-one Stories*, 1954; *A Visit to Morin*, 1959; *A Sense of Reality*, 1963; *May We Borrow Your Husband? and Other Comedies of the Sexual Life*, 1967; *Collected Stories*, 1972.

PLAYS: *The Heart of the Matter*, pr. 1950 (adaptation of his novel; with Basil Dean); *The Living Room*, pr., pb. 1953; *The Potting Shed*, pr., pb. 1957; *The Complaisant Lover*, pr., pb. 1959; *Carving a Statue*, pr., pb. 1964; *The Return of A. J. Raffles: An Edwardian Comedy in Three Acts Based Somewhat Loosely on E. W. Hornung's Characters in "The Amateur Cracksman,"* pr., pb. 1975; *For Whom the Bell Chimes*, pr. 1980; *Yes and No*, pr. 1980; *The Collected Plays of Graham Greene*, pb. 1985.

SCREENPLAYS: *Twenty-one Days*, 1937; *The New Britain*, 1940; *Brighton Rock*, 1947 (adaptation of his novel; with Terence Rattigan); *The Fallen Idol*, 1948 (adaptation of his novel; with Lesley Storm and William Templeton); *The Third Man*, 1949 (adaptation of his novel; with Carol Reed); *The Stranger's Hand*, 1954 (with Guy Elmes and Giorgino Bassani); *Loser Takes All*, 1956 (adaptation of his novel); *Saint Joan*, 1957 (adaptation of George Bernard Shaw's play); *Our Man in Havana*, 1959 (adaptation of his novel); *The Comedians*, 1967 (adaptation of his novel).

TELEPLAY: *Alas, Poor Maling*, 1975.

RADIO PLAY: *The Great Jowett*, 1939.

POETRY: *Babbling April: Poems*, 1925; *After Two Years*, 1949; *For Christmas*, 1950.

NONFICTION: *Journey Without Maps: A Travel Book*, 1936; *The Lawless Roads: A Mexican Journal*, 1939 (reissued as *Another Mexico*); *British Dramatists*, 1942; *Why Do I Write?: An Exchange of Views Between Elizabeth Bowen, Graham Greene and V. S. Pritchett*, 1948; *The Lost Childhood and Other Essays*, 1951; *Essais Catholiques*, 1953 (Marcelle Sibon, translator); *In Search of a Character: Two African Journals*, 1961; *The Revenge: An Autobiographical Fragment*, 1963; *Victorian Detective Fiction*, 1966; *Collected Essays*, 1969; *A Sort of Life*, 1971; *The Pleasure Dome: The Collected Film Criticism, 1935-40, of Graham Greene*, 1972 (John Russell-Taylor, editor); *Lord Rochester's Monkey: Being the Life of John Wilmot, Second Earl of Rochester*, 1974; *Ways of Escape*, 1980; *Getting to Know the General*, 1984.

CHILDREN'S LITERATURE: *The Little Train*, 1946; *The Little Fire Engine*, 1950 (also as

The Little Red Fire Engine); *The Little Horse Bus,* 1952; *The Little Steam Roller: A Story of Mystery and Detection,* 1953.

EDITED TEXTS: *The Old School: Essays by Divers Hands,* 1934; *The Best of Saki,* 1950; *The Spy's Bedside Book: An Anthology,* 1957 (with Hugh Greene); *The Bodley Head Ford Madox Ford,* 1962, 1963 (4 volumes); *An Impossible Woman: The Memories of Dottoressa Moor of Capri,* 1975.

MISCELLANEOUS: *The Portable Graham Greene,* 1973 (Philip Stout Ford, editor).

Bibliography

De Vitis, A. A. *Graham Greene.* Rev. ed. Boston: Twayne, 1986. This readable, well-organized treatment evaluates the different ways Greene seeks to embody his religious belief in his fiction. Establishes both the intellectual and the social setting in which he developed as a writer and includes detailed discussions of his novels, plays, and short stories. Places particular emphasis on publications after 1938 in which religious themes become clearly apparent. Includes a chronology, a selected bibliography, and an index.

Evans, Robert O., ed. *Graham Greene: Some Critical Considerations.* Lexington: University Press of Kentucky, 1963. This lively collection of fourteen critical essays offers a variety of approaches to Greene's novels along with frequent references to the "entertainments" and travel books. Topics include Greene's Catholicism, his similarities as a writer to François Mauriac, his intellectual background, and his accomplishments as a dramatist, short-story writer, and motion-picture critic. Includes a comprehensive bibliography of his works and the criticism of them published by 1963.

Hill, William Thomas. *Graham Greene's Wanderers: The Search for Dwelling–Journeying and Wandering in the Novels of Graham Greene.* San Francisco: International Scholars Publications, 1999. Examines the motif of the dwelling in Greene's fiction. Deals with the mother, the father, the nation, and the Church as the "ground" of dwelling.

Hoskins, Robert. *Graham Greene: An Approach to the Novels.* New York: Garland, 1999. An updated look at Greene's oeuvre. Includes bibliographical references and an index.

Sheldon, Michael. *Graham Greene: The Enemy Within.* New York: Random House, 1994. In this unauthorized biography, Sheldon takes a much more critical view of Greene's life, especially of his politics, than does Norman Sherry, the authorized biographer. A lively, opinionated narrative. Notes and bibliography included.

Sherry, Norman. *The Life of Graham Greene.* New York: Viking Press, 1989. This is the first part of what is certainly the most comprehensive, most authoritative account of Greene's life yet published, written with complete access to his papers and the full cooperation of family, friends, and the novelist himself. Leads the reader to 1939 to offer a rich account of the novelist's formative years, struggles, and experiences as a journalist. Includes a generous collection of photographs, a bibliography, and an index.

_____. *The Life of Graham Greene. Volume II: 1939-1955.* New York: Viking, 1995. Sherry continues his superb exploration of Greene's life and the sources of his fiction.

Turnell, Martin. *Graham Greene: A Critical Essay.* Grand Rapids, Mich.: Wm. B. Eerdmans, 1967. This brief study explores the factors which determine the quality of the religion in Greene's work from a Christian perspective. Discusses his novels and dramas, includes biographical background, and considers Greene's dilemma as a Christian writer along with those of François Mauriac and Jean Cayrol. A selected primary/secondary bibliography is included.

Wolfe, Peter. *Graham Greene the Entertainer.* Carbondale: Southern Illinois University Press, 1972. The first book-length treatment of Greene's "entertainments." Opens by discussing the varying critical approaches that his novels have received and then offers a readable, book-by-book analysis of each novel's characterization, plot, setting, themes, and style. Includes a selected primary/secondary bibliography and an index.

Thomas Hardy

Born: Higher Bockhampton, England; June 2, 1840
Died: Dorchester, England; January 11, 1928

Principal long fiction · *Desperate Remedies*, 1871; *Under the Greenwood Tree*, 1872; *A Pair of Blue Eyes*, 1872-1873; *Far from the Madding Crowd*, 1874; *The Hand of Ethelberta*, 1875-1876; *The Return of the Native*, 1878; *The Trumpet-Major*, 1880; *A Laodicean*, 1880-1881; *Two on a Tower*, 1882; *The Mayor of Casterbridge*, 1886; *The Woodlanders*, 1886-1887; *Tess of the D'Urbervilles*, 1891; *Jude the Obscure*, 1895; *The Well-Beloved*, 1897.

Other literary forms · In addition to his novels, Thomas Hardy published four collections of short stories, *Wessex Tales* (1888), *A Group of Noble Dames* (1891), *Life's Little Ironies* (1894), and *A Changed Man, The Waiting Supper and Other Tales* (1913). In the latter part of his life, after he had stopped writing novels altogether, he published approximately one thousand poems in eight separate volumes, which have since been collected in one volume by his publisher, Macmillan & Company. In addition to this staggering body of work, Hardy also published an epic-drama of the Napoleonic wars in three parts between 1903 and 1908 entitled *The Dynasts*, a one-act play entitled *The Famous Tragedy of the Queen of Cornwall* (1923), and a series of essays on fiction and other topics, which have been collected in individual volumes. All the novels and stories are available in a uniform library edition in eighteen volumes, published in the early 1960's by Macmillan & Company. Finally, *The Early Life of Hardy* (1928) and *The Later Years of Thomas Hardy* (1930), although ostensibly a two-volume biography of Hardy by his second wife, Florence Hardy, is generally recognized to be Hardy's own autobiography compiled from his notes in his last few years.

Achievements · Hardy is second only to Charles Dickens as the most written-about and discussed writer of the Victorian era. At least one new book and dozens of articles appear on his work every year. Certainly in terms of volume and diversity alone, Hardy is a towering literary figure with two admirable careers—one as novelist and one as poet—to justify his position.

Interest in Hardy's work has followed two basic patterns. The first was philosophical, with many critics creating metaphysical structures that supposedly underlay his fiction. In the late twentieth century, however, interest shifted to that aspect of Hardy's work most scorned before, his technical facility and generic experimentation. One hundred years after his heyday, what once was termed fictional clumsiness was reevaluated in terms of poetic technique.

Furthermore, Hardy's career as a poet, which has always been under the shadow of his fiction, has been reevaluated. Hardy was a curious blend of the old-fashioned and the modern. With a career that began in the Victorian era and did not end until after World War I, Hardy was contemporary both with Matthew Arnold and with T. S. Eliot. Critics such as Babette Deutsch and Vivian De Sola Pinto claim that Hardy bridged the gulf between the Victorian sensibility and the modern era. In his unflinching confrontation with meaninglessness in the universe, Hardy embodied Albert Camus's description of the absurd creator in *The Myth of Sisyphus* (1942); he rebelled

against the chaos of the world by asserting his own freedom to persist in spite of that meaninglessness.

Hardy was a great existential humanist. His hope for humanity was that people would realize that creeds and conventions which presupposed a god-oriented center of value were baseless. He hoped that humans would loosen themselves from those foolish hopes and creeds and become aware of their freedom to create their own value. If human beings would only realize, Hardy felt, that all people were equally alone and without hope for divine help, then perhaps they would realize also that it was the height of absurdity for such lost and isolated creatures to fight among themselves.

Biography · Thomas Hardy was born in the small hamlet of Higher Bockhampton in Stinsford parish on June 2, 1840. His father was a master mason, content with his low social status and at home in his rural surroundings. His mother, however, whom Hardy once called "a born bookworm," made Hardy aware of his low social status and encouraged his education. John Hicks, a friend of Hardy's father and a Dorchester architect, took the boy on as a pupil at the age of sixteen. The well-known poet William Barnes had a school next door to Hicks's office, and Hardy developed an influential friendship with the older man that remained with him. Another early influence on the young Hardy was Horace Moule, a classical scholar with a Cambridge education who was an essayist and reviewer. Moule introduced Hardy to intellectual conversation about Greek literature as well as contemporary issues; it was at Moule's suggestion that Hardy read John Stuart Mill as well as the infamous *Essays and Reviews* (1860, Reverend Henry Bristow Wilson, editor), both of which contributed to the undermining of Hardy's simple religious faith.

Hardy was twenty-two when he went to London to pursue his architectural training. By that time he also entertained literary ambitions and had begun writing poetry. The publication of A. C. Swinburne's *Poems and Ballads* in 1866 so influenced Hardy that he began a two-year period of intensive study and experimentation in writing poetry; none of the many poems he sent out was accepted, however, and he returned to Bockhampton in 1867. It was at this point that Hardy decided to turn to writing fiction. In his old age, he wrote in a letter that he never wanted to write novels at all, but that circumstances compelled him to turn them out.

Hardy's first fictional effort, *The Poor Man and the Lady*, based on the contrast between London and rural life, received some favorable responses from publishers, but after a discussion with George Meredith, Hardy decided not to publish it and instead, on Meredith's advice, wrote *Desperate Remedies* in imitation of the detective style of Wilkie Collins. Later, eager to publish works that would establish his career as a writer, Hardy took the advice of a reader who liked the rural scenes in his unpublished novel and wrote the pastoral idyll *Under the Greenwood Tree*. The book was well received by the critics, but sales were poor. One editor advised him to begin writing serials for periodical publication. With the beginning of *A Pair of Blue Eyes*, Hardy said good-bye to architecture as a profession and devoted the rest of his life to writing.

In 1874, Hardy married Emma Lavinia Gifford, a dynamic and socially ambitious young woman who shared his interests in books. In the meantime, *Far from the Madding Crowd* had appeared to many favorable reviews, and editors began asking for Hardy's work. While living with his wife in a cottage at Sturminster Newton, Hardy composed *The Return of the Native* and enjoyed what he later called the happiest years of his life. Hardy and his wife began a social life in London until he became ill and they decided to return to Dorset, where, while writing *The Mayor of Casterbridge*, he had his home, "Max Gate," built. For the next several years, Hardy continued his writing, traveled with his wife, and read German philosophy.

His enthusiasm for *Tess of the D'Urbervilles* was dampened when it was turned down by two editors before being accepted for serial publication by a third. The publication of the work brought hostile reaction and notoriety—a notoriety that increased after the publication of *Jude the Obscure*. Hardy was both puzzled and cynical about these reactions, but he was by then financially secure and decided to return to his first love:

After 1897 he wrote no more fiction but concentrated solely on poetry. His volumes of poetry were well received, and his experiment with metaphysics in the epic-drama, *The Dynasts*, brought him even more respect, honor, and fame. These final years of Hardy's life appear to have been spoiled only by the death of his wife in 1912. Within four years, however, he married Florence Dugdale, who had been a friend of the family and had done secretarial work for him. She cared for him for the remainder of his life. Hardy continued to write poetry regularly. His final volume of poems, *Winter Words*, was ready to be published when he died on January 11, 1928. His ashes were placed in Westminster Abbey.

Analysis · In *The Courage to Be* (1952), Paul Tillich has said that "the decisive event which underlies the search for meaning and the despair of it in the twentieth century is the loss of God in the nineteenth century." Most critics of the literature of the nineteenth century have accepted this notion and have established a new perspective for studying the period by demonstrating that what is now referred to as the "modern situation" or the "modern artistic dilemma" actually began with the breakup of a value-ordered universe in the Romantic period. Thomas Hardy, in both philosophical attitude and artistic technique, firmly belongs in this modern tradition.

It is a critical commonplace that at the beginning of his literary career Hardy experienced a loss of belief in a divinely ordered universe. The impact of this loss on Hardy cannot be overestimated. In his childhood recollections he appears as an extremely sensitive boy who attended church so regularly that he knew the service by heart, and who firmly believed in a personal and just God who ruled the universe and took cognizance of the situation of humanity. Consequently, when he came to London in his twenties and was exposed to the concept of a demythologized religion in the *Essays and Reviews* and the valueless nonteleological world of Charles Darwin's *On the Origin of Species by Means of Natural Selection* (1859), the loss of his childhood god was a traumatic experience.

What is often called Hardy's philosophy can be summed up in one of his earliest notebook entries in 1865: "The world does not despise us; it only neglects us." An interpretation of any of Hardy's novels must begin with this assumption. The difference between Hardy and other nineteenth century artists who experienced a similar loss of belief is that while others were able to achieve a measure of faith, William Wordsworth reaffirmed an organic concept of nature and of the creative mind which can penetrate it, and Thomas Carlyle finally entered the Everlasting Year with a similar affirmation of nature as alive and progressive—Hardy never made such an affirmative leap to transcendent value. Hardy was more akin to another romantic figure, Samuel Taylor Coleridge's Ancient Mariner, who, having experienced the nightmarish chaos of a world without meaning or value, can never fully get back into an ordered world again.

Hardy was constantly trying to find a way out of his isolated dilemma, constantly trying to find a value to which he could cling in a world of accident, chance, and meaningless indifference. Since he refused to give in to hope for an external value, however, he refused to submit to illusions of transcendence; the only possibility for him was to find some kind of value in the emptiness itself. Like the Ancient Mariner, all Hardy had was his story of loss and despair, chaos and meaninglessness. If value were to be found at all, it lay in the complete commitment to this story—"facing the worst," and playing it back over and over again, exploring its implications, making others aware of its truth. Consequently, Hardy's art can be seen as a series of variations in form on this one barren theme of loss and chaos—"questionings in the exploration of reality."

While Hardy could imitate popular forms and create popular novels such as *Desperate Remedies*, an imitation of Wilkie Collins's detective novel, or *The Hand of Ethelberta*, an imitation of the social comedy popular at the time, when he wished to write a serious novel, one that would truly express his vision of humanity's situation in the universe, he could find no adequate model in the novels of his contemporaries. He solved this first basic problem in his search for form by returning to the tragic drama of the Greek and Elizabethan ages, a mode with which he was familiar through extensive early reading. Another Greek and Elizabethan mode he used, although he was less conscious of its literary tradition, was the pastoral narrative—a natural choice because of its surface similarity to his own subject matter of isolated country settings and innocent country people.

Hardy's second problem in the search for form arose from the incompatibility between the classical tragic vision and his own uniquely modern view. The classical writers saw humanity within a stable and ordered religious and social context, while Hardy saw humanity isolated, alone, searching for meaning in a world that offered none. Because Hardy denied the static and ordered worldview of the past, he was in turn denied the broad context of myth, symbol, and ritual which stemmed from that view. Lost without a God-ordered mythos, Hardy had to create a modern myth that presupposed the absence of God; he needed a pattern. Hardy's use of the traditional patterns of tragedy and pastoral, combined with his rejection of the old mythos that formerly gave meaning to these patterns, resulted in a peculiar distortion as his novels transcended their original patterns.

Nature in Hardy's "pastoral" novels, *The Woodlanders* and *Far from the Madding Crowd*, is neither benevolent nor divinely ordered. Similarly, the human dilemma in his "tragic" novels, *The Return of the Native* and *The Mayor of Casterbridge*, is completely antithetical to what it was for the dramatists of the past. The Greek hero was tragic because he violated a cosmic order; Hardy's heroes are tragic precisely because there is no such order. For the Greek hero there is a final reconciliation which persuades him to submit to the world. For Hardy's hero there is only the never-ending dialectic between people's nostalgia for value and the empty, indifferent world.

In *Tess of the D'Urbervilles* and *Jude the Obscure*, Hardy rejected the traditional tragic and pastoral patterns and allowed the intrinsic problem of his two protagonists to order the chaotic elements of the works. The structure of these novels can be compared to that of the epic journey of Wordsworth in *The Prelude* (1850) and Coleridge in *The Rime of the Ancient Mariner* (1798). As critic Morse Peckham has said in *Beyond the Tragic Vision: The Quest for Identity in the Nineteenth Century* (1962), the task of the nineteenth century artist was no longer to find an external controlling form, but to "symbolize the orientative drive itself, the power of the individual to maintain his identity by creating order which would maintain his gaze at the world as it is, at things as they are." The loss of order is reflected in the structure of *Tess of the D'Urbervilles*, as the young heroine is literally evicted from the familiarity of her world and must endure the nightmarish wandering process of trying to get back inside. The structuring drive of *Jude the Obscure* is Jude's search for an external order that will rid him of the anguish of his own gratuitousness.

Far from the Madding Crowd · Hardy's first important novel, *Far from the Madding Crowd*, was the first in which he successfully adapted a traditional form, the pastoral, to his own purposes, greatly altering it in the process. In *Elizabethan Poetry: A Study in Conventions, Meaning and Expression* (1952), Hallet Smith has described the pastoral as constituting the ideal of the good life: In the pastoral world, nature is the true home of man; the gods take an active concern in man's welfare; the inhabitants of this world are content and self-sufficient. The plot complications of the pastoral usually arise by the intrusion of an aspiring mind from the outside, an antipastoral force which seeks to overthrow the idyllic established order. On the surface, *Far from the Madding Crowd* conforms perfectly to this definition of the pastoral. The story is set in an agricultural community, the main character is a shepherd, and the bulk of the inhabitants are content with their lives. The plot complications arise from the intrusion of the antipastoral Sergeant Troy and the love of three different men for the pastoral maid, Bathsheba. To see the novel as a true pastoral, however, is to ignore living form in order to see a preestablished pattern. The pastoral ideal cannot be the vision of this novel because Hardy was struggling with the active tension between human hopes and the world's indifference.

Far from the Madding Crowd begins in a lighthearted mood with the comic situation of Gabriel Oak's unsuccessful attempts to woo the fickle maid Bathsheba, but Oak, often called the stabilizing force in the novel, is an ambiguous figure. Although he is described as both a biblical and a classical shepherd, he is unequivocally neither. Moreover, the first section of the novel hovers between tragedy and comedy. Even the "pastoral tragedy," the "murder" of all of Gabriel's sheep by the foolish young dog, is equivocal; the dog is not so much destroyed for his crime as he is executed. Gabriel's character, as well as the entire tone of the novel, shifts after this short prologue. When he next appears he is no longer the contented shepherd with modest ambitions; rather, he has developed the indifference to fate and fortune which, Hardy says, "though it often makes a villain of a man, is the basis of his sublimity when it does not."

The change that takes place in Gabriel is caused by his loss and is more significant than the change in Bathsheba because of her gain of an inheritance. Bathsheba, a typical pastoral coquette in the prologue of the novel, makes an ostensible shift when she inherits a farm of her own, but she is still coquettish and vain enough to be piqued by Farmer William Boldwood's indifference to her charms and to send him the valentine saying "Marry Me." Boldwood, "the nearest approach to aristocracy that this remote quarter of the parish could boast of," is a serious, self-sufficient man who sees "no absurd side to the follies of life." The change the valentine causes in him is so extreme as to be comic.

The Bathsheba-Gabriel relationship is complicated by this new wooer. In this section of the novel, until the appearance of Sergeant Troy, there appears a series of scenes in which Gabriel, Boldwood, and Bathsheba are frozen into a tableau with the ever present sheep in the background. The death and physical suffering of the sheep take on a sinister, grotesque imagery to make an ironic commentary on the absurdity of humanity's ephemeral passions in a world dominated by cruelty and death. The irrationality of physical passion is more evident when Bathsheba is overwhelmed by Troy. Their relationship begins with the feminine frill of her dress being caught in his masculine spur and blossoms with her submission to his dazzling sword exercises. After Boldwood's complete demoralization and the marriage of Bathsheba and Troy, the antipastoral Troy corrupts the innocent harvest festival until it becomes a wild frenzy and then a drunken stupor. The pastoral world of the "good life" is turned upside down as the approaching storm transforms the landscape into something sinister. It is significant that the rustics are asleep during the storm, for they are truly unaware of the sickness of the world and its sinister aspect. Troy, too, is unaware of the storm, as he is always unaware of an incongruity between humanity and the indifferent world. Only Gabriel, Bathsheba, and Boldwood, the involved and suffering characters of the novel, react to this symbolic storm.

Just as the death of the sheep formed the ever present background to the first two parts of the novel, the death of Fanny Robin dominates the third section. From the time her body begins its journey in Joseph Poorgrass's wagon until the "Gurgoyle" washes Troy's flowers off her grave, death becomes the most important element in the book. By far the most important effect of Fanny Robin's death is on Bathsheba. When she opens the coffin to find out that Fanny was pregnant with Troy's child, the scene is "like an illusion raised by some fiendish incantation." Her running away to seclude herself in the wood is called by many critics her reconciliation with the natural world of the pastoral, but this view is wholly untenable: Her retreat is on the edge of a swamp of which the "general aspect was malignant." There is no pastoral goodness about the hollow in which she hides. It is a "nursery of pestilences. . . . From its moist and poisonous coat seemed to be exhaled the essences of evil things in the earth." This is one of those grotesque situations in which people become aware of their isolated state, when their need for solace in the natural world is met with only indifference, when they become aware of the absurdity of their demands on a barren and empty world. Bathsheba changes after her experience in this "boundary situation"; she gains the awareness which has characterized Gabriel all along.

After this climactic scene of confrontation with the indifferent world, the book loses its focus. In a diffuse and overlong denouement, Boldwood presses his advantage with Bathsheba until the night of the party, when she is on the point of giving in. Troy's return at this moment and his murder by Boldwood seems forced and melodramatic. Bathsheba's return to marry Gabriel is a concession to the reading public as much as it is to the pastoral pattern of the novel itself. *Far from the Madding Crowd*, a fable of the barrenness and death of the pastoral world and the tragic results of wrong choice through the irrationality of sexual attraction, truly ends with Bathsheba's isolation and painful new awareness in the pestilent swamp.

The Woodlanders · *The Woodlanders*, although more explicit in its imagistic presentation of the unhealthy natural world and more complex in its conflicts of irrational sexual attraction, manifests much of the same kind of formal distortion as is found in *Far from the Madding Crowd*. The world of Little Hintock, far from being the ideal pastoral world, is even more valueless, more inimical a world than Weatherbury. Instead of the grotesque death of sheep, trees become the symbolic representation of humanity's absurd situation in an empty world. Little Hintock is a wasteland, a world of darkness, isolation, guilt, and human cross-purposes. One's nostrils are always filled with the odor of dead leaves, fermenting cider, and heavy, blossomy perfume. One cannot breathe or stretch out one's arms in this world. The so-called "natural" inhabitants of the Wood are dissatisfied with the nature of the world around them. Grace's father, Mr. Melbury, cramped and crippled by his lifetime struggle to make his living from the trees, wants his daughter to be able to escape such a world by marrying an outsider. A conflict is created, though, by the guilt he feels for a wrong he did to Giles Winterborne's father; he tries to atone for it by promising Grace to Giles. John South, Marty's father, on whose life the landholdings of Giles depend, is neurotically afraid of the huge tree in his yard. The tree takes on a symbolic aura as representative of the uncontrollable force of the natural world.

Furthermore, the sophisticated outsiders in the novel are cut off from the world they inhabit and are imaged as "unnatural." Strange unnatural lights can be seen from the house of the young Dr. Fitzpiers, who is said to be in league with the devil. The bored Felice Charmond is so unnatural that she must splice on the luxuriance of natural beauty by having a wig made of Marty South's hair. The isolated and cramped Hintock environment creates a boredom and ennui in these two characters that serve to further the narrative drive of the novel.

Grace, the most equivocal character in the novel, is the active center of its animating conflicts. Her wavering back and forth between the natural world and the antinatural is the central tension that crystallizes the tentative and uncomfortable attitude of all the characters. It is her dilemma of choice that constitutes the major action, just as it was Bathsheba's choice that dominated *Far from the Madding Crowd.* The choices that the characters make to relieve themselves of tension are made through the most irrational emotion, love, in a basically irrational world. Grace marries Fitzpiers in an effort to commit herself to a solid world of value. Fitzpiers sees in Grace the answer to a Shelleyan search for a soul mate. To commit oneself to a line of action that assumes the world is ordered and full of value, to choose a course of action that hopes to lessen the tentativeness of life, to deceive oneself into thinking that there is solidarity—these are the tragic errors that Hardy's characters repeatedly make.

The marriage begins to break up when Fitzpiers, aware that Grace is not the ideal he desired, goes to the lethargic Mrs. Charmond, and when Grace, aware that her hope for solidarity was misdirected, tries to go back to the natural world through the love of Giles. Social conventions, however, which Hardy says are holdovers from outworn creeds, interfere. Grace is unable to obtain a divorce, for the law makes her irrational first choice inflexible. Despairing of the injustice of natural law as well as of social law, she runs away to Giles, who, too self-effacing to rebel against either code, lets her have his house while he spends the night in an ill-sheltered hut. At this point, confused and in anguish about what possibility there is left for her, uncertain of the value of any action, Grace confronts the true nature of the world and the absurdity of her past hopes for value in it. The storm that catches Grace alone in the house is a climactic representation for her of the inimical natural world, just as the pestilent swamp was for Bathsheba. "She had never before been so struck with the devilry of a gusty night in the wood, because she had never been so entirely alone in spirit as she was now. She seemed almost to be apart from herself—a vacuous duplicate only." Grace's indecision and absurd hopes have been leading to this bitter moment of realization in which she is made aware of the ephemeral nature of human existence and the absurdity of human hopes in a world without intrinsic value.

Just as in *Far from the Madding Crowd,* the tension of the action collapses after this confrontation. Giles dies, and Fitzpiers returns after having ended his affair with Mrs. Charmond. After a short period of indifference, Grace, still his wife by law, returns to him. In his customary ironic way, however, Hardy does not allow this reconciliation to be completely satisfying, for it is physical only. Grace, having narrowly missed being caught in a mantrap set for Fitzpiers, is enticingly undressed when Fitzpiers rushes to her and asks to be taken back. This physical attraction is the only reason that Fitzpiers desires a reconciliation. Grace is still indifferent to him, but it is now this very indifference that makes their reunion possible. Seeing no one reaction as more valuable than another, she takes the path of least resistance. The rural chorus ends the novel by commenting that they think the union will not last.

The Return of the Native · Although many critics have pointed out the formal framework of *The Return of the Native*–the classical five-act division; the unity of time, place, and line of action; and the character similarities to Oedipus and Prometheus–other studies have struggled with the book's ambiguities and the difficulties involved in seeing it as a classical tragedy. Certainly, the pattern is classical, but the distortion of the pattern becomes the more significant structuring principle. Egdon Heath is the landscape from which God has departed. People in such an empty world will naturally begin to feel an affinity with the wasteland, such as islands, moors, and dunes. Little more needs to be said here about the part the Heath plays in the action, for critics have called it the principal actor in the drama. Indeed, it does dominate the scene, for the actions of all the characters are reactions in some way to the indifference the Heath represents.

As in *Far from the Madding Crowd*, there is a chorus of rustics in *The Return of the Native*. They belong on the Heath because of their ignorance of the incongruity between human longing for meaning and the intractable indifference of the world. They still maintain a mythical, superstitious belief in a pagan animism and fatalistically accept the nature of things. The Druidical rites of the opening fires, the unimportance of Christian religion, the black mass and Voodoo doll of Susan Nonesuch: All these characterize the pagan fatalism of the rustics.

The main characters, however, do not belong with the rustics. They make something other than a fatalistic response to the Heath and are characterized by their various reactions to its indifference. Mrs. Yeobright is described as having the very solitude exhaled from the Heath concentrated in her face. Having lived with its desolation longer than any of the others, she can no longer escape, but she is desperate to see that Clym does. Damon Wildeve does not belong to the Heath but has taken over a patch of land a former tenant died in trying to reclaim. Although he is dissatisfied, he is not heroic; he is involved in no search, no vital interaction with the indifferent world. Tomasin Yeobright is characterized in a single image, as she is in the house loft, selecting apples: "The sun shone in a bright yellow patch upon the figure of the maiden as she knelt and plunged her naked arms into the soft brown fern." She aligns herself with the natural world through her innocence and consequently perceives no incongruity. Diggory Venn, the most puzzling figure in the novel, is an outcast. The most typical image of him is by his campfire alone, the red glow reflecting off his own red skin. He simply wanders on the open Heath, minding other people's business, and waiting for his chance to marry Tomasin.

These characters, regardless of their conflicts with the irrationality of human choice or the indifference of the Heath, are minor in comparison with the two antithetical attitudes of Eustacia Vye and Clym Yeobright. The most concrete image of Eustacia is of her wandering on the Heath, carrying an hourglass in her hand, gazing aimlessly out over the vast wasteland. Her search for value, her hope for escape from the oppressive indifference of the Heath, lies in being "loved to madness." Clym, however, sees friendliness and geniality written on the Heath. He is the disillusioned intellectual trying to make a return to the mythic simplicity of the natural world. Clym would prefer not to think, not to grapple with the incongruities he has seen. The very disease of thought that forces him to see the "coil of things" makes him desire to teach rather than to think. He is indeed blind, as his mother tells him, in thinking he can instill into the peasants the view that "life is a thing to be put up with," for they have always known it and fatalistically accepted it. Furthermore, he shows his blindness by marrying Eustacia, thinking she will remain with him on the Heath, while Eustacia reveals that she is as misdirected as he is by idealizing him and thinking that he will take her away from the Heath. Both characters search for a meaning and basis for value, but both are trapped by the irrationality of love and vain hopes in an irrational world.

At the beginning of book 4, Clym literally goes blind because of his studying and must actually look at the world through smoked glasses. He welcomes the opportunity to ignore the incongruities of the world by subsuming himself in the Heath and effacing himself in his furze-cutting. In his selfish attempt to "not think" about it, he ignores what this means to Eustacia. She can find no meaning at all in such self-effacing indifference; it is the very thing against which she is rebelling. She returns again to her old pagan ways at the village dance and considers the possibility of Wildeve once more.

Mrs. Yeobright's journey across the Heath, a trip colored by grotesque images of the natural world—the tepid, stringy water of nearly dried pools where "maggoty" shapes cavort; the battered, rude, and wild trees whose limbs are splintered, lopped, and distorted by the weather—is a turning point in the action of the book. In a concatenation of chance events and human misunderstanding, Eustacia turns Mrs. Yeobright away from the door, and the old woman dies as a result. At this point, Eustacia blames some "colossal Prince of the world for framing her situation and ruling her lot."

Clym, still selfish, ignores the problems of the living Eustacia and concentrates on the "riddle of death" of his mother. Had he been able to practice what he professed—human solidarity—he might have saved Eustacia and himself, but instead he bitterly blames her for his mother's death and is the immediate cause of Eustacia's flight. Eustacia's trip across the Heath to her death is similar to Mrs. Yeobright's in that the very natural world seems antagonistic to her. She stumbles over "twisted furze roots, tufts of rushes, or oozing lumps of fleshly fungi, which at this season lay scattered about the Heath like the rotten liver and lungs of some colossal animal." Her leap into the pool is a noble suicide. It is more a rebellion against the indifference of the world around her than it is a submission to its oppressiveness. It is the admission of the absurdity of human hopes by a romantic temperament that refuses to live by such absurdity.

The Mayor of Casterbridge · The tragic pattern of *The Mayor of Casterbridge* has been said by most critics to be more explicit than that of *The Return of the Native*; in the late twentieth century, however, critics were quick to point out that there are serious difficulties involved in seeing *The Mayor of Casterbridge* as an archetypal tragic ritual. Although Henchard is Oedipus-like in his opposition to the rational, Creon-like Farfrae, the plot of the novel, like that of *The Return of the Native*, involves the reactions of a set of characters to the timeless indifference of the world. In this case, the mute and intractable world is imaged in the dead myths and classical legends of Casterbridge. Secluded as much as Little Hintock, the world of *The Woodlanders*, Casterbridge is "huddled all together, shut in by a square wall of trees like a plot of garden by a box-edging." The town is saturated with the old superstitions and myths of the past. The primary image of the desolate world of the town and its dead and valueless past is the Casterbridge Ring, a relic of an ancient Roman amphitheater. The Ring is a central symbol which embodies the desolation of the old myths of human value. It formerly had been the gallows site, but now it is a place for illicit meetings of all kinds, except, Hardy notes, those of happy lovers. A place of man's inhumanity to man is no place for the celebration of love.

The inhumanity of one person to another and the human need for love play an important part in the action of the novel. While the classical Oedipus is guilty of breaking a cosmic law, Henchard is guilty of breaking a purely human one. By selling his wife, he treats her as a thing, not a human being. He rejects human relationships and violates human interdependence and solidarity. This is the sin that begins to find objectification years later when the blight of the bread agitates the townspeople and when his wife, Susan, returns.

It is not this sin alone that means tragedy for Henchard, just as it is not Oedipus's violation alone that brings his downfall. Henchard's character—his irrational behavior, his perverse clinging to the old order and methods, his rash and impulsive nature—also contributes to his defeat. Henchard is an adherent of the old ways. Though he is ostensibly the mayor, an important man, he is actually closer to the rustic, folk characters than the hero of any other Hardy novel. He is not a rebel against the indifference of the world so much as he is a simple hay-stacker, trying desperately to maintain a sense of value in the worn-out codes and superstitions of the past. In the oft-quoted "Character is Fate" passage in the novel, Hardy makes explicit Henchard's problem. He calls him a Faust-like character, "a vehement, gloomy being who had quitted the ways of vulgar men without light to guide him on a better way." Thus, Henchard is caught between two worlds, one of them dead and valueless, the other not worthy enough to be a positive replacement. The levelheaded business sense of Farfrae, the social climbing and superficiality of Lucetta, the too-strict rationality of Elizabeth-Jane—all who represent the new order of human attitudes—appear anemic and self-deceived in the face of Henchard's dynamic energy.

It often seems that the nature of things is against Henchard, but the nature of things is that events occur that cannot be predicted, and that they often occur just at the time when one does not want them to. Many such unpredicted and ill-timed events accumulate to cause Henchard's tragedy. For example, just when he decides to marry Lucetta, his wife Susan returns; just at the time of Susan's death, he is once more reminded of his obligation to Lucetta; just at the time when he tells Elizabeth-Jane that she is his daughter, he discovers that she is not; and just at the time when he calls on Lucetta to discuss marriage, she has already met and found a better mate in Farfrae.

Many of the events that contribute to his own downfall are a combination of this "unholy brew" and his impulsive nature. That the weather turned bad during his planned entertainment he could not prevent, but he could have been more prepared for the rain had he not been in such a hurry to best Farfrae. The unpredictable nature of the weather at harvest time was also beyond his control, but again had he not been so intent on ruining Farfrae he might have survived. He begins to wonder if someone is roasting a waxen image of him or stirring an "unholy brew" to confound him. Moreover, the attitudes of other characters accumulate to contribute to Henchard's downfall. Farfrae, as exacting as a machine, rejects Henchard's fatherly love and makes few truly human responses at all. Lucetta, once dependent on Henchard, becomes so infatuated with her new wealth that she no longer needs him. At the beginning of the novel, Susan's simple nature is incapable of realizing that Newsom's purchase of her is not valid, and at the end, her daughter, Elizabeth-Jane, is so coldly rational that she can cast Henchard off without possibility of reconciliation. None of these characters faces the anguish of being human as Henchard does.

The ambiguity that arises from the combination of all these forces makes it difficult to attribute Henchard's tragedy to any one of them. His death in the end marks the inevitable disappearance of the old order, but it is also the only conclusion possible for the man who has broken the only possible existing order when a cosmic order is no longer tenable—the human order. The reader is perhaps made to feel that Henchard has suffered more than he deserved. As a representative of the old order, his fall must be lamented even as the search is carried on for a new foundation of value and order. At the death of the old values in *The Mayor of Casterbridge*, a new order is not available.

Tess of the D'Urbervilles · The form and meaning of *Tess of the D'Urbervilles* springs from Tess's relation to the natural world. At the beginning of the novel she is a true child of nature who, although sensitive to painful incongruities in her experience, is confident that the natural world will provide her with a basis of value and will protect and sustain her. When nature fails her, her perplexity throws her out of the comfortable world of innocence and natural rapport. Tess then begins a journey both inward and outward in search of a stable orientation and a reintegration into a relationship with the natural world.

Tess first appears in her "natural home" in the small hamlet of Marlott, where her innocence is dramatized as she takes part in the May Day dance. There is a sensitivity in Tess that sets her apart from the other inhabitants. Shame for her father's drunken condition makes her volunteer to take the beehives to market, and despair for the laziness of her parents makes her dreamily watch the passing landscape and ignore where she is going. When, as a result, the horse Prince is killed, Tess's sense of duty to her family, now in economic difficulties, overcomes her pride, and she agrees to go to her aristocratic relatives for help. It is her first journey outside the little world of Marlott and her first real encounter with corruption. Alec, her cousin, is a stock figure of the sophisticated, antinatural world. Their first scene together is formalized into an archetypal image of innocence in the grasp of the corrupt.

Just as it is Tess's natural luxuriance and innocence that attracts Alec, it is also her innocence that leads to her fall. When he takes her into the woods, strangely enough she is not afraid of him as before. She feels that she is in her natural element. She so trusts the natural world to protect her that she innocently falls asleep and is seduced by Alec. The antinatural force that began with her father's alleged nobility, coupled with Tess's own innocence and sensitivity and her naïve trust in the world, all work together to make her an outcast. When her illegitimate child dies and the church refuses it a Christian burial, Tess unequivocally denies the validity of organized religion. She probes within herself to try to find some meaning in her despair. Suddenly she becomes quite consciously aware of the abstract reality of death: "Almost at a leap Tess thus changed from simple girl to complex woman." The facing of the idea of death without a firm hope for transcendence is the conclusion of Tess's inward search in this second phase of her experience, when, still maintaining a will to live and enjoy, she has hopes of submerging herself into the natural world again.

The Valley of the Great Dairies where Tess goes next is the natural world magnified, distorted, thrown out of proportion. It is so lush and fertile as to become a symbolic world. As Tess enters the valley, she feels hope for a new reintegration. For the time being, she dismisses the disturbing thought of her doubt in her childhood God and is satisfied to immerse herself within the purely physical world of the farm's lushness. She manages to ignore her moral plight until she meets the morally ambiguous Angel Clare. In contrast to Tess, Angel's moral perplexity arises from intellectual questioning rather than from natural disillusionment. Intellectually convinced that he has lost faith, Angel rebels against the conventions of society and the church and goes to the Valley of the Great Dairies where he believes innocence and uncontaminated purity and goodness prevail. For Angel, Tess represents the idealistic goal of natural innocence, but the natural world no more affirms this relationship than it did condemn the former one. On the first night of their marriage, Tess confesses to Angel her relationship with Alec. Angel, the idealist, has desired to see a natural perfection in Tess. Doubting that perfection, he rejects her as antinatural. Angel cannot accept the reality of what nature is truly like; he is tied to a conventional orientation more than he realizes.

After Angel leaves her, Tess wanders about the countryside doing farm work at various places until one morning on the road she awakes to find dead pheasants around her. At this point, Tess becomes aware that in a Darwinistic universe, without teleological possibility and without inherent goodness, violation, injury, even death are innate realities. Tess realizes that she is not guilty by the laws of such a world. After this realization she can go to the barren world of Chalk-Newton and not feel so much the incongruity of the place. With its "white vacuity of countenance with the lineaments gone," Chalk-Newton represents the wasteland situation of a world without order or value. Tess can remain indifferent to it because of her new realization of its indifference to her.

Cold indifference, however, offers no escape from her moral conflict. Alec D'Urberville comes back into her life, proclaiming that he has accepted Christianity and exorting her not to "tempt" him again. Ironically, by trying to convince him of her own realization of a world without God and by propounding Angel's uncommitted humanism to him, she only succeeds in reconverting Alec back to his old demonic nature and thus creates another threat to herself. When her father dies and the family loses its precarious freehold, Tess gives in to Alec's persistent urging once more. When Angel, in the rugged South American mountains, comes to the same realization that Tess experienced on the road, he returns to find that Tess has renounced life and self completely, allowing her body to drift, "like a corpse upon the current, in a direction dissociated from the living will." After the return of Angel, when Tess finds her last hopes dashed, she sees in Alec all the deception and meaninglessness of a world she trusted. When she kills him, she is transformed by her rebellion. Like Percy Bysshe Shelley's Beatrice Cenci, she is aware of no guilt; she transcends any kind of moral judgment. She acknowledges her absolute freedom, and in that fearful moment, she is willing to accept the human penalties for such freedom.

In the last part of the novel, when Angel and Tess wander without any real hope of escape, Tess is already condemned to die. Isolated in the awareness of her own ephemerality in a valueless world, Tess vows she is "not going to think of anything outside of now." The final scene at Stonehenge is a triumph of symbolic realization of place; the silent, enigmatic stones, mysterious and implacable, resist any attempt at explanation. Tess, in saying that she likes to be there, accepts the indifferent universe. Lying on the altar of a heathen temple, she is the archetypal sacrifice of human rebellion against an empty world. When the carriers of the law of nature and society arrive, Tess, having rebelled against these laws and rejected them, can easily say, "I am ready."

Tess's real tragedy springs from her insistent hope throughout the novel to find external meaning and justification for her life. Only at the end of the novel, when she rebels by killing Alec, does she achieve true awareness. Unlike the classical tragic hero, she is not reconciled to the world through an acceptance of universal justice.

Her very salvation, the only kind of salvation in Hardy's world, lies in her denial of such a concept.

Jude the Obscure · With some significant differences, *Jude the Obscure* is concerned with the same problem that animates *Tess of the D'Urbervilles*—the absurdity and tragedy of human hopes for value in an indifferent universe. As a literary creation, it is a "process" through which Hardy tries to structure the symbolic journey of every person who searches for a foundation, a basis for meaning and value. The problem, however, is that all the symbols that represent meaning to Jude—the colleges, the church, the ethereal freedom of Sue Bridehead, and even the physical beauty of his wife Arabella—are illusory. By contrast, those things that have real symbolic value in the world are the forbidding, sacrosanct walls of the college complex, which Jude cannot enter; the decaying materiality of the churches which he tries to restore; the neurotic irrationality of Sue, which he fails to understand; and his own body, to which he is inextricably tied. It is precisely Jude's "obscurity," his loss of "at-homeness" in the world, with which the novel is concerned. He is obscure because he is without light, because he tries in every way possible to find an illumination of his relation to the world, but without success.

It is significant that the novel opens with the departure of the schoolmaster Phillotson, for to Jude, orphaned and unwanted by his aunt, the teacher has been the center of the world. His leaving marks the necessity of Jude's finding a new center and a new hope to relieve his loneliness. The first projection of his hopes to find value is naturally toward Christminster, the destination of his teacher. In the first part of the book his dream is seen only as an indefinable glow in the distance that offers all possibilities by its very unknown nature. Although he consciously devotes himself to the Christian framework, one night after having read a classical poem, he kneels and prays to Diana, the goddess of the moon. Both of these value systems—Christian faith and Greek reason—are projected on his vision of Christminster, but both of them are temporarily forgotten when he meets Arabella, "a substantial female animal." Later, when she tells him that she is pregnant, although it destroys all his former plans, he idealizes the marriage state, calls his hopes for Christminster "dreams about books, and degrees and impossible fellowships," and dedicates himself to home, family, and the pedestrian values of Marygreen. His discovery that Arabella has deceived him is only the first reversal in his search for unity and value.

In the second phase of Jude's development, the long-planned journey to Christminster is prompted by the immediacy of seeing a picture of Sue Bridehead; she becomes a concrete symbol of his vision. His first glimpse of Sue has the quality of idealistic wish fulfillment. His growing desire for her expresses a need for an "anchorage" to his thoughts. He goes to the church she attends, and this church, associated with his vision of Sue, temporarily becomes that anchorage. Sue is not, however, representative of Christian values; she is rather the classical pagan. This dichotomy of values creates a recurring tension in Jude's search throughout the book.

Jude's first major disillusionment at Christminster comes when he is turned down by all five colleges to which he has applied. After this disappointment, he shifts his hopes from the reason and knowledge of the schools to the faith of the Church. This religious impulse dominates Jude's hopes in the third phase of his development. He practices the rituals of the Church in the hope that he can find a meaning for himself, but Sue, who laughed at his idealistic notions of the intellectual life, tells him that the Church is not the way either. Sue, who changes in Jude's eyes as his goals change, is always important to him as a symbol of his aspirations and ideals. When he loses her to Phillotson, he is struck even more by the "scorn of Nature for man's finer emotions and her lack of interest in his aspirations."

Phase four of Jude's search is a transition section presenting the decay of the values of the past. Jude, studying theology and church ritual with a last weakening hope, is only vaguely aware of the decay and aridity around him. His need for Sue, an ambiguous mixture of desire for the ideal and the physical, begins to take on more importance for him until he decides that he is unfit "to fill the part of a propounder of accredited dogma" and burns all his theology books. Sue, a spiritual creature, cannot live with Phillotson any longer. She goes to Jude, who, having rejected everything else, is ready to project his desires for meaning entirely on an ambiguous union with her as both physical wife and Shelleyan soul mate.

The fifth part of the novel is a phase of movement as Jude and Sue wander from town to town, living as man and wife in all respects except the sexual. Not until Arabella returns and Sue fears she will lose Jude does she give in to him, but with infinite regret. In the final phase of Jude's development, after the birth of his children, including the mysterious child named "Father Time," the family moves back to Christminster. Instead of being optimistic, Jude is merely indifferent. He recognizes himself as an outsider, a stranger to the universe of ideals and hopes of other men. He has undergone a process that has slowly stripped him of such hopes for meaning. He sees the human desire for meaning as absurd in a world that has no concern for humanity, a universe that cannot fulfill dreams of unity or meaning.

The tragedy of Father Time causes Sue to alter her belief that she can live by instinct, abjuring the laws of society. She makes an extreme shift, accepting a supreme deity against whose laws she feels she has transgressed; her self-imposed penance for her "sin" of living with Jude is to go back to Phillotson. After Sue leaves, Jude goes to "a dreary, strange flat scene, where boughs dripped, and coughs and consumption lurked, and where he had never been before." This is a typical Hardy technique for moments of realization: The natural world becomes an inimical reflection of the character's awareness of the absurd. After this, Jude's reaction to the world around him is indifference: He allows himself to be seduced by Arabella again and marries her. Jude's final journey to see Sue is a journey to death and a final rejection of the indifferent universe of which his experiences have made him aware.

In his relentless vision of a world stripped of transcendence, Hardy is a distinctly modern novelist. As Nathan A. Scott has said of him, "not only does he lead us back to that trauma in the nineteenth century out of which the modern existentialist imagination was born, but he also brings us forward to our own time."

Charles E. May

Other major works

SHORT FICTION: *Wessex Tales,* 1888; *A Group of Noble Dames,* 1891; *Life's Little Ironies,* 1894; *A Changed Man, The Waiting Supper and Other Tales,* 1913; *The Complete Short Stories,* 1989 (Desmond Hawkins, editor).

PLAYS: *The Dynasts: A Drama of the Napoleonic Wars,* pb. 1903, 1906, 1908, 1910 (verse drama), pr. 1914 (abridged by Harley Granville-Barker); *The Famous Tragedy of the Queen of Cornwall,* pr., pb. 1923 (one act).

POETRY: *Wessex Poems and Other Verses,* 1898; *Poems of the Past and Present,* 1901; *Time's Laughingstocks and Other Verses,* 1909; *Satires of Circumstance,* 1914; *Moments of*

Vision and Miscellaneous Verses, 1917; *Late Lyrics and Earlier,* 1922; *Human Shows, Far Phantasies: Songs and Trifles,* 1925; *Winter Words,* 1928; *Collected Poems,* 1931; *The Complete Poetical Works,* 1982-1985 (3 volumes; Samuel Hynes, editor).

NONFICTION: *Life and Art,* 1925 (E. Brennecke, editor); *The Early Life of Hardy,* 1928; *The Later Years of Thomas Hardy,* 1930; *Personal Writings,* 1966 (Harold Orel, editor); *The Collected Letters of Thomas Hardy,* 1978, 1980 (2 volumes; Richard Little Purdy and Michael Millgate, editors).

Bibliography

Bayley, John. *An Essay on Hardy.* Cambridge, England: Cambridge University Press, 1978. Gives a close reading of most of Hardy's major novels, stressing the instability in his style. Hardy's writing was often ambiguous and, by arousing uncertain expectations in the reader, he was able to enhance suspense. His later novels, culminating in *Jude the Obscure,* were more tightly organized, a feature not to Bayley's liking, who prefers the adventitious and unplanned. Also notes that Hardy's attitude toward his male heroes is often determined by their relations with the novel's central female personality.

Campbell, Matthew. *Rhythm and Will in Victorian Poetry.* Cambridge, England: Cambridge University Press, 1999. Examines the literature and poetry of Victorian greats Hardy, Robert Browning, Alfred, Lord Tennyson, and Gerard Manley Hopkins.

Kramer, Dale, ed. *The Cambridge Companion to Thomas Hardy.* Cambridge, England: Cambridge University Press, 1999. An indispensable tool for students of Hardy. Includes bibliographical references and an index.

_____. *Critical Essays on Thomas Hardy: The Novels.* Boston: G. K. Hall, 1990. Divided into a section of overviews and a section on individual novels: *Far from the Madding Crowd, The Return of the Native, The Mayor of Casterbridge, The Woodlanders, Tess of the D'Urbervilles,* and *Jude the Obscure.* Includes an introduction but no bibliography.

Millgate, Michael. *Thomas Hardy: A Biography.* New York: Random House, 1982. The most scholarly biography by one of Hardy's best critics. Includes detailed notes and bibliography.

Seymour-Smith, Martin. *Hardy.* New York: St. Martin's Press, 1994. An opinionated major biography, taking issue with but not superseding Michael Millgate's important work. No notes, brief bibliography.

Southerington, F. R. *Hardy's Vision of Man.* London: Chatto & Windus, 1971. Defends at considerable length a revolutionary account of Hardy. Most authorities see Hardy as a pessimist: His "President of the Immortals" is indifferent to human concerns. However, for Southerington, he is an optimist; his novels show that given appropriate attitudes, one need not be overcome by adversity. The novels also contain many autobiographical passages, which the book traces in detail.

L. P. Hartley

Born: Whittlesea, England; December 30, 1895
Died: London, England; December 13, 1972

Principal long fiction · *Simonetta Perkins*, 1925; *The Shrimp and the Anemone*, 1944; *The Sixth Heaven*, 1946; *Eustace and Hilda*, 1947; *The Boat*, 1949; *My Fellow Devils*, 1951; *The Go-Between*, 1953; *A Perfect Woman*, 1955; *The Hireling*, 1957; *Facial Justice*, 1960; *The Brickfield*, 1964; *The Betrayal*, 1966; *Poor Clare*, 1968; *The Love-Adept*, 1969; *My Sisters' Keeper*, 1970; *The Harness Room*, 1971; *The Collections*, 1972; *The Will and the Way*, 1973.

Other literary forms · L. P. Hartley published, in addition to eighteen novels, six collections of short stories: *Night Fears* (1924), *The Killing Bottle* (1932), *The Traveling Grave* (1948), *The White Wand* (1954), *Two for the River* (1961), and *Mrs. Carteret Receives* (1971). Reprinted in *The Complete Short Stories of L. P. Hartley* (1973), with the exception of ten apprentice pieces from *Night Fears*, the stories reveal Hartley's reliance on the gothic mode. At their least effective, they are workmanlike tales utilizing conventional supernatural machinery. At their best, however, they exhibit a spare symbolic technique used to explore individual human personalities and to analyze the nature of moral evil. The best of Hartley's ghost and horror stories include "A Visitor from Down Under," "Feet Foremost," and "W. S.," the last dealing with an author murdered by a character of his own creation. "Up the Garden Path," "The Pampas Clump," and "The Pylon" reveal a more realistic interest in human psychology, and they deal more directly with the theme central to Hartley's major fiction: the acquisition, on the part of an innocent, even morally naïve, protagonist, of an awareness of the existence of evil.

A frequent lecturer, and a reviewer for such periodicals as *The Observer, Saturday Review*, and *Time and Tide* from the early 1920's to the middle 1940's, Hartley published a volume of essays entitled *The Novelist's Responsibility: Lectures and Essays* (1967), in which he deplored the twentieth century devaluation of a sense of individual moral responsibility. These essays explain Hartley's fictional preoccupation with identity, moral values, and spiritual insight. His choice of subjects, particularly the works of Jane Austen, Emily Brontë, Nathaniel Hawthorne, and Henry James, suggests the origins of the realistic-symbolic technique he employs in both his short stories and his novels.

Achievements · While Hartley's novels from *Simonetta Perkins* to *Facial Justice* were published in the United States, they did not enjoy the popularity there which they earned in England. *The Go-Between*, for example, continued to be in print in England since its publication in 1953, and the *Eustace and Hilda* trilogy—composed of *The Shrimp and the Anemone, The Sixth Heaven*, and *Eustace and Hilda*—was given a radio dramatization by the British Broadcasting Corporation (BBC). In the course of a literary career of roughly fifty years, Hartley came to be a noted public figure, and his work received favorable attention from Lord David Cecil, Walter Allen, and John Atkins. Only in the United States, however, did his novels receive detailed critical attention. The three full-length studies of his fiction—Peter Bien's *L. P. Hartley* (1963), Anne Mulkeen's *Wild Thyme, Winter Lightning: The Symbolic Novels of L. P. Hartley* (1974), and Edward T. Jones's *L. P. Hartley* (1978)—are all American, as are the notable treatments of Hartley's work by James Hall and Harvey Curtis Webster.

Biography · Born on December 30, 1895, near Whittlesea in Cambridgeshire, Leslie Poles Hartley was named for Sir Leslie Stephen, the father of Virginia Woolf and himself a noted late Victorian literary man. Hartley's mother, Mary Elizabeth Thompson, according to Edward T. Jones, whose book on the novelist contains the most complete biographical account, was the daughter of a farmer named William James Thompson of Crawford House, Crowland, Lincolnshire. His father, H. B. Hartley, was a solicitor, justice of the peace, and later director of the successful brickworks founded by the novelist's paternal grandfather. This information figures as part of the background to Hartley's *The Brickfield* and *The Betrayal.*

Hartley was the second of his parents' three children; he had an older sister, Enid, and a younger, Annie Norah. None of the three ever married. Reared at Fletton Tower, near Peterborough, Hartley was educated at Harrow and Balliol College, Oxford, his stay at the latter interrupted by military service as a second lieutenant in the Norfolk Regiment during World War I. He was discharged for medical reasons and did not see action in France. In Oxford after the war, Hartley came into contact with a slightly younger generation of men, among them the future novelists Anthony Powell, Graham Greene, and Evelyn Waugh. His closest literary friend at this period, however, may have been Lord David Cecil. After leaving Balliol with a Second Honours Degree in 1921, Hartley worked as a reviewer for various periodicals, wrote the stories later collected in *Night Fears* and *The Killing Bottle*, and cultivated friendships with members of both Bohemian Bloomsbury and British society. His novella *Simonetta Perkins*, a Jamesian story of a young American woman's inconclusive passion for a Venetian gondolier, was published in 1925.

Hartley made many trips to Venice. From 1933 to 1939, he spent part of each summer and fall there, and he drew on this experience for parts of *Eustace and Hilda, The Boat*, and *My Fellow Devils*. Returning to England just before the start of World War II, Hartley started work on the series of novels which earned for him a place in the British literary establishment. Given the James Tait Black Memorial Prize for *Eustace and Hilda* in 1947 and the Heinemann Foundation Prize for *The Go-Between* in 1953, he served as head of the British Association of Poets, Playwrights, Editors, Essayists and Novelists (PEN) and on the management committee of the Society of Authors. In 1956, he was created a Commander of the British Empire by Queen Elizabeth II. In his later years, Hartley gave frequent talks, most notably the Clark Lectures delivered at Trinity College, Cambridge, in 1964. Joseph Losey won the Grand Prize at Cannes, France, in 1971 for a film version of *The Go-Between*, for which Harold Pinter wrote the script, and in 1973, Alan Bridges's film of *The Hireling*, from a script by Wolf Mankowitz, won the same prize. Hartley died in London on December 13, 1972.

Analysis · Indebted to Bloomsbury, as shown by a concern with personal conduct and a highly impressionistic style, L. P. Hartley betrays affinities with D. H. Lawrence, Aldous Huxley, and George Orwell in a more fundamental concern with larger social and moral issues. His best books argue for the existence of a spiritual dimension to life and demonstrate that recognition of its motive force, even union of oneself with its will, is a moral imperative. In this emphasis on connection, his novels recall those of E. M. Forster, but unlike his predecessor, Hartley insists that the nature of the motive force is supernatural, even traditionally Christian. In his most successful books, Hartley draws upon elements of both novel and romance, as Richard Chase defines them in *The American Novel and Its Tradition* (1957), and the uniqueness of the resulting hybridization precludes comparisons with the work of most of his contemporaries.

Hartley's moral vision, revealed by the gradual integration of realism and symbolism in his novels, is the most striking characteristic of his long fiction. In a book such as *The Go-Between*, he shows that all men are subject to the power of love, even when they deny it, and that achievement of insight into love's capabilities is a prerequisite to achieving moral responsibility. This pattern of growth at the center of Hartley's novels is conventionally Christian in its outlines. The protagonist of each book, beginning with Eustace Cherrington in the *Eustace and Hilda* trilogy, accepts his status as a "sinner" and experiences, if only briefly and incompletely, a semimystical transcendence of his fallen state. The epiphanic technique Hartley develops in the trilogy to objectify these moments of insight recurs in various forms in all of his novels, coming in time to be embodied not in symbolism but in the pattern of action in which he casts his plots. Without suggesting that Hartley's fiction is about theology, it is clear that his concern with the subject of morality cannot avoid having religious overtones. Like Nathaniel Hawthorne, he traces the process of spiritual growth in innocent, morally self-assured, and thereby flawed personalities who experience temptation, even commit sins, and eventually attain spiritual kinship with their fellow people. These encounters, in a book such as *Facial Justice*, occur in settings symbolic of traditional religious values, and so while Hartley's novels may be read from psychoanalytic or mythic points of view, they are more fully comprehended from a metaphysical vantage point.

There is a thematic unity to all of Hartley's longer fiction, but after 1960, there is a marked decline in its technical complexity. In one sense, having worked out his thematic viewpoint in the process of fusing realism and symbolism in his earlier books, Hartley no longer feels the need to dramatize the encounter of good and evil and to set it convincingly in a realistic world. His last novels are fables, and in *The Harness Room*, the most successful of them, the lack of realism intensifies his treatment of the psychological and sexual involvement of an adolescent boy and his father's slightly older chauffeur. This book brings Hartley's oeuvre full circle, back to the story of the American spinster and the Venetian gondolier he produced in *Simonetta Perkins* at the start of his career.

The Eustace and Hilda trilogy · The three novels constituting the *Eustace and Hilda* trilogy—*The Shrimp and the Anemone, The Sixth Heaven,* and *Eustace and Hilda*—objectify a process of moral growth and spiritual regeneration to be found in or behind all of Hartley's subsequent fiction. The process is not unlike that which he describes, in the Clark Lectures reprinted in *The Novelist's Responsibility*, as characteristic of Hawthorne's treatment of the redeeming experience of sin in *The Marble Faun* (1860). The epiphanic moments Hartley uses to dramatize his protagonist's encounters with Christ the Redeemer reveal truths which can be read on psychological, sociological, and theological levels.

In *The Shrimp and the Anemone*, Hartley depicts the abortive rebellion of Eustace Cherrington, aged nine, against the moral and psychological authority of his thirteen-year-old sister Hilda. Set in the summers of 1905 and 1906, the novel reveals young Eustace's intimations of a spiritual reality behind the surface of life. Unable to act in terms of these insights, for they are confused with his aesthetic sense, Eustace feeds his romantic inclination to construct an internal fantasy world and refuses to see the moral necessity of action. In *The Sixth Heaven*, Hartley details Eustace's second effort to achieve his freedom from Hilda, this time by engineering a socially advantageous marriage for her with Dick Staveley, a war hero and rising young member of Parliament. This novel focuses on a visit the Cherringtons make in June, 1920, to the Staveleys, acquaintances who live near their childhood home at Anchorstone. Eustace's adult epiphanic experiences are more insistent. Less tied to his childish aestheticism, they emerge in the context of the novel as hauntingly ambiguous intimations of a moral and spiritual realm which he unconsciously seeks to avoid acknowledging. In *Eustace and Hilda*, the final novel in the trilogy, Hartley brings his protagonist face to face with Christ during the Venetian Feast of the Redeemer, the third Sunday in July, 1920. This encounter leads to Eustace's return to Anchorstone and acceptance of moral responsibility for the emotionally induced paralysis Hilda experienced at the end of her love affair with Dick Staveley. Back in his childhood home, Eustace learns the lesson of self-sacrificial love in Christ's example, and he effects a cure for Hilda by staging a mock-accident for her at the edge of Anchorstone Cliff. Because of the strain this involves, he suffers a fatal heart attack, and the novel ends. His death signals the genuineness of the moral growth and spiritual regeneration which had begun in Venice. The interpenetration of realistic narrative and symbolic subtext which occurs by the end of the *Eustace and Hilda* trilogy objectifies Hartley's vision of the world.

The Boat · Hartley's equivalent of Ford Madox Ford's and Evelyn Waugh's treatments of men at war, *The Boat* presents the mock-epic struggle of Timothy Casson, a forty-nine-year-old bachelor writer, to gain permission to use his rowing shell on the fishing stream that runs through Upton-on-Swirrell. Timothy, settling back in England in 1940 after an eighteen-year stay in Italy, consciously attempts to isolate himself from the effects of the war in progress in the larger world. He devotes himself to collecting china, to cultivating friends, to raising a dog, and to forcing the village magnates to allow him to row on the Swirrell. In the process, Timothy violates his own self-interest, as well as that of his nation and his class, but he is not the tragicomic figure that Eustace Cherrington becomes in the trilogy. In Hartley's hands, Timothy achieves only a degree of the self-awareness that Eustace does, and this enables the novelist to label him the "common sinner" that all people are, a figure both sinned against and sinning.

Timothy's desire to take his boat out on the river is an assertion of individuality that polarizes the community. His attachment to his boat becomes a measure of his moral and political confusion, for Timothy is torn between the influences of Vera Cross, a Communist secret agent sent to Upton-on-Swirrell to organize unrest among the masses, and Volumnia Purbright, the wife of the Anglican vicar and an unconventional, perhaps mystical, Christian. The emblematic names suggest the comic possibilities Hartley exploits in his treatment of the two, but *The Boat* is a serious novel. Vera represents a social disharmony resultant upon the advocacy of ideology, while Volumnia reflects both social harmony and personal tranquillity resulting from sacrifice of self. Indeed, when Timothy persists in his protest against the prohibition against rowing and sets forth on the flooded Swirrell with two children and his dog as passengers, Volumnia confronts Vera on the riverbank. Vera attacks the vicar's wife, and the two women tumble into the water. When Vera drowns in the Devil's Staircase, Volumnia blames herself for the younger woman's death and subsequently dies from exposure and pneumonia. When at the end of *The Boat* Timothy, who had to be rescued from the river when his boat capsized in the flooded stream, dreams he receives a telephone call from Volumnia inviting him to tea, he hears Vera's voice as well as Volumnia's, and the two women tell him that they are inseparable, as are the moral and ethical positions they represent.

Near the end of the novel, Timothy prepares to leave Upton-on-Swirrell in the company of two old friends, Esther Morwen and Tyrone MacAdam. The two discuss the prospects for Timothy's acceptance of himself as an ordinary human being. At the time of the boating accident, he had managed to rescue one of the children with him, but he needed the fortuitous help of others to rescue the second child and to reach safety himself. Timothy is clearly partially responsible for the deaths of Vera Cross and Volumnia Purbright, and the "true cross" he must bear is an acceptance of moral complexity. Whether he will achieve this insight is an open question at the end of *The Boat*, and Hartley's refusal to make the book a neat statement reinforces its thematic point.

The Go-Between · Hartley's *The Go-Between*, arguably his finest novel, is the only one with a first-person narrator as protagonist. Leo Colston, like the focal characters of the *Eustace and Hilda* trilogy and *The Boat*, frees himself from psychological constraints and achieves a measure of moral insight. Indeed, Leo's story amounts to a rite of passage conforming to the pattern of initiation characteristic of the *Bildungsroman*. More significantly, *The Go-Between* is a study of England on the verge of its second Elizabethan Age, and the patterns of imagery which Hartley uses to reveal the personality of Leo suggest indirectly that the Age of Aquarius will be a golden one.

These linguistic patterns, introduced into the novel by Leo himself, derive from the signs of the zodiac. On one hand, they are a pattern manufactured by Leo as a schoolboy and utilized to explain his conviction that the start of the twentieth century, which he dates incorrectly as January 1, 1900, is the dawn of a second Golden Age. On the other hand, the zodiac motifs, as associated with Leo and other characters in the novel, underscore Hartley's thematic insistence on the power of self-sacrificial love to redeem both individuals and society from error. At the start of the novel in 1951 or 1952, Leo is an elderly man engaged in sorting through the accumulated memorabilia of a lifetime. Coming upon his diary for the year 1900, inside the cover of which are printed the zodiac signs, he recalls his experiences at Southdown Hill School and his vacation visit to a schoolmate, Marcus Maudsley. In the body of the novel, the account of that nineteen-day visit to Brandham Hall, the narrative voice is split between that of the thirteen-year-old Leo of 1900 and that of the aged man with which the book begins. Used by Marcus's sister Marian to carry messages to her lover, the tenant farmer Ted Burgess, Leo finds himself faced with the dubious morality of his actions when Marcus tells him that Marian is to marry Viscount Trimingham, the owner of Brandham Hall and a scarred veteran of the Boer War.

In Leo's mind, Marian is the Virgin of the zodiac, Trimingham the Sagittarian archer, and Burgess the Aquarian water-carrier. Determined to break the bond between Marian and Ted and to restore her to Viscount Trimingham, Leo resorts to the schoolboy magic with which he had handled bullies at school. He plans a spell involving the sacrifice of an *atropa belladonna* or deadly nightshade growing in a deserted outbuilding, but the ritual goes awry and he finds himself flat on his back with the plant on top of him. The next day, his thirteenth birthday, Leo is forced to lead Marian's mother to the spot where the girl meets her lover, and they discover the pair engaged in sexual intercourse. For Leo, whose adult sexuality has just begun to develop, this is a significant shock, and he feels that he has been defeated by the beautiful but deadly lady, both the deadly nightshade and Marian herself.

In the epilogue to *The Go-Between*, the elderly Leo Colston returns to Norfolk to find out the consequences of the mutual betrayal. Encountering Marian, now the dowager Lady Trimingham, once more, he undertakes again to be a messenger. This time he goes to her grandson Edward in an effort to reconcile him to the events of the fateful year 1900, to the fact that his father was really the son of Ted Burgess. This action on Leo's part embodies the theme of all of Hartley's fiction: The only evil in life is an unloving heart. At the end of his return journey to Brandham Hall, Leo Colston is a more vital man and a more compassionate one. Having faced the evil both inside and outside himself, he is open to love, and the Age of Aquarius can begin. That it will also be the age of Elizabeth II, given the political and sociological implications of the central action, gives Hartley's *The Go-Between* its particular thematic rightness.

Robert C. Petersen

Other major works
SHORT FICTION: *Night Fears*, 1924; *The Killing Bottle*, 1932; *The Traveling Grave*, 1948; *The White Wand*, 1954; *Two for the River*, 1961; *Mrs. Carteret Receives*, 1971; *The Complete Short Stories of L. P. Hartley*, 1973.
NONFICTION: *The Novelist's Responsibility: Lectures and Essays*, 1967.

Bibliography
Bien, Peter. *L. P. Hartley*. University Park: Pennsylvania State University Press, 1963. The first book on Hartley's fiction, important for its Freudian analysis of his novels; its identification of his indebtedness to Nathaniel Hawthorne, Henry James, and Emily Brontë; and its examination of Hartley's literary criticism. At its best when discussing the novels about the transition from adolescence to adulthood. Includes a brief bibliography.
Bloomfield, Paul. *L. P. Hartley*. London: Longmans, Green, 1962. An early short monograph by a personal friend of Hartley, coupled with one on Anthony Powell by Bernard Bergonzi. Focuses on character analysis and thematic concerns, providing a brief discussion of Hartley's novels. Laudatory, perceptive, and very well written.
Fane, Julian. *Best Friends*. London: Sinclair Stevenson, 1990. Contains a memoir of Hartley that helps to situate his fiction in terms of his sensibility and his time.
Hall, James. *The Tragic Comedians: Seven Modern British Novelists*. Bloomington: Indiana University Press, 1963. Claims that the Hartley protagonist possesses an inadequate emotional pattern that leads inevitably to failure. This neurotic behavior is discussed in his major fiction: *The Boat, Eustace and Hilda, My Fellow Devils*, and *The Hireling*. In these novels Hartley demonstrates that confidence is accompanied by a contradictory desire to fail.
Jones, Edward T. *L. P. Hartley*. Boston: Twayne, 1978. Provides an excellent analysis of Hartley's literary work, particularly of his novels, which are conveniently grouped. Also contains a chronology, a biographical introductory chapter, a discussion of Hartley's literary criticism, and an excellent annotated bibliography. Of special interest are Jones's definition of the "Hartleian novel" and his discussion of Hartley's short fiction.

Mulkeen, Anne. *Wild Thyme, Winter Lightning: The Symbolic Novels of L. P. Hartley.* Detroit, Mich.: Wayne State University Press, 1974. Focuses on Hartley's fiction until 1968, stressing the Hawthornian romance elements in his early novels. Particularly concerned with his adaptations of the romance and how his characters are at once themselves and archetypes or symbols. An extensive list of helpful secondary sources is provided.

Webster, Harvey Curtis. *After the Trauma: Representative British Novelists Since 1920.* Lexington: University Press of Kentucky, 1970. The chapter on Hartley, entitled "Diffident Christian," concerns his protagonists' struggles to distinguish between God's orders and society's demands. Discusses *Facial Justice, Eustace and Hilda, The Boat,* and *The Go-Between* extensively, concluding that Hartley merits more attention than he has been given.

Wright, Adrian. *Foreign Country: The Life of L. P. Hartley.* London: A. Deutsch, 1996. A good biography of Hartley for the beginning student. Includes bibliographical references and an index.

Aldous Huxley

Born: Laleham, near Godalming, Surrey, England; July 26, 1894
Died: Los Angeles, California; November 22, 1963

Principal long fiction · *Crome Yellow*, 1921; *Antic Hay*, 1923; *Those Barren Leaves*, 1925; *Point Counter Point*, 1928; *Brave New World*, 1932; *Eyeless in Gaza*, 1936; *After Many a Summer Dies the Swan*, 1939; *Time Must Have a Stop*, 1944; *Ape and Essence*, 1948; *The Genius and the Goddess*, 1955; *Island*, 1962.

Other literary forms · Besides the novel, Aldous Huxley wrote in every other major literary form. He published several volumes of essays and won universal acclaim as a first-rate essayist. He also wrote poetry, plays, short stories, biographies, and travelogues.

Achievements · Huxley achieved fame as a satirical novelist and essayist in the decade following World War I. In his article "Aldous Huxley: The Ultra-Modern Satirist," published in *The Nation* in 1926, Edwin Muir observed, "No other writer of our time has built up a serious reputation so rapidly and so surely; compared with his rise to acceptance that of Mr. Lawrence or Mr. Eliot has been gradual, almost painful." In the 1920's and the early 1930's, Huxley became so popular that the first London editions of his books were, within a decade of their publication, held at a premium by dealers and collectors. Huxley's early readers, whose sensibilities had been hardened by the war, found his wit, his iconoclasm, and his cynicism to their taste. They were also impressed by his prophetic gifts. Bertrand Russell said, "What Huxley thinks today, England thinks tomorrow." Believing that all available knowledge should be absorbed if humanity were to survive, Huxley assimilated ideas from a wide range of fields and allowed them to find their way into his novels, which came to be variously identified as "novels of ideas," "discussion novels," or "conversation novels." His increasing store of knowledge did not, however, help him overcome his pessimistic and cynical outlook on life.

Huxley's reputation as a novelist suffered a sharp decline in his later years. In *The Novel and the Modern World* (1939), David Daiches took a highly critical view of Huxley's novels, and since then, many other critics have joined him. It is often asserted that Huxley was essentially an essayist whose novels frequently turn into intellectual tracts. It has also been held that his plots lack dramatic interest and his characters are devoid of real substance. Attempts were made in the late twentieth century, however, to rehabilitate him as an important novelist. In any case, no serious discussion of twentieth century fiction can afford to ignore Huxley's novels.

Biography · Aldous Leonard Huxley was born at Laleham, near Godalming, Surrey, on July 26, 1894. His father, Leonard Huxley, a biographer and historian, was the son of Thomas Henry Huxley, the great Darwinist, and his mother, Julia, was the niece of Matthew Arnold. Sir Julian Huxley, the famous biologist, was his brother. With this intellectual and literary family background, Huxley entered Eton at the age of fourteen. Owing to an attack of *keratitis punctata*, causing blindness, he had to withdraw from school within two years, an event which left a permanent mark on his character, evident in his reflective temperament and detached manner. He learned to read Braille and continued his studies under tutors. As soon as he was able to read with the help of a magnifying glass, he went to Balliol College, Oxford, where he studied English literature and philosophy.

Huxley started his career as a journalist on the editorial staff of *The Athenaeum* under J. Middleton Murry. He relinquished his journalistic career when he could support himself by his writing. By 1920, he had three volumes of verse and a collection of short stories to his credit. He had also become acquainted with a number of writers, including D. H. Lawrence. While in Italy in the 1920's, he met Lawrence again, and the two became close friends. Lawrence exercised a profound influence on Huxley, particularly in his distrust of intellect, against his faith in

Library of Congress

blood consciousness. Later, Huxley became a disciple of Gerald Heard, the pacifist, and took an active part in Heard's pacifist movement. In 1937, he moved to California, where he came into contact with the Ramakrishna Mission in Hollywood. In Hinduism and Buddhism, Huxley found the means of liberation from man's bondage to the ego, a problem which had concerned him for a long time. To see if the mystical experience could be chemically induced, Huxley took drugs in 1953, and his writings concerning hallucinogenic drugs helped to popularize their use.

Huxley married Maria Nys in 1919. After her death in 1955, he married Laura Archera in 1956. On November 22, 1963, Huxley died in Los Angeles, where his body was cremated the same day. There was no funeral, but friends in London held a memorial service the next month.

Analysis · Aldous Huxley's novels present, on the whole, a bitterly satirical and cynical picture of contemporary society. A recurring theme in his work is the egocentricity of the people of the twentieth century, their ignorance of any reality transcending the self, their loneliness and despair, and their pointless and sordid existence. Devoid of any sense of ultimate purpose, the world often appears to Huxley as a wilderness of apes, baboons, monkeys, and maggots, a veritable inferno, presided over by Belial himself. The dominant negativism in the novelist's outlook on life is pointedly and powerfully revealed by Will Farnaby, a character in his book *Island*, who is fond of saying that he will not take yes for an answer.

Though Huxley finds the contemporary world largely hopeless, he reveals the possibility of redemption. Little oases of humanity, islands of decency, and atolls of liberated souls generally appear in his fictional worlds. A good number of his characters transcend their egos, achieve completeness of being, recognize the higher spiritual goals of life, and even dedicate their lives to the service of an indifferent humanity. Even Will Farnaby, who will not take yes for an answer, finally casts his lot with the islanders against the corrupt and the corrupting world. It is true that these liberated individuals are not, in Huxley's novels, a force strong enough to resist the onward march of civilization toward self-destruction, but they are, nevertheless, a testimony to the author's faith in the possibilities of sanity even in the most difficult of times. No one who agrees with Huxley's assessment of the modern world will ask for a stronger affirmation of faith in human redemption.

Huxley believed that man's redemption lies in his attainment of "wholeness" and integrity. His concept of wholeness did not, however, remain the same from the beginning to the end of his career. As he matured as a novelist, Huxley's sense of wholeness achieved greater depth and clarity. Under the influence of D. H. Lawrence, Huxley viewed wholeness in terms of the harmonious blending of all human faculties. Writing under the influence of Gerald Heard, he expanded his idea of wholeness to include a mystical awareness of the unity of man with nature. Coming under the influence of the Eastern religions, especially Hinduism and Buddhism, he gave his concept of wholeness further spiritual and metaphysical depth.

Crome Yellow · In *Crome Yellow*, his first novel, Huxley exposed the egocentricity of modern man, his inability to relate to others or recognize any reality, social or spiritual, outside himself, and the utter pointlessness of his life. Jenny Mullion, a minor character in the novel, symbolically represents the situation that prevails in the modern world by the almost impenetrable barriers of her deafness. It is difficult for anyone to carry on an intelligent conversation with her. Once early in the book, when Denis Stone, the poet, inquires if she slept well, she speaks to him, in reply, about thunderstorms. Following this ineffectual conversation, Denis reflects on the nature of Jenny Mullion.

> Parallel straight lines . . . meet only at infinity. He might talk for ever of care-charmer sleep and she of meteorology till the end of time. Did one ever establish contact with anyone? We are all parallel straight lines. Jenny was only a little more parallel than most.

Almost every character in the novel is set fast in the world that he has made for himself and cannot come out of it to establish contact with others. Henry even declaims, "How gay and delightful life would be if one could get rid of all the human contacts!" He is of the view that "the proper study of mankind is books." His history of his family, which took him twenty-five years to write and four years to print, was obviously undertaken in order to escape human contacts. If Henry is occupied with the history of Crome, Priscilla, his wife, spends her time cultivating a rather ill-defined malady, betting, horoscope reading, and studying Barbecue-Smith's books on spiritualism. Barbecue-Smith busies himself with infinity. Bodiham, the village priest, is obsessed by the Second Coming. Having read somewhere about the dangers of sexual repression, Mary Bracegirdle hunts for a lover who will provide her with an outlet for her repressed instincts. Denis constantly broods over his failure as a writer, as a lover, and as a man. Scogan, disdainful of life, people, and the arts, finds consolation only in reason and ideas and dreams about a scientifically controlled Rational State where babies are produced in test tubes and artists are sent to a lethal chamber.

Though there is a good deal of interaction among the guests at Crome, no real meeting of minds or hearts takes place among them; this failure to connect is best illustrated by the numerous hopeless love affairs described in the novel. Denis, for example, loves Anne, but his repeated attempts to convey his love for her fail. Anne, who is four years older than Denis, talks to him as if he were a child and does not know that he is courting her. Mary falls in love with Denis only to be rebuffed. Then, she makes advances to Gombauld, the painter, with no better result. Next, she pursues Ivor, the man of many gifts and talents, and is brokenhearted to learn that she means nothing to him. She is finally seen in the embrace of a young farmer of heroic proportions, and it is anybody's guess what comes of this affair. Even the relationship between Anne and Gombauld, which showed every promise of maturation into one of lasting love, meets, at the end, the same fate as the others.

Thumbing through Jenny's red notebook of cartoons, Denis suddenly becomes conscious of points of view other than his own. He learns that there are others who are "in their way as elaborate and complete as he is in his." Denis's appreciation of the world outside himself comes, however, too late in the novel. Though he would like to abandon the plan of his intended departure from Crome, particularly when he sees that it makes Anne feel wretched, he is too proud to change his mind and stay in Crome to try again with her. Thus, the characters in *Crome Yellow* remain self-absorbed, separated from one another, and hardly concerned with the ultimate ends of life. Scogan betrays himself and others when he says, "We all know that there's no ultimate point."

Antic Hay · *Antic Hay*, Huxley's second novel, presents, like *Crome Yellow*, an infernolike picture of contemporary society, dominated by egocentric characters living in total isolation from society and suffering extreme loneliness, boredom, and despair. Evidence of self-preoccupation and isolation is abundant. Gumbril Junior continually dwells on his failings and on his prospects of getting rich. He retires every now and then to his private rooms at Great Russell Street, where he enjoys his stay, away from people. Lypiatt, a painter, poet, and musician, is without a sympathetic audience. "I find myself alone, spiritually alone," he complains. Shearwater, the scientist, has no interest in anything or anyone except in the study of the regulative function of the kidneys. Mercaptan is a writer whose theme is "the pettiness, the simian limitations, the insignificance and the absurd pretentiousness of *Homo* soi-disant *Sapiens.*"

The men and women in *Antic Hay*, each living in his or her private universe, are unable to establish any true and meaningful relationships with one another. Myra Viveash is cold and callous toward men who come to her and offer their love: Gumbril Junior, Lypiatt, Shearwater, and others. She contemptuously lends herself to them. Lypiatt, hopelessly in love with her, finally takes his life. Gumbril, deserted by Myra, feels revengeful; in turn, he is cruelly cynical in his treatment of Mrs. Rosie Shearwater. Because of his carelessness, he loses Emily, who might have brought some happiness and meaning into his life. Engaged in his scientific research, Shearwater completely ignores his wife, with the result that she gives herself to other men. Men and women can easily find sexual partners, which does not, however, close the distance between them: They remain as distant as ever.

On the eve of Gumbril's intended departure from London for the Continent, Gumbril and Myra taxi the entire length and breadth of the West End to meet friends and invite them to a dinner that night. Their friends are, significantly enough, engaged in one way or another and shut up in their rooms—Lypiatt writing his life for Myra; Coleman sleeping with Rosie; and Shearwater cycling in a hot box in his laboratory. Despite the lovely moon above on the summer night and the poignant sorrow in their hearts, Gumbril and Myra make no attempt to take advantage of their last ride together and come closer. Instead, they aimlessly drive from place to place.

Those Barren Leaves · Huxley's next novel, *Those Barren Leaves*, shows how people who might be expected to be more enlightened are as self-centered as the mass of humanity. The setting of the novel, which deals with a circle of British intellectuals in Italy, immediately and powerfully reinforces the fact of their social isolation.

Mrs. Lilian Aldwinkle, a patroness of the arts and a votary of love, wants to believe that the whole world revolves around her. As usual, she is possessive of her guests who have assembled at her newly bought palace of Cybo Malaspina in the village of Vezza in Italy, and she wants them to do as she commands. She is unable, however, to hold them completely under her control. In spite of all her efforts, she fails to win the love of Calamy, and later of Francis Chelifer; Chelifer remains unmoved even when she goes down on her knees and begs for his love. She sinks into real despair when her niece escapes her smothering possessiveness and falls in love with Lord Hovenden. Well past her youth, Mrs. Aldwinkle finds herself left alone with nobody to blame but herself for her plight.

Miss Mary Thriplow and Francis Chelifer are both egocentric writers, cut off from the world of real human beings. Miss Thriplow is obsessed with her suffering and pain, which are mostly self-induced. Her mind is constantly busy, spinning stories on gossamer passions she experiences while moving, talking, and loving. Conscious of the unreality of the life of upper-class society, Chelifer gives up poetry and also the opportunity of receiving a fellowship at Oxford in favor of a job as editor of *The Rabbit Fanciers' Gazette* in London. The squalor, the repulsiveness, and the stupidity of modern life constitute, in Chelifer's opinion, reality. Because it is the artist's duty to live amid reality, he lives among an assorted group of eccentrics in a boardinghouse in Gog's court, which he describes as "the navel of reality." If Miss Thriplow is lost in her world of imagination and art, Chelifer is lost in "the navel of reality"—equidistant from the heart of reality.

Through the character of Calamy, Huxley suggests a way to overcome the perverse, modern world. Rich, handsome, and hedonistic, Calamy was once a part of this world, but he no longer enjoys running after women, wasting his time in futile intercourse, and pursuing pleasure. Rather, he spends his time reading, satisfying his curiosity about things, and thinking. He withdraws to a mountain retreat, hoping that his meditation will ultimately lead him into the mysteries of existence, the relationship between men, and that between man and the external world.

Calamy's withdrawal to a mountain retreat is, no doubt, an unsatisfactory solution, particularly in view of the problem of egocentricity and isolation of the individual from society raised in *Those Barren Leaves* and Huxley's two preceding novels. It may, however, be noted that Calamy's isolation is not a result of his egocentricity: He recognizes that there are spheres of reality beyond the self.

Point Counter Point · *Point Counter Point*, Huxley's first mature novel, is regarded by many critics as his masterpiece, a major work of twentieth century fiction. By introducing similar characters facing different situations and different characters facing a similar situation, a technique analogous to the musical device of counterpoint,

Huxley presents a comprehensive and penetrating picture of the sordidness of contemporary society.

Mark Rampion, a character modeled upon D. H. Lawrence, sees the problem of modern humanity as one of lopsided development. Instead of achieving a harmonious development of all human faculties—reason, intellect, emotion, instinct, and body—modern humankind allows one faculty to develop at the expense of the others. "It's time," Rampion says, "there was a revolt in favor of life and wholeness."

Huxley makes a penetrating analysis of the failure of his characters to achieve love and understanding. Particularly acute is his analysis of Philip Quarles, a critical self-portrait of the author. Since a childhood accident, which left him slightly lame in one leg, Philip has shunned society and has developed a reflective and intellectual temperament. As a result of his constant preoccupation with ideas, the emotional side of his character atrophies, and he is unable to love even his wife with any degree of warmth. In the ordinary daily world of human contacts, he is curiously like a foreigner, not at home with his fellows, finding it difficult or impossible to enter into communication with any but those who can speak his native intellectual language of ideas. He knows his weakness, and he tries unsuccessfully to transform a detached intellectual skepticism into a way of harmonious living. It is no wonder that his wife, Lilian, feels exasperated with his coldness and unresponsiveness and feels that she could as well love a bookcase.

Philip, however, is not as hopeless a case of lopsided development as the rest of the characters who crowd the world of *Point Counter Point*. Lord Edward Tantamount, the forty-year-old scientist, is in all but intellect a child. He is engaged in research involving the transplantation of the tail of a newt onto the stump of its amputated foreleg to find out if the tail will grow into a leg or continue incongruously to grow as a tail. He shuts himself up in his laboratory most of the day and a good part of the night, avoiding all human contact. Lady Edward, his wife, and Lucy Tantamount, his daughter, live for sexual excitement. Spandril, who prides himself on being a sensualist, actually hates women. Suffering from a sense of betrayal by his mother when she remarries, he attracts women only to torture them. Burlap wears a mask of spirituality, but he is a materialist to the core. Molly, pretty and plump, makes herself desirable to men but lacks genuine emotional interest. The novel contains an assortment of barbarians (to use the language of Rampion) of the intellect, of the body, and of the spirit, suffering from "Newton's disease," "Henry Ford's disease," "Jesus' disease," and so on—various forms of imbalance in which one human faculty is emphasized at the expense of the others.

Point Counter Point presents an extremely divided world. None of the numerous marriages, except that of the Rampions, turns out well, nor do the extramarital relationships. Both Lilian Quarles and her brother, Walter Bidlake, have problems with their spouses. Lilian plans to leave her husband, Philip Quarles, and go to Everard Webley, a political leader, who has been courting her, but the plan is terminated with Webley's murder. After leaving his wife, Walter lives with Marjorie Carling but finds her dull and unexciting within two years. Ignoring Marjorie, who is pregnant with his child, Walter begins to court Lucy Tantamount, a professional siren, who, after keeping him for a long time in a state of uncertainty, turns him away. John Bidlake, the father of Lilian and Walter, has been married three times and has had a number of love affairs. Sidney Quarles, the father of Philip, has had many secret affairs. Disharmony thus marks the marital world presented in the novel, effectively dramatized by means of parallel, contrapuntal plots.

Mark and Mary Rampion serve as a counterpoint to the gallery of barbarians and lopsided characters in the novel. Although Mary comes from an aristocratic family and Mark belongs to the working class, they do not suffer from the usual class prejudices. Transcending their origins, they have also transcended the common run of egocentric and self-divided personalities. They have achieved wholeness and integrity in personality and outlook. There is no dichotomy between what they say and what they do. Mark's art is a product of lived experience, and his concern for it is inseparable from his concern for life.

Though the dominant mood of Huxley's early novels is one of negativism and despair, the Rampions exemplify his faith in the possibility of achieving individual wholeness and loving human relationships. The Rampions may not be able to change the state of affairs in the modern world, but their presence itself is inspiring; what is more, they are, unlike Calamy of *Those Barren Leaves*, easily accessible to all those who want to meet them.

Brave New World · *Brave New World*, Huxley's best-known work, describes a centrally administered and scientifically controlled future society in A.F. 632 (A.F. standing for After Ford), around six hundred years from the twentieth century. It is difficult to recognize the people of Huxley's future World State as human beings. Decanted from test tubes in laboratories, the population of the Brave New World comes in five standardized varieties: Alphas, Betas, Gammas, Deltas, and Epsilons. Each group is genetically conditioned to carry out different tasks. By various methods of psychological conditioning, they are trained to live in total identification with society and to shun all activities that threaten the stability of the community. The State takes full care of them, including the emotional side of their life. All their desires are satisfied; they do not want what they cannot get. With substitutes and surrogates such as the Pregnancy Substitute and the Violent Passion Surrogate, life is made happy and comfortable for everyone. Although people have nothing of which to complain, they seem to suffer pain continually. Relief from pain is, however, readily available to them in *soma*, which is distributed by the State every day.

Sentiments, ideas, and practices which liberate the human spirit find no place in Huxley's scientific utopia and are, in fact, put down as harmful to the stability of the community. Parentage, family, and home become obsolete; sex is denuded of all its mystery and significance. Small children are encouraged to indulge in erotic play so that they learn to take a strictly matter-of-fact view of sex. Men and women indulge in copulation to fill idle hours. Loyalty in sex and love is regarded as abnormal behavior. Love of nature, solitude, and meditation are looked upon as serious maladies requiring urgent medical attention. Art, science, and religion are all considered threatening. Patience, courage, self-denial, beauty, nobility, and truth become irrelevant to a society that believes in consumerism, comfort, and happiness.

Huxley shows how some people in the Brave New World, despite every care taken by the State to ensure their place in the social order, do not fall in line. Bernard Marx yearns for Lenina Crowne and wants to take her on long walks in lonely places. Helmholtz Watson's creative impulses demand poetic expression. Even Mustapha Mond, the Resident Controller of Western Europe, is somewhat regretful over his abandonment of scientific research in favor of his present position. People who stubbornly refuse to conform to the social order are removed promptly by the State to an island where they can live freely according to their wishes.

It is through the character of John, the Savage, from the Reservation, that Huxley clearly exposes the vulgarity and horror of the Brave New World. Attracted to civilization on seeing Lenina, the Savage soon comes to recoil from it. In his long conversation with Mustapha Mond, he expresses his preference for the natural world of disease, unhappiness, and death over the mechanical world of swarming indistinguishable sameness. Unable to get out of it, he retires to a lonely place where he undertakes his purification by taking mustard and warm water, doing hard labor, and resorting to self-flagellation.

In *Brave New World*, Huxley presents a world in which wholeness becomes an object of a hopeless quest. Looking back at the novel, he observed that this was the most serious defect of the story. In a foreword written in 1946, he said that if he were to rewrite the book, he would offer the Savage a third alternative: Between the utopian and the primitive horns of his dilemma would lie the possibility of sanity—a possibility already actualized, to some extent, in a community of exiles and refugees from the Brave New World, living within the borders of the Reservation.

Eyeless in Gaza · In *Eyeless in Gaza*, Huxley returns to the subject of egocentric modern man deeply buried in intellectual preoccupations, sensuality, ideology, and fanaticism. Sensualists abound in *Eyeless in Gaza*. The most notorious among them are Mrs. Mary Amberley and her daughter, Helen Ledwidge, both mistresses at different times to Anthony Beavis, the central character in the novel. Believing in "sharp, short, and exciting" affairs, Mary keeps changing her lovers until she gets prematurely old, spent, and poor. When nobody wants to have her any more, she takes to morphine to forget her misery. Helen marries Hugh Ledwidge but soon realizes that he is incapable of taking an interest in anything except his books. To compensate for her unhappy married life, she goes from man to man in search of emotional satisfaction. Indeed, sensuality marks the lives of most of the members of the upper-class society presented in the novel.

In addition to sensualists, various other types of single-minded characters share the world of *Eyeless in Gaza*. Brian, one of Anthony's classmates and friends, suffers from a maniacal concern for chastity, and his mother shows a great possessiveness toward him. Mark, another of Anthony's classmates, becomes a cynical revolutionary. John Beavis, Anthony's father, makes philology the sole interest of his life. There are also Communists, Fascists, Fabians, and other fanatics, all fighting for their different causes.

Anthony Beavis is estranged early in his life from men and society after the death of his mother. He grows into manhood cold and indifferent to people. He finds it a disagreeable and laborious task to establish contacts; even with his own father, he maintains a distance. He does not give himself away to his friends or to the women he loves. *Elements of Sociology*, a book Beavis is engaged in writing, assumes the highest priority in his life, and he is careful to avoid the "non-job," personal relations and emotional entanglements which might interfere with his work's progress. As he matures, however, Beavis aspires to achieve a sense of completeness above the self: "I value completeness. I think it's one's duty to develop all one's potentialities—*all* of them." At this stage, he believes in knowledge, acquired by means of intellect rather than by Laurentian intuition. He is interested only in knowing about truth, not experiencing it like a saint: "I'm quite content with only *knowing* about the way of perfection." He thinks that experience is not worth the price, for it costs one's liberty. Gradually, he realizes that knowledge is a means to an end, rather than an end in itself, a means to achieve freedom from the self. After being so enlightened, he feels genuine love for Helen, who remains unmoved, however, because of her past experiences with him. From Dr. Miller, the anthropologist, Beavis learns how to obliterate the self and achieve wholeness through love and selfless service. He has a mystic experience of the unity of all life and becomes a pacifist to serve humankind.

After Many a Summer Dies the Swan · In *After Many a Summer Dies the Swan,* his first novel after his move to California, Huxley satirized the frenzied attempts made by men of the twentieth century to enrich their lives, stressing that the peace that comes with transcendence can bring an enduring joy. Huxley illustrates the vacuity of modern life through the character of Mr. Stoyte, an old California oil magnate living amid every conceivable luxury and comfort. With endless opportunities before him to make more money and enjoy life (he keeps a young mistress of twenty-two), Stoyte wants to live as long as he can. He finances Dr. Obispo's research on longevity in the hope that he will be able to benefit from the results of the doctor's experiments. He acquires the valuable Haubert Papers, relating to the history of an old English family, in order to discover the secret of the long life of the Fifth Earl, and he hires Jeremy Pordage, an English scholar, to arrange the papers. Dr. Obispo and his assistant, Pete, are basically no different from Mr. Stoyte in their outlooks. They believe that they will be rendering a great service to humanity by extending man's life, little realizing that growing up, as they conceive it, is really growing back into the kind of apelike existence represented by the life of the Fifth Earl. Jeremy Pordage has no real interest in anything except literature, and he too betrays a narrowness of outlook.

Propter exemplifies Huxley's dedicated search for more-than-personal consciousness. Retired from his university job, he spends his time helping poor migrant workers, trying to find ways of being self-reliant, and thinking about the timeless good. He argues that nothing good can be achieved at the human level, which is the level of "time and craving," the two aspects of evil. He disapproves most of what goes on in the name of patriotism, idealism, and spiritualism because he thinks that they are marks of man's greed and covetousness. One should, in his view, aim at the highest ideal: the liberation from personality, time, and craving into eternity.

Time Must Have a Stop · Bruno Rontini, the mystic saint in *Time Must Have a Stop,* observes that only one out of every ten thousand herrings manages to break out of his carapace completely, and few of those that break out become full-sized fish. He adds that the odds against a man's spiritual maturation today are even greater. Most people remain, according to him, spiritual children.

Time Must Have a Stop presents the obstacles that Sebastian Barnack has to face before he can reach full spiritual maturation. If egocentricity and single-mindedness were the main hurdles for Philip Quarles and Anthony Beavis, Sebastian's problems are created by his weak personality, shaped by his puritanical and idealistic father. He possesses fine poetic and intellectual endowments, but he is disappointed with his own immature appearance. Even though he is aware of his superior gifts, he looks "like a child" at seventeen. Naturally, his relatives and friends take an adoptive attitude toward him and try to influence him in different ways. Eustace, his rich and self-indulgent uncle, teaches him how to live and let live and enjoy life. Mrs. Thwale helps him to overcome his shyness in a most outrageous manner. There are many others who try to mold Sebastian's destiny and prevent him from true self-realization.

Huxley offers further insights into Propter's mystical faith through the character of Bruno Rontini, under whose guidance Sebastian finally receives enlightenment.

Bruno believes that there is only one corner of the universe that one can be certain of improving, and that is one's own self. He says that a man has to begin there, not outside, not on other people, for a man has to *be* good before he can *do* good. Bruno believes that only by taking the fact of eternity into account can one free one's enslaved thoughts: "And it is only by deliberately paying our attention and our primary allegiance to eternity that we can prevent time from turning our lives into a pointless or diabolic foolery." Under the guidance of Bruno, Sebastian becomes aware of a timeless and infinite presence. After his spiritual liberation, he begins to work for world peace. He thinks that one of the indispensable conditions for peace is "a shared theology." He evolves a "Minimum Working Hypothesis," to which all men of all countries and religions can subscribe.

Ape and Essence · Huxley's increasing faith in the possibility of man's liberation in this world did not, at any time, blind him to man's immense capacity for evil. *Ape and Essence* describes how man's apelike instincts bring about the destruction of the world through a nuclear World War III. New Zealand escapes the holocaust, and in A. D. 2108, about one hundred years after the war, the country's Re-Discovery Expedition to North America reaches the coast of Southern California, at a place about twenty miles west of Los Angeles, where Dr. Poole, the Chief Botanist of the party, is taken prisoner by descendants of people who survived the war. Though some Californians have survived the war, the effects of radioactivity still show in the birth of deformed babies, who are liquidated one day of the year in the name of the Purification of the Race. Men and women are allowed free sexual intercourse only two weeks a year following the Purification ceremony so that all the deformed babies that are born in the year are taken care of at one time. Women wear shirts and trousers embroidered with the word "no" on their breasts and seats, and people who indulge in sex during any other part of the year, "Hots" as they are called, are buried alive or castrated and forced to join the priesthood, unless they are able to escape into the community of "Hots" in the north. The California survivors dig up graves to relieve the dead bodies of their clothes and other valuable items, roast bread over fires fueled by books from the Public Library, and worship Belial.

Introducing the film script of *Ape and Essence*, Huxley suggested that present society, even under normal conditions, is not basically different from the society of the survivors depicted in the novel. Gandhi's assassination, he says, had very little impact on most people, who remained preoccupied with their own petty personal problems. Under normal conditions, this unspiritual society would grow into the kind of society represented by Dr. Poole and his team. Dr. Poole is portrayed as a middle-aged child, full of inhibitions and suppressed desires, suffering under the dominance of his puritanical mother.

Ironically, Dr. Poole experiences a sense of wholeness in the satanic postatomic world, as he sheds his inhibitions and finds a free outlet for his suppressed desires during the sexual orgies following the Purification ceremony. Declining the invitation of the Arch Vicar to join his order, Dr. Poole escapes with Loola, the girl who has effected his awakening, into the land of the "Hots." Through the episode of Dr. Poole, Huxley suggests that self-transcendence is possible even in the worst of times.

The Genius and the Goddess · *The Genius and the Goddess* describes how Rivers, brought up like Dr. Poole of *Apes and Essence* in a puritanical family, undergoes a series of disturbing experiences in the household of Henry and Katy Maartens, which apparently lead him into a spiritual awakening in the end. Rivers joins the Maartens household to assist Henry, the "genius," in his scientific research. He is shocked when Katy, the "goddess," climbs into his bed and shocked again when he sees Katy, rejuvenated by her adultery, performing her wifely devotions with all earnestness, as if nothing had happened. To his further bewilderment and shock, he discovers that he is sought by the daughter as well. The mother outwits the daughter, but Katy and Rivers face the danger of being exposed before Henry. Rivers is, however, saved from disgrace when the mother and daughter both are killed in a car accident. Rivers is an old man as he narrates the story of his progress toward awareness. Though his final awakening is not described, one can safely infer from his attitude toward his past experiences that he has risen above Katy's passion and Henry's intellect to a level outside and above time and has achieved a sense of wholeness. There is, indeed, no way of telling how grace comes.

Island · As previously noted, Huxley creates in almost every novel an island of decency to illustrate the possibility of achieving liberation from bondage to the ego and to time, even amid the chaos of modern life. This island is generally represented by an individual or a group of individuals, or it is simply stated to be located in some remote corner of the world. In his last novel, *Island*, Huxley offers a picture of a whole society that has evolved a set of operations, such as yoga, *dhyana* (meditation), *maithuna* (yoga of love), and Zen, to achieve self-transcendence and realize the Vedantic truth, *tat tvam asi*, "thou art That."

In Huxley's island of Pala, the chief concern underlying child care, education, religion, and government is to ensure among its citizens a harmonious development of all human faculties and an achievement of a sense of completeness. To save their children from crippling influences, the parents of Pala bring up one another's children on a basis of mutual exchange. In school, children are taught the important aspects of life from biology to ecology, from sex to religion. They are taken to maternity hospitals so that they can see how children are born; they are even shown how people die. No one subject or area is given exclusive importance. The credo is that "nothing short of everything will really do." When they come of age, boys and girls freely engage in sex. Suppressed feelings and emotions are given an outlet in a vigorous type of dance. An admixture of Hinduism and Buddhism is the religion of the people, but there is no orthodoxy about it. "Karuna" or compassion and an attention to "here and now," to what is happening at any given moment, are the basic tenets of their way of life. Moksha medicines are freely available to those who want to extend their awareness and get a glimpse of the Clear Light and a knowlege of the Divine Ground. As people know how to live gracefully, they also know how to die gracefully when the time for death comes. The country has followed a benevolent monarchy for one hundred years. The nation is aligned neither with the capitalist countries nor with the communists. It is opposed to industrialization and militarization. It has rich oil resources but has refused to grant licenses to the numerous oil companies that are vying to exploit Pala. Will Farnaby, the journalist who has managed to sneak ashore the forbidden island, is so greatly impressed by the imaginative and creative Palanese way of life that he abandons the mission for which he went to the island, which was to obtain, by any means possible, a license for the South East-Asia Petroleum Company to drill for oil on the island.

Huxley fully recognizes the extreme vulnerability of the ideal of integrity and wholeness in the modern world. The state of Pala has, for example, incurred the displeasure of both the capitalist and communist countries by its policy of nonalignment. Many big companies are resorting to bribery in an effort to get a foothold on the island. Colonel Dipa, the military dictator of the neighboring state of Randang-Lobo, has expansionist ambitions. While Pala is thus threatened by the outside world, corruption has also set in from within. Dowager Rani and Murugan, her son, disapprove of the isolationist policies of the island and want their country to march along with the rest of the world. On the day Murugan is sworn king, he invites the army from Randang-Lobo to enter the island and massacre the people who have been opposed to his progressive outlook.

Huxley's novels not only present the horrors of the modern world, but they also show ways of achieving spiritual liberation and wholeness. Huxley is among the few writers of the twentieth century who fought a brave and relentless battle against life-destroying forces. Untiringly, he sought ways of enriching life by cleansing the doors of perception, awakening his readers to the vital spiritual side of their beings.

S. Krishnamoorthy Aithal

Other major works

SHORT FICTION: *Limbo,* 1920; *Mortal Coils,* 1922; *Little Mexican and Other Stories,* 1924 (pb. in U.S. as *Young Archimedes, and Other Stories,* 1924); *Two or Three Graces, and Other Stories,* 1926; *Brief Candles: Stories,* 1930; *The Gioconda Smile,* 1938 (first pb. in *Mortal Coils*).

PLAYS: *The Discovery,* pb. 1924; *The World of Light,* pb. 1931; *The Gioconda Smile,* pr., pb. 1948.

POETRY: *The Burning Wheel,* 1916; *Jonah,* 1917; *The Defeat of Youth,* 1918; *Leda,* 1920; *Arabia Infelix,* 1929; *The Cicadas and Other Poems,* 1931.

NONFICTION: *On the Margin: Notes and Essays,* 1923; *Along the Road: Notes and Essays of a Tourist,* 1925; *Jesting Pilate,* 1926; *Essays New and Old,* 1926; *Proper Studies,* 1927; *Do What You Will,* 1929; *Holy Face and Other Essays,* 1929; *Vulgarity in Literature,* 1930; *Music at Night,* 1931; *Texts and Pretexts,* 1932; *Beyond the Mexique Bay,* 1934; *The Olive Tree,* 1936; *Ends and Means,* 1937; *Grey Eminence,* 1941; *The Art of Seeing,* 1942; *The Perennial Philosophy,* 1945; *Themes and Variations,* 1950; *The Devils of Loudun,* 1952; *The Doors of Perception,* 1954; *Heaven and Hell,* 1956; *Tomorrow and Tomorrow and Tomorrow,* 1956 (pb. in England as *Adonis and the Alphabet, and Other Essays,* 1956); *Brave New World Revisited,* 1958; *Collected Essays,* 1959; *Literature and Science,* 1963.

Bibliography

Baker, Robert S. *The Dark Historic Page: Social Satire and Historicism in the Novels of Aldous Huxley, 1921-1939.* Madison: University of Wisconsin Press, 1982. Devotes separate chapters to close readings of Huxley's novels, which are analyzed in terms of the protagonist's conflict with the prevailing secular society. Claims that Huxley is concerned with dystopian dilemmas and the price to be paid for the protagonist's losing struggle against change and society. Includes an excellent bibliography.

Bedford, Sybille. *Aldous Huxley: A Biography.* New York: Knopf, 1974. A superbly written life of the writer by one of England's renowned authors. In addition to the well-informed narrative, Bedford includes a chronology, a chronological list of Huxley's works, and a bibliography.

Bowering, Peter. *Aldous Huxley: A Study of the Major Novels.* New York: Oxford University Press, 1969. Treats Huxley as a novelist of ideas and attempts to treat the fiction and nonfiction as a whole. Each of his nine novels is analyzed in a separate chapter, and in a concluding chapter the complex relationship between the novelist and the artist is discussed. Well indexed.

Deery, June. *Aldous Huxley and the Mysticism of Science.* New York: St. Martin's Press, 1996. Discusses Huxley's use of science in his novels. Includes bibliographical references and an index.

Firchlow, Peter. *Aldous Huxley: Satirist and Novelist.* Minneapolis: University of Minnesota Press, 1972. Although the focus is on Huxley's novels, especially *Point Counter Point* and *Brave New World,* the book does provide a biographical chapter and one on his poetry, which is ignored by most writers. One of the highlights of the book is the parallel established between Huxley's *Island* and Jonathan Swift's book 4 of *Gulliver's Travels.*

May, Keith M. *Aldous Huxley.* New York: Barnes & Noble Books, 1972. Addresses the problem of how "novelistic" Huxley's novels are and concludes that it is language rather than structure that determines the meaning of each of his novels. The eleven novels, each of which is analyzed in a separate chapter, are divided into two chronological groups: novels of exploration and novels of certainty, with the dividing line coming between *Eyeless in Gaza* (1936) and *After Many a Summer Dies the Swan* (1939). Also contains a helpful bibliography.

Meckier, Jerome, ed. *Critical Essays on Aldous Huxley.* New York: G. K. Hall, 1996. Thoughtful essays on the author's oeuvre. Bibliographical references and an index are included.

Nance, Guinevera A. *Aldous Huxley.* New York: Continuum, 1988. Nance's introductory biographical chapter ("The Life Theoretic") reflects her emphasis on Huxley's novels of ideas. The novels, which are discussed at length, are divided into three chronological groups, with the utopian novels coming in the second group. Supplies a detailed chronology and a fairly extensive bibliography.

Watt, Donald, ed. *Aldous Huxley: The Critical Heritage.* London: Routledge & Kegan Paul, 1975. An invaluable chronological collection of book reviews and other short essays on Huxley's work and life. Among the literary contributors are Evelyn Waugh, E. M. Forster, William Inge, Stephen Spender, George Orwell, Thomas Wolfe, Ernest Hemingway, T. S. Eliot, and André Gide. The introduction traces the critical response to Huxley. Includes an extensive bibliography as well as information about translations and book sales.

P. D. James

Born: Oxford, England; August 3, 1920

Principal long fiction · *Cover Her Face,* 1962; *A Mind to Murder,* 1963; *Unnatural Causes,* 1967; *Shroud for a Nightingale,* 1971; *An Unsuitable Job for a Woman,* 1972; *The Black Tower,* 1975; *Death of an Expert Witness,* 1977; *Innocent Blood,* 1980; *The Skull Beneath the Skin,* 1982; *A Taste for Death,* 1986; *Devices and Desires,* 1989; *The Children of Men,* 1992; *Original Sin,* 1994; *A Certain Justice,* 1997.

Other literary forms · Though P. D. James is known principally as a novelist, she is also a short-story writer and a playwright. The great bulk of James's work is in the form of the long narrative, but her short fiction has found a wide audience through its publication in *Ellery Queen's Mystery Magazine* and other popular periodicals. It is generally agreed that James requires the novel form to show her literary strengths to best advantage. Still, short stories such as "The Victim" reveal in microcosm the dominant theme of the long works. James's lone play, *A Private Treason,* was first produced in London on March 12, 1985.

Achievements · James's first novel, *Cover Her Face,* did not appear until 1962, at which time the author was in her early forties. Acceptance of her as a major crime novelist, however, grew very quickly. *A Mind to Murder* appeared in 1963, and with the publication of *Unnatural Causes* in 1967 came that year's prize from the Crime Writers Association. In the novels which have followed, James has shown an increasing mastery of the labyrinthine murder-and-detection plot. This mastery is the feature of her work that most appeals to one large group of her readers, while a second group of readers would single out the subtlety and psychological validity of her characterizations. Critics have often remarked that James, more than almost any other modern mystery writer, has succeeded in overcoming the limitations of the genre. In addition, she has created one of the more memorable descendants of Sherlock Holmes. Like Dorothy Sayers's Lord Peter Wimsey and Agatha Christie's Hercule Poirot, James's Adam Dalgliesh is a sleuth whose personality is more interesting than his skill in detection.

Biography · Phyllis Dorothy James was born in Oxford, England, on August 3, 1920. She graduated from Cambridge High School for Girls in 1937. She was married to Ernest C. B. White, a medical practitioner, from August 8, 1941, until his death in 1964. She worked as a hospital administrator from 1949 to 1968 and as a civil servant in the Department of Home Affairs, London, from 1968 to 1972. From 1972 until her retirement in 1979, she was a senior civil servant in the crime department.

Although beginning her career as a novelist rather late in life, by 1997 James had authored fourteen books, nine of which were filmed for broadcast on television. In addition, her heroine, Cordelia Gray, was featured in a series of television dramas—not adapted from stories actually written by James—produced under the overall title *An Unsuitable Job for a Woman.* The temperament informing her fiction seems to be a conservative one, but she has stated that she belongs to no political party.

Nigel Parry

Although not overtly a Christian writer, James, a long-time member of the Church of England, frequently touches upon religious themes. This tendency is more marked in the later novels and is reflected in several of her titles.

Since her retirement from the Home Office, James has served as a magistrate in London and as a governor of the British Broadcasting Corporation. She has been the recipient of numerous literary prizes and other honors. In 1991, she was created Baroness James of Holland Park. Lady James is the mother of two daughters and has five grandchildren. She divides her time between homes in Oxford, her place of birth, and London, the city so intimately and lovingly described in her fiction.

Analysis · P. D. James's work is solidly in the tradition of the realistic novel. Her novels are intricately plotted, as successful novels of detection must be. Through her use of extremely well-delineated characters and a wealth of minute and accurate details, however, James never allows her plot to distort the other aspects of her novel. As a result of her employment, James had extensive contact with physicians, nurses, civil servants, police officials, and magistrates. She uses this experience to devise settings in the active world where men and women busily pursue their vocations. She eschews the country weekend murders of her predecessors, with their leisure-class suspects who have little more to do than chat with the amateur detective and look guilty.

A murder requires a motive, and it is her treatment of motivation that sets James's work apart from most mystery fiction. Her suspects are frequently the emotionally maimed who, nevertheless, manage to function with an apparent normality. Beneath their veneer, dark secrets fester, producing the phobias and compulsions they take such pains to disguise. James's novels seem to suggest that danger is never far away in the most mundane setting, especially the workplace. She avoids all gothic devices, choosing instead to create a growing sense of menace just below the surface of everyday life. James's murderers rarely kill for gain; they kill to avoid exposure of some sort.

Shroud for a Nightingale · The setting for *Shroud for a Nightingale* is a nursing hospital near London. The student nurses and most of the staff are in permanent residence there. In this closed society, attachments—sexual and otherwise—are formed, rivalries develop, and resentments grow. When a student nurse is murdered during a teaching demonstration, Inspector Adam Dalgliesh of Scotland Yard arrives to investigate. In the course of his investigation, Dalgliesh discovers that the murdered girl was a petty blackmailer, that a second student nurse (murdered soon after Dalgliesh's arrival) was pregnant but unmarried and had engaged in an affair with a middle-aged surgeon, that one member of the senior staff is committing adultery with a married man from the neighborhood and another is homosexually attracted to one of her charges. At the root of the murders, however, is the darkest secret of all, a terrible sin which a rather sympathetic character has been attempting both to hide and expiate for more than thirty years. The murder weapon is poison, which serves also as a metaphor for the fear and suspicion that rapidly spread through the insular world of the hospital.

Adam Dalgliesh carries a secret burden of his own. His wife and son died during childbirth. He is a sensitive and cerebral man, a poet of some reputation. These deaths have left him bereft of hope and intensely aware of the fragility of humanity's control over its own life. Only the rules that humankind has painstakingly fashioned over the centuries can ward off degeneration and annihilation. As a policeman, Dalgliesh enforces society's rules, giving himself a purpose for living and some brief respite from his memories. Those who commit murder contribute to the world's disorder and hasten the ultimate collapse of civilization. Dalgliesh will catch them and see that they are punished.

An Unsuitable Job for a Woman · In *An Unsuitable Job for a Woman*, published within a year of *Shroud for a Nightingale*, James introduces her second recurring protagonist. Cordelia Gray's "unsuitable job" is that of private detective. Gray unexpectedly falls heir to a detective agency and, as a result, discovers her vocation. Again, James avoids the formularized characterization. Gender is the most obvious but least interesting difference between Dalgliesh and Gray. Dalgliesh is brooding and introspective;

although the narratives in which he appears are the very antithesis of the gothic novel, there are aspects of the gothic hero in his behavior. Gray, on the other hand, is optimistic, outgoing, and good-natured, despite her unfortunate background (she was brought up in a series of foster homes). She is a truth seeker and, like William Shakespeare's Cordelia, a truth teller. Dalgliesh and Gray are alike in their cleverness and competence. Their paths occasionally cross, and a friendly rivalry exists between them.

Death of an Expert Witness · In *Death of an Expert Witness,* James's seventh novel, Dalgliesh again probes the secrets of a small group of coworkers and their families. The setting this time is a laboratory that conducts forensic examinations. James used her nineteen years of experience as a hospital administrative assistant to render the setting of *Shroud for a Nightingale* totally convincing, and she uses her seven years of work in the crime department of the Home Office to the same effect in *Death of an Expert Witness.* In her meticulous attention to detail, James writes in the tradition of Gustave Flaubert, Leo Tolstoy, and the nineteenth century realists. Because the setting, characterizations, and incidents of a James novel are so solidly grounded in detail, it tends to be considerably longer than the ordinary murder mystery. This fact accounts for what little adverse criticism her work has received. Some critics have suggested that so profuse is the detail, the general reader may eventually grow impatient, that the pace of the narrative is too leisurely. These objections from some contemporary critics remind the reader once more of James's affinity with the novelists of the nineteenth century.

The laboratory in which the expert witness is killed serves as a focal point for an intriguing cast of characters. Ironically, the physiologist is murdered while he is examining physical evidence from another murder. The dead man leaves behind a rather vacant, superannuated father, who lived in the house with him. The principal suspect is a high-strung laboratory assistant, whom the deceased bullied and gave an unsatisfactory performance rating. The new director of the laboratory has an attractive but cruel and wanton sister, with whom he has a relationship that is at least latently incestuous. In addition, Dalgliesh investigates a lesbian couple, one of whom becomes the novel's second murder victim; a melancholy physician, who performs autopsies for the police and whose unpleasant wife has just left him; the physician's two curious children, the elder girl being very curious indeed; a middle-aged baby-sitter, who is a closet tippler; and a crooked cop, who is taking advantage of a love-starved young woman of the town. In spinning her complex narrative, James draws upon her intimate knowledge of police procedure, evidential requirements in the law, and criminal behavior.

Innocent Blood · The publication in 1980 of *Innocent Blood* marked a departure for James. While the novel tells a tale of murder and vengeance, it is not a detective story. Initially, the protagonist is Philippa Rose Palfrey—later, the novel develops a second center of consciousness. Philippa is eighteen, the adopted daughter of an eminent sociologist and a juvenile court magistrate. She is obsessed with her unremembered past. She is sustained by fantasies about her real parents, especially her mother, and the circumstances which forced them to give her up for adoption. Despite these romantic notions, Philippa is intelligent, resourceful, and tenacious, as well as somewhat abrasive. She takes advantage of the Children Act of 1975 to wrest her birth record from a reluctant bureaucracy.

The record shows that she was born Rose Ducton, to a clerk and a housewife in Essex. This revelation sends Philippa rushing to the dreary eastern suburb where she was born, beginning an odyssey which will eventually lead to her mother. She discovers that her fantasies cannot match the lurid realities of her past. Her father was a child molester, who murdered a young girl in an upstairs room of his house. Her mother apparently participated in the murder and was caught trying to take the body away in her car. Her father has died in prison, and her mother is still confined. Though horrified, Philippa is now even more driven to find explanations of some sort and to rehabilitate the image of her mother. She visits Mary Ducton in prison, from which she is soon to be released, and eventually takes a small flat in London, where they will live together.

In chapter 8, James introduces the second protagonist, at which time the novel becomes as much his as it is Philippa's. Norman Scase is fifty-seven and newly retired from his job as a government accounts clerk. Scase is the widowed father of the murdered girl. He retires when he learns of Mary Ducton's impending release, for all of his time will be required to stalk her so that, at the appropriate moment, he may kill her. The murder of young Julia Mavis Scase robbed her father of the same years it stole from Philippa. Philippa is desperately trying to reclaim these lost years by learning to know, forgive, and love her mother. Scase is driven to a far more desperate act.

In form, *Innocent Blood* resembles Tolstoy's *Anna Karenina* (1875-1877). Like Anna and Levin, the dual protagonists proceed through the novel along separate paths. Philippa has no knowledge of Scase's existence, and he knows her only as the constant companion of the victim he is tracking all over London. James makes the city itself a character in the novel, and as Philippa shares her London with her mother, it is fully realized in Dickensian detail. Philippa is the more appealing protagonist, but Scase is a fascinating character study: the least likely of premeditating murderers, a little man who is insignificant in everything except his *idée fixe*. James created a similar character in "The Victim," a short story appearing seven years earlier. There, a dim and diffident assistant librarian stalks and murders the man who took his beautiful young wife away from him. The novel form, however, affords James the opportunity to develop completely this unpromising material into a memorable character. As Scase lodges in cheap hotels, monitors the women's movements with binoculars, and stares up at their window through the night, the reader realizes that the little man has found a purpose which truly animates his life for the first time. He and Philippa will finally meet at the uncharacteristically melodramatic climax (the only blemish on an otherwise flawless novel).

A Taste for Death · Commander Adam Dalgliesh returns in *A Taste for Death* after an absence of nine years. He is heading a newly formed squad charged with investigating politically sensitive crimes. He is assisted by the aristocratic chief inspector John Massingham and a new recruit, Kate Miskin. Kate is bright, resourceful, and fiercely ambitious. Like Cordelia Gray, she has overcome an unpromising background: She is the illegitimate child of a mother who died shortly after her birth and a father she has never known. The title of the novel is evocative. A taste for death is evident in not only the psychopathic killer but also Dalgliesh and his subordinates, the principal murder victim himself, and, surprisingly, a shabby High Church Anglican priest, reminiscent of one of Graham Greene's failed clerics.

When Sir Paul Berowne, a Tory minister, is found murdered along with a tramp in the vestry of St. Matthew's Church in London, Dalgliesh is put in charge of the investigation. These murders seem linked to the deaths of two young women previously associated with the Berowne household. The long novel (more than 450 pages) contains the usual array of suspects, hampering the investigation with their evasions and outright lies, but in typical James fashion, each is portrayed in three dimensions. The case develops an additional psychological complication when Dalgliesh identifies with a murder victim for the first time in his career and a metaphysical complication when he discovers that Berowne recently underwent a profound religious experience in the church, one reportedly entailing stigmata. Perhaps the best examples of James's method of characterization are the elderly spinster and the ten-year-old boy of the streets who discover the bodies in chapter 1. In the hands of most other crime writers, these characters would have been mere plot devices, but James gives them a reality which reminds the reader how deeply a murder affects everyone associated with it in any way. Having begun the novel with Miss Wharton and Darren, James returns to them in the concluding chapter.

Devices and Desires · *Devices and Desires* possesses the usual James virtues. The story is set at and around a nuclear power plant on the coast of Norfolk in East Anglia. The geographic details are convincing (even though the author states that she has invented topography to suit her purposes), and the nuclear power industry has obviously been well researched. Although the intricate plot places heavy demands of action upon the characters, the omniscient narrator analyzes even the most minor of them in such depth that they are believable. Finally, greater and more interesting than the mystery of "who did it" is the mystery of those ideas, attitudes, and experiences which have led a human being to murder. Ultimately, every James novel is a study of the devices and desires of the human heart.

In some ways, however, the novel is a departure. The setting is a brooding, windswept northern coast, the sort of gothic background which James largely eschewed in her earlier novels. *Devices and Desires* is also more of a potboiler than were any of its predecessors. As the story begins, a serial killer known as the Whistler is claiming his fourth victim (he will kill again during the course of the novel). A group of terrorists is plotting an action against the Larksoken Nuclear Power Station. The intrigue is so heavy and so many people are not what they seem that at one point the following tangled situation exists: Neil Pascoe, an antinuclear activist, has been duped by Amy Camm, whom he has taken into his trailer on the headland. Amy believes that she is acting as an agent for an animal rights group, but she has been duped by Caroline Amphlett, personal secretary to the Director of Larksoken. Caroline has, in turn, been duped by the terrorists for whom she has been spying, they plot her death when she becomes useless to them. Eventually, shadowy figures turn up from MI5, Britain's intelligence agency. In this instance, so much exposition and explication is required of James's dialogue that it is not always as convincing as in the previous books.

Adam Dalgliesh shares this novel with Chief Inspector Terry Rickards. Rickards is a mirror image of Dalgliesh. He is less intelligent and imaginative, but he has the loving wife and infant child whom Dalgliesh has lost. While Dalgliesh is on the headland, settling his aunt's estate, he stumbles upon a murder (literally–he discovers the body). Hilary Roberts, the beautiful, willful, and widely disliked and feared Acting Administrative Officer of the station, is strangled, and the Whistler's method is mimicked. As usual in a James novel, the suspects comprise a small and fairly intimate group. The author has totally mastered the detective story convention whereby at some point in the novel each of the suspects will seem the most plausible murderer.

The action of *Devices and Desires* affords James the opportunity to comment upon the use and potential misuse of nuclear power, the phenomenon of terrorism, the condition of race relations in London, even the state of Christianity in contemporary Britain. Still, what James always does best is to reveal, layer by layer, the mind which has committed itself to that most irrevocable of human actions, murder.

Original Sin · In *Original Sin,* Commander Dalgliesh's investigative team has changed: Although he is still assisted by Kate Miskin, John Massingham has been replaced by Daniel Aaron. Inspector Aaron is a Jew who is exceedingly uncomfortable with his Jewishness–Jewishness that will become a critical factor in the last quarter of the novel. *Original Sin* is replete with religious metaphors, beginning with its title. Again, the reader is reminded that Adam Dalgliesh is the "first," the dominant human being in each of the novels (despite the fact that he makes fewer and briefer appearances in *Original Sin* than in any novel heretofore). Dalgliesh is the son of a country rector. A minor character, a sister to one of the several members of the Peverell Press to die under mysterious circumstances, is also a sister in a larger sense: She is a nun in an Anglican convent. Frances Peverell, a major character, is a devout Catholic. She is also the near namesake of Francis Peverell, whose sin 150 years earlier has placed a sort of curse upon Innocent House, a four-story Georgian edifice on the Thames which serves as the home of the Peverell Press. Gabriel Dauntsey–a poet whose name suggests the Angel of Revelation–reveals the darkest secret of Innocent House toward the close of the novel.

Innocent House, dating from 1792, is reached by launch and exudes the atmosphere of a Venetian palace. It is the site of five deaths, all initially giving the superficial appearance of suicide. Four are eventually revealed to be murders. Thus, the very name of the building is heavily ironic. Inspectors Miskin and Aaron do most of the detecting, aided by an occasional insight shared or interview perceptively conducted by Commander Dalgliesh. Several of the characters bear the burden of original sin, the sins of their parents and ancestors. The motivation for multiple murders turns out to be events that occurred fifty years earlier in wartime France.

A Certain Justice · In her 1997 novel, *A Certain Justice,* P. D. James makes use of her whole bag of stylistic tricks, familiar but nevertheless effective. The appropriately ambiguous title refers to either, or both, justice of a particular sort and justice that is sure. The incidents of the novel support both interpretations. The conflicts within and between the members of Dalgliesh's investigative team continue. Kate Miskin is sexually attracted to her boss but dares not acknowledge this fact to herself. Daniel Aaron has left the force, presumably as a result of his unprofessional behavior at the conclusion of *Original Sin,* and has been replaced by Piers Tarrant. As usual, Kate is not sure that she likes her male partner. Also as usual, the murder suspects are members of a small, self-contained professional group–this time, from the Inns of Court, where London's lawyers practice.

As in other of her later novels, James introduces religious overtones. The chief suspect in the second murder, and the victim of the third (there are four, in all), is a vicar's widow who has lost her faith. Piers Tarrant has a theology degree from Oxford; he claims the study of theology is excellent preparation for police work. Detective Sergeant Robbins, who assists Kate and Piers in their enquiries, is a Methodist of impeccable Christian virtue. He combines two apparently paradoxical qualities, a benign view of his fellow human beings and a deeply sceptical view of human nature. The second quality makes him a very good detective. A key conflict in the latter part of the novel involves Father Presteign, a High Church Anglican priest. He initially receives crucial information about the second murder, but under the seal of the confessional.

A Certain Justice is marked by a parallel structure. As the novel begins, an accused killer is acquitted and so is free to kill again. An earlier such instance drives the main plot. Two characters, their intentions unknown to each other, set out to achieve a certain justice outside the law. Both attempts lead to violent death. James experiments with epistolary form in chapter 36, which is written in the form of a long letter left by a murder victim. In short, James continues to embellish her murder mysteries with the best features of the realistic literary novel.

Patrick Adcock

Other major works
PLAY: *A Private Treason*, pr. 1985.
NONFICTION: *The Maul and the Pear Tree: The Ratcliff Highway Murders, 1811*, 1971 (with T. A. Critchley); *Time to Be in Earnest: A Fragment of Autobiography*, 2000.

Bibliography

Bakerman, Jane S. "Cordelia Gray: Apprentice and Archetype." *Clues: A Journal of Detection* 5 (Spring/Summer, 1984): 101-114. A study of *An Unsuitable Job for a Woman*, which discusses James's female detective as the heroine of a *Bildungsroman*, or apprenticeship novel. Cordelia is only twenty-two when, almost by accident, she becomes a private investigator. Her first case is her rite of passage from girlhood to maturity and professionalism.

Barber, Lynn. "The Cautious Heart of P. D. James." *Vanity Fair* 56 (March, 1993): 80. A profile of James in her seventies—commercially successful, titled, and highly honored as a literary craftsman. Includes a contemporary portrait of the novelist.

Benstock, Bernard. "The Clinical World of P. D. James." In *Twentieth-Century Women Novelists*, edited by Thomas F. Staley. Vol. 16. Totowa, N.J.: Barnes & Noble, 1982. Benstock's essay is found on pages 104-129 of the volume. He discusses James's use of setting, her narrative technique, and the relationship between the two.

Gidez, Richard B. *P. D. James*. Boston: Twayne, 1986. An entry in Twayne's English Authors series. Chapter 1 examines James's place within the tradition of the English mystery novel. Chapters 2-10 discuss in chronological order her first nine novels. Chapter 11 is devoted to her handful of short stories, and chapter 12 summarizes her work through *The Skull Beneath the Skin*.

Hubly, Erlene. "Adam Dalgliesh: Byronic Hero." *Clues: A Journal of Detection* 3 (Fall/Winter, 1982): 40-46. The brooding Dalgliesh, aloof, often forbidding, constantly bearing the pain of a deep tragedy in his personal life, has often been likened to the heroes of nineteenth century Romantic fiction. Hubly's article treats the appropriateness of this comparison.

Macintyre, Ben. Review of *A Certain Justice*, by P. D. James. *New York Times Book Review*, Dec. 7, 1997, 26. Macintyre's review, as reviews often do with James's mysteries, praises her characterization, observing that each character is himself or herself an embryonic novel. He also notes that, as in other of the later novels, the protagonist, Dalgliesh, has become a token presence in the last two-thirds of *A Certain Justice*, "oddly distant and preoccupied."

Porter, Dennis. "Detection and Ethics: The Case of P. D. James." In *The Sleuth and the Scholar: Origins, Evolution, and Current Trends in Detective Fiction*, edited by Barbara A. Rader and Howard G. Zettler. Westport, Conn.: Greenwood Press, 1988. Pages 11-18 are devoted to Porter's essay on James, a writer for whom moral principles are an integral part of the crime and detection story. Porter concentrates upon *Death of an Expert Witness, An Unsuitable Job for a Woman,* and *Innocent Blood*. Robin W. Wink, who has written elsewhere on James, contributes a foreword to the book.

Siebenheller, Norma. *P. D. James*. New York: Frederick Ungar, 1981. The first four chapters discuss the eight novels, grouped by decades, that James had produced through 1980. Chapter 5 discusses the detective protagonists Adam Dalgliesh and Cordelia Gray. Chapter 6 takes up the major themes of the novels; chapter 7, the major characters other than the two detectives. The final chapter deals with the James "style," in the sense both of her craftsmanship and of her elegance.

Stasio, Marilyn. "No Gore, Please—They're British." *The Writer* 103 (March, 1990): 15-16. The basis of this article is an interview with James. In her questions and interpretations, Stasio stresses the elegant and highly civilized nature of James's crime fiction.

Ruth Prawer Jhabvala

Born: Cologne, Germany; May 7, 1927

Principal long fiction · *To Whom She Will,* 1955 (pb. in U.S. as *Amrita,* 1956); *The Nature of Passion,* 1956; *Esmond in India,* 1958; *The Householder,* 1960; *Get Ready for Battle,* 1962; *A Backward Place,* 1965; *A New Dominion,* 1972 (pb. in U.S. as *Travelers,* 1973); *Heat and Dust,* 1975; *In Search of Love and Beauty,* 1983; *Three Continents,* 1987; *Poet and Dancer,* 1993; *Shards of Memory,* 1995.

Other literary forms · Though Ruth Prawer Jhabvala is known mainly as a novelist, she is also an accomplished writer of short stories, film scripts, and essays. Among her collections of short stories are *Like Birds, Like Fishes, and Other Stories* (1963), *A Stronger Climate: Nine Stories* (1968), *An Experience of India* (1971), and *How I Became a Holy Mother and Other Stories* (1976); *Out of India* (1986) is a selection of stories from these volumes. *Shakespeare Wallah* (1965; with James Ivory), *Heat and Dust* (1983), and *A Room with a View* (1986; based on E. M. Forster's novel) are her best-known film scripts.

Achievements · Jhabvala has achieved remarkable distinction, both as a novelist and as a short-story writer, among writers on modern India. She has been compared with E. M. Forster, though the historical phases and settings of the India they portray are widely different. The award of the Booker Prize for *Heat and Dust* in 1975 made her internationally famous. Placing Jhabvala in a literary-cultural tradition is difficult: Her European parentage, British education, marriage to an Indian, and—after many years in her adopted country—change of residence from India to the United States perhaps reveal a lack of belonging, a recurring "refugee" consciousness. Consequently, she is not an Indian writing in English, nor a European writing on India, but perhaps a writer of the world of letters deeply conscious of being caught up in a bizarre world. She is sensitive, intense, ironic—a detached observer and recorder of the human world. Her almost clinical accuracy and her sense of the graphic, the comic, and the ironic make her one of the finest writers on the contemporary scene.

In 1984, Jhabvala won the British Award for Film and Television Arts (BAFTA) for Best Screenplay for the Ismail Merchant-James Ivory adaptation of *Heat and Dust,* and in 1986 she won an Academy Award for Best Adapted Screenplay for *A Room with a View.* In 1990, she was awarded Best Screenplay from the New York Film Critics Circle for *Mr. and Mrs. Bridge,* adapted from Evan S. Connell, Jr.'s novels. Jhabvala received an Academy Award for Best Adapted Screenplay in 1992 for Forster's *Howards End* and an Oscar nomination for her adaptation of Kazuo Ishiguro's *The Remains of the Day* in 1993. In 1984, Jhabvala won a MacArthur Foundation Award, and in 1994 she received the Writers Guild of America's Laurel Award.

Biography · Ruth Prawer was born in Cologne, Germany, on May 7, 1927, the daughter of Marcus and Eleonora Prawer; her family's heritage was German, Polish, and Jewish. She emigrated to England in 1939, became a British citizen in 1948, and obtained an M.A. in English from Queen Mary College, London, in 1951. That same year, she married C. H. S. Jhabvala, an Indian architect, and went to live in India.

Jhabvala formed a profound, albeit conflicted, relationship with the country. With her Indian husband and Indian-born children, Renana, Ava, and Feroza, she has had a unique opportunity of seeing the subcontinent from the privileged position of an insider but through the eyes of an alien. Thus, rootedness in a culture and people, an issue with which she is intimate, provides a wellspring for her screenplays, novels, and stories.

The author has returned to India, to millions a place of ancient wisdom and spiritual equilibrium, time and again. Her exposure to the waves of young foreigners who descended upon India in the 1960's only to be taken advantage of by unscrupulous "mystics," influenced such books as *Three Continents*. Indeed, the theme of religious charlatans permeates much of Jhabvala's work. While she would spend three months of each year in New Delhi, Jhabvala settled in New York in 1975, living near her friends and film colleagues, the Merchant-Ivory duo. Her work on film scripts with the team, which began in the 1960's, enriched her technique as a writer of fiction and widened her vision. One may well view this move to New York as initiating the second major influence on the author's body of work, giving rise to her collection of short stories, *East into Upper East: Plain Tales from New York and New Delhi* (1998). Jhabvala would contribute regularly to *The New Yorker*.

Analysis · Ruth Prawer Jhbavala's distinctive qualities as a novelist grow from her sense of social comedy. She excels in portraying incongruities of human behavior, comic situations which are rich with familial, social, and cultural implications. Marital harmony or discord, the pursuit of wealth, family togetherness and feuds, the crisis of identity and homelessness— these are among the situations that she repeatedly explores in her fiction. She writes with sympathy, economy, and wit, with sharp irony and cool detachment.

Jhabvala's fiction has emerged out of her own experience of India. "The central fact of all my work," she once told an interviewer, "is that I am a European living permanently in India. I have lived here for most of my adult life . . . . This makes me not quite an outsider either." Much later, however, in "Myself in India," she revealed a change in her attitude toward India: "However, I must admit I am no longer interested in India. What I am interested in now is myself in India . . . my survival in India."

This shift in attitude has clearly affected Jhabvala's fiction. There is

Jerry Bauer

a distinct Indianness in the texture and spirit of her first five novels, which are sunny, bright, social comedies offering an affirmative view of India. The later novels, darkened by dissonance and despair, reveal a change in the novelist's perspective.

In almost all of her novels, Jhabvala assumes the role of an omniscient narrator. She stands slightly aloof from her creations, an approach which has advantages as well as disadvantages. On the one hand, she does not convey the passionate inner life of her characters, many of whom are essentially stereotypes. Even her more fully developed characters are seen largely from the outside. On the other hand, she is a consummate observer. She has a fine eye for naturalistic detail, a gift for believable dialogue, but she is also an observer at a deeper level, registering the malaise that is characteristic of the modern world: the collapse of traditional values, the incongruous blending of diverse cultures: sometimes energizing, sometimes destructive, often bizarre. Thus, her fiction, while steeped in the particular reality of India, speaks to readers throughout the world.

Amrita · *Amrita* inaugurates Jhabvala's first phase, in which reconciliation between two individuals (symbolic as well of a larger, social integration) is at the center of the action. Amrita, a young, romantic girl, has a love affair with Hari, her colleague in radio. Their affair is portrayed with a gentle comic touch: She tells Hari of her determination to marry him at all costs; he calls her a goddess and moans that he is unworthy of her. Jhabvala skillfully catches the color and rhythm of the Indian phraseology of love.

While this affair proceeds along expected lines, Pandit Ram Bahadur, Hari's grandfather, is planning to get his grandson married to Sushila, a pretty singer, in an arranged match. When Hari confesses to his brother-in-law that he loves Amrita, he is advised that first love is only a "game," and no one should take it seriously. Hari then is led to the bridal fire and married to Sushila. He forgets his earlier vows of love for Amrita, even the fact that he applied for a passport to go with her to England.

The forsaken maiden, Amrita, finds her hopes for a happy union revived when another man, Krishna Sengupta, writes her a letter full of love and tenderness. Enthralled after reading his six-page letter, she decks her hair with a beautiful flower, a sign of her happy reconciliation with life. Amrita shares in the sunshine of love that comes her way.

The original title of the novel, *To Whom She Will* (changed to *Amrita* for the American edition), alludes to a story in a classic collection of Indian fables, the *Panchatantra* (between 100 B.C.E. and 500 C.E.; *The Morall Philosophie of Doni*, 1570). In the story, which centers on a maiden in love, a Hindu sage observes that marriage should be arranged for a girl at a tender age; otherwise, "she gives herself to whom she will." This ancient injunction is dramatized in the predicaments of Hari, Amrita, Sushila, and Sengupta, the four main characters. The irony lies in the fact that Amrita does not marry "whom she will." Nevertheless, the regaining of happiness is the keynote of Jhabvala's first novel of family relations and individual predicaments.

The Nature of Passion · Alluding to Swami Paramananda's translation of the *Bhagavad Gītā* (c. fifth century B.C.E.), which Jhabvala quotes, her second novel, *The Nature of Passion*, deals with one of the three kinds of passion which are distinguished in the *Bhagavad Gītā*: that which is worldly, sensuous, pleasure-seeking. This passion, or *rajas*, rules the world of Lalaji and his tribe, who represent the rising middle class and whose debased values become the object of Jhabvala's unsparing irony. She presents a series of vignettes of the life of the affluent—such as Lalaji and the Vermas—who migrated to India after the partition and continued to prosper. Here, Jhabvala's characters are not intended to be fully rounded individuals; rather, they play their parts as embodiments of various passions.

Lalaji's role is to illustrate the contagious effects of greed and corruption. An indiscreet letter written by his older son finds its way into a government file controlled by Chandra, his second son. When Lalaji asks Chandra to remove the incriminating letter, Chandra's self-righteous wife, Kanta, objects. She soon realizes, however, that their comforts and their holidays depend upon Lalaji's tainted money, and she relents, allowing the letter to be removed. Lalaji's daughter Nimmi, too, moves from revolt to submission. Lalaji's tenderness for Nimmi is conveyed beautifully. When she cuts her hair short, Lalaji accepts this sign of modernity. Nevertheless, despite her attraction to another young man, she accepts the marriage partner chosen for her by her family.

Jhabvala's irony is cutting, but her style in this novel has an almost clinical precision, a detachment that discourages reader involvement. By concentrating on social types rather than genuinely individualized characters, she limits the appeal of the novel, which already seems badly dated.

Esmond in India · Jhabvala's third novel, *Esmond in India*, as its title suggests, is concerned with the conflict between cultures. Esmond is an Englishman, a shallow man with a handsome face who tutors European women in Hindi language and culture and serves as a guide to visitors. He is an egotistic, aggressive colonial, and Jhabvala is relentless in her irony in sketching him, especially in a scene at the Taj Mahal where he loses his shoes. The pretentious Esmond is cut down to size and becomes a puny figure.

Esmond's relationship with his wife, Gulab, is the novel's central focus. She is a pseudoromantic Indian girl, very fond of good food. Their marriage is in ruins: Esmond feels trapped and speaks with scorn of her dull, alien mind, while she is keenly aware of his failure to care for her. Nevertheless, Gulab, as a true Hindu wife, bears Esmond's abuse and his indulgence in love affairs, until their family servant attempts to molest her. She then packs her bag and leaves Esmond.

Is Gulab a rebel or a complete conformist? In marrying Esmond, an Englishman, she surely seems to have become a rebel. Later, however, she is subservient in response to Esmond's cruelty; the servant assaults her because he knows that Esmond does not love his wife. This sets into motion her second rebellion: separation from Esmond. Gulab is a complex, memorable character.

Esmond, too, though he is drawn with sharp irony, is no mere caricature. At the heart of the novel is his overwhelming sense of a loss of identity, a crisis which grips his soul and makes him unequal to the task of facing India, that strange land.

The Householder · *The Householder* is perhaps Jhabvala's most successful, least problematic, most organically conceived novel. A true social comedy, it is a direct, simple "impression of life." It centers on the maturation of its likable central character, Prem, a Hindi instructor in Mr. Khanna's private college. Prem is a shy, unassuming young man, in no way exceptional, yet his growth to selfhood, presented with insight and humor, makes for compelling fiction.

The title *The Householder* is derived from the Hindu concept of the four stages of a man's life; the second stage, that of a family man, is the one which the novel explores.

Prem's relations with his wife, Indu, are most delicately portrayed. The scene of Prem loving Indu on the terrace in moonlight is both tender and touching. They both sense the space and the solitude and unite in deep intimacy. Prem realizes that Indu is pregnant and tenderly touches her growing belly, scenes that show Jhabvala at her best and most tender.

Prem's troubles are mainly economic—how to survive on a meager salary—and the comedy and the pathos which arise out of this distress constitute the real stuff of the novel. The indifference, the arrogance, and the insensitivity of the other characters are comically rendered, emphasizing Prem's seeming helplessness, as he struggles to survive and to assert his individuality. (A minor subplot is contributed by Western characters: Hans Loewe, a seeker after spiritual reality, and Kitty, his landlady, provide a contrast with Prem's struggle.) Nevertheless, Prem is finally able to overcome his inexperience and immaturity, attaining a tenderness, a human touch, and a balance which enable him to achieve selfhood and become a true "householder."

Get Ready for Battle · *Get Ready for Battle,* Jhabvala's fifth novel, resembles *The Nature of Passion.* Like that earlier novel, it pillories the selfish, acquisitive society of post-independence India. In particular, it shows how growing urbanization affects the poor, dispossessing them of their land. Like *The Nature of Passion, Get Ready for Battle* derives its title from the *Bhagavad Gītā,* alluding to the scene in which Lord Krishna instructs Arjuna to "get ready for battle" without fear; similarly, Jhabvala's protagonist, Sarla Devi, urges the poor to get ready for battle to protect their rights. *Get Ready for Battle* is superior to *The Nature of Passion,* however, in its portrayal of interesting and believable characters. While the characters in the later novel still represent various social groups or points of view, they are not mere types.

The central character, Sarla Devi, deeply committed to the cause of the poor, is separated from her husband, Gulzari Lal. They represent two opposite valuations of life: She leads her life according to the tenets of the *Bhagavad Gītā,* while he, acquisitive and heartless, is a worshiper of Mammon. The main action of the novel centers on her attempt to save the poor from being evicted from their squatters' colony and also to save her son from following her father's corrupt lifestyle. She fails in both these attempts, yet she is heroic in her failure.

Jhabvala brilliantly depicts the wasteland created by India's growing cities, which have swallowed farms and forests, at the same time destroying the value-structure of rural society. Yet *Get Ready for Battle* also includes adroitly designed domestic scenes. Kusum, Gulzari Lal's mistress, is shown with sympathy, while the relationship between two secondary characters, the married couple Vishnu and Mala, is portrayed with tenderness as well as candor. They show their disagreements (even speak of divorce), yet they are deeply in love. For them, "getting ready for battle" is a kind of game, a comic conflict, rather than a serious issue.

A Backward Place · Jhabvala's next novel, *A Backward Place,* initiated the second phase of her career, marked by dark, despairing comedies disclosing a world out of joint. In this novel, too, Jhabvala began to focus more attention on encounters between East and West and the resulting tensions and ironies. The novel's title, which refers to a European character's condescending assessment of Delhi, suggests its pervasive irony; neither Indians nor Europeans are spared Jhabvala's scorn. While it features an appealing protagonist, the novel is too schematic, too much simply a vehicle for satire.

Travelers · *A Backward Place* was followed by *Travelers*, a novel in the same dark mode, which presents the Western vision of contemporary India with telling irony. European girls seek a spiritual India, but the country that they actually experience is quite the opposite. Despite its satiric bite, the novel must be judged a failure: The great art of fiction seems to degenerate here into mere journalism, incapable of presenting a true vision of contemporary India.

Heat and Dust · This forgettable novel was followed by Jhabvala's most widely praised work, *Heat and Dust*, the complex plot of which traces parallels between the experiences of two Englishwomen in India: the unnamed narrator and her grandfather Douglas's first wife, Olivia. In the 1930's, Olivia came to India as Douglas's wife. Bored by her prosaic, middle-class existence, Olivia is drawn to a Muslim nawab with whom she enjoys many escapades. Invited to a picnic close to a Muslim shrine, Olivia finds the nawab irresistible. They lie by a spring in a green grove, and the nawab makes her pregnant. She then leaves Douglas, aborts her child, and finally moves to a house in the hills as the nawab's mistress.

After a gap of two generations, the narrator, who has come to India to trace Olivia's life story, passes through a similar cycle of experience. Fascinated by India, she gives herself to a lower-middle-class clerk, Inder Lal, at the same place near the shrine where Olivia lay with the nawab, and with the same result. The young narrator decides to rear the baby, though she gives up her lover; she also has a casual physical relationship with another Indian, Child, who combines sexuality with a spiritual quest.

Heat and Dust is an extraordinary novel. Unlike many of Jhabvala's novels, it has a strong current of positive feeling beneath its surface negativism. Olivia, though she discards her baby, remains loyal to her heart's desire for the nawab, and the narrator, while not accepting her lover, wishes to rear her baby as a symbol of their love. This note of affirmation heightens the quality of human response in *Heat and Dust*, which is also notable for its fully realized characterizations.

In Search of Love and Beauty · *In Search of Love and Beauty*, set primarily in the United States but ranging widely elsewhere, centers on the experience of rootlessness which Jhabvala knows so well, and which is so widespread in the twentieth century. The novel is a multigenerational saga, beginning with refugees from Nazi Germany and Austria and concluding in contemporary times. The rootlessness of that first generation to be dislocated from their culture is passed on to their children and their children's children, all of whom go "in search of love and beauty."

The first generation, represented by Louise and Regi, wishes to retain its German heritage, concretely symbolized by their paintings and furniture. The second generation, represented by Marietta, is partly Americanized. The restless Marietta travels to India, falls in love with Ahmad, an Indian musician, and befriends Sujata, a courtesan, sketched with deft accuracy. The image of India is lovable, vital, and glorious, and seems almost a counterpart to Germany's ideal image. The third-generation refugees, represented by Natasha and Leo, are more affluent and still more Americanized, yet they are trapped in drug abuse, depression, and meaninglessness.

Three Continents · *Three Continents* is the lengthiest and broadest in scope of Jhabvala's novels. Like the later *Shards of Memory*, the tale revolves around an Indian mystic and his followers. Young narrator Harriet Wishwell, the daughter of a rich but troubled

American family, and her gay twin brother, Michael, are raised by their grandfather after their parents' divorce. Educated at international schools, the twins go in search of a deeper meaning to life than what their American heritage provides. Their wishes are seemingly answered when they meet Rawul, whose movement, the Fourth World, is intended to transcend racial and political divisiveness and establish a state founded on peace and love. Michael believes he has found Nirvana in Rawul's son, Crishi, while Harriet also falls under his spell. The twins and Crishi form a sexual threesome, and eventually Harriet, besotted by Crishi, weds him, only to find herself continually frustrated by his lack of devotion to her. Rawul's, and by proxy Crishi's, charismatic hold on his devotees proves Harriet and her family's ultimate undoing.

Poet and Dancer and ***Shards of Memory*** · *Poet and Dancer* explores the dangers of love and commitment. Set in modern-day Manhattan, the novel explores the complex relations between two young cousins, Angel and Lara, as they become enmeshed in one another and lose touch with the realities of the outside world.

Shards of Memory concerns a young man, Henry, who has inherited all the correspondence and writings of a mysterious spiritual leader, known simply as the Master. It is with visits to his grandmother, Baby, in her Manhattan townhouse that Henry slowly uncovers bits and pieces of his family's past involvement with the Master's spiritual movement. Elsa, Baby's mother, married an Indian poet but spent her later years with her lesbian lover, Cynthia. Baby married Graeme, a standoffish British diplomat, but she later admits they had nothing besides their daughter, Renata, in common. As Graeme continues traveling the world, Baby gives over the raising of Renata to the child's grandfather, Kavi. Renata later falls in love with Carl, an idle German idealist. The son they produce, Henry, bears a striking resemblance to the Master. Baby sends young Henry from New York to London to be groomed by Elsa and Cynthia as the Master's heir. After a car accident there that kills the women and cripples Henry, he is returned to New York. As trunks full of the Master's writings arrive at the family apartment, Vera, the piano teacher's vibrant daughter, assists Henry in categorizing the vast quantities of work. There is a resurgence of interest in the Master after Henry publishes a book on his teachings, and eventually his parents purchase the Head and Heart House, which was intended as a center for the spiritual movement. Involvement with the Master, a plumb sensualist, takes over the followers' lives; parents become incapable even of rearing their children. Jhabvala's comment about such a spiritual movement has overtones of contempt. The zombielike groupies around the Master, as well as his own shady dealings in foreign countries, provide a clear warning against placing one's well-being in the hands of self-proclaimed gurus.

Vasant A. Shahane, updated by Nika Hoffman

Other major works

SHORT FICTION: *Like Birds, Like Fishes, and Other Stories,* 1963; *A Stronger Climate: Nine Stories,* 1968; *An Experience of India,* 1971; *How I Became a Holy Mother and Other Stories,* 1976; *Out of India,* 1986; *East into Upper East: Plain Tales from New York and New Delhi,* 1998.

SCREENPLAYS: *The Householder,* 1963; *Shakespeare Wallah,* 1965 (with James Ivory); *The Guru,* 1968; *Bombay Talkie,* 1970; *Autobiography of a Princess,* 1975 (with Ivory and John Swope); *Roseland,* 1977; *Hullabaloo over Georgie and Bonnie's Pictures,* 1978; *The Europeans,* 1979; *Quartet,* 1981; *The Courtesans of Bombay,* 1982; *Heat and Dust,* 1983 (based on her novel); *The Bostonians*, 1984 (with Ivory; based on Henry James's novel); *A Room with a View*, 1986 (based on E. M. Forster's novel); *Maurice*, 1987 (based on Forster's novel); *Madame Sousatzka*, 1988; *Mr. and Mrs. Bridge*, 1990 (based on Evan S. Connell, Jr.'s novels); *Howards End*, 1992 (based on Forster's novel); *The Remains of the Day*, 1993 (based on Kazuo Ishiguro's novel); *Jefferson in Paris*, 1995; *Surviving Picasso*, 1996; *A Soldier's Daughter Never Cries*, 1998 (based on Kaylie Jones's novel).

TELEPLAYS: *The Place of Peace*, 1975; *Jane Austen in Manhattan*, 1980; *The Wandering Company*, 1985.

Bibliography

Agarwal, Ramlal G. *Ruth Prawer Jhbavala: A Study of Her Fiction.* New York: Envoy Press, 1990. Contains good criticism and interpretation of the novels. Includes index and bibliography.

Booker, Keith M. *Colonial Texts: India in the Modern British Novel.* Ann Arbor: University of Michigan Press, 1997. Although discussion of the author is not central in this book, what proves engaging is the context into which Booker places Jhabvala's contribution to India's prominence in British literature.

Crane, Ralph J. *Ruth Prawer Jhabvala.* Boston: Twayne, 1992. Crane begins with discussion of Jhabvala's earliest novels and essays, then examines her American novels, then includes a section on Jhabvala and critics. Contains a valuable selected bibliography.

_____, ed. *Passages to Ruth Prawer Jhabvala.* New Delhi: Sterling Publishers, 1991. Features articles on Jhabvala's fiction. Includes index and bibliographic references.

Gooneratne, Yasmine. *Silence, Exile, and Cunning: The Fiction of Ruth Prawer Jhabvala.* Hyderabad, India: Orient Longman, 1983. A definitive work on Jhabvala, the title of which is taken from James Joyce's definition of a writer, with which Jhabvala concurs. Comments on the theme of loneliness and displacement that runs throughout Jhabvala's fiction as she explores the "sensibility of the Western expatriate in India." Biographical detail is interwoven with discussion of Jhabvala's fiction, including a chapter on her short stories and her writing for film. A strong critical study by an author who herself has a keen understanding of the India Jhabvala writes about.

Mason, Deborah. "Passage to America: *East into Upper East: Plain Tales from New York and New Delhi.*" *The New York Times*, November 29, 1998. An eloquent and appreciative analysis of Jhabvala's collection of stories, which squarely places her skills as a consummate storyteller at the forefront.

Pritchett, V. S. "Ruth Prawer Jhabvala: Snares and Delusions." In *The Tale Bearers.* London: Chatto & Windus, 1980. Discusses Jhabvala's novel *A New Dominion*, exploring both its satirical content and the author's role as "careful truth-teller." Hails Jhabvala as a writer who knows more about India than any other novelist writing in English. A short but interesting piece that compares Jhabvala's writing with that of Anton Chekhov.

Shahane, V. A. *Ruth Prawer Jhabvala.* New Delhi: Arnold-Heinemann, 1976. The first full-length study on Jhabvala, covering her novels up to *Heat and Dust* in 1975 and three short stories, including "An Experience of India." Shahane notes that Jhabvala's literary gift lies less in her unique insider-outsider status in India as it does in her awareness of human dilemma within the constructs of society. In a style both spirited and opinionated, Shahane contributes significant criticism to the earlier work of Jhabvala.

Sucher, Laurie. *The Fiction of Ruth Prawer Jhabvala.* New York: St. Martin's Press, 1989.
    In discussing Jhabvala's nine novels and four books of short stories, Sucher
    emphasizes Jhabvala's tragicomic explorations of female sexuality. Cites Jhabvala
    as a writer who deconstructs "romantic/Gothic heroism." A valuable contribution
    to the literary criticism on Jhabvala. Includes a useful bibliography.
Updike, John. "Louise in the New World, Alice on the Magic Molehill." Review of *In
    Search of Love and Beauty*, by Ruth Prawer Jhabvala. *The New Yorker* 59 (August 1,
    1983): 85-90. Updike likens the novel to Marcel Proust's "great opus concerning
    the search for lost time" but says it falls short of Proust in the flatness of its prose.
    Updike claims that, in spite of this, the novel contains many vivid scenes, and that
    "brilliance is to be found."

Samuel Johnson

Born: Lichfield, Staffordshire, England; September 18, 1709
Died: London, England; December 13, 1784

Principal long fiction · *Rasselas, Prince of Abyssinia: A Tale by S. Johnson*, 1759 (originally pb. as *The Prince of Abissinia: A Tale*).

Other literary forms · As the dominant figure of the mid-eighteenth century English literary world, Samuel Johnson's published works—both what he wrote under his own name and for others under their names—ranged throughout practically every genre and form. In verse, he wrote *London: A Poem in Imitation of the Third Satire of Juvenal* (1738) and *The Vanity of Human Wishes: The Tenth Satire of Juvenal Imitated* (1749); his poem "On the Death of Dr. Robert Levet, A Practiser in Physic" appeared first in *The Gentleman's Magazine* (August, 1783) and later in the *London Magazine* (September, 1783). His *Irene: A Tragedy*, performed at the Theatre Royal in Drury Lane in February, 1749, was printed later that same year.

The prose efforts of Johnson tend to generate the highest degrees of critical analysis and commentary. Biographical studies include *The Life of Admiral Blake* (1740), *An Account of the Life of Mr. Richard Savage* (1744), and *An Account of the Life of John Philip Barretier* (1744). His critical and linguistic works are by far the most important and extensive, of which the best known are *Miscellaneous Observations on the Tragedy of Macbeth* (1745), *The Plan of a Dictionary of the English Language* (1747), *A Dictionary of the English Language* (1755), and *Prefaces, Biographical and Critical, to the Works of the English Poets* (1779-1781). Also, Johnson's periodical essays for *The Rambler* (1750-1752), *The Adventurer* (1753-1754), and *The Idler* (1761) contain critical commentary as well as philosophical, moral, and religious observations.

A Journey to the Western Islands of Scotland (1775) is his major travel piece, while his political prose includes such essays as *The False Alarm* (1770), a pamphlet in support of the Ministerial majority in the House of Commons and its action in expelling a member of Parliament; *Thoughts on the Late Transactions Respecting Falkland's Islands* (1771), a seventy-five-page tract on the history of the territory and the reasons why England should not go to war with Spain; *The Patriot: Addressed to the Electors of Great Britain* (1774), in which Johnson defends the election of his friend Henry Thrale as MP for Southwark and writes to vindicate the Quebec Act; and *Taxation No Tyranny: An Answer to the Resolutions and Address of the American Congress* (1775). Finally, he edited the works of Richard Savage (1775) and the plays of William Shakespeare (1765); he also translated Father Jerome Lobo's *A Voyage to Abyssinia* (1735) and Jean Pierre de Crousaz's *Commentary on Pope's "Essay on Man"* (1738-1739).

Achievements · The quantity and quality of firsthand biographical material compiled during Johnson's life and immediately following his death have helped considerably in assessing the full measure of his contributions to British life and letters. Particularly through the efforts of James Boswell, John Hawkins, Hester Lynch Thrale Piozzi, and Frances Burney, the remarkable personality began to emerge. Through his early biographers, Johnson became the property of his nation, representing the most

positive qualities of the Anglo-Saxon temperament: common sense, honest realism, and high standards of performance and judgment. His critical judgments came forth as honest and rigorous pronouncements that left little room for the refinements and complexities of philosophical speculation; nevertheless, he must be considered a philosopher who always managed to penetrate to the essence of a given subject.

Perhaps Johnson's most significant contribution to eighteenth century thought focused upon what appeared to be a set of powerful prejudices that comprised the theses of his critical arguments. To the contrary, Johnson's so-called prejudices proved, in reality, to have been clearly defined standards or principles upon which he based his conclusions. Those criteria, in turn, originated from concrete examples from the classical and traditional past and actual experiences of the present. Johnson strived to distinguish between authority and rules on one side and nature and experience on the other. As the initial lesson of life, the individual had to realize that not all experience is of equal value–that instinctive and emotional activities, for example, cannot be placed above the authority of rational thought. In literary criticism, especially, Johnson's brand of classicism negated whim and idiosyncrasy and underscored the necessity for following universal nature–virtually the same criterion that gave strength to critical criteria during the earlier eighteenth century.

Johnson's domination of London intellectual life during the last half of the eighteenth century would by itself be sufficient to establish his reputation. As a writer, however, Johnson achieved distinction in several fields, and literary historians continue to cite him as a prominent poet, essayist, editor, scholar, and lexicographer. Although he failed to produce quality drama, he did succeed in writing a work of prose fiction that went through eight editions during his own lifetime and continues to be read. Certainly, his *A Dictionary of the English Language* has long since outlived its practical use; yet it, as well as *The Plan of a Dictionary of the English Language* that preceded it, remains an important work in the history and development of English lexicography. Principally, though, the achievement of Samuel Johnson focuses on his criticism, especially his sense of rhetorical balance, which causes his essays to emerge as valid critical commentary rather than as untrustworthy, emotional critical reaction.

Perhaps Johnson's greatest achievement is his prose style, which constitutes the essence of intellectual balance. The diction tends to be highly Latinate; yet, Johnson proved his familiarity with the lifeblood of his own language–its racy idiom. He possessed the ability to select the precise words with which to express exact degrees of meaning; he carefully constructed balanced sentences that rolled steadily forward, unhampered by parentheticals or excessive subordination. As writer and as thinker, Johnson nevertheless adhered to his respect for classical discipline and followed his instinct toward a just sense of proportion. His works written prior to 1760 tend to be stiff and heavy, too reliant upon classical and seventeenth century models. Later, however, in *The Lives of the Poets*, Johnson wrote with the ease and the confidence that characterized his oral, informal discussions with the famous intellectuals over whom he presided. Indeed, Johnson rose as a giant among the prose writers of his age when the strength of his style began to parallel the moral and intellectual strength of his own mind and personality.

In late February, 1907, Sir Walter Raleigh–professor of English literature at Oxford and respected scholar and critical commentator–delivered a lecture on Samuel Johnson in the Senate House at Cambridge. The final paragraph of that address is essential to any discussion of Johnson's literary and intellectual achievements. Raleigh maintained, principally, that the greatness of the man exceeded that of his works. In other words, Johnson thought of himself as a human being, not as an author; he thought of literature as a means and not as an end. "There are authors," maintained Raleigh, "who exhaust themselves in the effort to endow posterity, and distill all their virtue in a book. Yet their masterpieces have something inhuman about them, like those jewelled idols, the work of men's hands, which are worshipped by the sacrifice of man's flesh and blood." Therefore, according to Raleigh, humankind really seeks comfort and dignity in the view of literature that characterized the name of Samuel Johnson: "Books without the knowledge of life are useless; for what should books teach but the art of living?"

Biography · Born on September 18, 1709, in Lichfield, Staffordshire, England–the son of Michael and Sarah Ford Johnson–Samuel Johnson spent his formative years devouring the volumes in his father's bookshop. Although such acquisition of knowledge came about in haphazard fashion, the boy's tenacious memory allowed him to retain for years what he had read at a young age. Almost from birth, he evidenced those body lesions associated with scrofula; the malady affected his vision, and in 1710 or 1711, his parents took him to an oculist. Searches for cures even extended to a visit to London in 1712, where the infant received the Queen's Touch (from Anne) to rid him of the disease. The illness, however, had no serious effect upon Johnson's growth; he became a large man with enormous physical strength and, given the hazards of life during the eighteenth century, endured for a relatively long period of time.

Johnson's early education was at Lichfield and Stourbridge grammar schools, followed by his entrance to Pembroke College, Oxford, in 1728. Unfortunately, he remained at the university for only one year, since lack of funds forced him to withdraw. He then occupied a number of tutoring posts in Lichfield and Birmingham before his marriage, in 1735, to Mrs. Elizabeth Jervis Porter, a widow twenty years his senior to whom he referred as "Tetty." The following year, he attempted to establish a school at Edial, three miles to the southwest of Lichfield; despite his wife's money, the project failed. Thus, in 1737, in the company of David Garrick (a former pupil), Johnson left his home and went to London, where he found employment with Edward Cave, the publisher of *The Gentleman's Magazine*. His imitation of Juvenal's third satire, entitled *London*, appeared in 1738, and he followed that literary (but not financial) success with the biography of Richard Savage and *The Vanity of Human Wishes*, another imitation of a satire from Juvenal. By 1749, Garrick had established his reputation as an actor and then as manager of the Theatre Royal in Drury Lane, and he produced Johnson's tragedy of *Irene* as a favor to his friend and former teacher. The play, however, lasted for only nine performances and put to an abrupt end any hopes of Johnson becoming a successful dramatist.

Fortunately, Johnson's abilities could be channeled into a variety of literary forms. *The Rambler* essays appeared twice weekly during 1750-1752. In 1752, Elizabeth Johnson died, a severe loss to her husband because of his fear (terror, in fact) of being alone. Nevertheless, he continued his literary labors, particularly his dictionary, sustained in part by his sincere religious convictions and his rigorous sense of order and discipline. His adherence to the Church of England and to the Tory philosophy of government, both characterized by tradition and conservatism, grew out of that need to discover and to maintain stability and peace of mind. *A Dictionary of the English Language* was published in 1755, followed by essays for *The Idler* during 1758-1760. Another personal tragedy, the death of his mother in 1759, supposedly prompted the writing of *Rasselas* in the evenings of a week's time so that he could pay for the funeral expenses. By 1762, however, his fortunes turned for the better, motivated initially by a pension of three hundred pounds per year from the Tory ministry of King George III, headed by John Stuart, third Earl of Bute. Simply, the government wished to improve its image and to appear as a sincere but disinterested patron of the arts; the fact that *A Dictionary of the English Language* had become a source of national pride no doubt provided the incentive for bestowing the sum upon Johnson.

In mid-May of 1763, Johnson met young James Boswell, the Scotsman who would become his companion, confidant, and biographer—the one person destined to become the most responsible for promoting the name of Samuel Johnson to the world. The following year, the famous literary circle over which Johnson presided was formed; its membership included the novelist/dramatist/essayist Oliver Goldsmith, the artist/essayist/philospher Sir Joshua Reynolds, the politician/philosopher Edmund Burke, and, eventually, the actor/manager David Garrick and the biographer Boswell. Johnson further solidified his reputation as a scholar/critic with his edition of Shakespeare's plays in 1765, the same year in which he began his friendship with Henry and Hester Lynch Thrale—a relationship that was to remain of utmost importance for him throughout the next fifteen years. In 1781, Henry Thrale died; shortly thereafter, his widow married an Italian music master and Roman Catholic, Gabriel Piozzi, much against the wishes of Johnson. That union and Mrs. Piozzi's frequent departures from England brought to an end one of the most noteworthy intellectual and social associations of literary history.

In 1773, Boswell convinced his friend and mentor to accompany him on a tour through Scotland. Thus, the two met in Edinburgh and proceeded on their travels, which resulted, in January, 1775, in Johnson's *A Journey to the Western Islands of Scotland.* Later that same year (in March), he received the degree of Doctor in Civil Law (LL.D.) from Oxford University, after which he spent the three months from September through November touring France with the Thrales. His last major work—*Prefaces, Biographical and Critical, to the Works of the English Poets* (known popularly as *The Lives of the Poets)*—appeared between 1779 and 1781.

Johnson died on December 13, 1784, and he received still one final honor: burial in Westminster Abbey. The poet Leigh Hunt remarked:

> One thing he did, perhaps beyond any man in England before or since; he advanced by the powers of his conversation, the strictness of his veracity and the respect he exacted towards his presence, what may be called the personal dignity of literature, and has assisted men with whom he little thought of co-operating in settling the claims of truth and beneficence before all others.

Analysis · Although technically a work of prose fiction, *Rasselas* belongs to the classification of literature known as the moral tale. In Samuel Johnson's specific case, the piece emerges as an essay on the vanity of human wishes, unified by a clear narrative strand. Some critics have maintained that, in *Rasselas,* Johnson simply continued the same themes that he set forth ten years earlier in his poetic *The Vanity of Human Wishes* and then later in *The Rambler* essays. Essentially, in all three efforts, the writer focused on the problem of what it means to be human and of the psychological and moral difficulties associated with the human imagination. Johnson, both a classicist and a philosophical conservative, took his cue from the poet of Ecclesiastes, particularly the idea of the mind's eye not being satisfied with seeing or the ear with hearing. Instead, whatever the human being sees or possesses causes him only to imagine something more or something entirely different. Further, to imagine more is to want more and, possibly, to lose pleasure in that which is actually possessed. The inexhaustible capacity of the imagination (including specific hopes and wishes) emerges as the principal source of most human desires, an indispensable ingredient for human happiness. According to both the poet of Ecclesiastes and Samuel Johnson, however, human happiness must be controlled by reality, which is also the primary source of most human misery. Therefore, the line dividing happiness and enjoyment from pain, suffering, and torment remains thin and sometimes even indistinct.

Johnson chose to clothe his moral speculations in a form particularly popular among fellow eighteenth century speculators: the Oriental tale, a Western genre that had come into vogue during the earlier Augustan Age. Its popularity was based on the Westerners' fascination with the Orient: Writers set down translations, pseudo-translations, and imitations of Persian, Turkish, Arabic, and Chinese tales as backdrops for brief but direct moral lessons. Although the themes of Oriental tales tended toward the theoretical and the abstract, writers of the period tried to confront real and typical issues with which the majority of readers came into contact.

Rasselas · Originally published as *The Prince of Abissinia: A Tale*, 1759, Johnson's work of fiction is known simply as *Rasselas*. The common name, however, did not appear on the title page of any British edition published during the author's lifetime. The heading on the first page of both volumes of the 1759 edition, however, reads "The History of Rasselas, Prince of Abissinia." Not until the so-called eighth edition of 1787 does one find the title by which the work is generally known: *Rasselas, Prince of Abyssinia: A Tale by S. Johnson.*

Although Johnson once referred to *Rasselas* as merely a "little story book," the work enjoyed immediate and continuing success, which is an indication of its depth and seriousness of purpose. Literary historians agree that an English or American edition has appeared almost every year since the initial publication, while between 1760 and 1764, French, Dutch, German, Russian, and Italian editions were also released. Indeed, before long, Spanish, Hungarian, Polish, Greek, Danish, Armenian, Japanese, and Arabic translations were found, indicating clearly the universality of the piece.

The theme of the vanity of human wishes contributes heavily to the appeal of *Rasselas*, even though such a theme may tend to suffer from an emphasis on skepticism. Certainly, Johnson seems to have conveyed to his readers the idea that no single philosophy of life can sustain all cultures and that no particular lifestyle can become permanently satisfying. This philosophy might lead people to believe that life is essentially an exercise in futility and wasted energy. The vanity of human wishes theme, however, as manipulated by Johnson, also allows for considerable positive interpretations that serve to balance its darker side. In *Rasselas*, Johnson does not deny the value of human experience (including desires and hopes), but he frankly admits to its obvious complexity; man needs to move between conditions of rest and turmoil, and he further needs to experiment with new approaches to life. The admission of that need by the individual constitutes a difficult and complex decision, particularly in the light of the fact that absolute philosophies do not serve all people nor apply to all situations. In joining Prince Rasselas in his search for happiness, the experienced philosopher and poet Imlac reveals his understanding that a commitment to a single course of action constitutes a stubborn and immature attempt to settle irritating problems. Continued movement, on the other hand, is simply a form of escape. The philosopher well knows that all men require a middle ground that considers the best qualities of stability and motion.

What emerges from *Rasselas*, then, is a reinforcement of life's duality, wherein motion and rest apply to a variety of issues and problems ranging from the nature of family life to the creation of poetry. For example, the idea of the Happy Valley dominates the early chapters of the work to the extent that the reader imagines it as the fixed symbol for the life of rest and stability. Within the remaining sections, however, there exists a search for action covering a wide geographical area outside the Happy Valley. Johnson guides his reader over an unchartered realm that symbolizes the life of motion. Eventually, the two worlds unite. Before that can happen, however, Rasselas must experience the restlessness within the Happy Valley, while Pequah, the warrior's captive, must discover order in the midst of an experience charged with potential violence. In the end, Johnson offers his reader the simple but nevertheless pessimistic view that no program for the good life actually exists. In spite of that admission, though, humans will continue to perform constructive acts, realizing full well the absence of certainty. Rather than bemoan life, Johnson, through *Rasselas*, celebrates it.

Typical of the classic novel, the themes and plot of *Rasselas* are supported by its structure. The story is about Prince Rasselas who, with his sister Nekayah, lives in the Happy Valley, where the inhabitants anticipate and satisfy every pleasure and where the external causes of grief and anxiety simply do not exist. Rasselas becomes bored with his prison-paradise, however, and with the help of Imlac, a man of the world, he escapes to search for the sources of happiness. Johnson leads his characters through the exploration of practically every condition of life. The rich suffer from anxiety, boredom, and restlessness; they seek new interests to make life attractive, yet others envy them. Believing political power to be the means for doing good, Rasselas discovers that it is both impotent and precarious in its attempts to change the human condition. Learning, which he had thought of in terms of promise and idealism, suffers, instead, from petty rivalries and vested interests. Rasselas observes a hermit who, after having fled from the social world of emptiness and idle pleasure, cannot cope with solitude, study, and meditation. Finally, Rasselas and his companions return to Abyssinia—but not to the Happy Valley—and hope that they can endure and eventually understand the meaning and responsibilities of life.

Aside from its highly subjective moral issues and the variety of questions that the themes posed, *Rasselas* proved difficult for Johnson to write. Fundamentally an essayist, he belonged to a school of rhetoric that encouraged and even demanded formal argument; the task of developing fictional characters within a variety of settings, arranging various escapes and encounters, and then returning those same characters to or near their place of origin proved bothersome for him. To his credit, however, he carefully manipulated those characters into situations that would display the best side of his peculiar literary talents. As soon as Johnson's characters began to speak, to engage in elaborate dialogues, to position themselves for argument, and to counter objections to those arguments, his style flowed easily and smoothly. Thus, *Rasselas* consists of a series of dissertations, the subjects of which scan the spectrum of human experience: learning, poetry, solitude, the natural life, social amusements, marriage versus celibacy, the art of flying, politics, philosophy. Johnson applied a thin layer of fictional episodes to unify the arguments, similar to such earlier sources as Joseph Addison's *The Spectator* essays, Voltaire's *Candide* (published in the same year as *Rasselas*), and the early seventeenth century series of travelers' tales by Samuel Purchas known as *Purchas: His Pilgrimage.*

As Johnson's spokesmen, Rasselas and Imlac express the author's own fear of solitude and isolation, the supernatural, and ghosts. The Abyssinian prince and his philosopher guide also convey Johnson's horror of madness, his devotion to poetry, his thoughts on the relationship between hypocrisy and human grief, and his conviction (since the death of his wife and mother) that, although marriage can produce considerable trial and pain, celibacy evidences little or no pleasure.

In *Rasselas*, the loose fictional structure and the serious philosophic discussions combine to control the pessimism and to produce an intellectual pilgrimage upon which the travelers' questioning intellects and restless spirits seek purpose and meaning for life. In so doing, however, Johnson's Abyssinian pilgrims mistakenly associate happiness with any object or condition that suggests to them the presence of peace, harmony, or contentment. Rasselas, Nekayah, and even Imlac do not always understand that a human being cannot secure happiness simply by going out and looking for it. Johnson titled the final chapter "The Conclusion, in Which Nothing Is Concluded" probably because he sensed his own inability to suggest a solution to finding happiness, a condition he had not managed to achieve.

Outside the realm of its obvious moral considerations, *Rasselas* succeeds because of its attention to an analysis of a significant, universal, and timeless issue: education. Both Rasselas and his sister, Nekayah, are guided by the teacher, philosopher, and poet Imlac, whose principal qualification is that he has seen the world and thus knows something of it. Whether he serves as the knowledge and experience of the author does not appear as important as the reader's being able to recognize his function within the work and his contribution to the growth of the Prince and the Princess. At the outset, Imlac relates to Rasselas the story of his life, which serves as a prologue to what the young people will eventually come to know and recognize. Johnson knew well that the experience of one individual cannot be communicated to others simply; a person can only suggest to his listeners how to respond should they be confronted with similar circumstances. The Prince and Princess go forth to acquire their own experiences. They proceed to discover at first hand, to observe and then to ask relevant questions. Imlac hovers in the background, commenting upon persons and situations. As the narrative discussion goes forward, Rasselas and his sister gain experience and even begin to resemble, in their thoughts and statements, the sound and the sense of their teacher. Naturally, Imlac's motives parallel those of the title character, which make him seem more real and more human than if he were only a teacher and commentator. Simply, Imlac believes that diligence and skill can be applied by the moral and intelligent person to help in the battle with and eventual triumph over the life of boredom, waste, and emptiness.

In the development of the eighteenth century English novel, Johnson's contemporaries did not embrace *Rasselas* and accept it on the basis of its having met or failed to meet the standards for fiction. Although not a strong example of the form, Johnson does provide his characters with sufficient substance to support the moral purpose of his effort. Nekayah appears more than adequately endowed with grace, intelligence, and the ability to communicate; in fact, stripped of the fashions and the artificial conventions of her time and place (eighteenth century London), the Princess well represents the actualities of feminine nature. Certainly, the male characters speak and act as pure Johnsonian Londoners, clothed in the intellectual habits and language of the mid-eighteenth century. Johnson's intention was to convey the essential arguments of an intellectual debate, and his contemporary readers understood that *Rasselas* existed as nothing more or less than what its author intended it to be: a fictional narrative used as a vehicle for elevated style and thought.

The noted British essayist of the first half of the nineteenth century, Thomas Babington Macaulay, in his encyclopedic essay on Johnson, observed that a number of those who read *Rasselas* "pronounced the writer a pompous pedant, who would never use a word of two syllables where it was possible to use a word of six, and who could not make a waiting-woman relate her adventures without balancing every noun with another noun, and every epithet with another epithet." When considering the size of *Rasselas*, however, it seems the epitome of compression. By composing the work quickly, Johnson forced himself to ignore doubts or hesitations regarding the vanity of human wishes theme and to depend upon his experiences (as painful as they had been) and his skill in expressing them. The entire project also stood as a challenge to Johnson's imaginative and rhetorical artistry. Thus, he again confronted the major thesis of *The Vanity of Human Wishes* and *The Rambler* essays within the context of his own moral thinking.

Walter Jackson Bate, in his biography of Samuel Johnson, claimed that *The Vanity of Human Wishes* served as the prologue to the great decade of moral writing, while *Rasselas* was the epilogue. Indeed, such is the appropriate summation for any discussion of Johnson's moral writing as well as moral thought. The wisdom found within both works–as well as in *The Rambler, The Idler,* and *The Adventurer* essays–certainly solidifies a general understanding of Johnson's religious and moral views. *Rasselas,* in particular, however, gives dimension to those views, reflects the writer's acuteness, and displays the depth and meaning of his early disillusion with life. In writing *Rasselas,* Johnson sought to expose the exact nature of human discontent as it existed in a variety of specific contexts. Each episode in *Rasselas* proved worthy of serious consideration, and each instance revealed the extent to which Johnson could creatively apply his wisdom and his experience.

Samuel J. Rogal

Other major works

PLAY: *Irene: A Tragedy,* pr. 1749.

POETRY: *London: A Poem in Imitation of the Third Satire of Juvenal,* 1738; *The Vanity of Human Wishes: The Tenth Satire of Juvenal Imitated,* 1749; *Poems: The Yale Edition of the Works of Samuel Johnson,* 1965 (vol. 6; E. L. McAdam, Jr., and George Milne, editors).

NONFICTION: *Marmer Norfolciense,* 1739; *A Compleat Vindication of the Licensers of the Stage,* 1739; *The Life of Admiral Blake,* 1740; *An Account of the Life of John Philip Barretier,* 1744; *An Account of the Life of Mr. Richard Savage, Son of the Earl Rivers,* 1744; *Miscellaneous Observations on the Tragedy of Macbeth,* 1745; *The Plan of a Dictionary of the English Language,* 1747; essays in *The Rambler,* 1750-1752; *A Dictionary of the English Language: To Which Are Prefixed, a History of the Language, and an English Grammar,* 1755 (2 volumes); essays in *The Idler,* 1758-1760; preface and notes to *The Plays of William Shakespeare,* 1765 (8 volumes); *The False Alarm,* 1770; *Thoughts on the Late Transactions Respecting Falkland's Islands,* 1771; *The Patriot: Addressed to the Electors of Great Britain,* 1774; *Taxation No Tyranny: An Answer to the Resolutions and Address of the American Congress,* 1775; *A Journey to the Western Islands of Scotland,* 1775; *Prefaces, Biographical and Critical, to the Works of the English Poets,* 1779-1781 (10 volumes; also known as *The Lives of the Poets*); *The Critical Opinions of Samuel Johnson,* 1923, 1961 (Joseph Epes Brown, editor).

TRANSLATIONS: *A Voyage to Abyssinia,* 1735 (of Jerome Lobo's novel); *Commentary on Pope's "Essay on Man,"* 1738-1739 (of Jean Pierre de Crousaz).

Bibliography

Bate, Walter Jackson. *Samuel Johnson.* New York: Harcourt Brace Jovanovich, 1977. A magisterial biography which is readable and sympathetic. Frankly Freudian, the book presents a troubled Johnson who remains lovable despite his flaws. Devotes a chapter to *Rasselas,* which is viewed as a sensible, moral treatment of life.

Greene, Donald. *The Politics of Samuel Johnson.* 2d ed. Athens: University of Georgia Press, 1990. Divided into sections on his early years, first books, London career, and the reign of George III. Greene updated the scholarship of the first edition (1960) and included detailed notes and bibliography. Indispensable background reading for the Johnson student, written by one of the great Johnson scholars of the twentieth century.

Holmes, Richard. *Dr. Johnson & Mr. Savage.* New York: Pantheon, 1993. This distinguished biographer provides a fascinating insight into the origins of Johnson's prose by conducting a keen psychological investigation of Johnson's relationship with the controversial poet Richard Savage. This short book is ideal for the beginning student of Johnson, immersing him in Johnson's period and making Johnson a vivid presence as man and writer. Holmes provides a succinct and very useful bibliography.

Keener, Frederick M. *The Chain of Becoming: The Philosophical Tale, the Novel, and a Neglected Realism of the Enlightenment; Swift, Montesquieu, Voltaire, Johnson, and Austen.* New York: Columbia University Press, 1983. Argues for the psychological realism of philosophical tales like *Rasselas* and relates such works to the novels of Jane Austen.

Lipking, Lawrence. *Samuel Johnson: The Life of an Author.* Cambridge, Mass.: Harvard University Press, 1998. In Lipking's terms, he is writing a life of an author, not the life of a man–by which he means that he concentrates on the story of how Johnson became a writer and a man of letters. A superb work of scholarship, Lipking's book reveals a sure grasp of previous biographies and should be read, perhaps, after consulting Bate.

Reinert, Thomas. *Regulating Confusion: Samuel Johnson and the Crowd.* Durham, N.C.: Duke University Press, 1996. Reinert's fascinating work of scholarship should be consulted only after perusing earlier, introductory studies, for he is reexamining Johnson's views of human nature, urban culture, and individualism. "The crowd" of the book's title refers to Elias Canetti's theories of crowds and power, which Reinert applies to his reevaluation of Johnson.

Tomarken, Edward. *Johnson, "Rasselas," and the Choice of Criticism.* Lexington: University Press of Kentucky, 1989. After surveying the various critical approaches to *Rasselas*, offers a fusion of formalist and other theories to explain *Rasselas* as a work in which life and literature confront each other. The second part of the book argues that Johnson's other writings support this view.

Wahba, Magdi, ed. *Bicentenary Essays on "Rasselas."* Cairo: Cairo Studies in English, 1959. Issued as a supplement to *Cairo Studies in English,* this work collects a number of useful essays. Included are James Clifford's comparison of Voltaire's *Candide (1759) and Rasselas,* Fatma Moussa Mahmoud's *"Rasselas and Vathek,"* and C. J. Rawson's discussion of Ellis Cornelia Knight's *Dinarbas* (1790) as a continuation of Johnson's work.

Walker, Robert G. *Eighteenth-Century Arguments for Immortality and Johnson's "Rasselas."* Victoria, British Columbia: University of Victoria, 1977. Places Johnson's fiction "in the context of eighteenth century philosophical discussions on the nature of the human soul." Reads the work as an orthodox Christian defense of the soul's immortality and as a demonstration that happiness is not attainable in this world.

Elizabeth Jolley

Born: Birmingham, England; June 4, 1923

Principal long fiction · *Palomino,* 1980; *The Newspaper of Claremont Street,* 1981; *Mr. Scobie's Riddle,* 1983; *Miss Peabody's Inheritance,* 1983; *Milk and Honey,* 1984; *Foxybaby,* 1985; *The Well,* 1986; *The Sugar Mother,* 1988; *My Father's Moon,* 1989; *Cabin Fever,* 1990; *The Georges' Wife,* 1993; *The Orchard Thieves,* 1995; *Lovesong,* 1997.

Other literary forms · Elizabeth Jolley's reputation was first established by her short stories, one of which, "Hedge of Rosemary," won an Australian prize as early as 1966. The first works she ever published were her short-story collections *Five Acre Virgin and Other Stories* (1976) and *The Travelling Entertainer and Other Stories* (1979); although her novel *Palomino* won a prize as an unpublished work in 1975, it did not appear in print until 1980. A third volume of short stories, *Woman in a Lampshade,* was published in 1983. Her radio plays have been produced on Australian radio and on the British Broadcasting Corporation (B.B.C.) World Network.

Achievements · Jolley had been writing for twenty years before her first book, a volume of short stories, was published in 1976. In 1975, her novel *Palomino* was given the Con Weickhardt Award for an unfinished novel. *Palomino* was not published, however, until 1980, after a second volume of short stories had already appeared. Not until 1984 was Jolley widely reviewed in the United States. Her honors and awards include a 1986 nomination for the Booker Prize for *The Well,* the 1986 Australian Bicentennial Authority Literary Award for *The Sugar Mother,* the 1987 Miles Franklin Award for *The Well,* and the 1991 Australian Literary Society Gold Medal Award for *Cabin Fever.* She also won the 1993 inaugural France-Australia Award for Translation of a Novel for *The Sugar Mother* and the 1993 West Australian Premier's Prize for *Central Mischief.* In 1998 Jolley was named one of Australia's Living Treasures.

Sometimes compared to Muriel Spark and Barbara Pym, Jolley is unique in her characterization and tone. Critics variously refer to her novels as fantasy combined with farce, comedy of manners, moral satire, or black comedy. Although most reviewers see a moral dimension beneath the slapstick surface of her work, noting her compassion, her wisdom, and her penetration of complex human relationships, some have insisted that she is merely a comic entertainer. Yet to most thoughtful readers, it is obvious that Jolley's humor often derives from characters who refuse to be defeated by their destinies, who boldly assert their individuality, and who dare to dream and to love, however foolish they may appear to the conformists.

Biography · Elizabeth Monica Jolley was born in Birmingham, England, on June 4, 1923. Her mother, a German aristocrat, the daughter of a general, had married a young Englishman who had been disowned by his father because of his pacifist convictions. Privately educated for some years, Jolley and her sister were then sent to a Quaker school. Later, Jolley was trained as a nurse at Queen Elizabeth Hospital, Birmingham, and served in that capacity during World War II. In 1959, she moved to Western Australia with her husband and three children. After her move, Jolley began increasingly to divide her time between writing, tending to her farm, and conducting writing workshops.

Jolley was a tutor at the Fremantle Arts Centre and a writer-in-residence at the Western Australian Institute of Technology in the School of English. In 1996, her orchard and goose farm—the subject of her book *Diary of a Weekend Farmer* (1993)—was lost in bushfires that swept the area during the summer.

Analysis · In "Self Portrait: A Child Went Forth," a personal commentary in the one-volume collection *Stories* (1984), Elizabeth Jolley muses on the frequency with which the theme of exile appears in her works. Often her major characters are lonely, physically or emotionally alienated from their surroundings, living imaginatively in a friendlier, more interesting environment. Because of their loneliness, they reach out, often to grasping or selfish partners, who inevitably disappoint them. For Jolley's lonely spinster, widow, or divorcé, the beloved may be another woman. Sometimes, however, the yearning takes a different form, and the beloved is not a person but a place, like the homes of the old men in *Mr. Scobie's Riddle.*

If there is defeat in Jolley's fiction, there is also grace in the midst of despair. Despite betrayal, her characters reach for love, and occasionally an unlikely pair or group will find it. Another redeeming quality is the power of the imagination; it is no accident that almost every work contains a writer, who may, as in *Foxybaby*, appear to be imagining events into reality and characters into existence. Finally, Jolley believes in laughter. Her characters laugh at one another and sometimes at themselves; more detached, she and her readers laugh at the outrageous characters, while at the same time realizing that the characters are only slight exaggerations of those who view them.

Palomino · The protagonist of Jolley's novel *Palomino* is an exile desperate for love. A physician who has been expelled from the profession and imprisoned, Laura lives on an isolated ranch, her only neighbors the shiftless, dirty tenants, who inspire her pity but provide no companionship for her. Into Laura's lonely life comes Andrea Jackson, a young woman whom the doctor noticed on her recent voyage from England but with whom she formed no relationship. Up until this point, Laura's life has been a series of unsuccessful and unconsummated love affairs with women. At one time, she adored a doctor, to whom she wrote religiously; when the doctor arrived on a visit, she brought a husband. At another period in her life, Laura loved Andrea's selfish, flirtatious mother, who eventually returned to her abusive husband. Perhaps, Laura hopes, Andrea will be different. She is delighted when Andrea agrees to run off with her, ecstatic when she can install her on the ranch, where the women live happily, talking, laughing, and making love. In her new joy, Laura does not realize that, like her other lost lovers, Andrea is obsessed with a man—her own brother, Christopher. It is Christopher's marriage and fatherhood which has driven her into Laura's arms, but Andrea continues to desire Chris, even at moments of high passion. When Andrea admits that she is pregnant with Chris's baby and tries to use Laura's love for her to obtain an abortion, Laura is forced to come to terms with the fact that the love between Andrea and her is imperfect, as it is in all relationships, doomed to change or to dwindle. Obviously, loneliness is the human condition.

Although Jolley's characters must face hard truths such as the inevitability of loneliness, often they move through suffering to new understanding. This is the pattern of *Palomino.* The novel derives its title from the horses on a nearby ranch, whose beauty Laura can appreciate even though she does not possess them. Joy is in perception, not possession; similarly, joy comes from loving, not from being loved. When Andrea and Laura agree that they must part, for fear that their brief love will dwindle into dislike or indifference, they know that they can continue to love each other, even though they will never again be together.

Mr. Scobie's Riddle · In the graphic dialogue of Laura's tenants can be seen the accuracy and the comic vigor which characterize Jolley's later works. *Mr. Scobie's Riddle*, for example, begins with a series of communications between the matron of the nursing home where the novel takes place and the poorly qualified night nurse, whose partial explanations and inadequate reports, along with her erratic spelling, infuriate her superior. At night, the nursing home comes alive with pillow fights, medicinal whiskey, and serious gambling, at which the matron's brother, a former colonel, always loses. In the daytime, the home is a prison: Old people are processed like objects, ill-fed, ill-tended by two rock-and-rolling girls, and supervised by the greedy matron, whose goal is to part her new guest, Mr. Scobie, from his property. Yet if the patients are prisoners, so are their supervisors. Having lost her husband to an old schoolmate, the matron cannot ignore the fact that the couple cavorts regularly in the caravan on the grounds; in turn, the lonely matron saddles her schoolmate with as much work as possible. Meanwhile, the matron is driven constantly closer to bankruptcy by her brother's gambling and closer to a nervous breakdown by her inefficient and careless employees.

Some of the most poignant passages in *Mr. Scobie's Riddle* deal with the yearnings of two old men in Room One, who wish only to return to their homes. Unfortunately, one's has been sold and bulldozed down; the other's has been rented by a voracious niece and nephew. As the patients are driven toward their deaths, no one offers rescue or even understanding. There are, however, some triumphs. The would-be writer, Miss Hailey, never surrenders her imagination or her hope; ironically, her school-fellow, the matron, who has taken all her money, must at last turn to Miss Hailey for understanding and companionship. In the battle for his own dignity, Mr. Scobie wins. Even though he is returned to the nursing home whenever he attempts to go home, and even though his uncaring niece and nephew finally acquire his beloved home, he wins, for he never surrenders to the matron, but dies before she can bully him into signing over his property.

Miss Peabody's Inheritance · The unique combination of farcical humor, lyrical description, pathos, and moral triumph which marks Jolley's later work is also exemplified in *Miss Peabody's Inheritance*, published, like *Mr. Scobie's Riddle*, in 1983. In this novel, a woman writer is one of the two major characters. In response to a fan letter from a middle-aged, mother-ridden London typist, the novelist regularly transmits to her the rough episodes from her new novel, a Rabelaisian story of lesbian schoolmistresses and the troublesome, innocent girl whom they escort through Europe. When at last the typist travels to Australia to meet her writer-heroine, she finds that the writer, a bed-bound invalid, has died. Yet her courage, her imagination, and her manuscript remain for Miss Peabody, an inheritance which will enable her to live as fully and as creatively as the novelist.

Milk and Honey · In *Milk and Honey*, there is no triumph of love, of laughter, or of the imagination. Alone among Jolley's novels, *Milk and Honey* begins and ends in despair.

At the beginning, a door-to-door salesman with a poor, unhappy wife expresses his loneliness, his loss of the woman he loved and of the music he enjoyed. The rest of the novel re-creates his life, from the time when he went to live with his cello teacher and his seemingly delightful family, through the salesman's discovery that he was used and betrayed, to the final tragic climax, when his income vanished—his cellist's hand was charred in a fire—and the woman who made his life worth living was brutally murdered. Although many of the scenes in the novel are grotesque, they are devoid of the humor which is typical of Jolley and which often suggests one way of rising above despair. Nor does the protagonist's art—here, performing music, rather than creating fiction—enable him to transcend his situation. His love for his wife is destroyed with his illusions about her, his mistress is destroyed by his wife, and he and his wife are left to live out their lives together without love.

Foxybaby · *Foxybaby*, published in 1985, is as grotesque as *Milk and Honey*, but its characters move through desperation to humor, love, imagination, and hope. The setting is a campus turned into a weight-loss clinic. Typically, the characters are trapped there, in this case by the rascally bus driver, who ensures a healthy wrecker and garage business by parking so that all approaching cars plow into him. The central character of *Foxybaby* is, once again, a woman writer, Alma Porch, who along with a sculptor and a potter has been hired to take the residents' minds off food by submerging them in culture. Miss Porch's mission is to rehearse an assorted group of residents in a film which she is creating as the book progresses. Brilliantly, Jolley alternates the wildly comic events at the campus with the poignant story that Miss Porch is writing, an account of a father's attempt to rescue his young, drug-ruined, infected daughter and her sickly baby from the doom which seems to await them. From his affectionate nickname for her when she was a little girl comes the name of the book.

Like the love story in *Milk and Honey*, the plot in *Foxybaby* illustrates the destructive power of love. Well-meaning though he is, the father cannot establish communication with his daughter. The reason is unclear, even to the writer who is creating the story or, more accurately, is letting the characters she has imagined create their own story. Perhaps the father's love was crushing; perhaps in her own perverseness the daughter rejected it. At any rate, it is obvious that despite his persistence, he is making little headway in reaching the destructive stranger who is now his "Foxybaby" and who herself has a baby for whom she feels nothing.

Meanwhile, like Jolley's other protagonists, Porch considers escaping from the place which is both her prison and her exile but is prevented from doing so by the very confusion of events. Loquacious Jonquil Castle moves in with her; a Maybelle Harrow, with her lover and his lover, invites her to an orgy; and the indomitable Mrs. Viggars brings forth her private stock of wine and initiates Porch into the joys of the school-like midnight feast. Offstage, the bus driver is always heard shouting to his wife or his mistress to drop her knickers. Love, in all its variety, blooms on the campus, while it is so helpless in the story being shaped in the same place.

Although the campus trap will be easier to escape, bus or no bus, than the nursing home in *Mr. Scobie's Riddle*, Jolley stresses the courage of the residents, a courage which will be necessary in the lives to which they will return, whether those lives involve battling boredom and loneliness, like Miss Porch's, or rejection, like that of Jonquil Castle, the doting mother and grandmother, or age and the loss of love, like the lascivious Maybelle Harrow's. Just as they will survive the clinic, though probably without losing any weight, they will survive their destinies. At the end of the novel, there is a triumph of love, when Mrs. Viggars, admitting her loneliness, chooses to take a young woman and her three children into her home, in order to establish a family once again. There is also a triumph of imagination, when Miss Porch actually sees the characters whom she has created. For her loneliness, they will be companions.

At the end of the novel, the bus stops and Miss Porch awakes, to find herself at the school. Jolley does not explain: Has Porch dreamed the events of the book? Will they now take place? Or is the awakening misplaced in time, and have they already taken place? Ultimately, it does not matter. What does matter is the power of the imagination, which, along with humor and love, makes life bearable.

Hester Harper, another spinster protagonist, is somewhat like the doctor in *Palomino* in that she lives on an isolated ranch in Western Australia and yearns for love. In *The Well*, however, the beloved is an orphan girl, whom Hester takes home to be her companion. Refusing to admit her sexual desires, even to herself, Hester persuades herself that her feelings are merely friendly or perhaps maternal; yet she is so jealous of the orphan, Katherine, that she cannot bear to think of the friend who wishes to visit her or of the man who will ultimately take her away. The rival, when he appears, is mysterious, perhaps a thief, perhaps only an animal, whom Katherine hits on a late-night drive and whom Hester immediately buries in the well. Perhaps diabolical, perhaps distraught, Katherine insists that he is calling to her, demanding her love, threatening her and Hester. Although at last his voice is stilled, it is clear that Hester has lost control over Katherine, to whom the outside world of sexuality and adventure is calling with undeniable urgency. Unlike the doctor in *Palomino*, Hester cannot be contented with the memory of love. Imagination, however, once again mitigates the horror of life; at the end of the novel, Hester is making the mysterious nighttime adventure into a story to be told to children.

The Georges' Wife · In *The Georges' Wife*, Jolley repeats themes of earlier books, particularly *My Father's Moon* and *Cabin Fever*, themes of discord and harmony between brothers and sisters, husbands and wives, friends and lovers. As in earlier books, her spare prose is a dramatic contrast to the abundance of compassion and understanding she demonstrates for the complexities of human relationships. Focusing on the relationship between Vera and Mr. George, Jolley explores the life they attempt to create together, while Vera's mind continues to wander to her past and to her fear of repeating the past. The present and the past collide within her, just as the desire for peace collides with the reality of disharmony.

The Orchard Thieves · A similar theme of discord versus harmony is present in *The Orchard Thieves*. Characters in this novel are also haunted by times of discord which destroy their desire for calm. Every member of the household deals with this specter, especially the grandmother, a mother of three grown-up daughters, who understands that the unspoken and unrevealed either perplex or console people in their dealings with family. A middle sister returns home from England, with no explanations about her private life, thus jeopardizing the peace in the grandmother's house. In the face of this danger, the grandmother tries to rescue the situation and the people involved through her imagination, acceptance, and affection.

The title for this novel, the first part of which was originally published in *The New Yorker* in 1994 as "Three Miles to One Inch," is taken from a quotation from writer

Herman Melville: "The act of paying is perhaps the most uncomfortable infliction that the two orchard thieves entailed upon us." Uncomfortable inflictions do indeed intrude into the lives of Jolley's characters, especially those in this household.

Lovesong · Another tale about uncomfortable inflictions is *Lovesong*, a novel which explores another of Jolley's exiles, Thomas Dalton, who comes reluctantly to Mrs. Porter's establishment, a Home away from Home for Homeless Gentlemen. He wants a fresh start, as does Miss Emily Vales, a fellow lodger and recipient of the predictions found in Mrs. Porter's tea leaves. The study of these two wayfarers, typical examples of Jolley's characters who are struggling with their human mixture of pathos and nobility, echoes the same struggle poet T. S. Eliot describes in his own love song, "The Love Song of J. Alfred Prufrock" (1917).

Because she deals with cruelty, indifference, lust, greed, and, above all, with loneliness, Elizabeth Jolley cannot be considered a superficial writer. The great distances of her western Australia become a metaphor for the mysterious expanses of time; the small clumps of isolated individuals, trapped together on a ranch, on a weight-loss farm, or in a nursing home, represent society, as did Joseph Conrad's microcosmic ships on an indifferent ocean. Jolley makes it clear that love is infrequent and imperfect, that childhood is endangered by cruelty, and that old age leads through indignity to death. Yet most of her works are enlivened by comic characters who defy destiny and death by their very insistence on living. Some of her characters transcend their isolation by learning to love, such as the doctor in *Palomino* or Mrs. Viggars in *Foxybaby*. Others, such as Miss Peabody and Miss Porch, triumph through their imaginations. There is redemption in nature, whether in the beauty of palomino horses or the sunlit shore where Miss Porch sees her characters. There is also triumph in the isolated courage of a human being such as Mr. Scobie, who defies institutionalized and personal greed to save the beloved home to which he can return only in memory. If Elizabeth Jolley's characters are mixtures of the pathetic, the grotesque, and the noble, it is because they are human; if her stories keep the reader off balance between confusion, laughter, and tears, it is because they reflect life.

Rosemary M. Canfield Reisman,
updated by Marjorie Smelstor

Other major works

SHORT FICTION: *Five Acre Virgin and Other Stories*, 1976; *The Travelling Entertainer and Other Stories*, 1979; *Woman in a Lampshade*, 1983; *Stories*, 1984.

RADIO PLAYS: *Night Report*, 1975; *The Performance*, 1976; *The Shepherd on the Roof*, 1977; *The Well-Bred Thief*, 1977; *Woman in a Lampshade*, 1979; *Two Men Running*, 1981.

NONFICTION: *Central Mischief: Elizabeth Jolley on Writing, Her Past, and Herself*, 1992 (Caroline Lurie, editor), *Diary of a Weekend Farmer*, 1993.

Bibliography

Bird, Delys, and Brenda Walker, eds. *Elizabeth Jolley: New Critical Essays*. North Ryde, Australia: Angus and Robertson, 1991. Criticism and interpretation of Jolley's works. Includes bibliographic references.

Daniel, Helen. "A Literary Offering, Elizabeth Jolley." In *Liars: Australian New Novelists*. New York: Penguin Books, 1988. In this comprehensive study, Jolley's fiction is compared with a musical composition by Johann Sebastian Bach, consisting of component literary fugues. While each of her novels is separate, they all blend together to form a graceful totality, and Jolley's handling of theme, time, characterization, and narrative is discussed in this light. The essay appears in a book devoted to Jolley and seven other contemporary Australian novelists, and includes a primary and selected secondary bibliography.

Howells, Coral Ann. "In Search of Lost Mothers: Margaret Laurence's *The Diviners* and Elizabeth Jolley's *Miss Peabody's Inheritance.*" *Ariel* 19, no. 1 (1988): 57-70. This comparison of two novels, one Canadian, the other Australian, places them in the tradition of postcolonial writing by women who are concerned not only with their political dispossession as former colonials but with their gender dispossession as well. After a thorough discussion of the two works in this light, the conclusion is drawn that both writers claim their female literary inheritance by rejecting masculinist-inspired tradition and creating their own aesthetic.

Kirkby, Joan. "The Spinster and the Missing Mother in the Fiction of Elizabeth Jolley." In *Old Maids to Radical Spinsters: Unmarried Women in the Twentieth Century Novel,* edited by Laura L. Doan. Urbana: University of Illinois Press, 1991. Considers Jolley's use of single women in her fiction.

Manning, Gerald F. "Sunsets and Sunrises: Nursing Home as Microcosm in *Memento Mori* and *Mr. Scobie's Riddle.*" *Ariel* 18, no. 2 (1987): 27-43. This comparative study takes up the similarities in Muriel Spark's *Memento Mori* and Jolley's *Mr. Scobie's Riddle.* The two novels share setting (a nursing home) and theme (age, loneliness, and alienation), and both authors make imaginative use of tragicomic devices to enrich their tone. These works attempt to discover an answer that will lead to the acceptance of death.

Salzman, Paul. *Helplessly Tangled in Female Arms and Legs: Elizabeth Jolley's Fictions.* St. Lucia, Australia: University of Queensland Press, 1993. A small but useful book containing information about Jolley's fiction. Includes bibliographic references.

Westerly 31, no. 2 (1986). Entitled "Focus on Elizabeth Jolley," this special issue of an Australian journal provides essays on various aspects of Jolley's work, including one on the way her fiction connects to form a continuum, one on her novel *Milk and Honey,* and another on her handling of displaced persons. Also includes fiction by Jolley.

Willbanks, Ray. "A Conversation with Elizabeth Jolley." *Antipodes: A North American Journal of Australian Literature* 3 (1989): 27-30. While concentrating on Jolley's fiction—its characters, themes, background, and development—this interview offers some interesting information on the author's personal background. Jolley tells about her life in England, where she was born and lived to adulthood until she moved to Australia in 1959. She also recalls the impact Australia made on her when she first arrived and discusses its effect on her writing.

Rudyard Kipling

Born: Bombay, India; December 30, 1865
Died: Hampstead, London, England; January 18, 1936

Principal long fiction · *The Light That Failed,* 1890; *The Naulahka: A Story of East and West,* 1892 (with Wolcott Balestier); *Captains Courageous,* 1897; *Kim,* 1901.

Other literary forms · Best known for his short fiction, Rudyard Kipling wrote more than 250 stories. His style of leaving a story open-ended with the tantalizing phrase "But that's another story" established his reputation for unlimited storytelling. Although the stories are uneven in quality, W. Somerset Maugham considered Kipling to be the only British writer to equal Guy de Maupassant and Anton Chekhov in the art of short fiction.

His early stories both satisfied and glorified the Englishman in India. The empire builder, the man who devotes his life to "civilize the sullen race," comes off in glowing colors, as in the story "The Bridge Builders." Some of his best stories skillfully blend the exotic and the bizarre, and the early "The Man Who Would Be King" (1888), which is about two drifters and their fantastic dream to carve out a kingdom for themselves in Central Asia, best illustrates such a story. "A Madonna of the Trenches," with its strange, occult atmosphere; "The Children of the Zodiac," about a young poet who dreads death by cancer of the throat; and "The Gardener" (1926), with its unrelieved sadness and autobiographical reflections on the death of his son, reflect the pain, the suffering, and the dark melancholy of Kipling's later life.

The stories that make up *The Jungle Book* (1894) and *The Second Jungle Book* (1895) were written in Brattleboro, Vermont, when Kipling's mind "worked at the height of its wonderful creative power." They are in the class of animal and folktales that make up such world literary creations as the ancient folktales of *Aesop's Fables* (fourth century B.C.E.) and *The Jataka Tales.* Into the Jungle Book stories, Kipling incorporated not only the clear and clean discipline of the public school but also his favorite doctrine of the natural law. This law had a great impact on the Boy Scout movement and the origins of the Wolf Cub organization, found in the Mowgli tales.

Kipling was a prolific writer, and, as a journalist, he wrote a considerable number of articles, stories, and poems not only for his own newspapers but also for a variety of literary journals in England and the United States. In addition, he was a prolific letter-writer and carried on lengthy literary and political correspondence with such men as President Theodore Roosevelt, financier Cecil Rhodes, and writer H. Rider Haggard. His correspondence with Haggard has been collected in *Rudyard Kipling to Rider Haggard: The Record of a Friendship,* edited by Morton N. Cohen (1965). Two volumes of his *Uncollected Prose* were published in 1938, and even some of his desultory writing, such as *American Notes,* concerned with his travels in the United States in 1891, was reissued in the late twentieth century with editorial notes. Kipling personally supervised the publication of the Sussex edition of his work in thirty-five volumes (1937-1939). The Kipling Society, founded in 1927, publishes the quarterly *Kipling Journal,* which keeps Kipling enthusiasts informed of publications about Kipling. Biographical material on Kipling–including his autobiography, *Something of*

Myself: For My Friends Known and Unknown, published posthumously in 1937–is considerable, and the record of his literary achievement is now complete.

Achievements · Kipling's first book of fiction appeared in 1888. Since then, his works have undergone several editions, and several of his short stories and poems have found a permanent place in anthologies. Although England and India have both changed enormously since the turn of the twentieth century, Kipling's stories continue to attract and fascinate new readers. He was a best-selling author during his lifetime–one of his animal stories, *Thy Servant a Dog* (1930), sold 100,000 copies in six months in 1932–and he continues to be extremely popular in the English-speaking countries of the world. Several of his works, notably *Captains Courageous, Kim, The Jungle Book*, and some short stories, have been made into motion pictures.

Throughout his lifetime, and soon after his death, Kipling was associated with the British empire. He had become the laureate of England's vast imperial power, his first book was praised by the viceroy in 1888, and the king used Kipling's own words to address the empire on Christmas Day in 1932. The day Kipling's ashes were interred at Westminster Abbey–January 23, 1936–King George V's body lay in state in Westminster Hall and the comment that "the King has gone and taken his trumpeteer with him" appropriately described the image Kipling had projected.

Kipling wanted to serve the empire through the army or the civil service. Because he had neither family connections with which to obtain a civil service job nor strong eyesight, which barred him from military service, Kipling turned to writing. He wrote with a passionate intensity coupled with admiration for the soldiers, the bridge builders, the missionaries, and the civil servants in remote places who served the empire under "an alien sky." Many of the phrases he used to narrate their tales–"What do they know of England who only England know?," "East is East and West is West," "the white man's burden," "somewhere east of Suez"–have become part of the English language and are often repeated by those who are unfamiliar with his writings. To have used the pen in place of a gun to serve the imperial vision and have such lasting impact on British thinking constitutes a major achievement.

In 1890, Kipling published or republished more than eighty stories, including the novelette *The Light That Failed*. At twenty-five, he had become a famous literary figure. At forty-two, he became the first Englishman to win the Nobel Prize in Literature for "the great power of observation, the original conception and also the virile comprehension and art of narrative that distinguish his literary creations." He had also become a controversial personality, since critics and readers saw in his work the

effort to mix the roles of the artist and the propagandist. Kipling's writings would continue to be controversial and generate extremes of admiration or condemnation. He generates a love-hate response, and there are frequent Kipling studies that evaluate and interpret his writings from a new perspective. He is neither neglected nor ignored, which is a true testimony to his importance as a writer.

Biography · Rudyard Kipling was born in Bombay, India, on December 30, 1865. His father, John Lockwood Kipling of Yorkshire, was a scholar and an artist. The elder Kipling went to India as a professor of architectural sculpture in the Bombay School of Fine Arts and later became the Curator of the Lahore Museum, which Kipling was to describe meticulously in *Kim*. He also served as the Bombay correspondent of *The Pioneer* of Allahabad. In 1891, he published *Beast and Man in India* with the help of A. P. Watt, his son's literary agent. The book contains excerpts from Rudyard Kipling's newspaper reports to *The Civil and Military Gazette*. The book provided inspiration for Kipling's Jungle Books and several of his stories: "The Mark of the Beast," "The Finances of the Gods," and "Moti Guj, Mutineer" are some examples.

Kipling's mother, Alice Macdonald, was one of five Macdonald sisters, three of whom married into prominent families. Georgina Macdonald married the distinguished pre-Raphaelite painter Sir Edward Burne-Jones; Agnes Macdonald married another painter, Sir Edward Poynter, who was influential in helping John Kipling obtain a position in India; and a third sister married Alfred Baldwin, the railroad owner, whose son Stanley Baldwin became prime minister of England. Kipling was therefore connected with creative and intellectually stimulating families through his mother, while from his father, he inherited a strong Wesleyan tradition.

Rudyard and his sister, Trix, spent the first six years of their lives in India. Surrounded by Indian servants who told them Indian folktales, Kipling absorbed the Indian vocabulary and unconsciously cultivated the habit of thinking in that vocabulary, as illustrated in his short story "Tod's Amendment." Kipling recalls these early years in his posthumously published autobiography, *Something of Myself,* in which he recalls how he and his sister had to be constantly reminded to speak English to his parents, and that he spoke English "haltingly translated out of the vernacular idiom that one thought and dreamed in." This contributed to the great facility with which he uses Indian words as part of his style. Edmund Wilson, in his essay "The Kipling That Nobody Read," writes that Kipling even looked like an Indian as a young boy.

Like other Anglo-Indian children who were sent home to England for their education, Kipling and his sister were shipped to London to live with a relative of their father in Southsea. The pain and agony of those six years under the supervision of this sadistic woman in what Kipling calls "the house of desolation" is unflinchingly re-created in the early part of his novelette *The Light That Failed* and in the short story "Baa, Baa, Blacksheep." According to Edmund Wilson, the traumatic experiences of these six years filled Kipling with hatred for the rest of his life.

Kipling studied at the United Services College, a public school for children from families with a military background or with the government civil service. Kipling served as editor of the school newspaper, *The United Services College Chronicle*, to which he contributed several youthful parodies of poets Robert Browning and Algernon Charles Swinburne. One poem, "Ave Imperatrix," however, with its note of patriotism and references to England's destiny to civilize the world, foreshadows Kipling's later imperial themes. Although Kipling makes fun of flagwaving in "The Flag of Their Country," in *Stalky and Co.* (1899), he did imbibe some of his imperial tendencies at the school because there was an almost universal desire among the boys to join either the army or the civil service for the glory of the empire.

In 1882, when Kipling was sixteen, he returned to India, and his "English years fell away" and never "came back in full strength." Through his father's connections, Kipling had no difficulty in becoming assistant editor on *The Civil and Military Gazette* of Lahore at the age of eighteen. Two horror stories written during this period, "The Phantom 'Rickshaw" and "The Strange Ride of Morrowbie Jukes, C. E.," have found a place among his best-known stories.

After four years on *The Civil and Military Gazette*, Kipling moved to Allahabad as assistant editor to *The Pioneer*, and his writings began to appear in four major newspapers of British India. Young, unattached, with servants and horses at his disposal, enfolded in the warmth of his family, these years proved to be Kipling's happiest and most productive. He wrote to a friend, "I'm in love with the country and would sooner write about her than anything else." The poetry collection *Departmental Ditties* was published in 1886, and *Plain Tales from the Hills* in 1888. Soon, Kipling was known all over India, and a favorable review in the *Saturday Review* also created a demand for his writings in London.

In March, 1899, he left Lahore on a leisurely sea journey to London by way of Rangoon, Singapore, Hong Kong, Japan, and San Francisco. After making several stops across the United States, the twenty-four-year-old Kipling arrived in London in October, 1899. He has described this journey in *From Sea to Sea*, published the same year. In London, Kipling came into contact with the American Wolcott Balestier, whom he met in writer Mrs. Humphry Ward's drawing room. He collaborated with him on the novel *The Naulahka: A Story of East and West.* Balestier's sister Caroline was later to become Kipling's wife. Befriended by the poet W. E. Henley, Kipling published *Barrack-Room Ballads and Other Verses* in 1892. It was a completely new poetic voice in style, language, and content. Kipling won an audience, who were startled and shocked but fascinated and hypnotized by his style.

Kipling left for America in June, 1891, and the short visit brought him into conflict with certain members of the American press. He returned to England and went on a long sea voyage with a sentimental stopover in India, his last visit to the subcontinent. He returned to London hurriedly because of Wolcott Balestier's death, and a few weeks later, on January 18, 1892, he married Caroline Balestier. Henry James gave away the bride.

The newly married couple returned to the Balestier home in Brattleboro, Vermont, where Kipling wrote the Jungle Books and other stories. He also became a friend of Mark Twain. His desire for privacy, his recurrent conflicts with the press, the death of his eldest daughter, Josephine, his own illness, and the notorious publicity as a result of a quarrel with his brother-in-law all contributed to his decision to leave America in 1897, never to return.

Kipling went to South Africa during the Boer War (1899-1902) and became a good friend of another empire builder, Cecil Rhodes. It was during the war that Kipling completed his most important novel, *Kim.* Published in 1901, it was Kipling's farewell to India. In 1907, Kipling received the Nobel Prize. During World War I, Kipling lost his only son, John, and his melancholy deepened. The poem "My Boy Jack" (1916) articulates the grief and pain of that loss. In writing other works, he turned to the strange and the macabre, as in "A Madonna of the Trenches," "The Wish House," and "The Eyes of Allah."

Plagued by ill health during the last years of his life, he relied on his wife for support, but she also lost her health to the crippling effects of diabetes and rheumatism. Kipling published his last collection of stories, *Limits and Renewals*, in 1932 and continued to show interest in British and world affairs, angry at the complacency of his countrymen toward the growing fascism outside England. He died January 18, 1936, and his ashes were buried in Westminster Abbey.

Analysis · Rudyard Kipling wrote four novels, one of them, *The Naulahka*, in collaboration with Wolcott Balestier. Kipling was essentially a miniaturist, and his genius was for the short story, a single event dramatized within a specific time frame. His novels reflect an episodic quality, and although Kipling brings to them a considerable amount of technical information—about cod fishing in *Captains Courageous*, army and artistic life in *The Light That Failed*, authentic topography and local color in *The Naulahka*—he fails in the development of character and in evoking an emotional response from his readers. *Kim*, however, is an exception.

The Light That Failed · *The Light That Failed*, dedicated to his mother, has often been described by critics as "the book that failed." Kipling acknowledged a debt to the French novel *Manon Lescaut* (1731, 1733, 1753) by Abbé Prévost in writing the novel. It was first published in the January, 1891, issue of *Lippincott's Monthly Magazine* and was later dramatized and filmed. When Macmillan and Co. published it two months later, there were four new chapters, and the story concluded with a tragic ending and the note, "This is the story of *The Light That Failed* as it was originally conceived by the writer." The difference between the magazine version, with its more conventional ending, and the book version, with the sad ending, caused some consternation among readers and critics.

The *Light That Failed* has many autobiographical elements. The novel opens with two children brought up by a sadistic housekeeper; Kipling drew upon his own early life in "the house of desolation" for some of the harrowing experiences of Dick and Maisie in the novel. Dick and Maisie are not related but have an adolescent crush on each other. They are separated, and while Dick goes to the Far East to serve on the frontiers of the empire, Maisie pursues her dream of becoming an artist. Dick wants Maisie to travel with him, but Maisie, committed to her art, remains in England. Dick later moves to Egypt as a war artist. He returns to London, and after a period of frustration, he enjoys fame and success. Kipling draws on his familiarity with the art world to describe the life of Dick in London. He had never been to Africa, however, and for the realism of his African scenes, Kipling relied on information he obtained from his friends. When Dick expresses fury and anger at unscrupulous art dealers, Kipling is lashing out at the publishers in America who boldly pirated his works.

In Dick and Maisie's doomed love and its impact on Dick, readers see echoes of Kipling's own unrequited love for Violet Flo Garrard. Flo was a painter, like Maisie, and in the words of Kipling's sister, Flo was cold and obsessed with "her very ineffective little pictures." Writer Angus Wilson, in his study of Kipling, believes that Kipling found in Flo the quintessential *femme fatale*, "the vampire that sucks man's life away." Kipling has transferred some of the intensity of this feeling to Dick Heldar, almost his alter ego at certain times in the novel. Dick Heldar's obsession with the single life and his desire for military life also express Kipling's own passions. When Dick goes blind after being spurned by Maisie, Kipling is again drawing upon his own anxiety about the possible loss of his own vision.

The Light That Failed ends very melodramatically with Dick's death in the Sudanese battlefield amid bloody carnage. Apart from the autobiographical elements in the novel, *The Light That Failed* has little interest for the contemporary student of Kipling.

The Naulahka · Subtitled "A Story of East and West" and written in collaboration with Wolcott Balestier, *The Naulahka* compares the ways of the East, represented by the princely state of Rhatore in Central India, to those of the West, represented by the village of Topaz, Colorado. Balestier supplied the Western elements of the novel, and Kipling wrote the Eastern chapters. The result is a poorly written, melodramatic, and lackluster novel.

Naulahka is a priceless necklace owned by the Maharaja of Rhatore. Tarvin, an aggressive American entrepreneur, wants to bring the railroad to feudalistic Rhatore; he enlists the services of Mutrie, the wife of the president of the railroad company, to influence her husband. He promises to get her the Naulahka as a gift. Tarvin's fiancé, Kate, is also in India to help the Indian women. With her help, Tarvin tries to influence the Maharaja's son. Kate wants a hospital; Tarvin wants the railroad. Kate then breaks off her relationship with Tarvin; he secures the necklace but returns it in order to save Kate's life, which is threatened by a mad priest. Finally, Kate and Tarvin return to the United States.

The characters in *The Naulahka* are one dimensional, and the narrative style is very episodic. Kipling has drawn heavily from his earlier book *Letters of Marque* (1891), lifting entire passages and incidents.

Captains Courageous · A better novel than *The Light That Failed, Captains Courageous* is Kipling's only completely American book in character and atmosphere. Kipling made several visits to Gloucester, Massachusetts, with his friend Dr. John Conland to saturate himself with considerable technical information about cod fishing. He has used this information extravagantly in telling the story of *Captains Courageous.* The novel was published serially in *McClure's Magazine*, and Kipling was not pleased with its publication. In a letter to a friend, he wrote that the novel was really a series of sketches and that he had "crept out of the possible holes by labelling it a boy's story."

Captains Courageous is the story of Harvey Cheyne, the spoiled only son of a millionaire. On a voyage to Europe, Harvey falls overboard and is picked up by a fishing boat. He bellows out orders and insults the skipper, Disko. Disko decides to teach the boy a lesson and puts Harvey under a strict program of work and discipline. The plan succeeds, and Harvey emerges stronger and humanized. When the boat reaches Gloucester, laden with salted cod, a telegram is sent to Harvey's father, who rushes from San Francisco to retrieve his son. Harvey returns with his father to resume his studies and prepare himself for taking over his father's business empire.

"Licking a raw cub into shape," the central theme of *Captains Courageous*, is a favorite subject of Kipling. The technical knowledge about cod fishing is impressive, but the characters themselves have no individuality. Harvey Cheyne's transformation from a stubborn, spoiled young man into a mature, responsible individual is achieved too speedily. Kipling has used the story merely to illustrate what Birkenhead describes as "the virtue of the disciplined life upon a spoiled immature mind."

Kim · T. S. Eliot considered *Kim* Kipling's greatest work. Nirad C. Chaudhury, an Indian scholar, called *Kim* "not only the finest novel in English with an Indian theme but also one of the greatest of English novels in spite of the theme." Kipling wanted to write a major book about India, and he started the project in 1885, in "Mother

Maturin: An Anglo-Indian Episode." That work concerned itself with the "unutterable horrors of lower class Eurasian and native life as they exist outside reports and reports and reports." It was the story of an old Irishwoman who kept an opium den in Lahore but sent her daughter to study in London, where she marries, then returns to Lahore. Kipling's father did not like it, however, and Kipling dutifully abandoned the project. *Kim* emerged instead.

Published in 1901, *Kim* is Kipling's last book set in India. In *Something of Myself,* he tells readers how he had long thought of writing about "an Irish boy born in India and mixed up with native life." Written under the influence of his demon–Kipling's word to describe his guardian muse–*Kim* takes in all of India, its rich diversity and intensity of life.

In growing old and evaluating the past, Kipling turned to the best years of his life, his years in India. In *Kim,* Kipling relives his Indian years when everything was secure and his family intact. Kim's yearning for the open road, for its smells, sights, and sounds, is part of the longing of Kipling himself for the land that quickened his creative impulse and provided his literary success.

Kim is the story of an Irish orphan boy in India, a child of the streets. He grows up among Indian children and is aware of all the subtle nuances of Indian life. Yet, at the same time, he has the spirit of adventure and energy of his Irish ancestry. His joining the Red Lama from Tibet on his quest for the River of Healing, and Kim's fascination for the British Indian secret service, "the Great Game," results in his own self-discovery.

Kim has the characteristic features of a boy's story, the lovable boy involved in a quest filled with adventure and intrigue. One is reminded of Robert Louis Stevenson's *Treasure Island* (1881-1882) and *Kidnapped* (1886) and Mark Twain's *The Adventures of Tom Sawyer* (1876). *Kim,* however, rises above the usual boy's story in that it has a spiritual dimension. By coming into contact with the Lama, Kim emerges a sadder and wiser being at the end of the novel. Kim's racial superiority is emphasized throughout the novel, but after his association with the Lama, Kim is able to say, "Thou hast said there is neither black nor white, why plague me with this talk, Holy One? Let me rub the other foot. It vexes me, I am *not* a Sahib. I am thy chela, and my head is heavy on my shoulders." This is an unusual admission for Kim and Kipling.

Many of Kipling's earlier themes are elaborated and incorporated into *Kim.* There is the vivid picture of the Indian army; the tale of "Lispeth," from *Plain Tales from the Hills,* repeated in the story of the Lady of Shamlegh; and the Anglo-Indian, the native, and the official worlds providing backgrounds as they did in the short stories. Administering medicine in the guise of a charm to soothe and satisfy the Indian native, Jat is an echo from the earlier story, "The Tomb of His Ancestors." Buddhism, whose scriptural tales–*The Jataka Tales*–supplied Kipling with a wealth of source material for his two Jungle Books and *Just So Stories* (1902), supplies the religious atmosphere in *Kim.* Even Kim's yearning for the open road had been expressed previously in the character of Strickland, who, incidentally, makes a brief appearance in *Kim.*

Both Kim and the Venerable Teshoo Lama, the two main characters in *Kim,* emerge as distinctive individual characters and not mere types of the Asian holy man and the Anglo-Indian boy. They grow and develop an awareness of themselves and their surroundings. Kim realizes that his progress depends upon the cooperation of several people: the Lama, Mukherjee, Colonel Creighton, and Mahbub Ali. The Lama too undergoes a change of character. He realizes that his physical quest for the River of

Arrow has clouded his spiritual vision. The River of Arrow is at his feet if he has the faith to see it.

In selecting the Buddhist Lama as the main character, Kipling has emphasized the Middle Way. To the Lama, there is no color, no caste, no sect. He is also the tone of moderation without the extremes of Hinduism and Islam, the two main religious forces on the subcontinent.

In the relationship between Kim and the Lama, Kipling portrays an integral part of Indian spiritual life, the disciple and teacher relationship, the *guru* and *chela* interaction. It is not an ordinary relationship between a boy and a holy man; it is a special relationship, as the Lama notes, forged out of a previous association in an earlier life, the result of good karma. *Kim* is indeed a virtuoso performance; it is Kipling at his best.

K. Bhaskara Rao

Other major works

SHORT FICTION: *In Black and White*, 1888; *Plain Tales from the Hills*, 1888; *Soldiers Three*, 1888; *The Story of the Gadsbys*, 1888; *The Phantom 'Rickshaw and Other Tales*, 1888; *Under the Deodars*, 1888; *Wee Willie Winkie*, 1888; *Life's Handicap*, 1891; *Many Inventions*, 1893; *The Jungle Book*, 1894; *The Second Jungle Book*, 1895; *Soldier Tales*, 1896; *The Day's Work*, 1898; *Stalky and Co.*, 1899; *Just So Stories*, 1902; *Traffics and Discoveries*, 1904; *Puck of Pook's Hill*, 1906; *Actions and Reactions*, 1909; *Rewards and Fairies*, 1910; *A Diversity of Creatures*, 1917; *Land and Sea Tales for Scouts and Guides*, 1923; *Debits and Credits*, 1926; *Thy Servant a Dog*, 1930; *Limits and Renewals*, 1932.

POETRY: *Departmental Ditties*, 1886; *Barrack-Room Ballads and Other Verses*, 1892; *The Seven Seas*, 1896; *Recessional and Other Poems*, 1899; *The Five Nations*, 1903; *The Years Between*, 1919; *Rudyard Kipling's Verse*, 1940 (definitive edition).

NONFICTION: *American Notes*, 1891; *Beast and Man in India*, 1891; *Letters of Marque*, 1891; *The Smith Administration*, 1891; *From Sea to Sea*, 1899; *The New Army in Training*, 1914; *France at War*, 1915; *The Fringes of the Fleet*, 1915; *Sea Warfare*, 1916; *Letters of Travel, 1892-1913*, 1920; *The Irish Guards in the Great War*, 1923; *A Book of Words*, 1928; *Something of Myself: For My Friends Known and Unknown*, 1937; *Uncollected Prose*, 1938 (2 volumes); *Rudyard Kipling to Rider Haggard: The Record of a Friendship*, 1965 (Morton N. Cohen, editor).

MISCELLANEOUS: *The Sussex Edition of the Complete Works in Prose and Verse of Rudyard Kipling*, 1937-1939 (35 volumes).

Bibliography

Bauer, Helen Pike. *Rudyard Kipling: A Study of the Short Fiction*. New York: Twayne, 1994. Part 1 explores the major themes of Kipling's stories; part 2 examines his view of himself as a writer; part 3 provides examples from two particularly insightful critics. Includes chronology and bibliography.

Bloom, Harold, ed. *Rudyard Kipling*. New York: Chelsea House, 1987. Essays on Kipling's major work, his views on art and life, and his vision of empire. Includes introduction, chronology, and bibliography.

_____. *Rudyard Kipling's "Kim."* New York: Chelsea House, 1987. Nine essays ranging from general appreciation to detailed critical analysis, with an introduction, chronology, and bibliography.

Carrington, Charles. *Rudyard Kipling: His Life and Works*. London: Macmillan, 1978.

A standard biography with access to unique inside information. The appendices to the 1978 edition contain information previously suppressed by Kipling's heirs. Includes a chronology of his life and work as well as a family tree. Much stronger on his adult life than his childhood and concentrates on his life and the influences upon it rather than on literary critique.

Coates, John. *The Day's Work: Kipling and the Idea of Sacrifice.* Madison, N.J.: Fairleigh Dickinson University Press, 1997. Examines the themes of sacrifice and didacticism in Kipling's works. Includes bibliographical references and an index.

Knowles, Frederic Lawrence. *A Kipling Primer.* Reprint. New York: Haskell House, 1974. Chapter 1 concerns biographical data and includes personality traits. Chapter 2 elaborates on Kipling's literary techniques and critically examines the stages of his artistic development. Chapter 3 is an index to his major writings, with brief descriptions and criticisms of Kipling's works by other authors.

Laski, Marghanita. *From Palm to Pine: Rudyard Kipling Abroad and at Home.* New York: Facts on File, 1987. A lively, well-illustrated biography with a brief chronology, appendices on Kipling's major travels and his important works, a brief bibliography, and notes.

Orel, Harold, ed. *Critical Essays on Rudyard Kipling.* Boston: G. K. Hall, 1990. Sections on Kipling's poetry, his writing on India, his work as a mature artist, his unfinished memoir, and his controversial reputation. Introduced by a distinguished critic. No bibliography.

Arthur Koestler

Born: Budapest, Hungary; September 5, 1905
Died: London, England; March 3, 1983

Principal long fiction · *The Gladiators*, 1939; *Darkness at Noon*, 1940; *Arrival and Departure*, 1943; *Thieves in the Night: Chronicle of an Experiment*, 1946; *The Age of Longing*, 1951; *The Call Girls: A Tragi-Comedy with Prologue and Epilogue*, 1972.

Other literary forms · Arthur Koestler's first five novels, along with most of his other books, have been reissued in the Danube edition, published in England by Hutchinson and Company and in America by Macmillan Publishing Company. His nonfiction works include four autobiographical volumes—*Spanish Testament* (1937), abridged in the Danube edition as *Dialogue with Death* (1942); *Scum of the Earth* (1941); *Arrow in the Blue: The First Volume of an Autobiography, 1905-1931* (1952); and *The Invisible Writing: The Second Volume of an Autobiography, 1932-1940* (1954)–as well as an autobiographical essay on his disillusionment with Communism found in *The God That Failed* (1950), edited by Richard Crossman with additional essays by Richard Wright, Ignazio Silone, Stephen Spender, Louis Fischer, and André Gide. Koestler's nonfiction works exceed twenty-five volumes, divided roughly between social-historical commentary and the history of science. He also wrote one play, *Twilight Bar: An Escapade in Four Acts* (1945).

Achievements · Koestler will be remembered as an apostate to the Left who dramatized in *Darkness at Noon* and in his autobiographical works the integrity of many Communist intellectuals in the 1930's and the anguish they suffered under Soviet leader Joseph Stalin. As a novelist, he is generally a skilled storyteller, putting conventional techniques to the service of philosophical themes. Although none of his novels have been best-sellers in the usual sense, *Darkness at Noon*–translated into thirty-three languages–has been reprinted many times, and its appeal shows no sign of slackening. It continues to be read widely in college courses and is probably one of the most influential political novels of the twentieth century, despite the fact that comparatively little academic literary criticism has been devoted to it. Indeed, Koestler's novels, even *Darkness at Noon*, are perhaps kept alive more by political scientists and historians than by professional students of literature.

Besides being an accomplished novelist of ideas, Koestler was one of the finest journalists of his age, often producing works as controversial as his political fiction. Typical of his best essays is the piece in *The Lotus and the Robot* (1960) on "Yoga Unexpurgated" (noted as being "far too horrible for me to read" by William Empson in his review); like many other of his best essays, "Yoga Unexpurgated" will maintain its readability. *The Sleepwalkers: A History of Man's Changing Vision of the Universe* (1959), a survey of early scientific thought with emphasis on Renaissance astronomy, is part of a trilogy (with *The Act of Creation*, 1964, and *The Ghost in the Machine*, 1967) on the understanding of the human mind, and it ranks as Koestler's most suggestive effort at research and speculation. Even more controversial than his psychological studies, although a wholly different kind of work, is *The Thirteenth Tribe* (1976), which revived the thesis that the Jews of Eastern Europe are descended from the ancient Khazar

Empire. Scholarly reviews of Koestler's research tended to be severe. *The Case of the Midwife Toad* (1971) reveals sympathies for neo-Lamarckian philosophy, and *The Roots of Coincidence* (1972) surveys the claims of parapsychology, ending with a plea "to get out of the straitjacket which nineteenth-century materialism imposed on any philosophical outlook."

Although he flirted with crank notions, to the detriment of his credibility, Koestler was neither a crank nor a dilettante. His renegade vision has enlivened contemporary arts and letters for several decades, and it is likely that this force will continue to be felt for several more.

Biography · Arthur Koestler was born on September 5, 1905, in Budapest, Hungary, the only child of middle-class Jewish parents. He was precocious in math and science and closer to his mother than to his father, an eccentric, self-taught businessman. When Koestler was in his teens, the family moved to Vienna, and he attended the university there as a science student. After four years, he left school without a degree and went to Palestine, where he joined a Zionist movement for a while before obtaining a correspondent's job with the Ullstein newspapers of Germany. He advanced rapidly in journalism, becoming, in 1930, the foreign editor of *B.Z. am Mittag* and the science editor of *Vossische Zeitung* in Berlin, partly as a result of his success as a reporter on the *Graf Zeppelin* flight to the North Pole in 1931.

In December, 1931, Koestler became a member of the German Communist Party, and less than one year later he gave up his position with Ullstein and spent several weeks traveling in the Soviet Union. He then spent three years in Paris working for the Comintern, leaving for Spain at the outbreak of the Spanish Civil War in 1936.

His marriage to Dorothy Asher in 1935 lasted only two years before they were separated, eventually to be divorced in 1950. While in Spain for the Comintern in 1937, Koestler was captured by the Nationalists and sentenced to execution. Thanks to the British press, he was freed after three months, and he published an account of his experiences, *Spanish Testament* (1937). By the next year, he was in France again, where he resigned from the Communist Party in disillusionment with Stalinism and the show trials. During that time, he wrote *Darkness at Noon.* After escaping from Nazi internment in France, he fled to Britain and spent 1941 to 1942 in the British Pioneer Corps.

After *Darkness at Noon* was published, Koestler was in Paris at the center of the uproar it caused among members of the French

National Archives Left. (Simone de Beauvoir's *roman*

à clef, The Mandarins, in 1954, makes vivid this period in French intellectual life.) In the late 1940's, Koestler became a leader among anti-Communist voices in the West, twice visiting America to lecture, as well as enjoying an appointment between 1950 and 1951 as a Chubb Fellow at Yale University. After his divorce in 1950, he married Mamaine Paget. In 1952, he took up residence in America for two years, during which time he published his autobiographical volumes *Arrow in the Blue and The Invisible Writing.* He was divorced in 1953. One phase in his career ended in 1955, when he indicated in *Trial of the Dinosaur and Other Essays* that he was through writing about politics. At that time, his interest turned to mysticism and science, and he tried in his writings on extrasensory perception (ESP) to narrow the gap between natural and extrasensory phenomena. He married Cynthia Jefferies in 1965. After World War II, Koestler became a naturalized citizen of England, and his adopted country honored him by making him a Commander of the Order of the British Empire (C.B.E.) in 1972 and a Companion of Literature (C.Lit.) in 1974.

Koestler died in London, England, on March 3, 1983. His wife was found beside him, both victims of apparent suicide.

Analysis · All of Arthur Koestler's works, both fiction and nonfiction, reveal a struggle to escape from the oppressiveness of nineteenth century positivism and its later offshoots. *The Yogi and the Commissar and Other Essays* (1945) sums up the moral paradox of political action. The Yogi, at one extreme, represents a life lived by values that are grounded in idealism. The Yogi scorns utilitarian goals and yields to quietism; his refusal to intervene leads to passive toleration of social evil. The Commissar, committed to dialectical materialism, ignores the shallow ethical concerns of the historically benighted middle class and seeks to function as an instrument of historical progress. History replaces God, and human suffering is seen as an inevitable step toward the ultimate historical synthesis rather than as an element of God's mysterious purpose. For the Commissar, the end justifies the means, and it is this ethical position that is debated most effectively in *The Gladiators, Darkness at Noon,* and *Arrival and Departure.*

In his postscript to the Danube edition of *The Gladiators,* Koestler points out that these novels form a trilogy "whose leitmotif is the central question of revolutionary ethics and of political ethics in general: the question whether, or to what extent, the end justifies the means." The question "obsessed" him, he says, during the seven years in which he belonged to the Communist Party and for several years afterward. It was his answer to this question that caused him to break with the Party, as he explains eloquently in his essay in *The God That Failed.* The city built by the rebellious slaves in *The Gladiators* fails because Spartacus does not carry out the stern measures necessary to ensure the city's successful continuation. In *Darkness at Noon,* the old revolutionary Rubashov is depicted as trying to avoid the error Spartacus made, but ends up lost in a maze of moral and ethical complications that destroy him.

Behaviorist psychology is congenial to the materialism of Communist revolutionary ethics, and Koestler attacks its claims heatedly. Indeed, Koestler's interest in mysticism, the occult, and parapsychology was an attempt to find an escape route from the deadly rationalism that makes humans a mere clockwork orange. As far back as 1931, Koestler was investigating psychometry with as much curiosity as he brought to his journalistic accounts of the exploding universe. His answer to the behaviorists is laid out in *The Ghost in the Machine,* and it is clearly a theological answer. Koestler implies here that evolution is purposive, hence the theological nature of his understanding of life. A problem remains, however; Koestler argues that the limbic system of the brain is at odds with its neocortex, resulting in irrational decisions much of the time. Humans are thus as likely to speed to their own destruction as they are to their fulfillment. Koestler's unorthodox answer to humans' Manichaean internal struggle is deliberate mutation by chemical agents. The same topic is fictionalized quite successfully in *The Call Girls*.

The Gladiators · Koestler's first novel, *The Gladiators*, was written in German and translated into English by Edith Simon (his later novels were published in his own English). The source of the novel is the sketchy account–fewer than four thousand words all together–of the Slave War of 73-71 B.C.E. found in Livy, Plutarch, Appian, and Florus. Koestler divides his narrative into four books. The first, entitled "Rise," imagines the revolt led by the Thracian gladiator Spartacus and a fat, cruel Gaul named Crixus. They march through Campania looting and adding more defectors to their band. In book 2, "The Law of Detours," after the destruction of the towns Nola, Suessula, and Calatia, the rebels are twenty thousand strong, or more, and approaching the peak of their power. The unruly faction, however, has spoiled the movement's idealism by its ransacking of these towns, and Spartacus is faced with a decision: Should he let this group go blindly into a foolhardy battle with the forces of the Roman general Varinius, or should he counsel them and enforce a policy of prudence? In his deliberations he is aided by a wise Essene, a type of the imminent Christ, who tells him that of all God's curses on man, "the worst curse of all is that he must tread the evil road for the sake of the good and right, that he must make detours and walk crookedly so that he may reach the straight goal." He further tells Spartacus that for what the leader wants to do now, he needs other counselors.

Despite the Essene's warning, Spartacus follows the "law of detours." Later that night, he confers with Crixus, and although no details of their talk are given, it is clear that Crixus is going to lead the lawless to their unwitting deaths in a confrontation with Varinius. This sacrifice of the unruly faction, however justified, is a cynical detour from honor. Later, however, when the Thracian Spartacus, already pressed by food shortages in the Sun State after a double cross by the neighboring city, is faced with a rebellion against his policies by the Celts, he proves to be insufficiently ruthless: He still retains the idealism with which he began the revolution. Koestler sums it up in his 1965 postscript: "Yet he shrinks from taking the last step–the purge by crucifixion of the dissident Celts and the establishment of a ruthless tyranny; and through this refusal he dooms his revolution to defeat." Book 3, "The Sun State," recounts the conflicts that lead up to Spartacus's defeat, and the gladiators' humiliation and crucifixion are narrated in book 4, "Decline." Although Koestler's characters are wooden, *The Gladiators* is a satisfying historical novel; the milieu is well sketched, and Spartacus's dilemmas are rendered convincingly.

Darkness at Noon · *Darkness at Noon*, Koestler's masterpiece, is the story of an old Bolshevik, Rubashov, who is called before his Communist inquisitors on charges of heresy against the Party. He is interrogated first by Ivanov, who is himself executed, and then by Gletkin, and at the end he is killed by the inevitable bullet in the back of the neck. The novel is divided into three sections, one for each hearing Rubashov is given, and a short epilogue entitled "The Grammatical Fiction." Besides the confrontations between Rubashov and his questioners, there are flashbacks from Rubashov's past and extracts from his diary; the latter provide occasions for Koestler's meditations on history. The narrative is tight and fast moving, and its lucid exposition has surely made it one of the most satisfyingly pedagogic novels of all time. Many readers shared the experience of Leslie Fiedler, who referred to *Darkness at Noon* in his review of *The Ghost in the Machine*, admitting that "Koestler helped to deliver me from the platitudes of the Thirties, from those organized self-deceptions which, being my first, were especially dear and difficult to escape."

Speaking of the "historical circumstances" of *Darkness at Noon*, Koestler explains that Rubashov is "a synthesis of the lives of a number of men who were victims of the so-called Moscow Trials." Rubashov's thinking is closest to that of Nikolai Bukharin, a real purge victim, and Rubashov's tormentor, Gletkin, had a counterpart of sorts in the actual trial prosecutor Andrei Vishinsky. (Robert Conquest's *The Great Terror*, 1968, provides useful details of the real trials.)

Two main theses are argued in *Darkness at Noon:* that the end does not justify the means; and that the individual ego, the *I,* is not a mere "grammatical fiction" whose outline is blurred by the sweep of the historical dialectic. The events that cause Rubashov great pain and guilt involve two party workers whose devotion is sacrificed to the law of detours. Little Loewy is the local leader of the dockworkers' section of the Party in Belgium, a likable man whom Rubashov takes to immediately. Little Loewy is a good Communist, but he is ill used by the Party and eventually destroyed in an act of expediency. When the Party calls for the workers to resist the spreading Nazi menace, Little Loewy's dockworkers refuse to handle cargoes going out from and coming into Germany. The crisis comes when five cargo ships from Russia arrive in the port. The workers start to unload these boats until they discover the contents: badly needed materials for the German war effort. The workers strike, the Party orders them back to the docks, and most of the workers defect. Two years later, Mussolini ventures into Africa, and again a boycott is called, but this time Rubashov is sent in advance to explain to the dockworkers that more Russian cargo is on its way and the Party wants it unloaded. Little Loewy rejects the duplicity, and six days later he hangs himself.

In another tragedy of betrayal, Rubashov abandons his secretary, Arlova, a woman who loves him and with whom he has had an affair. When Arlova's brother in Russia marries a foreigner, they all come under suspicion, Arlova included. Soon after, she is called back to oblivion in Russia, and all of this happens without a word from Rubashov. As these perfidies run through his mind, Rubashov's toothache rages intensely. Ivanov senses Rubashov's human sympathies and lectures him on the revolutionary ethic: "But you must allow that we are as convinced that you and they would mean the end of the Revolution as you are of the reverse. That is the essential point. The methods follow by logical deduction. We can't afford to lose ourselves in political subtleties." Thus, Rubashov's allegiance to the law of detours leads him into a moral labyrinth. He fails to heed that small voice that gives dignity to the self in its resistance to the degrading impersonality of all-devouring history and the behaviorist conception of human beings.

Arrival and Departure · In *Arrival and Departure*, Koestler's third novel, Peter Slavek, twenty-two, stows away on a freighter coming from Eastern Europe and washes up in Neutralia (Portugal) in 1940. He is a former Communist who has been tortured by Fascists in his home country, and he is faced in Neutralia with four possibilities: reunion with the Party, with whom he is disillusioned; joining the Fascists, who present themselves as the shapers of the true brave new world; flight to America; or, finally, enlistment with the British, whose culture is maimed but still represents a "brake" on the madness overtaking Europe. Homeless and confused, he meets two women. Dr. Sonia Bolgar, a native of his country and friend of his family, gives him a room and looks after him while she is waiting for the visa that will take her to America. Her lover, Odette, is a young French war widow with whom Peter has a brief affair until Odette leaves for America. Her departure precipitates a psychosomatic paralysis of one of Peter's legs, symbolic of the paralysis of will brought on by his conflicting urges to follow her and to commit himself again to political action. Sonia, who is an analyst and reduces all behavior to the terms of her profession, leads Peter through a deconstruction of his motives that exposes their origins in childhood guilt feelings. His self-insight cures his paralysis, just as his visa for America is granted. He prepares to leave, but at the last moment he dashes off the ship and joins the British, who parachute him back into his own country in their service.

Much of *Arrival and Departure* is artistically inert, but it does have a solid point to make. Although Fyodor Dostoevski's name is never mentioned in *Arrival and Departure*, the novel is Koestler's response to Dostoevski's *The Possessed* (1871-1872), which depicts revolutionaries as warped personalities, dramatizing their neuroses and grudges in political action. For Koestler, human motives are more complex:

> "You can explain the messages of the Prophets as epileptical foam and the Sistine Madonna as the projection of an incestuous dream. The method is correct and the picture in itself complete. But beware of the arrogant error of believing that it is the only one."

Arrival and Departure is, then, a subtle commentary on the motivation of revolutionaries, rejecting any claims to exclusivity by psychoanalysis and psychobiography.

Thieves in the Night · A far more absorbing novel than *Arrival and Departure, Thieves in the Night* is an account of the establishment of the commune of Ezra's Tower in Palestine. Many of the events are seen from the perspective of one of the commune's settlers, a young man named Joseph who was born and educated in England. His father was Jewish, his mother English, and this mixed heritage justifies Koestler's use of him as a voice to meditate on the Jewish character and the desirability of assimilation. As a novelistic study of a single character, *Thieves in the Night* is incomplete, but as a depiction of the personal tensions within a commune and as an essay on the international politics wracking Palestine in the period from 1937 to 1939, it is excellent. The British policy formulated in the 1939 White Paper is exposed in all its cruelty. This policy—perhaps influenced by romantic conceptions of the Arab world—shut down the flow of immigrants into Palestine, leaving the Jews exposed and helpless in Europe. At the novel's end, Joseph has joined the terrorist movement and is engaged in smuggling Polish Jews off the Romanian cattle boats that are forbidden to unload their homeless cargo. In its musings on terrorism, *Thieves in the Night* seems to back off from the repudiation of the doctrine that the end justifies the means. Koestler always faced these issues honestly, and *Thieves in the Night* is as engrossing—and as cogent—in the twenty-first century as it was in 1946.

The Age of Longing · Published in 1951 and set in Paris in the mid-1950's, *The Age of Longing* describes a time of spiritual disillusionment and longing for an age of faith. The narrative opens on Bastille Day and focuses on three characters: Hydie, a young American apostate from Catholicism, who kneels on her prie-dieu and laments, "LET ME BELIEVE IN SOMETHING"; Fedya Nikitin, a security officer with a rigid commissar mentality; and Julien Delattre, poet and former Party member. The relationship between Hydie and Fedya occupies much of the novel, with Hydie's ache for religious solace played off against Fedya's unquestioning faith in Communism. Hydie is American, naïve, and innocent; she is seeking experience on which to base faith. Fedya is the son of proletarian revolutionaries from Baku, Azerbaijan, a son of the Revolution with the instincts of a true commissar. He seems to have been programmed with Party clichés. When the two become lovers, Fedya humiliates Hydie by treating her as a mere collocation of conditioned responses. She then turns against Fedya and, finally understanding his true assignment as a spy, tries to shoot him but botches the job. Regardless of whether their relationship has allegorical significance, the unfeeling commissar is one of Koestler's most effective characterizations. At one point, Fedya asks a young school friend why she likes him, and the answer is, "Because you are clean and simple and hard like an effigy of 'Our Proletarian Youth' from a propaganda poster."

The third main character, Julien Delattre, is in many ways Koestler's self-portrait. Delattre has given up his allegiance to the "God that failed," and he tells Hydie that "My generation turned to Marx as one swallows acid drops to fight off nausea." He finds his mission in warning others about the ideological traps that he has successfully escaped, and one of the best scenes in the novel comes when he takes Hydie to an evening meeting of the Rally for Peace and Progress. The centerpiece of the session is Koestler's satirical depiction of Jean-Paul Sartre, who appears as the pompous theoretician Professor Pontieux. Author of a fashionable work of postwar despair, "Negation and Position," Professor Pontieux "can prove everything he believes, and he believes everything he can prove." *The Age of Longing* ends with an image appropriate to its theme. A funeral party is proceeding past the graves of Jean de La Fontaine, Victor Hugo, and others when air-raid sirens start screaming. "The siren wailed, but nobody was sure: it could have meant the Last Judgment, or just another air-raid exercise."

The Call Girls · More than twenty years passed between the publication of *The Age of Longing* and that of *The Call Girls*, Koestler's last novel. During those two decades, Koestler's interests had shifted from ideology to science and human behavior. The "call girls" of the title are prominent intellectuals—mostly scientists but including a poet and a priest—nomads of the international conference circuit. Koestler puts them all together in a Swiss mountain setting and sets them to talking about ideas. They have been summoned by one of their members, Nikolai Solovief, a physicist, to consider "approaches to survival" and to send a message to the president of the United States. Unfortunately, the meeting degenerates into a series of uncompromising exchanges between behaviorists and nonbehaviorists. Only Nikolai and Tony, the priest, are able to accommodate themselves to the claims of both reason and faith, and rancor replaces the objective search for truth. *The Call Girls* is an entertaining exposition of the various options available to those seeking enlightenment today. Readers of *The Ghost in the Machine* and Koestler's work on ESP will recognize in the arguments of Nikolai and Tony those of Koestler himself. Koestler always staged his intellectual dramas in the dress of irreconcilable opposites—the Yogi and the Commissar, ends versus means—and here the protagonist is clearly spirit and the antagonist matter. His call girls demonstrate that there is still life in this old conflict.

Frank Day

Other major works

PLAY: *Twilight Bar: An Escapade in Four Acts*, pb. 1945.

NONFICTION: *Spanish Testament*, 1937; *Scum of the Earth*, 1941; *Dialogue with Death*, 1942; *The Yogi and the Commissar and Other Essays*, 1945; *Promise and Fulfillment: Palestine, 1917-1949*, 1949; *Insight and Outlook: An Inquiry into the Common Foundations of Science, Art, and Social Ethics*, 1949; *Arrow in the Blue: The First Volume of an Autobiography, 1905-1931*, 1952; *The Invisible Writing: The Second Volume of an Autobiography, 1932-1940*, 1954; *Trial of the Dinosaur and Other Essays*, 1955; *Reflections on Hanging*, 1956; *The Sleepwalkers: A History of Man's Changing Vision of the Universe*, 1959; *The Lotus and the Robot*, 1960; *Hanged by the Neck: An Exposure of Capital Punishment in England*, 1961 (with C. H. Rolph); *The Act of Creation*, 1964; *The Ghost in the Machine*, 1967; *The Case of the Midwife Toad*, 1971; *The Roots of Coincidence*, 1972; *The Challenge of Chance: Experiments and Speculations*, 1973 (with Sir Alister Hardy and Robert Harvie); *The Heel of Achilles: Essays, 1968-1973*, 1974; *The Thirteenth Tribe*, 1976; *Life After Death*, 1976 (with Arthur Toynbee, et al.); *Janus: A Summing Up*, 1978; *Bricks to Babel: Selected Writings with Comments*, 1981.

EDITED TEXTS: *Suicide of a Nation? An Enquiry into the State of Britain Today*, 1963; *Drinkers of Infinity: Essays, 1955-1967*, 1968 (with J. R. Smythies); *Beyond Reductionism: New Perspectives in the Life Sciences*, 1969 (with Smythies).

Bibliography

Cesarani, David. *Arthur Koestler: The Homeless Mind.* London: William Heinemann, 1998. A good examination of the writer and his works. Includes bibliographical references and an index.

Day, Frank. *Arthur Koestler: A Guide to Research.* New York: Garland, 1987. In addition to a listing of Koestler's publications, there are 518 entries for writings about him, many of them from newspapers and journals. Includes some foreign-language items, and the latest materials are from 1985.

Hamilton, Iain. *Koestler: A Biography.* New York: Macmillan, 1982. This lengthy biography, favorable to Koestler, is arranged year by year in the fashion of a chronicle and breaks off around 1970. Many events have been retold partly on the basis of interviews, Koestler's papers, and firsthand accounts.

Harris, Harold, ed. *Astride the Two Cultures: Arthur Koestler at Seventy.* London: Hutchinson University Library, 1975. This collection of essays by authors sympathetic to Koestler provides approximately equal coverage of the writer's involvement in literary and in scientific concerns.

Levene, Mark. *Arthur Koestler.* New York: Frederick Ungar, 1984. Koestler's own life is discussed in the first chapter, and his major literary works are considered in detail, but relatively little attention is given to his scientific writings. The chronology and bibliography are useful.

Pearson, Sidney A., Jr. *Arthur Koestler.* Boston: Twayne, 1978. Although a bit sketchy on matters of biography, this work deals with basic issues in Koestler's writings and has some trenchant and interesting discussion of political themes. Also helpful are the chronology and a selected annotated bibliography.

Perez, Jane, and Wendell Aycock, eds. *The Spanish Civil War in Literature.* Lubbock: Texas Tech University Press, 1990. Contains Peter I. Barta's essay "The Writing of History: Authors Meet on the Soviet-Spanish Border," which provides an excellent grounding in the political history from which Koestler's fiction evolved.

Sperber, Murray A., ed. *Arthur Koestler: A Collection of Critical Essays.* Englewood Cliffs,

N.J.: Prentice-Hall, 1977. Both positive and negative reactions appear in this fine sampling of critical work about Koestler's literary and scientific writings. Among those commentators represented by excerpts here are George Orwell, Saul Bellow, Edmund Wilson, Stephen Spender, and A. J. Ayer, as well as others. A chronology and bibliography have also been included.

Sterne, Richard Clark. *Dark Mirror: The Sense of Injustice in Modern European and American Literature.* New York: Fordham University Press, 1994. Contains a substantial discussion of *Darkness at Noon.*

D. H. Lawrence

Born: Eastwood, Nottinghamshire, England; September 11, 1885
Died: Vence, France; March 2, 1930

Principal long fiction · *The White Peacock,* 1911; *The Trespasser,* 1912; *Sons and Lovers,* 1913; *The Rainbow,* 1915; *Women in Love,* 1920; *The Lost Girl,* 1920; *Aaron's Rod,* 1922; *The Ladybird, The Fox, The Captain's Doll,* 1923; *Kangaroo,* 1923; *The Boy in the Bush,* 1924 (with M. L. Skinner); *The Plumed Serpent,* 1926; *Lady Chatterley's Lover,* 1928; *The Escaped Cock,* 1929 (best known as *The Man Who Died*); *The Virgin and the Gipsy,* 1930; *Mr. Noon,* 1984 (wr. 1920-1922).

Other literary forms · D. H. Lawrence was among the most prolific and wide-ranging of modern writers, a fact all the more remarkable considering that he spent so much time on the move, battling chronic tuberculosis, which cut short his life in his forty-fifth year. In addition to his novels, he published more than a dozen books of poetry, collected in *The Complete Poems of D. H. Lawrence* (1964); eight volumes of short fiction, including half a dozen novellas, collected in *The Complete Short Stories of D. H. Lawrence* (1961); and seven plays, collected in *The Complete Plays of D. H. Lawrence* (1965). He also wrote a wide range of nonfiction, including four fine travel books (*Twilight in Italy,* 1916; *Sea and Sardinia,* 1921; *Mornings in Mexico,* 1927; and *Etruscan Places,* 1932). *Movements in European History* (1921), published under the pseudonym Lawrence H. Davison, is a subjective meditation on historical cycles and Europe's decline, while *Psychoanalysis and the Unconscious* (1921) is a highly original and influential volume of literary criticism. Lawrence's religious vision, in the guise of a commentary on the Book of Revelation, is offered in *Apocalypse* (1931). Many other essays on diverse subjects appeared in periodicals during the last two decades of his life and were collected posthumously by Edward McDonald in *Phoenix* (1936), and by Warren Roberts and Harry T. Moore in *Phoenix II* (1968). Lawrence was also a formidable correspondent, and his letters are invaluable aids to understanding the man and the writer. Some 1,257 of the more than 5,500 known letters are available in a collection edited by Harry T. Moore. Several of Lawrence's fictional works—*Sons and Lovers, Lady Chatterley's Lover,* "The Rocking-Horse Winner," *Women in Love,* and *The Virgin and the Gipsy*—have been adapted to the motion picture medium, while his life is the subject of the 1981 film *The Priest of Love.*

Achievements · The running battle against censorship in which Lawrence engaged throughout most of his career undoubtedly performed a valuable service to subsequent writers and the reading public, though it cost him dearly both emotionally and financially. The essentially symbolic role of sexuality in his writing resembles some-what that found in Walt Whitman's, but Lawrence's more overt treatment of it— liberating as it was to a generation whose Victorian upbringing had been castigated by the Freudians—led to a general misunderstanding of his work that persisted for almost three decades after his death. The thirty-year suppression of *Lady Chatterley's Lover* backfired, as censorship so often does, attracting the public's attention to the object of the prohibition. Unfortunately this notoriety made the novel, far from

Courtesy D.C. Public Library

Lawrence's greatest, the one most commonly associated with his name in the popular mind. His reputation among more serious readers was not helped by the series of sensationalistic memoirs published by some of his more ardent followers in the 1930's and early 1940's. Championed as a prophet of free love and utopianism, repudiated as a crazed homosexual and protofascist, Lawrence the artist all but disappeared from view.

The appearance of several serious and sympathetic studies of Lawrence in the middle and late 1950's, by presenting a more accurate record of his life and a more discriminating assessment of his work, largely succeeded in salvaging Lawrence's stature as a major writer. Among those most responsible for the Lawrence revival were F. R. Leavis, Harry T. Moore, Edward Nehls, and Grahm Hough. Subsequent readers have been able to recognize more readily in the best of Lawrence's work what Leavis described as its "marked moral intensity," its "reverent openness before life."

In addition to his prophetic themes, Lawrence's technical innovations are now acknowledged as among the most important in modern fiction. He could convey a "ripping yarn" and portray lifelike characters when he chose, and parts of *Sons and Lovers* and *The Lost Girl,* among many other works, demonstrate his mastery of traditional realism in the representation of his native Midlands. More fundamentally, however, Lawrence's novels are triumphs of mood and sensibility; they seek (as Frank Kermode has said) less to represent life than to enact it. He has no peer in the evocative rendering of place, introducing poetic symbols that carry the meaning without losing sight of their basis in intensely observed, concrete details. His approach to characterization following *The Rainbow* was unconventional in that he avoided "the old stable ego" and pattern-imposed character types in an effort to go beneath the rational and articulate levels of consciousness to the nonhuman being in his characters. As Walter Allen has observed, for Lawrence "the value of people . . . consisted in how far mystery resided in them, how far they were conscious of mystery." The linear, cause-and-effect development of characters controlled by the rational intellect was for him a hindrance. He focused instead on the surging, dynamic forces—sexual impulses, the potency of nature and animals, the terrible allure of death—which in their purest form defy rationality and are communicated by a kind of unmediated intuition. His prose style was similarly subjective in emphasis. The frequent repetitiveness and inflated rhetoric can be tiresome, but at its best the prose is supple and sensuous, its dynamic rhythms incantatory, a powerful vehicle of Lawrence's vision. Further, he avoided the neat resolution of closure of traditional narratives, typically preferring the "open end" in which the vital forces operating in his characters are felt to be continuously and dynamically in process rather than subdued by the authorial imposition of finality. His comment on the bustling activities of Indian peasants on market day, in *Mornings in Mexico*, epitomizes his fictional method as well as his vitalist doctrine: "In everything, the shimmer of creation and never the finality of the created."

Lawrence's approach to fiction involved considerable risks, and many of his novels are seriously flawed. There are those who cannot read him at all. Nevertheless, the integrity of his vision and the sheer power with which he communicated it have made E. M. Forster's estimate (written shortly after Lawrence's death) stand up: "He was the greatest imaginative novelist of his generation."

Biography · David Herbert Lawrence was born on September 11, 1885, in the Midlands coal-mining village of Ad, Nottinghamshire. The noise and grime of the pits dominated Eastwood, but the proximity of fabled Sherwood Forest was a living reminder of what Lawrence would later call "the old England of the forest and agricultural past" upon which industrialization had been so rudely imposed. The contrast was to remain an essential element in his makeup. Allied to it was the equally sharp contrast between his parents. Arthur John Lawrence, the father, had worked in the coal pits from the age of seven. Coarse, semiliterate, intensely physical, a hail-fellow popular with his collier mates, he was prone to drink and to near poverty. Lydia (née Beardsall) Lawrence, his wife, was a former schoolteacher from a pious middle-class Methodist family, which counted among its forebears a noted composer of Wesleyan hymns. Along with his four siblings, young Lawrence was inevitably caught up in the frequent and sometimes violent strife between his mother and father. Delicate and sickly as a child, he could scarcely have emulated his father—not that he was inclined to do so. Instead, he sided with his mother. She in turn doted on him and encouraged him in his studies as a means of escape from the working-class life, thus further alienating him from his father. Only in later life would Lawrence come to see the dangerous liabilities of this overweening maternal bond and the counterbalancing attractiveness of his father's unassuming strength and vitality.

Lawrence was an outstanding student in school and at the age of twelve won a scholarship to Nottingham High School. After graduation in 1901, he worked for three unhappy months as a clerk in a surgical-appliance factory in Nottingham, until he fell seriously ill with pneumonia. About this time, he met Jessie Chambers, whose family lived on a small farm outside Eastwood. Over the next ten years his close relationship with the "spiritual" Jessie (the "Miriam" of *Sons and Lovers*) and her sympathetic family offered further stimulus to his fondness for the beauties of nature, for reading, and for ideas; eventually, with Jessie's encouragement and partial collaboration, he began to write stories and verse. The Chamberses' way of life and the bucolic scenery of Haggs farm, so tellingly unlike the ambience of Lawrence's own home, would later provide him with materials for his first novel, *The White Peacock*. After his prolonged convalescence from pneumonia, in 1903 he found a position as a "pupil-teacher" at an elementary school in nearby Ilkeston, Derbyshire. Two years there were followed by a third as an uncertified teacher in the Eastwood British School. In 1906, having won a King's Scholarship competition, he began a two-year course of study for his teachers' certificate at Nottingham University College. By 1908, he qualified to teach at Davidson Road School, a boys' elementary school in the London suburb of Croydon, where he remained until 1911.

Meanwhile Lawrence had published several poems in 1909 in the *English Review*, edited by Ford Madox Hueffer (later Ford), who introduced him to such established writers as H. G. Wells, Ezra Pound, and William Butler Yeats. Soon Lawrence was busily working at two novels, *The White Peacock* and the autobiographical *Paul Morel* (the working title of *Sons and Lovers*). While the former was still in press in December, 1910, his mother died of cancer, an event whose profound impact on him is duly commemorated in his poems and in *Paul Morel*, which he had already begun to rewrite. By this time his relationship with Jessie Chambers had diminished considerably, and he had had several brief affairs with other women. His ill health and his increasing commitment to writing (*The Trespasser*, his second novel, was to appear the following year) induced him to forgo teaching in the winter of 1911-1912. Back in Eastwood, in April, he met and fell in love with Frieda von Richthoven Weekley, the high-spirited daughter of a German baron, wife of a professor of philology at Nottingham University, and at thirty-two the mother of three small children. In May, Lawrence and Frieda eloped to the Continent. There, for the next six months, Lawrence wrote poems, stories, travel sketches (most of which were later collected in *Twilight in Italy*), and his final revision of the autobiographical novel. This writing, particularly the metamorphosis of *Paul Morel* into *Sons and Lovers* (with which Frieda assisted him by discussing her own maternal feelings and the theories of Freud), marked the true beginning of Lawrence's artistic maturity.

The advent of World War I coincided with what in many ways was the most crucial period of his development as a writer. By the end of 1914, Lawrence and Frieda had married, the critical success of *Sons and Lovers* had established his reputation, he had formed important associations with Edward Garnett, John Middleton Murry, and Katherine Mansfield, and he had begun to work on what many now consider his greatest novels, *The Rainbow* and *Women in Love* (originally conceived as a single work, *The Sisters*). Yet the triumph that might have been his soon turned to ashes. The official suppression of *The Rainbow* in November, 1916–the charge of "immorality" was leveled on both political and sexual grounds–was followed by a series of nightmarish episodes in which, largely because of Frieda's German origins, the Lawrences were hounded and persecuted as supposed enemy spies. Lawrence was reviled in the "patriotic" English press, and, after *The Rainbow* fiasco, in which many of his literary associates had failed to come to his defense, he found it increasingly difficult to publish his work and hence to make a living. Though he completed *Women in Love* in 1917, it did not appear until 1920 in the United States. Events seemed to conspire against him so that, by the end of the war, he could never again feel at home in his native land. This bitter severance motivated the "savage pilgrimage" that dominated the last decade of his life, driving him feverishly around the globe in search of some "ideal centre" in which to live and work in hope for the future.

Lawrence's travels were as much spiritual as geographical in character, and his quest became the primary focus of his writing after the war. The more than two years he spent in Italy and Sicily (1919-1921) provided him with the materials for the concluding chapters of *The Lost Girl* (which he had begun before the war and set aside to work on *The Sisters*) and for *Aaron's Rod*. Heading for America by way of Asia, the Lawrences briefly visited Ceylon and then Australia, where he wrote *Kangaroo* in just six weeks. In September, 1922, they arrived in the United States and soon settled near Taos, New Mexico, on a mountain ranch that was to be "home" for them during most of the next three years. Here Lawrence rewrote *Studies in Classic American Literature* (1923; begun in 1917) and produced such important works as "Eagle in New Mexico" and "Spirits Summoned West" (poems), "The Woman Who Rode Away," "The Princess," "St. Mawr," and half of the travel sketches that form *Mornings in Mexico*. During this period Lawrence also made three trips to Mexico, staying there a total of about ten months; his travel experiences, embellished by his rather extensive readings in Aztec history and archaeology, provided the sources for his novel of Mexico, *The Plumed Serpent*, his most ambitious creative undertaking of the postwar years. On the day he finished the novel in Oaxaca, he fell gravely ill with acute tuberculosis and nearly died. After convalescing in Mexico City and on the ranch in New Mexico, he returned with Frieda to Europe in the late fall of 1925, settling first in Spotorno on the Italian Riviera and later in a villa outside Florence.

Lawrence's last years were clouded by the inevitable encroachment of his disease, but he remained remarkably active. He toured the ancient Etruscan ruins; took up painting, producing some strikingly original works; and wrote three complete versions of what would become, in its final form, his most famous novel, *Lady Chatterley's Lover*. The book's banning and confiscation in 1928, reviving the old outcry of "obscenity," prompted several of his most eloquent essays on the subject of pornography and censorship. It was his final battle, save that which could not be won. Lawrence died in Vence, France, on March 2, 1930, at the age of forty-four.

Analysis · D. H. Lawrence occupies an ambiguous position with respect to James Joyce, Marcel Proust, T. S. Eliot, and the other major figures of the modernist movement. While, on the one hand, he shared their feelings of gloom about the degeneration of modern European life and looked to ancient mythologies for proto-types of the rebirth all saw as necessary, on the other he keenly distrusted the modernists' veneration of traditional culture and their classicist aesthetics. The mod-ernist ideal of art as "an escape from personality," as a finished and perfected creation sufficient unto itself, was anathema to Lawrence, who once claimed that his motto was not art for art's sake but "art for my sake." For him, life and art were intertwined, both expressions of the same quest: "To be alive, to be man alive, to be whole man alive: that is the point." The novel realized its essential function best when it embodied and vitally enacted the novelist's mercurial sensibility. His spontaneity, his limitations and imperfections, and his fleeting moments of intuition were directly transmitted to the reader, whose own "instinct for life" would be thereby quickened. Lawrence believed that at its best "the novel, and the novel supremely," could and should perform this important task. That is why he insisted that the novel is "the one bright book of life." One way of approaching his own novels–and the most significant, by general consen-sus, are *Sons and Lovers, The Rainbow, Women in Love, The Plumed Serpent*, and *Lady Chatterley's Lover*–is to consider the extent to which the form and content of each in turn rises to this vitalist standard.

To be "whole man alive," for Lawrence, involved first of all the realization of *wholeness*. The great enemy of human (and of aesthetic) wholeness, he believed, was modern life itself. Industrialization had cut man off from the past, had mechanized his daily life and transformed human relations into a power struggle to acquire material commodities, thereby alienating man from contact with the divine potency residing in both nature and other men and women. Modern Europe was therefore an accumulation of dead or dying husks, fragmented and spiritually void, whose inevi-table expression was mass destruction. For Lawrence, World War I was the apotheosis of modernization.

Yet contemporary history provided only the end result of a long process of atomization and dispersion whose seeds lay in ancient prehistory. In *Fantasia of the Unconscious* (1922), Lawrence formulated a myth of origins that sheds light on his quest for wholeness in his travels among "primitive" peoples as well as in his novels. He describes a kind of golden age before the flood, when the pagan world, both geo-graphically and culturally, was a single, unified entity. This *Ur*-culture, unlike the modern fragmented age, had developed a holistic knowledge or "science in terms of life." The primal wisdom did not differentiate among body, mind, and spirit; the objective and the subjective were one, as the reason and the passions were one; man and nature and the cosmos lived in harmonious relation with one another. Men and women all over the earth shared this knowledge. They "wandered back and forth from Atlantis to the Polynesian Continent. . . . The interchange was complete, and knowl-edge, science, was universal over the earth." Then the glaciers melted, whole conti-nents were drowned, and the monolithic world fragmented into isolated races, each developing its own culture, its own "science." A few refugees from the lost continents fled to the high ground of Europe, Asia, and America. There they "refused to forget, but taught the old wisdom, only in its half-forgotten, symbolic forms. More or less forgotten, as knowledge: remembered as ritual, gesture, and myth-story."

In modern Europe, even these vestiges of the old universal knowledge had largely become extinct, and with them died what was left of the unitary being of man. First Christianity, with its overemphasis on bodiless spirituality, and then modern science, with its excessive dependence upon finite reason as the instrument of control over a merely mechanistic world, had killed it. After the war Lawrence hoped, in traveling to lands where Christianity, modern science, and industrialization had not yet fully taken hold, to uncover the traces of the primal knowledge, if only "in its half-forgotten, symbolic forms." By somehow establishing a vital contact with "primitive" men and women and fusing his "white consciousness" with their "dark-blood consciousness," he hoped to usher in the next phase in the development of the human race. His novels would sound the clarion call—awakening the primordial memory by means of "ritual, gesture, and myth-story"—summoning "whole man alive" to cross over the threshold into the New World of regenerated being.

Although this myth of apocalypse and rebirth was fully articulated during Lawrence's "wander years" after the war, it was clearly anticipated in his earlier works. There the horror of the modern world's "drift toward death" and the yearning for some "holy ground" on which to begin anew were keenly felt. The initial experience of fragmentation in Lawrence's life was obviously the primal conflict between his mother and father, which among other things resulted in a confusion in his own sexual identity. In the fiction of this period, the stunting of life by fragmentation and imbalance is evident in the portrayal of such characters as Miriam Leivers in *Sons and Lovers*, Anton Skrebensky in *The Rainbow*, and Gerald Crich in *Women in Love*, just as the quest for vital wholeness is exemplified in the same novels by Paul Morel, Ursula Brangwen, and Rupert Birkin, respectively. If the secondary characters in Lawrence's novels tend in general to be static types seen from without, his protagonists, beginning with Ursula in *The Rainbow* and continuing through Constance Chatterley in *Lady Chatterley's Lover*, are anything but static. Rather, they are volatile, inconsistent, and sometimes enigmatic. In *The Plumed Serpent*, Kate Leslie vacillates between intellectual abstraction and immediate sensuous experience; between egotistic willfulness and utter self-abandonment to another; between withdrawal behind the boundaries of the safe and the known, and the passionate yearning for metamorphosis; and so on. There is a constant ebb and flow in Kate's behavior, even a rough circularity, that creates a spontaneous, improvisatory feeling in her narrative. Lawrence's protagonists are always in flux, realizing by turns the various aspects of their natures, and this dynamism is largely what makes them so alive. They are open to life: in themselves, in their natural environment, and in other vital human beings.

Lawrence believed that the novel was the one form of human expression malleable enough to articulate and dramatize the dynamic process of living. In his essay "Why the Novel Matters," he celebrates the novelist's advantage over the saint, the scientist, and the philosopher, all of whom deal only with parts of the composite being of humankind. The novelist alone, says Lawrence, is capable of rendering the whole of "man alive." He alone, by so doing, "can make the whole man alive [that is, the reader] tremble."

The priestly or prophetic function of the novelist is clearly central to this aesthetic doctrine. Lawrence is one of the very few modern writers to assume this role and to do so explicitly. At times, this very explicitness becomes problematic. His novels are quite uneven; most are marred in varying degrees by a hectoring didacticism that is less evident in his short fiction. Nevertheless, he needed the amplitude of an extended narrative to give voice to the several sides of his complex sensibility, as if to discover himself in the process. Perhaps that, as much as anything else, was the object of his quest. Collectively his novels represent a restless search for a form capable of rendering that sensibility fully and honestly.

Sons and Lovers · In a letter written a few months after the publication of *Sons and Lovers*, Lawrence made an admission which suggests that "art for my sake" could have been a cathartic as well as a heuristic function. "One sheds one's sickness in books," he wrote, "repeats and presents one's emotions, to be master of them." *Sons and Lovers*, his third novel, was the work that enabled Lawrence to come to terms, at least provisionally, with the traumas of his formative years. The more than two years he spent working and reworking the book amounted to an artistic and psychological rite of passage essential to his development as a man and as a writer.

The novel spans the first twenty-six years in the life of Paul Morel. Because of the obvious similarities between Paul's experiences and Lawrence's, and because the story in part concerns Paul's apprenticeship as an artist–or, more accurately, the obstacles he must overcome to be an artist–the novel has been seen as an example of a subspecies of the *Bildungsroman*, the *Künstlerroman*. Comparison with James Joyce's *Portrait of the Artist as a Young Man* (1916) suggests, however, how loosely the term applies to Lawrence's novel. Where Joyce scrupulously selects only those scenes and episodes of Stephen Dedalus's life that directly contribute to the young artist's development (his first use of language, his schooling, his imaginative transcendence of sex, religion, and politics, his aesthetic theories), Lawrence's focus is far more diffuse. The novel opens with a conventional set-piece description of the town of Bestwood (modeled on Eastwood) as it has been affected by the arrival and growth of the mining industry during the last half century. This is followed by an account of the courtship and early married life of Walter and Gertrude Morel, Paul's parents. Even after Paul's birth, the main emphasis remains for many chapters on the mother and father, and considerable space is devoted to their first child, William, whose sudden death and funeral conclude part 1 of the novel. Paul's interest in drawing is mentioned halfway through part 1, but it is not a major concern until he becomes friends with Miriam Leivers in part 2, and there the companionship itself actually receives more attention. Though the comparison does an injustice to the nature of Lawrence's real achievement in the novel, perhaps *Sons and Lovers* more nearly resembles *Stephen Hero* (1944), the earlier and more generally autobiographical version of Joyce's novel, than it does the tightly constructed *Portrait of the Artist as a Young Man.*

Yet, when in the late stages of revision Lawrence changed his title from *Paul Morel* to *Sons and Lovers*, his motive was akin to Joyce's when the Irishman discarded *Stephen Hero* and began to rewrite. The motive was form–form determined by a controlling idea. The subject of *Sons and Lovers* is not simply Paul's development but his development as an instance of the pattern suggested by the title; that pattern involves the Morels' unhappy marriage, the fateful experiences of Paul's brother William, Paul's frustrated relationship with Miriam, and his later encounters with Clara and Baxter Dawes, as well as Paul's own maturation. For Lawrence, the pattern clearly had wide application. Indeed, in a letter to Edward Garnett, his editor, written a few days after completing the revised novel, Lawrence claimed that his book sounded "the tragedy of thousands of young men in England."

This claim, along with the change in title and the late revisions designed to underscore a theme already present in the narrative, was probably influenced by the discussions that Lawrence and Frieda had in 1912 regarding Freud's theories, of which Frieda was then an enthusiastic proponent. (There is no evidence of Lawrence's awareness of Freud before this.) In a more general sense, the "tragedy" was rooted historically, as the novel shows, in the disruption of natural human relationships that was one of the by-products of modernization. Directly or indirectly, the characters in the novel are entrapped by the materialistic values of their society, unable even when they consciously reject those values to establish true contact with one another. Instead they tend to treat one another as objects to be possessed or manipulated for the purpose of self-gratification.

Thus Mrs. Morel, frustrated by her marriage to her coal-miner husband, transfers her affections to her sons, first to William, the eldest, and then to Paul after William's death. Walter Morel, the father, becomes a scapegoat and an outcast in his own home. Whether consciously or not, Mrs. Morel uses her sons as instruments to work out her own destiny vicariously, encouraging them in pursuits that will enable them to escape the socially confining life that she herself cannot escape, yet resenting it when the sons do begin to make a life away from her. Paul's fixation upon his mother–and his hatred of his father–contributes to a confusion of his sexual identity and to his inability to love girls his own age in a normal, healthy way. In the same letter to Edward Garnett, Lawrence characterized this inability to love as a "split," referring to the rupture in the son's natural passions caused by the mother's possessive love. The split causes Paul to seek out girls who perform the psychological role of mother-surrogates: Miriam, an exaggerated version of the spiritual, Madonna-like aspect of the mother image; and the buxom Clara Dawes, who from a Freudian viewpoint represents the "degraded sex-object," the fallen woman, equally a projection of the son's prohibited erotic desires for his mother. Because Paul's feeling for Miriam and Clara are thus compartmentalized and unbalanced, both relationships are unfulfilling, a fact which only reinforces his Oedipal bondage. At the same time, part of the responsibility for the unsatisfactory relationships belongs to Miriam and Clara themselves, both of whom exploit Paul to help them fulfill their own private fantasy lives. The world of *Sons and Lovers* is populated by isolated, fragmentary souls not unlike the inhabitants of T. S. Eliot's 1922 *The Waste Land* ("We think of the key, each in his prison/ Thinking of the key, each confirms a prison").

A decade after the appearance of *Sons and Lovers*, Lawrence declared that of all his books, it was the one he would like to rewrite, because in it he had treated his father unfairly. By then, of course, he was overtly committed to finding embodiments of "whole man alive" and, in retrospect, his father seemed to offer such an embodiment. When he wrote *Sons and Lovers*, however, he had not yet fully come to appreciate the importance of his father's unaffected male vitality. Although occasionally Walter Morel appears in a favorable light, the novel generally emphasizes his ineffectuality as a husband and father. The Oedipal conflict on which the story hinges perhaps made this unavoidable. In any event, the struggle to attain wholeness is centered in Paul Morel.

Because Paul's mother is "the pivot and pole of his life, from which he could not escape," her death amounts to the great crisis of the novel. The terrible spectacle of her agony as she lies dying slowly of cancer torments Paul until, by giving her an overdose of morphine, he commits a mercy killing. Unconsciously, the act seems to be motivated by his desire to release her from her debilitating "bondage" as wife and mother, the roles that have made her erotically unattainable to Paul. Her death is followed by an eerie, Poe-like scene in which the shaken Paul, momentarily imagining his mother as a beautiful young sleeping maiden, stoops and kisses her "passionately," as if to waken her like the handsome prince in a fairy tale, only to be horrified by her cold and unresponsive lips. It is a key moment, adumbrating as it does the writer's subsequent shift in allegiances to the "sensuous flame of life" associated with his father. For Paul, however, the loss of his mother induces a period of deep depression (interestingly enough, guilt is not mentioned) in which his uppermost desire is to reunite with his mother in death. This "drift towards death" was what Lawrence believed made Paul's story symptomatic of the times, "the tragedy of thousands of young men in England."

Nevertheless, the novel does not end tragically. Paul, on the verge of suicide, decides instead to turn his back on the "immense dark silence" where his lover/mother awaits him and to head toward the "faintly humming, glowing town"–and beyond it, to the Continent, where he plans to continue his artistic endeavors (just as Lawrence did). Some readers have found this last-minute turnabout implausible, a breakdown in the novel's form. Yet Lawrence anticipates Paul's "rebirth" by having him realize, after his mother's death, that he must finally sever his ties to both Miriam and Clara. For him to have returned to them then for consolation and affection would have meant that, inwardly, he was still cherishing some hope of preserving the maternal bond, even if only through his mother's unsatisfactory substitutes. When Paul effects a reconciliation between Clara and her estranged husband Baxter Dawes, who has been presented throughout in terms strongly reminiscent of Walter Morel, he is (as Daniel A. Weiss and others have observed) tacitly acting out a reversal of the original Oedipal conflict. If the primary emphasis of *Sons and Lovers* is on the tragic split in the emotional lives of the Morels, its conclusion finds Paul taking the steps necessary to begin to heal the split in himself. Only by so doing would Paul, like Lawrence, be able to undertake a quest for vital wholeness. That quest would become the chief subject of the novels following *Sons and Lovers.*

As sometimes happens to a writer after he has successfully struggled to transform autobiography into art, Lawrence reacted against *Sons and Lovers* almost as soon as he had finished it. The process of revaluating the influence of his parents, begun in his revisions of the novel and particularly evident in its concluding chapters, continued apace. His nonfiction of the period exhibits a growing hostility to women as spawners of intellectual and spiritual abstraction and the early traces of his interest in the reassertion of the vital male. Lawrence reacted also against certain aspects of the narrative technique used in *Sons and Lovers.* As he worked on his next novel, initially called *The Sisters*, he found that he was no longer interested in "visualizing" or "creating vivid scenes" in which characters revealed themselves through dramatic encounters and dialogue. The conventions of plot and the "furniture" of realistic exposition bored him. Moreover, the traditional methods of characterization were positively a hindrance to the kind of novel he felt he must write.

Lawrence had in fact embarked on a long and difficult struggle to create a new kind of novel, unprecedented in English fiction. When his publisher balked, Lawrence defended his experiment in an important letter that clarifies his intentions not only in what would eventually become *The Rainbow* and *Women in Love* but in most of his subsequent fiction:

> You mustn't look in my novel for the old stable *ego* of the character. There is another *ego*, according to whose action the individual is unrecognizable, and passes through, as it were, allotropic states which it needs a deeper sense than any we've been used to exercise, to discover are states of the same radically unchanged element. (Like as diamond and coal are the same pure single element of carbon.)

What all this suggests, and what is implicit in the novels themselves, is that the conventions of realism, which were developed preeminently in the English novel of the nineteenth century, are inadequate tools for use by a writer whose aim is the transformation of the very society whose values were embodied in realism. The "old-fashioned human element," "the old stable ego," the "certain moral scheme" prescribing "consistency" and linear development—these were relics of positivism, bourgeois humanism, and other ideologies of a dying culture. Lawrence gropes a bit in the attempt to describe their successors, but it is clear enough that the "other ego," the "physic" or nonhuman in humanity, and the "radically unchanged element" whose "allotropic" transformations determine a "rhythmic form" along lines unknown, are references to the mysterious source of vital energies capable (he believed) of regenerating both art and society.

The Rainbow · *The Rainbow* applies these ideas in a most interesting way. It is an elegiac study of the dying culture, written in Lawrence's revolutionary "new" manner. The story spans three generations of the Brangwen family, beginning with the advent of industrialism around 1840 in the rural Erewash valley—signaled by the construction of canals, the collieries, and the railroad—and continuing up to the first decade of the twentieth century. The theme is the destruction of the traditional way of life and the attempt, by the Brangwens, either to accommodate themselves to that loss or to transcend it by discovering a new basis for being.

The novel opens with a rhapsodic prose poem telescoping two hundred years of Brangwens into archetypal male and female figures living in "blood intimacy" with one another and with the land: "The pulse of the blood of the teats of the cows beat into the pulse of the hands of the men. [The men] mounted their horses and held life between the grip of their knees." Despite their "vital connection," however, there are opposing impulses in the male and the female principles that become increasingly important as the story proceeds. The Brangwen men, laboring in the fields of the Marsh Farm, are compared with the rim of a wheel revolving around the still center that is hearth and home; the women, like the axle of the wheel, live in the still center but always direct their gaze outward, beyond the wheel's rim toward the road, the village, the church steeple, "the spoken world" that is encroaching on the horizon. This tension between centripetal and centrifugal forces, the rim and the axle, is fruitful so long as the Brangwens live in harmony with the land, for it is a reflection of the cyclical processes of nature in which the clash of opposites generates change and growth. With the second generation, however, the principal Brangwen couple, Will and Anna, leaves the land and moves to the industrial town of Beldover, where Will works in a shop that produces machine-made lace. The seasonal cycle is replaced by the Christian liturgical calendar, in Lawrence's view a step toward abstraction. The old male-female opposition, having lost its former function as the means by which men and women participate in the dynamic rhythms of nature, becomes a destructive force. The marriage of contraries loses impetus because it now reflects not nature but the mechanisms that are dividing society. Husband and wife settle into a fixed domestic routine, typically Victorian, of piety (on Will's side) and child-rearing (on Anna's). Anna's "outward" impulse is thus sublimated, and, like Gertrude Morel in *Sons and Lovers*, she counts on her children to act out her frustrated quest beyond the pale.

Most important of these children is the oldest daughter, Ursula, who, with her sister Gudrun, will also figure prominently in *Women in Love*. Ursula has been called "the first complete modern woman" (Marvin Mudrick) and, even more sweepingly, "the first 'free soul'" (Keith Sagar) in the English novel. It is Ursula, a member of Lawrence's own generation, who finally breaks out of the old circle of life. As she grows into womanhood she challenges and ultimately rejects traditional views of religion, democracy, education, free enterprise, love, and marriage. She is the first Brangwen female to enter a profession and support herself (as a schoolteacher); she attends the university; she travels to London and the Continent. On several levels, then, her "centrifugal" movement takes her far afield. Yet despite her explorations she has no sense of who she really is. The traditional order, which formerly provided a living relationship with nature and with other men and women, has all but collapsed. Motivated only by her isolate will and unreciprocated by any meaningful male contrary—as is amply demonstrated by her unsatisfying love affairs with Winifred Inger, her schoolmistress, and the shallow Anton Skrebensky—Ursula's quest becomes a desperate exercise in redundancy and futility, her vital energies randomly dispersed.

The novel ends as it began, symbolically. In the last of a series of "ritual scenes," in which characters are suddenly confronted with the "physic" or nonhuman "ego" that is the mysterious life force, Ursula encounters a herd of stampeding horses. Whether hallucinatory or actual, the horses seem to represent the "dark" potencies which she has tried so long to discover on her quest and which have so far eluded her. Now, terrified, she escapes. Soon after, she falls ill with pneumonia, miscarries a child by Skrebensky, and lies delirious with fever for nearly a fortnight. All this is fitting as the culmination of Ursula's abortive, well-driven quest. Her "drift toward death," more like a plunge finally, is even more representative of her generation's crisis than Paul Morel's was in *Sons and Lovers*. As in the earlier novel, furthermore, Lawrence attempts to end *The Rainbow* on a hopeful note. After her convalescence, Ursula awakes one morning on the shores of what appears to be a new world, "as if a new day had come on the earth." Having survived the deluge, she is granted a vision of the rainbow—a symbol related to but superseding the old closed circle—which seems to offer hope for the regeneration not only of Ursula but also of her world.

On both levels, however, the symbolic promise is less than convincing. Unlike Paul Morel, Ursula has not performed any action or had any insight which suggests that her final "rebirth" is more than wishful thinking. As for the modern world's regeneration, when the novel appeared, in September, 1915, nothing could have been less likely. Lawrence hated the war, but like many other modern writers he saw it as the harbinger of the apocalypse, accelerating the advent of a new age. Before long he realized that he had "set my rainbow in the sky too soon, before, instead of after, the deluge." The furor provoked by the novel must have made the irony of his premature hopefulness all the more painful. In the teeth of that furor and the public persecution waged against Frieda and himself as supposed German spies, Lawrence set about writing *Women in Love*, considered by many today his greatest novel and one of the half-dozen or so masterpieces of modern fiction.

Women in Love · Whatever their differences with respect to the emphasis placed upon the operations of the "physic," or nonhuman, forces in humanity, *Sons and Lovers* and *The Rainbow* share several important traits that set them apart from most of Lawrence's subsequent novels, beginning with *Women in Love*. For one, they have in common a narrative structure that, by locating the action firmly within a social context spanning generations, subscribes to the novelistic convention of rendering the story of individuals continuous with the larger movements of history. *Women in Love* takes up the story of the "modern" Brangwens about three and one-half years after the end of *The Rainbow* but, in contrast to the earlier novel's sixty-six-year span, concentrates attention onto a series of loosely connected episodes occurring within a ten-month period, from spring to winter of 1909 or 1910. One result of this altered focus, at once narrower and relatively looser than that of the earlier novels, is that the social background seems far more static than before. The great transformation of society known as modernization has already occurred, and the characters move within a world whose ostensible change is the slow, inward process of decay. The shift of emphasis is evident also in the protagonists' attitudes toward society. The conclusions of the earlier novels–Paul's turning away from death toward the "humming, glowing town," and Ursula's vision of the rainbow offering hope that a corrupt world would "issue to a new germination"–imply that Western civilization could still respond to the most urgent needs of the individual. In *Women in Love* that assumption has completely vanished. Thus, although Lawrence originally conceived of *The Rainbow* and *Women in Love* as a single work and would later describe them as forming together "an organic artistic whole," the latter novel embodies a far darker view of the world. As Lawrence once said, *Women in Love* "actually does contain the results in one's soul of the war: it is purely destructive, not like *The Rainbow*, destructive-consummating."

The phrase "purely destructive" only slightly exaggerates the despairing nature of the novel's apocalyptic vision. Certainly its depiction of modern society as a dying tree "infested with little worms and dry-rot" suggests that the impetus toward death and destruction is so pervasive as to make the war all but inevitable. In the novel, the working class, far from resisting the dehumanizing mechanism of the industrial system, is "satisfied to belong to the great wonderful machine, even whilst it destroyed them." The leisure class is seen as similarly deluded and doomed. Hermione Roddice's chic gatherings at Breadalby, her country estate (modeled on Lady Ottoline Morrell's Garsington), offer no genuine alternative to the dying world but only a static image of the "precious past," where all is formed and final and accomplished–a "horrible, dead prison" of illusory peace. Meanwhile contemporary art has abdicated its time-honored role as naysayer to a corrupt social order. Indeed, in the homosexual artist Halliday, the promiscuous Minette, and the other decadent bohemians who congregate at the Pompadour Café in London, Lawrence clearly implicates intellectual and artistic coteries such as Bloomsbury in the general dissolution of modern society. That the pandering of the modern artist to the death-drive of mechanistic society was a general phenomenon and not limited to England is emphasized near the end of the novel with the appearance of Loerke, a German sculptor whose work adorns "a great granite factory in Cologne." Loerke, who asserts on the one hand that art should interpret industry as it had formerly interpreted religion and on the other that a work of art has no relation to anything but itself, embodies the amorality of modernist aesthetics from Lawrence's viewpoint. Dominated by "pure unconnected will," Loerke is, like Hermione, sexually perverse, and, like the habitués of the Pompadour, he "lives like a rat in the river of corruption."

All of these secondary characters in *Women in Love* exemplify the results of the displacement of the traditional order by industrialization, or what Lawrence terms "the first great phase of chaos, the substitution of the mechanical principle for the organic." Except for Hermione, they are consistently presented from without, in static roles prescribed for them by a static society. Against this backdrop move the four principal characters: Ursula and Gudrun Brangwen, who are sisters, and Rupert Birkin and Gerald Crich, who are friends. The interweaving relationships of these four, highlighted in scenes of great emotional intensity and suggestiveness, provide the "rhythmic form" of the novel. Notwithstanding their interactions with external society and their long philosophical arguments, they are chiefly presented in terms of a continuous struggle among the elemental energies vying for expression within them. Mark Schorer aptly describes the book as "a drama of primal compulsions." The "drama" concerns the conflict between the mechanical will and the organic oneness of being, between the "flux of corruption" or death and the regenerative forces of life, as these are variously embodied in the four main characters and their constantly shifting relationships.

Birkin, full of talk about spontaneity and "pure being" and the "blood-knowledge" available in sensuality, is clearly a spokesman for certain of Lawrence's favorite ideas. Considering this, it is interesting that from the outset the novel emphasizes his involvement in the death-fixation of modern society at large. He has been one of the "mud-flowers" at the Café Pompadour. In addition, he has been for several years involved in an affair with the perverse socialite Hermione, an affair that has degenerated into a hysterical battle of wills, sapping Birkin of his male vitality. As he tells Gerald, he wants above all to center his life on "the finality of love" for one woman and close relationships with a few other friends, but his goal is frustrated by the lingering parody of it represented in Hermione and the London bohemians. It is therefore significant that he is frequently ill and once goes to the south of France for several weeks to recuperate. His sickness is as much spiritual as physical. Dissatisfied with his prosaic career as a school inspector and frustrated in his relationships, he often finds himself "in pure opposition to everything." In this depressed state he becomes preoccupied with death and dissolution, "that dark river" (as he calls it) which seethes through all modern reality, even love. Not until after his violent break with Hermione, during which she nearly kills him, does Birkin begin to find his way back to life.

Unlike Birkin, Gerald does not believe that love can form the center of life. Instead he maintains that there is no center to life but simply the "social mechanism" which artificially holds it together; as for loving, Gerald is incapable of it. Indeed the novel everywhere implies that his inability to love derives from his abdication of vital, integrated being in favor of mere social fulfillment. As an industrial magnate (he is the director of the local coal mines and has successfully modernized them), Gerald advocates what Birkin calls the "ethics of productivity," the "pure instrumentality of mankind" being for him the basis of social cohesion and progress. If society is essentially mechanistic, Gerald's ambition is to be "the God of the machine" whose will is "to subjugate Matter to his own ends. The subjugation itself," Lawrence adds significantly, "was the point." This egotistic obsession is illustrated in a powerful scene in which Gerald rides a young Arab mare up to a railroad track and, while Gudrun and Ursula look on aghast, he violently forces the terrified mare to stay put as the train races noisily by them. The impact of this cruel assertion of will to power registers forcefully on Ursula, who is duly horrified and outraged, and on Gudrun, who is mesmerized by the "unutterable subordination" of the mare to the "indomitable" male.

After abortive affairs with other women, Birkin and Gerald are inevitably attracted to the Brangwen sisters. The protracted ebb and flow of the two relationships is tellingly juxtaposed in a series of scenes richly symbolic of the central dialectic of life and death. Meanwhile, not content with the romantic promise of finding love with a woman only, Birkin proposes to Gerald that they form a vital male bond as of blood brothers pledged to mutual love and fidelity. Whatever its unconscious origins, the intent of the offer is clearly not sexual. As the rest of the novel demonstrates (anticipating a theme that becomes more central and explicit in subsequent novels such as *Aaron's Rod* and *The Plumed Serpent*), Birkin is searching for a kind of pure intimacy in human relationships. He seeks with both men and women a bond of blood and mind and spirit—the integrated wholeness of being that for Lawrence was sacred—that when realized might form the nucleus of a new, vital human community. Because of Gerald's identification with the mechanism of industrial society, Birkin's repeated offer of a *Blutbrüderschaft* amounts to an invitation to a shared rebirth emblematic of epochal transfiguration, an apocalypse in microcosm. Because of that same identification, of course, Gerald, confused and threatened, must refuse the offer. Instead he chooses to die.

The choice of death is brilliantly dramatized in Gerald's impassioned encounters with Gudrun. Despite her earlier identification with the mare he brutally "subordinated," Gudrun might still have offered him the sort of vital relationship that both so desperately need. At any rate, had they been able to pursue their potential for love, the sort of shared commitment to mutual "being" that Birkin offers Gerald and that he eventually discovers with Ursula, regeneration, however painful and difficult, could have been realized. Rather than accept this challenge, however, Gerald falls back on his usual tactics and tries to subjugate Gudrun to his will. After his father's death, he becomes acutely aware of the void in his life and turns at once to Gudrun—walking straight from the cemetery in the rain to her house, up to her bedroom, his shoes still heavy with mud from the grave—not out of love but desperate need: the need to assert himself, heedless of the "otherness" of another, as if in so doing he could verify by sheer force of will that he exists. Yet, because this egotistic passion is a perversion of love as Lawrence saw it and because Gerald's yearning for ontological security is a perversion of the quest for true being, Gerald's anxieties are only made worse by his contact with Gudrun. For her part, Gudrun, unlike the helplessly dominated mare, never yields herself fully to Gerald. In fact, she does all she can to thwart and humiliate him, and their relationship soon becomes a naked battle of wills. It is redundant to say that this is a battle to the death, for, on the grounds that it is fought, the battle itself is death in Lawrencian terms. In the end, Gerald, whose aim all along as "God of the machine" had been to subjugate Matter to his will, becomes literally a frozen corpse whose expression terrifies Birkin with its "last terrible look of cold, mute Matter." Gudrun, headed at the end for a rendezvous with the despicable Loerke, arrives at a like consummation.

Whatever Lawrence might say about the "purely destructive" forces at work in *Women in Love*, in the relationship of Birkin and Ursula he finds a seed of new life germinating, albeit precariously, within the "dark river of dissolution." After the severance of his nearly fatal tie with Hermione, Birkin finds himself for a time in a quandary. Believing as he still does that the only means of withstanding dissolution is to center his life on close human ties, he casts about him to discover precisely the kind of relationship that will best serve or enact his quest for being. The "purely sensual, purely unspiritual knowledge" represented by a primitive statue of an African woman impresses Birkin but finally proves too remote a mystery for him to emulate; in any event, the modern female embodiments of this "mystic knowledge" of the senses are, like Hermione and Gudrun, will-dominated and murderous. A second way is that represented by the proposed bond with Gerald, the "Nordic" machine-god who for Birkin represents "the vast abstraction of ice and snow, . . . snow-abstract annihilation." When these alternatives both reveal themselves as mere "allotropic" variations of the flux of corruption from which he seeks release, Birkin finally hits upon a third way, "the way of freedom." He conceives of it in idealistic terms, as the paradisal entry into pure, single being, the individual soul taking precedence over love and desire for union, stronger than any pangs of emotion, a lovely state of free proud singleness, which accepted the obligation of the permanent connection with others, and with the other, submits to the yoke and leash of love, but never forfeits its own proud individual singleness, even while it loves and yields.

It is a difficult and elusive ideal, and when Birkin tries, laboriously, to describe it to Ursula—inviting her to join him in a new, strange relationship, "not meeting and mingling . . . but an equilibrium, a pure balance of two single beings" dynamically counterpoised as two stars are—she mocks him for dissimulating. Why does he not simply declare his love for her without "dragging in the stars"? She has a point, and Lawrence's art only benefits from such moments of self-criticism. Still, these paradoxical images of separateness in union, of a bond that finds its strength in the reciprocal affirmation of "otherness," do express, like the wheel's axle and rim in *The Rainbow*, Lawrence's essential vision of integrated, dynamic relationships. Furthermore, only by actively pursuing such a marriage of opposites, in which the separateness of each partner is necessary to the indissolubility of the bond, can both parties be caught up in something altogether new: "the third," which transcends individual selves in the oneness of pure being. For Lawrence this is the true consummation, springing up from "the source of the deepest life-force."

So polluted had the river of life become in modern Europe, however, that Lawrence could no longer bring himself to believe that this transcendence, ephemeral as it was to begin with, could survive the general cataract of dissolution. Moreover, even when Birkin and Ursula do find fulfillment together, it is not enough; for Birkin, at any rate, the new dispensation must involve other people as well as themselves. For both reasons, the quest for integrated wholeness of being, a mystery into which Birkin and Ursula are only new initiates, becomes translated into a pilgrimage through space. They must depart from the old, dying world and, like Lawrence and Frieda after the war, proceed in search of holy ground. The primary focus of subsequent novels, this quest is defined in *Women in Love* simply as "wandering to nowhere, . . . away from the world's somewheres." As *nowhere* is the translation of the word *utopia*, the social impetus of the search is implicit. "It isn't really a locality, though," Birkin insists. "It's a perfected relation between you and me, and others . . . so that we are free together." With this ideal before him, Lawrence was poised at the crossroads of his career.

In the postwar novels, which present fictionalized versions of his and Frieda's experiences in Italy (*Aaron's Rod*), Australia (*Kangaroo*), and Mexico (*The Plumed Serpent*), the quest translates increasingly into a sociopolitical doctrine projected onto whole societies. The bond between men and the fascination of powerful male leaders became more and more of an obsession in these novels. Lawrence tried mightily to remain faithful to the notion that the regeneration of societies should correspond to the "perfected relations" between individuals. The analogy presented difficulties, however, and the struggle to express his essentially religious vision in political terms proved fatal to his art. There are brilliant moments in all of these novels, especially in *The Plumed Serpent*, yet the alien aspects of the foreign lands he visited finally obscured the central issues in what was, at bottom, a quest for self-discovery. *Women in Love*, still in touch with the real motives of that quest and yielding immediate access to its first (and, as it turned out, finest) fruits, offers the richest rendering of both the modern drift toward death and its Lawrencian antidote, "whole man alive."

However ill-defined the object of his protagonists' plans for flight from Europe, ever since the cataclysm of 1914-1918, Lawrence himself had determined to relocate in the United States. Florida, California, upstate New York, New Mexico—all at one time or another figured as proposed sites of his American dream. In one of these areas, apart from the great urban centers, he would establish a utopian colony to be called Rananim. There he would start over again, free from the runaway entropy of modern Europe. In America, and more particularly aboriginal America, he believed that the Tree of Life remained intact, its potency still issuing "up from the roots, crude but vital." Nevertheless, when the war ended he did not go to America straightaway but headed east, not to arrive in the Western Hemisphere until late in 1922. During this prolonged period of yearning, his vision of America as the New World of the soul, the locus of the regeneration of humankind, took on an increasingly definite form. He was imaginatively committed to it even before settling near Taos, New Mexico, where he and Frieda lived on a mountain ranch for most of the next three years.

After studying the classic works of early American literature, he decided that he would write an "American novel," that is, a novel which would invoke and adequately respond to the American "spirit of place." For Lawrence the continent's daemon was the old "blood-and-vertebrate consciousness" embodied in the Mesoamerican Indian and his aboriginal religion. Because of four centuries of white European domination, that spirit had never been fully realized, yet despite the domination it still lay waiting beneath the surface for an annunciation. The terms of this vision, even apart from other factors having to do with his frustrating contacts with Mable Dodge Luhan and her coterie of artists in Taos, all but made it inevitable that Lawrence would sooner or later situate his American novel in a land where the Indian presence was more substantial than it was in the southwestern United States. The Pueblo Indian religion impressed him deeply with its "revelation of life," but he realized that for a genuine, large-scale rebirth to occur in America, "a vast death-happening must come first" to break the hold of the degenerate white civilization. It was natural enough that he turned his eyes south to Mexico, a land which actually had been caught up in revolution for more than a decade—a revolution moreover in which the place of the Indian (who constituted more than 30 percent of the population) in the national life was a central issue. Reading pre-Columbian history and archaeology, Lawrence found in Aztec mythology a ready-made source of symbols and in the story of the Spanish conquest an important precedent for his narrative of contemporary counterrevolution and religious revival.

The Plumed Serpent · Yet the writing of his *Quetzalcoatl,* the working title of what would become *The Plumed Serpent,* proved unusually difficult. *Kangaroo* had taken him only six weeks to write; *Aaron's Rod* and *The Lost Girl* were also composed in sudden, if fitful, bursts. In contrast, he worked on his "American novel" off and on for nearly two years, even taking the precaution of writing such tales as "The Woman Who Rode Away," "The Princess," and "St. Mawr" (all of which have much in common with the novel), and the Mexican travel sketches in *Mornings in Mexico,* as a kind of repeated trial run for his more ambitious project.

One reason the novel proved recalcitrant was that Lawrence became increasingly aware during his three journeys into the Mexican interior that his visionary Mexico and the real thing were far from compatible. The violence of the country appalled him; its revolution, which he soon dismissed as "self-serving Bolshevism," left him cold; and most important, its Roman Catholic Indians were demonstrably uninterested and seemingly incapable of responding to the sort of pagan revival called for by Lawrence's apocalyptic scheme. Yet so committed was he to his American "Rananim" that he was unwilling or unable to entertain the possibility of its failure. Rather than qualify his program for world regeneration in the light of the widening breach between his long-cherished dream and the disappointing reality, he elaborated the dream more fully and explicitly than ever, inflating his claims for it in a grandiose rhetoric that only called its sincerity into question. Had he been content with a purely visionary, symbolic tale, a prose romance comparable in motive with W. B. Yeats's imaginary excursions to "Holy Byzantium," such questions would probably not have arisen. Lawrence, however, could not let go of his expectation that in Mexico the primordial spirit of place would answer to his clarion call. At the same time, the realist in Lawrence allowed evidence to the contrary to appear in the form of his extraordinarily vivid perceptions of the malevolence of the Mexican landscape and its dark-skinned inhabitants. Yet even these were forced into the pattern of New World Apocalypse. In his desperation to have it both ways, doggedly asserting the identity of his own spiritual quest and the course of events in the literal, external world, he contrived a kind of symbolic or mythic formula in which sexual, religious, and political rebirth are not only equated but also presented as mutually dependent. The result, according to most critics, is a complicated muddle in which the parts, some of which are as fine as anything he ever wrote, do not make a whole. Yet for Lawrence the muddle itself would ultimately prove instructive.

In a sense *The Plumed Serpent* begins where *Women in Love* ends. The flow of Birkin and Ursula's relationship in the earlier novel is directed centrifugally away from England toward a nameless "nowhere" of shared freedom in pure being. In *The Plumed Serpent*, the protagonist, Kate Leslie, having heard the death-knell of her spirit in Europe, has arrived at the threshold of the New World of mystery, where a rebirth awaits her "like a doom." That the socialist revolution has addressed only the material needs of Mexicans and left their dormant spirit untouched suggests that Mexico is also in need of rebirth. Disgusted by the tawdry imitation of a modern European capital that is Mexico City, the seat of the failed revolution, Kate journeys westward to the remote lakeside village of Sayula. Sayula also happens to be the center of a new-Aztec religious revival led by Don Ramón Carrasco, who calls himself "the living Quetzalcoatl." The boat trip down the "sperm-like" lake to Sayula begins Kate's centripetal movement toward her destiny, and also Mexico's movement toward an indigenous spiritual reawakening; both movements are directed, gradually but inexorably, toward an "immersion in a sea of living blood."

Unlike Birkin and Ursula of *Women in Love*, Kate, a middle-aged Irish widow, wants at first only to be "alone with the unfolding flower of her own soul." Her occasional contacts with the provincial Indians inspire in her a sense of wonder at their "dark" mystery, but at the same time she finds their very alienness oppressive and threatening. She feels that the country wants to pull her down, "with a slow, reptilian insistence," to prevent her "free" spirit from soaring. Since Kate values her freedom and her solitude, she retreats periodically from the "ponderous, down-pressing weight" which she associates with the coils of the old Aztec feathered serpent, Quetzalcoatl.

Don Ramón explains to her that she must submit to this weight upon the spirit, for by pulling her down into the earth it may bring her into contact with the deep-rooted Tree of Life, which still thrives in the volcanic soil of primordial Mexico beneath the "paleface overlay" on the surface. This injunction is aimed not only at Kate but also at contemporary Mexico itself, which, beckoned by the pulsating drumbeats and hymns of the Men of Quetzalcoatl, is urged to turn its back on the imported white creeds (Catholicism and Bolshevism) and rediscover its indigenous roots. Only by yielding their hold on the conscious will can the "bound" egos of the Mexicans as well as of Kate achieve a transfiguration, symbolized in the novel by the Morning Star. Indeed, as a representative of white "mental consciousness," Kate is destined to perform an important role in the new dispensation in Mexico. Ramón's aim is to forge a new mode of consciousness emerging from the dynamic tension between the white and dark sensibilities. The new mode is embodied by Ramón himself, in his capacity to "see both ways" without being absorbed by either, just as the ancient man-god Quetzalcoatl united the sky and the earth, and as the Morning Star (associated with Quetzalcoatl) partakes of both night and day, moon and sun, yet remains itself.

Thus described, this doctrine may seem a welcome elaboration of the star-equilib-rium theory of human relationships advanced by Birkin in the earlier novel. The transcendent emergence of "the third," at best an elusive idea of divine immanence in *Women in Love*, seems to be clarified by the Aztec cosmogonic symbolism of *The Plumed Serpent*. Undoubtedly the latter novel is the fullest statement of Lawrence's vitalist religion. Yet there is something in the very explicitness of the religion in the novel that renders it suspect. As if in tacit acknowledgment of this, Lawrence, impatient with the slow progress of Don Ramón's appeal to the spirit, introduces a more overt form of conquest. When both Kate and Mexico fail to respond unequivo-cally to the invitation to submit voluntarily, Ramón reluctantly resorts to calling on the assistance of Don Cipriano Viedma, a full-blooded Indian general who commands a considerable army. Though Lawrence attempts to legitimize this move by having Ramón induct Cipriano into the neo-Aztec pantheon as "the living Huitzilopochtli" (the Aztec god of war) and by having Kate envision Cipriano as the Mexican Indian embodiment of "the ancient phallic mystery, . . . the god-devil of the male Pan" before whom she must "swoon," the novel descends into a pathological nightmare from which it never quite recovers.

It is not simply that Cipriano politicizes the religious movement, reducing it to yet another Latin American literary adventure which ends by imposing Quetzalcoatlism as the institutional religion of Mexico; nor is it simply that Cipriano, with Ramón's blessing, dupes Kate into a kind of sexual subservience that puts Gerald Crich's machine-god efforts with Gudrun (in *Women in Love*) to shame. The nadir of the novel is reached when Cipriano performs a public execution, stabbing to death three blindfolded prisoners who have betrayed Ramón. This brutal act is given priestly sanction by Ramón and even accepted by Kate, in her new role as Malintzi, fertility goddess in the nascent religion. "Why should I judge him?" asks Kate. "He is of the gods. . . . What do I care if he kills people. His flame is young and clean. He is Huitzilopochtli, and I am Malintzi." Their "godly" union is consummated at the foot of the altar in the new temple of Quetzalcoatl. At this point, if not before, the threefold quest for "immersion in a sea of living blood" ceases to serve a metaphorical function and becomes all too chillingly literal.

With its rigidified "mystical" doctrine, its hysterical rhetoric, and its cruelly inhu-man advocacy of "necessary" bloodshed and supermasculine dominance, *The Plumed Serpent* offers what amounts to a perfect Lawrencian hell but persists in celebrating it as if it were the veritable threshold of paradise. The novel has found a few defenders among critics enamored of "mythic design," but Harry T. Moore is surely correct in calling it "a tremendous volcano of a failure." Though for a short time he thought it his best novel, by March, 1928, Lawrence himself repudiated *The Plumed Serpent* and the militaristic "leader of men" idea that it embodies.

Nevertheless, *The Plumed Serpent* marks a crucial phase in Lawrence's develop-ment, for it carries to their ultimate conclusion the most disturbing implications of the ideas that had vexed his mind ever since the war. Submersion in the "dark blood," as the novel demonstrates, could lead as readily to wholesale murder in the name of religion as to vital and spontaneous relations between men and women. By coura-geously following his chimerical "Rananim" dream through to its end in a horrific, palpable nightmare, Lawrence accepted enormous risks, psychological as well as artistic. The effort nearly cost him his life, bringing on a severe attack of tuberculosis complicated by malaria. Yet, in the few years that remained to him, he was in a real sense a man reborn, able to return in imagination (in *The Virgin and the Gipsy* and *Lady Chatterley's Lover*, among other works) to his native Midlands, where he could once again take up the quest for "whole man alive," happily unencumbered by the grandiose political imperatives of world regeneration. Purging him of this ideological sickness, the writing of *The Plumed Serpent* proved as salutary to his later career as *Sons and Lovers* had been to his period of greatest accomplishment.

When Lawrence settled in southern Europe after leaving America in late 1925, he began to reshape his spiritual map in ways suggestive of his shifting outlook during his last years. The problem with the United States, he decided, was that everyone was too tense. Americans took themselves and their role in the world far too seriously and were unable to slacken their grip on themselves for fear that the world would collapse as a result. In contrast, the Europeans (he was thinking chiefly of southern Europeans rather than his own countrymen) were freer and more spontaneous because they were not controlled by will and could therefore let themselves go. At bottom, the European attitude toward life was characterized by what Lawrence called "insouciance." Relaxed, essentially free from undue care or fret, Europeans were open to "a sort of bubbling-in of life," whereas the Americans' more forthright pursuit of life only killed it.

Whether this distinction between America and Europe has any validity for others, for the post-America Lawrence it meant a great deal. In *The Plumed Serpent*, his "American novel," instead of realizing the free and spontaneous life flow made accessible by insouciance, he engaged in an almost hysterical striving after life writ large, resorting to political demagoguery and a formalized religion fully armed with rifles as well as rites. Apparently aware in retrospect of his error, he eschewed the strong-leader/submissive-follower relationship as the keynote to regeneration. In its place he would focus on a new relationship: a "sort of tenderness, sensitive, between men and men and men and women, and not the one up one down, lead on I follow, *ich dien* sort of business." Having discovered the virtues of insouciance and tenderness, Lawrence began to write *Lady Chatterley's Lover*, one of his most poignant, lyrical treatments of individual human relations.

Lady Chatterley's Lover · As always in Lawrence, the physical setting offers a crucial barometer of sensibility. In this case the treatment of setting is indicative of the novelist's loss of faith in the "spirit of place" as a valid embodiment of his quest. In comparison with his other novels, *Lady Chatterley's Lover* presents a scene much reduced in richness and complexity. Wragby Hall, the baronial seat of the Chatterleys, is described as "a warren of a place without much distinction." Standing on a hill and surrounded by oak trees, Wragby offers a view dominated by the smokestacks of the mines in and around the Midlands village of Tevershall. Like Shortlands, the Criches' estate in *Women in Love*, Wragby and its residents attempt through formal artifice to deny the existence of the pits from which the family income derives. The attempt is futile, however, for "when the wind was that way, which was often, the house was full of the stench of this sulphurous combustion of the earth's excrement," and smuts settle on the gardens "like black manna from skies of doom." As for Tevershall ("'tis now and 'tever shall be"), the mining village offers only the appalling prospect of "the utter negation of natural beauty, the utter negation of the gladness of life, . . . the utter death of the human intuitive faculty." Clearly Wragby and Tevershall are two sides of the same coin minted by the godless machine age. Between the two is a tiny, ever-diminishing remnant of old Sherwood Forest. The wood is owned by the Chatterleys, and many of its trees were "patriotically" chopped down during the Great War for timber for the allies' trenches.

It is here that Constance (Connie) Chatterley and her lover, Oliver Mellors, the gamekeeper, find—or rather create—life together. As Julian Moynihan has observed, the little wood symbolizes "the beleaguered and vulnerable status to which the vital career has been reduced" at the hands of modern civilization. The old centrifugal impulse for a faraway "nowhere" has yielded to a desperate centripetal flight toward refuge from the industrial wasteland. Yet try as they might to find sanctuary within the wood, the lovers must recognize that there is no longer any room in the world for true sanctuary, much less for a "Rananim." "The industrial noises broke the solitude," Lawrence writes; "the sharp lights, though unseen, mocked it. A man could no longer be private and withdrawn. The world allows no hermits." The geographical focus of the Lawrencian quest is no longer able to provide a modicum of hope and so yields to a new, scaled-down, more intimate image: the human body.

The sterility and spiritual paralysis of the modern world are embodied by Clifford Chatterley, Connie's husband. A paraplegic victim of the war, Clifford is both literally and symbolically deadened to the life of the passions. All his energy is directed to verbal, abstract, or social undertakings in which actual contact is minimal. Clifford believes in the form and apparatus of the social life and is indifferent to private feelings. A director of mines, he sees the miners as objects rather than men, mere extensions of the pit machinery. For him, "the function determines the individual," who hardly matters otherwise. Clifford also writes fashionably shallow stories and entertains other writers and critics to curry favor. He modernizes the coal mines with considerable success. Thus in broad outline he resembles Gerald Crich of *Women in Love*. Yet, in the far simpler world of *Lady Chatterley's Lover*, Lawrence chooses not to cloud matters by giving his antagonist any redeeming qualities. The reader is never invited to sympathize with Clifford's plight. Motoring around Wragby Hall in his mechanical wheelchair, Clifford coolly urges Connie to have a child by another man—the "sex thing" having been of no particular importance to him even before the war—so that he can have an heir to Wragby. By the end of the novel, he turns to his attendant Mrs. Bolton for the only intimacy left to him: a regressive, perverse form of contact. Such heaping of abuse onto Clifford, far in excess of what is needed to establish his symbolic role, undoubtedly detracts from the novel.

So long as she remains with Clifford, Connie finds herself in a condition of static bondage in which her individuality is circumscribed by the function identified in her title. A "lady" by virtue of her marriage, she is not yet truly a woman. Sex for her is merely a "thing" as it is for Clifford, an instrument of tacit control over men. She is progressively gripped by malaise. Physically she is "old at twenty-seven, with no gleam and sparkle in the flesh"; spiritually she is unborn. Her affair with Mellors is of course the means of her metamorphosis, which has been compared (somewhat ironically) with the awakening of Sleeping Beauty at the handsome prince's magical kiss. Less obvious is the overlapping of this fairy-tale pattern with a counterpattern of male transformation such as that found in the tale of the Frog Prince. For Mellors, too, is trapped in a kind of bondage, alone in his precarious refuge in the wood. The "curse" on him is his antipathy to intimate contacts, especially with women, after his disastrous marriage to the promiscuous Bertha Coutts.

The initial encounters between Connie and Mellors in the wood result only in conflict and hostility, as both, particularly Mellors, cling to their socially prescribed roles and resist the challenge of being "broken open" by true contact with another. Yet, when they finally do begin to respond to that challenge, it is Mellors who takes the lead in conducting Connie through her initiation into the mysteries of "phallic" being. With his "tender" guidance she learns the necessity of letting go her hold on herself, yielding to the "palpable unknown" beyond her conscious will. She discovers the importance of their "coming off together" rather than the merely "frictional" pleasures of clitoral orgasm (a notion acceptable within Lawrence's symbolic context if not widely endorsed by the "how-to" manuals of the Masters and Johnson generation, of which Lawrence would no doubt have disapproved). When she tries to get Mellors to tell her that he loves her, he rejects the abstract, overused word in favor of the earthier Anglo-Saxon language of the body and its functions. On one occasion he even introduces her to sodomy so as to "burn out the shames, the deepest, oldest shames, in the most secret places." The result of all this, paradoxically, is that the couple arrives at the state of "chastity." Having broken their ties to the sterile world, they are able to accept an imposed separation until it is possible, after a period of waiting for Mellors's divorce to occur, for them to live together in hope for their future.

In an aside in chapter 9, Lawrence, asserting that it is "the way our sympathy flows and recoils that really determines our lives," affirms that the great function of a novel is precisely to "inform and lead into new places the flow of our sympathetic consciousness" and to "lead our sympathies away in recoil from things gone dead." As a statement of intention, this will do for all of Lawrence's novels. Of course, even the best of intentions do not necessarily lead to artistic achievement. *Lady Chatterley's Lover*, though in many respects a remarkable recovery after the dead end that was the "leadership novels," is nevertheless flawed by the very directness with which it follows the "flow and recoil" idea. For one thing, the deck is too obviously stacked against Clifford. Lawrence never takes him seriously as a man; by making him the stationary target of so much scorn simply for what he represents, Lawrence in effect replicates Clifford's own treatment of people as mere objects or functions.

Because the "recoil" against Clifford as a "thing gone dead" seems facile and almost glib, Connie's counterflow toward Mellors seems also too easy, despite Lawrence's efforts to render her conflicting, vacillating feelings. Another part of the problem lies in the characterization of Mellors, who, after his initial reluctance, proves to be a tiresomely self-satisfied, humorless, "knowing" spokesman for the gospel according to Lawrence. Connie, however, is a marvelous creation, far more complex than even Mellors seems to realize. She is a worthy successor to Lawrence's other intriguing female characters: Gertrude Morel, Ursula and Gudrun Brangwen, Alvina Houghton (of *The Lost Girl*), and Kate Leslie.

At his best, in *Sons and Lovers, The Rainbow*, and especially *Women in Love*, Lawrence manages to enact the flow and counterflow of consciousness, the centrifugal dilation and the centripetal contraction of sympathies, in a far more complex and convincing way than he does in his last novel. Notwithstanding his battles with Mrs. Grundy, the underlying impulse of all his work is unquestionably moral: the passionate yearning to discover, celebrate, and *become* "whole man alive." The desperateness with which he pursued that elusive ideal in both his life and his art sometimes led him to resort to a bullying, declamatory didacticism, which took the chance of alienating his readers' sympathies.

Lawrence's moral vision was most compelling when embodied and rendered in dramatic or symbolic terms rather than externally imposed by "oracular" utterance and rhetorical bombast. Yet "art for my sake" necessarily involved him in these risks, of which he was fully aware. At a time when aesthetic objectivity and the deperson-alization of the artist were the dominant aims of the modernists, Lawrence coura-geously pursued his vision wherever it might lead.

Through his capacity for outrage against what he considered a dying civilization, his daring to risk failure and humiliation in the ongoing struggle to find and make known the "vital quick" which alone could redeem humanity and relocate human-kind's lost spiritual roots, Lawrence performed the essential role of seer or prophetic conscience for his age. Moreover, because subsequent events in the twentieth century more than confirmed his direst forebodings, his is a voice which readers today cannot afford to ignore. While many are decrying the death of the novel amidst the prolif-eration of the much-ballyhooed "literature of exhaustion," one could do worse than turn to Lawrence to find again the "one bright book of life."

Ronald G. Walker

Other major works

SHORT FICTION: *The Prussian Officer and Other Stories*, 1914; *England, My England*, 1922; *St. Mawr: Together with the Princess*, 1925; *The Woman Who Rode Away and Other Stories*, 1928; *Love Among the Haystacks and Other Stories*, 1930; *The Lovely Lady and Other Stories*, 1933; *A Modern Lover*, 1934; *The Complete Short Stories of D. H. Lawrence*, 1961.

PLAYS: *The Widowing of Mrs. Holroyd*, pb. 1914; *Touch and Go*, pb. 1920; *David*, pb. 1926; *A Collier's Friday Night*, pb. 1934; *The Complete Plays of D. H. Lawrence*, pb. 1965.

POETRY: *Love Poems and Others*, 1913; *Amores*, 1916; *Look! We Have Come Through*, 1917; *New Poems*, 1918; *Bay*, 1919; *Tortoises*, 1921; *Birds, Beasts, and Flowers*, 1923; *The Collected Poems of D. H. Lawrence*, 1928; *Pansies*, 1929; *Nettles*, 1930; *The Triumph of the Machine*, 1931; *Last Poems*, 1932; *Fire and Other Poems*, 1940; *Phoenix Edition of Complete Poems*, 1957; *The Complete Poems of D. H. Lawrence*, 1964 (Vivian de Sola Pinto and Warren Roberts, editors).

NONFICTION: *Twilight in Italy*, 1916; *Movements in European History*, 1921; *Psycho-analysis and the Unconscious*, 1921; *Sea and Sardinia*, 1921; *Fantasia of the Unconscious*, 1922; *Studies in Classic American Literature*, 1923; *Reflections on the Death of a Porcupine and Other Essays*, 1925; *Mornings in Mexico*, 1927; *Pornography and Obscenity*, 1929; *Á Propos of Lady Chatterley's Lover*, 1930; *Assorted Articles*, 1930; *Apocalypse*, 1931; *Etruscan Places*, 1932; *The Letters of D. H. Lawrence*, 1932 (Aldous Huxley, editor); *Phoenix: The Posthumous Papers of D. H. Lawrence*, 1936 (Edward McDonald, editor); *The Collected Letters of D. H. Lawrence*, 1962 (2 volumes; Harry T. Moore, editor); *Phoenix II*, 1968 (Moore and Roberts, editors).

Bibliography

Bloom, Harold, ed. *D. H. Lawrence*. New York: Chelsea House, 1986. A major compilation of critical commentary on Lawrence's writings, this collection of essays deals largely with his major novels and short stories and makes available varying assessments of philosophical and psychological concerns implicit in Lawrence's works. A chronology and short bibliography are also provided.

Ellis, David. *D. H. Lawrence: Dying Game 1922-1930.* Cambridge, England: Cambridge University Press, 1998. Volume 3 of the Cambridge biography of Lawrence (each volume is written by a different author). Ellis, like his Cambridge colleagues, has been criticized for use of excessive detail, but this biography is indispensable for students of specific periods of his life and work who wish a meticulous, accurate account. As Ellis remarks in his preface, more than most writers, Lawrence drew directly from his daily life, and only a minutely detailed biography can trace his creative process.

Heywood, Christopher, ed. *D. H. Lawrence: New Studies.* New York: St. Martin's Press, 1987. This work includes chapters on Lawrence's social origins, his poetry, his major novels, political thought, and "blood consciousness," but no bibliography.

Jackson, Dennis, and Fleda Brown Jackson, eds. *Critical Essays on D. H. Lawrence.* Boston: G. K. Hall, 1988. Various critical insights may be found in this collection of twenty essays, which includes articles by scholars and by well-known writers such as Anaïs Nin and Sean O'Casey. All literary genres in which Lawrence was involved are represented by one or more contributions here. Also of note is the editors' introduction, which deals with trends in critical and biographical literature about Lawrence.

Kinkead-Weekes, Mark. *D. H. Lawrence: Triumph to Exile 1912-1922.* Cambridge, England: Cambridge University Press, 1996. Volume 2 of the Cambridge biography of Lawrence. This is a massively detailed work, including chronology, maps, and notes.

Maddox, Brenda. *D. H. Lawrence: The Story of a Marriage.* New York: Simon & Schuster, 1994. As the subtitle indicates, Maddox focuses on Lawrence and his wife Frieda. A lively, deft writer, Maddox is not as meticulous as Lawrence's more scholarly biographers.

Meyers, Jeffrey. *D. H. Lawrence: A Biography.* New York: Alfred A. Knopf, 1990. The emphasis in this substantial and well-informed biography is on Lawrence's literary milieu and his development of themes and ideas in the broader intellectual context of his own time. Also provides some new interpretations of events in Lawrence's personal life.

Preston, Peter, and Peter Hoare, eds. *D. H. Lawrence in the Modern World.* Cambridge, England: Cambridge University Press, 1989. The worldwide dimensions of Lawrence's reputation are illustrated by this collection of papers from an international symposium which included scholars from France, Italy, Israel, and Korea, as well as from English-speaking countries.

Sagar, Keith. *D. H. Lawrence: Life into Art.* Athens: University of Georgia Press, 1985. This important literary biography by a specialist who has written several books about Lawrence sets forth the events of Lawrence's life alongside an exposition of themes and techniques which characterized the writer's work in several genres.

Schneider, Daniel J. *The Consciousness of D. H. Lawrence: An Intellectual Biography.* Lawrence: University Press of Kansas, 1986. Major themes in Lawrence's works reflected values and subjective responses developed over the course of the writer's life. Traces psychological concerns and modes of belief as they arose during Lawrence's career, without indulging in undue speculation or reductionism.

Squires, Michael, and Keith Cushman, eds. *The Challenge of D. H. Lawrence.* Madison:

University of Wisconsin Press, 1990. This group of essays, which deal both with individual works and with broader literary contexts, supplies some interesting and provocative insights. Of particular note is the first article, by Wayne C. Booth, a self-confessed "lukewarm Lawrentian" who maintains that Lawrence's works are better appreciated upon rereading and reconsideration.

Thornton, Weldon. *D. H. Lawrence: A Study of the Short Fiction.* New York: Twayne, 1993. Part 1 provides interpretations of Lawrence's most important stories; part 2 introduces Lawrence's own criticism; part 3 gives a sampling of important Lawrence critics. Includes a chronology and bibliography.

Worthen, John. *D. H. Lawrence: The Early Years, 1885-1912.* Cambridge, England: Cambridge University Press, 1991. This first volume in the Cambridge biography of Lawrence includes a family tree, chronology, and notes.

John le Carré

David John Moore Cornwell

Born: Poole, England; October 19, 1931

Principal long fiction · *Call for the Dead*, 1960; *A Murder of Quality*, 1962; *The Spy Who Came in from the Cold*, 1963; *The Looking-Glass War*, 1965; *A Small Town in Germany*, 1968; *The Naive and Sentimental Lover*, 1971; *Tinker, Tailor, Soldier, Spy*, 1974; *The Honourable Schoolboy*, 1977; *Smiley's People*, 1980; *The Quest for Karla*, 1982 (trilogy, includes *Tinker, Tailor, Soldier, Spy*, *The Honourable Schoolboy*, and *Smiley's People*); *The Little Drummer Girl*, 1983; *A Perfect Spy*, 1986; *The Russia House*, 1989; *The Secret Pilgrim*, 1991; *The Night Manager*, 1993; *Our Game*, 1995; *The Tailor of Panama*, 1996; *Single and Single*, 1999.

Other literary forms · John le Carré's reputation rests exclusively on his novels. He has published a handful of articles and reviews and two short stories but no book-length works in other forms.

Achievements · Espionage fiction, the spy thriller, has a large, worldwide audience; at the end of the twentieth century one out of every four contemporary works of fiction published in the United States belonged to this genre. Le Carré is preeminent among writers of espionage fiction. John Gardner, himself an espionage novelist and the author of the continuing James Bond saga, has called le Carré "the British *guru* of literary espionage fiction."

Le Carré not only constructs the intricate plots which have made his works international best-sellers but also raises complex and fundamental questions about human nature. Most espionage fiction has a rather simplistic frame of reference: right and wrong, good and evil, us and them. The hero battles it out, his victory assured as he prepares to take on another assignment to save the free world from total collapse. He is a superman, and his adventures are narrated with all the razzle-dazzle and pyrotechnics of escapist fiction.

Le Carré's novels undermine all the stereotypes of spy fiction. Instead of a clear-cut conflict between right and wrong, le Carré's novels offer subtle shades of grey. Instead of a dashing James Bond figure, le Carré's most representative hero is George Smiley, fat, short, and balding, who "entered middle age without ever being young." In novel after novel, le Carré is concerned with ends and means, with love and betrayal. He is concerned with character and motive, probing the agony and tragedy of the person who betrays his or her country not for personal profit but for a cause in which he or she believes. He dramatizes the dilemma faced by men and women involved in the monotonous and often inhuman work of espionage, which leads him to raise the uncomfortable yet fundamental question: How is it possible to defend humanity in inhuman ways? Like Graham Greene, le Carré compels one to go on a journey of self-exploration, to come to grips with one's own self-delusions, fears, and anxieties. In the words of George Grella (*The New Republic,* July 31, 1976), the novels of le Carré "are not so much spy thrillers as thoughtful, compassionate meditations on deception, illusion and defeat." Le Carré's major achievement is his remarkable ability to transform espionage fiction from cliché-ridden, escapist fare to the level of great literature.

Le Carré's novels take his readers to the nerve center of the secret world of espionage. His is an authentic voice, drawing upon his own experiences. Whether it is the minutiae about an agent's training in combat and radio transmitting technique in *The Looking-Glass War*, the subtleties of the "memory man" shredding classified documents in *A Small Town in Germany*, or the meticulous psychological and physical details involved in delivering a clandestine message in *Smiley's People*, le Carré's novels have, in the words of Melvyn Bragg, "the smell of insider lore . . . like a good wax polish." He gives a complete portrait of the intelligence community with all its warts and wrinkles, conveying the sheer monotony and the "measureless tedium of diplomatic life" which form the background of the deadly game of espionage. There is nothing glamorous in this limbo world of spies and double agents, a world chillingly described by Alec Leamas in *The Spy Who Came in from the Cold*: "What do you think spies are? They're a squalid procession of vain fools, traitors too, yes; pansies, sadists and drunkards, people who play cowboys and Indians to brighten their rotten lives." The British Foreign Service is involved not only in plots and counterplots to outwit the Soviets, but also in its own interdepartmental plots and counterplots within the Circus, the London headquarters of the intelligence establishment. In presenting such an uncompromisingly realistic portrait of the spy profession, le Carré has scored a significant achievement.

Finally, in his portrait of George Smiley, le Carré has created a major character in contemporary world literature. Smiley is "one of life's losers." A notorious cuckold who continues to love his beautiful, unfaithful wife, he "looks like a frog, dresses like a bookie," but has a brilliant mind. His vision of retirement is to be left alone to complete his monograph on the German baroque poet Martin Optiz. When he travels on a highly sensitive life-and-death mission, his fellow passengers think of him as "the tired executive out for a bit of fun." Smiley, however, is not one face but "a whole range of faces. More your patchwork of different ages, people and endeavours. Even . . . of different faiths." He is "an abbey, made up of all sorts of conflicting ages and styles and convictions." In spite of all the "information" the reader possesses about Smiley, he remains an elusive personality, thus reflecting a mark of great literary creations: a sense of mystery, of a life beyond the boundaries of the text.

Biography · John le Carré was born David John Moore Cornwell, the son of Ronald and Olive (Glassy) Cornwell, on October 19, 1931, in Poole, Dorset, England, "in a mouldering, artless house with a 'for sale' notice in the garden." He went to Sherborne School—where James Hilton's *Goodbye, Mr. Chips*, was filmed—but did not like Sherborne and attempted to run away. "I was not educated at all," le Carré writes in his essay "In England Now" (*The New York Times Magazine*, October 23, 1977), and speaks of his school as a prison. He spent much of his time "planning escapes across moonlit playing fields," thereby finding release from "those huge and lonely dormitories." He remembers the severity of the school crystallized in his being "sprawled inelegantly over the arm of the headmaster's small chair," to smart under blows from a small riding whip. Since young le Carré's father seldom paid the school fees, he was singled out even more for punishment. He was struck by the hand as well as whipped, and le Carré attributes his "partial deafness in one ear to a Mr. Farnsworth," a teacher in school at that time. The school atmosphere was violent: rugger wars were fought "almost literally to death," boxing was a religious obligation, and instructors drummed into their pupils the notion that "to die in battle" was the highest achievement to which they could aspire.

Le Carré's father was determined to make his two sons grow up independent, so he sent them to schools thirty miles apart. Young David and his brother Tony, two years his senior, made arduous journeys to meet each other on Sundays to find the emotional nourishment each so desperately needed. Le Carré quit Sherborne two years later.

Le Carré's father had dropped out of school at the age of fourteen and ever after, as le Carré said in an interview with *Time* magazine (October 3, 1977), "lived in a contradictory world," full of credit but no cash with a "Micawberlike tal-

The Douglas Brothers"

ent for messing up his business adventures." He finally ended up in prison for fraud. Le Carré's mother abandoned the children to live with a business associate of her husband. Le Carré did not see his mother until he was twenty-one. His father died in 1975 without reconciling with his sons. Without the support of his parents, le Carré had to depend on his elder brother. As children, they were ignorant of the whereabouts of their parents, and the young le Carré often wondered if his father were a spy on a crucial mission for England. False promises by his father made him distrustful of people, and he confesses that "duplicity was inescapably bred" into him. His childhood was therefore traumatic, and he draws upon this painful experience in *The Naive and Sentimental Lover* when he makes Aldo Cassidy, one of the heroes of the novel, tell Shamus how his mother abandoned him when he was a child. The loss "robbed him of his childhood," denying him "normal growth."

Le Carré's father was angry that his son had left Sherborne and, to punish him, sent him to Berne University in Switzerland; le Carré was sixteen at the time. At Berne, he studied German, French, and skiing. After completing his military service in Vienna with the army intelligence corps, he went to Lincoln College, Oxford, and studied modern languages, taking an honors degree in 1956. From 1956 to 1958, he taught languages at England's most prestigious public school, Eton.

Le Carré is fond of quoting Graham Greene's observation that "a writer's capital is his childhood." In his own case, the circumstances of his childhood led him to accept the "condition of subterfuge" as a way of life. In an interview with Melvyn Bragg (*The New York Times Book Review*, March 13, 1983), le Carré speaks again of the manner in which his childhood contributed to his secretive nature; he "began to think that [he] was, so to speak, born into occupied territory." Like the boy Bill Roach in *Tinker, Tailor, Soldier, Spy*, le Carré is the perennial clandestine watcher, observing, noting, analyzing, and piecing together the parts of the puzzle.

In 1954, le Carré married Alison Ann Veronica Sharp, daughter of a R.A.F. marshal. He has three sons from this marriage, which ended in divorce in 1971. He is now married to Jane Eustace, formerly an editor at his British publisher, Hodder and Stoughton; they have a son, Nicholas.

In 1960, le Carré entered the British Foreign Service and served as second secretary in Bonn from 1960 to 1963, and as consul in Hamburg from 1963 to 1964. Le Carré has been reticent about his actual work in the Foreign Office, and has been noncommittal about whether his Bonn and Hamburg posts were covers for duties as a secret agent. As Melvyn Bragg writes, "He used to deny having been a spy, but now it's out. He gives in gracefully–caught but too late for it to matter. His new line is a line in charming resignation, an admission of nothing very much." The tension, the drama, and the intense human conflict that pervade all his novels undoubtedly derive from le Carré's "insider lore."

Le Carré experimented with writing while he was a student at Sherborne, but abandoned it because he was discouraged in his creative attempts. After getting married and living in Great Missenden, he once again started writing. Frequently, he used the two-hour train journey he had to make every day to London to plot his stories and overcome his "restlessness as a diplomat." He chose the pseudonym "John le Carré" in order to satisfy the regulation of the British Foreign Service which forbids its employees to publish under their own names. Appropriately, the origin of le Carré's pseudonym is itself obscured in mystery and possible deception. Long ago, le Carré told interviewers that he had seen the name "Le Carré" ("The Square") on the window of a London shop, but diligent researchers have been unable to find any record of such a shop in the registry of London's businesses.

Le Carré's first two novels, *Call for the Dead*, which makes use of his German experience, and *A Murder of Quality*, which draws upon his Eton experience, had moderate success. It was with his third novel, however, *The Spy Who Came in from the Cold*, that le Carré won both fame and financial security. He gave up his job in the Foreign Office and became a full-time writer.

Le Carré leads a very private life in an elegantly furnished cliff house in Cornwall, near Land's End. He is a slow but eclectic reader and avoids novels in his own genre. He follows no writer as a model, but admires and enjoys good prose, clear, lucid, and full of subtle nuances. Joseph Conrad, Graham Greene, and V. S. Naipaul are among his favorite authors.

Le Carré emerged from the shadows somewhat in the 1990's, making himself available for interviews and addressing public issues. Of his time as a member of the secret world, he said in 1996: "I did nothing of significance. . . . I didn't alter the world order." He continued to travel extensively while researching his novels. When at home, he writes in the early morning and often walks along the beaches of Cornwall in the afternoons. He has grappled with the problem of writing novels about espionage in a post-Cold War world and has wondered how much he was affected by the great ideological clash of the superpowers–a clash that he helped to mythologize in his novels.

Concurrent with the release of his 1996 novel, *The Tailor of Panama*, le Carré treated the British reading public to a vituperative literary feud with the novelist Salman Rushdie. Speaking about his book to the Anglo-Israel Association in 1995, le Carré defended himself against charges of anti-Semitism, claiming that he "had become the victim of a witch-hunt by zealots of 'political correctness.'" Rushdie said that he wished le Carré had voiced a similar concern when his book *The Satanic Verses* (1988) prompted the Iranian regime of Ayatollah Ruhollah Khomeini to issue a *fatwa*, or death sentence, against him. Both writers quickly directed very personal attacks against each other in the letters section of the venerable British newspaper *The Guardian*. Le Carré wrote that "there is no law in life or nature that says that great religions may be insulted with impunity." Le Carré added in a later riposte that Rushdie's comments were "cultural intolerance masquerading as free speech."

Analysis · In his first novel, *Call for the Dead* (which took second place in the Crime Writers Association awards for 1961), John le Carré introduced George Smiley, not only his most important character, but also one of the most fascinating and complex characters in the world of fictional espionage. In the very first chapter of the novel, aptly entitled "A Brief History of George Smiley," the reader is offered more information about Smiley than is provided in any other novel in which he appears.

Call for the Dead · Cast in the form of a detective story, even though the theme—the control of Samuel Fennan, a British Foreign Service official, by East Germany—is one of international intrigue and espionage, *Call for the Dead* is a tight, short, well-constructed novel written against the background of Britain's postwar security crisis. There is a need for men of Smiley's experience because "a young Russian cypher-clerk in Ottawa" had defected. (The cypher-clerk to whom le Carré referred was Igor Gouzenko, author of *The Fall of a Titan*, 1954; his defection set in motion a number of arrests and other defections, including the notorious cases of Guy Burgess and Kim Philby, who were revealed to have been Soviet agents.)

Smiley, who "could reduce any color to grey," and who "spent a lot of money on bad clothes," has interviewed Samuel Fennan on the basis of an anonymous letter charging Fennan with Communist party affiliations. Soon after the interview, Fennan commits suicide in suspicious circumstances. In investigating Fennan's death, Smiley investigates himself. Smiley's self-exploration and the moral responsibility he accepts for having indirectly contributed to Fennan's death add strength to the novel. Years earlier, during a year in Germany in the Nazi era, Smiley had recruited a young man named Dieter Frey because the handsome young German had "a natural genius for the nuts and bolts of espionage." Smiley now has to confront Dieter, who turns out to be an East German agent involved in the Fennan case. When the confrontation takes place, Dieter, out of respect for their past friendship, does not fire his gun to kill Smiley, as he could. After that momentary hesitation, Dieter and Smiley struggle, and Smiley kills his former pupil. Ever the scholar-spy, Smiley recalls a line from Hermann Hesse, "Strange to wander in the mist, each is alone," and realizes that however closely one lives with another, "we know nothing."

Call for the Dead introduces and makes reference to a number of characters who become permanent citizens of le Carré's espionage world. There is Steed-Asprey, Smiley's boss, whose secretary, the Lady Ann Sercombe, Smiley married and lost. Le Carré makes a practice of alluding to Steed-Asprey in each subsequent novel, rewarding his faithful readers with sly bits of information; in *A Small Town in Germany*, for example, a character remarks with seeming irrelevance that Steed-Asprey has become ambassador to Peru. When Smiley is on his final hunt for Karla in *Smiley's People*, it is Steed-Asprey's training he recalls. The reader is also introduced to Peter Guillam, who plays a prominent part in assisting Smiley with tracking down the Soviet mole in *Tinker, Tailor, Soldier, Spy*. Mundt, who is a key character in *The Spy Who Came in from the Cold*, also makes a diabolical appearance in *Call for the Dead*. Le Carré's first novel makes it very clear that he was working to create a design, an oeuvre, and his later novels demonstrate that he succeeded in that attempt.

A Murder of Quality · Set in an English public school, le Carré's second novel, *A Murder of Quality* (which was a finalist for the Crime Writers Association Award for 1962), is a straight mystery novel with no element of espionage or international intrigue, except that the unofficial "detective" is George Smiley, brought into the case by a friend.

Stella, the wife of Stanley Rode, a teacher at Carne, a posh public school, feels threatened by her husband. Before Smiley can meet her and inquire as to the basis for her fear, Stella is murdered. In investigating Stella's death, Smiley meets a variety of characters both within and outside the school, reflecting the rigid class structure of British society. Le Carré draws upon his own teaching experience at Eton to present a convincing picture of a public school, with its inner tensions and nuances of snobbery and cruelty. "We are not democratic. We close the door on intelligence without parentage," says one of the characters. Stanley Rode is not considered a gentleman because he did not go to the right school. Life at the school is an intensely closed society, and hence, there has not been "an original thought . . . . for the last fifty years."

The least likely suspect turns out to be the murderer. Smiley faces a dilemma because the murderer is the brother of one of his best friends, a fellow agent who disappeared on a mission and is presumed dead. The irony of the situation makes Smiley say, "We just don't know what people are like, we can never tell. . . . We're the chameleons."

The Spy Who Came in from the Cold · Le Carré's third novel, *The Spy Who Came in from the Cold*, became an international best-seller and brought him fame and financial independence. Graham Greene called it "the best spy story I have ever read." Malcolm Muggeridge praised it for "the cold war setting, so acutely conveyed." It was made into a successful film, with Richard Burton as Alec Leamas. The novel was translated into more than a dozen languages and was called a masterpiece.

Le Carré has said that the novel was inspired by the sight of the Berlin Wall, which drew him "like a magnet." The plot was "devised in the shadow of the Wall." Written in a spare, athletic style (the first draft of 120,000 words was reduced to 70,000, while more than a dozen characters present in the first draft were eliminated in the final version), *The Spy Who Came in from the Cold* is the story of fifty-year-old Alec Leamas, "built like a swimmer," a veteran British agent who has lost his most important agent in East Germany. He is asked to take on one more assignment before coming "in from the cold." Tired and weary, almost burned out, Leamas accepts his terminal assignment: to get a British agent, "a mole," out of East Germany. It is, however, not until the very end that Leamas, a master spy himself, realizes that he is not involved in a mere double cross, but in a triple cross, and that *he* is to be sacrificed. *The Spy Who Came in from the Cold* is also a touching love story of two of society's outcasts, Leamas and Liz. Both are betrayed by the men and institutions in whom they have faith and hope, and to whom they have given their loyalty.

The moves and countermoves in the novel are plotted with the intricacy of a masterly chess game. "I wanted to make an equation and reverse it," le Carré has said, "make another equation and reverse that. Finally, let him think he's got nearly to the solution of the main equation, and then reverse the whole thing."

In Alec Leamas, le Carré creates a stunning portrait of an antihero. "Not accustomed to living on dreams," Leamas is a citizen of the amoral world of espionage, who practices the art of self-deception so completely that he is unable to distinguish where his life begins and his deception ends. "Even when he was alone he compelled himself to live with the person he had assumed." Leamas is needed by the British Foreign Service because he is the expendable man. His boss asks him if he is tired of spying because "in our world we pass so quickly out of the register of hate or love. . . . All that is left in the end is a kind of nausea." Leamas has a sharp-edged cynicism, but when he meets Liz, a devoted but naïve Communist, in the London Library, he feels for her, believing that she can give him "faith in ordinary life." She is his tender spot; she also becomes his Achilles heel. The Service has no qualms about using her to discredit and destroy Leamas, because "In the acquisition of intelligence, the weak and even the innocent must suffer."

Le Carré makes the telling point that in condoning the sacrifice of the individual, without his consent, for the good of the masses, both East and West use the same weapons of deceit and even the same spies. Le Carré's judgment on this murky world is not reassuring: "There is no victory and no virtue in the cold war, only a condition of human illness and misery."

Mundt, whom the reader met in *Call for the Dead*, has a prominent role in the novel as the second man in the *Abteilung*, the East German Secret Service. A loathsome figure, an ex-Nazi, he turns out to be a double agent serving the British. To rescue him is Leamas's task, and in the process, two decent human beings, both Jews, are destroyed. "I used Jewish people," le Carré writes in his article "To Russia, with Greetings" (*Encounter*, May, 1966), "because I felt that after Stalin and Hitler they should particularly engage our protective instincts." Smiley makes a brief appearance in the novel in a somewhat menacing role, the only such appearance in all of le Carré's novels, Smiley without his humane personality. There are other references to Steed-Asprey, Peter Guillam, and to the Samuel Fennan case, echoes from *Call for the Dead*.

The Looking-Glass War · The time frame of le Carré's next novel, *The Looking-Glass War*, is twenty years after that of *The Spy Who Came in from the Cold*. The British Military Intelligence unit, which during World War II has been vibrant, proud, and respectable, now exists as a mere remnant. Its officers and agents, nostalgic for the old days, wait for an incident to happen that could summon them to relive the past glory and regain their identity and honor. The head of this outfit is Le Clerc, a bland "precise cat of a man." When one of his agents stumbles across evidence pointing to the possible Soviet smuggling of nuclear rockets to the East Germans, Le Clerc is overjoyed. It is a British version of the Bay of Pigs. Le Clerc wants to stage an overflight to photograph the incriminating evidence. He goes about his mission with messianic zeal, because to him, the enemy is not only the Soviet Union, but the Circus—the rival British intelligence agency—as well. The Circus could take the mission away from him and destroy his unit's moment of glory. In *The Looking-Glass War*, le Carré reveals the Cold War professionals' lack of "ideological involvement." In his own words, "Half the time they are fighting the enemy, a good deal of the time they are fighting rival departments."

Taylor, the man sent to pick up the secret film, is killed, and Le Clerc recruits Avery, untrained for such work, to go undercover to bring back Taylor's body. Avery is a true believer; he attributes legendary qualities to his unit. He is faced with reality when he bungles the recovery mission and is saved only by a seasoned and contemptuous British diplomat, but he falls under Le Clerc's spell again in an ambitious project to train an agent—one of their own, not a Circus man—to send into East Germany to gather evidence of the rockets. His true moment of disillusionment comes when Fred Leiser, the agent in whose training he has participated, is caught inside East Germany. The Department refuses to help Leiser, who is left to fend for himself because of "some squalid diplomatic reason."

Leiser, an immigrant from Poland with wartime espionage experience, is another one of le Carré's rootless spies who is given a prepackaged identity and then discarded. Leiser's training provides the Department with its "carefree exciting days," yet in spite of his loyalty and his gentlemanly dress, Leiser is not considered by the Oxonians who run the show as "one of us." "He is a man to be handled, not known," says Haldane, a friend of Smiley. Leiser is not from the proper class nor from the proper school and hence cannot be a member of the privileged caste to which Haldane and Smiley belong. Through the character of Leiser, le Carré again analyzes the subtle nuances of the British class system.

A Small Town in Germany · The "town" of *A Small Town in Germany* is Bonn, "a very metaphysical spot" where "dreams have quite replaced reality." Britain is eager to get into the Common Market, so eager that she is prepared to shake hands with the devil. The devil in this case is Karfeld, a demogogue with Hitlerian overtones, fanatically anti-British and involved in forging a Russo-German alliance. Of more immediate concern to the British, however, is Leo Harting, second secretary in the political section of the British embassy. Because of his refugee background—like that of Leiser in *The Looking-Glass War*—Harting is in an "unpromotable, unpostable, unpensionable position."

At the beginning of the book, Harting is missing along with some top-secret files. Information in these files could destroy British chances to join the Common Market and compromise British-German relations. Harting must be found, but the files are more important than the man. To lead this urgent manhunt, Alan Turner is sent from London. Most of the events in the novel are seen through Turner's eyes.

"A big lumbering man," Turner walks "with the thrusting slowness of a barge; a broad aggressive policeman's walk." Like Leamas, Turner is a professional. Tough, acerbic, with a passionate obsession to get the job done, Turner shakes up the inefficient officials of the British embassy. In his pursuit of Harting, Turner begins to see a mirror image of himself. Both are underground men. "I'll chase you, you chase me and each of us will chase ourselves," Turner soliloquizes. In Turner's view, Harting must not only be found but also protected, because he is "our responsibility." To the Oxonians, Harting, although he dresses in British style and "uses our language," is "only half tamed." He is, like Leamas and Leiser, expendable. In his minute analysis of the British embassy officials in Bonn, le Carré portrays what Raymond Sokolov aptly calls "an encyclopedia of the English class system."

Both as an exciting tale of suspense and as a novel exploring the moral dilemma confronting men and women involved in defending Western freedom, *A Small Town in Germany* further advanced le Carré's reputation as an able chronicler of a murky world.

Tinker, Tailor, Soldier, Spy · *Tinker, Tailor, Soldier, Spy*, the first volume in the trilogy concerning Smiley's pursuit of his Soviet counterpart, Karla, is the story of the exposure of a Soviet "mole" burrowed deep within the Circus. Smiley, who has been fired (officially, he has "retired") because of his close association with Control, the former head of the Circus, now dead, who was discredited by the mole because he was coming too close to the truth, is summoned "to come out of his retirement and root out as unobtrusively as possible" the Soviet mole. Smiley begins his meticulous search through the "long dark tunnel." Proust-like, he indulges in remembrance of things past to trace the identity of the mole. He even questions his own motives, part of the subtle pressure exerted on him by his adversary Karla. The search in memory takes him to Delhi, India, where the reader meets Karla for the first time. Karla, "a little wiry chap, with silvery hair and bright brown eyes and plenty of wrinkles," is imprisoned under the name of Gerstman. With characteristic frankness, Smiley tells Karla, "I can see through Eastern values just as you can through our Western ones." Trying vainly to persuade Karla to defect, Smiley offers him cigarettes and hands him his lighter, a gift inscribed with love from his wife, Ann. Karla keeps the lighter when he returns, unpersuaded, to his cell. Echoes of this prison meeting between Karla and Smiley reverberate effectively in *The Honourable Schoolboy* and *Smiley's People*.

Smiley finally captures the mole: He is suave, handsome Bill Haydon, who comes from the right background and the right school. Haydon has turned mole because he could no longer be an empire builder. Haydon not only has betrayed his country, but also has betrayed his friend Jim Prideaux by setting him up for Soviet cruelty. Further, at the command of Karla, Haydon has slept with Smiley's wife, Ann, thereby creating a doubt in Smiley's mind concerning his own motives for ferreting out Haydon. The bureaucratic world of official secrets is linked with the private world of emotional betrayal, giving le Carré's work a universality which transcends its genre.

Kim Philby, the British defector, was the prototype of Bill Haydon. In his introduction to *The Philby Conspiracy* (1968), le Carré writes that the British secret services are "microcosms of the British condition, of our social attitudes and vanities." *Tinker, Tailor, Soldier, Spy* portrays such a microcosm.

Tinker, Tailor, Soldier, Spy was a successful television miniseries with Alec Guinness as George Smiley. Le Carré admired the production, but he has remarked that Guinness "took the character away from me. Writing Smiley after Smiley-through-Guinness had entered the public domain was very difficult. In a sense his screen success blew it for me."

The Honourable Schoolboy · Set in Southeast Asia at the time of America's disastrous retreat from Vietnam, *The Honourable Schoolboy*, the second volume in the trilogy *The Quest for Karla*, is a stunning novel of contemporary history. In *The Honourable Schoolboy*, Smiley steps out of Europe: The action of the novel ranges across Southeast Asia and is centered in Hong Kong. There are two spheres of action: the Circus, where one encounters the familiar faces of Peter Guillam, Sam Collins, and Toby Esterhase; and Southeast Asia, where Smiley has sent Jerry Westerby to track down a high-ranking Chinese who is a top Soviet agent. As the novel progresses Smiley must also contend with the machinations of the "cousins" (the American Central Intelligence Agency).

Jerry Westerby is the honorable schoolboy, so called because he was called "schoolboy" in the Tuscan village where he was trying to write a novel, and given the honorific "the Honorable" because he is the son of a Press Lord. Le Carré had introduced Westerby in *Tinker, Tailor, Soldier, Spy*, and in making him the major figure in *The Honourable Schoolboy*, he demonstrated one of his techniques for developing characters. In an interview with Michael Barber (*The New York Times Book Review*,

September 25, 1977), le Carré explained that he gives some of his minor characters "a variety of qualifications" so that he can later "turn them from two dimensional characters into three dimensional characters." He had provided Westerby with a Far Eastern background in the earlier novel, making him a natural for a leading role in a novel with that setting.

In *The Honourable Schoolboy*, Smiley feels compelled to restore the dignity of the Circus, lost in the aftermath of the exposure of Bill Haydon. When he spots large amounts of money from Russia pouring into Southeast Asia, his curiosity is aroused. He recruits Westerby, a newspaper writer and an "occasional" for the Circus, to go to Hong Kong. Westerby's targets are two Chinese brothers, Drake Ko and Nelson Ko. In dealing with them, Westerby is fatally attracted to Drake Ko's mistress Lizzi Worthington. Westerby, by allowing his passion—and compassion—to intrude on his sense of duty, pays a heavy price for his weakness.

The Honourable Schoolboy is a very complex novel, and there are plots within plots like ingenious Chinese boxes. Any attempt at a synopsis would be futile, and it is difficult to capture the rich texture of the novel. Le Carré peoples it with a multitude of characters, each bursting with possibilities for a separate novel. There is Craw, the Australian journalist, an old China hand, based on the London *Sunday Times* correspondent Richard Hughes (who also appears as Dikko Henderson in Ian Fleming's *You Only Live Twice*, 1964); Connie Sachs, the Circus Sovietologist; Fawn, the professional killer; and the mercenary pilot Ricardo, to mention but a few. They interact with one another in a variety of ways to dramatize a labyrinthine maze of involved relationships, both personal and political. Within this framework, le Carré again poses the questions with which he continues to be concerned: What is honor? What is loyalty? These questions, as Eliot Fremont-Smith noted, "provide the tension in the book, and are its engines of suspense."

Smiley's People · *Smiley's People*, the final volume in the trilogy *The Quest for Karla*, opens with the knowledge that one of Smiley's most valued and loyal "people," Vladimir, alias Colonel Miller, has been murdered. He had a message for Smiley concerning the Sandman (a code name for Karla). Once again, Smiley is called back from retirement. Smiley's quest is to find a weak spot in Karla, his Soviet counterpart. In Karla, Smiley sees his own dark and mysterious side. As Connie Sachs says to him, "You and Karla, two halves of the same apple."

In this novel, Smiley is the detective *par excellence*. He stalks Vladimir's killer with the skill and acumen of Sherlock Holmes. No James Bond, Smiley is the philosopher-spy who wants to find Karla's Achilles heel. He is convinced that Karla is not "fireproof." The tender spot turns out to be Karla's mentally defective daughter, Alexandra. Smiley plays upon this weakness, this aspect of a Karla "flawed by humanity."

Karla yields, and the final tense scene of *Smiley's People* is acted out on the same site as le Carré's masterpiece, *The Spy Who Came in from the Cold*—the Berlin Wall. Smiley sees the face of the man whose photograph had hung on the wall in the Circus, constantly reminding him of his unfinished business. They face each other, "perhaps a yard apart," Smiley hears the sound of Ann's gold cigarette lighter fall to the ground, and Karla crosses over to give Smiley the victory he has sought for so long.

In *Smiley's People*, the reader meets Ann for the first time, "beautiful and Celtic." When Smiley sees her, "Haydon's shadow" falls "between them like a sword." In the end, Smiley is alone, as he had been in his first appearance in *A Call for the Dead*, "without school, parents, regiment or trade," a man who has invested his life in institutions and realizes philosophically that all he is "left with is myself."

The women in *Smiley's People* are more fully delineated than in le Carré's previous novels. He attributes this to his second marriage. After completing *Smiley's People*, le Carré expressed the hope that the "emergence of female strength" in that novel could be carried into later writing. In *The Little Drummer Girl*, he fulfilled that ambition.

The Little Drummer Girl · Charmian ("Charlie"), an English actress–incidentally inspired by le Carré's own sister Charlotte, a Shakespearean actress–is the heroine of *The Little Drummer Girl*. Charlie is a promoter of many causes, a grab-bag of the serious and the fashionable, "a passionate opponent of apartheid . . . a militant pacifist, a Sufist, a nuclear marcher, an anti-vivisectionist, and until she went back to smoking again, a champion of campaigns to eliminate tobacco from theatres and on the public underground." The resemblances to Vanessa Redgrave are unmistakable.

Kurtz, an Israeli intelligence agent, offers Charlie the most spectacular role of her career–an opportunity to perform in "the theatre of the real." She is transformed into a successful double agent with the task of cracking "the terror target." The target is Khalil, a Palestinian guerrilla who is bombing Jews and Israelis in Bonn and various other European cities. In her attempt to get Khalil out into the open, Charlie undergoes an astonishing change in her own character. It is hard to think of another novel that has so masterfully portrayed the destruction and reconstruction of the psyche of a person in the process of being turned into a double agent.

The Little Drummer Girl is a departure for le Carré. There are no moles here, but rather terrorists, and Britain and the Soviet Union are replaced by Israelis and Palestinians. Le Carré made several trips to the Middle East, talking with members of Israeli intelligence and with Yasser Arafat to soak up the atmosphere and allow his characters to develop and determine the action of the novel. The characters are not only authentic but also credible. In Charlie's switching of roles and loyalties, le Carré has the opportunity to present both viewpoints, the Israeli and the Palestinian. While le Carré admires all that Israel stands for, in this book he is a partisan for the needs of the Palestinians. In *The Little Drummer Girl*, le Carré skillfully weaves a suspense tale taken from newspaper headlines, seeking out the universal themes of loneliness, alienation, exile, love, and betrayal of human beings behind those headlines. The result is a great novel.

A Perfect Spy · In his next two novels, le Carré returned to the world of British espionage. *A Perfect Spy* centers on Magnus Pym, a British double agent. Here, as in previous works, le Carré considers the meaning of loyalty and betrayal, not only among spies but also in everyday life; in much of the book, espionage is peripheral. The character of Rick Pym, Magnus's charming but untrustworthy father, is clearly based on le Carré's own father, and the novel is his most autobiographical to date.

The Russia House · With *The Russia House*, le Carré became one of the first masters of espionage fiction to reckon with the changes wrought by Mikhail Gorbachev's policy of *glasnost*. Published in the spring of 1989, shortly before the momentous events in Germany and Eastern Europe, *The Russia House* suggests that powerful factions in the United States intelligence community and military establishment might well contrive to keep the Cold War going.

A Perfect Spy and *The Russia House* demonstrate le Carré's continuing determination to extend the boundaries of the espionage novel. Indeed, le Carré's career offers proof—if further proof is needed—that great fiction can be written in any genre, that genius is no respecter of critical categories.

The Secret Pilgrim · The occasion of le Carré's next novel, *The Secret Pilgrim*, is the end-of-term dinner at the Circus's training center, Sarratt. The guest of honor, the legendary George Smiley, makes his last appearance in le Carré's work, imparting his wisdom to the spies in training and to Ned, previously Barley Blair's case officer in *The Russia House*. Ned listens to Smiley's recollections, feeling "that he was speaking straight into my heretical heart."

Smiley's comments propel Ned into a deep retrospection of the thirty years of secrecy and betrayal that have constituted his life in the Service. *The Secret Pilgrim* progresses not so much as an integrated whole but as a series of short stories. At the end of the evening's celebration, Smiley flatly states that "It's over, and so am I. . . . Time you rang down the curtain on yesterday's cold warrior. . . . The worst thing you can do is imitate us." Jauntily, as a parting note, Smiley says to "tell them to spy on the ozone layer, will you, Ned?"

The Night Manager · A problem that le Carré faced in the 1990's was what to write about after the end of the Cold War, which had been so central to his work. He solved this problem in his next novel, *The Night Manager*, his mostly richly textured and intricately plotted book since *The Honorable Schoolboy*. Jonathan Pine, one-time British soldier and itinerant hotelier, is haunted by the death of Sophie, an Egyptian woman he had tried to save from her brutal arms-dealing lover. Pine volunteers his services to British intelligence after he encounters Dicky Roper, the man who is ultimately responsible for Sophie's death. Pine becomes a pawn in a struggle between the "enforcement" operatives who control him, and who wish to prosecute Roper, and the "Pure Intelligence" services of the "River House" who have a secret understanding with Roper. A further complication is Pine's love for Roper's mistress, Jemima. Infiltrating Roper's household, Pine eventually becomes involved in Roper's arms deals until his cover is blown. The conclusion of the novel is a clear homage to Joseph Conrad's "The Secret Sharer"; Pine and Jemima are helped off Roper's yacht, while Roper sadly watches from the rail.

Our Game · *Our Game*, a play on the British expression "the Great Game," pits two Cold War colleagues against each other. Timothy Cranmer, a retired case officer, now a winemaker, pursues his agent, Larry, who has disappeared with Cranmer's girl-friend, Emma. Tracing Emma to Paris, Cranmer continues to follow Larry, first to Moscow, then to Chechnya during its civil war. While he arrives too late to confront his former colleague, Cranmer is not too late to redeem his own and Larry's legacy. He joins the Chechen guerrillas.

The Tailor of Panama · Le Carré's only comic novel, *The Tailor of Panama*, recalls Graham Greene's *Our Man in Havana*. Harry Pendel, a former convict and "bespoken tailor," is suborned as a source by British intelligence. Unfortunately he has no intelligence to impart, so he invents it. Fueled by this source, the intelligence community in Panama contrives an American coup, while the British ambassador elopes with his secretary. Le Carré's darkly humorous vision of intelligence gathering is juxtaposed against the real problems of contemporary Panamanians.

K. Bhaskara Rao, updated by James Barbour

Bibliography

Barley, Tony. *Taking Sides: The Fiction of John le Carré.* Philadelphia: Open University Press, 1986. This work applies a somewhat esoteric critical examination to the problems of morality and reality in le Carré's work up to *The Little Drummer Girl.* It is a thorough text, but it suffers from being too academic.

Beene, Lynn Diane. *John le Carré.* New York: Twayne, 1992. This is a very useful biography of David Cornwell's life before he adopted the pseudonym John le Carré, and his career since becoming a writer. Following the biography, the author provides a detailed and well-referenced analysis of le Carré's novels through *Smiley's People.*

Cobbs, John, L. *Understanding John le Carré.* Columbia: University of South Carolina Press, 1998. This is a thorough and comprehensive critical work about John le Carré's novels, all of which, through *The Tailor of Panama,* are analyzed.

Lewis, Peter E. *John le Carré.* New York: Frederick Ungar, 1985. An extensive critique of John le Carré's work, with special mention of its political context. The material is well organized and includes a useful bibliography.

Monaghan, David. *The Novels of John le Carré: The Art of Survival.* New York: Basil Blackwell, 1985. Provides book-by-book coverage of all of le Carré's novels through *The Little Drummer Girl.* Also includes an insightful chapter on George Smiley.

——————. *Smiley's Circus.* London: Orbis Press, 1986. A wonderful illustrated index of characters from all the novels through *A Perfect Spy,* particularly focusing on the Karla trilogy of novels. Includes chronologies of the plots of the novels, maps, and photographs of some of the more famous British landmarks featured in le Carré's work. This is an invaluable tool for untangling the byzantine complexity of George Smiley's world. Its careful compilation of characters is testament not only to Monaghan's skill as a researcher but also to le Carré's deeply textured work.

Sauerberg, Lars Ole. *Secret Agents in Fiction.* New York: St. Martin's Press, 1984. A criticism and comparison of John le Carré, Ian Fleming, and Len Deighton. Although there are references to le Carré throughout the text, one chapter, "The Enemy Within," is devoted solely to his work.

Wolfe, Peter. *Corridors of Deceit: The World of John le Carré.* Bowling Green, Ohio: Bowling Green University Popular Press, 1987. An in-depth probing of le Carré's writing, this work contains many interesting insights into the author's characters but lacks a bibliography.

Joseph Sheridan Le Fanu

Born: Dublin, Ireland; August 28, 1814
Died: Dublin, Ireland; February 7, 1873

Principal long fiction · *The Cock and Anchor*, 1845; *Torlogh O'Brien*, 1847; *The House by the Churchyard*, 1863; *Wylder's Hand*, 1864; *Uncle Silas*, 1864; *Guy Deverell*, 1865; *All in the Dark*, 1866; *The Tenants of Malory: A Novel*, 1867 (3 volumes); *A Lost Name*, 1868; *The Wyvern Mystery*, 1869; *Checkmate*, 1871; *The Rose and the Key*, 1871; *Morley Court*, 1873; *Willing to Die*, 1873 (3 volumes).

Other literary forms · Joseph Sheridan Le Fanu is better known today as a short-story writer than as a novelist. His many tales first appeared in periodicals, later to be combined into collections. In addition to having genuine intrinsic merit, the stories are important to an understanding of Le Fanu the novelist, for in them he perfected the techniques of mood, characterization, and plot construction that make his later novels so obviously superior to his early efforts. Indeed, Le Fanu seems to have recognized little distinctive difference between the novel and the tale; his novels are often expansions of earlier stories, and stories reissued in collections might be loosely linked by a frame created to give them some of the unity of a novel. The major collections, *Ghost Stories and Tales of Mystery* (1851), *Chronicles of Golden Friars* (1871), *In a Glass Darkly* (1872), and *The Purcell Papers* (1880), reveal an artist who ranks with Edgar Allan Poe, Ambrose Bierce, M. R. James, and Algernon Blackwood as one of the masters of supernatural fiction in the English language. One story from *In A Glass Darkly*, "Carmilla," is reprinted in almost every anthology of horror stories and has inspired numerous film versions, the most famous being Carl-Theodore Dreyer's *Vampyr* (1931).

Le Fanu wrote verse throughout his literary career. While unknown as a poet to modern audiences, in his own day at least one of his compositions achieved great popularity in both Ireland and the United States. "Shamus O'Brien" (1850) is a fine ballad that relates the adventures of the title character in the uprising of 1798.

Achievements · In the preface to his most famous novel, *Uncle Silas*, Le Fanu rejects the claim of critics that he is a mere writer of "sensational novels." Pointing out that the great novels of Sir Walter Scott have sensational elements of violence and horror, he denies that his own work, any more than Scott's, should be characterized by the presence of such elements; like Scott, Le Fanu too has "moral aims."

To see the truth in this self-appraisal requires familiarity with more than one of Le Fanu's novels. Singly, each of the major works overwhelms the reader with the cleverness of its plot, the depravity of its villain, the suspense evoked by its carefully controlled tone. Several novels together, however, recollected in tranquility, reveal a unity of theme. Moreover, each novel can then be seen as not merely a variation on the theme but also as a deliberate next logical step toward a more comprehensive and definitive statement. The intricacies of plot, the kinds of evil represented by the villains, the pervasive gothic gloom are to Le Fanu more than story elements; they are themselves his quite serious comment on the nature of human existence, driven by natural and social forces that leave little room for the effective assertion of free will toward any beneficial end.

In Le Fanu's short stories, more often than in his novels, those forces are embodied in tangible supernatural agents. "Carmilla," for example, is the tale of a real female vampire's attack on a young woman, but seen in the context of the larger theme, it is more than a bit of occult fiction calculated to give its readers a scare. With her intense sexuality and lesbian tendencies, the vampire is nothing less than the embodiment of a basic human drive out of control, and that drive–like the others that move society: self-preservation, physical comfort–can quite unpredictably move toward destruction. Le Fanu's most significant achievement as a novelist was to show how the horror genre could be used for serious purposes–to show that monsters are not as horrible as minds that beget monsters, and that ghosts are not as interesting as people who are haunted.

Biography · Joseph Sheridan Le Fanu was descended from a Huguenot family that had left France for Ireland in the seventeenth century. Both his grandfather, Joseph, and great uncle, Henry, had married sisters of the famous playwright, Richard Brinsley Sheridan. His father, Philip Le Fanu, was a noted scholar and clergyman who served as rector at the Royal Hibernian School, where Le Fanu was born, and later as Dean of Emly. His mother was from all accounts a most charming and gentle person, an essayist on philanthropic subjects and a leader in the movement for humane treatment of animals. With loving and indulgent parents and the excitement of life at the school, where military reviews were frequent, Le Fanu's childhood was a happy one.

In 1826, the family moved to Abington in county Limerick. Le Fanu and his brother, William, were not sent to a formal school but were tutored by their father with the help of an elderly clergyman, who gladly excused the boys from their lessons so he could pursue the passion of his life: fishing. Walking tours through the wild Irish countryside, conversations with friendly peasants, who told of fairies and pookhas and banshees, shaped very early the imagination of the boy who would become the creator of so many tales of the mysterious and supernatural. The Tithe Wars of 1831 and the resulting animosity of the peasants to the Le Fanus, who were seen as representative of the Anglo-Irish establishment, forced the young Le Fanu to examine his own Irishness. On the one hand, he was intellectually supportive of the union and convinced that the British rule was in the best interests of the Irish people; on the other, the courage and sacrifices of the bold Irish nationalists filled him with admiration and respect.

In 1837, Le Fanu was graduated from Trinity College, Dublin. He took honors in classics and was well-known for his fine orations before the College Historical Society. Called to the Irish Bar in 1839, he never practiced law but entered a productive career in journalism. His first published work, "The Ghost and the Bonesetter," appeared in the *Dublin University Magazine* in January, 1838. That magazine was to publish serially eight of Le Fanu's fourteen novels after he became its owner and editor in 1861. During the early 1840's, Le Fanu became proprietor or part-owner of a number of journals, including *The Warder, The Statesman, The Protestant Guardian*, and the *Evening Mail.*

In 1844, Le Fanu married Susan Bennett. The union was a happy one; the Le Fanus had two sons and two daughters. One son, George, became an artist and illustrated some of his father's works. Le Fanu's novels published in the 1840's, *The Cock and Anchor* and *Torlogh O'Brien*, received poor reviews, and Le Fanu turned from writing fiction to concentrate on his journalistic work. With the death of his beloved wife in 1858, he withdrew from society and became a recluse. Only a few close friends were allowed to visit "the invisible prince" at his elegant home at Merrion Square, Dublin. Emerging only occasionally to visit booksellers for volumes on ghosts and the occult, Le Fanu established a daily routine he was to follow for the remaining years of his life: writing in bed by candlelight from midnight till dawn, rising at noon, and writing all afternoon at a prized, small desk once owned by Richard Brinsley Sheridan. In this manner was produced the greatest share of a literary canon that rivals in quantity the output of the most prolific authors of the Victorian age.

At the end, under treatment for heart disease, troubled by nightmares—especially one recurring scene of a gloomy, old mansion on the verge of collapsing on the terrified dreamer—Le Fanu refused the company of even his closest friends. On the night of February 7, 1873, his doctor found him in bed, his arms flung wide, his unseeing eyes fixed in terror at something that could no longer do him harm. "I feared this," the doctor said; "that house fell at last."

Analysis · After writing two novels that failed to impress the critics, Joseph Sheridan Le Fanu left that genre for approximately fifteen years. In his reclusive later life, he returned to long fiction to produce the fine work for which he is remembered. Le Fanu's career as a novelist reveals a marked change in his perception of humanity and the very nature of the universe itself. The development of the author's major theme can be illustrated by a survey of the major novels in his quite extensive canon.

The Cock and Anchor · The early works, *The Cock and Anchor* and *Torlogh O'Brien*, are both historical novels dealing with the Ireland of the late seventeenth and early eighteenth centuries, the turbulent time of the Williamite wars (1689-1691). *The Cock and Anchor* presents a slice of Irish life that cuts across events and persons of real historical significance and the personal misfortunes of one fictional couple, Mary Ashewoode and Edmund O'Connor. The story of these ill-fated lovers has nothing special to recommend it. Mary is kept from Edmund first by her father, Sir Richard, who would marry her for a fortune to Lord Aspenly, a conventional fop, and then by her brother, Henry, who would see her wed to one Nicholas Blarden, a conventional villain. Mary escapes these nefarious designs and flees to the protection of Oliver French, the conventional benevolent uncle. There is, however, no happy ending: Mary dies before Edmund can reach her. The designing Sir Richard suffers a fatal stroke; brother Henry finally finds the destiny for which he was born, the hangman's noose; and even Edmund's unlucky life ends on the battlefield of Denain in 1712. More interesting to the modern reader are the historical characters. The haughty Lord Warton, Viceroy of Dublin, personifies power and Machiavellian self-interest. Joseph Addison and young Jonathan Swift are also here in well-drawn portraits that demonstrate considerable historical research. Still, the novel is at best uneven, the work of an author with promise who has more to learn about his craft.

The technical obstructions, however, cannot hide Le Fanu's message: The problems of Ireland are profound and rooted deep in a history of conflict. The Anglo-Irish establishment, represented by the Ashewoode family, has lost sight of the values needed to end the strife and move the society toward peace and prosperity, values such as personal responsibility, compassion, and even love within the family. Le Fanu was unwilling to risk clouding his theme by allowing the happy marriage of Mary and Edmund, the conventional ending to which the conventional plot could be expected to lead. They die to prove the point. The Ashewoodes's decay is really Ireland's decay, and the wage is death.

Torlogh O'Brien · *Torlogh O'Brien*, Le Fanu's second novel and the last he was to write for sixteen years, is set a few years before *The Cock and Anchor*, during the Williamite wars. Again, most critics have found little to admire in the work. The historical scenes and characters show that once more Le Fanu thoroughly researched his subject, but the fictional characters reveal little improvement in their creator's art. The plot, except for some unusually violent scenes, would hold no surprises for a reader of romances. The villainous Miles Garret, a traitor to the Protestant cause, wishes to take Glindarragh Castle from Sir Hugh Willoughby, a supporter of William of Orange. Arrested on false charges created by Garret, Sir Hugh and his daughter, Grace, are taken to Dublin for trial. Their escort is Torlogh O'Brien, a soldier in the army of King James II, whose family originally held the estate. O'Brien and Sir Hugh, both honorable men, rise above their political differences to gain mutual respect. Finally, it is O'Brien who intervenes to save the Willoughbys from the designs of Garret, and of course his bravery is rewarded by the love of Grace.

From the first novel to the second, villainy—Nicholas Blarden or Miles Garret—remains a constant, and the agony of a torn Ireland is the common background against which Edmund O'Connor and Torlogh O'Brien act out their parts. The social cancer that blighted the love of Mary and Edmund is, however, allowed a possible cure in *Torlogh O'Brien*. As the deaths of the lovers in the first novel showed Ireland as a sterile wasteland, so the union of the Willoughbys and O'Briens in the second promises restoring rain, but when after the long hiatus Le Fanu returned to novel writing, he chose to let the promise go unfulfilled.

The House by the Churchyard · Held by many critics to be Le Fanu's finest work, *The House by the Churchyard*, the first novel of his later period, appeared in the *Dublin University Magazine* in 1861; two years later, it was published in London as a book. The story is set in late eighteenth century Chapelizod, a suburb of Dublin. As in the earlier historical romances, there are villains, lovers, and dispossessed heirs. A major plot concerns the righting of an old wrong. Eighteen years after the death of Lord Dunoran, executed for a murder he did not commit, his son, using the name Mr. Mervyn, returns to the confiscated family lands hoping to establish his father's innocence. The real murderer, Charles Archer, has also returned to Chapelizod under the alias of Paul Dangerfield. He is soon recognized by a former accomplice, Zekiel Irons, and a witness, Dr. Barnaby Sturk. Sturk attempts blackmail, only to have Archer beat him severely. His victim in a coma, Archer plays benefactor and arranges for a surgeon he knows to be incompetent to perform a brain operation, supposedly to restore Sturk to health. To Archer's surprise, the operation gives Sturk a period of consciousness before the expected death. Irons joins Sturk in revealing Archer as the murderer, Lord Dunoran's lands and title are restored to Mervyn, and the family name is cleared at last.

This, however, is only one of several interrelated plots that make *The House by the Churchyard* a marvel of Victorian complexity. To label the Archer mystery as the major story line would be to mislead the reader who has yet to discover the book. More accurately, the novel is about Chapelizod itself. The discovery of a murderer stands out in the plot as, to be sure, it would in any small community, but Le Fanu is reminding his readers that what immediately affects any individual—for example,

Mervyn's need to clear his father's name—no matter how urgently, is of limited interest to other individuals, who are in turn preoccupied with their own concerns. Mrs. Nutter has her own problem with protecting her inheritance from wicked Mary Matchwell. Captain Devereux and Lilias Walsingham have their doomed romance to concern them, as, on a more humorous note, Captain Cuffe is preoccupied with his love for Rebecca Chattesworth, who is finally joined with Lieutenant Puddock, the former suitor of Gertrude Chattesworth, who in turn has a secret romance with Mervyn. Indeed, the unsolved murder cannot totally dominate even the life of Lord Dunoran's son.

Some of the characters serve a comic purpose, and with so many complex entanglements, the comic could easily slide into complete farce. Le Fanu avoids caricature, however, by providing each comic figure with some other distinguishing quality—wit, compassion, bravery. In *The House by the Churchyard,* Le Fanu, already a master of description and mood, added the one needed skill so obviously absent in his early novels, the art of characterization.

The characterization of Archer, alias Dangerfield, is by itself sufficient to demonstrate Le Fanu's growth as a novelist. Dangerfield's evil is almost supernatural; he describes himself as a corpse and a vampire, a werewolf and a ghoul. He is incapable not only of love but also of hate, and he calmly announces before his suicide that he "never yet bore any man the least ill-will." He has had to "remove two or three" merely to ensure his own safety. The occult imagery used to define Dangerfield also links him to the microcosm of Chapelizod, for Mervyn's Tiled House is reputedly haunted; the specter of a ghostly hand has frightened more than one former resident. Le Fanu allows Mervyn, like Torlogh O'Brien, his happy ending, but so powerful is the hold of Dangerfield on the novel that the possibility of colossal evil that he personifies is not totally exorcised even by his death. The fact that he was not really supernatural but was the embodiment of human depravity in no way diminishes the horror.

Wylder's Hand • With his fourth novel, *Wylder's Hand,* Le Fanu left historical romances and social panoramas to study evil with a closer eye. The story, certainly Le Fanu's finest mystery, concerns the strange disappearance of young Mark Wylder, a lieutenant in the navy and rival of Captain Stanley Lake for the hand of Dorcas Brandon, a rich heiress. From several locations in Europe, Wylder has sent letters containing instructions for the conduct of his business and releasing Dorcas to marry Lake. The suspicions of Larkin, a family attorney, are aroused by a problem with the dating of certain letters, but then Wylder returns to Brandon Hall, where he is actually seen in conversation with Lake. The very next day, however, Lake is thrown from his horse as the animal is startled by the pointing hand of Mark Wylder's corpse protruding from the ground, exposed by a heavy rain. Dying, Lake confesses to having murdered his rival and arranging for the posting of forged letters. In fact, it was not Wylder who appeared the preceding night at Brandon but one James Dutton, the unwitting accomplice who had posted the letters and who happens to resemble Wylder. Only one person knew of Wylder's fate, having witnessed his midnight burial: Rachel Lake, the murderer's sister. Devotion to her brother and to Dorcas Brandon, who really loves Lake, compelled her silence.

The plot is a masterpiece of suspense, but still more impressive are the characterizations. Each figure is finely drawn and fits into a mosaic of human types which together pictures a species ill equipped to deal with evil. Wylder is a swaggering braggart, crude, unfeeling, with a general air of disreputability that seems to promise some future act of monstrous brutality had not a violent death cut short his career. Like two vicious dogs claiming the same territory, Wylder and Lake cannot exist in the same world without one destroying the other. Lake's evil, however, is of a quite different nature. In many respects, he is Le Fanu's most interesting study. Wylder's is a rather directionless evil; it could as easily manifest itself in one abhorrent action as another. Dangerfield was simply amoral. Born without any sense of restraint, his natural selfishness led to murder for convenience. Lake's evil is weakness. Greed for property and position seems almost an outside force, a part of human society that can compel even murder in those who lack the strength to resist. He experiences guilt and fear and never is able to derive satisfaction from his villainy. Considering that the murdered man was certainly no credit to the human race, the reader may actually feel sympathy for Lake. In him, Le Fanu presents the criminal as victim, but the consequences of Lake's weakness affect others as well. Rachel's knowledge of the secret and Dorcas's ignorance isolate them from the man they love, much as Lake is himself isolated. Gloom, a sense of a scheme of things not quite right, permeates the texture of the entire novel. There is no happy ending. Years later, Rachel and Dorcas are seen in Venice, sad and alone.

Uncle Silas · In *Uncle Silas*, Le Fanu continued his investigation of the terrible yet tragic evil represented by Lake. Two earlier tales, "An Episode in the Secret History of an Irish Countess" (1838) and "The Murdered Cousin" (1851) provided a basic plot structure for the study, and in 1864, the same year that *Wylder's Hand* was published, a bound edition in three volumes with the title *Uncle Silas: A Tale of Bartram-Haugh* appeared. Considered by most critics Le Fanu's finest novel, it brings all the skill acquired over a productive career to a definitive study of the themes that interested its author most: the nature of evil, and the hereditary aristocracy as a paradigm for the effects of that destructive force. As usual, the study is conducted through carefully drawn characters and a plot filled with mystery and suspense.

In compliance with the will of the deceased Austin Ruthyn, his daughter, Maud, is made the ward of Austin's brother, Silas, a sinister man suspected but never convicted of a past murder. The suspicions are well founded, for Uncle Silas will stop at nothing to gain full ownership of Maud's estate. When an arranged marriage between Maud and Silas's son, Dudley, proves impossible–the scoundrel is discovered to be already married–murder seems the only solution. Dudley botches the job, however, and kills Madame de la Rougierra, another of Silas's agents, by mistake. Maud flees to a kindly relative; Dudley flees to Australia; and Uncle Silas dies that same night from an overdose of opium.

Le Fanu called *Uncle Silas* a "tragic English romance," and indeed the novel does depict a truly tragic situation. The Ruthyns stumble blindly through situations and realities they can hardly perceive, much less understand. Austin Ruthyn, heedless of the suspicions surrounding his brother, sends his daughter into the wolf's lair. Dudley, purposeless and crude, sees only the moment, and this he addresses with instinct rather than intelligent consideration of consequences. Even Maud Ruthyn, the heroine and narrator, is unaware of her perilous situation until it is almost too late. Gothic heroines are expected to be naïve, and Le Fanu uses that trait in his narrator to good advantage. Maud often tells more than she realizes, and the reader sensitive to the unspoken messages that careful diction can convey sees the closing circle of predators before she does. The rhetorical effect is a sense of foreboding, a tension that charges the entire novel.

Despite his avoidance of prosecution for an earlier crime and his careful designs for his niece's downfall, Silas is as blind as any of the lesser characters. His lust for wealth and property is virtually inherited: Similar drives have directed his family for generations. His body a slave to narcotics, his mind to religious fanaticism, he is the aristocracy in decay. Le Fanu surrounds him with appropriate death imagery, and his loutish son, Dudley, married without Silas's knowledge to a barmaid, is final evidence of the collapse of the Ruthyn line. Silas's first murder victim had been a Mr. Charke, to whom he owed gambling debts, but with the planned murder of Maud, the violence turns in upon the Ruthyns themselves. Austin's blind trust puts Maud in harm's way, and Silas's blind greed would destroy her; *Uncle Silas* is ultimately nothing less than a portrait of the aristocratic class cannibalizing itself. Maud survives and eventually marries a young lord, but her concluding words speak more of hope for happiness than happiness realized, and the death of her first child, sorrowfully remembered, strikes at the last the same note sounded throughout the novel.

Willing to Die · That note of futility is heard most clearly in Le Fanu at the end of his career as a novelist. *Willing to Die*, first published serially in *All the Year Round* (1872-1873), is by no means his finest effort. The story, while complex, lacks the gothic excitement of the works for which he is remembered. Still, the novel is important in a thematic study.

Ethel Ware, the heroine, is allowed to sample a full range of life's possibilities. Poverty, loneliness, love, all contribute to the growth of her character; she surmounts all obstacles to achieve great material wealth and an understanding of the meaning of life. This is a new picture; in Ethel, the reader does not meet yet another aristocrat beaten by an ignorance of the forces at work in human society. Ethel wins, in the sense that Silas Ruthyn and Stanley Lake would have liked to win, but the mature vision that comes with the material victory only shows that the quest is pointless and the victory hollow. Isolated in her accomplishment as the protagonists of earlier novels were most often isolated in their failures, Ethel sees that the human struggle is manipulated by forces of society and chance, and whether the struggle culminates in a moment that might be called success or failure is finally irrelevant, for the last force to affect the struggle, death, affects the Wares and the Ruthyns alike.

The novels of Le Fanu are the record of an artist exploring social structures and individual minds in quest of horrors natural and supernatural. With his final entry in that often brilliant record, *Willing to Die*, he penetrated at last to the very heart of darkness to discover the ultimate horror: the utter futility of it all.

William J. Heim

Other major works

SHORT FICTION: *Ghost Stories and Tales of Mystery*, 1851; *Chronicles of Golden Friars*, 1871; *In a Glass Darkly*, 1872; *The Purcell Papers*, 1880; *The Watcher and Other Weird Stories*, 1894; *A Chronicle of Golden Friars*, 1896; *Madam Crowl's Ghost and Other Tales of Mystery*, 1923 (M. R. James, editor); *Green Tea and Other Ghost Stories*, 1945; *Best Ghost Stories of J. S. Le Fanu*, 1964.

POETRY: *The Poems of Joseph Sheridan Le Fanu*, 1896.

Bibliography

Begnal, Michael. *Joseph Sheridan Le Fanu*. Lewisburg, Pa.: Bucknell University Press, 1971. Sketches Le Fanu's life up to the death of his wife in 1858 and the beginning of his seclusion in Dublin. Analyzes his work as part of the gothic tradition to which Le Fanu makes a serious contribution, though he breaks from it to relate his ideas to his contemporary society. Focuses on his last four novels, presented as his best, which he published after emerging from his seclusion, beginning with *The House by the Churchyard*, in 1863. A brief study with a chronology and a selected bibliography.

Crawford, Gary William. *J. Sheridan Le Fanu: A Bio-Bibliography*. Westport, Conn.: Greenwood Press, 1995. Part 1 discusses Le Fanu's biography; part 2 is a primary, annotated bibliography of magazines, books, anthologies, and manuscripts; part 3 is an annotated secondary bibliography. The beginning student of Le Fanu will find this book an indispensable tool, which includes an appendix on films and plays based on Le Fanu's work. Also contains two useful indexes.

McCormack, W. J. *Dissolute Characters: Irish Literary History Through Balzac, Sheridan Le Fanu, Yeats, and Bowen*. Manchester, England: Manchester University Press, 1993. The section on Le Fanu discusses his relationship to the English novel, the development of his fiction, his treatment of characters, and his drawing on history. Includes notes but no bibliography.

_____. *Sheridan Le Fanu and Victorian Ireland*. Oxford, England: Clarendon Press, 1980. After a short introductory note, analyzes Le Fanu's life and career, examining the special conditions in Victorian Ireland behind his writing. These include the clerical world of Dublin during the struggles for Catholic emancipation, his Irish political background, and his own changing opinions with regard to the repeal of the Act of Union. Includes a close analysis of the symbolism of *Uncle Silas* as his most complex novel. McCormack acknowledges that his late writing is not good, but argues that study of his entire career is fundamental to study of Anglo-Irish literature. Contains illustrations, two appendices, a substantial bibliography with manuscript sources, and an index.

Melada, Ivan. *Sheridan Le Fanu*. Boston: Twayne, 1987. After summarizing Le Fanu's life, concentrates on his writing and concludes with an assessment of his literary achievements. Discusses Le Fanu's early short fiction, then his historical novels, followed by a sustained analysis of *Uncle Silas*, and then the late short fiction; Le Fanu's poetry and periodical fiction are saved for a final word on the variety of his work. Estimates his achievement by arguing that *Uncle Silas* shows him to be a master of terror literature, that his cinematic style should be attractive to a modern audience, and that his canon makes Le Fanu a major author in the gothic tradition. Provides a prefatory chronology, supplementary notes, a selected annotated bibliography, and an index.

Doris Lessing

Born: Kermanshah, Persia; October 22, 1919

Principal long fiction · *The Grass Is Singing*, 1950; *Martha Quest*, 1952; *A Proper Marriage*, 1954; *Retreat to Innocence*, 1956; *A Ripple from the Storm*, 1958; *The Golden Notebook*, 1962; *Landlocked*, 1965, 1991; *The Four-Gated City*, 1969; *Briefing for a Descent into Hell*, 1971; *The Summer Before the Dark*, 1973; *The Memoirs of a Survivor*, 1974; *Shikasta*, 1979; *The Marriages Between Zones Three, Four, and Five*, 1980; *The Sirian Experiments*, 1981; *The Making of the Representative for Planet 8*, 1982; *Documents Relating to the Sentimental Agents in the Volyen Empire*, 1983; *The Diary of a Good Neighbour*, 1983 (as Jane Somers); *If the Old Could . . .* , 1984 (as Somers); *The Diaries of Jane Somers*, 1984 (includes *The Diary of a Good Neighbour*, and *If the Old Could . . .*); *The Good Terrorist*, 1985; *The Fifth Child*, 1988; *Playing the Game*, 1995; *Love, Again*, 1996; *Mara and Dann*, 1999; *Ben, in the World*, 2000.

Other literary forms · Doris Lessing has published numerous volumes of short stories. She has also written memoirs, documentaries, essays, plays, reviews, and a book of poems.

Achievements · Lessing has been one of the most widely read and influential British novelists of the second half of the twentieth century. Her works have been translated into many languages and have inspired critical attention around the globe. Generally serious and didactic, Lessing's fiction repeatedly urges the human race to develop a wider consciousness that would allow for greater harmony and less violence. Although known particularly as a master of realism, Lessing is often experimental or deliberately fantastic, as shown in her science-fiction novels. Her interests are far-ranging, from Marxism and global politics to the mystical teachings of Sufism to the small personal voice of the individual. Her awards include the Somerset Maugham Award, the German Shakespeare Prize, the Austrian Prize for European Literature, and the French Prix Médicis for Foreigners. In 1995 she won the James Tait Black Prize and a *Los Angeles Times* Book Prize for her 1994 autobiography, *Under My Skin*.

Biography · Doris May Lessing was born in Kermanshah, Persia (later Iran), in 1919, the first child of Alfred Cook Tayler and Emily Maude McVeagh Tayler, who had emigrated from England to Persia shortly after World War I. A brother, Harry, was born two years later, and in 1925 the family moved to a farm in Southern Rhodesia (later Zimbabwe). Her parents were never financially successful. Her father was a dreamer who became a cynic after he failed at maize farming; her mother was domineering but ineffective. Despite Lessing's love of the African landscape and the isolated veld, she was eager to leave her family behind. She attended a Catholic convent school in Salisbury (now Harare) but left when she was fourteen, saying that she had eye problems, though she continued her voracious reading.

Lessing left home when she was fifteen to become a nursemaid and moved to Salisbury to work in various jobs, mostly clerical, and began writing fiction. She was married to Frank Charles Wisdom, a minor civil servant, in 1939, and had a son, John, and a daughter, Jean. Divorced in 1943, she was remarried two years later to a German-Jewish refugee, Gottfried Lessing. They had a son, Peter, in 1947. She divorced Gottfried Lessing in 1949 and that same year moved to England, settling in London; in 1950 she published her first novel. After that she continued to live in London and to make her living as a professional writer, publishing reviews, media scripts, and nonfiction in addition to novels, short stories, drama, and poetry.

Ingrid Von Kruse

Lessing's interest in politics began with a Marxist group in Rhodesia, and in England she was briefly a member of the Communist Party, leaving it officially in 1956. In the late 1950's she participated in mass demonstrations for nuclear disarmament and was a speaker at the first Aldermaston March in 1958. During the early 1960's she worked in the theater, helping to establish Centre 42, a populist art program, and writing her own plays. In the late 1960's Lessing's thinking began to be heavily influenced by the mystical teachings of Indries Shah and Sufism, which emphasizes conscious evolution of the mind in harmony with self and others. Although for many years Lessing resisted the role of public persona, in the mid-1980's she began to make numerous public appearances in many countries.

Lessing's work was recognized several times in 1995. She received an honorary degree from Harvard University that year and was also welcomed back into South Africa, which she had been forced to leave in 1956. She went to visit her daughter and grandchildren and was received with open arms by the country. In 1995, her autobiography won the prestigious James Tait Black Memorial Prize for best biography and a *Los Angeles Times* Book Prize.

Lessing has remained one of the most prolific writers of the twentieth century, and many of her books have won critical acclaim. In the 1990's she made fewer public appearances, devoting herself to more writing. Although she made a fourteen-week tour to promote her autobiography, Lessing has stated that she is more useful to her publisher when she stays at home and writes. When her novel *Love, Again* was published in 1996, she made no public appearances to promote the book.

Analysis · Doris Lessing is a powerful writer committed to the lofty goal of changing human consciousness itself. The narrative voice that weaves throughout her prolific fiction is that of an intense thinker who observes, explores, and describes the contemporary world but whose ultimate sense of human life is that the individual, and indeed the human race, is meant to go beyond mere recognition of perceived reality and to struggle with visions of the possible. Her novels repeatedly suggest that changes in the way humans view themselves, their world, and their relationships with others are imperative if life on this planet is to survive.

Lessing's scope is wide. Her creative imagination is able to provide a close analysis of a character with all that individual's fears, longings, and contradictions and to relate that individual not only to his or her circle of acquaintances but to patterns of global economics and politics as well, and then to sweep beyond even this planet to the cosmos and a perspective that encompasses the metaphysical questions of existence. Her fictional explorations are multiple, multidimensional, and overlapping, suggesting that no one viewpoint is adequate or complete. This range is also reflected in her varied narrative forms, which include realism, naturalism, science fiction, utopianism and dystopianism, fantasy, fable, transcultural postmodernism, and experimental combinations of these. This heterogeneity of themes, techniques, and perspectives illustrates Lessing's overriding premise that truth and substance cannot easily be compartmentalized or assigned fixed labels: Existence is always process, always in flux.

Lessing's position as an exile is a prominent aspect of her work, both in content and in theme. Born in the Middle East of English parents, she spent her adolescence in Southern Rhodesia, first with her family on an isolated and impoverished farm whose workers were all native black Africans, and then on her own in Salisbury. In the city she became involved with a group interested in international politics whose most specific focus was increased rights for black Rhodesians. Her experiences there in the 1940's, including two marriages and three children, became material for nearly all of her novels for the first twenty years of her writing career.

The Grass Is Singing · In 1949 Lessing arrived in London with her youngest son and the manuscript of *The Grass Is Singing.* In many ways this first book established a pattern for subsequent novels. Her manuscript was accepted for publication within three days of her submitting it to a publisher. The novel was well received and went through seven reprintings within five months. The title comes from part 5 of T. S. Eliot's *The Waste Land* (1922); Lessing's wide reading included the twentieth century writers as well as the great British, French, and Russian novelists of the nineteenth century. She most admired those writers with a sense of moral purpose, a sense of commitment to all humanity. *The Grass Is Singing* clearly shows the horrific effects of apartheid and racial prejudice on both the white colonial rulers and the black people who make up the overwhelming majority of the populations of southern Africa.

In a stylistic technique directly opposite to that of a stereotypical detective story, the third-person narrator reveals at the outset of *The Grass Is Singing* that Mary Turner, the wife of a poor farmer, has been killed by a houseboy, Moses, who confessed to the crime. The opening chapter shows the confusion and emotional collapse of Mary's husband, Dick Turner, and the reactions of Charlie Slatter, a neighbor, and Tony Marston, a young recent immigrant from England. The plot then becomes straightforward as it gives the background and chronology of events that led to the murder.

Mary grew up in the city and had established a pleasant though rather meaningless life after the death of her parents. At age thirty she begins to overhear acquaintances' disparaging remarks about the fact that she has never married. Suddenly seeing herself as a failure, she agrees to marry virtually the first man available, an impractical farmer who comes to town for supplies. Dick Turner immediately takes her to his isolated shack, where they are surrounded by black workers; the nearest white neighbor is many miles away. Mary is unprepared for marriage and totally inept at dealing with the series of houseboys Dick brings from the field to do cooking and housework. In exile from her city life, Mary is further hampered by the typical white Southern Rhodesian belief that natives are basically nonhuman, or at least subhuman and destined to inferiority. She cannot handle the intimate day-by-day contact with the native houseboys who seem so alien to her, and with the advent of the arrogant Moses, the many psychological strains lead inexorably to her almost invited death. Mary and all of white culture are guilty, but it is the black Moses who will be hanged.

Mary's failures are also a result of her inability to understand herself. She is not a reader. She has dreams and nightmares but makes no exploration of their possible significance. She has never examined social and political realities and has no one with whom to discuss her problems. She is unable to adjust to her current reality and unable to create any alternative reality.

The Children of Violence series · *Martha Quest, A Proper Marriage, A Ripple from the Storm, Landlocked,* and *The Four-Gated City* trace in detail the growth and development of Martha Quest, an autobiographical character who, unlike Mary Turner, is intensely interested in knowing herself and making sense of the world. Together these novels make up the Children of Violence series. The first four are set in Africa, while *The Four-Gated City,* which nearly equals in length the preceding four, is set in London and traces Martha Quest's life from her arrival there around 1949 to the late 1990's. The novels set in Africa are categorized as social realism, while *The Four-Gated City* moves beyond that to discuss what are often considered paranormal capacities, and the work concludes after some unspecified disaster has destroyed much of life on earth. The futurist world Lessing depicts here is neither entirely utopian nor dystopian, and despite forces beyond the control of the individual, Martha Quest and some of the other inhabitants of the postcatastrophic world epitomize the continuing need for individual responsibility and commitment to a more harmonious world.

Martha Quest, as her surname suggests, is a quintessential Lessing heroine, always examining the human condition and searching for a higher consciousness to change herself and her world. The characterization is detailed and frank, including descriptions of Martha's sexual relationships and, in *A Proper Marriage,* a lengthy and explicit description of childbirth. Yet Martha's perceptions and innermost thoughts also provide a historical overview of an entire era and a challenge to the status quo. Central to all Martha's struggles is her determination to grow and to envision a freer and more responsible world.

The Golden Notebook · It is good to note that Lessing interrupted the writing of the Children of Violence series to work on *The Golden Notebook,* published in 1962 and generally acknowledged as her most impressive and influential novel. "The two women were alone in the London flat," begins the long novel, and from this simple statement Lessing creates a fascinating portrait of the modern world. The protagonist is Anna Wulf, a writer who says that she is suffering from writer's block after a successful first novel about racial problems in Africa. Anna's friend Molly is a divorced mother trying to make a life for herself. Through them Lessing perceptively examines the problems of the intelligent and disillusioned modern woman. Anna tries to create order out of chaos by keeping a diary, which she divides into four notebooks: a black notebook recounting her experiences as a young woman in Africa; a red notebook for her Communist and political activities; a yellow notebook, which includes her fictional attempts to understand herself, including the creation of an autobiographical character named Ella, who is also writing a novel; and a blue notebook to record the factual details of her daily life and her relationships with men. Sections of these notebooks are repeated sequentially four times and are finally superseded by another notebook, the golden one of the novel's title, in which Anna attempts to integrate these compartmentalized and often-conflicting aspects of her life. In the golden notebook section, influenced by the mental breakdown of one of her lovers, Saul Green, Anna goes through layers of madness in herself and questions the idea of reality itself.

The shape of this pivotal metafictional novel is further complicated by sections called "Free Women," which open and close the book as well as separate the repeated sections of the black, red, yellow, and blue notebooks. The five "Free Women" sections together form a conventional novel about sixty thousand words long. Although it deals with the same characters and events recounted in the various notebook sections, it does so in a reductive and more structured way. It is as though the "Free Women" novel were what Anna is able to produce to end her writer's block, but a novel that shows that fiction is unable to capture the intricacies and complexities of actual existence. Since the sections of this conventional novel frame and appear throughout the larger work, the contrasts and variations with the notebook sections make *The Golden Notebook* as a whole a complex structural and stylistic achievement.

While *The Golden Notebook* elaborates Lessing's attitudes toward racism, sexism, and the interconnections between the personal and the political, it also shows the development of Lessing's thinking to include the benefits of the irrational and the necessity of exploring areas beyond the layers of social pretense and conventionality. These areas are further addressed in *The Four-Gated City* and in three subsequent novels, *Briefing for a Descent into Hell, The Summer Before the Dark,* and *The Memoirs of a Survivor.* Each of these novels breaks from traditional versions of realism and insists upon a wider definition of the possible.

Briefing for a Descent into Hell · *Briefing for a Descent into Hell,* one of the very few Lessing novels with a male as the central character, presents Charles Watkins, a classics professor at the University of Cambridge, who is found wandering incoherently in the streets and is hospitalized for treatment of a mental breakdown. While in the hospital, Watkins, who has forgotten even his name, imagines himself taken away in a spaceship, and most of the book relates his various encounters with unfamiliar creatures and situations that seem almost mythological. Many of these experiences are painful or frightening. Often he is alone, yet he feels a sense of urgency and intense anxiety: He must accomplish certain tasks or risk total failure for himself and others. He also has times of exceptional joy, as he sees the beauty of creation and has revelations of a harmony that could prevail if each creature accepted its part in the scheme of things and made its responsible contribution. In the final pages of the book, Watkins is given electroshock treatment and yanked back into his old life, but both he and the reader are left with the sense that compared with his previous insights he has been forced back to a shallow and hollow "normalcy."

The Summer Before the Dark · In *The Summer Before the Dark,* Kate Brown, a woman in her early forties, also goes through a period of "madness," which reveals the extent to which she has previously succumbed to the pressures to become only roles: wife, mother, sex object, efficient organizer, selfless caregiver. During the summer that is the time frame of the novel, Kate's husband and grown children are away from home; at loose ends, Kate accepts a position as translator for an international food organization. She soon finds herself traveling and organizing global conferences. She spends some time in Spain with Jeffrey Merton, a young man whose psychosomatic and psychological illnesses spill over into her own life, and she returns to London to deal with her doubts and confusions. She stays for a while in a flat with Maureen, a twenty-two-year-old who is establishing her own identity. Through her reactions to Maureen, Kate comes to understand much about herself and her own family, and she finally grasps the relevance of a recurring dream about a seal. The seal dream appears fifteen times in the novel, and the basic image is of Kate struggling to return an abandoned seal to the ocean. When Kate is finally able to finish the dream and return the seal to water, she realizes that what she has been burdened with is her own ego and that she must fight against the power of repressive institutions and roles.

The Memoirs of a Survivor · Lessing again shows the conjunction between the individual and the larger society, including the importance of responsibility and direction, in *The Memoirs of a Survivor*. In this dystopian rendering of the "near future," the unnamed first-person narrator records her observations of a world in a state of cultural and social decline following an unexplained catastrophe. A stranger consigns into the narrator's care a girl of about twelve, Emily, who has with her Hugo, an ugly cat/dog creature. Much of the novel describes Emily's accelerated development through puberty and her association with Gerald, a young gang leader who, with Emily's help, tries to rebuild some semblance of order or at least some system of survival in a degenerated and nonfunctional society. From the window of her flat the narrator watches groups abandon the city, never to be heard of again, and she witnesses the collapse of civilization, demonstrated particularly in the very young children who fend for themselves and who have only fleeting connections to others for immediate gain. In these children, not only respect for others but also language itself has broken down, and they attack their victims or one another with barbaric yaps.

In the midst of all this collapse, the narrator has become aware of another layer of reality in and through the walls of her flat. When she enters this space, she is confronted with a variety of scenes from the past, not necessarily her own past, and usually she sees something that she must do. On one journey through the walls she glimpses a figure of a woman, perhaps a goddess or some aspect of herself, who fills her with a sense of hope. Surrounded by despair in the present world, the narrator constructs an alternative visionary world, and at the end of the novel, when even the air is unbreathable, the collapsed world is left behind as the narrator steps through the wall through both a willed and a magical transformation. She takes with her Emily and Gerald and their group of youngsters as well as Hugo, transformed from an ugly beast into something shining with hope and promise.

The Canopus in Argos series · After a rare gap of five years without a novel, Doris Lessing burst forth with *Shikasta*, which she announced was the first in a series called Canopus in Argos: Archives, and in the next four years she published the other four books in the series. A number of loyal readers were disappointed with what Lessing called her "space fiction," with its undeveloped, stylized characters and strangely unexciting interplanetary rivalries. Yet the series attracted a new audience of science-fiction readers, and, taken as a whole, the series continues Lessing's themes: the individual versus the collective, political systems and their interference with racial and sexual equality, the interconnectedness of all life, and the need for a more enlightened consciousness.

Some of the terms used to describe the varied genres in the Canopus in Argos novels include outer space fiction, science fiction, fantasy, psychomyth, allegory, utopian and indicate the variety within and among these books. They do not even comfortably fit the classification of series, or *roman-fleuve*, since traditionally a series centers on a single character, as Lessing's Children of Violence had centered on Martha Quest. *Shikasta* is filled with reports, journals, and interviews by aliens who discuss the fate of Earth, or Shikasta. *The Marriages Between Zones Three, Four, and Five* does not seem to be set on another planet so much as in the realm of myth and legend as Al·Ith moves between the zones in search of her destiny. *The Sirian Experiments* is told by a woman named Ambien II, who is a leading administrator in the Sirian Colonial Service. She discovers that the rival Canopean Empire is actually in advance of Sirius in every way and more deserving of conducting experiments on Shikasta than is her own empire, though the Sirians certainly do not want to hear this. *The Making of the Representative for Planet 8* is the story of a small planet whose inhabitants live comfortably until the time of The Ice begins, with ice and snow covering most of the globe. The inhabitants are unable to emigrate, but a few of them survive in some nonphysical but essential existence. *Documents Relating to the Sentimental Agents in the Volyen Empire* uses testimonies and histories to show that the Volyen Empire has failed to keep its promises to its inhabitants and to the cosmos. The empire suffers a rhetoric-induced downfall, as its leaders had become enamored with the sound of their grand ideas rather than performing the actions that should have accompanied them.

None of the narrators and voices in the Canopus in Argos series is entirely reliable, and many questions are left unanswered. Perhaps this confusion is itself Lessing's goal: to make her readers question and reconsider ideas and actions. As Johor, an emissary to Shikasta, comments on the very first page of the series: "Things change. That is all we may be sure of. . . . This is a catastrophic universe, always; and subject to sudden reversals, upheavals, changes, cataclysms, with joy never anything but the song of substance under pressure forced into new forms and shapes."

The Diaries of Jane Somers · The same year the final volume of Canopus in Argos was published, another novel appeared, titled *The Diary of a Good Neighbour*, purportedly by a new British writer, Jane Somers. It was not until the following year, and after the publication of another Jane Somers novel, *If the Old Could . . .*, that Lessing publicly revealed her authorship with the publication of the two novels together as *The Diaries of Jane Somers*. In her introduction to the book Lessing discusses some of her reasons for having used a pseudonym. One was to create a new persona as the narrator: How would a real Jane Somers write? Another was to show the difficulties unestablished writers have in getting published, and indeed the first manuscript was rejected by several publishers before it was printed by Michael Joseph in London, the same firm that had accepted the unknown Doris Lessing's *The Grass Is Singing* nearly four decades earlier. Lessing also says that she wanted the novels to be judged on their own merit, apart from the Lessing canon. When the Jane Somers novels first appeared, they sold in only modest numbers and received favorable but very limited attention from reviewers. Lessing notes that the modern publishing business markets high-volume, high-profile authors with the planned expectation that the novels will have a short shelf life as big sellers for a few weeks but soon are replaced and out of print; such policies do not favor new and experimental novelists.

The Diaries of Jane Somers focuses on old age, especially the relationship that develops between the middle-aged Jane Somers, head of a high-fashion magazine, and Maudie Fowler, a poor but proud woman in her nineties. Set in a realistic London, the novels, particularly *The Diary of a Good Neighbour*, give an insightful analysis of contemporary health-care services and again show the impact of social attitudes and governmental policies on the individual. The social realism of the novel, with its discussions of aging and dying, is given contrast by the summaries of novels Jane writes about Maudie's life. Maudie tells stories of her long, hard life, and Jane transforms them into successful romanticized fictions, which Maudie then enjoys hearing. Jane, whose friends call her Janna, is repeatedly mistaken for a "Good Neighbour," a social worker, as though there could be no other explanation for her friendship with Maudie. The layers of illusion and reality, fictions and lives, add to the emotional power of the novel and make it an important addition to Lessing's later works.

The Good Terrorist and The Fifth Child · *The Good Terrorist* shows rather stupid and totally unsympathetic would-be revolutionaries who move from city to city in England planning random bombings. Contrary to the title, there is no good terrorist in the novel, and it is just as well that these characters have a tendency to blow up themselves accidentally rather than killing others. A much more interesting novel is *The Fifth Child*, which can be read as an accurate and realistic account of an unfortunate English family, but which to other readers is a science-fiction fantasy, a tale of an alien being born into a human family. The novel hovers on some point that embraces both readings. The setting is England in the 1960's. Harriet and David Lovatt want a big family and a settled home life. Everything seems to be working according to their plan until the birth of their fifth child. Ben has nothing childlike about him: He is gruesome in appearance, insatiably hungry, abnormally strong, demanding, and violent. In no way does he fit into the happy home. Yet Harriet, steeped in the idea of motherhood, cannot bear to abandon him in some mental institution and insists on keeping him with her. As the years pass, the older children escape though already harmed by Ben's weirdness and violence, and even David finally recognizes that he cannot continue to live with such a creature. The novel ends in despair, the problems unresolved. Ben is well on his way to becoming a fully grown criminal, a rapist and murderer, with no one able to subdue him. The story of the Lovatts becomes a parable of the modern world, the vision of a simple and happy existence shattered within the family itself and a society unwilling to confront and unable to control its own most brutal aspects.

Love, Again · Lessing's novel *Love, Again* confronts the uncertainty of love and the decisions made because of love. Sarah, an aging theater manager, writes a play based on the true story of a young, beautiful French mulatto named Julie Varion. Julie has many eligible suitors in her life, but none commits himself to her because of family pressures of status and community responsibility. Julie finally becomes engaged to an older gentleman, but she mysteriously dies before the wedding. Writing about this alluring character and her life is emotionally trying for Sarah, who feels she, unlike Julie, is unable to act upon her love interests because of her age. Unable to act on her feelings, Sarah suffers silently through her painful longings for a twenty-eight-year-old actor and a thirty-five-year-old director. Sarah eventually comes to terms with her age through painful moments of realization and acceptance.

All the characters are seen through the eyes of a narrator who focuses primarily on Sarah and reveals the characters as Sarah sees them. Like Julie and her suitors, Sarah and her friends are bound by obligations and social rules which affect the decisions they make for their own lives. Sarah is faced with decisions of loving but letting go. Sarah's brother, Hal, realizes that his future only holds loneliness because of his inability to see others and their needs. Stephen, a dear friend of Sarah's, ultimately commits suicide over his preoccupation and obsession with the deceased Julie Varion, which only become more intense as the production of the play about her continues.

Mara and Dann · *Mara and Dann* is an exciting adventure story set thousands of years in the future. The two main characters, Mara and her brother Dann, were kidnapped from their home with the Mahondi tribe when Mara was seven and Dann was four. In order to stay alive, the two are forced to change their names when they are taken to a village of the Rock People, a tribe considered less advanced than the Mahondi. Mara stays in the village until she becomes a strong young woman who desires to learn as much as possible even as she faces starvation and drought; she is sold into slavery and taken prisoner to be a breeder for other tribes. Dann suffers through abductions and addictions and becomes divided in his desires and duties toward his sister. Through his dream world, Dann faces his fears and eventually accepts his past experiences. Although the two are separated many times, they never stop searching for each other even at the risk of slavery and death.

The novel is an interesting tale of survival of the human mind and spirit even through the most severe times a new world can encounter after an ice age. Mara and Dann's characters are well developed, and they change and learn from their experiences. Mara learns to love and to trust but also learns the price she must pay to survive in the world outside her home. Lessing portays issues of racism, greed, and power as they have affected every generation throughout time.

Lessing has had a wide readership. For many years she has been on best-seller lists, and her novels have been translated into many languages. Her work is widely anthologized and has been closely read by many contemporary authors, particularly women writers. The number of critical articles, books, and sections of books about her work is enormous and international in scope, reflecting the wide diversity of readers and the serious attention her work has commanded throughout her writing career.

Lessing's novels, far-ranging in scope and treatment, resist any easy labels. Still, her major themes, though presented in a variety of ways, have been remarkably consistent. The individual has responsibilities, Lessing always shows, not only to achieve self-knowledge and inner harmony but to contribute to the greater harmony of society as well. Human consciousness must expand, and people's attitudes and actions must change if human life is to survive.

Lois A. Marchino, updated by Mary A. Blackmon

Other major works

SHORT FICTION: *This Was the Old Chief's Country*, 1951; *Five: Short Novels*, 1953; *The Habit of Loving*, 1957; *A Man and Two Women*, 1963; *African Stories*, 1964; *The Temptation of Jack Orkney and Other Stories*, 1972 (also known as *The Story of a Non-Marrying Man and Other Stories*); *This Was the Old Chief's Country: Volume 1 of Doris Lessing's Collected African Stories*, 1973; *The Sun Between Their Feet: Volume 2 of Doris Lessing's Collected African Stories*, 1973; *Sunrise on the Veld*, 1975; *A Mild Attack of Locusts*, 1977; *To Room Nineteen/Her Collected Stories*, 1978; *The Temptation of Jack Orkney/Her Collected Stories*, 1978; *Stories*, 1978; *London Observed: Stories and Sketches*, 1991 (pb. in U.S. as *The Real Thing: Stories and Sketches*, 1992); *Spies I Have Known and Other Stories*, 1995.

PLAYS: *Each His Own Wilderness*, pr. 1958; *Play with a Tiger*, pr., pb. 1962; *Making of the Representative for Planet 8*, pr. 1988 (libretto); *Play with a Tiger, and Other Plays*, pb. 1996.

POETRY: *Fourteen Poems*, 1959.

NONFICTION: *Going Home*, 1957; *In Pursuit of the English: A Documentary*, 1960; *Particularly Cats*, 1967; *A Small Personal Voice*, 1974; *Prisons We Choose to Live Inside*, 1987; *The Wind Blows Away Our Words*, 1987; *African Laughter: Four Visits to Zimbabwe*, 1992; *Under My Skin*, 1994; *A Small Personal Voice: Essays, Reviews, Interviews*, 1994; *Doris Lessing: Conversations*, 1994 (pb. in England as *Putting the Questions Differently*); *Shadows on the Wall of the Cave*, 1994; *Walking in the Shade*, 1997.

MISCELLANEOUS: *The Doris Lessing Reader*, 1988 (selections).

Bibliography

Fishburn, Katherine. *The Unexpected Universe of Doris Lessing: A Study in Narrative Technique*. Westport, Conn.: Greenwood Press, 1985. This study considers Lessing's science fiction from *Briefing for a Descent into Hell* through the Canopus in Argos series. It argues that the science fiction has the purpose of transforming reality and involving the reader in ideas and the intricacies of the texts rather than in characterization. Fishburn also published *Doris Lessing: Life, Work, and Criticism* (Fredericton, New Brunswick, Canada: York Press, 1987), which provides a brief overview of Lessing's life and works, including literary biography, critical response, and an annotated bibliography.

Galen, Muge. *Between East and West: Sufism in the Novels of Doris Lessing*. Albany: State University of New York Press, 1997. This text applies the ideas of Sufism and its influence on Lessing and her novels. An introduction to Sufism and to Doris Lessing is included to help the reader understand the basic ideas of Sufism. Emphasis is placed on her space-fiction utopias as an alternative to the current Western lifestyles.

Greene, Gayle. *Changing the Story: Feminist Fiction and the Tradition*. Bloomington: Indiana University Press, 1991. Lessing's works are repeatedly referred to throughout the text. *The Golden Notebook* is covered extensively in a chapter titled "Naming a Different Way," which concentrates on how the novel was very differently received and understood by male and female readers. The essay focuses on the form and structure of the story as well as character development.

_____. *Doris Lessing: The Poetics of Change*. Ann Arbor: University of Michigan Press, 1997. Greene centers this study on how Lessing's novels are concerned with change. Several different critical approaches to Lessing's works, including Marxist, feminist, and Jungian, are included in the study.

Kaplan, Carey, and Ellen Cronan Rose, eds. *Doris Lessing: The Alchemy of Survival*. Athens: Ohio University Press, 1988. Eleven essays that display a variety of approaches to Lessing's works. The approaches and various perspectives are as diverse as her readership. The essays were gathered from Modern Language

Association conventions from 1971 to 1985. The introduction includes a brief history of the development of the Doris Lessing Society and notes how Lessing criticism has grown within the MLA convention each year.

Robinson, Sally. *Engendering the Subject: Gender and Self-Representation in Contemporary Women's Fiction.* Albany: State University of New York Press, 1991. A chapter of this book is devoted to Lessing and her works. Primary focus is placed on the Children of Violence series: *Martha Quest, The Four-Gated City, Landlocked, A Proper Marriage,* and *A Ripple in the Storm.* Robinson focuses on Lessing's desire to present a humanist view in her characters and themes and how the female main characters tend to create contradictions when trying to reach their goals.

Rubenstein, Roberta. *The Novelistic Vision of Doris Lessing: Breaking the Forms of Consciousness.* Urbana: University of Illinois Press, 1979. This volume shows the cyclic design in Lessing's repeated themes, particularly the mind discovering, interpreting, and ultimately shaping its own reality. In a comprehensive chronological approach through 1978, it examines the relationship between fictional structure and meaning, the purpose of doubling, and the relationship between fiction and reality.

Seligman, Dee. *Doris Lessing: An Annotated Bibliography of Criticism.* Westport, Conn.: Greenwood Press, 1981. Seligman incorporates earlier checklists and bibliographies and provides a comprehensive annotated bibliography through 1978. She includes a bibliography of research and teaching suggestions, interviews with Lessing, and book reviews. Marshall Tymn draws on Seligman's bibliography and updates it to 1988 in the *Journal of the Fantastic in the Arts* special issue on Doris Lessing, edited by Nicholas Ruddick (volume 2, no. 3, 1990).

Sprague, Claire, and Virginia Tiger, eds. *Critical Essays on Doris Lessing.* Boston: G. K. Hall, 1986. This collection includes review essays and various other articles plus a general introduction to Lessing and a chronology of her works. It is divided into sections entitled "Politics and Patterns," "Female (Other) Space," "Inner and Outer Space," and "Reception and Reputation."

Whittaker, Ruth. *Modern Novelists: Doris Lessing.* New York: St. Martin's Press, 1988. This resource provides a brief biography and insightful background information into Lessing and how her works have been influenced by her past. Major focus is given to her novels and a discussion of how Lessing excels as a modern novelist.

C. S. Lewis

Born: Belfast, Northern Ireland; November 29, 1898
Died: Oxford, England; November 22, 1963

Principal long fiction · *Out of the Silent Planet*, 1938; *Perelandra*, 1943; *That Hideous Strength: A Modern Fairy Tale for Grownups*, 1945; *The Lion, the Witch, and the Wardrobe*, 1950; *Prince Caspian*, 1951; *The Voyage of the Dawn Treader*, 1952; *The Silver Chair*, 1953; *The Horse and His Boy*, 1954; *The Magician's Nephew*, 1955; *The Last Battle*, 1956; *The Chronicles of Narnia*, 1950-1956 (includes the 7 previous titles); *Till We Have Faces: A Myth Retold*, 1956.

Other literary forms · Though his novels for adults and children continue to be widely read and admired, C. S. Lewis is also well known as a religious essayist and literary scholar-critic. His religious writings of three decades include autobiography (*The Pilgrim's Regress*, 1933; *Surprised by Joy: The Shape of My Early Life*, 1955; *A Grief Observed*, 1961) and essays in varying lengths and forms. Some of his essays include *The Personal Heresy* (1939, with E. M. W. Tillyard), *Rehabilitations* (1939), *The Problem of Pain* (1940), *The Screwtape Letters* (1942), *The Abolition of Man* (1943), *Miracles: A Preliminary Study* (1947), *Mere Christianity* (1952), *Reflections on the Psalms* (1958), and *The Four Loves* (1960). Posthumous works of a religious nature include *Letters to Malcolm: Chiefly on Prayer* (1964), *Letters to an American Lady* (1967), *God in the Dock* (1970), and *The Joyful Christian: 127 Readings from C. S. Lewis* (1977).

Lewis's criticism, focused primarily on medieval and Renaissance studies, includes *The Allegory of Love* (1936), *A Preface to "Paradise Lost"* (1942), *English Literature in the Sixteenth Century, Excluding Drama* (1954), *Studies in Words* (1960), *An Experiment in Criticism* (1961), and *The Discarded Image* (1964). Several posthumous volumes of criticism appeared, including *Spenser's Images of Life* (1967), *Selected Literary Essays* (1969), and *Present Concerns* (1986).

Less widely known are Lewis's early volumes of poetry, *Spirits in Bondage* (1919), a collection of lyrics; and *Dymer* (1926), a narrative. The posthumous *The Dark Tower and Other Stories* (1977) includes an unpublished fragment of a novel. This collection and one other, *Of Other Worlds: Essays and Stories* (1966), contain the only extant fictional pieces not printed during Lewis's lifetime. The Wade Collection at Wheaton College (Illinois) and the Bodleian Library, Oxford, hold many volumes of Lewis papers, including eleven volumes of Lewis family letters written from 1850 to 1930.

Achievements · Lewis's achievements as a novelist are hard to separate from his role as a Christian apologist and from his impeccable literary scholarship. Many of Lewis's readers believe that his greatness lies in the unusually wide scope of his work: He wrote so much so well in so many forms. His *Mere Christianity*, for example, is a superb primer on Christian ideas, while *The Four Loves* and *A Grief Observed* are powerful explorations of the endurance of love despite doubt and deep pain. *The Screwtape Letters*, Lewis's most popular book in America, still enthralls new readers with its witty yet serious study of the war between good and evil in the contemporary world. Among his critical writings, *The Allegory of Love* remains a classic study of medieval literature and society, while *The Discarded Image* is one of the very best discussions of the contrast between the medieval worldview and the modern mind.

The popularity of Lewis's novels for adults (*Out of the Silent Planet, Perelandra,* and *That Hideous Strength*—known as the space trilogy—and *Till We Have Faces*) owes more perhaps to their treatment of themes also developed in his nonfiction than to their literary excellence, although the space trilogy is widely read among devotees of fantasy and science fiction who have little acquaintance with Lewis's other works. The extraordinary appeal of Lewis's fiction for children, the Narnia books, is undisputed. Each year, these seven novels gain thousands of new readers of all ages and are, for many, the introduction to Lewis which inspires them to delve into his other works. Indeed, had Lewis never published another word, the Narnia books would have ensured his reputation with both critics and the public.

Biography · Born in Belfast in 1898, the son of Albert Lewis, a successful lawyer, and Flora Hamilton Lewis, a writer and mathematician, Clive Staples Lewis spent his early childhood in an atmosphere of learning and imagination. His mother tutored him in French and Latin before he was seven; his nurse, Lizzie Endicott, taught him the folktales of Ireland. Clive and his brother, Warren, devoted long, often rainy afternoons to exploring the book-lined corridors of Little Lea, their home. As small children, the brothers invented their own country, Boxen, for which they wrote a four-hundred-year chronicle and which they peopled with animal characters who became subjects of individual stories. These early childhood adventures were of incalculable influence on Lewis's long fiction, written almost half a century later.

With his mother's death from cancer in 1908, Lewis's life changed drastically and irrevocably. A disconsolate, bewildered Albert Lewis sent his sons to boarding school in England, the first of several cruel experiences before age sixteen that nurtured in Lewis a hatred for public-school education. At last persuading his father to place him with the demanding but kind tutor W. T. Kirkpatrick in 1914, Lewis developed his great scholarly talents and won a scholarship to University College, Oxford, two years later. Before taking his entrance exams, however, Lewis was recruited into the army and served as a second lieutenant on the front lines in France during World War I.

Surviving a wound and the mental shocks of war, Lewis happily entered Oxford life in 1919, his education financed by his father—whose support in other ways would always be lacking. Perhaps to compensate for this lack of parental affection, Lewis developed a steadfast friendship with a Mrs. Moore, the mother of a friend who had died fighting in France. With Mrs. Moore and her young daughter, Maureen, Lewis set up housekeeping, this arrangement continuing thirty years, until Mrs. Moore's death in 1951. Lewis's tenure at Oxford, as student, tutor, and fellow of Magdalen College, lasted even longer, ending in 1954 with his acceptance of the chair of Medieval and Renaissance Literature at Magdalene College, Cambridge. During the Oxford years, he wrote and published most of his fifty-eight books of adult and children's fiction, literary criticism, essays, Christian apologetics, and poetry. It was there also that Lewis, influenced by such close friends as J. R. R. Tolkien, underwent his conversion to Christianity.

Lewis's Christian fervor led to widely read publications and to a long series of radio talks before and during World War II. His faith also inspired fictional works, including his space trilogy, written during the war, and his Narnia books for children. Many of his Oxford colleagues, however, were offended by his overt religiousness—and his popularity. Through these years, they thus denied Lewis the Magdalen professorship that his eminence as a literary scholar warranted.

With his rise to a more esteemed position in the more congenial atmosphere of Cambridge, Lewis completed, among other projects, the books of Narnia, the first of which had been published in 1950, and wrote perhaps his finest novel, *Till We Have Faces*. This last work of fiction was dedicated to Joy Davidman Gresham, an American admirer with whom he had corresponded for several years and who came to England to join him in 1955. They were married in 1956, and, according to Lewis, "feasted on love" for the four years they shared before Joy's death from bone cancer in 1960. Despite his own worsening health, Lewis continued to produce autobiographical and critical works until suffering a heart attack in 1963. He died on November 22, the date of President John F. Kennedy's assassination and of the death of writer Aldous Huxley.

Analysis · The happy fact of C. S. Lewis's creation of long fictional works is that the more of them he wrote, the better he became as a novelist. This is not to say that with each book from *Out of the Silent Planet* to *Till We Have Faces* he measurably improved, but from the early space trilogy (1938-1945) through the Narnia tales (1950-1956) to his last novel, there is a clear change in Lewis's conception of fiction. In the early books, characters exemplify definite sides in an ethical debate, and plot is the working out of victory for Lewis's side. In the later books, however, character becomes the battleground of ambiguous values, and plot takes place more and more within the minds of the characters.

The space trilogy · The hero of the space trilogy, Cambridge don Elwin Ransom, is often less the protagonist of novels than an embodiment of the Christian and intellectual virtues that Lewis recommended in his essays. Throughout the trilogy, Ransom represents Lewis's ideal of the relentless intellectual, his learning solidly founded on respect for great ideas from earlier ages, who valiantly maintains his integrity despite the powerful temptations posed by modern materialism. In both *Out of the Silent Planet* and *Perelandra*, Ransom's journeys to Mars (Malacandra) and Venus (Perelandra), respectively, Ransom's adversary is as clearly villainous as Ransom himself is heroic. The antagonist is Edward Weston, a brilliant physicist, who represents for Lewis that most insidious modern outgrowth of Renaissance humanism: the belief that the highest goal of humankind is to establish its dominance over all forms of life in as many worlds as it can conquer. This view, which Lewis saw as the root of the boundless ambition of political leaders Adolf Hitler, Joseph Stalin, and Benito Mussolini, is exemplified in Weston's misuse of technology to build a spacecraft that enables him to reach other planets, so that he might make them colonies of Earth. By moving the scene of this attempt away from Earth, Lewis can manipulate material reality so that the limitations of Weston's philosophy become obvious and his actions ludicrous. Assuming the innate superiority of man over all other forms, and thus a perpetual state of war between man and nature, Weston fails to see the simplest, most significant facts of the new worlds he intends to conquer. As Ransom, the Christian student of myths and languages, easily perceives, the forces that rule Mars and Venus are both fully hospitable to humankind and infinitely more powerful. Thus, Weston shoots gentle creatures because they appear strange and, in a parody of the European explorers, tries to bribe with shiny trinkets the Oyarsa of Malacandra, who, as Ransom learns, is second only in power and wisdom to Maleldil, ruler of the universe.

In contrast to Weston, Ransom—a far truer scientist than his opponent—learns the language of and befriends these extraterrestrials; hence, mysteries are opened to him. In *Out of the Silent Planet*, he learns that only Earth (Thulcandra), long under the dominance of the "bent eldil," is deprived of clear knowledge of the Oyarsa and Maleldil; Thulcandrans believe themselves enlightened above all others, when in reality they are the most benighted. He learns also that the universe is in a state of becoming: that the creatures of old worlds, such as Malacandra, can no longer be endangered by such forces as those which guide Weston, but that newer worlds, such as Thulcandra, are still theaters of contending principles, while the youngest worlds, such as Perelandra, have yet to achieve spiritual identity.

This is vital knowledge for Ransom, who realizes, in the second book, that he has been given wisdom because he has also been given the responsibility of helping to bring about Maleldil's reign on Perelandra, which places him in open confrontation with Weston, now clearly the mere instrument of the bent eldil. In a probing recapitulation of the temptation of Eve, Lewis has Ransom and Weston contend, somewhat in the mode of the medieval *psychomachia*, for the mind of Tinidril, the first woman of Perelandra. As the confoundingly subtle arguments of the Unman (the spirit that controls Weston) begin to conquer Tinidril, Ransom at last understands that he must physically fight, to the death, his adversary. Despite his slim chance of survival, Ransom attacks the Unman; he ultimately defeats him, though suffering wounds, incredible fatigue, and near despair. It is an epic battle, reminiscent of the Pearl-Poet's fourteenth century manuscript *Sir Gawain and the Green Knight* and Edmund Spenser's *The Faerie Queene* (1590, 1596); Ransom's faith and courage in the fight prepare the reader for his apotheosis in the final chapters, wherein Lewis's paradisiacally lush description of Perelandra takes on an almost beatific vividness and illumination.

In novelistic terms, *Perelandra* surpasses *Out of the Silent Planet* in its attention to the development of Ransom's awareness of his role and his struggle to maintain his integrity in the face of fears and misleading appearances. Nevertheless, its extraterrestrial setting and its clearly demarcated hero and villain make *Perelandra* more an epic romance than a novel. This is not to prefer one book to the other, but it is to distinguish them both from the third part of the trilogy, *That Hideous Strength*, which may be Lewis's most interesting fiction, although not his most consistent. *That Hideous Strength* tries to harmonize heterogeneous elements of romance, epic, and novel. Following the novelist's impulse, Lewis brings his setting back to earth and localizes it in the sort of place he knew best, a venerable English college town, which he calls Edgestow. He also centers the reader's interest on two authentic protagonists, Jane and Mark Studdock, whose story is their painful, humiliating, sometimes dangerous progress toward faith and self-awareness. They act bravely in the ultimate crisis, both risking torture and death, but they engage in nothing like the epic struggle of Ransom and the Unman.

Still, the events in which they engage are of epic magnitude, and in this thrust of the book Lewis returns to familiar fictional territory. The plot concerns a powerful conspiracy to turn Britain into a totalitarian state. This conspiracy is opposed most strenuously by a small underground directed by Elwin Ransom, now a heroic, almost godlike leader, whose powers are spiritual rather than physical. His main adversaries are men who, like Weston, call themselves scientists, but whose distinguishing traits are lust for power, deviousness, and cruelty. Having established a research institute called the National Institute of Co-ordinated Experiments (N.I.C.E.), these men use the press, political infiltrators, and their own "police" to avoid, placate, or squash opposition to their Nazi-like program of "social planning." Mark Studdock is one of the bright but indecisive minds easily co-opted by the N.I.C.E. Lewis shows convincingly how the leaders play on his ego and his fears of rejection in order to exploit his talent as a journalist. Conversely, Jane Studdock falls in with the resistance group; she weighs its values against those of her husband and gradually comes to see that whichever road she chooses will mean great danger for both of them. She chooses the resistance.

Had Lewis limited the book to the clash between political philosophies and its impact on two ordinary people, he would have had a conventional novel, but he wanted to portray this clash as occurring on a cosmic level, as a war between pure good and pure evil. Since the combatants in this novel are the human representatives of these supernatural forces, the reader necessarily finds himself once more in the realm of romance. Aware of his mixing of genres in *That Hideous Strength*, Lewis called the amalgam a fairy tale, arguing that his work fell into that long tradition in which supernatural events subsume the ordinary activities of realistic characters. What fairy tale means here is that when the N.I.C.E. performs such blatant works as the turning of rivers from their courses, the trapping of huge numbers of animals for vivisection, and the deforestation of ancient preserves, they call down on themselves the wrath of nature, personified in a resurrected Merlin, who pledges allegiance to Ransom as the spiritual successor of Arthur. His obedience allows Ransom to reinvest him with eldilic power, which enables him single-handedly to destroy the N.I.C.E. Add to the appearance of Merlin such important romantic elements as Jane Studdock's clairvoyance and the veneration of a talking head by the N.I.C.E., and *That Hideous Strength* seems almost more romance than novel.

The book should be judged as a fairy tale. Lewis warns the reader in his preface not to be deceived by the "hum-drum scenes and persons" into thinking this a realistic fiction. He merely intends the familiar names and places to heighten the reader's appreciation of the importance of the spiritual battles occurring around and within each individual. Indeed, one explicit purpose of the book is to warn England—here Lewis was prophetic—that radical social evil would not be eradicated with Hitler's defeat. The formal problem, however, is that a bit of realism begets the expectation of total realism, and so readers accustomed to novels will naturally look askance at Merlin's return and the survival of the severed head, while they will accept the generic consistency of the floating islands in *Perelandra*. Even if Lewis had deleted these effects from the third book, however, he would have had to substitute other supernatural manifestations in order to be consistent not only with the pattern of the first two books but also, more important, with his religious conviction of the immanence of the supernatural in everyday life. Viewing the book as a fairy tale, Lewis felt, would allow the reader sufficient suspension of disbelief to become involved with the characters. Nevertheless, the reader would still face, as in all of Lewis's other works, the challenge of accepting or rejecting Lewis's position on God, nature, and humanity.

The Chronicles of Narnia · Lewis actually began the first book of the Narnia series, *The Lion, the Witch, and the Wardrobe*, in 1939, when four children, inspiration for the Pevensie children in the stories, were evacuated to his home at the start of the war. Returning ten years and many books later to the idea of writing for children, Lewis found the fictional form perhaps best suited to his genius. These tales of ordinary boys and girls transported to another world allowed Lewis to relive in some sense the childhood idyll at Little Lea that had been cut short by his mother's death; moreover, they let him put directly into prose the fantastic images—fauns, castles, golden lions—that came to him, without his having to adapt them, as he had in the space trilogy, to the narrower tastes of adult readers. The fairy-tale form restricted him to simpler vocabulary and syntax, as well as to a more exclusively narrative and descriptive mode, but these restrictions freed him to do what he did best in fiction: dialogue, action narrative, and vivid description of select detail. More than anything else, however, the form let him depict given characters as essentially good or evil, though careful readers will observe that these qualities are consistently dramatized in action, not merely posited by authorial fiat. One of the many virtues of these stories is that appearance never defines character; the reader likes or dislikes persons or animals in these books only when he has come to know them.

The seven books traverse some sixty years of English time, roughly between 1895 and 1955, and more than one thousand years of time in Narnia, a land which is the home of Aslan, the Golden Lion, as well as talking animals, dwarves, fauns, satyrs, witches, men and women, boys and girls. The chronicle begins with *The Magician's Nephew* (the sequence of publication differs from the internal chronology of the series), in which young Digory Kirke and Polly Plummer magically enter Narnia at the time of its creation by Aslan. Unfortunately, the curious Digory inadvertently breaks the spell that has bound Jadis, the White Witch, who becomes the main enemy of the Narnians.

In *The Lion, the Witch, and the Wardrobe*, almost fifty English years have passed, but an untold number in Narnia. The visitors are now the four Pevensie children, who enter Narnia through a magical wardrobe in the spacious country home of an old friend of their parents—Professor Digory Kirke. They find a cold world in terror of the Witch. The children eventually join those who are still rebelling against her, and their faith is rewarded when Aslan returns. His conquest is not complete, however, until he has been ritually murdered by the Witch, only to be reborn in far greater splendor. The four children are crowned kings and queens of Narnia.

The Horse and His Boy occurs during the reign of Peter Pevensie as High King of Narnia. It concerns Shasta, a boy of neighboring Calormen, who through various adventures is revealed to be the true prince of Archenland, another Narnian neighbor. The fourth part of the chronicle, *Prince Caspian*, takes place a thousand years forward in Narnian time, but only two or three years after the adventure through the wardrobe. The four children are transported to Narnia from a railway bench, only to find all record of their reign obliterated by time and by the purposeful lies told by invaders. The children's arrival, however, coincides with another coming of Aslan, who, aided by an alliance of all the creatures of Narnia, restores to the throne the true heir, Caspian. He is still king of Narnia when the fifth adventure, *The Voyage of the Dawn Treader*, occurs. This time, the two younger Pevensies, Edmund and Lucy, accompanied by a recalcitrant friend, Eustace Scrubb, reenter Narnia to help Caspian sail the farthest seas to find seven Narnian lords banished by the invaders. On their voyage, they discover lands beyond imagining, including Aslan's country itself. The sixth chronicle, *The Silver Chair*, is another story of a search, this time by Eustace and a friend, Jill Pole, who are called to Narnia to find the dying Caspian's long-lost son, Rilian. Despite many deceptions and dangers, the children eventually discover the prince, by then the rightful king of Narnia.

The chronicles end with *The Last Battle*, the apocalypse of Narnia. King Tirian, Rilian's descendant, is joined by Eustace and Jill in a final battle to save Narnia from invading hordes of hostile neighbors. As they go to certain death, they are suddenly greeted by Aslan, who ushers them into the real Narnia, of which the mere parody is now disappearing as quickly as it had been born centuries before. There they are joined by all the friends of Narnia, including three of the four Pevensies, who, with their parents, have come to the real Narnia thanks to a railway accident in "their" world. Aslan tells them that this Narnia is forever, and that they need never leave: "The term is over; the holidays have begun. The dream is ended; this is the morning."

Till We Have Faces · Almost nothing of the style of the space trilogy is recognizable in *Till We Have Faces*, Lewis's first novel for adults after 1945, and the last of his career. Though Lewis here was reworking an ancient myth, that of Cupid and Psyche, this book can be unambiguously called a novel, in the full modern sense of that word. It begins and ends in the spiritual turmoil of the mind of the narrator, Orual, Queen of Glome, a tiny state somewhere north of Greece, sometime in the centuries just preceding the birth of Christ. The novel is the story of her life, told in two parts. The first, much the longer, is Orual's complaint against the gods for their hatred of humankind, hatred shown most obviously in their failure ever to make themselves clearly known. The second part, a few brief chapters hastily penned by the dying queen and ended in midsentence by her death, repents for the slanders of part 1 and tells of a few pivotal encounters and an extraordinary dream that have resolved her anger.

Part 1 recalls a lifelong source of her rage, her ugliness, which has made Orual hated by her father, the king, and shunned by most others. A far greater injury, however, is the sacrifice of her wonderfully beautiful sister, Psyche, whom the head priest of Glome offers to the god of the Grey Mountain in hopes of ending a drought. Orual cannot forgive the gods for taking the only joy of her life. What irritates her most, however, is her discovery that Psyche has not been devoured by the god of the mountain, as most people believe, but that he has wedded her. Moreover, Psyche is happy. Convincing herself that her sister's happiness can only be a fatal delusion, Orual persuades Psyche, with a threat of suicide, to disobey her lord's one command: that she never look at him. The result is that Psyche is banished and forced to undergo ordeals. Orual is also punished: The god tells her, cryptically, "You also will be Psyche." Never fully comprehending this sentence, and enraged by the ambiguity of the portent, Orual passes the years, eventually succeeding her father and distracting her thoughts by careful attention to government of her people. Orual becomes a wise and masterful ruler, but her mind remains troubled. When, by chance, she discovers that the story of Psyche has given rise to a cult of worshipers, she decides finally to spill her anger and doubt onto paper. The story the sect tells is false, she feels: In it, Psyche's sister is accused of deliberately plotting her fall. She feels that she must write to clear the record, to exonerate herself.

In part 2, she repents. She admits that the very writing of part 1 has brought back disquieting memories: Perhaps she had been jealous of Psyche. Her self-awareness grows when two meetings with longtime observers of her life convince her that her perspective on people and events has always been narrow and selfish. Finally, two terrible dreams—visions, she realizes—bring her crime before her eyes; she understands the sentence of the god. She has indeed been Psyche, in that while her sister has performed the ordeals assigned her, Orual, in her years of suffering, has borne all the anguish of them. Thus, she has both committed the crime and expiated the guilt. Her confession in part 2 gives way to thanksgiving, as she discovers that, washed clear of her guilt, she is as beautiful as the sister whom she is at last free to love.

The richness of Orual's character has been likened by critics to the increasing depth of compassion in Lewis's essays of these later years. The striking resonance of these works has been attributed, at least in part, to the influence on Lewis's life at this time of Joy Davidman, to whom he dedicated *Till We Have Faces.* That Lewis's renunciation of bachelorhood late in his life signaled an opening of himself, and his prose, to emotions and ways of seeing that he had not before allowed himself seems plausible; nevertheless, the simple design and straightforward nature of this last novel can as easily be explained as further developments of Lewis's style in the direction taken by the Narnia books. Perhaps the exploration of his own childhood necessitated by writing these books taught him lessons about his writing as profound as those Orual learned in trying to recapture her past. Perhaps he learned that he was truly happy as a writer when he could explore the curious corridors of his personality, just as he had loved to explore the rooms and passages of his boyhood home. It is surely no coincidence that the first part of his autobiography, *Surprised by Joy,* was published in 1955, while he was at work not only on *Till We Have Faces* but also on *The Last Battle.* All three books reveal an exquisite sensitivity which can be attributed to his deep introspection at this time. This sensitivity, this honesty, makes these books far more memorable in themselves than his more clever experiments in less traditional forms.

Christopher J. Thaiss

Other major works

SHORT FICTION: *The Dark Tower and Other Stories,* 1977.

POETRY: *Spirits in Bondage,* 1919; *Dymer,* 1926; *Poems,* 1964; *Narrative Poems,* 1969.

NONFICTION: *The Pilgrim's Regress,* 1933; *The Allegory of Love,* 1936; *The Personal Heresy,* 1939 (with E. M. W. Tillyard); *Rehabilitations,* 1939; *The Problem of Pain,* 1940; *The Screwtape Letters,* 1942; *Broadcast Talks,* 1942; *A Preface to "Paradise Lost,"* 1942; *Hamlet: The Prince or the Poem,* 1942; *Christian Behaviour,* 1943; *The Abolition of Man,* 1943; *Beyond Personality,* 1944; *The Great Divorce,* 1945; *Miracles: A Preliminary Study,* 1947; *Arthurian Torso,* 1948; *The Weight of Glory, and Other Addresses,* 1949; *Mere Christianity,* 1952; *English Literature in the Sixteenth Century, Excluding Drama,* 1954; *Surprised by Joy: The Shape of My Early Life,* 1955; *Reflections on the Psalms,* 1958; *The Four Loves,* 1960; *The World's Last Night, and Other Essays,* 1960; *Studies in Words,* 1960; *An Experiment in Criticism,* 1961; *A Grief Observed,* 1961; *The Discarded Image,* 1964; *Letters to Malcolm: Chiefly on Prayer,* 1964; *Studies in Medieval and Renaissance Literature,* 1966; *Letters of C. S. Lewis,* 1966; *Christian Reflections,* 1967; *Letters to an American Lady,* 1967; *Spenser's Images of Life,* 1967; *Selected Literary Essays,* 1969; *God in the Dock,* 1970; *The Joyful Christian: 127 Readings from C. S. Lewis,* 1977; *They Stand Together: The Letters of C. S. Lewis to Arthur Greeves, 1914-1963,* 1979; *On Stories, and Other Essays on Literature,* 1982; *C. S. Lewis: Letters to Children,* 1985; *Present Concerns,* 1986; *Letters: C. S. Lewis and Don Giovanni Calabria, a Study in Friendship,* 1988.

MISCELLANEOUS: *Of Other Worlds: Essays and Stories,* 1966; *The Business of Heaven,* 1984; *Boxen: The Imaginary World of the Young C. S. Lewis,* 1985.

Bibliography

Carpenter, Humphrey. *The Inklings: C. S. Lewis, J. R. R. Tolkien, Charles Williams, and Their Friends.* Boston: Houghton Mifflin, 1979. A major study of the lives and works of the "Inklings," a name first applied by Lewis, perhaps as early as 1933, to a group of literary friends who met regularly together at Oxford University. Capsule biographies of the Inklings, bibliographies of their major works, a section of photographs, extensive notes, and an index enhance an illuminating exploration of Lewis's literary milieu.

Downing, David C. *Planets in Peril: A Critical Study of C. S. Lewis's Ransom Trilogy.* Amherst: University of Massachusetts Press, 1992. The introduction contains a concise, insightful view of Lewis's varied career as literary critic, novelist, philosopher, and theologian. The first chapter shows how his early life influenced the writing of his trilogy. Subsequent chapters explore his Christian vision, his use of classicism and medievalism, his portraits of evil, his treatment of the spiritual pilgrimage, and the overall achievement of his trilogy. Includes notes and bibliography.

Gilbert, Douglas, and Clyde S. Kilby. *C. S. Lewis: Images of His World.* Grand Rapids, Mich.: Wm. B. Eerdmans, 1973. Photographer Gilbert's several hundred color and black-and-white portraits of friends of Lewis, as well as the British countryside that was his continual inspiration, are coupled with excerpts of Lewis's published and unpublished writings. Kilby, curator of the Lewis collection at Wheaton College in Illinois, has added a chronology of Lewis's life. Lewis family pictures and photographs of his juvenilia complement this visually impressive volume.

Holbrook, David. *The Skeleton in the Wardrobe: C. S. Lewis's Fantasies: A Phenomenological Study.* Lewisburg, Pa.: Bucknell University Press, 1991. Of use mainly to advanced students, Holbrook provides a probing reading of Lewis's fiction for children and for adults. He explores the thesis that the Narnia stories make disturbing reading for children. Bibliography included.

Manlove, C. N. *C. S. Lewis: His Literary Achievement.* New York: St. Martin's Press, 1987. An explication of Lewis's major works of fiction, from *The Pilgrim's Regress* (1933) to *Till We Have Faces: A Myth Retold* (1956), including an analysis of each of the Narnia books (published between 1950 and 1956). Representative of a subgenre of Lewis studies, and easily accessible is its consideration of narrative, structure, and theme in Lewis's stories. Finds Lewis's use of imagery and analogy a potent means of giving literary vitality to traditional Christian doctrines, though his complexly patterned works raise him above facile religious apologist.

Sayer, George. *Jack: C. S. Lewis and His Times.* San Francisco: Harper & Row, 1988. An intimate biography by a former pupil and lifelong friend of Lewis. Assesses Lewis's experience of grade-school life as less abnormal than that portrayed in his own autobiography, suggests that Lewis and Mrs. Moore were not lovers, and provides a personal account of the last years of Lewis's life. Lewis emerges a gifted and sincere nonsectarian Christian. A section of black-and-white photographs, a classified bibliography, and an extensive index are included.

Smith, Robert Houston. *Patches of Godlight: The Pattern of Thought of C. S. Lewis.* Athens: University of Georgia Press, 1981. A scholarly but accessible analysis of Lewis's philosophy of religion, linking what is dubbed his Christian "Objectivism" to the profound influence of Platonism on his views of the nature of humanity and of God. A sympathetic treatment which nevertheless finds Lewis to have been flawed as a philosopher, a rational mystic torn between a romantic vision of the absolute and the boundaries of a reasoned faith. Extensive notes, a bibliography, and an index add to the worth of the study.

Wilson, A. N. *C. S. Lewis: A Biography.* New York: W. W. Norton, 1990. An important interpretation of Lewis and his work from a Freudian perspective. Paints Lewis as neither a saint nor a full-time Christian apologist but as a man of real passions and a contradictory nature unbefitting the cult following that developed after his death. The chronological biography traces many of his adult preoccupations to the sometimes traumatic experiences of his early childhood and comes to some controversial conclusions regarding several of Lewis's relationships (especially regarding Mrs. Moore). Black-and-white photographs, a select bibliography, and an index complete what turns out to be an iconoclastic portrait of the creator of Narnia.

Matthew Gregory Lewis

Born: London, England; July 9, 1775
Died: At sea, near Jamaica; May 14, 1818

Principal long fiction · *The Monk: A Romance*, 1796 (also published as *Ambrosio: Or, The Monk*).

Other literary forms · Matthew Gregory Lewis's work in genres other than fiction deserves more critical attention than it has generally received. In his own day, his reputation as a dramatist almost equaled his fame as the author of *Ambrosio: Or, The Monk*, commonly referred to simply as *The Monk*. *The Castle Spectre* (1797), a gothic drama, was a major success. Clearly the work of the author of *The Monk*, the drama is populated by stock characters who move through an intricate plot decorated with ghosts and spectacle. *The Castle Spectre* allowed Lewis to show what *The Monk* would only let him describe. *Alfonso, King of Castile* (1801), a tragedy, was much hailed by critics, and helped establish Lewis's reputation as a major figure in the literary world of the early nineteenth century.

Lewis also wrote poetry. Some of his finer pieces appear in the text of *The Monk*. One, "Alonzo the Brave and the Fair Imogine," is still read as an excellent example of the then-popular gothic ballad and is included in *The Oxford Book of Eighteenth Century Verse* (1926). Lewis is also highly respected as a writer of nonfiction. *Journal of a West India Proprietor, Kept During a Residence in the Island of Jamaica* (1834) is a detailed and vivid account of Jamaica in the days of slavery and of the reactions of a genuinely humane person to this environment.

Achievements · Lewis's outstanding achievement is his famous novel, *The Monk*. Often mentioned but seldom read today, this work helped to define a particular type of gothic novel that is still popular today. Rather than merely suggesting a dangerous supernatural presence by the careful use of tone, *The Monk* relies upon graphic description and bold action. Lewis's imagination worked with clear visual images rather than with hints and elusive impressions. Indeed, he has contributed more to the gothic conventions of stage and cinema than he has to later horror fiction. The great gothic writers of the nineteenth century—Nathaniel Hawthorne, Edgar Allan Poe, Emily Brontë—relied more on psychological effects and less on graphic horror than did Lewis. Lewis's true successors are contemporary novelists such as Stephen King and Peter Straub, who have taken the graphic depiction of horror to new extremes.

Among the countless readers of *The Monk*, perhaps none has enjoyed the book so thoroughly as Lewis himself did. In September, 1794, he announced in a letter to his mother that he had produced "a romance of between three and four hundred pages octavo" in a mere ten weeks. With the outrageous immodesty of youth, he proclaimed, "I am myself so pleased with it, that, if the Booksellers will not buy it, I shall publish it myself." Two years later, the novel was published with a preface in imitation of Horace: "Now, then, your venturous course pursue,/ Go, my delight! dear book, adieu!" *The Monk*'s course has been "venturous" indeed. An immediate success, it went into a second edition the same year it was published, and by 1800, readers were buying the fifth edition. The first edition had been published anonymously; the second, however, not only bore the proud author's name but also his title of MP (Member of Parliament).

While the earliest reviews of *The Monk* had been generally favorable—the book was deemed artful, skillful, interesting—the second wave of criticism brought judgments less kind. *The Monk* was "a poison for youth, and a provocative for the debauchee," said poet Samuel Taylor Coleridge in the *Critical Review* for February, 1797. Moreover, the poison had been brewed by a Member of Parliament, the critics were fond of noting. Such criticism did no harm to the sale of the book, but an embarrassed Lewis expurgated later editions of *The Monk*.

Biography · Matthew Gregory Lewis was the oldest of four children born to Matthew Lewis and Frances Maria Sewell. Both families were quite prominent: Frances was the daughter of Sir Thomas Sewell, master of the rolls, and Matthew, born in Jamaica to a landed family, was deputy-secretary at war. They were an ill-matched pair, the elder Matthew being distant and austere, his wife delighting in gay times and the company of musical and literary people. The marriage failed, and the Lewises separated. While loyal to both parents, young Lewis was his mother's favorite, and he returned her affection in full.

From an early age, Lewis showed a great love for music and drama. At fifteen, he submitted a farce to the Drury Lane Theatre; it was rejected, but this did nothing to curb his industry. He sent his mother numerous songs and poems and outlined his plan to write a two-volume novel, burlesquing popular novels of sensibility. His father intended for him to have a diplomatic career, and in preparation, Lewis spent school vacations in Europe, where he soon mastered German. Through his father, he received a position as an attaché to the British embassy in Holland. While at The Hague, he completed *The Monk*. Lewis returned to England, and his novel was published in March, 1796.

Library of Congress

Still in his early twenties, "Monk" Lewis became one of the most popular writers in England. In the following few years, this popularity was reinforced by some noteworthy successes on the stage. *The Castle Spectre* enjoyed a long run at Drury Lane; *Alfonso* played to enthusiastic audiences at Covent Garden. In the later years of his short life, Lewis turned away from literary effort. Having achieved great prominence at an early age, he seems to have found little reason to continue in an activity which could bring him no greater fame and which he did not need to pursue for a livelihood. "The act of composing has ceased to amuse me," he wrote in the preface to the play *Venoni* (1808).

Lewis's father provided more than adequate support, and after his death in 1812, the son inherited substantial fortune and property. Modest in his own needs and habits, he was known to his friends (who included poets Percy Bysshe Shelley, Lord Byron, and Sir Walter Scott) as a man of generosity and deep concern for the oppressed. In 1815, he sailed for Jamaica to do all he could to improve the conditions of the slaves on his estates. He was responsible for important reforms and improvements, including a hospital and a humane code regulating punishments for crimes. After a brief return to England and then to Italy to visit Shelley and Byron, Lewis sailed again for Jamaica. During a five-month stay, he continued to work for better conditions for slaves. He left the island on May 4, 1818. Already sick with yellow fever, his health declined over the next several days. He died on shipboard, on May 14, and was buried at sea. According to witnesses, the coffin was wrapped in a sheet with sufficient ballast to make it sink. The plunge caused the weights to fall out, however, and the loose sheet caught the wind. The body of "Monk" Lewis, the author of one of the most fantastic books in the English language, was last seen in a sailing coffin headed for Jamaica.

Analysis · While *The Monk* is seldom read today, few students of English literature have not heard of this scandalous example of the gothic novel. While the modern devotee of popular gothic literature and film whose sensitivity has long since been dulled by graphic, technicolor horrors may find *The Monk* mild stuff indeed, the novel is not without excitement, and its relation to modern gothic cinema is closer than that of most other classic gothic novels, especially those of Ann Radcliffe. Radcliffe would not allow her imagination to break free from eighteenth century rationalism; the supernatural, in the end, had to be given a natural explanation. Matthew Gregory Lewis's gothic vision looked toward nineteenth century Romanticism. He endowed certain characters with total confidence in tangible reality only to deflate their skepticism with head-on encounters with the supernatural that defy reason's best efforts at explanation. Magic works in *The Monk*; the ghosts are real and interfere with human destiny; demons interact with men, and Satan himself, as a *deus ex machina*, finally resolves the plot.

The Monk · The plot of *The Monk*, like the plot of most classic gothic novels, is not easily summarized. Father Ambrosio, a renowned priest and orator of Madrid who symbolizes all that is chaste and holy, falls in love with an innocent girl in his congregation, Antonia. He is, at the same time, pursued by the bolder Matilda, who enters the order disguised as a novice in order to be near Ambrosio. She and Ambrosio become passionate lovers, and Matilda, seeing that Ambrosio still pines for the young Antonia, promises to grant her to him by the aid of magic. Ambrosio bungles the staged seduction, kills Antonia's mother, Elvira, by mistake, and is forced to abduct Antonia to the dungeon of the monastery, where he drugs and rapes her. Seized with remorse and fear of exposure, he drives a knife in her heart when she returns to consciousness and begins to cry out. Imprisoned and faced with an Inquisitional investigation, he yields to Matilda's entreaties to sell his soul to the Devil in exchange for release from prison. He soon bitterly realizes that he faces far worse punishment at the Devil's hands than he would have, had he faced the Inquisitors, who were preparing to pardon him.

A subplot of the novel involves Agnes, a youthful nun who has given birth to the child of her lover, Raymond. She and the child are condemned to languish without food or water in the deepest part of the dungeon. In the final chapters of the book, she is discovered, half dead, and restored to Raymond.

Perhaps the most important thing to remember about Lewis the novelist is that he was also a successful playwright for the popular stage. Readers of *The Monk* do not have to concern themselves with questions of interpretation; they need not be bothered with understanding complex characters and subtle motivations. Lewis has made all the important decisions, principally that the supernatural is not only real but also a controlling force in human affairs, and with that decision, complex characterization becomes impossible and unnecessary. While Lewis denied his creation some of the elements that make a novel great, he added enough action to produce a good story.

Critics in Lewis's time generally agreed that the disreputable member of Parliament who authored *The Monk* had indiscriminately heaped immoral action upon blasphemous action to create a plot utterly devoid of moral purpose. Such a charge is not entirely fair, for *The Monk* obviously teaches a number of moral lessons. Antonia demonstrates that innocence alone is no defense against evil. The adventures of Agnes could hardly be said to promote promiscuity, and the decline and fall of Ambrosio, the monk, provides the major theme: Pride is a vice that can pervert all virtues, even religious piety.

Nevertheless, those early critics were not altogether unfair in their severe judgment, for Lewis's morality is only shallowly rooted in his plot. Antonia, a model of virtue, is forcibly raped and then stabbed to death by the panic-stricken monk. Agnes, in the heat of passion, gives herself to Raymond; her reward, after suffering the loss of her child and imprisonment in a subterranean crypt, is finally to be united in matrimony with her dashing and well-to-do lover. Ambrosio is proud of the spirituality and dedication to priestly celibacy that sets him above men bound to the flesh. A truly tragic Ambrosio would finally come to understand that his pride was misplaced, for, indeed, he is a man like his fellows. In fact, the events of the book viewed in the light of the revelations at the conclusion may even support Ambrosio's original pride. The monk is enticed to damnation by the personal attention of the Devil himself, who is apparently unwilling to trust this prize to the temptations that are sufficient to damn normal men.

Until the final two or three pages of the novel, Ambrosio seems quite capable of damning himself with no outside help, and more than one sentence would be helpful in understanding why this particular monk is deserving of such special demoniac effort. Lust, perfidy, rape, and murder so much direct his actions that the reader is at a loss to understand how Ambrosio has ever been considered virtuous. Those last pages, however, cast the preceding four-hundred in a quite different light. After revealing that Elvira and Antonia (the murdered mother and daughter) were, in fact, Ambrosio's own mother and sister, the Devil goes on to brag,

> "It was I who threw Matilda in your way; it was I who gave you entrance to Antonia's chamber; it was I who caused the dagger to be given you which pierced your sister's bosom; and it was I who warned Elvira in dreams of your designs upon her daughter, and thus, by preventing your profiting by her sleep, compelled you to add rape as well as incest to the catalogue of your crimes."

The prior existence of that virtue is suddenly given credibility by this surprise revelation of the total manipulation that was necessary for its destruction.

These concluding revelations come as such a surprise that some critics regard them as merely tacked on to the action of the novel. In particular, the revelation of Matilda's true nature suggests that the conclusion was a kind of afterthought. Early in the novel, disguised as a young monk, she wins the friendship of Ambrosio. When she reveals her true sex, friendship turns to lustful love, and when Ambrosio's lust cools, her love becomes utter dedication to satisfying his every desire, even his desire for Antonia. Matilda is, in some ways, the most interesting and complex character in the novel. In the conclusion, however, Lewis does his readers the dubious favor of unraveling her complexity by having the Devil finally announce that she is not a woman at all but a lesser demon in human form, whose every action has followed the Devil's own blueprint for Ambrosio's destruction. This is especially puzzling for the careful reader, who remembers that in earlier pages, Matilda professed love for Ambrosio while thinking him asleep, and that on more than one occasion, even the narrator presented her affection as sincere.

The Monk's conclusion, then, both damages the credibility of the narrator and clouds whatever moral might be found in the fall of Ambrosio. More accurately, he does not fall; he is pushed. Those late eighteenth and early nineteenth century critics for whom morality was a measure of artistic accomplishment had some cause for their attack on *The Monk*. A more generous interpretation will allow that Lewis did not construct his plot or characters to illustrate morals; he only tried to salvage what morality he could from a plot that was allowed to go its own way in search of excitement and adventure.

While there was much in *The Monk* to surprise and shock readers of the day, the novel was, in many ways, highly conventional. For example, the death of Antonia was demanded by convention. Once deflowered, an unmarried female character was useless as a symbol of virtue. Although the woman was raped against her will, her very participation in an extramarital sex act destroyed her aura of purity for eighteenth century audiences. If the association of purity with that particular character was still needed to move the plot or motivate other characters, as Antonia's purity is clearly still needed as a contrast to Ambrosio's final sin, the selling of his soul, then something must be done to remove the taint of sex and reestablish the woman in her former symbolic role. She must pay for her unintentional sin through sacrifice, and Lewis's audience expected the ultimate sacrifice: death. After her rape, Antonia, alive, is of no use to the novel; her marriage to her sweetheart, Lorenzo, a man of wealth and breeding, would be unthinkable. Dead, however, her purity is restored and can effectively serve as a foil to Ambrosio's depravity. Antonia's fate could not have been otherwise.

Romantic conventions also demanded a happy ending for the characters left alive. Lorenzo's all too rapid recovery from the loss of his beloved Antonia and his speedy attachment to Virginia, a minor character introduced late in the plot as an obvious replacement, is perhaps Lewis's most awkward attempt to satisfy convention.

His handling of Agnes, the other major female character, is considerably more skillful. In a cast of one-dimensional characters, Agnes stands out, if only as a slightly more believable human being. She displays moral frailty without becoming a caricature of lust; she is possessed of a sense of humor and at least enough intelligence to remind the reader that the quality is generally lacking among the other characters. Agnes, like Antonia, loses her virginity. That she does so with her own true love, Raymond, whom she hopes to marry, helps only a little. Lewis recognized that it would be awkward indeed to kill off Agnes in addition to Antonia. He would then be forced to end his story with a miserable Raymond or to find some way to kill him as well. Either solution would detract from the utter misery of the monk, whose fate is seen as all the more wretched in contrast with the final happiness of the other characters. Another Virginia created in the last pages to help Raymond forget his lost love would be more than even a reader of romances could accept. Forced by his plot to allow Agnes to live, Lewis at least attempted to satisfy his audience's predictable indignation at her indiscretion by bringing her as close to death as possible.

Before her happy reunion with Raymond, Agnes passes through a purgatory as horrible as any in literature. Thought dead by all but a very few, the pregnant Agnes is imprisoned by the evil prioress in a hidden dungeon under the convent's crypt. There, alone, with barely enough bread and water to sustain her, she gives birth. The child soon dies, and the nearly insane Agnes is left to lavish a mother's love on its putrefying corpse until her rescue by Lorenzo. Lewis was certainly aware that here he was walking a fine line between pity and disgust. If the audience reacts with repugnance, Agnes would acquire a new taint that would make her happy union with Raymond unacceptable. To avoid this, Lewis carefully chooses his words when Lorenzo comes upon the despairing Agnes. The dead baby is only a "bundle" with which Agnes refuses to part, and while the bundle's contents is obvious, Lewis wisely—and uncharacteristically—renders the scene vague and withholds description. Several pages later, a fully recovered and quite sane Agnes is allowed to tell her own story, and she tells it with such sensitivity and self-understanding as to convince the audience that she has passed through the fire, learned from the experience, and is now a proper wife for Raymond.

The destinies of the individual characters—Antonia, Lorenzo, Agnes, the monk himself—show that Lewis was not naïve. He knew what his readers demanded to satisfy their moral expectations and sense of justice, and as far as was convenient, he was willing to comply, but if popular expectation conflicted with his own sense of what made a good story—adventure, graphic detail, action rather than characterization, and no rationalization of the fantastic—then he was committed to disappointing expectation.

William J. Heim

Other major works

PLAYS: *Village Virtues*, pb. 1796; *The Castle Spectre*, pr. 1797; *The Twins: Or, Is It He or His Brother?*, pr. 1799, pb. 1962 (adaptation of Jean François Regnard's *Les Ménechmes: Ou, Les Jumeaux*); *The East Indian*, pr. 1799; *Adelmorn the Outlaw*, pr., pb. 1801; *Alfonso, King of Castile*, pb. 1801; *The Captive*, pr. 1803 (dramatic monologue); *The Harper's Daughter: Or, Love and Ambition*, pr. 1803 (adaptation of his play *The Minister*); *Rugantino: Or, The Bravo of Venice*, pr., pb. 1805 (two acts; adaptation of his play *The Bravo of Venice*); *Adelgitha: Or, The Fruits of a Single Error*, pb. 1806; *The Wood Daemon: Or, "The Clock Has Struck,"* pr. 1807; *Venoni: Or, the Novice of St. Mark's*, pr. 1808, pb. 1809 (adaptation of Jacques Marie de Monvel's play *Les Victimes cloîtrées*); *Temper: Or, The Domestic Tyrant*, pr. 1809 (adaptation of Sir Charles Sedley's translation, *The Grumbler*, of David Augustin Brueys and Jean Palaprat's play *Le Grondeur*); *Timour the Tartar*, pr., pb. 1811; *One O'Clock: Or, The Knight and the Wood Daemon*, pr., pb. 1811 (music by Michael Kelly and Matthew Peter King; adaptation of his play *The Wood Daemon*); *Rich and Poor*, pr., pb. 1812 (music by Charles Edward Horn; adaptation of his play *The East Indian*).

DRAMA TRANSLATIONS: *The Minister*, pb. 1797 (Friedrich Schiller's play *Kabale und Liebe*); *Rolla: Or, The Peruvian Hero*, pb. 1799 (August von Kotzebue's play *Die Spanier in Peru: Oder, Rollas Tod*).

POETRY: *The Love of Gain: A Poem Initiated from Juvenal*, 1799; *Tales of Wonder*, 1801 (with Sir Walter Scott, Robert Southey, and John Leyden); *Monody on the Death of Sir John Moore*, 1809; *Poems*, 1812; *The Isle of Devils: A Metrical Tale*, 1827.

NONFICTION: *Journal of a West India Proprietor, Kept During a Residence in the Island of Jamaica*, 1834 (also as *Journal of a Residence Among the Negroes in the West Indies*, 1861).

TRANSLATIONS: *The Bravo of Venice: A Romance*, 1805 (of J. H. D. Zschokke's novel *Abällino der Grosse Bandit*); *Feudal Tyrants: Or, The Counts of Carlsheim and Sargans: A Romance, Taken from the German*, 1806 (four volumes; Christiane Benedicte Eugénie Naubert's novel *Elisabeth, Erbin von Toggenburg: Oder, Geschichte der Frauen in der Schweiz*).

EDITED TEXTS: *Tales of Terror*, 1799 (also as *An Apology for Tales of Terror*; includes work by Sir Walter Scott and Robert Southey); *Tales of Wonder*, 1801 (2 volumes; includes work by Scott, Southey, Robert Burns, Thomas Gray, John Dryden, and others).

MISCELLANEOUS: *Romantic Tales*, 1808 (4 volumes; includes poems, short stories, and ballads); *Twelve Ballads, the Words and Music by M. G. Lewis*, 1808; *The Life and Correspondence of M. G. Lewis, with Many Pieces Never Before Published*, 1839 (2 volumes; Margaret Baron-Wilson, editor).

Bibliography

Cox, Jeffrey N. *Seven Gothic Dramas: 1789-1825*. Athens: Ohio University Press, 1992. See part 6 of Cox's introduction for a discussion of "Lewis and the Gothic Drama: Melodrama, Monodrama, and Tragedy."

Howard, Jacqueline. *Reading Gothic Fiction: A Bakhtinian Approach*. Oxford, England: Clarendon Press, 1994. See chapter 5, "Anticlerical Gothic: Matthew Lewis's *The Monk*." Recommended for advanced students with some grounding in literary theory.

Irwin, Joseph James. *M. G. "Monk" Lewis*. Boston: Twayne, 1976. Presents the life and writings of Lewis, with a concluding overview of his achievements. Discusses his family background, the beginning of his literary career in Paris, and the consequences of his second journey to Jamaica. Concentrates on *The Monk*, which brought Lewis fame and notoriety and set the standard for tales of terror. Also surveys his success and failure in the theater, with attention to his nongothic plays, such as *The East Indian*, and his poetry, praised by Sir Walter Scott and Samuel Taylor Coleridge. One chapter argues that *Journal of a West India Proprietor* is about self-discovery and has humanitarian and social importance, anticipating critical study of slavery. Includes notes, an annotated bibliography, and an index.

Kiely, Robert. *The Romantic Novel in England*. Cambridge, Mass.: Harvard University Press, 1972. An important book on Romantic prose fiction, including Lewis's gothic romances, which analyzes in depth twelve Romantic novels to define the intellectual context of the era. Notes that concepts of reality were tested and changed by Romantic novels, and Edmund Burke's ideas of the sublime modified aesthetic forms. Lewis is given a prominent place in this general thesis, and *The Monk* is analyzed in detail as the focus of his chapter. Proposes that Ambrosio is a symbol of the artist and concludes that the novel is a nightmare vision of the chaos beneath the appearance of order. Finds a common drift toward death in most novels of this genre. Includes notes and an index.

Peck, Louis F. *A Life of Matthew G. Lewis.* Cambridge, Mass.: Harvard University Press, 1961. This first modern full-length biography of Lewis uses materials not available to earlier biographers, such as diaries, memoirs, and the correspondence of Lewis's contemporaries. Chapter 1 details his background and early life up to 1796 and devotes attention to *The Monk,* arguing that it was published in 1796 rather than 1795. Follows Lewis from his membership in Parliament in 1796 to the beginning of the Kelly affair in 1810, and also examines his dramas and his other prose and verse. Narrates Lewis's affairs in Jamaica and his death on board the ship returning him to England. Contains a collection of selected letters, a list of his principal works, a bibliography of works cited, notes, and an index.

Summers, Montague. *The Gothic Quest: A History of the Gothic Novel.* 1938. Reprint. New York: Russell & Russell, 1964. A pioneer study, placing gothic in the Romantic movement and examining its popularity from the success of publishers and circulating libraries. After cataloging the influences of Continental literature on English gothic writers, examines novels in the mode of the historical gothic. Gives sustained attention to Lewis's career, sketching his life, summarizing his plots, describing the public's response to each novel, and suggesting various works directly influenced by his novels and dramas. Lewis is also cited throughout the book as a major contributor to the gothic tradition. Contains sixteen illustrations, including, as a frontispiece, a portrait of Lewis, end notes for each chapter, and two indexes, one general and one for novels.

Varma, Devendra P. *The Gothic Flame.* London: Arthur Barker, 1957. A classic historical study of the gothic novel in England, which examines the origins of the gothic and analyzes Horace Walpole's *The Castle of Otranto* as the first novel in the genre. The study of Lewis is focused on, though not limited to, *The Monk,* showing how it derives from the taste for horror and how his writings influenced authors after him, including twentieth century American writers. Lewis was one of the earliest authors in the school of horror, emphasizing psychology, which combined with Sir Walter Scott's historical school and Ann Radcliffe's school of terror to produce Charles Robert Maturin and others. Includes three appendices, a bibliography, and an index.

Penelope Lively

Born: Cairo, Egypt; March 17, 1933

Principal long fiction · *The Road to Lichfield*, 1977; *Treasures of Time*, 1979; *Judgement Day*, 1980; *Next to Nature, Art*, 1982; *Perfect Happiness*, 1983; *According to Mark*, 1984; *Moon Tiger*, 1987; *Passing On*, 1989; *City of the Mind*, 1991; *Cleopatra's Sister*, 1993; *Heat Wave*, 1996; *Spiderweb*, 1998.

Other literary forms · While Penelope Lively is known primarily as a novelist, she first earned an international reputation in the early 1970's as a writer of literature for children. Readers see in these early stories strong traces of the concerns subsequently explored in her adult fiction. The most widely known of her children's books, *The Ghost of Thomas Kempe* (1973), describes the experiences of young James Harrison as he encounters the ghost of a seventeenth century former inhabitant of the cottage in which James now lives. Blamed for the poltergeist's mischievous actions, James discovers the significance of historical perspective in explaining the world at large. Here, as in many of Lively's works for children, most notably *A Stitch in Time* (1976), the supernatural is the medium by which the past comes into contact with the present.

Along with many stories for older children, Lively has written one picture book for infants, *The Cat, the Crow, and the Banyan Tree* (1994; illustrated by Terry Milne). She has produced three short-story collections for adults and two full-length works of nonfiction: *The Presence of the Past* (1976), a study of landscape history, and *Oleander, Jacaranda* (1994), a personal memoir in which Lively looks back to her early childhood in Egypt. She has also written radio and television scripts, book reviews, and other articles for academic and nonacademic publications, including travel articles for *The New York Times*.

Achievements · Lively's work has earned her a number of literary accolades. With *Moon Tiger*, she won Britain's most prestigious literary award, the Booker-McConnell Prize, an award for which two previous novels, *The Road to Lichfield* and *According to Mark*, were shortlisted. *Moon Tiger* also received the 1988 *Los Angeles Times* Book Award. *Treasures of Time*, Lively's second work of long fiction for adults, received the British Arts Council's inaugural National Book Award in 1979. She won the Carnegie Medal, the top children's literature award in Britain, for *The Ghost of Thomas Kempe*, and the Whitbread Prize for *A Stitch in Time*. In 1985, Lively was named a Fellow of the Royal Society for Literature, and four years later, she became an officer of the Order of the British Empire (O.B.E.) by Queen Elizabeth II. In general, her body of work qualifies her as one of Britain's most popular, prolific, and influential late twentieth century novelists.

Biography · Born of British parents Vera and Roger Low, Lively spent her childhood in the suburbs of Cairo, where her father worked for the National Bank of Egypt. An only child, she received no formal education but was taught at home by a personal tutor in an apparently rather haphazard fashion. The young Lively was encouraged, however, to read voraciously the great classics of children's literature, as well as the

Miriam Berkley

Bible and ancient mythology. The ardent interest in the past that Lively exhibits in all her works may well have been engendered by the family's weekly visits to the Egyptian pyramids.

After her parents divorced in 1945, she was sent at the age of twelve to live with her grandmother in rural Somerset, England, and soon after, to an austere English boarding school. Although the school emphasized physical over intellectual activity–she once was admonished by the headmistress for reading poetry outside of the classroom–Lively continued to read widely and obtained a place at St. Anne's College of Oxford University. Here, Lively felt a sense of liberation among Britain's best scholars and students. Her field was history, but she also read a good deal of contemporary fiction. She graduated in 1954 with a B.A. in modern history.

After working for a short time as a secretary for an Oxford University professor, in 1957 Lively married research fellow Jack Lively, who later became a professor of politics at the University of Warwick. They had two children, Josephine and Adam, whom Lively stayed home to raise. She read to them often and soon became interested in writing children's stories of her own. Her first, *Astercote*, appeared in 1970, and others followed in quick succession. While continuing to publish works for children, in the late 1970's Lively turned to adult fiction–short stories and novels–and subsequently earned both critical acclaim and popular success. From 1985, Lively became active in the International Association of Poets, Playwrights, Editors, Essayists, and Novelists (PEN), and for a long period of time she chaired the Society of Authors. She also lectured in various countries for the British Arts Council. In the 1990's, Lively's time was divided between London and her farmhouse in Oxfordshire, and she continued to publish fiction for children and adults.

Analysis · Lively is one of a number of British novelists who emerged in the late 1970's and early 1980's to reaffirm the English novel's capacity to express postmodernist themes without sacrificing its roots in the eighteenth and nineteenth century realist tradition. Her fictional worlds are predicated on the conventions of realist fiction, but these conventions are transformed both by perceptual shifts in the consciousness of her characters–a technique strongly reminiscent of modernists such as Virginia Woolf–and by her self-conscious examination of the nature of language.

In a manner characteristic of postmodernist British fiction, Lively's choice of characters demonstrates her fascination not only with the past but also with the ways in which it is reconstituted in and refracted by the present. Her novels introduce us to archaeologists, paleontologists, architects, biographers, historians, and teachers of history; all these occupations have in a common a concern for the meaning and the weight of the past. Lively is less experimental in terms of technique than some of her fellow writers in Britain and elsewhere; however, her theoretical interest in the workings of history and memory, and the intersections between the two, aligns her with such notable contemporaries as Julian Barnes, A. S. Byatt, and Salman Rushdie. Collectively, then, her novels stress the palimpsest quality of a narrative present ineluctably underwritten by the presence of the past.

The Road to Lichfield · *The Road to Lichfield* marked Lively's shift from children's stories to adult fiction. The novel records the experiences of a middle-aged history teacher, Anne Linton, whose dying father, she learns, has been having an affair for many years. On train trips to visit her father, Anne meets schoolteacher David Fielding, and they begin an affair of their own. Her father's clandestine past, and her own clandestine activities in the present, force her to recognize the subjective quality of memory and perception. Marked by Lively's characteristically polished style, *The Road to Lichfield* employs a shifting third-person perspective to portray events from a number of different points of view. This technique recurs consistently in Lively's subsequent novels.

According to Mark · Lively's second novel earned her a second appearance on the Booker Prize shortlist. *According to Mark*, like much of Lively's subsequent work, is concerned with whether the attempt to re-create the past is closer to the order of fiction than to that of objective truth. Here, she tells the story of a literary biographer embarked on a project to write the life of a 1920's man of letters. The novel's title alludes to one of four biblical versions of the gospel, and her protagonist shares with Lively herself a concern for the nature and validity of historical evidence in re-creating the past. During the course of his research, the protagonist determines that uncovering the truth is impossible. The novel itself, though, qualifies this rather nihilistic conclusion in the sense that what the protagonist fails to re-create in the dead subject of his biographical research—"life"—he discovers for himself through his growing love for his subject's daughter.

Moon Tiger · "I am writing a history of the world," the elderly Claudia Hampton announces on her deathbed at the beginning of Lively's Booker Prize-winning novel, "and in the process my own." With these words, Lively's narrator, a former war correspondent and popular historian, establishes *Moon Tiger*'s preeminent concern: What is the relationship between world history and the span of an individual's life? As Claudia looks back on her past, she is periodically interrupted by the narrative present, in the form of the overheard voices of medical staff discussing her case. The rich and full life she fleshes out, though, during the course of the novel, stands in sharp contrast to their dismissive clinical remarks.

In typically postmodernist fashion, history is inescapable in this novel, but it takes on many diverse forms. Claudia's childhood interest in fossils and rock formations, for example, draws our attention to the scale of geological time, while in witnessing some of the crucial moments of World War II she points to the historical significance of global events and to those, such as German general field marshal Erwin Rommel, who apparently are history's central players. However, as the novel's opening lines suggest, these conventional conceptions of what constitutes history are overshadowed by the story of Claudia's own life. Combining personal recollections with ruminations on the nature and purpose of history, Claudia's story stresses the significance of imagination and memory over hard historical evidence. This is typified by Claudia's strategy of imagining "real" events from the different points of view of those involved; in such cases, the details remain broadly the same, but their meaning and context differ markedly according to the perspective from which they are perceived. In employing such techniques, Claudia's narration criticizes implicitly the conventional historian's faith in empirical evidence, objectivity, and linear cause-and-effect patterns.

The structure of *Moon Tiger* is, like memory itself, fragmentary and achronological, but the kaleidoscopic representation of Claudia's life is brought into focus when she recalls her brief affair in Egypt during World War II with Tom, a doomed British tank commander. This pivotal moment in the novel at once underscores and explains Claudia's perception of history: Tom's untimely death in a German air attack is in one respect utterly peripheral, hardly a footnote in the record of the twentieth century's central historical event, and yet Tom has, in effect, played the central role in Claudia's autobiography. In this way, the novel affirms the significance of the individual life in relation to history's larger forces. Such a conclusion is characteristic of Lively's work as a whole, but in *Moon Tiger* it receives perhaps its fullest and most evocative expression. *Moon Tiger* remains, for many readers, Lively's best novel, and it is certainly her most widely read and most widely taught.

City of the Mind · Following the enormous success of its predecessor, *City of the Mind* explores the history and geography of the city of London through the mind of the protagonist, Matthew Halland, an architect who contemplates the impact of his buildings on the centuries-old cityscape of England's capital city. Set against the backdrop of history on a grander scale—an array of the city's inhabitants going back to Elizabethan times—are the smaller experiences of an individual life: Halland's divorce, losing custody of his daughter, the commercial pressures imposed on him by a greedy developer, and his encounter with an expert glass engraver and Holocaust survivor. Ultimately, Halland's faith in human relations is restored when he meets and falls in love with the editor of an art magazine, Sarah Bridges. All these events influence in significant and unexpected ways Halland's minor contribution to the redevelopment of London's docklands that took place in the 1980's. *City of the Mind* examines the nature of historical continuity and historical change and asks, what is our debt to the past?

Cleopatra's Sister · This novel is in some ways Lively's most ambitious, in the sense that she creates an imaginary history not simply for her characters but for an entire country. *Cleopatra's Sister* tells the story of Lucy Faulkner, a relatively unsuccessful freelance journalist. On her way to Kenya, Lucy meets Howard Beamish, a paleontologist fascinated by different conceptions of time. Their airplane is grounded in the fictitious African nation of Callimbia and subsequently hijacked by Callimbian freedom fighters. The novel is concerned with the growing love between the two characters as they become enmeshed in unpredictable political circumstances. Interestingly, though, the narrative that traces this developing relationship periodically is interrupted by chapters such as "A Brief History of Callimbia," in which Lively creates a fictional history of the country from ancient times to the present day. Reviewers of

Cleopatra's Sister found this element of the novel rather contrived or improbable, which is a fairly valid response. However, the novel does affirm the primacy of individual over national histories and individual relationships over political relationships, and in that sense it remains true to Lively's abiding concerns.

John L. Marsden

Other major works

SHORT FICTION: *Nothing Missing but the Samovar and Other Stories*, 1978; *Corruption and Other Stories*, 1984; *Pack of Cards: Stories 1978-86*, 1986; *The Five Thousand and One Nights*, 1997.

NONFICTION: *The Presence of the Past: An Introduction to Landscape History*, 1976; *Oleander, Jacaranda: A Childhood Perceived, a Memoir*, 1994.

CHILDREN'S LITERATURE: *Astercote*, 1970; *The Whispering Knights*, 1971; *The Wild Hunt of Hagworthy*, 1971 (published in the U.S. as *The Wild Hunt of the Ghost Hounds*); *The Driftway*, 1972; *The Ghost of Thomas Kempe*, 1973; *The House in Norham Gardens*, 1974; *Boy Without a Name*, 1975; *Going Back*, 1975; *A Stitch in Time*, 1976; *The Stained Glass Window*, 1976; *Fanny's Sister*, 1976; *The Voyage of QV66*, 1978; *Fanny and the Monsters*, 1979; *Fanny and the Battle of Potter's Piece*, 1980; *The Revenge of Samuel Stokes*, 1981; *Fanny and the Monsters and Other Stories* (containing the three *Fanny* stories), 1982; *Uninvited Ghosts*, 1984; *Dragon Trouble*, 1984; *Debbie and the Little Devil*, 1987; *A House Inside Out*, 1988; *The Cat, the Crow, and the Banyan Tree*, 1994 (illustrated by Terry Milne).

Bibliography

Jackson, Tony E. "The Consequences of Chaos: *Cleopatra's Sister* and Postmodern Historiography." *Modern Fiction Studies* 42, no. 2 (Summer, 1996). The theme of historiography in another of Lively's novels is taken up by Jackson.

LeMesurier, Nicholas. "A Lesson in History: The Presence of the Past in the Novels of Penelope Lively." *New Welsh Review* 2 (Spring, 1990). In a less theoretical vein than Jackson, LeMesurier discusses more generally the influence of the past on Lively's characters and settings.

Lively, Penelope. "An Interview with Penelope Lively." Interview by Amanda Smith. *Publishers Weekly* 232, no. 12 (March, 1988). Those interested in hearing what Lively has to say about her own life and work should begin by consulting this informative article.

Moran, Mary Hurley. *Penelope Lively*. New York: Twayne, 1993. Offers brief but useful critical readings of each of Lively's first nine novels for adults.

_____. "Penelope Lively's *Moon Tiger*: A Feminist 'History of the World.'" *Frontiers: A Journal of Women Studies* 11, no. 2/3 (1990). This essay takes a radical feminist approach to Lively's most well-known novel.

Raschke, Debrah. "Penelope Lively's *Moon Tiger*: Reexamining a 'History of the World.'" *ARIEL* 26, no. 4 (October, 1995). Examines Lively's treatment of history and personal identity as unstable. Raschke argues that the novel represents a liberation from the traditional limits of women's participation in historiography.

Malcolm Lowry

Born: Liscard, England; July 28, 1909
Died: Ripe, England; June 27, 1957

Principal long fiction · *Ultramarine*, 1933, revised 1962; *Under the Volcano*, 1947; *Lunar Caustic*, 1968; *Dark as the Grave Wherein My Friend Is Laid*, 1968; *October Ferry to Gabriola*, 1970.

Other literary forms · All but two of the volumes now attributed to Malcolm Lowry were published after his death at the age of forty-seven. During the last decade of his life, after the publication of *Under the Volcano*, Lowry worked more or less concurrently on numerous projects but was unable to finish any of them before his death. The one closest to completion when he died was *Hear Us O Lord from Heaven Thy Dwelling Place* (1961), a collection of seven interrelated tales. Additional short fiction has been collected in *Malcolm Lowry: Psalms and Songs* (1975), edited by Margerie Bonner Lowry. A selection of poems, edited by Earle Birney, appeared in 1962. *Lunar Caustic*, a novella edited from two earlier versions by Birney and Margerie Bonner Lowry, was published in 1968. Throughout his career, Lowry elaborated and reelaborated a massive scheme of interlocking narratives called, collectively, "The Voyage That Never Ends," which, had he lived to complete it, would have included all of his longer works, with *Under the Volcano* at the center of the "bolus," as he called it. The *Selected Letters of Malcolm Lowry*, edited by Harvey Breit and Margerie Bonner Lowry, appeared in 1965 and played a large part in the revival of interest in Lowry during the 1960's and 1970's. Lowry was also much interested in the cinema and, in collaboration with his second wife Margerie Bonner (herself a published novelist), prepared a screenplay for an adaptation of F. Scott Fitzgerald's *Tender Is the Night* (1934); the film was never produced, but the Lowrys' notes for the film script were published in 1976. Malcolm Lowry's life is the subject of the film *Volcano: An Inquiry into the Life and Death of Malcolm Lowry* (1977), directed by Donald Brittain.

Since so many of Lowry's works were left unfinished at his death, and since even the works published posthumously are selections from numerous versions Lowry left behind, selections made and pieced together by editors, the authenticity of the texts published after 1957 is at least questionable. The special collection of Lowry manuscripts housed at the University of British Columbia Library in Vancouver is, therefore, very important.

Achievements · The only Lowry novel to attract any notable attention during his lifetime was *Under the Volcano*, which was in general very warmly received (in France and the United States at any rate, though curiously it was all but ignored in England) upon its appearance in 1947. During the ten years following, however, no extended works of fiction by Lowry appeared in English, and by the time of his death, even *Under the Volcano* was out of print. Nevertheless, an underground following quietly persisted in its admiration for what must then have seemed, to most, a cometlike blaze of genius revealed in that one novel, appearing out of nowhere and as suddenly disappearing from sight.

The situation altered with the posthumous publication of other Lowry works in the 1960's, beginning with *Hear Us O Lord from Heaven Thy Dwelling Place*. By 1965, a selection of poems had appeared, *Ultramarine* and *Under the Volcano* had been reissued, the *Paris Review* offered a new edition (the first to appear in English) of *Lunar Caustic*, and *Selected Letters of Malcolm Lowry* was published to largely favorable reviews. Lowry was belatedly "discovered" in England, and *Under the Volcano* was hailed as "one of the great English novels of this century" (Philip Toynbee). With the appearance at the end of the decade of the heavily edited, fragmentary novels *Dark as the Grave Wherein My Friend Is Laid* and *October Ferry to Gabriola*, however, a reaction set in. Both books were widely regarded as failures, and Lowry's tendency toward solipsism was judged to have gotten the better of him in his abortive later works. This view probably does an injustice to Lowry. First, works never brought to completion by Lowry cannot be justly measured against a fully realized work on which the author lavished almost ten years of concerted labor. Even so, Douglas Day's long awaited authorized biography, published to nearly universal acclaim in 1973, seemed to legitimize the view of Lowry as an artist *manqué* whose single triumph amounted to a kind of fluke accomplished despite its author's compulsive tendencies to self-destruction and willed failure. In the late twentieth century, there were salutary signs of a reassessment of the Lowry canon as a whole, with such critics as Muriel C. Bradbrook, Ronald Binns, and Sherrill Grace arguing persuasively against the distortions of the "one-book author" label.

Biography · The youngest of four brothers, Clarence Malcolm Lowry was born at Warren Crest, North Drive, Liscard, Cheshire, England, on July 28, 1909. His father, Arthur O. Lowry, was a wealthy cotton broker of sturdy Victorian probity; his mother, Evelyn Boden, was the daughter of Captain Lyon Boden of Liverpool. A prominent shipowner and mariner, Captain Boden had died of cholera while homeward bound from Calcutta in 1880. This part of the family legacy, so unlike that of the paternal side, would provide Malcolm Lowry with the doom-tinged romantic yearning for the sea much in evidence in his fiction.

At fourteen, Lowry was sent to a public school, The Leys, from which he was expected to proceed to Cambridge University, as his brothers had done. It was during his four years at The Leys, however, that he began to engage in what amounted to a subtle subterfuge of the respectable middle-class life that his father had prescribed for him. He became infatuated with jazz and took up playing the "taropatch," or tenor ukulele. Enthusiastic readings of Herman Melville, Joseph Conrad, Jack London, and the early Eugene O'Neill fed his dreams of adventure at sea. Meanwhile, encouraged by one of his schoolmasters (the model for James Hilton's "Mr. Chips"), he began to write his own stories for the school's literary magazine. At this time, too, he began, surreptitiously at first, what would become his lifelong addiction: alcohol.

By 1927, the conflict with his father had become overt, but Lowry finally agreed to go to Cambridge—after going to sea. In May, he shipped as deckboy aboard the SS *Pyrrhus*, bound for the Far East. This experience, which lasted about six months and was to provide the raw material for *Ultramarine*, punctured at least some of his youthful illusions about the sea. It was followed, in the summer of 1928, by another pilgrimage, this time to New England, where he went to pay homage to Conrad Aiken. The American writer's experimental novel of the sea, *Blue Voyage* (1927), was the catalyst of a kind of private tutorial (Lowry being already engaged in the writing of *Ultramarine*). The two got on famously, beginning a literary kinship—and, later a competition—as father and son, which would last in one form or another for thirty years.

At Cambridge, Lowry scarcely applied himself to his formal studies. Instead, he played the role of the loutish yet brilliant sailor, took up jazz again, became a connoisseur of avant-garde German silent films, drank, ran with an "advanced" circle of friends, and continued to work on *Ultramarine*. In November, 1929, one of his friends, Paul Fitte, committed suicide. The circumstances remain uncertain, but it is clear from the obsessive references to this event in his later fiction that Lowry felt partly responsible for it. The other significant occurrence of this time came in the summer of 1930, when Lowry again shipped out, this time as fireman on a Norwegian tramp steamer bound for Archangel in the White Sea. His purpose was to pay a visit to Norwegian author Nordahl Grieg, whose novel *The Ship Sails On* (translated in 1927) seemed to Lowry as important a precursor as Aiken's *Blue Voyage*. This journey and the eventual meeting between the two men gave Lowry the idea for another novel, *In Ballast to the White Sea*, on which he worked intermittently for the next fourteen years until the manuscript (running to some one thousand pages) was destroyed in a fire at his home in Canada in 1944.

After graduating with third-class honors in English, Lowry traveled on the Continent, meeting Aiken in Spain in the spring of 1933. There he also met and soon married Jan Gabrial, formerly a stunt woman in Hollywood films. It was an unhappy match, and Jan left him only a few weeks after their marriage in January, 1934. She returned to the United States, Lowry following her by ship the next autumn. In June, 1935, after a particularly severe bout of drinking, he was admitted to the psychiatric ward of Bellevue Hospital in New York. Upon his release ten days later, he began, between further drinking marathons, to write the first draft of *Lunar Caustic*. When an attempt to find a job in Hollywood proved fruitless, Jan and Lowry sailed to Mexico in November, 1936, settling soon after in Cuernavaca, where he began to write *Under the Volcano*. In December of the following year, Jan, who had never been faithful to the unstable Lowry, left him permanently. He drifted south to Oaxaca, where he spent some days in jail and formed an important friendship with a Mexican named Juan Fernando Márquez. Almost continually drunk, Lowry, with the assistance of "agents" sent by his father, was at length put on a train out of the country in July, 1938.

Back in California, Lowry met and fell in love with another American, Margerie Bonner. By the end of 1940, divorced from Jan and remarried to Margerie, Lowry had moved with Margerie into a squatter's shack in Dollarton, on Burrard Inlet, British Columbia. Here they would remain, with occasional trips to Mexico, Haiti, and Europe, for the next fourteen years. It was by far the happiest, most sober (comparatively speaking), and most productive period of Lowry's life. By December, 1944, he had completed the fourth and final version of *Under the Volcano*. A five-month return visit to Mexico between 1944 and 1945 had nearly disastrous consequences—a suicide attempt, more drinking, the discovery that his Mexican friend, Juan Fernando Márquez, had been killed, trouble with the Mexican authorities, and finally deportation—but from these experiences Lowry gained most of the materials for *Dark as the Grave Wherein My Friend Is Laid* and the unpublished fragment *La Mordida*. By 1950, he was working, as it were, simultaneously on these novels, the stories to be collected in *Hear Us O Lord from Heaven Thy Dwelling Place*, the film script for *Tender Is the Night*, his poems, and *October Ferry to Gabriola*.

This period of intense creative effort came to an end in 1954, when Lowry's American publisher, out of patience with his proliferating but seemingly unproductive schemes for his "bolus," severed their contract. Another severance occurred when the Lowrys left their "northern paradise" in Dollarton. After a final, brief reunion with

Aiken in New York, they sailed for Italy. In late 1955, Lowry was admitted to a hospital in London for psychiatric treatment. Released in February, 1956, he settled with Margerie in the village of Ripe, Sussex, where he resumed his work. His sudden death, on June 27, 1957, caused by a fatal combination of alcohol and barbiturates, was officially termed "death by misadventure." Not surprisingly, Lowry had long since arrived at his own verdict:

> Malcolm Lowry
> Late of the Bowery
> His prose was flowery
> And often glowery
> He lived, nightly, and drank, daily,
> And died playing the ukulele.

Analysis · Like most artists, Malcolm Lowry was always fascinated by the mystery of the creative process. Unlike many other modern writers, however, he was little inclined to the explicit formulation of aesthetic theories. Still, his attitudes toward art, particularly his own art, are frequently embodied in his fiction. In the opening chapter of *Under the Volcano*, for example, one of the main characters, a film director named Jacques Laruelle, sees a drunken horseman "sprawling all over his mount, his stirrups lost, . . . barely managing to hold on by the reins, though not once . . . [grasping] the pommel to steady himself." Hurtling at breakneck speed through the narrow, winding streets of a Mexican village, the rider slips to one side, nearly falls, rights himself, almost slides off backward, and barely regains his balance, "just saving himself each time, but always with the reins, never the pommel." A closer look reveals a machete in one of the rider's hands, used to beat the horse's flanks furiously. It is, as M. Laruelle reflects, a "maniacal vision of senseless frenzy, but controlled, not quite uncontrolled, somehow almost admirable." This image serves, *mutatis mutandis*, as an epitome of Lowry's art: full of high risk, willfully unstable, disdainful of conventional controls, precariously balanced–but balanced all the same.

Obviously, such balance is achieved, when it is achieved, with great difficulty. This was particularly true for Lowry, whose inclination was always to follow the minutest divagations of the mind. His is an art of excess, in several senses. The composition of a novel, for him, meant continual amplification and expansion, patiently adding layer after layer of meaningful reference and telling detail, until the structure of the whole fairly exploded with a rich profusion of reverberating meanings. Such "overloading," to use Lowry's own word describing his technique, is felt at every level. His prose style, for example, is characterized by wheeling complex sentences, rife with qualifications, suspensions, and parentheses. Brian O'Kill has aptly described this style as "expansive" and "centrifugal," persistently "avoiding the closed unit of the periodic sentence in favor of an open form with an almost infinite capacity for addition and reduplication."

Lowry's range of tone is also unusually wide and varied. As Robert B. Heilman observed,

> In recording a disaster of personality that is on the very edge of the tragic, [Lowry] has an extravagant comic sense that creates an almost unique tension among moods. Desperation, the ludicrous, nightmare, the vulgar, the appalling, the fantastic, the nonsensical, and the painfully pathetic coexist in an incongruous melange that is still a unity.

In a famous letter defending *Under the Volcano* against various suggestions for further revision, Lowry argued that the book could be regarded as a symphony, an opera, a jazz break, a poem, a tragedy, a comedy, a farce, a Churrigueresque cathedral, a wheel, a cryptogram, a prophecy, a film, and a kind of machine. If this claim sounds extravagant, it should be remembered that Lowry believed, with Charles Baudelaire, that "life is a forest of symbols." Virtually everything in this novel, from a theater marquee to items on a menu, newspaper advertisements, an armadillo digging a hole, a cat chasing a dragonfly, amusement park rides, a travel brochure, a urinal—*everything* signifies. Appearing amid profuse allusions to the Bible, Christopher Marlowe, Dante, the Cabbala, John Bunyan, Sophocles, William Shakespeare, Herman Melville, and T. S. Eliot, among many others, these "found objects" in the setting gradually develop into a vast network of the protagonist's plight, elevating it to the level of a modern myth, indeed a tragedy for modern times.

In these respects, as in many others, Lowry resembles no one so much as Melville. (Lowry once admitted, characteristically with irony at his own expense, that he identified himself with the American novelist for several reasons but "mostly because of his failure as a writer and his whole outlook generally." Both novelists were acutely aware of the monstrous potencies of the human imagination, which could envision—and proceed resolutely to enact—apocalyptic destruction as readily as it could create life-serving works of art. Both knew well the dangers involved in unleashing those potencies, particularly in the service of a narcissistic quest for what Melville's Ishmael calls "the ungraspable phantom of life," the self.

Such a view of the imagination, overtly Romantic and possessed by the seductive demoness of an artistic ego of leviathan, of volcanic, proportions, is clearly fraught with risk. Lowry, like Melville, accepted the risks involved, not the least of which was the gamble that the reader would go along, entertaining the terms of the risk. There are times when, inevitably, the gamble fails. "Overloading"—the Melvillian tendency in Lowry to pile on six portents or allusions or symbols to evoke something that another writer would either summarize in a simple declarative sentence or else not attempt to say at all—sometimes threatens to sink the vessel. Reading the work of both men requires the granting of far more than the usual share of indulgences before the bountiful aesthetic rewards can be reaped.

Some readers, however, do not find such tolerance of unevenness to their taste, and *Under the Volcano* is on the way to becoming one of the least read of great novels, in company with *Moby Dick* (1851). Lowry's other works (like Melville's *Pierre*, 1852, and *The Confidence Man*, 1857) are so much the more neglected, despite the efforts of later critics to call attention to their worth. One can only regret this aesthetic stinginess, along with the more commonplace preference for readily accessible, streamlined fictions. In Lowry's case, the reader who gives himself to the experience proffered, accepting the terms of risk including the excesses involved, and the occasional failings, is likely to find that the gamble more than justifies itself. For, as Matthew Corrigan has aptly observed, when such "writing works for us, it does so . . . because it entails a vision of a higher order of creative existence altogether than we ordinarily get in modern literature."

Under the Volcano · *Under the Volcano* is a book of wonders, a grand testament to the undiminished plentitude of the English language and the prodigious powers—both creative and destructive—of the human imagination. Not the least of its wonders is that Malcolm Lowry began writing it while he was in Mexico suffering through the personal anguish of a failed marriage, chronic alcoholism, and a terror of life so pervasive that it is a minor miracle he survived at all, much less that he was able to write. The novel went through at least four complete drafts in nine years (the third draft having been rejected by no fewer than thirteen publishers) and was finally completed in December, 1944. By that time, Lowry, from the far more stable perspective provided by living simply on the beach in Dollarton with his second wife Margerie, had succeeded in sufficiently harnessing his inner demons so as to transform his earlier sufferings into art. He described the work in an important letter to his British publisher, Jonathan Cape, as a "drama of . . . man's struggle between the powers of darkness and light," but it would be more precise to call it a "Bible of Hell" written by one who had been a member of the devil's party and knew it well.

One index of Lowry's ability to amplify his experience, transmuting it into a pattern with universal implications, is his management of setting. While the fictional village of Quauhnahuac is loosely modeled on Cuernavaca, where Lowry lived between 1936 and 1938, there is no attempt at documentary realism. To be sure, Lowry selects elements from the real town—the surrounding mountains dominated by the great volcano, Popocatepetl, the Cortes palace with its revolutionary frescoes, the Hotel Casino de la Selva, the dilapidated Borda Gardens of Maximilian and Carlota, the winding cobbled streets, the quaintly named cantinas, the fetid barranca or ravine winding through the town—but his rendering of them emphasizes not mere "local color" but the power of the mind to metamorphose external reality into an interlocking set of correspondences to the inner life of man. One of Lowry's strongest convictions was that life was, as Charles Baudelaire said, a forest of symbols. Thus, Hernando Cortes's palace and the Diego Rivera frescoes adorning it suggest the Spanish Conquest and the Mexican Revolution of 1910-1920, which in turn suggest both the endless internecine conflicts of history and the perpetual battle of the individual human soul against the powers of darkness. The Borda Gardens embody similar meanings, along with the aura of doomed love.

The volcano literally looms large over the entire novel, its snowy summit serving as a symbol of the characters' spiritual aspiration toward ascent, while at its base winds the ubiquitous barranca, suggestive of an alternative destination awaiting the wayward soul. The proximity of the barranca to the totemic volcano and to the many gardens in the novel (most of them, like the Borda Gardens, overgrown, untended, and ruined) calls attention to one of Lowry's central themes: the "infernal paradise" that is the essence of Mexico and, by extension, the modern world itself. This oxymoronic image owes something to D. H. Lawrence, whose novel *The Plumed Serpent* (1926) similarly links the contradictions endemic to revolutionary Mexico with the struggle of his protagonist to undergo a kind of rebirth of spirit. In Lowry, however, the allure of the infernal paradise does not liberate his protagonist from the despoiled garden of life and propel him toward redemption; rather, it arrests him in a state of prolonged inertia, a paralysis of will which renders him finally incapable of actively pursuing the spiritual ascent he so often imagines for himself. In Lowry's version of the myth, at least in *Under the Volcano*, man is condemned to inhabit a garden gone to seed, bereft of its creator: Paradise, surviving only as an image of longing, is irretrievably lost. Solipsistic dreams of ascent succeed only in preventing the upward progress of the soul and, indeed, in promoting its gradual descent into the infernal abyss.

Lowry's narrative, like his setting, is designed to encourage the reader to view the events in broadly symbolic terms. Apart from the opening chapter, which is set one

year to the day after the events recounted in the rest of the novel, the narrative's
present action is confined to the events of a single day, November 2, 1938, the last
day in the life of the protagonist Geoffrey Firmin, a British ex-Consul and an
alcoholic's alcoholic. It is also the last day in the life of his wife, Yvonne. The Firmins
have been divorced for nearly a year, but on this holiday, known to all in Mexico as
the Day of the Dead (All Soul's Day), Yvonne has returned to try to reconcile with
Geoffrey. He realizes, however, that such a reconciliation—which he himself has
desperately longed for during her absence—would require that he give up drinking,
and this he cannot bring himself to do. They quarrel, fail at making love, and part for
a time, the Consul to the company of a bottle, Yvonne to that of Geoffrey's half
brother Hugh, formerly her lover. Later, the threesome make a day trip "downhill"
by bus to Tomalín, where, as Hugh makes a spectacle of himself at an event called a
"bull-throwing," Yvonne fervently proposes to Geoffrey that they leave Mexico and
try to make a new life together in some "northern paradise" (clearly a reference to
Dollarton).

At length, after more drinking and more quarreling, the Consul emphatically
refuses and runs off alone, claiming that he prefers "hell" to her offer of a "sober"
northern paradise. Pursuing Geoffrey in the darkness through the woods, Yvonne
encounters a spooked horse and is trampled to death. The Consul, meanwhile, has
gone to the lurid Farolito cantina in Parián, where, after a series of misunderstandings
and mescal-inspired blunders—culminating in his freeing of a tethered horse (the same
animal that tramples Yvonne in the forest), an act of fuddled yet genuine protest—he
is accused of being a Communist spy and is shot to death by Fascist "irregular police."
His body is thrown down into the barranca along with that of a dead dog. In the
novel's opening chapter, these tragic events, along with many earlier incidents in the
lives of the doomed Firmins, are recollected on the Day of the Dead one year later
by Jacques Laruelle, a retired French film director who had once been the Consul's
closest friend as well as another of Yvonne's lovers.

Such a summary is inevitably misleading, for *Under the Volcano*, like most of
Lowry's fiction, really offers little in the way of conventional plot. For one thing, the
story is deliberately deprived of any ordinary sort of suspense by the disclosure of its
tragic outcome in the first chapter. What this curiously epiloguelike prologue accom-
plishes, among other things, is a displacement of emphasis away from the sequence
of events themselves to their causes and, in the grief of M. Laruelle, some of their
effects. Other disruptions of the superficial story interest stem from the frequent use
of flashbacks (although strictly speaking, the entire novel after the first chapter is a
flashback), as the characters brood on their past lives leading up to this day of crisis;
from ellipses caused by the Consul's passing out or hallucinating; and from the
constantly shifting narrative viewpoint. Five of the novel's twelve chapters are presented from the Consul's perspective, three from Yvonne's, three from Hugh's, and
one from Laruelle's. The focus is thus chiefly inward, on the embattled consciousness
of the characters.

Even the characters' surroundings in the external world—Laruelle's bizarre
mosquelike house with the oracular inscription on one of the towers (*no se puede vivir
sin amar,* "one cannot live without loving"); the municipal garden with its equally
oracular warning sign (*¿Le gusta este jardín que es suyo? ¡Evite que sus hijos lo de-
struyan!*—"Do you like this garden that is yours? See that your children do not destroy
it!"); the amusement park rides, including a loop-the-loop contraption called (after a
play by Jean Cocteau) *La Máquina Infernal* and a "luminous wheel" that is as much

time or fortune as a ferris wheel; the advertisements for a horror film, *The Hands of Orlac,* about an artist-turned-murderer; a cantina called *La Sepultura,* and another called *Salón Ofelia;* the forest around Quauhnahuac and Parián equated repeatedly with Dante's dark wood–all these external places or objects (and there are many other examples) are essentially coordinates on the map of the mind that the novel traces. Indeed, so densely overgrown is Lowry's "forest of symbols" that one can sometimes lose sight of the immediate or human level of the story. At such junctures, time seems to be arrested or abolished by the "self-reflexive" play of images and motifs, just as it does in *The Waste Land* (1922) and other great "spatializing" works in the modernist tradition. Yet in *Under the Volcano,* the force of time is powerfully affirmed at the bottom of the reeking barranca.

Despite the novel's inward focus, Lowry manages to achieve an ironic detachment from his characters. This is no mean feat, not only because of the autobiographical origins of the story, but also because the Consul himself lays claim to ironic detachment even as he observes his own downfall. Lowry's detachment is achieved precisely through the form of the novel, an exceedingly complex design which includes but is finally larger than even the Consul and his remarkably resourceful capacity to transform his life into species of "quixotic oral fiction." Even though the Consul's tragedy in a moral sense is of his own making, it is made by Lowry to resonate like a central melodic pattern within an enormous surrounding symphonic structure. In part, this resonance derives from the novel's frequent echoing of its own infernal music–the leitmotifs mentioned previously. Equally important are the allusive echoes to literature, myth, and history.

The novel teems with allusions direct and implicit to the Bible, the Cabala, Sophocles, Ovid, Dante, Christopher Marlowe, William Shakespeare, Johann Wolfgang von Goethe, William Blake, Percy Bysshe Shelley, Edgar Allan Poe, Herman Melville, Joseph Conrad, and T. S. Eliot, among others. Persistently, the Consul's situation is compared (often by the Consul himself) with that of Oedipus, Prometheus, Adam, Christ, Judas, the Fisher King, Faust, and Hamlet. These allusions, moreover, are not gratuitous. Individually and collectively, they amount to a kind of running commentary on the pattern of heroism to which the Consul, and sometimes the other characters, aspire, and against which his downfall may be measured. What is one to make, for example, of a hero who, at one moment, proclaims in impressive Promethean tones that "the will of man is unconquerable. Even God cannot conquer it," and who collapses "with a crash," unconscious, the next?

Even more tellingly ironic are the historical analogues that Lowry draws between the Consul and such figures as Cortés, William Blackstone the explorer, Maximilian, and General Victoriano Huerta. All of the latter were men of action, which the Consul emphatically is not; yet, like him, they all became involved, sooner or later, in nefarious political intrigues whose result–sometimes unwittingly–was the exploitation of a subject people, usually of another nation or race. During World War I, Geoffrey, then lieutenant commander of a Q-boat, the SS *Samaritan,* was obscurely implicated in the murder of captured German officers; and as Lowry wrote to Cape, "you can even see the German submarine officers taking revenge on the Consul in the form of the *sinarquistas* and semi-fascist *brutos* at the end." However absurd on the face of it, the political pretexts for the murder of the Consul by the pro-Fascists carry a certain underlying truth.

In an important episode in chapter 8, a wounded Mexican Indian is found by the roadside. Because of a Mexican law prohibiting any interference in a crime, even after the fact, the Consul prevents Hugh from attempting to help the dying man. *"Compañero,"* the Indian says, appealing to them, but all they can do is ruminate on the horror of it all, even as another traveler on the bus to Tomalín openly steals the dying man's money. Clearly, there is but a small difference between this sin of commission, the theft, and the Consul's sin of omission, so that in the last chapter, it is fitting that *he* should be "the one dying by the wayside and no good Samaritan would halt." "We evict those who destroy," warns the terrible sign in the garden (as meaningfully mistranslated by the Consul) and, like Cortés, Huerta, and no doubt every other man, in one diluted way or another, Geoffrey Firmin stands guilty at heart: *"No se puede vivir sin amar."*

Yet while Lowry more than encourages the reader to see his characters against this elaborate backdrop of interrelated allusions, symbols, and motifs, it would be a mistake to overemphasize the backdrop at the expense of the foreground figures. The Consul, Hugh, Yvonne, and Laruelle are the cynosures through whose eyes the reader is allowed to glimpse the "massive interests" of a world sliding into the abyss beneath the volcano. At the same time, there is admittedly a deficiency in Lowry's portrayal of character, if by "portrayal" one has in mind the conventions of realistic characterization such as found in Henry James. Lowry was well aware of this deficiency. "The truth is," he wrote to Jonathan Cape, "that the character drawing [in *Under the Volcano*] is not only weak but virtually nonexistent, save with certain minor characters, the four main characters being intended, in one of the book's meanings, to be aspects of the same man, or of the human spirit." Lowry seems almost to be opting for a kind of allegorist's stance when he adds that there "are a thousand writers who can draw adequate characters till all is blue for one who can tell you something new about hell fire. And I am telling you something new about hell fire." This is, as it were, Lowry's *donnée*. He is not particularly interested in his characters as fully realized individuals whose development over the course of time is gradually presented.

The four main characters are all, as he said to Cape, "aspects of the same man." Hugh is "Everyman tightened up a screw . . . the youth of Everyman"; Yvonne is "the eternal women," the anima principle; Laruelle is the Consul's *Doppelgänger*, a surrogate for the artist/betrayer with blood on his hands. Although Lowry has provided glimpses into these characters' past lives, his purpose is less to trace the etiology of, for example, the Consul's alcoholism, than it is to locate key moments that chime with the present situation or offer ironic contrast to it. As Terence Wright has noted, "Lowry is not concerned with the Consul's fall as a *process*, nor with the attempts to save him as a thing which may or may not be accomplished, but with the *contemplation* of a state of affairs–the state of affairs being that a man is in Hell."

Notwithstanding the Consul's grandiose gestures toward Promethean rebellion, what is really most remarkable about him is his readiness to embrace his own death and damnation. This is perhaps what Lowry was referring to when he claimed to be teaching the world "something new about hell fire." The Consul *knows*, as his very utterance indicates ("A corpse will be transported by express!"), that his "glorious" descent is nearing its conclusion and that death is imminent, just as the reader knows, from the opening chapter, that Geoffrey has *already* succeeded in finding the disaster he has so ardently courted. This curious sense that everything has already happened conditions the whole feeling of the book and makes possible a range of effects–including moments of wild comedy and soaring lyricism–that one would not ordinarily expect to find in a tragic tale. It is as if the Consul, having resigned himself to the inevitability of his downfall, having indeed long since chosen the "hell" of addiction, solipsism, and despair represented for him by the Farolito, can undergo his descent and simultaneously observe himself descending, even deriving a certain amusement from the spectacle. The Consul's semidetachment from his own suffering derives in part from his very awareness of the paradigms of tragic downfall in literature, above all Marlowe's Doctor Faustus, whose despairing quest for forbidden knowledge he deliberately emulates. At the same time, indulging in this "heroic" despair, he seems to harbor the illusion (derived this time from Blake) that "right through hell there is a path" leading to a "new life" beyond: By sinking as low as it is possible for a man to sink, giving himself over to complete damnation, he will somehow be saved in the end.

Salvation, however, will come, if it comes, not in the form of a loving union with Yvonne in some sober northern paradise but in the form of mystical vision, a state of mind for which, he believes, alcohol is *"absolutamente necesario."* The Consul regards his drinking as a religious exercise comparable to the partaking of an eternal sacrament. His determination to resist the meddling "salvage operations" of Hugh and Yvonne takes on the significance of a kind of holy war, an anticrusade, so to speak. As he tells Jacques Laruelle, he is fighting for nothing less than "the survival of the human consciousness." The fact that these are, on one level, an alcoholic's rationalizations, does not alter the issue. Drink, as the principal means of access to the visionary state, has become an integral part of his quest for occult knowledge and, as such, is immutably associated with a peculiar kind of fulfillment that the Consul has actually known, ". . . how, unless you drink as I do, can you hope to understand the beauty of an old woman from Tarasco who plays dominoes [in the cantina] at seven o'clock in the morning?"

This mixture of attitudes accounts for the "tragic joy" that, for a time, mitigates the gathering darkness of *Under the Volcano.* The Consul's vision at such moments is of genuinely heroic proportions, for he succeeds not merely in embracing Faustian despair but in transcending it, albeit fleetingly. The Consul is a man of awesome imaginative energies and tremendous resources of humor and intelligence, so that when he dies, the reader experiences that sense of immense waste that accompanies the deaths of great tragic heroes such as Doctor Faustus. Yet the very qualities that set him apart contribute directly to his downfall. The ultimate irony here is that even though he succeeds in finding at the Farolito the "hell" he has sought all along, he succeeds "in a manner somewhat outside his calculations." He finds that damnation is not so ennobling—much less is it an amusing object for detached contemplation—after all. Knocked flat on his face by the shots of a Chief of Rostrums (of all people), the Consul is disappointed, as he was bound to be: "Christ . . . this is a dingy way to die," he tells himself. At this point, the Consul in effect sloughs off the trappings of a borrowed literary heroism and achieves his own "autochthonous" stature as a hero. He dies not as a modern-day Faustus but as Geoffrey Firmin, self-evicted from the potential satisfaction of living in even an infernal paradise. Nevertheless, as he lies dying, shorn of all vestiges of grandiosity, he recognizes what, in his solipsism, he has become. He acknowledges the tragic error of attempting to live without loving—faces, that is, his own essential humanity—though, as his final vision of climbing the volcano only to find himself hurtling down into it makes clear, it is too late for him to act on this new awareness. Moreover, even if he could somehow act, Yvonne is no longer attainable, thanks to his last defiant gesture of releasing the horse.

The novel closes with the Consul's final vision (chorically echoed by the oracular warning sign in the ruined garden), at once the culminating comment on his life of solipsistic denial and a vision of apocalyptic destruction:

The world itself was bursting, bursting into black spouts of villages catapulted into space, with himself falling through it all, through the inconceivable pandemonium of a million tanks, through the blazing of ten million burning bodies, falling, into a forest, falling.

Although *Under the Volcano* is Lowry's best and most highly regarded work, his other pieces have received more sympathetic treatment. Muriel C. Bradbrook was the first to call attention to Lowry's early experiences on the Wirral Peninsula, in public school, and at Cambridge as in many ways the crucial source of his mature vision, an emphasis that nicely balances Douglas Day's excessive dwelling on the last, doom-haunted years. Ronald Binns is one of several critics to examine Lowry's fiction after *Under the Volcano* both seriously and sympathetically, finding in it evidence of a new direction toward the metafictional mode of such postmodernists as Samuel Beckett, Vladimir Nabokov, and Jorge Luis Borges, rather than mere failed attempts to repeat the "high modernist" performance that links *Under the Volcano* with the older tradition of James Joyce and Marcel Proust. For her part, Sherrill Grace maintains that *Under the Volcano* is "best viewed as the magnificent Popocatepetl among lesser, but by no means uninteresting, peaks." In short, although *Under the Volcano* still stands as Lowry's undisputed masterpiece, an adequate appreciation of his complex achievement finally depends on a firm understanding of his "bolus" as a whole. When this understanding occurs, there is reason to believe that Lowry will be recognized as one of the greatest of modern visionary artists.

Ronald G. Walker

Other major works

SHORT FICTION: *Hear Us O Lord from Heaven Thy Dwelling Place,* 1961; *Malcolm Lowry: Psalms and Songs,* 1975 (Margerie Bonner Lowry, editor).

POETRY: *Selected Poems,* 1962 (Earle Birney, editor).

NONFICTION: *Selected Letters of Malcolm Lowry,* 1965 (Harvey Breit and Margerie Bonner Lowry, editors).

MISCELLANEOUS: *Notes on a Screenplay for F. Scott Fitzgerald's "Tender Is the Night,"* 1976 (with Margerie Bonner Lowry).

Bibliography

Asals, Frederick. *The Making of Malcolm Lowry's "Under the Volcano."* Athens: University of Georgia Press, 1997. Discusses Lowry's themes in his major work. Includes bibliographical references and an index.

Binns, Ronald. *Contemporary Writers: Malcolm Lowry.* London: Methuen, 1984. Discusses the Lowry "myth," with emphasis given to *Under the Volcano* and the autobiographical elements in his writing. The chapter on metafictions is a particularly useful survey of Lowry's late experimental novels and stories. A valuable guide for the beginning reader of Lowry.

Bowker, Gordon. *Malcolm Lowry Remembered.* London: British Broadcasting Corp., 1985. A readable collection of reminiscences that attempt to "penetrate the myth and reach the man." Some of the essays are published here for the first time. Also includes interviews with Lowry's two wives and many of his friends and admirers.

_____. *Pursued by Furies: A Life of Malcolm Lowry.* New York: HarperCollins, 1993. A comprehensive, scholarly biography. See especially the preface for pithy comments on the relationship between Lowry's life and fiction. Includes a brief bibliography.

Costa, Richard Hauer. *Malcolm Lowry*. New York: Twayne, 1972. The second half of this study deals with Lowry's work during his fifteen years in Canada. Costa approaches his study of Lowry from a Jungian perspective and looks at this author's "mystical-messianic aspects."

Grace, Sherrill, ed. *Swinging the Maelstrom: New Perspectives on Malcolm Lowry*. Montreal: McGill-Queen's University Press, 1992. Grace's introduction is a useful guide to Lowry's reputation. Part 1 contains essays on the relationship between his life and his fiction. Part 2 concentrates on *Under the Volcano*; part 3 on Lowry's subsequent fiction; part 4 on assessments of his body of work. Includes notes but no bibliography.

Markson, David. *Malcolm Lowry's Volcano: Myth, Symbol, Meaning*. New York: Times Books, 1978. An in-depth critical study of Lowry's *Under the Volcano*, considered his masterpiece and recognized by many critics as a major novel of this century. Indispensable to the serious scholar of Lowry.

Rose Macaulay

Born: Rugby, England; August 1, 1881
Died: London, England; October 30, 1958

Principal long fiction · *Abbots Verney*, 1906; *The Furnace*, 1907; *The Secret River*, 1909; *The Valley Captives*, 1911; *The Lee Shore*, 1912; *Views and Vagabonds*, 1912; *The Making of a Bigot*, 1914; *Non-Combatants and Others*, 1916; *What Not: A Prophetic Comedy*, 1918; *Potterism: A Tragi-farcical Tract*, 1920; *Dangerous Ages*, 1921; *Mystery at Geneva*, 1922; *Told by an Idiot*, 1923; *Orphan Island*, 1924; *Crewe Train*, 1926; *Keeping up Appearances*, 1928 (pb. in U.S. as *Daisy and Daphne*, 1928); *Staying with Relations*, 1930; *They Were Defeated*, 1932 (pb. in U.S. as *The Shadow Flies*, 1932); *Going Abroad*, 1934; *I Would Be Private*, 1937; *And No Man's Wit*, 1940; *The World My Wilderness*, 1950; *The Towers of Trebizond*, 1956.

Other literary forms · Though principally a novelist, Rose Macaulay wrote prolifically in several genres. Early in her career, she published two slim volumes of verse, *The Two Blind Countries* (1914) and *Three Days* (1919), both of which earned favorable reviews in the British press. For many years, Macaulay contributed reviews and essays to such publications as *The Spectator, The Guardian*, and the *New Statesman*; she produced two generally well-received book-length critical studies, *Milton* (1934, revised 1957) and *The Writings of E. M. Forster* (1938). Some of Macaulay's best prose can be found in two of her widely acclaimed travel books, *Fabled Shore: From the Pyrenees to Portugal* (1949) and *Pleasure of Ruins* (1953).

Achievements · Throughout much of her lifetime, Macaulay was one of Great Britain's best-known authors. Many of her lighter sketches and essays appeared in the *Daily Mail*, the *Evening Standard*, and other newspapers and periodicals aimed at large, general audiences; some of her fiction appeared in serialized form in *Eve*, a popular English magazine aimed at women and filled mainly with froth. Yet Macaulay's more serious works consistently earned high praise in Great Britain's most respected literary publications; her twenty-third and final novel, *The Towers of Trebizond*, won the prestigious James Black Tait Memorial Prize. In 1951, Macaulay was awarded an honorary doctorate of letters from Cambridge University; in 1958, she was named a dame commander of the British Empire. Her death from heart seizure in 1958 brought forth warm and respectful tributes from many leading literary figures, including Harold Nicolson, Rosamond Lehmann, and Anthony Powell.

Biography · Emilie Rose Macaulay was born in Rugby, England, on August 1, 1881. Her father, George Macaulay, was a schoolmaster and Latin scholar; her mother, the former Grace Conybeare, was a bright, energetic, but rather severe woman who sought to impart to her children a High Church interpretation of Anglican Christianity. Rose Macaulay was related to a long line of ministers, teachers, and authors (the celebrated historian Thomas Babington Macaulay was her paternal grandfather's first cousin); not surprisingly, she was so well schooled by her parents that, by early adolescence, she was already on very familiar terms with, among other classics,

Dante's *Divine Comedy* (c. 1320) and Shakespeare's plays. Because doctors prescribed warmth and sunshine as a means of treating her mother's tuberculosis, Macaulay spent the better part of her childhood in Varazzo, Italy–a place she would later recall with considerable fondness. In 1900, she entered Oxford's Somerville College, where she studied modern history and became, as her biographer Constance Babington Smith records, "a chatterbox who gabbled away so fast that at times she was hardly intelligible, a ready speaker who made lively contributions to undergraduate debates." Soon after completing her studies at Oxford, Macaulay–while living with her parents in Wales–began work on her first novel, *Abbots Verney*, which critics praised for its artistic promise. In 1915, Macaulay acquired a flat of her own in London, where she quickly developed friendships with such influential literary figures as J. C. Squire, Hugh Walpole, and Walter de la Mare, and where, in 1917, she entered into what became a twenty-five-year love affair with Gerald O'Donovan, a married man and a former Catholic priest who was himself well known in London's literary circles as the author of the highly autobiographical and anticlerical novel *Father Ralph* (1913). Though she traveled frequently, widely, and often intrepidly to locations that saw little tourist activity, Macaulay continued to make her home in London, where even in old age she was seen, as one friend recalled, "at every party, every private view, protest meeting, cruise, literary luncheon, or ecclesiastical gathering." Macaulay openly began to identify herself as an agnostic during her university days; much of her fiction pokes generally gentle fun at organized religion. After O'Donovan's death in 1942, however, she experienced a renewed interest in orthodox Christianity, an interest much in evidence in her later novels.

Analysis · Over a writing career that spanned fifty years, Rose Macaulay produced twenty-three novels. She understandably came to regard the earliest of these–including *The Furnace, The Secret River*, and *The Valley Captives*–as immature and rather badly made, and she did nothing to encourage their republication. In her novels, Macaulay utilizes a wide variety of carefully rendered settings (some of which are quite exotic); her prose is beautifully cadenced and richly detailed. Occasionally, however, the exuberance and ornateness of Macaulay's prose can be distracting, and, occasionally, her plots bog down beneath the weight of the descriptive digressions and authorial intrusions that pepper her texts. Many of Macaulay's characters are both convincing and memorable. Some, however, are both stereotypical and stiff and appear to be exchanging speeches rather than engaging in spontaneous conversation. Macaulay recognized that, as a novelist, she was least skilled at characterization; indeed, she was sometimes urged by friends and critics to concentrate on the essay form. Yet Macaulay also recognized that her fiction had a large and rather devoted readership and that, moreover, fiction could provide her with an entertaining vehicle for disseminating, and dissecting, a wide range of stimulating ideas.

As a novelist, Macaulay returned again and again to the same themes. It is plain that, on the whole, she very much liked human beings. Still, she was critical of the intellectual laziness that she found epidemic in the human race. Repeatedly, her novels mock and sometimes savage characters who unthinkingly digest easy answers to the questions of life and who are prone, then, to sentimentality and cant. Though she is not generally ranked among her generation's more overtly feminist authors, Macaulay frequently reveals in her work a deep disdain for a social system that continued to deny women equal access to education and adventure. She regularly features as central figures young women who are witty, well read, and intellectually ambitious.

Many of Macaulay's recurring concerns are overtly stated in *Potterism*, one of her most enduring novels–and the first to sell impressively in the United States. *Potterism* is, in fact, dedicated to "the unsentimental precisians in thought, who have, on this confused, inaccurate, and emotional planet, no fit habitation." It features among its five epigraphs Dr. Johnson's injunction to "clear your mind of cant. . . . Don't *think* foolishly." At the core of *Potterism* is the abrupt death of a young newspaper editor recently wed to Jane Potter, whose father is the publisher of a string of superficial, cant-spewing newspapers, and whose mother, under the pseudonym of Leila Yorke, churns out foolish and schmaltzy novels that enjoy huge sales. In order to discuss and analyze this somewhat suspicious demise from varying perspectives, Macaulay presents "extracts" from the "private journals" of several characters who knew the young editor, including his novel-writing mother-in-law. Employing clichéd and rather empurpled prose, Mrs. Potter shows herself to be quite capable of the sort of over-emotionalism and muddled thinking that Macaulay, throughout her career, so thoroughly disdained. The three authors of the other journal entries are the friends of the Potter twins, Johnny and Jane, who have sought to distance themselves from what they disparagingly refer to as the "Potterism" of their parents. Macaulay demonstrates that Johnny and Jane and their university-trained friends are not without their own pretensions and illusions, but she makes it clear that their crusade against vulgarity and stupidity, though quite probably quixotic, is well worth the taking.

Told by an Idiot · Macaulay's thirteenth novel, the highly praised *Told by an Idiot*, is set in England between 1879 and 1927 and takes its title, and its epigraph, from Macbeth's well-known observation that life is a "tale told by an idiot, full of sound and fury,/ Signifying nothing. . . ." In this work, Macaulay focuses on the family of Maurice Garden, whose continuing struggles with faith and doubt have made him at various times a Catholic, a Baptist, a Positivist, an Anglican, "a plain agnostic," and, when the novel opens, an enthusiastic member of the Ethical Society. Garden's theological gyrations are well tolerated by his calm wife and his bright children, whose ranks include lively daughters named Imogen, Stanley, and Rome. Through her portrait of Maurice, Macaulay not only conveys something of her sense of the futility of most conflicting "isms" but also provides an acute portrait of the mental landscape of Victorian England. Through her depiction of the Gardens' daughters, she is able to portray young women who, though by no means perfect, possess energy, perspicacity, and a desire for independence.

Orphan Island · In *Orphan Island*, perhaps Macaulay's most satisfactorily plotted novel, she harshly satirizes the sort of narrow-minded smugness that was not uncommon among influential people in the Victorian age. In the novel's early chapters, Macaulay describes how in 1855 a ship carrying dozens of young English orphans is blown off its California-bound course during a violent storm and winds up wrecked along the coast of a small, uncharted island in the South Pacific. In succeeding chapters, she shows how the prim and proper Miss Charlotte Smith, the orphans' supervisor, gradually turns the island into a model of Victorian England and establishes herself as its stern and platitudinous queen. In the 1920's, Miss Smith's island is rediscovered by a team headed by Mr. Thinkwell, a Cambridge lecturer in sociology. Thinkwell is astonished to discover that, in the remotest part of the South Pacific, Victorian England–complete with pronounced social inequities and an obsession with propriety–is, in effect, frozen in time. Still, Thinkwell enjoys the island's remarkable beauty, which Macaulay effectively renders through frequent and detailed descriptions of its sunny skies, lush plant life, and exotic vegetation. He also becomes attached to his growing status as a man of great intelligence and learning. In fact, near the novel's close and soon after the ancient Miss Smith's long-expected death, he becomes the island's prime minister, bent on reforming the corrupt monarchy into a republic where freedom and social justice can thrive. Macaulay does not reveal whether Thinkwell succeeds, though she does point out that, in the end, human folly has a way of winning out, and that the island is "likely" to become "as tyrannous, as unfair, as oligarchic in constitution and economic condition" as it was during Miss Smith's curious reign.

They Were Defeated · Macaulay's sole historical novel is *They Were Defeated*, called *The Shadow Flies* in its American edition, which takes place in England and covers an eight-month period beginning in the fall of 1640. Essentially, the novel centers on the often bloody and self-defeating religious conflicts that were then taking place between Puritans, Anglicans, and Roman Catholics. Among its characters are several well-known historical and literary figures, including the poets Robert Herrick, John Cleveland, and John Suckling. The scholarly and highly analytical Dr. Conybeare, himself based on one of Macaulay's distant relations, is one of the many central characters in her fiction who finds himself struggling with religious doubts. Similarly, his daughter Julian is a recognizable Macaulay "type": She bears what is commonly regarded as a male name and desires for herself the male prerogative to ask questions and obtain knowledge. In a prefatory note to this long, intricately plotted, and largely convincing book, Macaulay explains,

> I have done my best to make no person in this novel use in conversation any words, phrases, or idioms that were not demonstrably used at the time in which they lived; though I am aware, for all the constant and stalwart aid of the Oxford Dictionary, and the wealth of literature, letters and journals of the period that we possess for our guidance, that any such attempt must be extremely inadequate; or, at least, that mine is so.

In fact, after the publication of *The Shadow Flies*, Macaulay received assurances from several students of the language that her errors in word usage were both minor and few.

Going Abroad · *Going Abroad*, Macaulay's next novel, represents a decided change of pace. Dedicated to two friends "who desired a book of unredeemed levity," *Going Abroad* is set largely in Zarauz, a coastal resort town in the Basque country of Spain. It features a large cast of British eccentrics, including a Dante scholar, a young aesthete, a rigid colonel, and a woman schooled in the classics who seeks to relocate and re-create the Garden of Eden. Also featured in *Going Abroad* is a pair of vulgarians who run a string of beauty parlors and a group of hearty Oxford students who seek to spread goodness and religion through the Moral Re-armament Movement, and who are successfully portrayed by Macaulay as both foolish and, in their own sort of way, admirable. By focusing on the often strained interaction of these diverse types, Macaulay created a highly successful comic novel set in an appealingly sunny climate—one that deserves to be ranked among the most amusing of its time.

The World My Wilderness · During the 1950's, Rose Macaulay produced two novels that are generally placed among her most accomplished. The first of these, *The World*

My Wilderness, draws heavily upon the recent events of World War II. Its central figure, a seventeen-year-old girl named Barbary, spent the war years in France, where she witnessed or was touched by a host of brutalities, including her stepfather's murder by Resistance fighters who believed, wrongly, that he collaborated regularly with the Nazis. After the war, Barbary moves to London to live with her father, a wealthy barrister. She studies art and tries to start a more ordered life. As Macaulay repeatedly emphasizes, however, the ruins of war still dominate London: Blocks and blocks of buildings have been shattered, and so have innumerable lives. Thus, Barbary and her brother Raoul eventually fall in with a group of young Londoners who have been similarly affected by the recent violence and chaos and who spend their days wandering around in the city's many ruins, their energies focused on petty crime. During the war, Macaulay's small flat was itself destroyed by German bombs; she lost all of her letters, manuscripts, and books. Certainly, much of her sense of loss and despair informs *The World My Wilderness*.

The Towers of Trebizond · *The Towers of Trebizond*, Macaulay's final novel, begins with the delightful and arresting words, "Take my camel, dear." This work, which is set principally in Turkey, along the Mediterranean coast, seems at first glance to be an outrageous and funny farce in the manner of *Going Abroad*. For example, one of its main characters, the camel-riding Aunt Dot, is immediately recognizable as yet another of Macaulay's eccentric—and harmless—fanatics. Her goal is to spread single-handedly the doctrine of female emancipation throughout Islamic Turkey, while along the way bringing wayward Muslims into the Anglican fold. She is accompanied on her trip by a priggish, relic-scavenging High Church priest, and by a niece, Laurie, who relates the novel's action.

Like many of Macaulay's earlier novels, *The Towers of Trebizond* pokes gentle, rather affectionate fun at zealous churchgoers. Like many of her novels, it displays a subtle, complex, and rhythmical prose style that sometimes dazes and more frequently dazzles. Laurie, its narrator, is certainly very much in keeping with Macaulay's earlier central figures. She is witty, intelligent, and widely read. In the final analysis, Laurie's observations on many serious matters give *The Towers of Trebizond* a far less farcical tone than *Going Abroad*. Indeed, Laurie—Macaulay's last heroine—is, perhaps appropriately, her most autobiographical. She not only freely expresses a mixture of guilt and joy at having maintained a long and intimate relationship with a married man, but, like Macaulay after Gerald O'Donovan's death, she repeatedly reveals a deep desire to return to the Church that she denied for so many years. Even more revealing, however, is her zest for life. Like Macaulay, Laurie has read and traveled and carefully observed because, as she points out,

> life, for all its agonies of despair and loss and guilt, is exciting and beautiful, amusing and artful and endearing, full of liking and of love, at times a poem and a high adventure, at times very gay; and whatever (if anything) is to come after it, we shall not have this life again.

Brian Murray

Other major works

POETRY: *The Two Blind Countries*, 1914; *Three Days*, 1919.

NONFICTION: *A Casual Commentary*, 1925; *Catchwords and Claptrap*, 1926; *Some*

Religious Elements in English Literature, 1931; *Milton*, 1934, revised 1957; *Personal Pleasures*, 1935; *The Writings of E. M. Forster*, 1938; *Life Among the English*, 1942; *They Went to Portugal*, 1946; *Fabled Shore: From the Pyrenees to Portugal*, 1949; *Pleasure of Ruins*, 1953; *Letters to a Friend, 1950-1952*, 1961; *Last Letters to a Friend, 1952-1958*, 1962; *Letters to a Sister from Rose Macaulay*, 1964.

Bibliography

Bensen, Alice. *Rose Macaulay*. New York: Twayne, 1969. This standard account is especially valuable because there are few books devoted to Macaulay. Offers a survey of her widely varied output: novels, short stories, historical works, travel books, essays, and book reviews. Her tolerance for and sympathy with others are brought out. Macaulay belonged to the species of "gifted amateurs," and her carefully wrought style was sometimes too arch.

Crawford, Alice. *Paradise Pursued: The Novels of Rose Macaulay*. Madison, N.J.: Fairleigh Dickinson University Press, 1995. Explores Macaulay's beginnings as an Edwardian novelist, her World War I novels, her treatment of women and civilization in the 1920's, her novels of the 1930's, and her final novels. Includes appendices on Macaulay's childhood reading and on other writings. Provides notes and bibliography.

Emery, Jane. *Rose Macaulay: A Writer's Life*. London: John Murray, 1991. The standard biography of Macaulay, written with grace and sensitivity to the life and the work. See especially the introduction, "Three Voices of Rose Macaulay." Includes notes and bibliography.

Passty, Jeanette. *Eros and Androgyny: The Legacy of Rose Macaulay*. London: Associated University Presses, 1988. Sees Macaulay as a feminist pioneer who repudiated the traditional pattern of the male-dominated family in favor of an androgynous ideal, arguing that people should pursue their aims in a gender-free way. Gives an account of Macaulay's work, the most comprehensive available, with the feminist theme always in the forefront. Her correspondence with Father Hamilton Johnston and its importance for her work receive detailed attention.

Smith, Constance Babington. *Rose Macaulay*. London: Collins, 1972. The standard (and only) biography of Macaulay. Presents a detailed account of her family background and sheds light on key episodes in her life, such as her unrequited love for Rupert Brooke. Gives synopses of most of her major works. A useful feature is an appendix that contains tributes to Macaulay from a number of her friends, including Harold Nicolson and Rosamond Lehmann.

Sir Thomas Malory

Born: Warwickshire (?), England; early fifteenth century
Died: London (?), England; March 14, 1471

Principal long fiction · *Le Morte d'Arthur*, 1485.

Other literary forms · *Le Morte d'Arthur* is the only work attributed to Sir Thomas Malory. It was published in 1485 by William Caxton, England's first printer. The 1485 edition, for centuries the only source of Malory's tale, is a continuous narrative of twenty-one "books," though at the end of some books that clearly complete a larger grouping or "tale," Caxton included "explicits" (concluding comments) by the author. These explicits indicate that Malory may have intended the work to be organized in a fashion somewhat different from that of the published version. A manuscript of *Le Morte d'Arthur* discovered in 1934 at Winchester Cathedral indicates that Malory did not write it as a single long work, but rather as a series of eight separate tales, each of which deals with some aspect or character of the Arthurian legend.

Achievements · Any assessment of Malory's achievement as a literary artist is inevitably bound up with a judgment of the form of *Le Morte d'Arthur*: Is it a single story or eight separate tales? As critic Stephen Knight points out, this question of form is central to critical inquiry, for "if we are not clear whether we have before us one book or eight, or something in between, then our attitude towards the work or works must be obscure and tentative." That Malory's *Le Morte d'Arthur* should be considered a series of separate "works" is argued forcefully by Eugène Vinaver, editor of the modern standard edition, conspicuously entitled *The Works of Sir Thomas Malory* (1947, 3 volumes). Vinaver argues in the introduction to his edition that the unity that scholars have found in *Le Morte d'Arthur* was imposed by Caxton, not intended by Malory, and his edited text, based on the Winchester manuscript, restores many passages excised by Caxton in the 1485 edition. Vinaver's opinion has been challenged by several critics, most notably by R. M. Lumiansky, who has argued that even in the Winchester manuscript one can see a unity of design and a progression from early to late tales, suggesting that Malory himself conceived of his eight tales as forming a single "work."

Unfortunately, although this issue has been debated at length, it has not been settled with any real certainty, and any final judgment of Malory's talents as an original artist may remain in abeyance for some time. Yet, whether one considers the Caxton edition of *Le Morte d'Arthur*, where a stronger sense of unity is prevalent, or the Winchester manuscript, from which the argument for eight separate tales can be made more forcefully, one can see an unmistakable unity imparted by the ordering of the tales. Malory's story moves progressively from the birth of Arthur to his assumption of kingship and defeat of all opposition, through the numerous stories depicting the adventures of knights in service to him, to his death at the hands of his traitorous, illegitimate son, Mordred. This kind of chronological progress is noticeably absent in the romances which Malory used as sources for his work. In the romances, especially that amorphous collection known as the French Vulgate Cycle, from which Malory borrowed much of his materials, there is often little sense of direction or completeness to the knights' adventures. From the modern reader's point of view, Malory deserves special credit for unifying these disparate tales and arranging them in an order that lends motivation to certain characters' actions and–perhaps more important–gives the reader a sense of the cause-and-effect relationship between certain incidents that is lacking in the "French books" from which Malory says he has "drawn out" his tales.

Malory's achievement in condensing and organizing his sources has also been a matter of debate. Nineteenth century scholars, possessed of newly discovered Arthurian manuscripts of the twelfth through fifteenth centuries, were divided on the issue. Several noted medievalists branded Malory as a mere "compiler"; others, equally respected, praised him for his originality. Perhaps the most laudatory comment was offered by George Saintsbury, who claimed that in *Le Morte d'Arthur*, Malory made a significant advance over the romance tradition by developing a firm sense of narrative purpose, akin to that of the modern novelist. Saintsbury sees Malory exhibiting "the sense of *grasp*, the power to put his finger, and to keep it, on the central pulse and nerve of the story." Saintsbury and others, notably W. P. Ker, also praised Malory for his strong, original prose style. T. S. Eliot has called Malory "a kind of crude Northern Homer," a fine prose stylist.

Regardless of the criticisms leveled at Malory's tale as an artistic achievement in its own right, there can be little question about the importance of *Le Morte d'Arthur* in literary history. Since its publication, it has stood as the preeminent English-language document to which readers of succeeding centuries have turned to learn of the Arthurian legend. Caxton's edition was followed by two others early in the sixteenth century, attesting to Malory's immediate popularity. Intellectuals during the Renaissance may have agreed with Roger Ascham, who commented in *The Scholemaster* (1570) that the chief pleasure of *Le Morte d'Arthur* lay in two points, "open manslaughter and bold bawdy." Nevertheless, the appearance of still more editions of the work and the numerous references to the Arthurian legend in the literature of the period offer further proof of the influence of Malory's work long after its publication. When English society developed a renewed interest in chivalric materials and especially in the Arthurian legend, *Le Morte d'Arthur* was the work to which writers from Sir Walter Scott to Alfred, Lord Tennyson turned as the *locus classicus* of the legend. It was by comparison to Malory that Tennyson's *Idylls of the King* (1859-1885) and the Arthurian poems of A. C. Swinburne, William Morris, and Matthew Arnold were judged by their contemporaries, and all openly acknowledged their debt to the author of *Le Morte d'Arthur*.

In part, *Le Morte d'Arthur*'s influence as a source for Arthurian adventure and chivalric virtue may be attributed to the good fortune of its having been printed, while hundreds or even thousands of Arthurian tales existed only in manuscript until the late nineteenth or even the twentieth century. Nevertheless, even after scholarly and popular bookshelves began to be filled with other versions, Malory's work continued to be regarded as the premier English rendition of the Arthurian story. In the twentieth century, T. H. White, who had at his disposal both medieval and modern accounts of the legend numbering in the hundreds, turned to Malory for inspiration in writing what is no doubt the most important twentieth century Arthurian tale, *The Once and Future King*. John Steinbeck, whose accomplishments as a novelist earned him the Nobel Prize, began a modern adaptation of Malory because he wanted to bring to "impatient" modern readers the "wonder and magic" of *Le Morte d'Arthur*. While the literary purist may question the value of modernizing Malory, one cannot quarrel too much with Steinbeck's motive, for he speaks truly when he observes that these stories "are alive even in those of us who have not read them." To write a work that becomes a part of the cultural heritage of one's country, and a classic of one's language and literature, is an achievement few writers accomplish; Malory is one of the exceptions.

Biography · Though it is clear that "Sir Thomas Malory, knight prisoner" wrote *Le Morte d'Arthur*, there is serious debate about which Thomas Malory actually authored the work. Records of fifteenth century England contain references to more than a dozen Thomas Malorys. Most modern scholars believe that the author of *Le Morte d'Arthur* was Sir Thomas Malory of Newbold Revell, Warwickshire, in southern England, but there are other candidates, most notably Thomas Malory of Hutton and Studley, Yorkshire, in the north.

That Thomas Malory of Newbold Revell was the author of *Le Morte d'Arthur* was first proposed in 1894 by George L. Kittredge, who examined both the Caxton text and historical records and deduced that the Newbold Revell knight met all the necessary criteria for authorship. From the explicit at the end of book 21 of *Le Morte d'Arthur*, Kittredge concluded that Thomas Malory was a knight, that he was in prison (he prays for "good delyveraunce"), and that the book was concluded in the ninth year of the reign of Edward IV, that is, March, 1469, to March, 1470. Extant records indicated that the Malory from Newbold Revell was the son of a gentleman and therefore probably received the education requisite to produce the work. He had been exposed to knightly virtues while in service to Richard Beauchamp, earl of Warwick, who was said to have embodied the knightly ideals of the age. He is reported to have died on March 14, 1471, after the *terminus ad quem* of the book's composition.

Kittredge's identification of Malory was reinforced when, in the early 1920's, Edward Cobb found an indictment consisting of eight charges against the Newbold Revell knight. Although it is not clear that Malory was ever found guilty on any of the charges, it is certain that he spent time in jail; in fact, it appears that between 1460 and 1471, the Newbold Revell knight spent most of his time at Newgate prison. His presence there would explain his having access to the books upon which he based *Le Morte d'Arthur*, because Newgate was situated near a monastery with an excellent library. Malory may well have bribed his keepers to allow him to borrow the books.

The Winchester manuscript, discovered in 1934, contains several new explicits that provide additional information about the author. For example, at the end of the "Tale of Sir Gareth," Malory petitions his readers to pray that God will send him "good delyveraunce sone [soon] and hastely." Even more clear is the explicit at the end of the "Tale of King Arthur," in which the author says that "this was drawyn by a knyght presoner sir Thomas Malleorre." On this evidence, the knight from Newbold Revell has emerged as the leading candidate for the authorship of *Le Morte d'Arthur*.

The primary arguments discrediting the Newbold Revell knight have been made by William Matthews in *The Ill-Framed Knight* (1965). According to Matthews, no evidence suggests that this Malory had any familiarity with northern poetry, yet the dialect of *Le Morte d'Arthur* and its English sources (especially the alliterative *Morte Arthure*) are clearly northern. Further, none of the references to real places (many are mentioned in the text) are to locations near Warwickshire. Matthews contends, too, that it is doubtful that a criminal would have had access under any circumstances to the library near Newgate, and that there is no evidence that the monastery's library had the books upon which *Le Morte d'Arthur* is based. At the time the work was completed, Thomas Malory of Newbold Revell could have been seventy-five years old, much too old to have completed such an arduous task. Finally, the Newbold Revell knight's political alliances were Yorkist, and *Le Morte d'Arthur* is distinctly Lancastrian in outlook. Kittredge had also cited two documents to support his claim, but this documentary evidence is discounted by Matthews. Matthews says that Kittredge's Malory was too old to have participated in a 1462 winter siege in which a Malory is recorded to have taken part. Similarly, the Newbold Revell knight could not have been the one named in the pardon made by Edward IV in 1468, since the pardon applied to political prisoners, and the Warwickshire man was a common criminal.

Matthews has proposed a second candidate, Thomas Malory of Hutton and Studley in Yorkshire. This Malory was a member of an eminent northern family; it is realistic to assume that he could read French, had access to the necessary source documents, was familiar with northern poetry and places, and spoke the northern dialect prominent in *Le Morte d'Arthur*. In addition, he supported the Lancastrian cause. The objections to his candidacy for authorship are that he is not described in family genealogies as a knight or chevalier, and there is no record of his ever being a prisoner. Matthews argues, however, that these are not serious discrepancies. Many men who could do so did not claim the title of knight. That there is no record of the Yorkshire Malory being a prisoner is also explainable. Although records abound detailing the imprisonment of criminals, it was not a fifteenth century custom to keep records of prisoners of war. These prisoners often had some measure of freedom and several wrote books while in captivity. It seems more likely that a work the scope of *Le Morte d'Arthur* would be written under these conditions than under those imposed on criminals. Further, the expression "knight-prisoner," used by Malory to refer to himself in the explicits, is applied in *Le Morte d'Arthur* to Lionel, Lancelot, and Tristram when they become prisoners of war. Similarly, "good deliverance" is used when Malory speaks of Tristram's trials in prison. Thus, the term "knight-prisoner" is used in a somewhat complimentary fashion as the epithet of a prisoner of war, not a common criminal. The claim for Thomas Malory of Studley and Hutton rests on these grounds.

Other candidates have been proposed as the author of *Le Morte d'Arthur*, but few can be considered seriously. Thomas Malorys appear in the records of English courts and parishes as laborers, armigers—and one as a member of Parliament (though he is mentioned only once, and nothing else is known about him). What is known for certain about the author of *Le Morte d'Arthur* can only be gleaned from the text of the work itself, and then verified—with much conjecture—by searching the records of fifteenth century England.

**Analysis · ** The modern reader approaching Sir Thomas Malory's *Le Morte d'Arthur* may be perplexed at first reading, for while the story of Arthur and his knights has the appearance of a novel, it is certainly far removed from representatives of the genre with which today's reader is more familiar. Though there is an overarching structure to the work, provided by the chronology of Arthur's reign, individual stories often seem mere appendages that add little to the major plot and seldom seem to have concrete beginnings or endings themselves. The "fault" for this apparent lapse into chaos lies not so much with Malory (though too close a reliance on his sources does tend to cause the story to branch off in several directions that lead nowhere), but rather with the reader who is not familiar with medieval techniques of storytelling. It is not uncommon to find medieval romances that simply begin *in medias res* and seem to end there as well. That form of narrative technique has been supplanted in today's literary world by the "well-made story," whose beginning, middle, and end are clearly defined, and whose parts are clearly integrated into the whole. The medieval audience demanded neither tight concentration on a single story line nor analysis of cause-and-effect relationships; to appreciate Malory and his achievement in the chain of events leading to the modern novel one must first appreciate that for writers before him, and for Malory himself, emphasis on the event itself, rather than on its consequences or on the role of characters, was of primary importance. Malory, in fact, was one of the first writers to delve into the minds of his characters and achieve a certain degree of verisimilitude in presenting the people who appear in his story.

Malory lacks originality in the modern sense, since almost everything he recounts in *Le Morte d'Arthur* is taken from medieval romances popular for centuries before his. His accomplishments as a storyteller and his claim to literary greatness lie in the artistry with which he wove together the elements of the Arthurian legend and in the insight he presents into the meaning of the story both for his contemporaries and for readers throughout the centuries. Beneath the surface chaos of the tales that make up the work, Malory has presented a unified vision of a society in triumph and in decay; his is a complex work with a complex purpose. As D. S. Brewer explains in his introduction to *Malory: The Morte Darthur* (1968), the work was "a part of the movement that transformed the medieval knight into the English gentleman." Through this story of the "ideal society," Malory presents the enduring dilemma of man's attempt to reconcile individual demands with those of the society in which he lives and those of the God he worships.

Le Morte d'Arthur · *Le Morte d'Arthur* consists of eight tales, which Caxton divided into twenty-one books in his edition. The story itself divides into three large sections. The first, consisting of books 1 through 5 in the Caxton text, details the coming of Arthur and the establishment of the Round Table. It begins with the adulterous conception of the King, tells the now popular story of the sword in the stone, and continues with an account of the early battles and adventures of Arthur and his knights in their effort to subdue external threats to the realm. Always the careful craftsman where larger issues of plot and motivation are concerned, Malory skillfully interweaves into this larger story details that become important in later episodes: the "dolorous stroke" wielded by Balin that initiates in a curious way the Holy Grail quest, the hatred felt by Morgan le Fay for her brother Arthur, and the power of Excalibur and its symbolic significance. In the final book of this section, Arthur is hailed as the conqueror of Rome and welcomed into the city by the pope himself; the last great external challenge to this new order of society has been met and overcome.

The main books of *Le Morte d'Arthur* (11-17) deal with the adventures of Arthur's knights. Included are tales of the prowess of Sir Lancelot, the dedicated idealism of Sir Gareth ("Beaumains"), and the accomplishments and deceptions of Sir Tristram and his paramour, La Beal Isould. In these accounts, the court of King Mark is established as a kind of counterculture to that of Arthur, and the reader is made to feel the imminent doom that awaits Arthur's kingdom should the knights falter in their loyalty to their leader and the virtues he upholds. The final books of this section recount the quest of the Sangreal (Holy Grail), a devastating undertaking that strips

Arthur of many of his knights and exposes the shortcomings of many of those considered the best in the realm. The quest marks the beginning of the end of the Round Table, for through vain pursuit of this holy artifact, the knights reveal their spiritual imperfection and perhaps their inherent imperfectability.

The third and final section of the work tells of the decay of Arthur's kingdom, a process that begins when the knights return from the unsuccessful Grail quest. Lancelot, by his actions, reveals that his dedication to the Queen is greater than his devotion to God, his personal needs more important than his public duties. Arthur becomes unable to effect a suitable compromise between public and private life, and as incident after incident forces him to choose between his queen and his knights, he reluctantly is forced to opt for the latter. His sad statement after the civil war has begun in his kingdom reflects his inability to maintain a balance between his private and public lives: "Much more I am sorrier for my good knights' loss than for the loss of my fair queen; for queens I might have enough, but such a fellowship of good knights shall never be together in no company." This conflict between public and private virtues, a universal condition of humankind that Malory perceived at the heart of the Arthurian tale that he was transcribing, is the cause of the tragic development in the story.

The essence of the conflict Malory portrays in *Le Morte d'Arthur* has been described by D. S. Brewer as "the divergence of the values of honour and goodness from each other." The concept of honor is the paramount public virtue, informing the code of chivalry and motivating actions of those who were proponents of knighthood. Goodness, on the other hand, is a private virtue, and in *Le Morte d'Arthur* it is specifically identified as a Christian attribute. Hence, the conflict between honor and goodness is elevated beyond the level of individuals struggling within themselves to choose the proper path in life; it becomes, under Malory's skillful handling of individual tales from Arthurian romances, a larger conflict between two modes of living–the way of the good knight and the way of the good Christian.

The public virtue of honor had been the hallmark of chivalry for centuries before Malory brought it under scrutiny in *Le Morte d'Arthur*, and his characters all place great emphasis on winning and maintaining it. The promise of honor brings the knights to court; the chance to increase one's honor motivates them to accept the most impossible quests and to battle against the most insurmountable odds. The preservation of honor demands strict obedience to one's lord, unswerving fidelity to one's lady, and unshakable loyalty to one's brother knights. By striving for honor, the knights make the Round Table great, and paradoxically, by striving to maintain their honor, they destroy it.

In the society that Malory's Arthur imagines and attempts to build, honor and goodness are inseparable. In a passage not in any of Malory's sources, the King charges all his knights "never to do outrageousity nor murder, and always to flee treason [that is, to avoid committing it]; also, by no mean to be cruel, but to give mercy unto him that asketh mercy, upon pain of forfeiture of their worship . . . and always to do ladies, damosels, and gentlewomen succour, upon pain of death." By their honor, the knights are committed to doing good deeds. As the story progresses, however, the requirements of honor and goodness begin to diverge, and the inability of the knights and ladies to reconcile the two leads to the tragic demise of Arthur's society.

Malory highlights the growing divergence throughout a number of stories in *Le Morte d'Arthur*, but in none more clearly than "The Poisoned Apple" (book 18,

chapters 1-7). In this vignette, Guinevere is accused by Sir Mador of poisoning Sir
Patrice, his cousin. Mador demands justice: Either the queen is to be executed, or her
champion must defeat Mador in battle. Arthur cannot fight, as he is to sit in judgment
of the case, and Lancelot is not at court. Clearly this is a matter of honor—the king's
lady is to be shamed, bringing dishonor on the entire court—and yet all of the knights
present at court suspect Guinevere and refuse to fight in her behalf. In desperation,
Arthur and Guinevere send for Sir Bors. They appeal to him to champion the queen
not because she is to be shamed, and through her the court, but rather because he has
an obligation to uphold the honor of his kinsman Lancelot, who no doubt would fight
for the queen were he at court. Bors tells Arthur he will fight "for my Lord Launcelot's
sake, and for your sake." Bors then appeals to other knights, claiming that "it were
great shame to us all" should the wife of Arthur be "shamed openly"; he is rebuked
by many who, while acknowledging their respect for the king, have no love for
Guinevere because she is a "destroyer of good knights." Though Lancelot eventually
arrives in time to fight for Guinevere and save her from this charge, of which she is
innocent, the implication here—borne out later in *Le Morte d'Arthur*—is that the prowess
that wins honor may also allow one to win when the cause for which one is fighting
is on the wrong side of justice; it might may indeed prevail for evil instead of
goodness.

This sad fact is brought home to the reader in Malory's account of Lancelot's
battles for the queen when she is accused of adultery. Lancelot is forced to come to
Guinevere's rescue, even at the expense of creating strife within Arthur's realm,
because his honor is at stake. "Whether ye did right or wrong," Bors advises him, "it
is now your part to hold with the queen, that she be not slain . . . for and she so die
the shame shall be yours." In the final chapters of *Le Morte d'Arthur*, Malory presents
Lancelot fighting reluctantly against truth to preserve his honor. Arthur, too, fights
reluctantly, even though he is on the side of truth, for he would rather preserve his
noble society of knights than save his queen, and he appears willing to be cuckolded
rather than have the Round Table destroyed by internal strife.

The clear dichotomy between knightly and Christian virtues is made evident at
several points in *Le Morte d'Arthur*, but Malory makes his most forceful statement
about the problem in "The Maid of Astolat" (book 18, chapters 9-20). Lancelot,
fighting in disguise against his own kinsmen and the other knights of the Round Table,
is wounded and taken to a hermitage to heal. The hermit attending him asks who this
knight is, and when he learns it is one who fought against Arthur, remarks: "I have
seen the day . . . I would have loved him the worse because he was against my lord,
King Arthur, for sometime I was one of the fellowship of the Round Table, but I thank
God now I am otherwise disposed." The hermit has renounced his former calling,
perhaps because he has seen where the path of honor leads and has adopted a new
path and a new Lord. Lancelot, who recovers from his wound while at the hermitage,
comes to a momentary realization of his folly and bitterly acknowledges that his
"pride" has led to his being thrown into this lowly condition. Only much later,
however, does he abandon the pursuit of honor through the chivalric code, and by
then Arthur is dead, Guinevere has entered a nunnery, and the kingdom is in ruins.
The sense that one gets from reading Malory's account of the last days of Arthur's
realm is that even the most chivalric society is doomed to failure, and that humanity's
only hope lies in adopting values and goals that transcend worldly ideals.

What, then, has Malory accomplished in telling this tale? In the strife that tears
Arthur's kingdom apart, fifteenth century readers saw mirrored their own griefs over

the demise of feudal England, ravaged by the bloody struggle for the English throne that became known as the Wars of the Roses. *Le Morte d'Arthur* offered these readers faith, in a curious way, because in his work Malory has shown that, despite the collapse of an ideal society, lives and societies continue.

Even in their failures, the characters of *Le Morte d'Arthur* appear as larger-than-life personages who speak to the reader of the potential greatness of humankind. If honor can somehow be wedded to goodness, if the public virtues that gave the knights their sense of purpose can be married to the private virtues that cause humans to rise above societal bonds when necessary, the ideal society can be created. To his contemporary readers, Malory's story no doubt offered this note of special hope. Thus, *Le Morte d'Arthur* speaks not only to its fifteenth century readers, but through the story of Arthur and his knights, Malory also speaks to all peoples of all nations and times of the possibility of greatness, the inevitability of failure, and the glory that humankind achieves by striving for the impossible.

Laurence W. Mazzeno and Sarah B. Kovel

Bibliography
Archibald, Elizabeth, and A. S. G. Edwards, eds. *A Companion to Malory*. Woodbridge, England: D. S. Brewer, 1996. Part of the Arthurian Studies series, this volume examines the Arthurian legend in Malory's seminal work. Includes bibliographical references and an index.
Field, P. J. C. *The Life and Times of Sir Thomas Malory*. Cambridge, England: D. S. Brewer, 1993. A very detailed, scholarly retelling of Malory's life. Recommended for advanced students and scholars.
Ihle, Sandra Ness. *Malory's Grail Quest: Invention and Adaptation in Medieval Prose Romance*. Madison: University of Wisconsin Press, 1983. Examines "The Tale of the Sangreal" from *Le Morte d'Arthur*, looking both to its thirteenth century French source and to Malory's own structural and thematic adaptation. Gives insight into medieval literary theory and the underlying intentions of Malory's distinctive Grail quest.
McCarthy, Terence. *An Introduction to Malory*. Reprint. Cambridge, England: D. S. Brewer, 1991. McCarthy provides very ample discussions of how to read Malory, exploring, in depth, characters such as Lancelot, Tristram, and Arthur and the world of romance that Malory creates. McCarthy takes many different critical approaches, and he includes a section of background and biography as well as a very useful bibliographical essay.
_____. *Reading "The Morte Darthur."* Cambridge, England: D. S. Brewer, 1988. A study intended to assist the newcomer to Malory's work. Follows Eugène Vinaver's division of this work into eight books. Presents various contexts through which to view *Le Morte d'Arthur*. A useful and accessible reader.
Merrill, Robert. *Sir Thomas Malory and the Cultural Crisis of the Late Middle Ages*. New York: Peter Lang, 1987. An original inquiry into the psychology of the knights of Arthurian romance and the impact of the Round Table on their lives. Traces the formation of medieval institutions and explores the personal and social tensions in the Middle Ages that led to the Protestant Reformation.
Parins, Marilyn Jackson. *Malory: The Critical Heritage*. New York: Routledge, 1988. An important collection of early criticism and commentary on Malory's *Le Morte d'Arthur* in chronological order, beginning with William Caxton's preface to the

first edition and ending with remarks by influential literary critic George Saintsbury in 1912.

Riddy, Felicity. *Sir Thomas Malory.* New York: E. J. Brill, 1987. An excellent critical
commentary that examines *Le Morte d'Arthur* from a number of perspectives. This
scholarly work contains much useful information.

Charles Robert Maturin

Born: Dublin, Ireland; September 25, 1780
Died: Dublin, Ireland; October 30, 1824

Principal long fiction · *Fatal Revenge: Or, The Family of Montorio*, 1807; *The Wild Irish Boy*, 1808; *The Milesian Chief*, 1812; *Women: Or, Pour et Contre*, 1818; *Melmoth the Wanderer*, 1820; *The Albigenses*, 1824.

Other literary forms · In addition to his novels, Charles Robert Maturin also wrote plays, three of which were performed and published during his lifetime: *Bertram: Or, The Castle of St. Aldobrand, a Tragedy* (1816), *Manuel* (1817), and *Fredolfo* (1819). A fourth, *Osmyn, the Renegade: Or, The Siege of Salerno, a Tragedy*, written sometime between 1817 and 1821, was produced in Dublin in 1830. It was never published in its entirety; excerpts were printed in *The Edinburgh Literary Journal* (April 24, 1830). Of these plays, only *Bertram* was financially successful. When it first appeared, it was one of the most talked about plays of the season, and today it is noted for being one of the first dramatic portrayals of the brooding, sinned against, and sinning figure who has come to be called the Byronic hero.

Two short fictional pieces were published posthumously: "Leixlip Castle: An Irish Family Legend" appeared in *The Literary Souvenir: Or, Cabinet of Poetry and Romance* of 1825, and "The Sybil's Prophecy: A Dramatic Fragment" was printed in the 1826 edition of the same publication. Both these pieces are in the gothic style.

Achievements · Maturin is best known for the fifth of his six novels, *Melmoth the Wanderer*. Although, when it first appeared, many critics viewed it merely as an unfortunate attempt to revive the gothic novel, a form earlier made popular by such authors as Ann Radcliffe and Matthew Gregory Lewis, scholars now consider *Melmoth the Wanderer* one of the finest examples of its genre. It is judged to be not only a culmination of the gothic novel but also a forerunner of the psychological novels of such writers as Fyodor Dostoevski and Franz Kafka. Although Maturin's handling of narrative structure is often awkward and confusing, and although he borrowed so closely from the works of others that he can be accused of plagiarism, his novels are original in their depiction of extreme states of mind, especially those engendered by fear.

Maturin himself was aware of his major strength. In the prefatory pages of *The Milesian Chief*, he wrote: "If I possess any talent, it is that of darkening the gloomy, and of deepening the sad; of painting life in extremes, and representing those struggles of passion when the soul trembles on the verge of the unlawful and the unhallowed." His settings of mazelike madhouses and dungeons lead the reader into the dark places of the human soul. This particular aspect of his novels fascinated and influenced many other authors. Edgar Allan Poe, Robert Louis Stevenson, Oscar Wilde, Christina and Dante Gabriel Rossetti, Honoré de Balzac, and Charles Baudelaire were all impressed by Maturin's attempt to penetrate the mystery of evil. Critical attention has been given to Maturin's role in Irish literary history. In such novels as *The Milesian Chief* and *The Wild Irish Boy*, descriptions of Irish settings and character

Library of Congress

play an important part. More study needs to be done to evaluate fully this contribution to the development of the Irish regional novel; whatever the outcome, Maturin's place among the significant writers of the English gothic novel is assured.

Biography · Charles Robert Maturin was born in 1780, one of several children born to William Maturin and his wife, Fidelia Watson. The Maturin family was of French descent. One of their ancestors was a Huguenot priest who was forced to leave France because of religious persecution during the reign of Louis XIV. This aspect of his family history strongly impressed the young Maturin, and throughout his life he was fond of relating how his ancestors had suffered for their faith. He himself was strongly anti-Catholic and especially opposed to the rule of monastic life, which he considered dangerously repressive. His novels contain many scenes and descriptions of monasteries as sadistic places where virtue turns to vice.

When in Ireland, Maturin's family became closely connected with the Anglican Church. Maturin's great-grandfather, Peter Maturin, was Dean of Killala from 1724 to 1741, and his grandfather, Gabriel James Maturin, succeeded Jonathan Swift as Dean of St. Patrick's in Dublin in 1745. Following this tradition, Maturin entered Trinity College in 1795 to study theology, and in 1803 he took holy orders. In the same year, he married Henrietta Kingsbury, a daughter of the Archdeacon of Killala. From all reports, the couple were well suited and happily married. After ordination, Maturin served as curate in Loughrea, Galway, for two years. He then returned to Dublin to become curate of St. Peter's, a position he held for the rest of his life. Unfortunately, his small income from this curacy was insufficient to support his family, especially after his father was accused of fraud and dismissed from his position with the Irish post office in 1809. Later, he was cleared and given another position, but for a time the family struggled in severe poverty. In fact, Maturin was continually troubled by financial difficulties. To supplement his income, he ran a school to prepare boys for college, and later he turned to novel writing.

The prefaces of his novels and the styles of romance he chose to employ indicate that he wanted very much to become a popular writer. Because he realized that many of his parishioners and superiors might not approve of a minister writing novels, he used the pseudonym of Dennis Jasper Murphy, publishing three novels under that name. When it was discovered that he was the author of the play *Bertram*, a play involving adultery and an amoral hero, he was for a time in danger of losing his curacy. Apparently, friends intervened to soothe the necessary bishops. After this incident, since his identity was known, he published his next novels and plays under his own name. It is quite possible that his literary activities did prevent his advancement in the clerical profession. There were those who interpreted the beliefs of his characters, some of which were atheistic and heretical, as Maturin's own.

His novels did gain him one very influential friend, Sir Walter Scott. In 1810, Scott wrote a generally favorable review of *Fatal Revenge* for *The Quarterly Review*. Encouraged, Maturin wrote to him, and a correspondence was begun which lasted until Maturin's death. Although the two men never actually met, Scott did assist Maturin with encouragement and advice, and he was instrumental in Maturin's one financial success; he recommended *Bertram* to George Gordon, Lord Byron, who was then responsible for play selection at Drury Lane Theatre. Byron was favorably impressed, and the famous actor Edmund Kean agreed to play the lead. The play's success earned Maturin one thousand pounds, most of which paid a relative's debt. Earlier, Maturin had been able to sell the copyright of his third novel, *The Milesian Chief,* for eighty pounds (the first two novels he had printed at his own expense), and later he was advanced five hundred pounds for *Melmoth the Wanderer,* but his literary efforts never brought the long-sought and often desperately needed financial stability. Up until his death, he continually tried to write in a style that would sell. *The Albigenses* is a historical romance, a type Scott had established and made quite popular. This novel was the first in what was to be a trilogy depicting European manners in ancient, medieval, and modern times. Soon after *The Albigenses* was completed, Maturin died in his home on October 30, 1824, apparently after a long period of ill health. The exact cause of his death is not known. He left a wife and four children who were still in desperate need of financial assistance.

Analysis · In his preface to *Fatal Revenge,* Charles Robert Maturin stresses the fear of the unknown as essential in man's emotional and spiritual life: "It is *not* the weak and trivial impulse of the nursery, to be forgotten and scorned by manhood. It is the aspiration of a spirit; 'it is the passion of immortals,' that dread and desire of their final habitation." In one of his sermons, he focuses on the same theme:

> The very first sounds of childhood are tales of another life—foolishly are they called tales of superstition; for, however disguised by the vulgarity of narration, and the distortion of fiction, they tell him of those whom he is hastening from the threshold of life to join, the inhabitants of the invisible world, with whom he must soon be, and be for ever.

These quotations indicate a major aspect of Maturin's perception of human existence; the haunted and the sacred are interwoven and share a common ground. Human fascination with the supernatural, the world of demons and ghosts, springs from the same source as the desire to believe in salvation and a return to paradise. In fact, the road to salvation leads through the dark places of the soul where individuals must admit their fallen state, their own guilt. The theme of guilt is common in all of Maturin's novels. His major characters must struggle with the serpents in their own hearts, their own original sin. In keeping with this theme, the settings of his novels are generally those of a fallen world; dungeons and underground passages are common backgrounds for the action. Even in those novels that contain descriptions of more natural surroundings, storms and earthquakes are common occurrences, always reminding people that they have been exiled from paradise. Harmony with nature, with humanity, and with God has been lost.

Maturin develops this theme of guilt, which brings exile and separation, through his handling of character. The divided nature of humanity is represented by the pairing of characters, especially brothers: Ippolito and Annibal in *Fatal Revenge*, Connal and Desmond in *The Milesian Chief*, Paladour and Amirald in *The Albigenses*. These brothers are described in such a way as to suggest one identity fragmented into two opposing selves. Ippolito is passionate, Annibal rational; Desmond is the soft flower, Connal the proud oak. Often a character is torn in two opposing directions and does not know how to reconcile them: Connal between his Irish pride and his realization that the Irish peasants are not yet ready to govern themselves; Charles in *Women* between his love for Eva, a shy quiet girl, and Zaira, a worldly and more accomplished woman. At times, a character seems pursued by a dark, sinister double: Montorio by Schemoli in *Fatal Revenge*; Alonzo by the parricide in *Melmoth the Wanderer*. By far the most striking and powerful example of this is the character of the wanderer himself. Melmoth represents the potential for evil which can be found in all humans. In developing Melmoth's character, Maturin echoes the warning in Genesis against too much curiosity about the tree of knowledge of good and evil. Melmoth has sold his soul for increased knowledge; his sin is one of "pride and intellectual glorying," the sin of Lucifer and of the first mortals.

As Maturin's characters wander in a fallen world, little guidance is provided. Especially weak and ineffective are the parental figures. In fact, a distinguishing trait of this fallen world is the disintegration of the family. In all of Maturin's six novels, there are parents who are woefully irresponsible. They are often self-centered, putting their own greedy desires before their children's welfare, or they seek to expiate their own guilt by placing the burden of their sin upon their children. This selfish turning inward and transference of guilt to another is also found in Maturin's representations of larger structures of authority, especially the Catholic Church. As the divided soul wanders in a fallen world, parent and church offer little hope.

Maturin reserves the role of spiritual guide for the female characters who either love or are loved by the hero (such love is not always fulfilled or requited). Often his women are idealized creatures who can reconcile within themselves all conflicting opposites: in *Melmoth the Wanderer*, Immalee embodies passion and purity; in *The Albigenses*, Genevieve is a "mixture of strengh and purity that is never to be found but in woman." Even if a woman finds herself hurled into a world of experience and corruption, as Zaira is in *Women*, her heart remains pure. At times, Maturin uses his female characters to symbolize self-sacrificing love that, although never placing the beloved before God, does place the beloved before the self. Despite Maturin's emphasis on such redeeming love, however, when domestic happiness is found by his characters it seems contrived and imposed upon them by others. Maturin is undoubtedly at his best when depicting people lost and searching for wholeness, not in actually finding it.

Fatal Revenge · Maturin titled his first novel *The Family of Montorio*, but the publisher changed the title to *Fatal Revenge*, hoping to attract readers who would be interested in a gothic tale. The novel is definitely written in the style of Ann Radcliffe—one of its central figures, a ghostlike monk who calls himself Schemoli, is clearly patterned after Radcliffe's Schoedoni in 1797's *The Italian*—but Maturin uses what he borrows to develop his own characteristic theme with originality. Although he follows Radcliffe's technique of revealing the supernatural events as merely the result of disguise and charade, his descriptions of aberrant states of mind, to which all are subject, go beyond her handling of evil, and beyond the mere cataloging of grotesque horrors used by those writers who chose to imitate the more sensational style of Matthew Gregory Lewis. Annibal concludes after a brief period of solitary confinement that an "inward acquaintance" delights one not with tranquillity but, on the contrary, with "the grave of the mind." In describing the anguish of his guilt, Montorio cries, "the worm within me never dieth; and every thought and object it converts into its own morbid food." In Maturin, the evil within is quite real.

The plot of this novel is complicated, and Maturin's narrative is at times twisted and confusing. The tale relates the vengeful machinations of Schemoli, the once noble Count Montorio. He is seeking revenge for the wrongs his younger brother committed against him by manipulating Ippolito and Annibal, two young men he believes are his brother's sons, into believing that they are fated to murder their father. In part, the novel's convoluted structure works to Maturin's advantage, for it helps create a nightmare quality that suits this theme of revenge and guilt. By the end of the novel, after several brutal crimes, it is clear that the words of Ippolito to the Inquisition accurately represent human nature as portrayed in the novel: "There is no human being fully known to another . . . [t]o his own consciousness and recollection, a man will not dare to reveal every thought that visits his mind; there are some which he almost hopes are concealed from the Deity."

The Wild Irish Boy · Maturin's second novel, *The Wild Irish Boy*, although often following the style of the sentimental, regional novel, still has some of the same motifs and themes as those of the gothic *Fatal Revenge*. The novel does have many flaws and is probably Maturin's poorest work: There are long pointless digressions, a decidedly awkward handling of point of view, and an ineffective mixture of literary techniques. Nevertheless, when Maturin touches upon those subjects that most fascinated him, he does so with some success. The novel's most interesting character is Lady Montrevor, a strong, compelling woman who through her own foolish vanity allows herself to be trapped into a loveless marriage, thus sacrificing the sincere love of a good man. She must bear the anguish of her loss and the knowledge of her guilt. She does so grandly, wanting no man's pity. Maturin often alludes to John Milton's fallen angel when describing her: She is "no less than archangel ruined." In many ways, she is a female Byronic hero who knows that evil is more than appearance. This type of female character clearly interested Maturin. Zaira in *Women* and Armida in *The Milesian Chief* are similarly delineated, and all three are quite unlike the sentimental heroines so typical of the other novelists of the day.

The Milesian Chief · In Maturin's third novel, *The Milesian Chief,* his interest in the anguish of the proud heart reveals itself in his portrayal of the hero as well as of the heroine. Connal, the Irish rebel, is the once-great angelic chief fallen among lesser spirits, an appropriate male partner for the melancholy Armida, who is shaded by a "proud dejection, like that of an abdicated monarch." The novel is set in Ireland during an uprising against the British in 1798. As the plot unfolds, it becomes clear that Maturin is more successful in handling narrative structure and point of view than in his previous works, and although the final scene, in which the four major characters (Connal, Armida, Desmond, and Ines) all die more or less at the same time in the same place, seems contrived, it is psychologically appropriate. Throughout the novel, these four personalities have been interwoven. Connal and Desmond function as opposites linked in one identity, and each female character both mirrors and complements her male counterpart. Again, even when trying to write a regional novel, Maturin shows that his main interest lies in depicting the individual lost and searching for a way back to some longed-for paradise.

Women: Or, Pour et Contre · In his preface to *Women: Or, Pour et Contre*, Maturin writes that he believes his previous novels failed to win popular approval because they lacked reality. He indicates that in this novel he has fashioned his characters to resemble those of "common life." This intention does not, however, cause any significant change in his major theme. Again, through his three central characters, Maturin depicts human nature as torn and guilt ridden. Charles vacillates between his love for Eva, a shy innocent girl, and Zaira, the older, more accomplished woman. He is never able to commit himself fully to loving one or the other until it is too late. Only when Eva is dying of consumption brought on by Charles's abandoning her for Zaira does he desert Zaira to return to Eva. Throughout the novel, Eva has struggled with her love for Charles, for in her heart it conflicts with her love for God. On her deathbed, she rejects Charles completely, refusing even to see him, and she dies at peace with God. Zaira undergoes a similar ordeal after Charles abandons her. She turns to God, hoping for consolation, yet she continues to see Charles's image before her eyes. After Eva's death, Charles dies from fever and madness. As the novel closes, Zaira becomes the primary figure of guilt. She lives on, always holding her hand to her heart, accusing herself of having murdered her daughter. She has discovered that Eva was the child taken from her at birth, the child she has been trying to find. This discovery is not made until it is too late to remedy the painful consequences of the mother and daughter loving the same man. Maturin concludes the novel with an image typical of his style: "The serpents that devour us, are generated out of our own vitals."

Melmoth the Wanderer · Although Maturin's preface to *Melmoth the Wanderer* suggests that what follows will show the reader the enemy of humankind in the form of Satan, the tales within tales that constitute the novel show instead that this enemy lies within each individual. By combining the qualities of Faust, Mephistopheles, and the Wandering Jew, Maturin fashioned a hero-villain suitable for leading the reader through the maze of tales that takes him into the obscure recesses of the human soul. Melmoth is Maturin's most compelling and powerful character; he is an embodiment of the dark side of each human being, the shadow that each person casts. Thus, it is particularly appropriate that in the narrative frame of these tales of human malignity, John Melmoth, who bears the same name as the mysterious wanderer, inherits the task of dealing with the molding manuscript that will set him on his own journey into the mystery of evil. His withdrawal at midnight into a closed room, sealed off from society, to read the manuscript, disregarding his uncle's warning that perhaps he should destroy it unread, suggests a type of original sin. Indeed, as he pursues knowledge of the wanderer's life, he learns that all people are potential agents of Satan. After all, Melmoth the Wanderer did not spring from the fires of hell, but from his own family.

The hope that Maturin offers in his guilty state is to be found in self-sacrificing love; yet to love in this manner one must believe in the potential for goodness in humankind, the possibility of redemption. Melmoth is finally damned not because of his original bargain to sell his soul but because of his own misanthropy. He believes in nothing but the hostility and evil of human nature. Immalee, the island maiden who learns of suffering by loving him, was his hope. If he had chosen to trust in her love, seeing in it the essence of the greater self-sacrificing love of Christ, he might have been saved.

The Albigenses · Maturin's last work, *The Albigenses,* is a historical novel that focuses on the crusade in 1208 against the Albigenses, a Manichaean sect declared heretical by the Catholic Church. Maturin, however, follows the historical facts only roughly, altering events and chronology to suit plot and character. Again, he portrays two brothers, Paladour and Amirald, and their two loves, Isebelle and Genevieve. Although the theme of the fragmented self is not as predominant as in his previous novels, it is present. Paladour and Amirald were separated at birth, and for most of the novel neither knows the other is his brother; they are characterized in such a way as to suggest differing aspects of one personality. Paladour is associated with iron and Amirald with flowers, yet they are bound together through suffering. In choosing their brides, they also reveal complementary personality traits: Paladour marries the noble Lady Isebelle, and Amirald chooses the simple peasant girl Genevieve. When the novel ends, the reader is left with the impression that all four live together in absolute harmony.

Such an easy resolution does seemed contrived, for *The Albigenses* begins with Paladour's sinister encounter with a seemingly demonic lady of the lake. He believes there is a curse upon him and that he is fated to murder his bride on their wedding night. When the effects of these dark tones are no longer wanted, Maturin quickly resolves all with rational explanations. Paladour is then free to live as a very natural husband. Part of the dissatisfaction the reader feels with this happy ending may be accounted for by the fact that the novel bristles with gothic motifs that are not smoothly integrated into the historical aspects of the novel.

Despite Maturin's own belief that the day of the gothic novel had already passed when he began writing, and his repeated attempts to use whatever narrative form might suit the reading public, he was continually drawn to the techniques of the gothic tale. Whether it be a mysterious monk haunting underground passages or a madwoman raving prophetic truths, all his novels have gothic elements. The gothic novel provided him with a literary world suitable for the images of evil and suffering that populated his own mind, a mind repeatedly drawn to the problems of human guilt and the divided soul. The body of Maturin's work, although uneven, offers ample proof of his ability to shape these dark themes with power and originality.

Diane D'Amico

Other major works

PLAYS: *Bertram: Or, The Castle of St. Aldobrand,* pr., pb. 1816; *Manuel,* pb. 1817; *Fredolfo,* pb. 1819.

Bibliography

Bayer-Berenbaum, Linda. *The Gothic Imagination: Expansion in Gothic Literature and Art.* Rutherford, N.J.: Fairleigh Dickinson University Press, 1982. A sympathetic study of gothicism, the essence of which is its confrontation with evil and feelings of doom. Contains chapters on literary gothicism and Gothic art and its relationship to literature, as well as focused analyses of particular works of literature. As one of the central writers of gothicism, Maturin is given considerable attention, including an extensive analysis of *Melmoth the Wanderer* that examines the novel as a pattern of expulsions and expansions. The conclusion sees a correlation between the gothic urge for expansion and its style of intensification. Includes a bibliography and index.

Kiely, Robert. *The Romantic Novel in England.* Cambridge, Mass.: Harvard University Press, 1972. An important book on Romantic prose fiction, including Maturin's gothic romances, which analyzes in depth twelve Romantic novels to define the intellectual context of the era. Notes that concepts of reality were tested and changed by Romantic novels and Edmund Burke's ideas of the sublime modified aesthetic forms. Maturin has an important place in this general thesis, and *Melmoth the Wanderer* is analyzed in detail as the focus of his chapter. Finds this novel more emotionally involved with Roman Catholicism and rebellious against authoritarian political systems than other gothic fiction, believing it to be a journey into the darkness of the mind. Finds a common drift toward death in most novels of this genre. Includes a set of notes and an index.

Kramer, Dale. *Charles Robert Maturin.* New York: Twayne, 1973. Analyzes Maturin's personality, describes the conditions of his life, and indicates his innovations in the gothic tradition. Examines his early novels from *Fatal Revenge* to *The Wild Irish Boy*, then looks at Maturin's experiments on the stage, where he achieved popular success with *Bertram* but hardly any with *Manuel* and *Fredolfo*. Analyzes *Women*, Maturin's novel of "real life," and devotes a chapter to *Melmoth the Wanderer* as his most successful writing, favorably comparing it to Mary Shelley's *Frankenstein* and William Godwin's *Adventures of Caleb Williams*. Also examines *The Albigenses* as a descendant of Sir Walter Scott's historical romances and sketches Maturin's place in the history of literature. A chronology, notes and references, a selected annotated bibliography, and an index are included.

Lougy, Robert E. *Charles Robert Maturin.* Lewisburg, Pa.: Bucknell University Press, 1975. An insightful review of Maturin's life and writings, dividing his career into early, middle, and later years. *Fatal Revenge* is analyzed for his characteristic themes: fear and guilt. His other writings are placed in the context of his biography but also receive critical attention in comparison with one another, as well as with other works in the gothic and Irish traditions. Focuses on *Bertram*, which benefited from the popularity of Lord Byron's *Childe Harold's Pilgrimage*, and concentrates on *Melmoth the Wanderer* as a unique adaptation of the legends of the Wandering Jew and Faust. Although *The Milesian Chief* and *Women* deserve credit and Maturin's other writings are given some attention, his reputation rests on *Melmoth*. Includes a chronology and a selected bibliography of primary and secondary works.

Tinkler-Villani, Valeria, Peter Davidson, and Jane Stevenson, eds. *Edited by Candlelight: Sources and Developments in the Gothic Tradition.* Amsterdam: Editions Rodopi, 1995. See Anthony Johnson's essay, "Gaps and Gothic Sensibility: Walpole, Lewis, Mary Shelley, and Maturin," for a learned and clear discussion of how Maturin handles the gaps in reality that gothic fiction exploits.

W. Somerset Maugham

Born: Paris, France; January 25, 1874
Died: Saint-Jean-Cap-Ferrat, France; December 16, 1965

Principal long fiction · *Liza of Lambeth,* 1897; *The Making of a Saint,* 1898; *The Hero,* 1901; *Mrs. Craddock,* 1902; *The Merry-Go-Round,* 1904; *The Bishop's Apron,* 1906; *The Explorer,* 1907; *The Magician,* 1908; *Of Human Bondage,* 1915; *The Moon and Sixpence,* 1919; *The Painted Veil,* 1925; *Cakes and Ale,* 1930; *The Narrow Corner,* 1932; *Theatre,* 1937; *Christmas Holiday,* 1939; *Up at the Villa,* 1941; *The Hour Before Dawn,* 1942; *The Razor's Edge,* 1944; *Then and Now,* 1946; *Catalina,* 1948; *Selected Novels,* 1953.

Other literary forms · A professional man of letters whose work spanned more than six decades, W. Somerset Maugham published in a wide range of literary forms, the significant exception being poetry. He first won success, fame, and wealth in the theater; his most acclaimed dramas were performed on the London stage during the first three decades of the twentieth century. He produced more than a hundred short stories, largely written during the period from 1921 to 1950; his collected short stories include four of the best-known stories of the twentieth century: "Rain," "The Outstation," "The Letter," and "The Colonel's Lady." Fifteen or more additional volumes are devoted to autobiography, literary and aesthetic criticism, and travel. Among these, the most useful for students are *The Summing Up* (1938), *Great Novelists and Their Novels* (1948), and *A Writer's Notebook* (1949).

Achievements · Maugham's twenty novels are exceptionally uneven; the first eight, though interesting, suggest the efforts of a young novelist to discover where his talent lies. From the publication of *Of Human Bondage* (1915) through *The Razor's Edge* (1944), he produced his most significant prose works. During this period, he was a world-famous man of letters with a following of many thousands who would buy and read anything he wrote; however, a few novels that he produced, such as *Then and Now* and *Up at the Villa,* were not in his best vein.

The novels brought Maugham acclaim and recognition both from a general audience and from the intelligentsia. Among common readers, he was perhaps the most successful English novelist of the twentieth century, and, as Samuel Johnson pointed out, the common reader is not often wrong. Yet, it must be admitted that Maugham's detractors, such as Edmund Wilson, present valid criticism: One expects a serious artist to exert an important influence, either thematic or formal, upon his medium. The symphony was forever altered by Ludwig van Beethoven; no similar statement can be made about Maugham and the novel. He sought to tell a story with clarity and grace, to embody a set of attitudes and values, and to entertain his readers with insights into character and life.

Biography · William Somerset Maugham, son of an English solicitor, was born in the British Embassy in Paris and spent his early childhood in France, learning French as his first language. Following the early death of both parents, Maugham went at age ten to England to live with his uncle, the Reverend Henry Maugham, Vicar of

Library of Congress

Whitstable, and his German-born wife. The rigid routine and disciplined family life of the Whitstable rectory contrasted with the casual, carefree existence and close warmth that Maugham had known in France. He was enrolled in the King's School, Canterbury, where he spent several unhappy years. A permanent stammer that developed during this period of his life destroyed any possibility of following the profession of his father and two of his brothers. Instead of enrolling in a university, Maugham chose to travel abroad to Germany, where at Heidelberg he saw Henrik Ibsen's dramas and attended lectures by Kuno Fischer on the philosophy of Arthur Schopenhauer. Returning to London, he enrolled in the medical school at St. Thomas's Hospital, where he received his M.D. in 1897.

Maugham's stronger interests, however, were literary and aesthetic, and when his first novel, *Liza of Lambeth*, achieved a modest success, he resolved to enter upon a career as a writer. None of the novels that Maugham wrote during the following decade repeated the success of *Liza of Lambeth*, yet he achieved sudden and unexpected acclaim through a series of plays, modern comedies of manners, beginning with *Lady Frederick* (1907). In 1908, four of his plays were running in London simultaneously. During World War I, Maugham served with British Intelligence in Switzerland and Russia. In 1915, he married Syrie Bernardo Wellcome, a marriage that ended in divorce in 1927. Following World War I, Maugham traveled to more remote areas of the world: the South Seas, Southeast Asia, and America, accompanied by his secretary, a gregarious American named Gerald Haxton, who aided the author in finding material for his fiction. Maugham acquired the Villa Mauresque on the French Riviera in 1928, an estate that became his home for the remainder of his life, though he continued his frequent travels and spent several years during World War II living in the United States. Creative work during his later years centered principally upon short stories, novels, and autobiography.

Analysis · W. Somerset Maugham's novels are written in a style highly idiomatic and fluent, revealing the qualities of simplicity, lucidity, and euphony which the author sought to attain. Content to narrate an interesting story from his own unique angle of vision, he brought to the genre a gift for creating interesting characters who reflect life's ironies. In his later works, Maugham's narrative persona is a character interested in people, yet detached and somewhat clinical in his analysis of their actions and motives. The narrator demonstrates an unusual degree of tolerance for human peccadillos and incongruities and is reluctant to judge the actions of human beings. He writes primarily of adults in conflict with one another and with social mores. Frequently, his characters grow in tolerance and acceptance of human life, which is portrayed somewhat pessimistically. Maugham based his characters upon people whom he had known or whose lives he had somehow come to know; their actions are presented with consummate realism. They are motivated by their passions or emotions and by their attempts to control their destinies, not by an ideology or set of ideals. Though they may experience inner turmoil and conflict, they are seldom tormented by such emotions. Like their creator-narrator, the characters often have the ability to view themselves with clinical detachment and objectivity, to cast a cold eye on life.

Liza of Lambeth · Among the early novels of Maugham, *Liza of Lambeth*, published when the author was only twenty-three, is probably the best known. Set in the Lambeth slum along Vere Street, London, it depicts naturalistically the lives of people in a state of poverty, characters such as those whom the author had come to know at first hand as an obstetric clerk at St. Thomas's Hospital. In its depiction of character, *Liza of Lambeth* fits the tradition of the naturalistic novel, somewhat in the manner of George Gissing, whose work Maugham knew well. The Cockney dialogue that pervades the novel is accurately represented, both in its pronunciation and in its slang or colloquial expressions. As is typical of naturalistic fiction, the characters are generally without hope, yet even in a naturalistic tradition Maugham reveals an original perspective. Unlike much naturalism, *Liza of Lambeth* does not urge social reform; the characters exhibit more hostility toward one another than toward any system. They generally accept their lot, which would be bearable but for their own mistakes. Liza Kemp's friend Sally enters marriage with hope, only to find her chances for happiness shattered owing to her husband's bad temper following drinking bouts, a weakness he had previously concealed. Liza, brimming with life and energy, spurns the devotion of a staid suitor, Tom, and finds excitement in an affair with an older, married neighbor, Jim Blakeston. By allowing passion to dominate their lives, the characters create undue hardships for themselves. This theme is commonly found in Maugham's work.

Just as *Liza of Lambeth* represented an effort at producing a naturalistic novel, Maugham's other early novels give the impression of deliberate attempts at imitating well-established forms. In *The Making of a Saint*, he wrote a brief historical novel with a late fifteenth century Florentine setting. A story of intrigue, assassination, and revenge, it is derived from a brief passage in a work by Niccolò Machiavelli. *Mrs. Craddock* is set in rural England of the late nineteenth century, a novel of manners depicting provincial life, much in the manner of Arnold Bennett; *The Merry-Go-Round* belongs to a similar tradition. In *The Magician*, Maugham incorporates the conventions of the gothic genre, though there is perhaps too much realism for this work to be designated a true gothic novel.

Of Human Bondage · In *Of Human Bondage*, Maugham's longest novel and his masterpiece, he turned to the well-known form of the *Bildungsroman*, the novel of a young person growing to maturity. *Of Human Bondage* is highly autobiographical, although it departs significantly from autobiographical accuracy in places. With the aid of an omniscient narrator, the reader follows the life of Philip Carey from his mother's death when he was only nine until he becomes a doctor and resolves to marry. Numerous characters in the novel are based upon people the author knew. The Reverend William Carey and his wife Louisa are based upon Maugham's uncle and aunt with whom he lived; Lawson is his friend Sir Gerald Kelly; Cronshaw derives from the eccentric poet Aleister Crowley, who had also been the model for Oliver Haddo in *The Magician*; and Hayward is based upon Maugham's friend Ellington Brooks. In a similar manner, Maugham incorporates descriptions of places that he knew well, with names only slightly altered (Whitstable to Blackstable, Canterbury to Tercanbury) or not altered at all, as the countryside of Kent or the cities of London and Paris.

In *Of Human Bondage*, Maugham sees three forces impinging upon Philip, shaping and influencing his life, forces that the novel emphasizes strongly: passion, disillusionment, and the quest for purpose in life. Philip is ill-equipped to cope with passion. Having been born with a clubfoot, which becomes a source of ridicule among school boys, and having lost both parents in childhood, he becomes overly sensitive. He takes pleasure in the solitary pursuit of reading and is less in the company of others than most boys; as a result, he has little understanding of the world at large. He finds that women who adore him arouse in him no passion in return, whereas he falls irrationally and inexplicably in love with the common and venal Mildred Rogers. Only after a long period of bondage, humiliation, and pain can he free himself from this attachment, which he comes to regard as degrading. At the end of the novel, he proposes marriage to Sally Athelney, not because he feels passion for her but because he believes she will be a good wife. Maugham's view of romance in this work is consistent with the view presented in his other works and with Arthur Schopenhauer's pessimistic outlook—that romantic passion is a kind of trick played upon people by nature to foster procreation, that it does not last, that it is irrational, and that it represents a poor basis for marriage.

To express the necessity for disillusionment, Maugham depicts Philip as growing up in an atmosphere of illusion involving religious beliefs and assumptions about the code of an English gentleman. When Philip arrives in Germany, it becomes awkward to continue to maintain that a gentleman necessarily belongs to the Church of England. He encounters a diversity of religious beliefs, all sincerely held and advocated through conflicting arguments. The result is that he loses his religious faith, though he assumes that the actual cause of the loss is that he lacks the religious temperament. Losing a framework so basic, he experiences a sense of liberation, yet he finds his new freedom uncomfortable as well, lacking in certainties.

Philip clings to one certainty: He assumes without question that he must earn his living through some profession, and he begins to explore various unsuitable paths. He rejects the idea of becoming a clergyman, quits a career in accounting, abandons the struggle to become an artist after studying in Paris, and finally decides to pursue medicine. He does not escape hardship, for at one point he loses the money provided for his education and must work at a department store until his uncle's death brings a small inheritance.

Reflecting upon happiness, Philip is puzzled as to how this quality fits as a purpose in life, since his own is unhappy. He observes that happiness eludes people such as the dancers at the Bal Bullier in Paris who pursue it frenetically. Those who seek happiness through the enjoyment of art waste their lives, and those who struggle to create art seldom find happiness, even when they succeed. Yet, the paintings of El Greco suggest to Philip that the will of humankind is powerful, that life can be made meaningful through struggle. After this realization, Philip comes to understand the secret of a piece of Persian rug given him by an eccentric poet. The poet told him that the rug held the key to the meaning of life, but he refused to explain the puzzle to

Philip. The solution becomes apparent to Philip years later, after much searching for it: Life has no meaning. There is no set of obligations by which a person must live, no certain path to follow. With this bleak conclusion, Philip comes to another realization: Like the weaver of the carpet, a person may choose the strands that please his aesthetic sense and make a pattern of his life satisfying to his own taste. Happiness and pain are important only as strands in the design. Though people are under no obligation to create a design, they are free to do so if they choose; or, if they reject freedom of the will, it may seem that they are free. Life for Philip, then, has purpose because he wills to endow it with purpose—a conclusion primarily existential but also in accord with Schopenhauer's view of people's will.

The Moon and Sixpence · In *The Moon and Sixpence*, a novel that relies somewhat upon autobiographical materials used in *Of Human Bondage,* Maugham narrates a portion of the life of his hero Charles Strickland, a stockbroker turned artist whose character is based upon that of the artist Paul Gauguin. The narrator, or the Maugham persona, is a successful author who enjoys access to high society and, like Maugham, travels extensively around the world. He is detached and analytical in his attitudes, revealing a fondness for the maxims of Blaise Pascal and La Rochefoucauld. He prefers to permit the story to unfold in an episodic way by letting others whom he meets tell him what they know or think about Strickland. Maugham sees in Strickland the frustrated genius, a moderately successful businessman who, at age forty, decides to become an artist, ruthlessly throwing over everything to pursue his ambition, and succeeding.

The action occurs over a period of more than twenty years, with the setting shifting from London to Paris to Tahiti and back to London. As in the earlier *Of Human Bondage* and later in *Christmas Holiday,* art is an important theme, and allusions to paintings and painters are numerous. At the beginning of the novel, Maugham invents a "scholarly" tradition on Strickland, complete with footnotes, to enhance the realism. In the concluding segment set in Tahiti, he introduces characters who had known Strickland during his final years and who report on his decline and death. They are modeled after characters whom Maugham met in Tahiti and who told him about Gauguin. With references to actual people whose identities the author does not very much bother to conceal, *The Moon and Sixpence,* then, is a *roman à clef,* as are its two most important successors, *Cakes and Ale* and *The Razor's Edge.*

Cakes and Ale · In *Cakes and Ale,* the most "literary" of Maugham's novels, the narrator assumes the name Willie Ashenden, one that Maugham had used in his collection of short stories based upon his work as an intelligence agent (*Ashenden,* 1928). Ashenden is a novelist in his fifties who during the course of the narrative has several meetings with another novelist and critic, Alroy Kear. Kear, about the same age as Willie Ashenden, represents the Edwardian novelist Hugh Walpole. The unflattering portrait of Walpole, recognizable to many contemporaries and to Walpole himself, contributed to an attack on Maugham by Evelyn Wiehe in *Gin and Bitters* (1931), where he is given the name Leverson Hurle. Besides the narrator and Kear, another author plays a major role in the novel. Edward Driffield, the grand old man of Victorian literature, is based upon the character of Thomas Hardy. Rosie Gann, Driffield's first wife, is modeled after the actress Ethelwyn Sylvia Jones, to whom Maugham once proposed.

Alroy Kear, who is writing a biography of Driffield, discovers that Ashenden has been a longtime acquaintance of the Driffields. The Driffields once lived in Ashenden's village of Blackstable, where they were regarded with suspicion by the villagers, especially by Ashenden's uncle, the vicar, who represents the epitome of Victorian propriety and prudery. The villagers' suspicions are confirmed when the Driffields move to London, leaving behind debts to most of the merchants.

Later, Ashenden renews his acquaintance with the Driffields in London, gradually losing touch with them after Rosie leaves Driffield for a Blackstable coal merchant, Lord George Kemp. Ashenden's knowledge of all these details merges in flashbacks that go back as far as his childhood. Ashenden knows that a tactful biographer such as Kear, who has secured the approval of Driffield's second wife, cannot include such revealing recollections, and thus he tells them to the reader. He concludes his narrative with an account of meeting Rosie, then more than seventy years old, in New York. She confesses to Ashenden that she ran off with Lord George because "He was always such a perfect gentleman," a judgment with which every other character in the novel would have disagreed.

Except for one brief episode that occurs in New York, the novel is set either in London or in the nearby villages and countryside. Maugham relies heavily on flashbacks ranging over a period of some forty years; *Cakes and Ale* is a novel cast in the form of reminiscences of a character, which assuredly would conflict with the "official" biography of Driffield as recorded by Alroy Kear. Its appeal lies primarily in its allusions to actual persons, its behind-the-scenes literary gossip, and the creation of Rosie Gann, probably the most appealing of Maugham's female characters—a wholesome, agreeable, and vivacious woman utterly lacking in pretense.

The Razor's Edge · In *The Razor's Edge*, the narrator becomes "Mr. Maugham," a celebrated author and world traveler. With characters such as the urbane and aristocratic art agent, Elliott Templeton, he exchanges views and pleasantries in an attitude of amusement and tolerance. To younger characters such as Sophie Macdonald he offers sage advice. To readers he offers a variety of wry comments on the art and craft of the novel. He speculates as to why people whom he barely knows divulge their life stories so readily to him. He admits the reader behind the scenes of the writer's study with such unguarded comments as the famous opening, "I have never begun a novel with more misgiving," and such wry asides as "I feel it right to warn the reader that he can very well skip this chapter without losing the thread of [the] . . . story. . . . I should add, however, that except for this conversation I should perhaps not have thought it worthwhile to write this book." Usually "Mr. Maugham" limits his involvement to conversation; his own actions, where they are noted (as when he withdraws to write a novel or takes his boat to Toulon), do not advance the plot. Occasionally, he does involve himself in the plot in some minor way. He contrives for the dying Elliott Templeton to receive an invitation to a party given by the Princess Novemali after she had deliberately snubbed Elliott, and he is on hand to identify the body of Sophie Macdonald.

"Mr. Maugham" reports the story as the major characters reveal it in their conversations. Isabel Bradley is in love with Larry Darrel but sensibly marries the successful Gray Maturin, only to find that after Gray loses his assets during the Depression, she and her husband and their two daughters must live on the generosity of her uncle Elliott. Larry, whose main interest in life is the study of philosophy and religion, attempts to marry Sophie Macdonald to save her from a dissolute life, an effort that Isabel shrewdly thwarts. Larry goes to a Benedictine monastery in France, later leaving it to study the Hindu religion in India. Returning from India at the end of the novel, he gives up his independent income and resolves to find work in New York driving a taxi. The Maturins move from Paris to Dallas, where Gray has secured an executive position in an oil company. The plot covers more than a decade, with the settings in France, England, and America. "Mr. Maugham," like the young Philip Carey, seeks a pattern in the lives of those he has met, and he finds that each life in *The Razor's Edge* has been a success. Even Sophie Macdonald, whose trauma caused her to seek death, found what she was seeking.

Maugham's three most significant novels following *Of Human Bondage* explore ideals that he considered in the final chapters of his autobiography, *The Summing Up*–truth, beauty, goodness. In *The Moon and Sixpence*, Charles Strickland represents the true genius whose work survives and speaks to posterity, even though his talent surfaced late in life and he violated accepted standards to advance it. In him, truth is neither obvious nor pleasant, but its existence can be confirmed by those who have felt the power of his work. Even the wife he abandoned displays reproductions of his paintings in her home and takes pride in his attainments. In *Cakes and Ale*, the ideal is beauty, which readers and critics find in the style, characters, and descriptions of Edward Driffield's novels. The narrator Willie Ashenden rejects this aesthetic beauty in favor of a more realistic beauty. He discovers the ideal in the warmth and charm of Rosie Gann, Driffield's first wife, who possessed neither fidelity nor business ethics but whose character brought others a wholesome sense of well-being. In *The Razor's Edge*, Larry Darrel reveals a basic goodness, a difficult quality to depict, partly because it may be attributed to the absence of either appetites or temptations. Though not an ascetic, Larry keeps passion and ambition in check and pursues his own spiritual development. He readily sacrifices himself for others, making a futile effort to save Sophie Macdonald from self-destruction through an offer of marriage, yet his sacrifices do not appear quixotic. A generous amount of modesty enables him to make the best of a life that reveals only goodness as an extraordinary element.

In each character, the ideal is neither obvious nor probable in the conventional sense. Its existence is ironic, and it might be overlooked were not the Maugham persona on hand to define it. Not even the narrator, however, can explain or account for it; the reader savors its presence without fully understanding its origin.

Among the remaining novels of Maugham, one finds works of literary merit and appeal, though they represent lesser achievements. A reader of Maugham would not want to miss novels such as *The Painted Veil* and *The Narrow Corner*, which narrate suspenseful and intense conflicts. Works such as these differ from the better-known novels in several important respects. First, the Maugham persona is either absent or less intrusive. In *The Narrow Corner*, for example, the author's viewpoint is usually expressed through Dr. Saunders, who lives on a Pacific island and has no literary interests or ambitions. Further, the settings are usually foreign or exotic–European or Asian rather than American or English. Instead of spanning decades, the plots narrate events that occur during a few months; novels such as *Up at the Villa*, for example, differ little from some of Maugham's short stories.

Significantly, in Maugham's major novels, the important characters–Philip Carey, Larry Darrel, Rosie Gann, and Charles Strickland–either embody an ideal or achieve some measure of success in pursuit of an ideal, whereas idealism in the minor works is usually crushed and defeated. Fred Blake and Erik Christensen in *The Narrow Corner* find only disappointment, disillusionment, and early death, as does the unfortunate Karl Richter in *Up at the Villa*. Those who survive are worldly-wise and detached characters who can regard life as Maugham's spokesman Dr. Saunders does:

Life is short, nature is hostile, and man is ridiculous but oddly enough most misfortunes have their compensations and with a certain humour and a good deal of horse-sense one can make a fairly good job of what is after all a matter of very small consequence.

The minor works reward the reader with their depiction of the ironies of human life, the eccentricities of human beings, and the unusual settings and universal conflicts, yet, however rewarding, they lack the thematic richness and emotional concentration of Maugham's best novels.

Stanley Archer

Other major works

SHORT FICTION: *Orientations,* 1899; *The Trembling of a Leaf: Little Stories of the South Sea Islands,* 1921; *The Casuarina Tree: Six Stories,* 1926; *Ashenden: Or, The British Agent,* 1928; *Six Stories Written in the First Person Singular,* 1931; *Ah King: Six Stories,* 1933; *East and West: The Collected Short Stories,* 1934; *Cosmopolitans,* 1936; *The Favorite Short Stories of W. Somerset Maugham,* 1937; *The Round Dozen,* 1939; *The Mixture as Before: Short Stories,* 1940; *Creatures of Circumstances: Short Stories,* 1947; *East of Suez: Great Stories of the Tropics,* 1948; *Here and There: Selected Short Stories,* 1948; *The Complete Short Stories,* 1951; *The World Over,* 1952; *Seventeen Lost Stories,* 1969.

PLAYS: *A Man of Honor,* wr. 1898-1899, pr., pb. 1903; *Loaves and Fishes,* wr. 1903, pr. 1911; *Lady Frederick,* pr. 1907; *Jack Straw,* pr. 1908; *Mrs. Dot,* pr. 1908; *The Explorer,* pr. 1908; *The Noble Spaniard,* pr. 1909; *Penelope,* pr. 1909; *Smith,* pr. 1909; *Landed Gentry,* pr. 1910 (as *Grace*); *The Tenth Man,* pr. 1910; *The Land of Promise,* pr. 1913; *Caroline,* pr. 1916, pb. 1923 (as *The Unattainable*); *Our Betters,* pr. 1917; *Caesar's Wife,* pr. 1919; *Home and Beauty,* pr. 1919 (also known as *Too Many Husbands*); *The Unknown,* pr., pb. 1920; *The Circle,* pr., pb. 1921; *East of Suez,* pr., pb. 1922; *The Constant Wife,* pr., pb. 1926; *The Letter,* pr., pb. 1927; *The Sacred Flame,* pr., pb. 1928; *The Breadwinner,* pr., pb. 1930; *The Collected Plays of W. Somerset Maugham,* pb. 1931, 1952 (3 volumes; including 18 plays); *For Services Rendered,* pr., pb. 1932; *Sheppey,* pr., pb. 1933.

SCREENPLAY: *Trio,* 1950 (with R. C. Sherriff and Noel Langley).

NONFICTION: *The Land of the Blessed Virgin: Sketches and Impressions in Andalusia,* 1905 (also known as *Andalusia,* 1920); *On a Chinese Screen,* 1922; *The Gentleman in the Parlour: A Record of a Journey from Rangoon to Haiphong,* 1930; *Don Fernando,* 1935; *The Summing Up,* 1938; *Books and You,* 1940; *France at War,* 1940; *Strictly Personal,* 1941; *Great Novelists and Their Novels,* 1948; *A Writer's Notebook,* 1949; *The Writer's Point of View,* 1951; *The Vagrant Mood: Six Essays,* 1952; *The Partial View,* 1954 (includes *The Summing Up* and *A Writer's Notebook*); *Ten Novels and Their Authors,* 1954 (revision of *Great Novelists and Their Novels*); *The Travel Books,* 1955; *Points of View,* 1958; *Looking Back,* 1962; *Purely for My Pleasure,* 1962; *Selected Prefaces and Introductions,* 1963.

Bibliography

Cordell, Richard A. *Somerset Maugham, a Writer for All Seasons: A Biographical and Critical Study.* 2d ed. Bloomington: Indiana University Press, 1969. A valuable discussion of Maugham's philosophy, which Cordell finds in the "writings of wise men of all ages." Considers both sides, sympathetic and unsympathetic, to Maugham while focusing on his novels, short stories, plays, and nonfiction (briefly). The best of his work is *Of Human Bondage, The Moon and Sixpence,* and *Cakes and Ale.* Indexed.

Holden, Philip. *Orienting Masculinity, Orienting Nation: W. Somerset Maugham's Exotic Fiction.* Westport, Conn.: Greenwood Press, 1996. Examines the themes of homosexuality, gender identity, and race relations in Maugham's works.

Loss, Archie K. *"Of Human Bondage": Coming of Age in the Novel.* Boston: Twayne, 1990. One of Twayne's masterwork studies, this is an excellent analysis.

Maugham, Robin. *Somerset and All the Maughams.* New York: New American Library, 1966. Maugham's complex personality is illuminated in this intriguing study of his ancestors and immediate family members. An index is included.

Morgan, Ted. *Maugham.* New York: Simon & Schuster, 1980. The first full-scale biography of Maugham and therefore an essential text in all studies of the man and his work. Unlike previous biographers, Morgan enjoyed the cooperation of Maugham's literary executor and, therefore, is able to correct many distortions in previous studies. Offers the most comprehensive account yet of the private man, including photographs, a complete primary bibliography, and an index.

Naik, M. K. *William Somerset Maugham.* Norman: University of Oklahoma Press, 1966. Argues that a conflict between "cynicism" and "humanitarianism" kept Maugham from literary success. Only in *Cakes and Ale*, his short stories, and his travel books does he balance the two points of view.

Rogal, Samuel J. *A William Somerset Maugham Encyclopedia.* Westport, Conn.: Greenwood Press, 1997. Contains information on Maugham's life as well as his works. Includes bibliographical references and an index.

George Meredith

Born: Portsmouth, England; February 12, 1828
Died: Box Hill, England; May 18, 1909

Principal long fiction · *The Shaving of Shagpat*, 1855; *Farina*, 1857; *The Ordeal of Richard Feverel*, 1859; *Evan Harrington*, 1861; *Emilia in England*, 1864 (as *Sandra Belloni: Or, Emilia in England*, 1886); *Rhoda Fleming*, 1865; *Vittoria*, 1867; *The Adventures of Harry Richmond*, 1871; *Beauchamp's Career*, 1874-1875 (serial), 1876 (book); *The Egoist*, 1879; *The Tragic Comedians*, 1880; *Diana of the Crossways*, 1885; *One of Our Conquerors*, 1891; *Lord Ormont and His Aminta*, 1894; *The Amazing Marriage*, 1895; *Celt and Saxon*, 1910 (unfinished).

Other literary forms · Ironically, George Meredith, one of nineteenth century England's greatest novelists, actually considered himself a poet. Regrettably, the several volumes of poetry he published during his lifetime went largely unnoticed. Even though Alfred, Lord Tennyson, praised "Love in the Valley," published in his first volume, *Poems* (1851), dedicated to his then father-in-law, Thomas Love Peacock, it was as a novelist that Meredith achieved recognition in his own time. Undaunted, nevertheless, Meredith continued to write poems and, in keeping with his stated vocation and with his aspiration, both his first and his last published books were collections of poems.

Modern Love and Poems of the English Roadside (1862) represents Meredith's lyric and dramatic power at its height, especially in the sequence of fifty sixteen-line lyrics, *Modern Love*. In these poems, Meredith traces the dissolution of a marriage with an unrestrained candor that is more like the attitudes toward marital relationships of the late twentieth century than the straight-faced, closed-lipped Victorian notions. At the lowest point in the sequence, the persona exclaims, "In tragic life, God wot,/ No villain need be! Passions spin the plot;/ We are betrayed by what is false within." Herein Meredith seems to capture with great precision the essence of tragedy. Meredith's poetic vision is not always dark; light imagery, in fact, plays a significant role in his poetry.

The thinking man appears often in Meredith's works, but he is perhaps most prominent in the 1877 essay "The Idea of Comedy and the Uses of the Comic Spirit." This essay is significant enough to be included in many contemporary collections of criticism, especially in those that pertain to drama. Acknowledging that the muse of comedy has never been "one of the most honored of the Muses," Meredith submits that it is the "Comic Spirit" that civilizes man. By means of thoughtful laughter, the Comic Spirit corrects and checks the foibles of all the men who exceed the bounds of temperance and indulge in excessive behavior. Although Meredith opened himself to censure in his own day, his ideas about women and their roles in comedy are particularly interesting to today's reader. Indeed, comedy, "the fountain of common sense," teaches that men and women are social equals and that women are often men's superiors.

Achievements · In the late nineteenth century, Meredith achieved the status of a literary dictator or arbiter of taste. The path toward this recognition was, however, a

long and arduous one. For years, Meredith received little to no recognition, and he had to wait for the publication of *The Ordeal of Richard Feverel* before he enjoyed the limited appreciation of Algernon Charles Swinburne, Dante Gabriel Rossetti, and others among the pre-Raphaelites. Not until the appearance of *The Egoist* in 1879 did Meredith's literary reputation reach its zenith.

During his last years, Meredith received many awards and honors, including the succession of Alfred, Lord Tennyson, as the president of the Society of British Authors and election as one of the original members of the Order of Merit. Within twenty years after Meredith's death in 1909, nevertheless, his literary reputation began to suffer a partial eclipse, from which it began to recover in the 1970's. One explanation for Meredith's decline in reputation is simple: His turgid style and complex plots demand more from the average reader than he or she is often willing to give. C. L. Cline's three-volume edition of *The Letters of George Meredith*, which appeared in 1970, and Phyllis B. Bartlett's two-volume collection of *The Poems of George Meredith* (1978) have done much to reawaken interest in Meredith's work, particularly in his poetry, which seems to appeal to modern readers much more markedly than it had to those of his own time. Even so, the influence of Meredith the novelist on such younger writers as Thomas Hardy was decisive, and Meredith's theory of the Comic Spirit as the civilizing force of all thoughtful men speaks to all cultures of all times.

Biography · Born the son and grandson of tailors, George Meredith appears to have rejected his humble origins. Indeed, he once threatened that he would "most horribly haunt" any who attempted to reconstruct his biography. Despite his modest heritage, legacies from his mother and an aunt permitted him to attend private schools, St. Paul's Church School, Southsea, and the Moravian School of Neuwied, Germany. His objective in formal training was to become a lawyer, and he was apprenticed to a London solicitor in 1845. Young Meredith soon became dissatisfied with the legal profession, however, and began to seek a career as a journalist, a vocation which he pursued throughout most of his life, since he was never quite able to survive financially as an author of novels and poems.

From at least 1845 until his marriage in 1849 to Mary Ellen Nicolls, a widow and the daughter of Thomas Love Peacock, Meredith appears to have read widely and deeply in the literature of Greece, Rome, Germany, France, and England. The first few years of his marriage appear to have been ones of continued intellectual growth. The Merediths lived either with or near the aspiring young author's famous father-in-law. Meredith made good use of Peacock's extensive and often arcane library, whose shelves included volumes on such Near Eastern religions as Zoroastrianism, a faith that was later to have a profound influence on Meredith's novels and poems.

The first few years of apparent bliss were soon terminated, however, when Mary eloped in 1858 with the painter Henry Wallis to the isle of Capri. Meredith was consequently left alone to rear his son Arthur; the author later wrote about these unhappy times both in the novel *The Ordeal of Richard Feverel* and in the lyric sequence *Modern Love*. After Mary's death in 1861, Meredith married, within three years, Marie Vulliamy; this match proved to be both enduring and much happier. After serving as war correspondent, he and his new wife moved to Flint Cottage, Box Hill, Surrey, where he lived the remainder of his life. Box Hill is where admiring and enthusiastic young authors went to seek Meredith's sage counsel.

Analysis · Although George Meredith's works all emphasize the corrective, civilizing influences of the Comic Spirit, his novels, as well as his poems, forcefully work out a sort of theodicy which is consistently informed by the Near Eastern religion Zoroastrianism. This philosophy that treats the being and government of God and the immortality of the soul displays the theme of the struggle between good and evil in the early work *Farina*.

Farina **and** *The Ordeal of Richard Feverel* · In the novel, surrounded by the trappings of medieval Germany, Farina, the hero of the tale, is left to contend with the evil effects of a bout between a monk and Satan. The monk represents the Zoroastrian god of light or good, Ormuzd, and Satan, the god of darkness or evil, Ahriman. In the later, much more successful novel *The Ordeal of Richard Feverel*, this dialectic is seen in the sixth chapter, "The Magian Conflict" (the magi were ancient priests of Zoroaster). In this case, Meredith assigns the roles of the two opposing parties of the struggle to a Tinker and a Yeoman; the witness to this debate is the adolescent Richard Feverel, whose father, Sir Austin, has attempted unsuccessfully to shield him from any introduction to the world's forces of good and evil.

The Tinker, who appears to be a faithful follower of Zoroaster, the ancient prophet of the faith, asserts that the Good Spirit reigns supreme. The Yeoman, whom Meredith playfully calls Speed-the-Plough, protests, because of his recent misfortune of having lost several jobs, that the Evil Spirit dominates. The Yeoman is particularly hostile to Farmer Blaize, with whom Richard and a companion have also had an unpleasant encounter. Farmer Blaize is responsible for the beginning of the Yeoman's misfortunes. Tinker and Yeoman discuss the universal strife between good and evil in Zoroastrian terms, wherein the Good Spirit is supposed to hold dominion for a two-thousand-year period and the Evil Spirit is believed to assume dominion for a like period of two thousand years. Clearly, then, this debate challenges the young Richard to side with Ahriman (darkness) or to join the legions of Ormuzd (light).

Richard later relates the details of this encounter to Adrian Harley, a sort of tutor and confidant of the young Mr. Feverel, who is actually a disciple of the Comic Spirit and whom the narrator addresses as the Wise Youth. Adrian explains to Richard that "I'm perfectly aware that Zoroaster is not dead. You have been listening to a common creed. Drink the Fire-worshippers, if you will." Adrian recognizes the nature of the timeless controversy and applies to it the synecdoche, "Zoroaster," to point out the age of the struggle. Adrian also emphasizes that this struggle is a universal one, the result of a "common creed," regardless of Sir Austin's refusal to acknowledge it.

Adrian's comic toast to the Fire-worshippers is also ironic in that Richard and Tom Bakewell, the ploughman, have plotted to burn Farmer Blaize's hayracks. That night, Richard and his friend Ripton Thompson watch the fiery destruction resulting from the match of Tom Bakewell, whose last name is comically appropriate to his role. This "Bakewell Comedy," however, has serious overtones when seen in the light of the Zoroastrian metaphor. The fire of the boys' vision is not a pure one, for there are "dense masses of smoke" amid the flames which leap into the darkness like "snakes of fire." In Zoroastrianism, Ahriman (Evil) is responsible for this corruption of the pure flame.

The chapter's title, "Arson," which initiates the Bakewell Comedy, effectively points out the boys' error. The boys are, like Tom Bakewell, not good Zoroastrians because the fire they are worshiping reflects the evil nature of their revenge. Adrian sees through their conspiracy; however, he does not expose the boys. Rather, in the true manner of the Zoroastrians, he believes that the most effective punishment would be a spiritual, inner conflict. "The farmer's whip had reduced them to bodily contortions; these were decorous compared with the spiritual writhings they had to perform under Adrian's skillful manipulation." Adrian knows the true value of fire to the Zoroastrians: it is a symbol of the inner light of the soul, which glows brightest when fired by Ormuzd. If the soul is possessed by the evil Ahriman, the spiritual light is contaminated and burns, if at all, with a dim, impure glimmer.

Richard's next crucial encounter intensifies the glow of the purer fire burning within him. He meets Lucy Desborough, destined to be his wife. The imagery used to describe this encounter is filled with references to light. Nature herself has provided "a Temple for the flame" of love. From a boat, Richard first sees Lucy pictured in an idyllic scene of radiant sunshine reflecting from the "green-flashing plunges of a weir." Lucy's face is shaded from the sun's illumination mysteriously but compellingly "by a broad straw hat with a flexible brim that left her lips and chin in the sun, and sometimes nodding, sent forth a light of promising eyes." Her hair was "golden where the ray touched" it. Even her name is derived from the Latin word for light: *lux.* Richard's soul is filled with the light of passionate love, but he has another journey to the vision of the celestial light of the Zoroastrians.

Other references to Zoroastrianism abound in the novel. For example, at a later point, Sir Austin yields to the dark force of Ahriman when he chooses to "do nothing" at a time when his son needs his counsel most. Consequently, he turns his son away from him, perhaps forever, thus proving that a father with a "system" for child rearing cannot meet that system on its own terms.

Viewed within the bounds of the magian conflict, *The Ordeal of Richard Feverel* is seen as a novel about the inevitability of the human strife between good and evil, both of which are inextricably mixed within the soul of every human being. Some measure of hope is given the novel, however, when the reader learns that, finally, Richard does view, if but for a moment, the celestial light of Ormuzd through the aid of a truly devoted wife.

It is this hope that raises *The Ordeal of Richard Feverel* to the level of true tragedy, which must in some measure be positive. Although Sir Austin falls victim to Ahriman, his son, Richard, has seen the vision of Ormuzd. By the use of Zoroastrian imagery, Meredith has greatly intensified his conviction that the ultimate destiny of humankind is unity with the light of the spirit or, more realistically for Meredith, unity with the great "Over Reason" of the universe. This unity directs man along the path of spiritual evolution and is the apex of Meredith's developing doctrine about man: blood (perfection of the body), brain (perfection of the mind), and spirit (perfection of the needs of man's spiritual consciousness by means of realizing his intrinsic independence and freedom).

The tone of the first half of *The Ordeal of Richard Feverel* is predominantly one of comic irony; the latter half of the novel, however, assumes tragic dimensions. Meredith's later novels display a much greater reliance upon the comic mood. Even so, the essence of "The Magian Conflict" is never lost; rather, Meredith wields the forces of darkness against those of light to accentuate the balancing, equalizing role of his emerging Comic Spirit, whose seeds have been planted in the wise youth, Adrian Harley. The struggle to reach the evolutionary apex, the light of the spirit, assumes a background role in the novels following *The Ordeal of Richard Feverel* and is treated later most directly in the poetry. In his novels, Meredith becomes increasingly more concerned with the question of how one should meet the vicissitudes of everyday life.

Meredith published his essay "The Idea of Comedy and the Uses of the Comic Spirit" in 1877. *Beauchamp's Career* appeared the year before; quite naturally the novel portrays many of the theories Meredith proposed in his essay. In 1879, Meredith completed *The Egoist*, which the author named "a comedy in narrative." Meredith's last great achievement in the novel genre appeared in 1885 and was entitled *Diana of the Crossways*. The novels provide interesting examples of the working out of Meredith's theories centered in the Comic Spirit, and they demonstrate some degree of the use of Zoroastrian imagery. *Beauchamp's Career* employs the Zoroastrian contrast of light and dark to a much greater extent than the other two novels. Meredith draws from Zoroastrianism to a noticeable degree, however, in each of these three novels in order to make the instructive character of his Comic Spirit more emphatic.

Beauchamp's Career · Meredith makes repeated references to fire, sun, and light throughout *Beauchamp's Career*, which undoubtedly reflects his prior use of Zoroastrianism in *The Ordeal of Richard Feverel*. Meredith's dependence upon Zoroastrianism is most pronounced, however, in his characterization of Dr. Shrapnel. Nevil Beauchamp is ambitious and wants to be a politician; he plans to exercise his philanthropic desire to "save the world." He joins a radical political party in order to battle the more conservative Tory Party and to oppose the vehement objections of his Uncle Everard Romfrey, a hater of radicals. After Nevil loses an election for a seat in Parliament, he comes under the tutelage of Dr. Shrapnel, a professed Fire-worshipper.

Since "Fire-worshippers" is a name that Zoroastrians were often mistakenly called, when Dr. Shrapnel testifies "I am a Fire-worshipper," the reader perceives already an element of Meredith's comedy. Dr. Shrapnel, whose name calls to mind a number of images, all of which indicate either potential destruction or active destruction, has obviously become enamored of the mystic, esoteric nature of the religion and hence has adopted certain of its tenets to his own philosophy. Basically Shrapnel's personal doctrine is, in his own words: "That is our republic: each one to his work; all in union! There's the motto for us! *Then* you have music, harmony, the highest, fullest, finest!"

Admittedly, Shrapnel's philosophy is good, or superior in its idealism, and it represents a direct restatement of Meredith's own philosophy (expressed in many of his poems). At this point in the novel, however, the philosophy is stated by an extremist; hence, there is a touch of the comic which becomes more apparent as the novel progresses. Meredith's infrequent use of the exclamation point and his almost negative use of italics make this particular passage stand out as the radical view of an extremist.

Rosamund Culling, the future wife of Nevil's uncle, thinks of Shrapnel as "a black malignant . . . with his . . . talk of flying to the sun." As may be expected from Rosamund's tone, Dr. Shrapnel has at some time in her company been overzealous in the expression of his republican sentiments. News of Dr. Shrapnel's inflammatory radicalism soon reaches Nevil's Uncle Romfrey, who proceeds to horsewhip Shrapnel to the point of severe injury. Lack of understanding by his fellowman appears to be Shrapnel's failing and provides the occasion for comment from the Comic Spirit, who judges that Shrapnel must suffer for his intemperance, for his imbalance. Compromise should be man's objective.

Both in *The Egoist* and in *Diana of the Crossways*, the part played by Zoroastrian imagery is greatly reduced from that which it played in *The Ordeal of Richard Feverel* and *Beauchamp's Career*. Meredith's Comic Spirit, however, comes to the front in full array; the increased subordination of Zoroastrian imagery to Meredith's portrayal of his Comic Spirit indicates that Meredith's theories and understanding of the purpose of his literary art were expanding and maturing. In the later novels, Meredith's Zoroastrian and classical images become frequently and inseparably fused, a combination which further exemplifies Meredith's artistry and more significantly indicates that Meredith's philosophy was progressively becoming more distinct. His thinking was beginning to become a cultivated doctrine.

The Egoist · *The Egoist* characterizes the egocentric element in Meredith's theory of high comedy. Sir Willoughby Patterne, who thinks himself the epitome of goodness and excellence in the world, surrounds himself with admirers and sycophants who satisfy his compulsion to be adored. In creating Patterne, Meredith has taken the next logical step from his production of Beauchamp. Patterne does not merely aspire to goodness and excellence; he actually believes himself to be the embodiment of these qualities.

Patterne attempts to satisfy his ego chiefly by involving himself with three women whom he manipulates with promises of marriage. His first "pretender," Constance Durham, sees through Patterne's facade of greatness with some degree of alacrity and leaves him. The lovely Clara Middleton, however, is not so insightful. She experiences a great deal of emotional turmoil, first in ascertaining the truth of Patterne's pose and then in distinguishing the light of "her sun" from that of Patterne's less self-assured cousin, Vernon Whitford, "a Phoebus Apollo turned Fasting Friar."

Here, Meredith gives more attention to extravagances so that he may better reveal the necessity for the corrective influence of his Comic Spirit. Sir Willoughby Patterne burns; he does not merely reflect. His fire is the product of his own egotism, which burns with an outer brilliance but promises no inner flame. Meredith may well be recalling satirically the Western world's traditional misconception of the importance of fire to the Zoroastrians, who do not worship fire for itself but only as a symbol of the light of the inner spirit.

The character of Vernon presents a striking contrast to that of Patterne. His light is the light of Apollo, who is not only the Greek god of poetry but also the classical god of the sun. Meredith has fused classical allusion with the Zoroastrian importance placed upon fire. Vernon's flame is one of inner strength, for he burns with the light of poetic truth as well as with physical fire. He is also a Fasting Friar, however, a characteristic that raises doubt about the nature of his fire, since Meredith was not an ascetic. In effect, he has achieved in the characterization of Vernon the moderation that Dr. Shrapnel's explosive goals denied him, since Vernon's flame is tempered with some degree of asceticism. Vernon has measured life for what it is, but he has not given up the light of hope for what life can become. Meredith has achieved in his image of the contrast of the two fires the blending of Zoroastrian, classical, and Christian elements.

Laetitia Dale, the third of Patterne's "adorers," presents an interesting foil to Patterne's character. At the beginning of the novel, she is described as a delicate, misled woman, a "soft cherishable Parsee." The Zoroastrian connection is obvious: The Parsees are a modern sect of the Zoroastrians. Indeed, within Meredith's comic framework, Laetitia worships "her sun" much as the Parsees were reputed to worship a "god of fire."

Laetitia gradually becomes a strong, practical Parsee, however, as she, like the other two women in Patterne's egotistic design, begins to see that the source of Patterne's fire is not from within. Patterne is left in the end with Laetitia and is forced to accept her on her own terms. No reader of *The Egoist* can claim its conclusion as romantic or condemn it as pessimistic; rather, Meredith has achieved a noble expression of the corrective power of his Comic Spirit.

Diana of the Crossways · Meredith creates in *Diana of the Crossways* a character who faces decisions similar to those of the women in *The Egoist*. Even Diana's superior wit and intellect do not prevent her from battling the forces of darkness. Meredith prepares the reader for Diana's struggle in the introductory chapter of the novel. He develops a light image, "rose pink," which "is rebuked by hideous revelations of filthy foul," a likeness of darkness. Meredith opens this novel with a discussion of the same subject he had treated in his other novels. For man to think himself already a part of the celestial light at his present step on the evolutionary ladder is surreptitious folly. The future holds for him only "hideous revelations of filthy foul." The narrator further asserts that it is not within the capacity of man to suppress completely the evil forces of darkness. The duality of good and evil inevitably creeps into life.

Having established an atmosphere of foreboding, the narrator sets out to explore Diana's mental processes. Diana quickly becomes disillusioned by a mismatched marriage. Her husband, Warwick, is a man of limited intelligence. As a consequence, Diana becomes drawn to ideas outside the rigid, Victorian system of mores. Her desires strongly urge her to take leave of her witless, insensitive husband, who has accused her of infidelity. She experiences a night of conflict in which she fights like "the Diana of the pride in her power of fencing with evil."

Meredith's presentation of the strife between good and evil by his mixing of classical mythology with overtones of the Zoroastrian duality creates a sense of the universal nature of Diana's struggle. Diana must decide whether to remain loyal to her marriage vows or to strike out on her own and obey her inner compulsions. She finds the impetus for her escape in Dacier, a character who is associated with devil imagery. Indeed, Dacier is the embodiment of Meredith's assertion that there is "an active Devil about the world."

Dacier is a lure to Diana in her desire to escape. His devilish character, however, is ironically exposed by his sanctimonious friend, Sir Lukin. Lukin declares that no man should be fooled by masks of goodness that seem to cover the bad in the world. Dacier, who presents every indication of virtuous conduct, is compared to the old Jewish Prince of Devils, Asmodeus, who spurs on appetite and uproarious activities of all sorts. Although the name Asmodeus appears in the Apocrypha, it also bears connotations to Eshina-Dewa, a wicked spirit of ancient Persian mythology. This is one of Meredith's clearest fusions of Zoroastrianism with Christianity.

Dacier is thwarted in his evil intentions to seduce Diana. An acceptable guide appears for Diana in Thomas Redworth, a character capable of controlling Diana's energetic impulses. Dacier does obtain a prize, however, in the lovely but naïve Constance Asper. Constance is "all for symbols, harps, effigies, what not" and believes that brains in women are "devilish." Constance is perhaps the ideal mate for *The Egoist*'s Sir Willoughby Patterne, and she presents no problems for Dacier's devious motivations. Constance, along with Dr. Shrapnel and Patterne, has failed to see the smoke for the fire. All three are so enamored of the physical brilliance of the flames that they cannot see the subtle glow of spiritual truth within the heart of the blaze.

In *Diana of the Crossways*, Meredith suggests that the endurance of life is perhaps more replete with task than with play. The individual is forced to make a distinction between good and bad, which life seldom presents in a clear-cut fashion. Constance and Dacier somewhat ironically indulge each other in their ostensibly opposing forces. The subtle comment of the Comic Spirit is that both approach life with attitudes of excess; hence, both have lost contact with the steady movement toward self-improvement. Diana and Redworth offer hope to the reader, however, because they have accepted the moderation that the Comic Spirit has taught them and that is necessary for the future success of the human spirit.

These novels present Meredith's concern with the inevitability of "The Magian Conflict" in the life of each man. They also present Meredith's keen observation that this conflict is never one from which one emerges successfully with ease. The struggle makes man's attempt to choose an acceptable path—a way which is acceptable both to him and to his society—extremely difficult. The conflict is presented in terms of Zoroastrian, Christian, and classical myth; Meredith borrows from each in order to make his presentation of this undeniable, unavoidable battle assume universal dimensions. Meredith's Comic Spirit attempts to aid man in his struggle, but it is not always successful in exposing man's shortcomings, excesses, and refusal to see himself in a true light. In the fullest meaning of Meredith's doctrine, however, the individual is also instrumental in the greater, universal struggle of humankind to move up the evolutionary ladder.

Meredith demonstrates in his attitude toward humankind and nature the belief that humans can achieve their evolutionary destiny by conforming to the lessons and demands of nature. His philosophy is universal in scope and implies a comprehensive fusion of nearly all the ethical ideals that people have gathered from the beginning of time. Although Meredith does not discard all the dogma or the moral ideals of the many religious philosophies he studied, he does select with careful scrutiny those elements that he feels contribute to his own doctrines. Indeed, he demonstrates that he is vitally affected by all the religious thought known to him.

John C. Shields

Other major works

SHORT FICTION: *The Case of General Ople and Lady Camper*, 1890; *The Tale of Chloe*, 1890.

POETRY: *Poems*, 1851; *Modern Love and Poems of the English Roadside*, 1862; *Poems and Lyrics of the Joy of Earth*, 1883; *Ballads and Poems of Tragic Life*, 1887; *A Reading of Earth*, 1888; *Selected Poems*, 1897; *A Reading of Life, with Other Poems*, 1901; *Last Poems*, 1909; *The Poems of George Meredith*, 1978 (2 volumes; Phyllis B. Bartlett, editor).

NONFICTION: *On the Idea of Comedy and the Uses of the Comic Spirit*, 1877; *The Letters of George Meredith*, 1970 (3 volumes; C. L. Cline, editor).

Bibliography

Beer, Gillian. *Meredith: A Change of Masks.* London: Athlone Press, 1970. Attempts one of the first modern appraisals of Meredith's art, seeing him as a novelist anticipating twentieth century concerns and techniques, as well as questioning Victorian certitudes. Includes an index.

Muendel, Renate. *George Meredith.* Boston: Twayne, 1986. Chapters on Meredith's poetry, his early fiction, his novels of the 1870's and 1880's, and his last novels. A beginning chapter sums up his biography. Includes chronology, notes, and an annotated bibliography.

Pritchett, V. S. *George Meredith and English Comedy.* Toronto: Clarke, Irwin, 1970. A very readable introductory account of Meredith, constituting the five Clark lectures for 1969.

Roberts, Neil. *Meredith and the Novel.* New York: St. Martin's Press, 1997. A good study of Meredith's long fiction. Includes bibliographical references and an index.

Shaheen, Mohammad. *George Meredith: A Re-appraisal of the Novels.* Totowa, N.J.: Barnes & Noble Books, 1981. Suggests that traditional Meredith criticism has viewed his fiction too much in the light of *The Egoist.* Concentrates on Meredith's other major works as more representative of his true independent mind and specifically explores how character expresses theme for Meredith. Contains selected bibliography.

Stevenson, Lionel. *The Ordeal of George Meredith.* London: Peter Owen, 1954. A straightforward, readable biography of Meredith. Includes a bibliography.

Williams, Ioan, ed. *Meredith: The Critical Heritage.* London: Routledge & Kegan Paul, 1971. A collection of reviews and essays showing the critical reception of Meredith's work from 1851 through 1911. Contains indexes of his work, periodicals, and newspapers.

Iris Murdoch

Born: Dublin, Ireland; July 15, 1919
Died: Oxford, England; February 8, 1999

Principal long fiction · *Under the Net*, 1954; *The Flight from the Enchanter*, 1956; *The Sandcastle*, 1957; *The Bell*, 1958; *A Severed Head*, 1961; *An Unofficial Rose*, 1962; *The Unicorn*, 1963; *The Italian Girl*, 1964; *The Red and the Green*, 1965; *The Time of the Angels*, 1966; *The Nice and the Good*, 1968; *Bruno's Dream*, 1969; *A Fairly Honourable Defeat*, 1970; *An Accidental Man*, 1971; *The Black Prince*, 1973; *The Sacred and Profane Love Machine*, 1974; *A Word Child*, 1975; *Henry and Cato*, 1976; *The Sea, the Sea*, 1978; *Nuns and Soldiers*, 1980; *The Philosopher's Pupil*, 1983; *The Good Apprentice*, 1985; *The Book and the Brotherhood*, 1987; *The Message to the Planet*, 1989; *The Green Knight*, 1993; *Jackson's Dilemma*, 1995.

Other literary forms · Iris Murdoch produced a considerable amount of work in areas other than fiction, particularly in the areas of literary criticism, drama, and, most important, philosophy. Her first book, *Sartre: Romantic Rationalist* (1953), was a critique of Jean-Paul Sartre's philosophy as it appears in his novels. She wrote three plays for the theater and adapted several of her novels for the stage. *The Servants and the Snow* was first performed at the Greenwich Theatre in 1970, and *The Three Arrows* at the Arts Theatre, Cambridge, in 1972; the two plays were published together in 1973 as *The Three Arrows, and The Servants and the Snow: Two Plays.* Another play, *Art and Eros*, was performed at the National Theatre in 1980. Murdoch collaborated with J. B. Priestley to adapt her novel *A Severed Head* for the stage in 1963 (published in 1964), and with James Saunders to adapt *The Italian Girl* in 1967 (published in 1969). *The Black Prince* has also been adapted for the stage and was performed at the Aldwych Theatre in 1989.

Murdoch also produced books on the subject of philosophy: *The Sovereignty of Good* (1970), which consists of three essays on moral philosophy, "The Idea of Perfection," "On 'God' and 'Good,'" and "The Sovereignty of Good Over Other Concepts"; and *The Fire and the Sun: Why Plato Banished the Artists* (1977), a study of Plato's objections to art and artists. Murdoch added to her work on Plato in the form of two "platonic dialogues" entitled "Art and Eros: A Dialogue About Art" and "Above the Gods: A Dialogue About Religion," which she combined in a 1986 book entitled *Acastos: Two Platonic Dialogues. Metaphysics as a Guide to Morals* appeared in 1992, and a collection of essays entitled *Existentialists and Mystics: Writings on Philosophy and Literature* was published in 1997. She also published several philosophical papers in the Proceedings of the Aristotelian Society and other important articles on philosophy and aesthetics, including "The Sublime and the Good" (*Chicago Review*) and "The Sublime and the Beautiful Revisited" (*Yale Review*). Her best-known essay, "Against Dryness: A Polemical Sketch," which appeared in the January, 1961, issue of *Encounter*, is a work of literary criticism that urges a return to the capacious realism of the great nineteenth century novelists.

Achievements · Murdoch, who is universally acknowledged as one of the most important novelists of postwar Britain, combined a prolific output with a consistently high level of fictional achievement. From the beginning of her career as a novelist, she was a critical and popular success in both Great Britain and the United States. In general, Murdoch is thought of as a "philosophical novelist," and despite her objections to this description, she attempted a fusion of aesthetic and philosophical ideas in her fiction. Including her first novel, *Under the Net*, published in 1954, she published twenty-six novels and received a variety of literary awards and honors. In 1973, she was awarded the James Tait Black Memorial Prize for Fiction for *The Black Prince* and in 1974 received the Whitbread Literary Award for Fiction for *The Sacred and Profane Love Machine*. *The Sea, the Sea* won the Booker Prize for Fiction in 1978. Murdoch became a member of the Irish Academy in 1970 and an honorary member of the American Academy of Arts and Letters in 1975; she was awarded the honorary title of Commander of the British Empire in 1976. She was made a Dame of the Order of the British Empire in 1987, and in 1990 she received the Medal of Honor for Literature from the National Arts Club in New York.

Biography · Jean Iris Murdoch was born in Dublin, Ireland, on July 15, 1919, to Anglo-Irish parents, Wills John Hughes Murdoch and Irene Alice Richardson. The family later moved to London, where Murdoch attended the Froebel Education Institute; she finished her secondary education at the Badminton School, Bristol, in 1937. From 1938 to 1942, she attended Somerville College at Oxford University, studying classical literature, ancient history, and philosophy. After obtaining a first-class honors degree, she worked from 1942 to 1944 as the assistant principal in the British Treasury, and from 1944 to 1946 served as an administrative officer with the United Nations Relief and Rehabilitation Administration in England, Austria, and Belgium.

After the war, an interest in existentialism led Murdoch to turn her attention to philosophy. She was unable to accept a scholarship to study in the United States because she had become a member of the Communist Party while an undergraduate at Oxford, and instead attended Newnham College at Cambridge University from 1947 to 1948 after receiving the Sarah Smithson Studentship in philosophy. In 1948, she was made a fellow of St. Anne's College, Oxford, where she lectured in philosophy until 1963, when she was named an honorary fellow of the college. In 1956, she married John Bayley, the author of many books of literary criticism and many book reviews. For many years Bayley was the Thomas Warton Professor of English Literature at Oxford. He has also written several novels, including *The Queer Captain* (1995).

From 1963 to 1967, Murdoch lectured at the Royal College of Art in London, after which she stopped teaching to devote all her time to writing fiction and philosophy. Her novels have won many awards, including the Book of the Year Award from the Yorkshire *Post* (1969), the James Tait Black Memorial Prize (1974), and the Booker Prize (1978). Murdoch became a Commander of the Order of the British Empire (CBE) in 1976 and a Dame of the same order (DBE) in 1987. Oxford University awarded her an honorary D.Litt. in 1987; Cambridge University followed in 1993. In 1992, she published her major philosophical work, *Metaphysics as a Guide to Morals*, a brilliant and sometimes garrulous survey of her ideas about many more topics than its title indicates. In 1997, many of her writings on philosophy and literature were collected in *Existentialists and Mystics*.

At one time Murdoch maintained a London flat in the Earls Court area, but she and her husband always had their primary residence in or near Oxford. In the mid-1990's, Murdoch was diagnosed as suffering from Alzheimer's disease. Her husband described their life together, including how they coped with her mental condition, in *Iris: A Memoir* (1998), published in the United States as *An Elegy for Iris* in 1999, the year Murdoch died.

Thomas Victor

Analysis · A knowledge of Iris Murdoch's philosophical and critical essays is invaluable for the reader wishing to understand her fiction. Her moral philosophy, which entails a rejection of existentialism, behaviorism, and linguistic empiricism, informs her fiction throughout and provides a basis for an interpretation of both the content and the form of her work. Although early influenced by Sartrean existentialism, she developed a radically different view of the human condition. The major disagreement she had with the existentialist position is its emphasis on choice, a belief Murdoch characterizes as "unrealistic, over-optimistic, romantic" because it fails to consider the true nature of human consciousness and what she called "a sort of continuous background with a life of its own." Existentialism, which she called "the last fling of liberal Romanticism in philosophy," presents humanity with "too grand" a conception of itself as isolated from its surroundings and capable of rational, free choice. She describes this picture of humankind as "Kantian man-gods" who are "free, independent, lonely, powerful, rational, responsible, and brave." Although Murdoch denied being a Freudian, Sigmund Freud's "realistic and detailed picture of the fallen man" is much closer to her own conception of human nature, and she agreed with what she called Freud's "thoroughly pessimistic view" in which the psyche is described as an "egocentric system of quasi-mechanical energy" determined by its individual history; the natural attachments of this psyche are "sexual, ambiguous, and hard for the subject to control." The most important dimension of this description of the individual is his lack of rational free will, and Murdoch's statement in "Against Dryness" that "we are not isolated free choosers, monarchs of all we survey, but benighted creatures sunk in a reality whose nature we are constantly and overwhelmingly tempted to deform by fantasy" is perhaps her tersest summary of the human condition.

Murdoch's philosophical position is the basis for her choice of prose fiction as the most realistic literary genre. The novelist's advantage is his "blessed freedom from rationalism," and she saw the novel as the literary form which, because of its lack of formal restrictions, could best portray the "open world, a world of absurdity and loose ends and ignorance." Although she had reservations about modern literature and believed that the twentieth century novel tends either to be "crystalline" (self-contained, mythic, sometimes allegorical, and frequently neurotic) or "journalistic" (semi-documentary, descriptive, and factual), the nineteenth century novel as written by Leo Tolstoy, Jane Austen, and George Eliot remains the best example of how fiction can create free, independent characters who are not "merely puppets in the exteriorization of some closely-locked psychological conflict" of the author. The nineteenth century novel, because it "throve upon a dynamic merging of the idea of person with the idea of class," was not simply a representation of the human condition but rather contained "real various individuals struggling in society"; in other words, it presented characters *and* the "continuous background with a life of its own."

Murdoch believed that the most important obligation for the novelist is the creation of particularized, unique, and ultimately indefinable human beings, characters who move outside the novelist's consciousness into an independent ontological status. This aesthetic theory has its corollary in Murdoch's moral philosophy, in which she stresses the need for the individual to recognize the "otherness" of other individuals. The great novelist, like the "good" person, has an "apprehension of the absurd irreducible uniqueness of people and of their relations with each other," an apprehension she castigates Sartre for lacking. Recognition of otherness is, to a degree, dependent upon the individual's ability to "attend" to other individuals, a concept Murdoch derives from the philosophy of Simone Weil. Murdoch describes attention as a "patient, loving regard, directed upon a person, a thing, a situation" and believes that we *"grow by looking"*; morality, both for the individual and the novelist who is attempting a realistic portrayal of human beings in the world, is an endless process of attending to a reality outside the individual consciousness. Attention is seeing, "a just and loving gaze directed upon an individual reality," and as such is an effort to counteract "states of illusion" brought about by selfish fantasy. For Murdoch, attention is also another name for love, and "the ability to direct attention is love." Imaginative prose literature, Murdoch believed, is the best medium in which to focus attention on the individual because it is *"par excellence* the form of art most concerned with the existence of other persons."

In "The Sublime and the Good," Murdoch defines love as "the perception of individuals. Love is the extremely difficult realization that something other than oneself is real. Love, and so art and morals, is the discovery of reality." She has also said that the main subject of her fiction is love, and her novels usually depict the difficulties involved in recognizing the uniqueness and independence of other human beings. In *The Bell,* the Abbess tells Michael Meade that "all of our failures are ultimately failures in love," a statement that neatly describes Murdoch's fictional world. The enemy of love in her novels is the propensity of the individual to fantasize and to create false pictures of reality, particularly distorted conceptions of other people. As a result, her novels frequently present situations in which characters are forced to confront the "otherness" of those around them, situations which often involve a realization of the past or present sexual involvements of other persons. The comfort and safety of the "old world," as it is called by many Murdoch characters, is destroyed by a discovery about the past or by characters suddenly falling passionately in love with each other. *A Severed Head*, in which Martin Lynch-Gibbon is shocked by a series of revelations about his wife and friends and falls precipitately and unpredictably in love with Honor Klein, is one of the best examples of this recurring pattern in Murdoch's work.

Murdoch believed that the experience of art can serve to shock the individual into an awareness of a reality outside the personal psyche, and her novels contain several scenes in which characters who gaze upon paintings are able to escape temporarily from solipsistic fantasy. Dora Greenfield in *The Bell*, Harriet Gavender in *The Sacred and Profane Love Machine*, and Tim Reede in *Nuns and Soldiers* each experience what Murdoch calls "unselfing" and Harriet Gavender describes as "not being myself any more"; in fact, Dora Greenfield notes that paintings give her "something which her consciousness could not wretchedly devour. . . . The pictures were something real outside herself." Murdoch, in "The Sublime and the Beautiful Revisited," calls art "spiritual experience" because it can bring out this radical change in perception, and in *The Fire and the Sun: Why Plato Banished the Artists*, she claims that in an unreligious age good art provides people with "their clearest experience of something grasped as separate and precious and beneficial and held quietly and unpossessively in the attention."

Murdoch's ambivalent attitudes about the role of art and artists are present in both her fiction and her philosophy. In an interview with Michael Bellamy, in *Contemporary Literature* (1977), she described art as a "temptation to impose from where perhaps it isn't always appropriate," and in the same discussion noted that "morality has to do with not imposing form, except appropriately and cautiously and carefully and with attention to appropriate detail." Murdoch suggested to several interviewers that the basis of her novels is what she calls the conflict between "the saint and the artist," or the dichotomy between the "truthful, formless figure" and the "form-maker." She mentioned Tallis Browne and Julius King in *A Fairly Honourable Defeat*, Ann and Randall Peronett in *An Unofficial Rose*, and Hugo Belfounder and Jake Donaghue in *Under the Net* as examples. She believes that Plato's life exemplifies this conflict: "We can see played out in that great spirit the peculiarly distressing struggle between the artist and the saint." The true or "good" artist must avoid the "ruthless subjection of characters" to his will and should use symbolism judiciously in a "natural, subordinate way" that attempts to be "perfectly realistic." In her fiction, Murdoch's artist-figures are often demonic individuals who manipulate people in real life without regard for their well-being or independence as persons. Her "saint" figures have a corresponding lack of form, or sense of self, and are frequently unable or unwilling to act in any way. Douglas Swann's comment in *An Unofficial Rose* that "nothing is more fatal to love than to want everything to have form" is also true of Murdoch's attitude toward art.

Many of Murdoch's characters attempt to find form in their own lives in order to explain the apparent chaos that surrounds them. In her essay "Vision and Choice in Morality," Murdoch talks about the need at times to stress "not the comprehensibility of the world but its incomprehensibility" and says that "there are even moments when understanding *ought* to be withheld." In *The Flight from the Enchanter*, John Rainborough experiences a moment of joy when he feels "how little I know, and how little it is possible to know," but this happiness in a lack of knowledge is rare in Murdoch's fiction. In the same novel, Rosa Keepe, a much more representative Murdoch character, listens to the sound of the machines in the factory, hoping to hear a "harmonious and repetitive pattern," just as Michael Meade in *The Bell* expects to find "the emergence in his life of patterns and signs." At the end of the novel, he regretfully concludes that the apparent pattern he had observed in his life was merely his own "romantic imagination. At the human level there was no pattern."

The search for rational, discernible causal relationships is the major structuring principle in *An Accidental Man*, a novel concerned with the discovery of, in Gracie Tisbourne's words, "a world . . . quite without order." In "The Sovereignty of Good over Other Concepts," Murdoch says that "there are properly many patterns and purposes within life, but there is no general and as it were externally guaranteed pattern or purpose of the kind for which philosophers and theologians used to search," and she has also stated her desire to write novels that, because they contain more of the contingent, accidental dimensions of life, are more realistic than "patterned" fiction.

Murdoch's reservations about form in life and art are paralleled by her suspicions about language. A fervent defender of literature and language who said in "Salvation by Words" that "words constitute the ultimate texture and stuff of our moral being. . . . The fundamental distinctions can only be made in words" and in *The Fire and the Sun* that "the careful responsible skillful use of words is our highest instrument of thought and one of our highest modes of being," Murdoch also voiced suspicions about the ironic nature of language, its potential to distort the truth and to create false pictures of reality. This distrust of language is evident in her first novel, *Under the Net*, and continued to inform her fiction. In this respect, Murdoch was greatly influenced by Ludwig Wittgenstein; direct references and sly, sometimes ironic allusions to Wittgenstein appear repeatedly in her novels.

In spite of these reservations, however, Murdoch mounts one of the most eloquent defenses of art and literature in modern times in *The Sovereignty of Good* and *The Fire and the Sun*. She claims in "The Sovereignty of Good over Other Concepts" that art "can enlarge the sensibility of its consumer. It is a kind of goodness by proxy," and in "On 'God' and 'Good,'" she asserts that art, rather than being any kind of playful diversion for the human race, is "the place of its most fundamental insight." According to Murdoch, literature is the most important art because of its unique ability to shed light on the human condition: "The most essential and fundamental aspect of culture is the study of literature, since this is an education in how to picture and understand human situations." This statement in "The Idea of Perfection" obviously places an enormous burden on the novelist, a burden which Murdoch's prolific output, technical virtuosity, and moral vision appear to be capable of bearing.

Under the Net · Jake Donaghue, the narrator-protagonist of *Under the Net*, informs the reader early in the novel that the story's central theme is his acquaintance with Hugo Belfounder. The relationship between the two men illustrates Murdoch's philosophical and aesthetic concerns, for the Hugo-Jake friendship represents the saint-artist dichotomy; this "philosophical novel" allows her to explore the problem of theoretical approaches to reality, the issue of contingency, the realization of the otherness of individuals, and the ambiguities of language and art.

The character of Hugo Belfounder is based in part on that of the enigmatic Elias Canetti, winner of the Nobel Prize in Literature in 1981; the Bulgarian-born Canetti, who has lived in England since 1939, appears in various guises in several of Murdoch's early novels. Hugo, some of whose precepts also suggest the influence of Wittgenstein, is Murdoch's first "saint" figure, and he embodies many of the qualities of the "good" characters who appear later in her fiction. Hugo's saintliness is a result of his truthfulness and his lack of desire for form or structure in life and art. Opposed to him is Jake, who, fearing that he may actually tell the truth to Mrs. Tinckham about being evicted by Madge, delays telling his story until he can present it in a "more dramatic way . . . as yet it lacked form." Form, as Jake tacitly admits, is a kind of lying, an imposition of structure that distorts reality. Hugo, on the other hand, is attracted by the ephermerality and formlessness of the firework displays he has created, and he abandons them when they receive the attention of art critics who begin to classify his work into styles. Hugo is also characterized by a selflessness that Jake finds astonishing: It does not occur to him that he is responsible for the concepts discussed in Jake's book *The Silencer*, or that Anna Quentin's mime theater is based upon her interpretation of his beliefs.

The difference between the two men is also evident in their attitude toward theory. After his conversations with Hugo, Jake concedes that his own approach to life is "blurred by generalities," and he is entranced by Hugo's refusal to classify the world around him or to adopt any kind of theory about it. Annandine, Hugo's persona in *The Silencer*, says that "the movement away from theory and generality is the movement towards truth. All theorizing is flight. We must be ruled by the situation itself and this is unutterably particular." Theories, like form, distort what they attempt to explain and understand. Hugo's lack of a general theoretical framework for his ideas, the "net" of the novel's title, makes everything he encounters "astonishing, delightful, complicated, and mysterious."

Part of Jake's education and development as a potential artist is dependent upon relinquishing the need for theories and generalizations. In his first meeting with Anna, he notices that she is in "the grip of a theory," and one of the most important episodes in the novel is Jake's realization that Jean-Pierre Breteuil, whose work he has previously translated into English, has finally written a good novel, a feat Jake had believed impossible. He understands that he has incorrectly "classed" Jean-Pierre and says that "It wrenched me, like the changing of a fundamental category." Similarly, when Jake becomes aware that Hugo is in love with Sadie Quentin rather than Anna, he says that "a pattern in my mind was suddenly scattered and the pieces of it went flying about me like birds." At the end of the novel, Jake has abandoned attempts to impose his own ideas onto his environment; rather, he decides to sit quietly and "let things take shape deeply within me," noting that he can "sense," beneath the level of his attention and without his conscious aid, "great forms moving in the darkness."

Jake's initial need to perceive form and to create theories is paralleled by his fear of contingency. One of Murdoch's major quarrels with Sartre is his inability to deal with the contingent, or, in her words, the "messiness" and "muddle" of human existence. Rather than rejecting Sartre's concept of viscosity, Murdoch frequently forces her characters to come to terms with the physical world and the accidental and apparently chaotic nature of reality. Early in the novel, Jake announces that "I hate contingency. I want everything in my life to have a sufficient reason," and later, in a reference to Sartre's *La Nausée* (1938; *Nausea*, 1949), observes that Hugo's Bounty Belfounder film studio is situated in a part of London "where contingency reaches the point of nausea." The novel ends with Jake laughingly admitting that he does not know the reason why Mrs. Tinckham's kittens look as they do. "I don't know why it is," he says, "It's just one of the wonders of the world." In this scene, Jake focuses on the particular–the kittens–and is able to accept that their appearance cannot be explained by him, two actions which show that he has moved much closer to Hugo's position. Hugo had earlier advised Jake that "some situations can't be unravelled" and, as a result, should be "dropped."

This acceptance of contingency implies a realization that life cannot be completely controlled by human will. Jake also learns that other individuals exist independently of him and resist his efforts to explain and categorize their behavior. When he introduces his close friend Peter O'Finney to the reader, he claims that "Finn has very little inner life," and that, while Finn is an inhabitant of his universe, "I . . . cannot conceive that he has one containing me." Events in the novel force Jake to move out of his solipsistic consciousness, and at the conclusion he acknowledges that for the first time Anna exists "as a separate being and not as a part of myself," an experience he finds "extremely painful." She becomes "something which had to be learnt afresh," and he then asks if it is possible ever to know another human being. He answers himself in a statement that clearly belongs to his author: "Perhaps only after one has realized the impossibility of knowledge and renounced the desire for it and finally ceased to feel even the need of it." In the same way, Jake also grants Hugo a final mysteriousness and impenetrability, comparing him to a monolith whose purpose remains obscure.

Murdoch's suspicions about the nature of language are also evident in *Under the Net*. In a conversation between Hugo and Jake, Hugo maintains that, by definition, language lies: "The whole language is a machine for making falsehoods." Language is also vulnerable because of humanity's tendency to distort and to exaggerate experiences when attempting to articulate them; Hugo notes that when he speaks he does not state precisely what he thinks but rather what will impress Jake and force him to respond. Only actions, says Hugo, do not lie. This is not, however, Murdoch's final word on language and literature, for Jake's development as a human being during the course of the novel culminates in his realization that he will be able to write creatively. The "shiver of possibility" that he feels at the novel's conclusion is his knowledge that his earlier writing has been merely a preparation for his emergence as a novelist.

Murdoch's first novel is clearly a *Künstlerroman* and her most overtly "philosophical" novel. In an interview in 1978 with Jack Biles, in *Studies in the Literary Imagination*, she said that she does not want to "promote" her philosophical views in her novels or to allow them to "intrude into the novel world." This attitude certainly seems more descriptive of the novels written after *Under the Net*. Although she paints an ironically amusing portrait of the novel's only professional philosopher, Dave Gellman, her major concerns in her first novel are clearly philosophical; *Under the Net* contains in more obvious form the philosophical issues which are transmuted into the fictional material of her subsequent work.

A Fairly Honourable Defeat · Speaking of *A Fairly Honourable Defeat* in her interview with Michael Bellamy, Murdoch said that the "defeat" of the novel's title is the defeat of good by evil. She calls the novel a "theological myth" in which Julius King is Satan, Tallis Browne is a Christ-figure, and Leonard Browne is God the Father. Another trichotomy, however, is suggested in *A Fairly Honourable Defeat*, for Julius and Tallis, like Ann and Randall Peronett in *An Unofficial Rose*, embody the saint-artist opposition that is so common in Murdoch's fiction; and Rupert Foster represents the rationalist philosopher's approach to experience, an approach which ultimately fails because it does not take into consideration the reality of evil and the formlessness of good. The relationship among these three men is one of the most important thematic concerns of the novel.

A Fairly Honourable Defeat begins with Hilda and Rupert Foster enacting a scene common in Murdoch's fiction, that of the happily married couple whose contentment has insulated them from their less fortunate friends. Like Kate and Octavian Gray in *The Nice and the Good,* Rupert and Hilda feel as if their happiness has granted them a privileged and protected status. Rupert's statement that "Anything is permitted to us," ominously similar to Friedrich Nietzsche's "all is permitted," signals that for the moment they live in the "old world" of pleasure and stability that is so frequently shattered in the course of a Murdoch novel. The agent of destruction in *A Fairly Honourable Defeat* is Julius King, a scientist who considers himself an "artist" whose art works consist of manipulating the lives of people around him, forcing them to "act parts" and in the process become "educated" about their moral failures.

Julius King's reaction to Rupert's philosophy of life is the catalyst for the events of the novel. Although Rupert, like Murdoch, calls human existence "jumble" and castigates his sister-in-law Morgan Browne for her "love and do as you please" attitude toward people, Rupert believes that "complete information and straight answers and unambiguous positions . . . clarifications and rational policies" are possible and desirable; for Rupert, goodness is a fairly simplistic concept that can be experienced directly and articulated eloquently. His statement to Morgan after Julius has orchestrated their ostensible "love affair" that "nothing awful can happen" summarizes his inability to grasp the kind of evil that Julius represents, and the destruction of the manuscript of his book on moral philosophy symbolizes the fragility of his worldview, a fragility underscored by his death. Rupert's major error is believing that his own rationality can prevail; he hypocritically thinks that "the top of the moral structure was no dream, and he had proved this by exercises in loving attention: loving people, loving art, loving work, loving paving stones and leaves on trees." In reality, as Julius later observes, Rupert is in love with his own image of himself as a good, loving, and rational man who can control any urge that threatens the "moral structure" of his world; while he espouses many theories about the nature of love, he lacks the "direct language of love" that makes real action possible.

Unlike Rupert, who believes that his duty is to love others, Julius's attitude toward human beings is one of contempt, an emotion the narrator describes as "the opposite extreme from love: the cynicism of a deliberate contemptuous diminution of another person." One of the major reasons for his low valuation of people is the very quality that makes them vulnerable to his manipulation—their malleability, or, as he phrases it, the easiness with which they are "beguiled." In a conversation with Tallis, Julius says that most individuals, motivated by fear and egotism, will cooperate in almost any deception. The most obvious examples of his theory in *A Fairly Honourable Defeat* are Morgan Browne and Simon Foster. Morgan, titillated by Julius's boast that he can "divide anybody from anybody," first encourages him in his plan to separate Simon and Axel and later unknowingly becomes one of his victims; Simon, afraid that Julius will destroy his relationship with Axel, unwillingly allows Julius to "arrange" a relationship between Rupert and Morgan. In fact, Julius's claim that he is an "artist" and a "magician" depends upon the moral weaknesses of the characters whose lives he carefully "plots."

Both Leonard Browne and Julius King mount verbal assaults on the world; in some respects, their diatribes sound remarkably similar. Like Leonard, Julius believes that the human race is a "loathesome crew" who inhabit a "paltry planet"; he goes further than Leonard, however, in his statement that human beings "don't deserve to survive," and, more important, in his desire to see the reification of his ideas. Julius's theory that people are merely puppets who need to be educated becomes, in practice, a tragedy. Although, like Hugo Belfounder, he claims that philosophy is the subtlest "method of flight" from consciousness and that its attempted truths are "tissues of illusions," in *Theories*, he is entranced with his own theorizing, as is Rupert. Good, he says, is dull, and what passes for human goodness is a "tiny phenomenon" that is "messy, limited, truncated." Evil, by comparison, "reaches far far away into the depths of the human spirit and is connected with the deepest springs of human vitality." Good, according to Julius, is not even a "coherent concept; it is unimaginable for human beings, like certain things in physics."

One of Murdoch's saintlike characters, James Tayper Pace in *The Bell*, also discusses the difficulty of comprehending goodness while he emphasizes the need for the individual to seek the good beyond the confines of his own consciousness: "And where do we look for perfection? Not in some imaginary concoction out of our own idea of our own character—but in something so external and so remote that we can get only now and then a distant hint of it." In "The Sovereignty of Good over Other Concepts," Murdoch talks about contemplating goodness, and, like James Tayper Pace, defines it as "an attempt to look right away from self towards a distant transcendent perfection, a source of uncontaminated energy, a source of *new* and quite undreamt-of virtue." Unlike Pace and Murdoch, Julius is unwilling to waste his energies in the contemplation of a concept so "remote" and "transcendent" and is instead beguiled by the immediacy and vitality of evil.

Tallis Browne, the "saint" of *A Fairly Honourable Defeat*, is one of the strangest characters in Murdoch's fiction. Early in the novel, his wife Morgan, talking about the human psyche, complains that "it stretches away and away to the ends of the world and it's soft and sticky and warm. There's nothing real, no hard parts, no centre." This description of human consciousness also explains Morgan's dissatisfaction with her husband, who is completely lacking in the qualities she so admires in Julius King: form and myth. With Tallis, says Morgan, "there were no forms and limits, things had no boundaries"; he lacks any kind of personal "myth," while she characterizes Julius as "almost all myth." Like Julius, Tallis does not believe in theories, and at one point he correctly accuses Morgan of being "theory-ridden" and chasing "empty abstractions"; unlike Julius, however, he has no theories about human nature or behavior, a fact that Julius acknowledges when he tells Tallis that Rupert probably feels that "theorizing would be quite out of place with you." While Julius manipulates the relationships of those around him according to his ideas about human weakness and Rupert writes a text on morality and goodness, Tallis nurses his dying father and helps to feed and shelter the poverty-stricken immigrants in his neighborhood.

The formlessness of Tallis's goodness causes him to have no desire to analyze the tragedy of Rupert's death or to assign reasons or blame. He grieves "blankly" over what appears to have been a "disastrous compound" of human failure, muddle, and sheer chance, and mourns Rupert by attempting to remember him simply with a kind of mindless pain. His reaction to the loss of his wife is similar. Rather than indulging in anger, grief, or speculations about their future relationship, he simply lets her "continue to occupy his heart." His unwillingness to impose any kind of form or to structure his surroundings in any way extends to his feelings for his father Leonard, who is dying of cancer. Tallis cannot find the appropriate moment to tell his father of his impending death because, as he tells Julius, "It seems so arbitrary, at any particular instant of time, to change the world to that degree." Rather than seeing human beings as puppets, as does Julius, Tallis has reached a crisis state in which he fears that any action may have a deleterious effect on those around him. Significantly, however, in spite of Tallis's passivity he is the only character in the novel who is capable of positive action. As Axel phrases it, he is "the only person about the place with really sound instincts." In the Chinese restaurant, he strikes the young man who is abusing the Jamaican, and later he forces Julius to telephone Hilda Foster to explain that it is Julius who has created the "affair" between Morgan and Rupert.

At the end of the novel, Tallis has abandoned the idea of prayer, which the narrator notes could only be a "superstition" for him at that point, and has instead become a completely passive and receptive consciousness. He catches hold of objects "not so as to perform any act himself, but so as to immobilize himself for a moment to be, if that were possible, perhaps acted upon, perhaps touched." The similarity of this statement to Simone Weil's definition of "attention" in *Waiting for God* (1951), where she describes the act of attention as "suspending our thought, leaving it detached, empty, and ready to be penetrated by the object . . . our thought should be empty, waiting, not seeking anything," is clear. Much earlier in the novel, Morgan has grabbed an object, a green paperweight belonging to Rupert, in an attempt to escape from the formlessness of the psyche. Tallis, on the other hand, uses objects as a way to attend to reality, as a means of opening himself up to the world outside himself.

A Fairly Honourable Defeat ends with Tallis weeping over his father's approaching death and Julius, after contemplating his choices of Parisian restaurants, concluding that "life was good." The conversation between the two men which precedes this, however, is much more ambiguous. Julius, in an apparent attempt to win Tallis's approbation for his actions, reveals a great deal about himself personally and asks Tallis to agree that he is "an instrument of justice." Tallis's attitude toward Julius is one of detached tolerance, and his response to Julius's statement is merely to smile. A parallel to his calm acceptance of Julius's evil is his response to the "weird crawling things," apparently rats, mice, and insects, which inhabit his house; he feels for them "pity rather than disgust" and has advanced far beyond Rupert's claim to love "paving stones and leaves on trees." Tallis's acceptance of the world, which has grown to embrace even its most despicable and horrible elements, makes him the most saintlike character in Murdoch's fiction. He is her answer to Sartre's Roquentin in *Nausea*: Instead of becoming nauseated by the world's plethora of objects and the muddle of existence, as does Roquentin, Tallis, at the end of *A Fairly Honourable Defeat*, is capable of feeling only pity and acceptance for everything that surrounds him.

An Accidental Man · In *An Accidental Man*, Murdoch presents a chaotic world of accident and unpredictability in which several of her characters search for—and fail to find—any kind of pattern or causal relationships in their lives. Perhaps Murdoch's fear that form in fiction can hinder the characters' development as complex and fully realized individuals and that intricately patterned fiction sometimes prevents the author from exploring "the contradictions or paradoxes or more painful aspects of the subject matter" led her to write a novel in which the narrative voice is almost completely absent: In *An Accidental Man*, the characters appear to have taken over the novel. In an interview with W. K. Rose, in *Shenandoah* (Winter, 1968), Murdoch expressed the desire to write a novel "made up entirely of peripheral characters, sort of accidental people like Dickens's people," and mentioned that the author "might go so far as starting to invent the novel and then abolishing the central characters." *An Accidental Man* is the result of these speculations about fiction, for it contains a Dickensian sweep of characters and lacks any kind of "protagonist." The inclusion of more "accident" in Murdoch's work is one aspect of her wish to write realistic fiction, for she believes that the novelist should portray the world as "aimless, chancy, and huge." *An Accidental Man*, a brittle comedy of manners which contains four deaths, two attempted suicides, and more than twenty characters, some of whom are suffering from mental retardation, schizophrenia, and brain damage, is Murdoch's vision of a contingent, random, and godless world.

Many characters in the novel share this vision. At the conclusion, Matthew Gibson Grey notes that Austin's appropriation of Mavis Argyll "has been, like so many other things in the story, accidental." Charlotte Ledgard, contemplating suicide, sees herself as "the slave of chance" and the world as being made up of "chaos upon which everything rested and out of which it was made." Ludwig Leferrier senses that "human life perches always on the brink of dissolution," and Gracie Tisbourne, who is usually not given to philosophical speculations, has "a sense of the world being quite without order and of other things looking through." The characters in *An Accidental Man* wander through mazes in which they lack important information about their own and others' lives, or they become the victims of "accidents" which radically transform their existence. London's labyrinthine streets become symbolic of their ignorance and blindness as they pass and miss one another, and, in the instance of Rosalind Monkley, symbolic of accidental death itself. Garth Gibson Grey, Matthew Gibson Grey, Ludwig Leferrier, and Mavis Argyll all hope to find some kind of logical order and rationality in the world, but are finally defeated by the "absolute contradiction . . . at the heart of things," and instead encounter what Garth calls "the rhetoric of the casually absent god."

Although Murdoch is generally not interested in experimentation in form, *An Accidental Man* shows her moving beyond the traditional narrative form of her earlier work in search of new structures to embody the philosophical assumptions that underlie the novel. Conspicuously missing in this novel is an authoritative narrative voice; instead, one tenth of the book is in epistolary form and a significant portion consists of chapters of untagged dialogue. In *An Accidental Man*, Murdoch, who has stated her wish to expel herself from her fiction in order to avoid imposing "the form of one's own mind" on the characters, creates a work in which the narrator is frequently not privy to the inner thoughts or reactions of the characters and can only report their spoken and written words without comment or elucidation. The disappearance of the narrator in certain sections of the novel parallels the absence of god; Murdoch creates a novelistic world in which the reader must search for his own patterns and conclusions without the guiding presence of the authorial voice which was present in her earlier fiction. In addition, the narrator's refusal to pass judgments or give information about the thoughts of the characters, despite the fact that he has shown himself to be omniscient in certain situations, results in a coldly detached tone which refuses to grant a fundamental importance to any act.

Like the chapters of dialogue, the epistolary sections of the novel create a voyeuristic situation for the reader that parallels the voyeurism that takes place several times during the narrative. The reader is privileged to read correspondence and to overhear important conversations while being denied access to the characters' thoughts, just as the characters in *An Accidental Man* have a noticeable penchant for eavesdropping on one another's conversations and reading other people's letters. The epistolary sections also create comically ironic effects because the reader knows more about the entire situation than any of the individual letter-writers, and the ignorance, lies, and exaggerations of the writers are juxtaposed in ways that underscore the limited and fallacious viewpoint of each individual. These chapters also give Murdoch an opportunity to open up the novel, expanding its boundaries to encompass more and more territory—a narrative technique that corresponds to her desire to write fiction that depicts reality as "a rich receding background" with "a life of its own."

The widening framework of the novel creates a constantly changing perspective, for when the narrator withdraws from a direct presentation of events in order to present the reactions of peripheral or uninvolved characters, the importance of these events is reduced through distancing and in the process rendered comic. The same technique is used in the chapters of pure dialogue, where events which have been treated seriously in earlier episodes become the subject of comically trivial cocktail-party conversations. The dialogic and epistolary sections are central elements in the novel, for Murdoch uses them to advance the narrative through fragmentary bits of information which are often necessary for a complete understanding of what is happening; her belief that "reality is not given whole" is expressed in her narrative technique.

The self-acknowledged "accidental man" of the novel's title is Austin Gibson Grey. Neurotically obsessed with his older brother, Matthew, and unable to keep either his wife or his job, Austin is nevertheless a survivor who depends upon his own egotism for his continued well-being. One aspect of Austin's ability to survive is his refusal to allow the catastrophes of others to affect him. He observes that "a man can see himself becoming more callous to events because he has to survive," and his reaction to the death of Rosalind Monkley, whom he has killed in an automobile accident, is typical. He writes to his wife, Dorina, that "I will survive and recover, I have had worse blows than this"; he does not mention any guilt he may feel about the incident or the pain Rosalind's death may have caused her family. Similarly, after Dorina's accidental death, Austin tells Matthew that "Poor old Dorina was just a sort of half person really, a maimed creature, she had to die, like certain kinds of cripples have to. They can't last." In spite of Austin's selfishness, however, he is merely the most exaggerated example of egotism in *An Accidental Man*. The statement by an unnamed character at the novel's conclusion that "Austin is like all of us only more so" is, unfortunately, correct.

Austin Gibson Grey resembles several other characters in Murdoch's fiction, all of whom show a talent for survival and an ability to turn unfortunate incidents to their account. In the same way, Austin's wife Dorina is representative of another character-type which recurs throughout Murdoch's novels: the individual who functions as a scapegoat or assumes the consequences of the sins of others. Frequently, through no fault of their own, such characters cannot cope with the events happening around them and either choose suicide or become the victims of an "accidental" death that appears to be inevitable. Traditionally, the scapegoat or *pharmakos* figure is an individual who must be expelled from society in order to maintain its continued existence and vitality. Dorina Gibson Grey is a *pharmakos* who manifests all these characteristics. Early in the novel, she feels as if "something were closing in for the kill," and after her death, her sister Mavis voices the opinion that "she has died for me," telling Matthew that "she has somehow died for us, for you and me, taking herself away, clearing herself away, so that our world should be easier and simpler." Dorina's death enables Garth Gibson Grey to feel love once again for his father. Her death also rejuvenates her husband, as Matthew ironically observes: "Something or other had . . . done Austin good. Perhaps it was simply Dorina's death." Her death has an almost ritualistic dimension in *An Accidental Man*, and it ensures the rejuvenation of several of the characters.

The ending of *An Accidental Man* is one of the darkest in Murdoch's fiction, and very few of the defeats suffered in this novel can be termed "honourable." In fact, several characters, including Matthew Gibson Grey, Garth Gibson Grey, and Charlotte Ledgard, appear to have settled for what Julius King in *A Fairly Honourable Defeat* calls a "sensible acceptance of the second rate." Matthew, en route with Ludwig Leferrier to the United States, where Ludwig will receive a prison sentence for refusing to fight in Vietnam, realizes that "he would never be a hero. . . . He would be until the end of his life a man looking forward to his next drink"; Garth is metamorphosed into a self-satisfied, successful novelist whose former social conscience and pursuit of goodness have been abandoned in favor of marriage to Gracie Tisbourne and all that she represents; and Charlotte chooses to remain with Mitzi Ricardo in spite of her knowledge that what she feels for Mitzi is merely "a fake dream love." These failures contrast with the fates of Austin and Clara Tisbourne, both of whom are described as looking "radiantly juvenile." Austin, in particular, has been completely rejuvenated by the misfortunes of others and is finally able to move his fingers, which have been rigid since his childhood "accident"; his inability to do this heretofore has symbolized his problems with dealing with the world, just as his new physical flexibility reflects the rebirth of his psyche.

The darkly comic final chapter of *An Accidental Man*, which consists solely of untagged dialogue, furnishes important information while it trivializes the events of the entire novel. The fact that Ludwig Leferrier is now in prison in the United States after his decision to leave his idyllic and protected situation in England, the real moral dilemma of the novel, is mentioned in passing and then dropped by an unnamed character who incorrectly says that he has been imprisoned for "Drugs or something." In this final section of the novel, unlike the earlier chapters of letters and dialogue, the reader becomes less and less certain about who is actually speaking. In fact, the dialogue appears to be spoken by a group of eerie, disembodied voices which create an ominous atmosphere from which the narrator and the main characters have departed, leaving the reader to overhear the mindless gossiping of strangers. At the conclusion of *An Accidental Man*, contingency and "the rhetoric of the casually absent god" have triumphed.

The Sea, the Sea · In *The Sea, the Sea*, Murdoch focuses on a type of character who has appeared throughout her fiction, the artist or would-be artist who confuses life and art with unfortunate (and sometimes tragic) consequences. In Murdoch's earlier novel, *The Black Prince*, Bradley Pearson's quiet life is suddenly shattered by a series of revelations and catastrophes which include an affair with the teenage daughter of his best friend. These real-life events cause Bradley to create the novel he had been unable to write previously; at the same time, Bradley is consciously aware of his movement from experience to the expression of experience in aesthetic form and realizes the difference between the two, even though he takes great pride in his "artistic" consciousness throughout the story. In *The Sea, the Sea*, however, Charles Arrowby, the famous and ostensibly "retired" theatrical director who is unable to leave behind the artifice and dramatic structure of the stage, begins to "direct" life offstage, ignoring the boundaries between fact and fiction. His theater becomes the small seaside village to which he has moved, and his actors are the people around him.

Published one year before *The Sea, the Sea*, *The Fire and the Sun*, Murdoch's study of Plato's objections to art and artists, is instructive to read in the light of her portrayal of Charles Arrowby. Although Murdoch disagrees with several of Plato's fundamental assumptions about the nature of art, her narrator in *The Sea, the Sea*, embodies many of Plato's—and Murdoch's—suspicions about the artistic sensibility. In *The Fire and the Sun*, Murdoch discusses the Platonic doctrine that art and the artist "exhibit the lowest and most irrational kind of awareness, *eikasia*, a state of vague image-ridden illusion"; in Plato's myth of the cave, this state corresponds to the prisoners who, facing the wall, can see only the shadows cast by the fire. Charles Arrowby, called the "king of shadows" several times in the novel, exemplifies the "bad" artist, the "naive fantasist" who "sees only moving shadows and construes the world in accordance with the easy unresisted mechanical 'causality' of his personal dream life." Throughout the novel, James Arrowby, Charles's cousin and the "saint" figure in *The Sea, the Sea*, tries to convince Charles that the woman he is pursuing is only a "dream figure," just as Hartley Fitch, the sixty-year-old woman who was Charles's adolescent girlfriend and is now married to another man, tells Charles that their love is a "dream" that does not belong in the real world. Near the end of the novel, Charles acknowledges the truth of their interpretations, calling his novel "my own dream text."

Charles Arrowby's psychological state, one that combines tremendous egotism with an obsessional need to control other people while remaining almost completely deluded about what is happening around him, closely resembles Murdoch's description of Plato's idea of the "bad" man. The "bad" or mediocre man is "in a state of illusion, of which egoism is the most general name. . . . Obsession, prejudice, envy, anxiety, ignorance, greed, neurosis, and so on *veil* reality." Similarly, Plato says that the human soul desires "omnipotence" and erects barriers between itself and reality so that it can remain comfortably within a "self-directed dream world." Although on the novel's first page Charles claims that he has come to his retirement home "to repent of egoism," his realization that Hartley is living in the same village results in his jealously obsessional need to "capture" her from her husband. Although he views himself as a Prospero-like magician-artist who can effect any kind of magical transformation, he gradually reveals his incorrect evaluations of himself and others. Charles's novel, the chronicle of his delusions and errors, is a portrait of the "bad" man who refuses to acknowledge the unpredictability and intransigence of reality.

Charles tells the reader that his last great role as an actor was as Prospero in William Shakespeare's *The Tempest* (1611), and he believes he has much in common with Shakespeare's magician. Despite his statement early in the novel that "Now I shall abjure magic and become a hermit," he soon begins the direction of his final "drama." His theatrical vision of the world often obscures reality; not surprisingly, he is overjoyed to discover that what he first called a "diary," "memoir," and "autobiography" has become a novel. The change from a journalistic mode of writing to a fictional one parallels his growing tendency to dramatize and fictionalize events, and soon after his announcement that he is indeed writing a novel, he begins to construct an elaborate "story" about Hartley and her marriage. James fails in his attempt to convince his cousin that he is fighting for a "phantom Helen" and that his wish to rescue her is "pure imagination, pure fiction." Although Charles later admits to the reader that he has created an "image" of Hartley which does not correspond to reality, he denies that his "image" is untrue. His kidnapping of Hartley reveals his need to hold her prisoner in his imagination, to create an aesthetic image he can manipulate for his own purposes. Unlike Bradley Pearson, who finally admits that any kind of final possession of human beings is impossible, Charles continues to believe that he can force Hartley to concede to the planned denouement of his "drama."

Charles's attitude toward his novel is related to his dramatic theories, and both have implications for the way his story is interpreted by the reader. He defines the theater as "an attack on mankind carried on by magic," and its function as being "to victimize an audience every night, to make them laugh and cry and suffer and miss their trains. Of course actors regard audiences as enemies, to be deceived, drugged, incarcerated, stupefied." Although he claims to take painstaking care to relate events in his novel as truthfully as possible, at one point even reassuring the reader that he is rendering the dialogue almost verbatim, he is delighted by his sudden discovery that language, like dramatic art, can create illusion and veil truth. He says that anything written down is "true in a way" and gloats over the fact that he could write down "all sorts of fantastic nonsense" in his memoir and be believed because of "human credulity" and the power of the written word. He takes an increasing pleasure in fictionalizing his life and in transforming the people around him into "stylish sketches," acts which reveal his desire to cast his friends and enemies into a drama he can both write and direct. Like Bradley Pearson in *The Black Prince*, he finds that verbalizing experience can be a way to control what is happening; he also believes that he can dramatically intensify his feelings by writing them out "as a story." When he writes out his account of the visit of another former girlfriend, Lizzie Scherer, he observes that it would be "rewarding" to "write the whole of one's life thus bit by bit as a novel. . . . The pleasant parts would be doubly pleasant, the funny parts funnier, and sin and grief would be softened by a light of philosophic consolation." Murdoch, who has said that the function of art is to reveal reality rather than to console its creator or consumer, portrays Charles as the "bad" artist who attempts to use art and the creative process for solace instead of revelation.

Just as Murdoch's characters often misuse art and their own creative impulses, they frequently fall in love suddenly and violently, an experience that produces a state of delusion and neurotic obsession. Although she says in *The Fire and the Sun* that the "lover" can be shocked into an awareness of "an entirely separate reality" during the experience of love, the lover's ego usually causes him to wish to "dominate and possess" the beloved. The lover, rather than wishing to "serve and adore," instead wants "to de-realize the other, devour and absorb him, subject him to the mechanism of . . . fantasy." Charles Arrowby's "Quest of the Bearded Lady," as one character terms his pursuit of Hartley, exemplifies this dimension of falling in love; his feelings for her are typical of the obsessive, self-centered, fantasy-ridden love that Murdoch believes is antithetical to an objective, free apprehension of others. He admits that he is "like a madman" and compares himself to a "frenzied animal." Later, he says that "I was sane enough to know that I was in a state of total obsession and that I . . . *could only* run continually along the same rat-paths of fantasy and intent." Unlike his cousin James, who has cultivated the intellectual and spiritual detachment of Eastern philosophy combined with a concern for the well-being and "otherness" of individuals, Charles's passion for Hartley Fitch is, at bottom, an obsession with his own past and loss of innocence.

In two earlier novels, *An Accidental Man* and *The Black Prince*, Murdoch uses narrative devices such as epistolary and dialogic chapters and the addition of "postscripts" by other characters to alter the reader's perspective and interpretation of events. In *The Sea, the Sea,* she allows Charles Arrowby to add a "revision" to his novel that qualifies and contradicts much of his earlier narrative. At the end of the "History" section of *The Sea, the Sea,* he closes his story on a note of repentance and revelation, goes to sleep hearing "singing," and awakens to see the seals he had previously been unable to sight.

Murdoch believes that fiction should reflect the "muddle" of reality, and thus she adds a postscript by the narrator appropriately entitled "Life Goes On." Charles begins by mocking his "conclusion" and observing that life, unlike art, "has an irritating way of bumping and limping on, undoing conversions, casting doubt on solutions"; he then decides to continue his story a while longer, this time in the form of a "diary" in which he alters his own version of events and reveals that he has learned very little from them. In this way, Murdoch further reduces the stature of her "failed Prospero," and the picture of Charles that emerges in the postscript is that of a rapidly aging man with an incipient heart condition. Another addition to the group of "power figures" in Murdoch's fiction who believe that they can "invent" reality and manipulate other people for aesthetic purposes, Charles Arrowby represents Murdoch's belief in the final impossibility of one human being's controlling another. In *The Sea, the Sea,* the would-be director who thought himself a "god" or "king" is revealed as a relatively powerless individual over whom the formlessness and unpredictability of "transcendent reality" triumphs.

The Good Apprentice · Murdoch's most critically acclaimed novel of the 1980's is *The Good Apprentice,* a novel that reflects her continuing desire to write fiction whose length and complexity embody her belief in a contingent, infinitely particularized universe in which goodness is easily discussed but achieved, if at all, with great difficulty and pain. The "good apprentice" can refer to either of two characters in the novel. Edward Baltram has recently been responsible for the death of his best friend and is attempting to deal with his resulting guilt and self-hatred; Stuart Cuno, his stepbrother, is, like many other Murdochian characters, seeking goodness and finding it a problematical goal.

Murdoch makes Stuart Cuno the mouthpiece of some of her most cherished ideas about the nature of goodness. Like Murdoch, Stuart acknowledges that goodness is often an unimaginable concept that involves inaction rather than action, and several times in the story he is referred to as a "negative presence." Stuart has rejected the entire concept of God and instead attempts to meditate blankly, to empty his mind out in order to perceive clearly, what Murdoch calls "an instinctive craving for nothingness which was also a desire to be able to love and enjoy and 'touch' everything, to *help* everything." Psychoanalyst Thomas McCaskerville, who stands in direct opposition to Stuart's nontheoretical approach to goodness, catechizes the younger man at length in an important conversation that reveals Thomas's dependence on the cozy theories of psychoanalysis that Murdoch has mocked in her earlier novels. Thomas has a conceptual framework for almost any idea or event, and his discovery that his wife Midge has been having an affair with Stuart's father Harry Cuno only temporarily shocks him out of his comfortable mental and emotional world. His further realization that his supposedly psychotic patient Mr. Blinnet is actually quite sane and has been faking mental illness for years is another blow at Thomas's carefully constructed theoretical world.

It is the artist Jesse Baltram, Edward's father, who best represents one of the most enduring and interesting figures in Murdoch's fiction, the magician-artist power figure who mysteriously spellbinds those around him and functions as a catalyst for many important events. Edward goes to Seegard, Jesse's home, to be "healed" and "purified" of his friend's death. In the process he meets May Baltram, Jesse's wife, his two half sisters, and, finally, his father, who has been reduced by an unspecified illness to childlike behavior and incoherence. Jesse's difficulty in making rational conversation is another alternative in the novel to Stuart's "blankness" and "whiteness" and Thomas's frenziedly articulate philosophizing: It signifies that the logical ordering principle of language ultimately cannot describe or explain a reality that is always "boiling over" with energy and creativity. Jesse's description of the world and the relationship between good and evil, in which syntax and logic break down, is directly opposed to the other characters' slick facility with language. He tells Edward,

> "What I knew once—about good and evil and those—all *those* things—people don't really have them, meet them—in their lives at all, most people don't—only a few—want that—that fight, you know—think they want—good—have to have evil—not real, either—of course—all inside something else—it's a dance—you see—world needs power—always round and round—it's all power and—energy—which sometimes—rears up its beautiful head—like a dragon—that's the meaning of it all—I think—in the shadows now—can't remember—doesn't matter—what I need—is a long sleep—so as to dream it all—over again."

Jesse's connection with the supernatural and paranormal dimension of Edward's stay at Seegard reveals Murdoch again experimenting with the limits of realistic fiction. As in *The Sea, the Sea*, she is willing to force the reader to accept the unexplained and acknowledge the thin line between the natural and the supernatural, between distortion of perception and a glimpse into another world where the usual rational rules no longer apply. *The Good Apprentice* shows Murdoch at the height of her powers as a novelist, combining her "moral psychology" with her long-held aesthetic theories in a work that proves the undiminished fecundity of her imagination and intelligence.

The Book and the Brotherhood · In another important novel of the 1980's, *The Book and the Brotherhood*, Murdoch's power-figure is as charismatic as Jesse but is neither impotent nor incoherent. David Crimond is an intellectual of the far Left (the communists kicked him out for being too radical). Years ago at Oxford, a group of Crimond's friends pledged to support him while he wrote the volume of revolutionary economic and social philosophy they thought the world needed. Years later, although Crimond's book remains unpublished, his intellectual, personal, and even sexual power over the group remains undiminished. The novel shows how the friends try to define their moderating political views in relation to Crimond's.

The novel also shows how the friends and *their* friends try to make peace with the world. Each yearns for fulfillment, though in widely different ways—some of them touching, some admirable, some reprehensible. Gerard, perhaps the novel's central character, yearns for a vague something (his yearning began with his affection for his pet parrot, as described in one of Murdoch's most brilliant passages). Rose, a passive woman, yearns for Gerard. Duncan yearns for his wife, who yearns for Crimond. Jenkins, a saintly schoolmaster, yearns for a perfect act. Other characters are less important but stranger. At the end of an Oxford party, Gulliver is awakened by a deer's kiss; later he has a paranormal experience in a London railway station. Other inexplicable forces are exerted by buried Roman roads and by Church rituals performed by an unbelieving priest.

The Book and the Brotherhood offers no certainties, for neither Crimond's ideas nor Gerard's refutations are convincing. It shows a wide spectrum of memorable characters yearning earnestly and sometimes comically toward some things they cannot fully define.

The Green Knight · Murdoch's last great novel, *The Green Knight*, is one of her most perplexing. The story is bizarre. It often resembles (but does not strictly parallel) that of the medieval narrative poem *Sir Gawain and the Green Knight*. In its central act, Murdoch once again pushes the bounds of realism. One dark night in a public park, Lucas Graffe, while attempting to kill his brother Clement with a baseball bat, hits a third man instead and kills him. Later, like the medieval Green Knight, the supposedly dead man reappears. His name is Peter Mir, and he is this novel's powerful magician; he is alive and demands justice. His demand is worked out in a way that also recalls *Sir Gawain and the Green Knight*. (Mir also is said to resemble Mr. Pickwick, Prospero, the Minotaur, and Mephistopheles.)

The stories of other characters encircle the central one. Clement hopelessly loves Louise Anderson, whose magical house contains three wonderful daughters who are about to begin life's journey. The most mysterious is Moy, who can move small stones at a distance. The Andersons keep a dog named Anax, one of Murdoch's finest animal creations. His master, Bellamy, gave him away to embark on a spiritual quest for which he is ill suited. At one point Anax, who may embody the goodness of the flesh, escapes and tries to find his master in an anxious lope through the streets of London.

Murdoch's conclusion of this novel may not satisfy everyone, but the journey through the novel is exciting and rewarding. Her last novel, *Jackson's Dilemma*, has many high spots, but it is often confusing. By the time the reviews appeared, her Alzheimer's disease had progressed so far that she could not understand them.

Angela Hague, updated by George Soule

Other major works

PLAYS: *A Severed Head*, pr. 1963 (with J. B. Priestley); *The Italian Girl*, pr. 1967 (with James Saunders); *The Servants and the Snow*, pr. 1970; *The Three Arrows*, pr. 1972; *The Three Arrows, and The Servants and the Snow: Plays*, pb. 1973; *Art and Eros*, pr. 1980; *The Black Prince*, pr. 1989; *Joanna Joanna*, pb. 1994; *The One Alone*, pb. 1995.

NONFICTION: *Sartre: Romantic Rationalist*, 1953; *The Sovereignty of Good*, 1970; *The Fire and the Sun: Why Plato Banished the Artists*, 1977; *Acastos: Two Platonic Dialogues*, 1986; *Metaphysics as a Guide to Morals*, 1992; *Existentialists and Mystics: Writings on Philosophy and Literature*, 1997 (edited by Peter Conradi).

Bibliography

Bloom, Harold, ed. *Iris Murdoch*. New York: Chelsea House, 1986. Bloom's collection of essays, a representative selection of some of the best articles and book chapters on Murdoch, includes his introductory analysis of *The Good Apprentice* and Murdoch's essay "Against Dryness."

Bove, Cheryl K. *Understanding Iris Murdoch*. Columbia: University of South Carolina

Press, 1993. A lucid and valuable handbook for college students. Early chapters summarize Murdoch's philosophical ideas.

Byatt, Antonia S. *Degrees of Freedom: The Novels of Iris Murdoch.* New York: Barnes & Noble Books, 1965; expanded edition, London: Vintage, 1994. This important study focuses on the degrees of freedom that characters have in Murdoch's early novels and notes Murdoch's failings. The expanded edition reprints the original edition and adds a foreword, the entire text of Byatt's pamphlet *Iris Murdoch* (1976), a review of Byatt's first book, and Byatt's own reviews of many of Murdoch's later novels.

Dipple, Elizabeth. *Iris Murdoch: Work for the Spirit.* Chicago: University of Chicago Press, 1982. A valuable and essential study of the aesthetic, moral, and philosophical dimensions of Murdoch's works through *Nuns and Soldiers.* Dipple discusses Murdoch's use of Plato's concept of the Good and perhaps overemphasizes the bleak Buddhist elements in the novels.

Gordon, David J. *Iris Murdoch's Fables of Unselfing.* Columbia: University of Missouri Press, 1995. Gordon discusses many of Murdoch's ideas, especially those concerning power and human motives.

Heusel, Barbara. *Patterned Aimlessness: Iris Murdoch's Novels of the 1970's and 1980's.* Athens: University of Georgia Press, 1995. Heusel analyzes Murdoch's relation to many philosophers, Wittgenstein in particular. She uses Bakhtin's dialogic method to illuminate how Murdoch's characters interact.

Johnson, Deborah. *Iris Murdoch.* Bloomington: Indiana University Press, 1987. Johnson uses Anglo-American and French feminist theories to analyze Murdoch from a feminist perspective, focusing on Murdoch's male narrators, the issue of confinement, the symbol of the cave, and the problem of endings in the fiction.

Soule, George. *Four British Women Novelists: Anita Brookner, Margaret Drabble, Iris Murdoch, Barbara Pym, an Annotated and Critical Secondary Bibliography.* Lanham, Md.: Scarecrow Press, 1998. An analysis of most critical books and articles on this author through 1996, with evaluations.

Todd, Richard. *Iris Murdoch: The Shakespearian Interest.* New York: Barnes & Noble Books, 1979. Murdoch's frequently noted debt to Shakespeare is explored in this study, which pays particular attention to *The Black Prince, Bruno's Dream, A Word Child, The Nice and the Good,* and *A Fairly Honourable Defeat.*

George Orwell

Eric Arthur Blair

Born: Motihari, India; June 25, 1903
Died: London, England; January 21, 1950

Principal long fiction · *Burmese Days*, 1934; *A Clergyman's Daughter*, 1935; *Keep the Aspidistra Flying*, 1936; *Coming Up for Air*, 1939; *Animal Farm*, 1945; *Nineteen Eighty-Four*, 1949.

Other literary forms

Since the mid-1940's, George Orwell has been considered one of the world's premier essayists. Combining reportage, the polemical essay, fictional techniques, and refracted autobiographical detail, his works defy precise generic definition. Orwell's numerous nonfiction works have been compiled in *The Collected Essays, Journalism, and Letters of George Orwell* (1968), edited by Sonia Orwell and Ian Angus.

Achievements · Although Orwell is widely recognized as one of the best essayists of the twentieth century, his reputation as a novelist rests almost entirely on two works: the political allegory *Animal Farm* and the dystopian *Nineteen Eighty-Four*. Both have been translated into so many other languages and have been so widely read that the adjective "Orwellian" has international currency, synonymous with the "ghastly political future," as Bernard Crick has pointed out (*George Orwell: A Life*, 1980). Indeed, Jeffrey Meyers is convinced that Orwell, the writer of essays, political tracts, and fiction, "is more widely read than perhaps any other serious writer of the twentieth-century" (*A Reader's Guide to George Orwell*, 1975).

Biography · George Orwell was born Eric Arthur Blair, the son of Richard Walmesley Blair and Ida (Limouzin) Blair. Orwell was born in India and lived there for four years, until his father moved the family back to England, to a small house named "Nutshell" in Henley-on-Thames. After a short leave, Orwell's father returned alone to India, leaving his wife and children in England and rejoining them later, upon his retirement. With his father's return, Orwell, like most male members of the upper middle class, was sent away to boarding school, St. Cyprian's, located at Eastbourne on the Sussex Coast. After several miserable years, as Orwell described them in his autobiographical *Such, Such Were the Joys* (1953), he won a scholarship to Eton, the public school that would forever set him apart from the working classes about which he was so concerned during most of his adult life.

Considered rather unacademic at Eton, Orwell was graduated in December, 1921, and, after a decision not to attend the university, he applied to the India Office for the position of Imperial Police Officer. Five years in Burma, from 1922 to 1927, shaped the impressionable young man so as to make him forever sympathetic to individuals victimized by governmental bureaucracy and imperialistic power. Orwell left Burma in the summer of 1927, ostensibly on sick leave (he suffered from a lung condition most of his life). At some point early in his leave, Orwell wrote a letter of resignation to the India Office and explained to his skeptical parents that all he really wanted was to write.

In 1928, Orwell commenced a long, five-year apprenticeship as a writer, time spent as a tramp in both Paris and London, and in the writing and rewriting of countless manuscripts. By 1933, he had assumed the name by which he is known and had produced, in addition to at least two destroyed novels, the nonfictional *Down and Out in Paris and London* (1933) and his first novel, *Burmese Days*, published one year later.

From 1933 to 1937, Orwell continued to develop his literary talents, producing two more novels, a book about his experiences with poverty-stricken coal miners in Wigan (*The Road to Wigan Pier*, 1937), and several essays, occasional pieces, and book reviews. By the end of this period, he had also married, for the first time, and, within a year or so of that, gone to Spain. Perhaps the most singular experience of his life to date, the Spanish Civil War found Orwell on the front lines, a member of a *Partido Obrero de Unificación Marxista* (a Marxist worker's party) brigade; henceforth, Orwell passionately declared himself a fighter for "democratic Socialism" and, in that context, wrote his most famous nonfictional work, *Homage to Catalonia* (1938). After being wounded (and nearly imprisoned), Orwell escaped Spain with the help of his wife, returned to England, and continued his literary career. Within another year, his lungs still causing problems, Orwell moved to the dry climate of Morocco, where he wrote much of *Coming Up for Air.*

His fourth novel was buried under mounting war concerns and preparations. Orwell, unable to join the military because of health, became a spokesman for the British Broadcasting Corporation. During the last years of the war, Orwell finished writing *Animal Farm*, only to see it rejected by almost every major publisher in England and America. Finally brought out in August, 1945, during the last days of the Pacific War, *Animal Farm* was a work of near-perfection, making Orwell's name internationally known, so that when *Nineteen Eighty-Four* was published four years later, the world came to realize that both works would henceforth be considered literary classics, satires ranking with Thomas More's *Utopia* (1516) and Jonathan Swift's *A Tale of a Tub* (1704). Orwell's death in 1950 at the age of forty-six was a tragic loss to the world of letters and to the larger world with which he always kept in touch.

Analysis · Excepting *Animal Farm*, most critics view George Orwell's fictions as aesthetically flawed creations, the work of a political thinker whose artistry was subordinate to his intensely didactic, partisan passions. This reaction to Orwell's novels was generally promoted posthumously, since his fiction in the 1930's was often ignored by the larger reading public and panned by those reviewers who did pick up one of his books. The early academic critics—up to the late 1960's—were often Orwell's personal friends or acquaintances, who tended to see his early novels as conventionally realistic and strongly autobiographical. Even his masterpieces, *Animal Farm* and *Nineteen Eighty-Four*, were viewed as formally undistinguished, however powerful their message. It was not until the second generation of critics began looking at Orwell's fiction that a more balanced assessment was possible.

Burmese Days · Orwell's first published novel, *Burmese Days*, concerns the life of John Flory, an English policeman in Burma during the early 1920's. The plot is fairly straightforward. After a lengthy introduction to Flory's personality and daily life, Orwell dramatizes him as a man blemished with a physical stigma, a birthmark, and puzzled by a moral dilemma, how to deal with the increasingly rebellious natives, to whom he is secretly sympathetic but against whom he must wield the club of imperialistic authority. In the middle of this dilemma, Elizabeth arrives, a young English woman who is fresh faced but decidedly a traditional "burra memsahib." Flory attempts to win both her heart and mind—much to the dismay of his Burmese mistress, Ma Hla May—and succeeds in doing neither, even though he manages to half-succeed in proposing marriage during an earthquake. With a mind too closed to anything not properly British, and a heart only to be won by someone very English, Elizabeth forgets Flory's attentions with the arrival of Verrall, an English military policeman, who will in turn reject her after his billet is completed. A humble Flory waits for Elizabeth, and after Verrall has left takes her to church services, confident that he has out-

Library of Congress

lasted his rival. Unfortunately, Flory is humiliated by Ma Hla May, is repulsed yet again by Elizabeth, and, in a mood of despair, commits suicide, killing both his dog and himself.

Burmese Days is interesting for its accurate psychological portrayal of a man trapped between two worlds: loving England, yet hating English imperialistic politics; loving and hating the subject people, the Burmese, yet fascinated by their culture and the beauty of their environment. Flory is strangely sympathetic to their struggle for independence while doing everything possible to keep it in check.

In such a world, Flory is emphatically not meant to be a sympathetic character, but rather a victim of the very political order he has sworn to uphold. In effect, Orwell has laid a trap for the unwary reader. Too close an identification with Flory, too intense a desire to have him succeed in marrying Elizabeth—an unholy alliance of imperialistic Englishwoman and revolutionary, thinking pariah—will prevent the reader from recognizing the irreconcilable contradictions inherent in the British presence in Burma.

Coming Up for Air · Orwell's fourth published novel, *Coming Up for Air*, was written in Marrakesh, Morocco, shortly after he had recovered from yet another bout with tubercular lesions of the lungs. Although the novel sold moderately well for the time (a first printing, according to Bernard Crick, of two thousand copies and a second printing of one thousand), many critics were vaguely condescending toward the hero, George Bowling, a middle-class insurance salesman who longs for the golden country of the past while simultaneously dreading the horrors of a second world war, then only months away. Many of the themes more fully developed in *Nineteen Eighty-Four* find their initial expression in Orwell's last conventional novel, set before the outbreak of the devastation that the next six years would bring.

Coming Up for Air is set in London during the late 1930's; Orwell employs a first-person narrative to describe the life of George Bowling, a middle-aged, middle-class salesman, whose first set of false teeth marks a major milestone in his life. Musing in front of a mirror while he prepares for work one morning, George's mind wanders back to the past, the golden England of thirty years earlier when he was growing up. As he goes about his day, disgusted with all the evidence of modern life in front of him—the casual brutalities, the tasteless food, the bombers overhead—George forms a plan to return to Lower Binfield, his childhood home, and, by extension, the simple life he had once led. Unfortunately, his return only confirms the all-pervasive slovenliness of the modern world: Lower Binfield has been swallowed by a sprawling suburb, his adolescent sweetheart has become a frowsy old married woman (she is all of two years older than he), and the fishing hole (once filled with huge finny dreams) has been emptied of water and filled with trash. Shocked and completely disenchanted, Bowling makes plans to get at least a relaxing few days from the trip when a bomber accidentally drops a bomb close by, killing and wounding several people. In thorough disgust, Bowling packs, leaves, and returns home to face his wife, who has somehow found out where he has gone, although his motives for going will be forever incomprehensible to her.

A plot summary of the novel fails to do justice to the subtle tonal shifts and complicated psychological changes Orwell employs in presenting his portrait of the average man waiting for the apocalypse. Orwell has used the ancient theme of the double (or *Doppelgänger*) to illustrate the self-fragmentation of European man prior to the outbreak of the war. George Bowling is divided into two "selves." Tubby is the outwardly fat, insensitive insurance tout who is able to function successfully in a fast-paced, competitive world that would eat up less hardened personalities, but his character can only survive at the cost of any sort of satisfying inner life. Georgie, on the other hand, would be lost in the modern rat race and so is protected by Tubby; nevertheless, Georgie can give expression to the memories, the sensitivities, the love for natural pleasures that Tubby (and George Bowling) would have to forgo to remain functional. Thus, George Bowling devised a strategy for living both materially successfully and psychologically well in the modern world, doing so by splitting his identity into Tubby and Georgie. *Coming Up for Air* details the ongoing dialogue between these two "selves"—a conversation that reflects the strains of modern living as well as any other novelist has done in the twentieth century.

Furthermore, Orwell has modified the literary conventions of the *Doppelgänger* to suit his own needs. Whereas the death of one-half of the double usually means the destruction, ultimately, of both, Orwell has Tubby live on after Georgie is symbolically destroyed by the bombing plane. The tonal change at this point, rather like the tonal change in Joseph Heller's *Catch-22* (1961) with the death of Kid Sampson, shows the reader the world that Orwell envisioned between 1938 and 1939, one horrible enough to prevent total escape even by death. It is, however, typically Orwellian that however horrible human bondage can make the cultural world, nature, of which humankind is a part, has enough ebullient energy to wait out any social mess—a wait without immediate hope, without idols, but also without hopeless despair. George Bowling leaves Lower Binfield, returning to his scold of a wife, Hilda; to the everlasting round of bills, worries, war clouds on the horizon, and a death-in-life without Georgie; but, as the novel's epigraph states, "He's dead, but he won't lie down."

Animal Farm · *Animal Farm* is one of those rare books before which the critic lays down his pen. As a self-contained "fairy story," the book can be read and understood by children not old enough to pronounce most of the words in an average junior high school history text. As a political satire, *Animal Farm* can be highly appreciated by those who actually lived through the terrible days of World War II. As an allegory concerned with the limitations and abuses of political power, the novel has been pored over eagerly by several generations of readers.

The novel is built around historical events in the Soviet Union, from before the October Revolution to the end of World War II; it does this by using the frame of reference of animals in a farmyard, the Manor Farm, owned by a Mr. Jones. Drunk most of the time and, like Czar Nicholas of Russia in the second decade of the twentieth century, out of touch with the governed, Jones neglects his farm (allegorically representing the Soviet Union, or by extension, almost any oppressed country), causing much discontent and resentment among his animals. One day, after Jones does his nightly rounds, Major, an imposing pig (V. I. Lenin), tells the other animals of a dream he has had concerning theories about the way they have been living. Animals have been exploited by Mr. Jones and humankind generally, but Major has dreamed of a time when they will throw over their yokes and live free, sharing equally both the profits and the hazards of their work. Major teaches the animals the words to a song, "Beasts of England" (The Internationale), and tells them to look to the future and the betterment of all animals; three days later he dies.

The smartest of the animals, the pigs, are aroused by his speech and by the song; they secretly learn to read and write, developing a philosophical system called animalism (Communism, Bolshevism) whose principles are taught to all the animals. When Jones forgets one day to feed them (as Russians starved near the end of their involvement in World War I), the animals revolt spontaneously, driving out Jones, his wife (Russian nobility), and Moses, the raven (the Russian Orthodox Church). The animals rejoice, feeling a sense of camaraderie and *esprit de corps*, and set about to build a new life.

The pigs, however, by taking on the responsibility of organization, also take over certain decision-making processes—as well as all the milk and apples; in fact, Orwell has himself stated that the first sign of corruption, the taking of the cow's milk, led to the inevitable destruction of everything else. Two pigs in particular, Snowball (Leon Trotsky) and Napoleon (Joseph Stalin), argue constantly, while a third, Squealer (*Pravda*, Tass) appears more than happy to endorse any course of action with his adroit use of language and his physical habit of skipping from side to side as he speaks. After changing the name from Manor Farm to Animal Farm, the pigs paint on the the side of the barn the seven commandments of animalism, the most important being "All animals are equal." Meanwhile, Napoleon has been privately raising puppies born on the farm after the overthrow of Jones, puppies that develop into savage attack dogs (secret police, People's Commissariat of Internal Affairs [NKVD]); with these, he will one day drive off the farm all of his personal enemies, especially the brilliant theoretician, Snowball. Also soon to be lost to Animal Farm is Mollie (the bourgeoisie), who shows up at Pilkingtons (the West, England).

At this point, the work becomes more difficult, the pigs assume practical control, and the arguments become more intense. Even though Benjamin, the donkey (Tolstoyan intellectuals), remains cynical about the supposed heaven on earth, Boxer, the horse (the peasantry), vows to work harder; nevertheless, the animals continue to lose their spirit and cohesiveness until attacked by Farmer Jones, who tries to regain the Farm. Because of Snowball's brilliant strategy, Jones is driven off in what is thereafter called the Battle of the Cowshed (the Civil War).

Following the victory celebration, Snowball and Napoleon move toward a decisive parting: The former wants to move full speed ahead with the building of the windmill (permanent revolution), while the latter thinks the most important task immediately ahead is the increase in food production (develop socialism in Russia first). After much debate and just before what could be an affirmative vote for Snowball's policies, Napoleon unleashes his secretly kept dogs on his rival, chasing him out of Animal Farm forever. Henceforth, the unchallenged leader abolishes Sunday meetings, increasingly changes rules at will, and even announces that the building of the windmill was his idea.

The animals continue to work hard, still believing that they are working for themselves. The changes Napoleon institutes, however, are so at variance with the initial rules of Animal Farm, and life gets to be so much drudgery, that no one has the memory to recall the ideals of the past, nor the energy to change the present—even if memories were sound.

Very soon, life at Animal Farm seems indistinguishable from the life the animals led at Manor Farm. Orwell is not so much ultimately pessimistic as he is realistically moral: Institutionalized hierarchy begets privilege, which begets corruption of power. The first mistake of the animals was to give over their right to decide who got the the milk and apples. Lord Acton's famous statement could not be more appropriate: "Power tends to corrupt; absolute power corrupts absolutely."

Nineteen Eighty-Four · *Nineteen Eighty-Four* is Orwell's most famous work. As a fantasy set in the future, the novel has terrified readers for more than fifty years—frightened them into facing the prospect of the ultimate tyranny: mind control. As a parody of conditions in postwar England, it is, as Anthony Burgess has argued in *1985* (1978), a droll, rather Swiftean exaggeration of then current trends straining the social and political fabric of British culture. As a critique of the way in which human beings construct their social reality, the novel has so affected the modern world that much of its language (like that of its predecessor, *Animal Farm*) has entered into the everyday language of English-speaking peoples everywhere: *doublethink, newspeak, thoughtcrime,* and *Big Brother.* Bernard Crick argues that the novel is intimately related to *Animal Farm*—more so than most critics have hitherto acknowledged—and that both works convey Orwell's most important message: Liberty means telling people what they do not want to hear. If the vehicle for the telling gets corrupted, then the message itself will always be corrupted, garbled; finally, the very thoughts which led to the utterances in the first place will be shackled, constrained not only from the outside but also from the inside. To think clearly, to speak openly and precisely, was a heritage Englishmen received from their glorious past; it was a legacy so easily lost that it needed to be guarded fiercely, lest those who promulgated ideologies of right or left take away what had been won with such difficulty. That was where the danger lay, with those who practiced the "smelly little orthodoxies" that are still "contending for our souls."

The story begins with a man named Winston Smith who is hurrying home on a cold, windy April day as the clocks are striking thirteen. With this ominous beginning, the reader is quickly plunged into a gritty, decaying world where the political order so dominates everyday life that independent thought is a crime, love is forbidden, and language seems to say the opposite of what one has normally come to expect. As Winston's daily life unfolds, the reader quickly learns that the whole world has been divided into three geographical areas: Oceania, Eurasia, and Eastasia. All are engaged in perpetual warfare with one or both of the others, not for territorial or religious reasons but primarily for social control. At some point, atomic warfare had made total war unthinkable, yet it suits the political leaders of Oceania (the same is also true of the other two political areas) to keep the population in a general state of anxiety about foreign attack. Under the guise of national concern, Oceania's leaders keep the population under their collective thumb by the use of propaganda (from the Ministry of Truth), by outright, brutally applied force (from the Ministry of Love), by eternally short rations (Ministry of Plenty), and by the waging of perpetual war (Ministry of Peace). The ruling elite, called the Inner Party, makes up only two percent of the population; the Outer Party, the next thirteen percent. The remainder, some eighty-five percent of the population, are called Proles, the oppressed masses.

Winston, a member of the Outer Party, has been disturbed by strange thoughts of late, and one day he purchases a small, bound volume of blank paper, a diary where he can record his most private thoughts without being observed by the omnipresent telescreen, manned by members of the Thought Police. In his diary, he records his first thought: "Down with Big Brother!" To compound such a heinous thoughtcrime, he begins a liaison with a pretty young woman, a member of the Anti-Sex League, named Julia. After their affair has progressed for some time, they are contacted by a man named O'Brien, who enlists their aid in combating Big Brother by joining a group called the Brotherhood. O'Brien gives Winston a book, written by a man named Emannuel Goldstein, called *The Theory and Practice of Oligarchical Collectivism.* Having made love to Julia in a room rented from an old Prole (secretly a member of the Thought Police), Winston begins reading to her from Goldstein's book, actually an exposition of the theory that Orwell has used to construct *Nineteen Eighty-Four.*

Although Winston is fascinated, Julia, a rebel from the waist down only, falls asleep, and, after a while, so does Winston. They awake many hours later, are captured by the Thought Police, who apparently knew of their hideaway from the first, and are taken to rooms in the Ministry of Love. There, they find that O'Brien is in reality a member of the Thought Police; he alternately tortures and debates with Winston, trying to convince him that he must love Big Brother.

When torture fails, Winston is taken to Room 101, where he will be subjected to that which he fears most—in his case, rats. He gives in, begs them to "do it to Julia," and is ultimately convinced that he loves Big Brother. The novel ends as Winston, having exchanged mutual conversations of betrayal with Julia, sits at the Chestnut Café, drinking Victory Gin, completely brainwashed and committed to Big Brother.

Much has been said about the ultimate pessimism of *Nineteen Eighty-Four* being related to Orwell's fatal illness, which he fought unsuccessfully during the composition of the novel. If, however, one thinks of Orwell's fiction less in biographical terms and more in relation to artistic intention, then such a conclusion could be subject to argument. Although the novel ends with Winston in what Northrop Frye calls the sixth level of irony, unrelieved bondage, one should draw a distinction, as Orwell does in his other writings (most notably in the essay "A Good Word for the Vicar of Bray"), between humans' actions as cultural beings and their activities as creatures of planet Earth, natural beings.

As political creatures, people and their purely cultural institutions could, Orwell believes, develop a world such as the one portrayed in *Nineteen Eighty-Four*. As biological residents of the planet Earth, however, this would be impossible. Humankind never displays hubris more graphically than does O'Brien in his speech about the party's supposed control of nature. In Orwell's view, humans will never fully control nature, because they are only a part of that which they wish to control. The great chestnut tree blossoming over Winston and his degeneration as a free being is Orwell's symbol indicating that the natural world can outlast society's cultural and political aberrations. "The planting of a tree," says Orwell, "if [it] takes root . . . will far outlive the visible effect of any of your other actions, good or evil." If there is hope for Oceania in the Proles, perhaps it is because they are instinctively closer to the natural world symbolized by the chestnut tree. Nevertheless, whether one thinks there is any hope for the people of that world or not, their existence has served as a warning to the larger world: The price of the right to tell people what they do not want to hear is never too high to pay.

John V. Knapp

Other major works

NONFICTION: *Down and Out in Paris and London,* 1933; *The Road to Wigan Pier,* 1937; *Homage to Catalonia,* 1938; *Inside the Whale and Other Essays,* 1940; *The Lion and the Unicorn,* 1941; *Critical Essays,* 1946 (published in the U.S. as *Dickens, Dali, and Others*); *Shooting an Elephant and Other Essays,* 1950; *Such, Such Were the Joys,* 1953; *The Collected Essays, Journalism, and Letters of George Orwell,* 1968 (4 volumes; Sonia Orwell and Ian Angus, editors); *Orwell: The War Commentaries,* 1986.

MISCELLANEOUS: *Orwell: The Lost Writings,* 1985.

Bibliography

Bloom, Harold, ed. *George Orwell.* New York: Chelsea House, 1987. This compilation includes thirteen articles from leading critics and scholars which deal for the most part with major themes and well-known novels. A short bibliography and chronology are also included.

Crick, Bernard. *George Orwell: A Life.* Boston: Little, Brown, 1980. The most important full-scale effort so far, considering all phases of Orwell's career and pointing out some odd contrasts and anomalies that lay beneath what was outwardly very much a private life. The first biography to benefit from unlimited rights of quotation from Orwell's works held under copyright. Based upon extensive use of the writer's archives and other manuscript sources, as well as numerous publications.

Davison, Peter. *George Orwell: A Literary Life.* New York: St. Martin's Press, 1996. This book follows the course of Orwell's career as a writer. Although it does contain background chapters explaining his origins, it is chiefly concerned with his literary influences and relationships, including those with his publishers and editors. Davison served as the editor of *The Complete Works of George Orwell,* an experience that makes him particularly suited to the task of writing a literary biography that is something other than the usual "life and works."

Gardner, Averil. *George Orwell.* Boston: Twayne, 1987. This interesting and sensible summary treatment of Orwell's career and literary contributions takes note of areas where interpretive controversies have arisen. The chronology and the annotated selected bibliography are also useful.

Holderness, Graham, Bryan Loughrey, and Nahem Yousaf, eds. *George Orwell.* New York: St. Martin's Press, 1998. Essays on Orwell's novels; his use of allegory; his politics; his handling of form, character, and theme; and his view of England. Includes a bibliography.

Reilly, Patrick. *"Nineteen Eighty-Four": Past, Present, and Future.* Boston: Twayne, 1989. This spirited defense of Orwell's last novel upholds his conceptions against the claims of modern detractors. Contains a detailed chronology and an annotated bibliography. Reilly also wrote an earlier critical study of Orwell's fiction, *George Orwell: The Age's Adversary* (New York: St. Martin's Press, 1986).

Rodden, John. *The Politics of Literary Reputation: The Making and Claiming of "St. George" Orwell.* New York: Oxford University Press, 1989. Essentially a study of publications about Orwell rather than of the writer himself. Points to the seemingly ubiquitous impact of phrases and concepts associated with his ideas, many of which have been used in recent contexts that Orwell himself scarcely could have foreseen. The breadth of Rodden's research, in more obscure newspapers and journals, is impressive.

Sandison, Alan. *George Orwell After "Nineteen Eighty-Four."* London: Macmillan, 1986. This interpretive effort, based on an earlier work, regards Orwell's writings as a reflection of a long intellectual tradition of religious and philosophical individualism. A lengthy postscript presents Sandison's views on other works about Orwell.

Sheldon, Michael. *Orwell: The Authorized Biography.* New York: HarperCollins, 1991. A major biography, with extensive notes and bibliography.

Slater, Ian. *Orwell: The Road to Airstrip One.* New York: W. W. Norton, 1985. This attempt to trace the events of Orwell's life by way of his major works becomes slightly awkward in places but also reaches some interesting conclusions on matters of politics and literature.

Stansky, Peter, and William Abrahams. *Orwell: The Transformation.* London: Constable, 1979. Deals with Orwell's work through his period of combat service in the Spanish Civil War, discussing the origins of five early works. Concludes that Orwell's political point of view had begun to take a definite shape by 1937 as a result of his own experiences.

_____. *The Unknown Orwell.* London: Constable, 1972. Orwell's early years in India, at Eton, in Burma, in Paris, and in London are considered in the light of his decision to become a writer in the period leading up to the publication of his first book in 1933. Information provided by those who had known him personally has supplied details about Orwell's education and the beginning of his literary career.

Walter Pater

Born: London, England; August 4, 1839
Died: Oxford, England; July 30, 1894

Principal long fiction · *Marius the Epicurean: His Sensations and Ideas*, 1885 (two volumes); *Gaston de Latour: An Unfinished Romance*, 1896.

Other literary forms · Walter Pater is principally remembered as a critic. His most influential work, *Studies in the History of the Renaissance* (1873; revised as *The Renaissance: Studies in Art and Poetry*, 1877, 1888, 1893), decisively changed the Victorian conception of art as a vehicle for the expression of uplifting sentiments or edifying ideals. Pater, whose unnamed antagonist was John Ruskin, argued that art is preeminently concerned with the dextrous elaboration of its own sensuous ingredients. Form, color, balance, and tone: These are the elements of which art is constituted. Hence, the imposition of a moral upon a painting, a poem, or a musical composition subverts the integrity of the work and distorts the function of criticism. The genuine critic begins with an analysis of the impression which a painting or a poem communicates and then endeavors to trace that impression to the structural elements of which the work is composed. Ultimately, as the notorious conclusion to *The Renaissance* makes clear, art is chiefly to be cherished as a means of enhancing, expanding, and enlarging the faculties of sensuous apprehension and as a catalyst in the pursuit of more varied, exquisite, and complex sensations. In the last analysis, Pater was inclined to evaluate and judge life itself as an aesthetic phenomenon.

Pater qualified this position in his later works, however, and since *Marius the Epicurean*—his one completed novel—was expressly written to revise and reevaluate the conclusion of *The Renaissance*, it is necessary to acquire some preliminary understanding of Pater's earlier and less complex point of view.

By way of preparation for *Marius the Epicurean*, Pater composed a series of stories that foreshadow the mature techniques of his novel. The best of these stories, "The Child in the House," traces the influence of a child's environment upon the formation of his sensibility and character. Here, in a statement which may be regarded as a keynote to the author's subsequent utterances, Pater expresses through the character of Florian Deleal the distinguishing quality that informs not only his own sensibility but also the sensibility of Marius and, indeed, of all his protagonists: "For with the desire of physical beauty," observes Pater of Florian, "mingled itself early the fear of death—the fear of death intensified by the desire of beauty."

Before examining the implications of this sentiment in the context of *Marius the Epicurean*, it is interesting to note that virtually all of Pater's other works—in both criticism and fiction—are meditations on the propinquity of beauty and death and on the desire that this meditation engenders in Pater to conceive of an absolute which defines itself in and gives broader significance to the sensuous flux of existence. As Pater observes in his study of Plato, "to realize unity in variety, to discover *cosmos*, an order that shall satisfy one's reasonable soul—below and within apparent chaos: is from first to last the continuous purpose of what we call philosophy."

In addition to *The Renaissance*, then, Pater's other works are briefly these: *Imaginary*

Portraits (1887), a collection of stories that prefigure *Marius the Epicurean* in their emphasis on the aesthetic quality and philosophical repercussions of experience upon a sensitive and circumspect temperament rather than with the dramatization of experience itself; *Appreciations* (1889), a heterogeneous collection of literary criticisms that apply the principles adduced in *The Renaissance* to the examination of English and French literary figures; *Plato and Platonism* (1893), the philosophical and theoretical counterpart to *Marius the Epicurean,* which examines the respective relations between the temporal and the eternal, the relative and the absolute, the ideal and the real in the works of Plato; *Greek Studies* (1895), an examination of the myths of Dionysus and Persephone and their symbolic relation to the spirit of art; and *Miscellaneous Studies* (1895), a grouping of Pater's most important writings on figures of literary, religious, and artistic significance. Of special interest in the latter is the short essay "Diaphaneite," wherein Pater delineates those attributes that go into the making of an ideal and yet realizable humanity. Finally, *Essays from the "Guardian"* (1896) is a collection of Pater's reviews on the writers of his day.

Achievements · Pater's achievement as a novelist and a critic is central to the modern vision of art. Though he was not always edified by the scandalous manner in which his disciples interpreted his message, nor gratified by the distortion of his ideas by an entire generation of aesthetes and decadents, Pater, when he is fully understood, emerges as a figure of incalculable importance in the evolution of twentieth century literature. In the first place, he did away with much of the fustian that obscured the appreciation of art in his own day, and he left a critical legacy, which extended into the present century in the works of Bernard Berenson and Roger Fry. Moreover, as Harold Bloom observes of Pater's most memorable character, "Marius, more than any fictional character of our age, is the representative modern poet as well as the representative man of literary culture who remains the only audience for that poet." As a stylist, too, Pater was wonderfully suggestive and original. Adapting the rich and ornate cadences of Ruskin to his more subtle purpose, Pater evolved a style that is the last word in delicacy, refinement, and understated eloquence. His sentences are characterized by elaborate parentheses, delicately wrought rhythms, and mannered circumlocutions—annoying to some readers—and his prose matches with minute accuracy the uncertainties, doubts, and deliberations of a mind in debate with itself, a mind fastidiously alive to the full complexity of human

experience and scrupulously intent upon a verbal music that, in its hesitant rhythms, remains faithful to that experience. In this regard, he clearly anticipates Marcel Proust.

It is not, however, on the level of style alone that Pater's influence has been indelible. *Marius the Epicurean*, in the role which it assigns to memory, its tone of melancholy retrospect, its analysis of a highly developed sensibility enamored of perfection yet resigned to uncertainty, anticipates, to a remarkable degree, the structural, tonal, and thematic underpinnings of Proust's novels. When one adds to this Pater's lasting influence on Oscar Wilde, James Joyce, André Gide, and William Butler Yeats—the last of whom claimed that *Marius the Epicurean* is "the only great prose in modern English"—one is compelled to admit that Pater was one of the first major sensibilities of the modern age.

Biography · For a writer who was to become the subject of numerous debates and controversies regarding the tendency of his works, the quality of his influence, and the dubiety of his doctrines, Walter Horatio Pater's life seems, at first glance, a singularly colorless affair. The youngest son of a dedicated physician who died prematurely, Pater was reared in a household dominated by his sisters, his mother, and his godmother. He remained, throughout childhood, indifferent to the activities or sports of his peers, preferring to imagine a world of ceremonious gallantry and hieratic ritual. He manifested a deep attachment to the solemn devotions and sumptuous worship of the Anglican Church. A need to remain true to the irrepressible skepticism and intellectual scrupulousness of his own nature prevented him, at the last, from acting upon his early impulses and taking orders. With a temperament more than commonly inclined to self-analysis and introspection, Pater, following his matriculation at Queens College, Oxford, chose to pursue an academic career. He was elected a junior fellow at Brasenose College in 1864.

From the first, the young don was regarded with certain suspicions, "having acquired," as Humphry Ward observed, "a new and daring philosophy of his own, and a wonderful gift of style." Benjamin Jowett, the famous translator of Plato, was acutely displeased with the seemingly subversive conclusion to *The Renaissance* and successfully hindered Pater's advancement at Oxford. In defiance, however, of Jowett's reprobations, Pater continued to enjoy a steady advance in influence and reputation. Ultimately, his increased fame warranted the taking of additional rooms in London, and there, in the company of sisters and friends, Pater enjoyed the sympathy and civility which were sometimes denied him at Oxford. Modest, retiring, elusive, and enigmatic: These are the epithets that most frequently occur in contemporary portraits of Pater. It was doubtless these qualities that won him the admiration of his most famous pupil: Gerard Manley Hopkins. It is interesting to note (and much to Pater's credit) that, in the surcharged evangelical atmosphere of Oxford, where professors more often strove to win converts than to foster independence of mind, Pater was the single instructor who continued to be loyal to Hopkins after his embrace of Catholicism. Indeed, Pater's elasticity and insouciance, his careful cultivation of what John Keats called "negative capability," were as characteristic of the man as they were of the artist. Pater died as a result of a heart attack in 1894.

Analysis · Walter Pater's *Marius the Epicurean* is the culminating expression of a fictional genre that began in the 1830's and continued until the turn of the century. This genre, a peculiar mixture of religious speculation and personal confession, developed almost synchronously with the assault of science against traditional Christianity, beginning with the publication, in 1832, of Sir Charles Lyell's *Principles of Geology.* Lyell's book, which exploded the biblical account of creation, was the first of several–the most famous being Charles Darwin's–that shook Western culture to its foundations. The passage of the Reform Bill, the theories of Darwin and Karl Marx, the development of the so-called "higher" criticism in the exegesis of biblical texts, the rise in population, and the spread of revolution were but a few events that challenged the inherited certainties of Victorian England. Men were forced to reevaluate old beliefs, to doubt discredited traditions, to revise social policies, to change moral valuations. It is not surprising that the confessional novel, the novel of doubt and faith, should acquire an unprecedented significance during such a period. The absence of reliable guideposts threw men back upon themselves and obliged them to search for unity, purpose, and direction in the kaleidoscopic sequence of their own lives.

Marius the Epicurean · *Marius the Epicurean* is one of the finest offshoots of a literary tradition inaugurated by Thomas Carlyle's *Sartor Resartus* (1835) and sustained in such works as John Henry Newman's *Loss and Gain* (1848), William Hale White's *The Autobiography of Mark Rutherford* (1885), and Mrs. Humphry Ward's *Robert Elsmere* (1888). Pater chose to set his search for meaning and purpose amid the disintegrating spectacle of Antonine Rome, but its bearing on the condition of late Victorian England is emphatically underlined: "Let the reader pardon me if here and there I seem to be passing from Marius to his modern representatives–from Rome, to Paris or London," Pater interpolates at one point. Marius is clearly meant to be prototypical: He dramatizes a quest for religious values that satisfies the demands of modern consciousness and reflects the ambiguity of a shattered world.

This is not to say that his growth is haphazard or random; on the contrary, Pater implies an underlying teleology in Marius's development: However dim and faint the sense of a superintending providence, his life is oriented toward the climactic moment of self-sacrifice with which the novel ends. Marius does not, however, fully resolve the conflicting calls of conscience and sensation, beauty and duty, engagement and withdrawal, in the fulfillment of that end. Though Pater evidently sees Marius's entire existence as an elaborate preparation for the revelatory moment in which his moral and spiritual being are ultimately defined, critics have generally judged that this is accomplished, if at all, without dramatic conviction.

Marius's youth is characterized, as was Pater's, by a more than common susceptibility to sensuous impressions. His home, "White Nights," a villa with adjacent farm, contributes to these susceptibilities. The note of grave beauty, of life lived under the conditions of animal sacrifice and seasonal change, develops in the boy a wistful reverence and wonder, which deepen with the passage of years. The Wordsworthian element in all this is not fortuitous, for Marius is destined to enact precisely that pattern of spiritual growth enunciated in "Lines Composed a Few Miles Above Tintern Abbey" and "Ode: Intimations of Immortality"–a pattern that involves a gradual conversion from the sensory to the spiritual planes of existence, a slow but steady ascension from the "aching joys" and "dizzy raptures" of his first impulsive response to beauty to the sober steadfastness of a mind that recognizes "a sense sublime of something far more deeply interfused." This conversion, if such it may be called, does not, for Marius, issue in the renunciation of his former pleasures, but rather a deepening awareness of their ultimate origin and tendency. In brief, Marius comes to dwell consciously in the presence of a spirit which is implied in his first naïve responses to nature and beauty. Hence, the pagan ceremonies, which solicit Marius's devotion and awe, already foreshadow "certain heavy demands" that will not become apparent to the lad until he acquires the mature self-consciousness of adulthood. It is then, on the level of discursive thought, that he will begin to recognize "some ampler vision, which should take up into itself and explain this world's delightful shows." "White Nights" is, therefore, as Pater suggests, not only a domestic dwelling place but also a state of mind peculiar to youth and prior to the self-dedication that maturity exacts.

In any event, it is not long before Marius is obliged to abandon the "world's delightful shows" in the pursuit of a more bracing conception of beauty. To cure a childhood illness, Marius is sent to the Temple of Aesculapius. The process of healing is complemented by meditations on Platonic texts. While these constitute a cherishable legacy for Marius, the boy reacts against a world of abstract essences. The impalpable ideas of Plato attract him only insofar as they fuse with the world of spatiotemporal objects, "green fields, for instance, or children's faces." Here, Pater is clearly attempting to revise the "impressionism" of his youth, itself a recrudescence of the Heraclitean theory of perpetual flux, with a Symbolist theory of correspondences. Beauty will no longer be an end in itself but "an outward imagery identifying itself with unseen moralities." While Marius does not achieve such an identification at once or without great difficulty, Pater clearly intends that the boy's unthinking empiricism should be shaken and unsettled. In a word, the exhortation "to burn with a hard gem-like flame," which Pater formerly enunciated in *The Renaissance*, is now being duly qualified by an obligation "to discriminate, ever more and more fastidiously, select form and colour in things from what was less select." Pater is avid to demonstrate, through his hero Marius, the correct application of the aesthetic theory to life, an application that requires a transvaluation of the concept "Beauty" to include "not pleasure, but fulness of life, and insight as conducting to that fulness . . . whatever form of human life, in short, might be heroic, impassioned, ideal." Marius's stay at the temple initiates an intellectual or moral awakening, a search for a hieratic order of conduct and beauty that is truly serviceable to that ideal. Dissatisfied with the abstractness of the Platonic method, Marius rejects the world of ideal forms in the pursuit of its equivalent in a living community, a veritable body of fellow aspirants. His search for this community determines the subsequent shape of the novel.

Immediately prior to his departure from the temple, Marius is vouchsafed a distant view of a city which appears to be an earthly incarnation of the Platonic archetype he is seeking. This first glimpse of Rome kindles in Marius the illusion that it, perhaps, is that "new city coming down 'like a bride out of heaven,'" of which Plato discoursed so eloquently. Accordingly, Marius takes practical steps to bring him closer to "the most religious city in the world." He moves next to Pisa, preparing for his future obligations as secretary to the Emperor Aurelius. He is soon befriended by an aspiring youth of literary ambitions by the name of Flavian—a character who clearly represents one aspect of Marius's own divided consciousness.

Flavian's function in the novel is to bear involuntary witness to the limitations of aesthetic hedonism. Pater clearly intends through this subordinate character to disabuse his devotees of the notion that burning with a hard, gemlike flame is equivalent to self-indulgent dissipation. Beneath "the perfection of form" that Flavian achieves in his bearing and his poetry, Marius recognizes "a depth of corruption," which compels him to follow his friend only so far. Pater anticipates, here, to a remarkable degree the theme of Thomas Mann's *Death in Venice* (1912): the awareness that an exclusive preoccupation with artistic form may have the effect of neutralizing both good and evil by reducing them to complementary colors, lights, and shades in a composition. Nevertheless, Flavian performs a vital role in the drama of Marius's development: It is he who introduces Marius to the "golden book" of Apuleius.

At this point, Pater reproduces in full Apuleius's tale of Cupid and Psyche. Through subtle and strategic modifications of the original, Pater conceives of the tale as a presentiment of Marius's spiritual development. Evoking the solemn harmonies of the King James version of the Bible and softening the racy idiom of Apuleius, Pater endows the story of Cupid and Psyche with a "gentle idealism" and facilitates its interpretation as an allegory. Just as Psyche, symbol of the human soul, is redeemed from death by the intervention of Cupid, so Marius—bewildered, distracted, and divided by the contradictory sects and philosophical schools of decadent Rome—is presumably redeemed from despair by the appearance of a community that claims to satisfy the deepest needs of the human spirit. The road to that community is, however, difficult, uncertain, and devious.

Flavian's life is prematurely ended by an outbreak of plague. Marius, who remains, as ever, faithful to the evidence of his senses, is convinced of "nothing less than the soul's extinction." It may be parenthetically observed that despite his later sympathy with the Christian response to suffering, Marius never fully abandons those scruples "which can make no sincere claim to have apprehended anything beyond the veil of immediate experience." With his departure for Rome, he remains in a state of suspended judgment with regard to the ultimate destiny appointed for the human soul.

The actual journey to the capital of the ancient world includes a number of incidents that undermine the philosophic detachment of the young Marius. Notwithstanding the glory of the Roman *campagna*, the many idyllic details of which Marius, with his habitual eye for the concrete, discerns with "a fresh, primeval poetry," he is plunged, following a scarcely averted accident, into further uncomfortable wrestling with the eternal questions. This accident—a loosened boulder falls from a wall beside the path Marius is following—has the effect of shaking him into a recognition that "his elaborate philosophy had not put beneath his feet the terror of mere bodily evil." The force, however, that is destined to correct the deficiencies in Marius's scheme of existence is not far away. Stopping at an inn to revive his spirits, Marius orders a glass of wine and muses vacantly over the "ring of delicate foam" that sparkles in his cup. Presently, his attention is arrested by a voice—"a youthful voice, with a reassuring clearness of note, which completes his cure." As he will soon learn, it is the voice of Cornelius, a young Roman soldier whose influence is destined to supersede that of Flavian. It is not, however, until much later in his pilgrimage that Marius discovers that the origin of Cornelius's gracious alacrity of spirit is traceable to "some new knighthood or chivalry, just then coming into the world."

Marius, however, is not yet in a position to be irresistibly won over to that knighthood. He must first extend his philosophical hypotheses beyond the immediate circle of his own sensations; the role of Marcus Aurelius in the novel is to facilitate this extension. Unlike Flavian and Cornelius, the philosophical emperor of Rome is more than merely a shadowy personification of Marius's fractured ego: Aurelius is a figure of vital warmth and sympathy who encourages Marius to enlarge his spiritual perspective and to discover that an exclusive preoccupation with the passing moment may actually narrow the range of experience, curtail the development of character, and inhibit the acquisition of wisdom. The upshot of Aurelius's teachings is to reinforce Marius's search for a "comely order . . . to which, as to all other beautiful phenomena in life, he must, for his own peace, adjust himself."

While his influence is certainly salutary, Aurelius remains, in the final analysis, incapable of reconciling his devotion to that "comely order" with the debased reality of Antonine Rome. It is not long before Marius discovers a number of serious shortcomings in Aurelius's view of existence. To be sure, Marius accepts the merits of a philosophical scheme that posits a universal reason, or *logos,* a point of rest and a center of calm from which to withstand the vertiginous whirl of feelings and events, the traumatic blows of fate and destiny. Unfortunately, such a scheme, as Marius equally recognizes, may easily devolve into a pretext for neglecting one's peers in the present, for averting one's eyes from the plenitude and plurality of the living world. While freely granting the efficacy of believing in a "universal commonwealth of mind"–the sense of expanded horizons, the freedom from petty vexations, the glimpse of imperishable ideals that it allows–Marius rejects the concomitant calm and serenity that Aurelius, for example, maintains in the midst of human misery.

Two episodes in particular underline the deficiencies of the Stoical system. The first of these occurs during a performance at the Colosseum over which Aurelius, notwithstanding his own aversion to the gladiatorial games, presides with an air of tolerance. This indifference to the unspeakable butchery of men and animals, a consequence of the Stoic divorce of reason from reality, provokes Marius "to mark Aurelius as his inferior, now and for ever, on the question of righteousness." When it comes, however, to the suffering and death of his son, Lucius Verus, Aurelius is presented in a more sympathetic light. This episode, too, leaves an indelible mark in Marius's consciousness. The disparity between the imperturbable calm of the professed Stoic and the irrepressible grief of the stricken parent is poignantly dramatized when the boy, after an operation of surpassing agony, lapses into a coma from which he never recovers.

The chapter that immediately follows this episode signals the direction that Marius henceforth will take. An epigraph from the Psalms–"My heart is ready, O God, a ready heart is mine"–clearly enunciates the imminence of that spiritual crisis toward which his whole life has been moving. It would be a mistake, however, to construe this crisis as a sudden shattering encounter with the divine. On the contrary, nothing in the sense of a clear dramatic conversion may be said to happen. The epiphany that Marius is vouchsafed has all the character of a Wordsworthian "spot of time." In one of his vagrant wanderings on the outskirts of Rome, Marius pauses at an outdoor inn to gaze at the extensive Roman *compagna.* His attention is divided among a number of apparently trivial and unrelated details–"a bird came and sang among the wattled hedge-roses: an animal feeding crept nearer: the child who kept it was gazing quietly"–when, suddenly, the entire scene presents itself as the outward and tangible emblem of "that . . . Ideal, to which the Old Testament gives the name of Creator, which for the philosophers of Greece is the Eternal Reason, and in the New Testament the Father of Men." The mundane world is transfigured and transvalued in a moment of privileged perception: no less and no more. The departure of this mood is as quiet and unobtrusive as its inception, but it leaves Marius with the firm conviction that the remainder of his life must be "a search for the equivalent of that Ideal . . . a gathering together of every trace and token of it, which his actual experience might present." The event is clearly something of a watershed.

At this juncture, Marius is given the opportunity to visit a pair of houses that represent two opposing visions of reality. The first house represents the finest flowering of classical antiquity. It is here that Marius meets his former idol, the poet Apuleius; enjoys the refined pleasures and urbane conversation of the Roman intelligentsia; and delights in the delectations of a banquet replete with music, dance, and fine condiments. The whole proceedings, however, are tainted by a certain foppish connoisseurism, a pampered elegance, a "facility" and "self-complacency" in the exchange of ideas. Marius departs with a nagging sense of weariness and disillusion.

The second house, to which he is introduced by Cornelius, is that of the Christian saint, Cecilia. It is characteristic that Pater should choose the canonized patroness of music as the agent of Marius's contact with Christianity. Presumably, if art can obscure the moral being of man, as in the case of Flavian, it can also reveal that moral being. The grave, refined, and simple dignity of the Christian community—its air of domestic and filial piety, its comely rectitude of spirit, its solicitude for the departed, care for the living, and faith in things to come—stands in favorable contrast to the enervating amusements and facile wit of the Roman upper crust. Yet it is important to note that the early Church, as Pater presents it, has nothing of that apocalyptic fervor that looks forward to the end of the world and the last things. On the contrary, "the contrast between the church and the world," Pater tells us, "was becoming less pronounced." By far the largest part of Marius's attraction to this community derives from his contemplation of "the beautiful house of Cecilia, its lights and flowers, of Cecilia herself, moving among the lilies, with an enchanted grace."

The fact is that Marius remains ultimately indifferent to the dogmatic foundations of Christianity. To be sure, he returns to his childhood home and supervises the reburial of his ancestors according to the usages of the early Church. Furthermore, he willingly intercedes on Cornelius's behalf following an officially sanctioned purge of the growing Christian community. There is, however, a considerable degree of ambiguity involved in Marius's position vis-à-vis the Christian faith. Marius is arrested along with Cornelius for being present at a community act of worship. An outbreak of plague shatters the fragile tolerance extended to the Church and initiates widespread persecution of the Christians. On the strength of his relations with Aurelius, Marius contrives to have Cornelius released. He is compelled, however, to give a deposition on his friend's behalf and to join the other prisoners in the long and arduous journey to Rome. This generosity of spirit on the part of Marius is prompted by a mistaken notion that Cornelius is Cecilia's intended: The latter's vows of chastity entirely elude Marius's understanding. Traveling to Rome in company with the other captives, Marius is stricken with plague and abandoned at a neighboring farm which, as it turns out, is the dwelling of some recent converts. Lying in a state of semidelirium for several days, he finds consolation, during the lucid intervals allowed him, in "the scent of newmown hay . . . and the sounds of cattle . . . from the green places around." The occupants, erroneously assuming that he is a Christian, administer to the dying Marius the last rites of their faith.

Is Marius, then, a Christian? This question has been the subject of critical debate since the novel's appearance. For Paul Elmer More, *Marius the Epicurean* is "only another manifestation of that aestheticism which Pater sucked from the Romantic school of his century and disguised in the phraseology of ancient faith." He further adds, "to write thus was to betray Christianity with a kiss." T. S. Eliot has no hesitation in asserting that "of the essence of the Christian Faith . . . Pater knew almost nothing." Arthur Benson is equally forthright in claiming that "the very peace which Marius discerns in Christianity is the old philosophical peace over again." The point is that Marius fails to grasp and remains largely indifferent to the theoretical foundations of Christianity. "Our creeds," as Pater observes, "are but the brief abstract of our prayer and song." Inasmuch as Christianity invests that song with a deeper pathos, frees the mind from its empirical trammels, and endows existence with a warmer hope, it is clearly a serviceable hypothesis for the questing human spirit. Its dogmatic underpinnings, however, are of secondary importance.

Some might claim that Pater's enterprise in *Marius the Epicurean* is fundamentally affiliated with the Christian existentialism of Søren Kierkegaard. There is, however, one signal and important difference. Unlike Kierkegaard, who posits a leap of faith in which reason is virtually annihilated, Pater viewed all such leaps as a source of potential fanaticism. Christianity, for Pater, is clearly a stage in the development of human potential, but he would jealously protect that potential from any claim that might threaten its autonomy. The Church of Cecilia is, at bottom, a fictive structure in which there is "no forced opposition between soul and body, the world and the spirit." It is even identified, at one point, with that "half-humorous placidity of soul, of a kind illustrated later very effectively by Montaigne." Just as modern-day theologians who attempt to gerrymander Christianity into the camps of Karl Marx, Sigmund Freud, Friedrich Nietzsche, or Ludwig Feuerbach, Pater has created a church of his own making—distinctly unrecognizable to the average believer. From the perspective of Christ's statement, "He who is not with me is against me," Marius is most certainly not a Christian; on the other hand, if one considers the earlier phrasing of this statement in the gospel of Mark, "He who is not against us is for us," then the question of Marius's death as "a kind of sacrament with plenary grace" remains open.

Gaston de Latour · Moreover, as Pater was to recognize in *Gaston de Latour*, institutional Christianity, insofar as it defines itself in what a man professes rather than in what he is, is as prodigal of sectarian bigotry and bloodshed as the worst excesses of pagan Rome. Like *Marius the Epicurean, Gaston de Latour* examines the situation of faith in an "age of transition . . . when the problem of man's destiny and his relations to the unseen was undergoing a new solution." Though Pater never lived to complete the novel—it remains, at best, a series of discontinuous meditations on the religious and political ferment of the Reformation—its essential outlines are as follows. Born in the midst of growing strife between Huguenots and Catholics, Gaston comes of age in "the cornlands of France," in close proximity to the cathedral of Chartres and amid the luxuries of his rustic manor house. He becomes acquainted with King Charles the Ninth, joins the "episcopal household of Chartres as a page," and falls under the influence of the poetry of Pierre de Ronsard. Like Marius, in a different context, he becomes the votary of a great philosopher: in this instance, Michel de Montaigne. He eventually travels to Paris and takes up with a spirited Huguenot girl; under the pressure of her brothers, he marries her in a Protestant ceremony which exerts no real claim upon him: "The transaction seemed to have but that transitoriness as also the guilt of a vagrant love." Miscalculating the forces of destruction gathered on the eve of St. Bartholomew, Gaston returns to his homestead at Deux-manoirs, "his wife left behind there in Paris." He later learns of the death of his wife "while the stairways of the Louvre, the streets, the trap-doors of Paris, run blood." Following the banishment of King Charles, Gaston returns to Paris and falls under the influence of the heterodox monk Giordano Bruno. Here the novel abruptly ends.

What is clearly significant about this work is its relation to *Marius the Epicurean.* Just as Marius qualifies the hedonism of *The Renaissance,* so *Gaston de Latour* qualifies the Christianity of *Marius the Epicurean.* Indeed, of Gaston himself the reader is told that "the very genius of qualification followed him through his keen, constant, changeful consideration of men and things."

Pater's attitude is obvious. He clearly distrusts the external machinery of a church that absorbs the individual conscience and resolves all doubts in cozy conformity, irresponsible anonymity, and superstitious fear. Pater rejects dogmatic formulations and ideologies of any kind, especially insofar as these inhibit the cultivation of human sympathy or the development of individual character. "The man who never alters his opinion is like standing water, and breeds reptiles of the mind," wrote William Blake, and Pater would have most certainly agreed. Indeed, the true saint of the Reformation, for Pater, is Montaigne, and the legitimate attitude in all matters speculative and religious is not the intransigence of the doctrinaire but the suspended judgment of a humanist. "It was something to have been," writes Pater of Montaigne, "in the matter of religious tolerance, as in so many other matters of justice and gentleness, the solitary conscience of the age."

In the final analysis, the question of whether Pater's protagonists are ultimately Christian pales before the question of whether they are comprehensively human. Thoughtful, but without energy; sensitive, but without resolve; scrupulous, but without conviction; both Marius and Gaston remain imprisoned, each in his own consciousness and incapable of genuine community with others. The essentially selfish conviction that informs these novels and that may be taken as a motto for Pater's life and work is perhaps stated most succinctly in one of the Pythian Odes of the Latin poet Pindar: "O my soul, do not aspire to immortal life, but exhaust the limits of the possible." Pater once remarked of Marius that his was a philosophy that at least guaranteed its possessor of living a life without harm to others. The question remains, however, whether such a philosophy is adequate to the full range of human experience. In the absence of more solid and substantial convictions than those which Pater demonstrates in his writings, this question remains a point of legitimate concern in any final estimate of his achievement.

Stephen I. Gurney

Other major works

SHORT FICTION: *Imaginary Portraits,* 1887.

NONFICTION: *Studies in the History of the Renaissance,* 1873 (rev. as *The Renaissance: Studies in Art and Poetry,* 1877, 1888, 1893); *Appreciations: With an Essay on Style,* 1889; *Plato and Platonism: A Series of Lectures,* 1893; *Greek Studies: A Series of Essays,* 1895; *Miscellaneous Studies,* 1895; *Essays from the "Guardian,"* 1896.

Bibliography

Bloom, Harold, ed. *Modern Critical Views: Walter Pater.* New York: Chelsea House, 1985. Bloom has compiled what he considers some of the best criticism available on Pater. The introduction by Bloom provides a useful overview of Pater's work and contains much insight. Also includes a reprint of an unabridged pamphlet on Pater by Ian Fletcher, a highly respected critic of Pater. A valuable and well-rounded study.

Brake, Laurel, and Ian Small, eds. *Pater in the 1990's.* Greensboro, N.C.: ELT Press, 1991. This collection of fifteen critical essays was culled from papers offered at a 1988 Pater conference at Oxford University. The editors note that while half of the essays they include reflect the older New Criticism approach to literature, the other half demonstrate the shift in Pater criticism toward consideration of his works in historical and biographical contexts. Topics range from editing Pater to his friends

and literary influences to his own lasting influence on writers such as James Joyce.
Buckler, William E. *Walter Pater: The Critic as Artist of Ideas.* New York: New York University Press, 1987. This scholarly study examines the breadth and depth of Pater's prose and poetry, as well as his role as a critic, acknowledging him as a major but underrated writer. The work focuses on Pater's aestheticism in his work, and chapter 8 examines Pater's *Plato and Platonism,* which has been generally ignored by critics.
Court, Franklin E. *Walter Pater: An Annotated Bibliography of Writings About Him.* De Kalb: Northern Illinois University Press, 1980. This volume includes a checklist of a representative body of criticism on Pater from 1871 through 1973. Contains abstracts of critical articles, reminiscences, biographies, and letters to editors. A rich source of bibliographical information for the Pater scholar.
Levey, Michael. *The Case of Walter Pater.* London: Thames and Hudson, 1978. An appreciative study of Pater, largely biographical and executed with thoroughness. Levey promotes Pater's case but alludes to the difficulty in placing Pater's writing because he moved so fluidly from fiction to fact.
Moliterno, Frank. *The Dialectics of Sense and Spirit in Pater and Joyce.* Greensboro: ELT Press, University of North Carolina at Greensboro, 1998. Compares themes and aesthetics in Pater and James Joyce. With bibliographical references and an index.
Monsman, Gerald. *Walter Pater.* Boston: Twayne, 1977. A chronological look at Pater's work and life. Examines the heroes in his works, in particular the hero in *Marius the Epicurean.* A useful study for the beginning reader of Pater. A selected bibliography is provided.
Shuter, William. *Rereading Walter Pater.* New York: Cambridge University Press, 1997. Part of the Cambridge Studies in Nineteenth Century Literature series, this volume examines Pater's works with a critical eye.